Cycles of Conquest

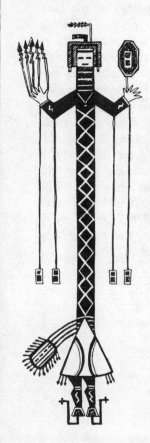

Cycles of Conquest

*The Impact of Spain, Mexico,
and the United States on the
Indians of the Southwest,
1533–1960*

by

EDWARD H. SPICER

Drawings by Hazel Fontana

THE UNIVERSITY OF ARIZONA PRESS, TUCSON

About the Author ...

EDWARD H. SPICER has combined field experience with scholarly research to become one of the foremost authorities on present-day Indian tribes. Professor of anthropology at the University of Arizona, he has served as president of the American Anthropological Association and was selected for membership in the National Academy of Sciences and the American Philosophical Society. Spicer's firsthand acquaintances with Southwestern Indians began in the 1930s and he has continued his close association ever since. He did field research among the Indians of Mexico while working in that country on two Guggenheim fellowships, and spent still another year in Mexico, Peru, and Bolivia on a National Science Foundation senior post-doctoral fellowship for the study of Indian community development. He also was chosen a National Endowment for the Humanities senior fellow. Spicer holds his Ph.D. in anthropology from the University of Chicago and his master's from the University of Arizona. He is editor of the University of Arizona Press book *Ethnic Medicine in the Southwest* as well as author of a number of other books and articles.

Seventh printing 1981

THE UNIVERSITY OF ARIZONA PRESS

I.S.B.N. 0-8165-0021-5
L.C. No. 61-14500

To Lawson and Carlos

Preface

THIS BOOK WAS CONCEIVED in the summer of 1953 as I was driving from Tucson to Window Rock, Arizona, to join a party of technicians from India. M. L. Wilson, formerly director of Agricultural Extension in the United States Department of Agriculture, had arranged a study tour of the Southwest for the purpose of pointing out factors for success and failure in government programs among the Indians of the region. I had been searching for books and articles which would help us to tell the story. There was no one book which attempted even an introduction to the dramatic record of the impact of European civilization on the Indian cultures. Despite the fact that there were reasonably good descriptions of almost every Indian culture in New Mexico, Arizona, Chihuahua, and Sonora, and adequate accounts of most of the important events affecting Indian-White relations from the time of the entrance of the Spaniards, there was almost nothing which attempted to interpret these facts and events in terms of cultural processes or the response of one people to the culture of another. Apart from some recent figures on the growth of livestock and agriculture on several reservations, and a few admirably detailed studies of some introduced crafts, such as Navajo rug-weaving and silverworking, no author had set out to present the fascinating narrative of the acceptance, modification, and spread of any one cultural trait or complex. Abundant facts had been gathered, but interpretation from any viewpoint which might make possible and profitable a comparison of cultural development in the Southwest with any other region of the world remained unaccomplished.

The rich store of information in scientific journals and monographs seemed to be crying for some attempt at synthesis. The kind of interpretation attempted in this volume grew out of a search for answers to the following question: What are the chief ways in which Indians have responded to Western civilization and what has happened to their cultures as a result of contact? Such questions keep us focused on cultural change and the processes of growth and development stimulated by the advent of white men. The present volume attempts to answer the questions in a broad way for the region as a whole, but with sufficient detail to provide a sense of concreteness regarding the experience of each of the major Indian groups.

A feature of the basic conception of the study is that there has been a similarity in the results of culture contact over a wide area which is called, for want of a better name, the Southwest. This region extends from the southern Sierra Madre Mountains in Mexico to the San Juan River in Utah, and from the Pecos River in New Mexico to the Gulf of California. It is a region in which at the time of the arrival of the Spaniards the Indians were predominantly agricultural, but their level of political organization was much below that of the Aztecs and Tarascans who adjoined them to the south. The plan of the book called for inclusion of all the native people of this region, but this plan has not been fully carried through. When I began to write, information was not available concerning the Mayos of the Fuerte River Valley in Sinaloa, the Tepehuanes of Durango and Chihuahua, the Huicholes of Jalisco, or the Coras of Nayarit. At least what came to my hand did not permit parallel treatment with the more northern tribes. Meanwhile, more and better information has become available, but not in time for inclusion in this volume. Moreover, the Warihios of the southern border between Chihuahua and Sonora have also been excluded because I could not satisfy myself that the data available were satisfactory. The original plan also included the Eastern Apaches — Jicarilla, Mescalero, and Lipan — but the task of becoming sufficiently familiar with them seemed too formidable and I gave up. These omissions make the book incomplete in terms of the conception which guided its writing, but I nevertheless believe that what is presented provides a framework for understanding cultural processes in the region as a whole.

The region dealt with, from the point of view of the Mexican reader, might be called the "Northwest." The term Southwest is used with apologies and in full awareness that for historians like Othón de Mendizábal the region with which we are concerned is the Northwest. Yet it is also the southwestern part of the North American continent, and that offers some justification for holding that my preference for "Southwest" is not based entirely on ethnocentric considerations. Ralph Beals's term, "the Greater Southwest," served its purpose in enlarging the rather restricted horizon of North American ethnologists and in emphasizing the fact of cultural unity from Nayarit to New Mexico, but I see no reason for continuing to use the adjective "greater" in historical and anthropological discussions of the region. We still await the scholar with a fine sense for terms who hits upon the right designation for this cultural-geographical entity.

If I have any credentials for having attempted a study of this scope, they are to be found chiefly in a thirty-year residence in the region, and close acquaintance with individuals among a number of Indian groups. I have carried out intensive field work among Yaquis, Seris, Western Apaches, and Papagos. I have had more limited, but still fairly intimate contacts with Mayos, Gila Pimas, Hopis, Navajos, Yavapais, Yumas, and some of the Eastern Pueblos. The only Indian group among whom I have nòt at least visited is the Tarahumara.

As might be expected in a work of this kind, the listing of materials consulted has presented problems. Because I had in mind a book that would be inviting to many different kinds of readers and because I conceived of it as presenting facts already well known to students of the region, I felt justifièd in avoiding footnotes and detailed bibliographic references. Yet it seems to me that I owe it to the reader to point out materials which can carry him more deeply into the story of any one tribe or process of change. Also, I owe it to the specialist, who may be critical of my interpretation, to indicate the chief sources of my inferences. I have tried to meet this dual obligation by listing for each chapter those works on which I have leaned most heavily and on which I think a reader might also most profitably rely in pursuing a theme. These, it will be noted, are rarely primary sources. I have taken advantage wherever I could of already accomplished work of synthesis, such as that of Bandelier, of Bolton, of Scholes, or of Underhill. For better or worse, I have tried to build understanding on such work and believe that others may do likewise.

I am indebted to the John Simon Guggenheim Memorial Foundation which gave me a fellowship during the year 1955-56, to The University of Arizona which gave me sabbatical leave during the same year and provided much aid in the preparation of the manuscript, and to the Social Science Research Council which provided funds to enable me to write during the summer of 1957. I am also grateful to the following persons who read parts of the manuscript and gave me the benefit of critical comments: Robert P. Armstrong, Harry Behn, Henry F. Dobyns, Edward P. Dozier, Paul Ezell, Mary Frobisher, James E. Officer, Rosamond B. Spicer, and Evon Z. Vogt. And I am further grateful for the sympathetic aid, far beyond the call of editorial duty, of Kit Scheifele and Jack L. Cross.

Edward H. Spicer

Tucson, Arizona

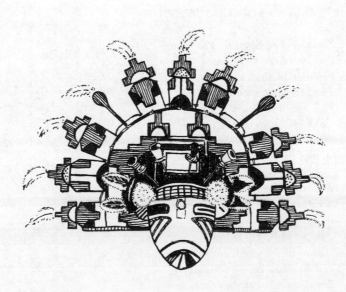

Table of Contents

List of Maps

INTRODUCTION

Cultural Frontiers

THE SCOPE of the modern European expansion which began in the fifteenth century far exceeded that of any previous "world" conquest. During the 1500's and 1600's it proceeded to enmesh in its web of domination the natives of the Americas, Africa, southern Asia, and the islands of the South Seas. The Indians of North America were the first to feel the full impact, as the Spaniards moved with surprising success to add a New Spain to their empire. Rapidly a New France and a New England likewise took form as vast appendages of the little nations of western Europe. The lives of the several million natives of North America were steadily transformed through systematic efforts to involve them in the European trade lines and political systems and to replace their religions with the various forms of Christianity.

The transformation of Indian life was not, however, a simple process. It did not consist of an even and progressive replacement of Indian with European customs and ways of thought. On the contrary, as in the wake of other conquests, there were many different trends and counter-trends with respect to the acceptance and rejection of what the conquerors offered as a new and superior way of life. One development which characterized European expansion not only in the Americas but also in Oceania and Africa was the formation of enclaved groups of natives. Where the land and other resources were regarded as undesirable by the invaders or where, through a variety of circumstances ranging from exceptional tribal cohesion to unusual natural barriers, the natives were able to resist successfully, the processes of extermination and cultural absorption did not take place. In such areas small groups of native peoples maintained in some degree their own ways of life as cultural islands in the midst of the European societies expanding around them.

The fate of such people who survived the first vigorous phase of conquest is today doubtful. Their future turns on a far more complex set of circumstances than did that of people who were earlier submerged or extinguished. No longer important in the strategy of the expanding Western nations, the enclaved peoples have persisted as distinct entities on sufferance of the dominant societies. In most cases, after the native peoples were subjugated, strong sentiment grew up in the

[1]

conquering nation regarding the injustice of the original conquest. The native survivors assumed a symbolic significance as reminders of a ruthless past and as representatives of a lost, and better way of life, pre-urban and pre-industrial. Associated with this symbolism strong feelings developed for preservation of the native peoples and their ways, but only a segment of the dominant nation was influenced by such sentiments. In contrast in every country stood those generally classed as practical people who remained dominated by the old urge for conquest, but now expressed in new terms, such as political integration and cultural assimilation. Continuation of the cultural enclaves was regarded as somehow against natural law, and problems respecting them were phrased simply in terms of economic and social welfare. National policy regarding the native peoples alternated between these two positions in such regions as the United States, Mexico, and New Zealand in response to the views of the different interested segments, depending on which gained political influence. These opposing influences in national policy have made the future of the native peoples equivocal.

It was under such circumstances that some two hundred thousand Indians existed as late as 1960 in northwestern Mexico and southwestern United States. In terms of climate and other natural influences, as well as in terms of historical relations between Europeans and natives, this region, spanning two modern nations, was a single entity. It was a major area of native enclavement in North America. Twenty-five Indian groups, sometimes referred to as "tribes," survived here as people with some degree of distinctive custom. They represented more than half the Indian cultures which existed in the region in the early 1500's when the Spaniards first began explorations.

The fact that the Indians all constituted enclaves in the midst of the dominant Mexicans and Anglo-Americans did not mean that their places in the enveloping societies were identical. They lived under a tremendous variety of conditions. The smallest group — the Seris — consisted of two hundred persons; they eked out a living by fishing and turtle hunting on the desert shores of the Gulf of California where, the dominant peoples agreed, their condition was one of grinding poverty. The largest group — the Navajos on the Colorado Plateau in the north — numbered over eighty-four thousand, and in the single year 1958 received over twenty-nine million dollars in royalties or lease bonuses on oil and gas resources. In Sonora the Yaquis, who as late as 1927 were regarded as a serious military threat by the Mexican government, still maintained a dedicated standing army. On the other hand, their nearest neighbors and long-time allies — the Mayos — were described in the textbooks of the Sonora school system as inherently peaceful and obedient to Mexican desires. The Pueblo Indians of New Mexico were pointed to in the literature of America as classic examples of the small democratic city-state providing its citizens with the satisfactions of integrated community living. Yet Western Apaches, close by in Arizona, presented an equally classic example of the thoroughly disorganized Indian tribe, successively subverted by well-meaning government programs.

This variety gave color and interest to the life of the region. It led students and creative artists, over two generations, to intensive study and interpretation

1. INDIANS OF ARIZONA, NEW MEXICO, CHIHUAHUA, SONORA, 1960

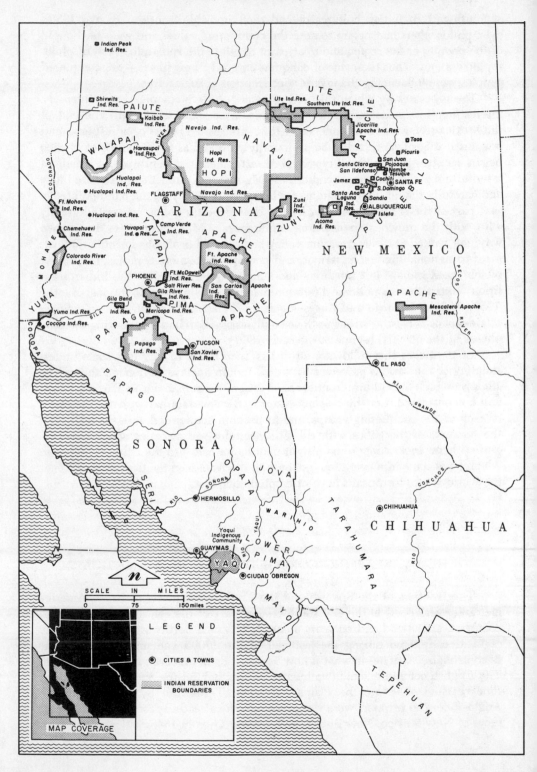

of Southwestern Indian cultures behind their invisible frontiers. By the 1950's even philosophers had begun to note the contrasting values and ways of thought of the peoples of the region and to attempt to relate the Indian to Western philosophic systems. Thus the cycle of conquest entered a new phase — the conquered peoples were influencing the invaders' conception of themselves.

The processes by which this had come about were complex and immensely interesting. Indian contacts with Spaniards from about 1533 until the end of the Mexican War for Independence in 1821 established habits of adjustment and new institutions which had to be profoundly modified as the Republic of Mexico began its struggle for stability. By 1960, after nearly a century and a half of intermittent and destructive conflicts, the Mexican government had initiated new and carefully thought out programs for bringing Indians into the national life. In that part of the region taken over by the United States policy contrasted greatly with both the previous Spanish and contemporary Mexican policies. In its own way, the United States reservation policy had created problems in Indian adjustment to national life just as serious, and perhaps even more complex, than those which faced Indians in Chihuahua and Sonora. Over the region the Indian transition from tribal to national life veered in many different directions. By the 1950's Indian, Mexican and Anglo-American dissatisfaction with the adjustment attained was at least as strong as Spanish dissatisfaction had been during the final phases of the colonial regime in the early 1800's.

In the pages that follow an effort has been made to arrive at some understanding of the various processes by which Indian enclavement came about. The steps by which the cultural frontiers have arisen, become intensified, or weakened will be considered. For this it is necessary to become familiar with the programs of each of the conquering groups, and to become acquainted with the history of the contacts of the tribes with the European-derived societies which have engulfed them. In so doing some insight may be gained into the cultural processes which have come into operation, not only in the American Southwest but all over the world where Europeans have attempted conquest.

THE OVERLAPPING CONQUESTS OF NORTH AMERICA

The frontiers of the Spanish and the English conquests of North America met and overlapped in the arid southwestern part of the continent. The Spanish conquest, after two hundred years of steady advance northward from the Valley of Mexico, faltered during the last half of the 1700's and, in the face of the uncontrollable Apaches in what is now Sonora, began to recede a little southward. The English conquest, some two hundred years behind the Spanish, had by this time reached only into the Plains states and Texas; but by the early 1800's Anglo-American trappers were venturing into the already Spanish-explored provinces of New Mexico, New Biscay, and Sonora. Then in 1848, with the Treaty of

Guadalupe Hidalgo closing the war between Mexico and the United States, the latter took over the frontier which Spain had never quite been able to control. As the region was partitioned into the modern states of Chihuahua, Sonora, New Mexico, and Arizona, the two new nations of Mexico and the United States resumed Spain's wavering efforts to conquer and make over the Indians.

From the first, beginning in the late 1500's, the Spaniards identified their attempts to change the Indians of this region as a mission for civilizing a savage people. The missionaries, the military captains, and the colonial administrators were very conscious of this mission and of themselves as bearers of civilization. Again and again they used the word "civilization" and instituted changes in everything from clothing to religious practice in its name. What they regarded as "civilization" was not necessarily what a modern student of human history would regard as such. The Spaniards identified civilization with specific elements of the Spanish culture of the period. They identified it by and large with the Castilian variety of the Spanish language, with adobe and stone houses, with men's trousers, with political organization focused through loyalty and obedience to the King of Spain, and with the Roman Catholic form of Christianity. For more than two hundred years after 1540 the Spaniards in northwestern New Spain sought by various means to replace corresponding features of Indian cultures with these and other elements of Spanish culture.

Later, in the early 1800's, when Mexicans assumed control of the region, they too thought of themselves as bearers of civilization. Yet the program for changing the lives of the Indians which they instituted was by no means identical with that of the Spaniards. Like the Spanish, they too called it "civilization" in their reports and state documents, but it was obviously considerably different. They still regarded Castilian Spanish, or at least what had become the Mexican variety of the language, as an important element, and they still emphasized rectangular houses of some sort and men's trousers, but their emphasis on other elements was quite different. They sought with determination to introduce individual landholding among the Indians; a representative, elective, and constitutional form of government with no king; and equality in citizenship rights which the Spaniards had proposed in theory but had not instituted. They also proposed, if they did not push at first, elementary schools without religious instruction; they had no program for promulgating the Roman Catholic or any other religion. Here was a new set of economic, political, and religious values. The Mexicans nevertheless were just as certain as the Spaniards that their own kind of culture was civilization and that they had a mission to civilize the Indians.

The Anglo-Americans, when they came into possession of the northern part of New Spain, thought of civilization at first as something peculiarly their own and not for the Indians. They began by setting up reservations as places where Indians could be isolated from the requirements of civilization. But speedily, as settlers encircled the reservations, the Anglo-Americans also began to think of themselves as bearers of civilization. They identified civilization with the American variety of the English language, the agricultural technology of the United States at that time, elementary schools with religious instruction, the holding of land by individual title, and usually some one of the Protestant varieties of Christianity. It was by no means the case that they regarded representative, constitutional forms of political organization as an essential of civilization; at least they did not systematically introduce their form of government among Indians until more than a half century later.

It is apparent that the changes in Indian cultures attempted successively by the three dominant peoples differed in important ways. It is doubtful that the Anglo-Americans would have considered the Spanish program as a truly civilizing one, and vice versa. Yet the members of each group spoke repeatedly of themselves as bringers of civilization and justified most of their actions towards Indians on that basis.

The fact is, however, that these efforts did bring civilization to the Indians, even if the ethnocentrically oriented bearers of civilization differed among themselves as to its nature. Spanish culture was not in itself civilization, but it was nevertheless a civilized Western culture. It was a culture which made use of writing and was in process of being secularized as a result of that revolution in communication which we know as literacy; and this literacy, however reluctantly and imperfectly, was transmitted partially to the Indians. Spanish culture was one in which the specialization of labor, and therefore the differentiation of social roles, had been carried as far as in any culture in the world of the sixteenth and seventeenth centuries; and Spaniards made some effort to introduce their craft and governmental specialties. It was also a culture which had carried the supremacy of the state over the family even further than had Rome, and thereby had begun the release of the individual from the limited sphere of kinship status to the vastly expanded role of citizen. Moreover, Spain was a nation whose experience had acquainted her vividly with the possibility of variety in religious belief, and thus her tradition embodied, if her rulers did not officially accept, that heterogeneity of thought and practice which characterizes civilization. In these respects, Spanish culture had elements of civilization, and Spaniards whether they realized it or not brought civilization to the Indians.

The Spaniards, however, did little more than lay the foundations. To the extent that they introduced a new religion among the many religions of the Indians of northwestern New Spain, to the extent that they introduced some conception of a wider state organization, to the extent that they introduced new occupations such as metalworking and animal husbandry, to the extent that they introduced a small measure of literacy — they brought civilization. But by the time the Spaniards had spent their conquering energy in the late 1700's, many Indians of the region still had only the barest acquaintance with these things, and the great majority had embraced them either not at all or in a very partial and tentative fashion. The civilizing of the Indians, in the sense that we have defined that process, was well started, but two hundred years of contacts with the Spaniards had brought nothing like the almost immediate transformation which missionaries and government officials seemed to expect.

It remained for the successors of the Spaniards to carry the process further. The Mexicans appear to have had a conception of civilization closer to the one we have suggested. They dreamed, at least, of a scheme for making Indians literate, and urged, in the new laws of the states of Sonora and Chihuahua, the formation of schools in the Indian villages. They sought immediately to impose representative government and to make the Indians functioning citizens of the new national system. They were content to let Roman Catholicism assume whatever place it could in the national growth and they made no systematic effort to revitalize the missionary program of the Spaniards. But the Mexicans had no economic means, for over a hundred years, either for industrializing Indian life, or for making their literacy program effective. In these respects, until the twentieth century was well advanced, the mission for civilizing the Indians was carried no further than Spain had carried it. Moreover, the means that the Mexicans employed for integrating Indians into the state for the most part aroused resistance. As the Mexicans resorted to force, they defeated their own ends, and their program for political integration largely failed. It was not until the 1930's that the Mexicans introduced a further element of civilization into their program for changing the Indians, namely, the freedom to choose from among a variety of alternative courses. As this was introduced into government plans for education and economic development among the Tarahumara Indians in Chihuahua, the process of civilizing the Indians took on a new character. But meanwhile force had stimulated counter-processes and the direction of cultural change became uncertain.

The Anglo-Americans, after a slow start complicated by the necessity for completing the conquest of the Navajos, Apaches, and Yuman-speaking tribes which neither Spain nor Mexico had been able to dominate, began after 1870 to put into operation their conception of the civilizing process. Much later than the Mexicans they conceived of literacy as an essential element in this process, but because of more means for doing so put a school program into operation some fifty years earlier than the Mexicans. They also undertook much sooner than the Mexicans to introduce economic specialization and technological improvement into Indian life, including craft and trades training in their earliest schools. It is true that little was accomplished for a long time in relating such training to the social roles of Indian children, but economic elements of civilization were thus nevertheless introduced. The Anglo-Americans further showed some insight into the process of civilization in not imposing a single set of religious beliefs and practices. Nevertheless, even though they permitted the Indians enrolled in the schools some degree of choice among the various Christian denominations, until the 1930's they sought to suppress Indian religions. Yet with this apparent insight into the economic, communicative, and even to some extent religious aspects of civilization, the Anglo-Americans maintained one peculiar blind spot. In an area where one would expect that their culture would have influenced them otherwise, the government officials in charge of Indian affairs continued until the 1930's without any effective program for the development of national citizenship among Indians. The process of political integration remained suspended, even after a beginning was made in the 1930's. Thus, after four hundred years, the Anglo-Americans as well as the Mexicans, and like the Spaniards before them, had still not carried through their mission as they saw it.

Many cultural changes had taken place. Undeniably the condition of civilization, as we have defined it, had increased among the Indians of the region. But the expectations of the invaders were not realized. Indian cultures did not disappear through replacement by Spanish, Mexican, or Anglo-American cultures. In the sense that the programs of the invaders did not produce the results expected, they failed; but in the sense that these programs set in motion the processes of civilization, they did not fail. Even though complete cultural conquest was not achieved by the three successive invasions, cultural growth nevertheless went on apace. It was continuing in a milieu of cultural frontiers and heterogeneity, not in one of cultural unity as the first Spaniards to enter the region had hoped.

To some extent the causes of what had happened lay in the nature of the invaders' own programs. These consisted of three distinct conceptions of what the Indians should become. They varied in intensity and in the means employed for bringing about the changes. The variety of approaches could hardly have been expected to produce uniformity of results. Moreover, the Indians on whom the invaders had expected to impose their varied programs of change were not culturally identical peoples.

THE INDIANS OF NORTHWESTERN NEW SPAIN IN 1600

GENERAL CHARACTERISTICS — The people of this region were as varied in their ways of life as the face of the rugged and desert land in which they lived. Yet there was a general similarity. Their houses ranged from the simplest of brush shelters to masonry-walled apartment buildings. Their gods varied from ill-defined animal spirits to organized companies of beneficent ancestral deities. Their languages presented a dismaying diversity to the Spaniards. What they had in common was a level of economic and political development which marked them off from the Indians of central Mexico.

It quickly became apparent to the northward-pushing Conquistadores that they had here entered a different cultural world from the Aztec-dominated one which they had first encountered in Mexico. Coronado, in his search for the Seven Golden Cities of Cibola, was responsible for the first clear account of its extent after his fifteen hundred-mile journey in 1540. Systematic exploration began, however, from Zacatecas three hundred miles northwest of Mexico City. Here Spaniards opened a spectacular silver mine in 1546. Swinging out in wider and wider arcs from Zacatecas, missionaries and prospectors steadily became aware that the Indians to the northwest had built up no empires comparable to those of the Aztecs and Tarascans to the south. As they came to know these people of simpler culture better, they could distinguish them on many counts from neighboring peoples. It became clear that they constituted a cultural region of their own, bounded roughly on the east by the upper Rio Grande River system and on the north and west by the San Juan and Colorado rivers.

The family resemblance of the Indians of this region rested chiefly on their common practice of agriculture. All but a few hundred people on the coast of the Gulf of California and some others at the north end of the Sierra Madre Mountains had knowledge of domestic plants and raised at least the native American staples: corn, beans, and squash. They differed in the extent to which they relied on these crops and consequently in the importance which they attached to farming as a way of life, but agriculture was definitely the hallmark of the overwhelming majority. It was this which distinguished them from the buffalo-hunting nomads of the Great Plains to the east, the seed-gatherers and rabbit-hunters of the basin and range country to the north, and the acorn-gatherers of California to the west. The practice of agriculture was also the one obvious cultural link which they shared with the Aztecs and other peoples of central Mexico.

They differed, however, from the Aztecs in the simplicity of their economy. Whether agriculture was merely a supplement to gathering and hunting or the primary basis of life, the economy of every group in the region was simple. Every community was self-sufficient, economically independent of every other community. There was trade, to be sure, which extended widely through the region, but there was no system of markets to encourage individual or areal specialization. The trade goods were rarely food or basic tools, but rather luxury and ceremonial items, such as paints, feathers, shells, semiprecious stones, and other unique products of localized areas. Rather than a regularized system of exchange of good products and handicrafts, trading was a small-scale and rather sporadic enterprise.

Accompanying this economic self-sufficiency of communities was a political self-sufficiency. With one possible and long-since-extinct exception in the Gila River Valley, the region had never known any state organization. No one of the Indian communities at the time of the Spanish entry maintained any military or administrative control over any other community. It is true that some who spoke the same dialect united for purposes of warfare, but such common action was temporary and the organization formed for fighting purposes dissolved when the fighting was over. Moreover, the kind of warfare indulged in did not involve conquest and subjugation of one group by another. Widely extended political organization and conquest were unknown institutions. It was a region of small, autonomous, local communities, economically and politically independent of one another. In these respects the Indians presented a quite different set of problems to the Spaniards than did those of central Mexico, where the existence of already developed states simplified conquest and subsequent cultural domination.

These general characteristics were common to people who otherwise differed from one another in many ways. Of these differences the Spaniards became increasingly aware. In the fifty years between 1533, when Diego de Guzmán the slave-raider penetrated as far north as the Yaqui River, and 1582, when Espejo the prospector visited the Indians of what later became central Arizona, the Spaniards made at least passing contact with most of the peoples of the region. It required another two hundred years, however, before the northwesternmost mission was planted on the Colorado River and before it could be said that

Spanish exploration had revealed with much clarity the locations of all the inhabitants of the vast area. During this period of scores of exploratory expeditions and the growth of communication lines in many directions across the region, the Spaniards came to distinguish at least forty-five different groups of Indians for whom they employed distinct names.

The fact that Spaniards found it convenient to use such a large number of names for reporting on and dealing with the Indians was some indication of the cultural variety which existed. One of the important and, to the Spaniards, frustrating differences was in regard to language. Moving northward from group to group, trying at first to use interpreters who spoke Aztec, the Spaniards found that communication depended on acquaintance with a whole series of Indian languages. In the south as they moved up through the Sierra Madre Mountains and out into the deserts of the west, they learned that there were six major languages spoken within the areas of modern Chihuahua and Sonora. For these they adopted names: Tarahumara, Concho, Opata, Pima, Cahita, and Seri. They were mutually unintelligible and, moreover, there were several dialects of each, often also mutually unintelligible.

Key to Map on Page 11

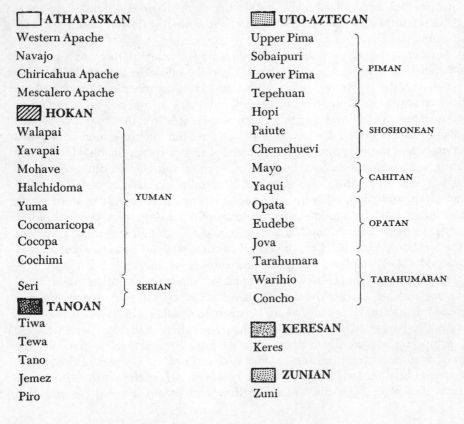

☐ ATHAPASKAN
Western Apache
Navajo
Chiricahua Apache
Mescalero Apache

▨ HOKAN
Walapai ⎤
Yavapai ⎟
Mohave ⎟
Halchidoma ⎬ YUMAN
Yuma ⎟
Cocomaricopa ⎟
Cocopa ⎟
Cochimi ⎦

Seri ⎫ SERIAN
▓ TANOAN ⎭
Tiwa
Tewa
Tano
Jemez
Piro

▨ UTO-AZTECAN
Upper Pima ⎤
Sobaipuri ⎟ PIMAN
Lower Pima ⎬
Tepehuan ⎦
Hopi ⎤
Paiute ⎬ SHOSHONEAN
Chemehuevi ⎦
Mayo ⎫ CAHITAN
Yaqui ⎭
Opata ⎤
Eudebe ⎬ OPATAN
Jova ⎦
Tarahumara ⎤
Warihio ⎬ TARAHUMARAN
Concho ⎦

▓ KERESAN
Keres

▨ ZUNIAN
Zuni

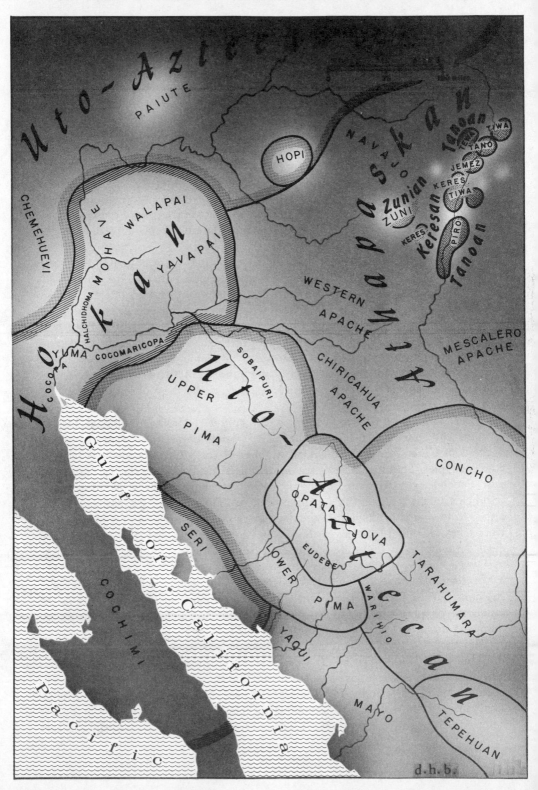

The situation was even more complicated in the area now comprising New Mexico and Arizona. Eventually the Spaniards identified some fourteen different languages there which they called Piro, Tiwa, Tewa, Keres, Jemez, Zuni, Moqui, Navajo, Apache, Maricopa, Yuma, Mohave, Yavapai, and Walapai, plus some others which soon became extinct. Most of these, too, had dialect divisions.

Much later, linguists discovered that many of these languages were related to one another and that only three distinct language families were represented. These relationships were of no significance, however, from the point of view of the Spaniards. They were concerned with establishing some kind of working relationships with people who spoke some twenty different languages and among whom there was no lingua franca.

The Indians also differed with respect to their economies, ranging from those who did no farming to those for whom the planting and raising of crops was the very focus of life and religion. There were four different types of economy.

THE RANCHERÍA PEOPLES — The great majority of people of the region in the early 1600's were called by the Spaniards "ranchería" people. That is, they had fixed points of settlement and were not free rovers, but their settlements or "rancherías" were not compact and closely built. Houses were scattered as much as a half mile apart, and the group occupying the scattered houses often shifted from one ranchería location to another in the course of the year. The ranchería peoples were all agriculturalists and for them farming was a major activity. Three-quarters of all the Indians in the region, or nearly one hundred fifty thousand, were ranchería farmers. However, to list them all together in this way obscures some important differences.

Most of the ranchería peoples spoke languages which belonged to the Uto-Aztecan stock, and it may be said that the dominant culture patterns of the Indians of Chihuahua and Sonora were those of the Uto-Aztecan-speaking ranchería peoples. There were three major groups. In the east were the Tarahumaras and Conchos who lived in the highlands of the Sierra Madres, planting small cornfields in the summer on the ridges and in mountain valleys, and retreating either to lowlands or down into the deep gorges during the severe winters. They were scattered widely over a very large area and lived in shelters that ranged from cave excavations in the cliffs of gorges to stone masonry houses. Despite such variations, however, these peoples had fairly uniform culture patterns, including as most distinctive very widely dispersed settlements and influential individual shamans, rather than priests, as the important religious leaders. Like the other ranchería peoples, the Tarahumaras relied almost as much on wild foods as on domestic crops, yet agriculture was basic and important in their lives.

Farther west, and ranging in an irregular belt from the high Sierras through the valleys of Sonora up into the deserts of southwestern Arizona lived other ranchería peoples, who spoke dialects of the Uto-Aztecan language of Piman, not mutually intelligible with Tarahumaras. Piman settlements were a little more compact than those of the Tarahumara; but many Pimans moved from mountain villages in the winter to valley settlements for the raising of corn, squash, and beans in the summer. They, too, had shamans rather than priests and in most respects were otherwise like the Tarahumaras. It might be said that they represented an adaptation of the same culture pattern to a mode of living somewhat more town-like, but they were still far from being subject to classification as a town-dwelling people.

Still farther along this continuum toward town-like settlements were the people of southern Sonora, and those parts of central Sonora not occupied by the Pimans — in the south the Cahitans, and north of them the Opatans, both groups speaking Uto-Aztecan languages. The Cahitans, comprising such tribes as the Mayos and Yaquis, lived near the mouths of large rivers where the water supply was regular and abundant. Favorable agricultural conditions permitted and encouraged somewhat more concentrated settlements than did the dry-farming country of the Tarahumaras or the more desert country of many of the Pimans. (However, some Pimas lived under very similar conditions in certain areas, as on the Gila and its tributaries in what became southern Arizona.) In fact, insofar as settlement pattern and concentration of population went, there was probably an equal range among Piman, Cahitan, and Opatan. It was merely that the Cahitans and some Opatans had more large rancherías concentrated in less space than the Pimans. The density of Cahitan population was such that they developed tribal organization for warfare, embracing all the rancherías of a tribe. This wider integration for war purposes and the somewhat denser and more compact settlements were accompanied by permanent, organized ceremonial groups. The presence of these groups added another aspect to religious life besides that of the shamanistic and gave rise to at least rudimentary forms of priesthood. Thus the Uto-Aztecan-speaking ranchería tribes constituted peoples with similar economies, but with a considerable range in type of community structure.

To the northwest were other ranchería peoples. Their language belonged to a totally different stock — Hokan. They constituted a range comparable to that of the Pimas, but seem not to have developed communities as large or as concentrated as the Opatans or Cahitans, despite the fact that many of them lived along the constantly flowing waters of the lower Colorado River. The Yumans, as this branch of the Hokan speakers came to be called, differed from the Piman ranchería peoples chiefly in that they habitually organized themselves as total tribal units for warfare. Despite the strong tribal feeling among the Yumans, tribal organization did not exist, save for warfare, however, and there were no settlements so large or so dense as those of the Yaquis and Mayos. They relied more heavily on wild foods than the Pimans, but in other respects their culture resembled in its greater simplicity that of the Pimans rather than the Cahitans.

These four sub-types of the ranchería peoples constituted the bulk of all the people in the region with whom the Spaniards had to deal. Situated along river bottoms or in well watered mountain areas, their lands had the greatest potential for agricultural development. Wherever the Spanish program of reduction, that is, concentration of people into towns around churches, was actually put into effect among them, they moved further than any other Indians of the region toward the acceptance of Spanish forms of religious and social life.

THE VILLAGE PEOPLES — The second major type of economy that existed in the region was that of intensive irrigated and dry farm agriculture, practiced by people living in very compact small villages. This was the economy of the Indians who lived along the Rio Grande River in New Mexico — the Eastern Pueblos — and on the great plateau drained by the Colorado River — the Western Pueblos. Already compact village dwellers, they provided no scope for the Spanish program of reduction. Their villages consisted of contiguous masonry or sun-dried mud houses in fixed locations. Each village was a tightly organized unit with an elaborate ceremonial life under the direction of priesthoods. There were probably not more than forty thousand people living under these conditions in the whole region when the Spaniards first began to establish colonies among them about 1600. Their similarity of way of life was not matched by similarity of language, since there was almost as much language diversity among them as among the whole one hundred fifty thousand of the ranchería peoples. In their villages seven distinct languages were spoken, about the same number as among the rancherías. Their role in the drama of cultural conflict and change which began to unfold after the Spanish arrival was one chiefly of a tenacious and, for the most part, passive resistance.

THE BAND PEOPLES — The third type of economic life which had evolved in the region was that of bands with no very fixed settlement locations. They practiced agriculture along with hunting and wild-food gathering, but for them agriculture was a relatively minor source of subsistence. These were the Athapaskan-speaking tribes of the northeast. After the arrival of the Spaniards they came to be called the Navajos and the Apaches. The Apaches ranged from nonagricultural groups like the Mescaleros and Chiricahuas of the east to bands of Western Apaches who, like the Navajos farther north, had given small-scale farming a secure, if subordinate, place in their economy. These bands had not long been residents of the region, but had been pushing southwestward since the 1300's. They were still in process of this migration when the Spaniards arrived, although probably by that time most of the Navajos and Western Apaches had identified themselves with particular localities over which they had ranged for some time. Some of these claimed territories were of very great extent. They usually were dotted with spots sacred to the bands which ranged them, and, rather than a fixed point of settlement, it was devotion to these places which gave the band its roots. All such localities were, seasonally and annually, temporary places of residence for these nomadic agriculturalists. There may have been as many as fifteen thousand people in these agricultural bands at the time the Spaniards arrived in the region. It was they more than any other groups whose way of life was most radically altered by Spanish contact.

NONAGRICULTURAL BANDS — The fourth economy of the region was nonagricultural. Based on simple utilization of wild foods, it was exceptional in the region and only a few thousand people existed at this level of economic development. The roving bands later known as the Seris, who roamed the coast of Sonora, were the principal nonagriculturalists. They hunted deer and rabbits, caught fish and sea turtles, and gathered the abundant cactus fruits, greens, and seaweed seeds of the desert coast and adjacent islands. The Spaniards could not conceive of "civilizing" them until they were brought in from the gulf and settled as farmers on an inland river. The Seris and the other nonagriculturalists were few in numbers and isolated from the main theaters of the expansion of Spanish life in the region, yet they played an important role in the complicated pattern of events in Sonora history.

Although three-fourths of these varied tribes maintained their identities during the 350 years following 1600, none did so without experiencing important changes in their ways of life. For a few, like the nomadic Seris, the changes consisted chiefly of the adoption of new tools for carrying on their fishing and hunting, while their social and religious life remained almost as it was when they first met Spaniards on the deserts of western Sonora. For many, such as the Yaquis in the fertile river lands of southern Sonora, the whole structure of their society as well as their world of religious belief was transformed into something new, so that a Yaqui of 1600 would have had to undergo an intensive period of re-education in order to live comfortably with Yaquis of 1950. For still others, like the Eastern Pueblos in their well organized little villages along the Rio Grande, the considerable changes in their tools and village organization seemed to result in no basic alteration in way of life. They gave the appearance of a peculiar stability in the midst of the successive changes around them.

There was no single, uniform pattern in the way the cultures changed or the way the people preserved their identities. Nevertheless in the various reactions to the programs for civilizing them, one could see a few general patterns not unique to Indians but to be found also among other peoples enclaved by Western nations.

REACTIONS TO CONQUEST

In the 1950's, a quarter of a century after the last Indian uprising, the prevailing views among white men of the region in both Mexico and the United States, insofar as they were conscious at all of the Indian population, were that complete submergence was only a matter of time and that Indians were a pitiable people meriting help in their inevitable progress toward cultural assimilation.

The long struggle of nearly every Indian group for self-determination had been largely forgotten. Some romantic memory of the last phases of the Apache wars was kept alive by popular and historical writers in the United States, and the Yaqui wars were recent enough to have left an aftermath of bitterness and hatred among old families of Sonora. But on the whole the White population was relatively new and had not experienced the hostility of the Indians. Since little or nothing of Indian history was taught in either the Mexican or the United States schools, Whites knew Indians only in the short perspective of current contacts. It would have been a great surprise to all but scholars to learn that those Indians whose reputation for peacefulness was widely accepted, such as the "industrious" Pueblos of New Mexico, the "gentle" Papagos of Arizona, and the "peaceful" Mayos of Sonora, had waged war against the Whites as bitterly, if not so successfully, as the Apaches and the Yaquis.

Probably the easiest generalization to make which would apply to all the Indians of the region is that all offered resistance, and at some time fought to maintain their independence of White domination. It is true that among surviving groups the Arizona Pimas had no record of ever having fought the Spaniards, the Mexicans, or the Anglos. But the so-called "Pimas" were the descendants of one small local segment of the widespread Upper Pimas; and the Upper Pimas had attempted in 1751, and before, to fight off the control of the Spaniards. Again, those Indians known as the Havasupai seem not to have taken up arms against Whites, but they too were a small segment of the upland Yuman-speaking peoples who, as Walapais and Yavapais, had their record of armed resistance to the Anglos. Even the Hopis of northern Arizona, who maintained in the 1950's that their native religion forbade war, had participated in the Pueblo Indian Rebellion of 1680, killing the missionaries assigned to them, as well as many converted Hopis. Further, in the 1890's, they certainly offered physical, if not armed, resistance to the Anglo-American efforts to take their children forcibly to boarding schools.

Although direct resistance was a universal reaction to contact with the Whites, it did not always come first. There were many tribes whose first reaction was one of friendly curiosity and there were others who sought the advantage of alliance with the Spaniards, or later with Anglo-Americans, against Indian enemies. In fact, a majority of the Indian groups offered no initial resistance to the Spaniards. The most general pattern consisted of three phases: an early period of friendly relations, during which the Spaniards established themselves in presidio and mission; then a brief violent outbreak against the controls set up, followed, in a greater or less period of time, by Spanish demonstration of their full military power; and finally, acceptance of domination. This pattern was repeated again and again in the region throughout the period of Spanish control. With some tribes, such as the Tarahumaras who were scattered widely over the Sierra Madre highlands, a single demonstration of Spanish military force was not sufficient and the subjugation efforts were repeated periodically over as much as a century. In most cases, once revolt flared up the Spaniards retaliated with sufficient ruthlessness so that, even though a number of years were required for restoration of peace, Indians were convinced of the futility of further armed resistance.

Following the capitulation to armed force, the immensely varied reactions of the Indians to White contact began to take shape. No two groups seemed to follow the same course of adjustment to the programs for change which Spain and the later nations put into effect. While the Opata Indians of central Sonora almost immediately intermingled and intermarried with Spanish settlers, and as a result adopted Spanish ways, the Pueblo Indians of New Mexico devised means for fending off the Spanish contacts, continuing to move in the old ways with as little influence as possible from the invaders. Between these extremes there were a dozen different kinds of response. For some, geographical isolation fostered independent development; for others, close association with the newcomers fostered an antipathy and consequent social isolation which had almost the same effects. The differences in the results of contact could not be explained by any simple formula.

The causes for the diversity of reactions were many. To understand them it is necessary to trace the history of each tribe in an attempt to see the connections between the conditions of contact and the patterns of response. It is also necessary to keep in mind the differences between the programs of the dominant societies. We shall examine the Spanish program and the reactions to it first, and then the later Mexican and Anglo programs and reactions to them. However, we shall endeavor to keep the whole of the Southwest in view, and thus to understand the cultural history of the region in the light of the whole set of circumstances touched off by the Spanish Conquest.

PART I

THE EVENTS OF CONTACT:
SPANISH-INDIAN RELATIONS

Introduction

THE EXPANSION of Spain in the New World, like the expansion of other European nations in the Americas, Africa, and Asia, is a series of events the record of which will remain forever incomplete. No amount of inference from the meager facts recorded can ever establish the full nature of the events. It is not that there was any lack of European commentators—there were many. But the natives of the invaded regions were not literate people, and therefore what they thought and said about what was happening to them was never adequately recorded. Especially in the earlier periods, there are no accounts by natives of their reactions to the contacts with the invaders. It is true that the words of some native leaders and occasionally even the comments of some common man were set down, but the recording was done by Europeans and the accounts thus bear the mark of European interpretation. Again and again, what purports to be a record of the native viewpoint is actually what the European writers thought the natives were thinking.

This situation prevails in the records of contacts in the region with which this volume is concerned. It was a rare Spanish chronicler who was equipped for the exacting task of even moderately objective reporting. Although often sympathetic, Spanish accounts have the inevitable bias of writers from one culture looking through the barriers of language and cultural difference at the members of another. There is no way in which this bias can be corrected. Thus, it is when the question is raised as to what Indians thought about Spaniards and Spanish culture that the great void in the record appears. This void seriously impairs our understanding of these instances of human development.

It is especially in the earliest phases of contact that the record is so one-sided. One searches in vain for records of the Indians' first impressions of the Spaniards to match the Spaniards' first impressions of the Indians. As the contacts continued, some Spaniards learned something about the Indians, but even so they rarely recorded much more than descriptions of externals such as clothing and the reactions to Spanish behavior — which were usually mistaken for normal Indian behavior. Fortunately, however, some Indians appeared in court — either to testify against some missionary on charges of mistreatment of Indians, to answer for themselves on charges of insubordination or insurrection, to testify against some civil governor on charges brought against him by the missionaries, or on some other account. Insofar as the northwest of New Spain is concerned, it is almost entirely in such court records that the authentic voices of the Indians are heard. However, this setting is so alien, so framed in terms of Spanish culture, that often too little that is revealing emerges. Indeed, until well into the nineteenth century the records are nearly mute on the subject of Indian viewpoints and feelings about the transformation being wrought in their lives.

The names of a few distinguished Indians were recorded, and occasionally a writer attempted a sympathetic appraisal — such as Andrés Pérez de Ribas' remarkable sketch of the Opata leader Sisibotari. But for the most part there is really no history of the Indians, only the history of the Spaniards in their contacts with the Indians. Through a glass darkly, something — and probably the main outline — of what was taking place can be discerned. However, insofar as the Indians are concerned, it is history without letters written by the principals, without a single state document, without diaries, notebooks, newspapers, or memorandums! Only the last hundred years of our epoch can be regarded as providing records for Indian life in any way comparable to those for the history of the invaders.

There is little that can be done to correct the lens, but at least it can be kept in mind that there is a distortion. Nothing brings the fact home more definitely than to remember that none of the major tribes enters or maintains a place in history under its own name. The names used are misnomers of one sort or another bestowed by Spaniard or Anglo-American. Even the villages of the Pueblo Indians, where one might have expected the invaders to adopt the native place names, were renamed or, with one or two exceptions, inaccurately recorded.

It is in full recognition of the fact that the information about the Indians themselves is secondhand and terribly biased that the exposition of the "history" of the contacts of the Indians of northwestern New Spain with the Spaniards is undertaken in the pages which follow.

The history of Indian-Spanish contacts presented here opens in the last decade of the 1500's. Sixty years have elapsed since Coronado's journey of exploration and his harsh subjection of the Indians on the Rio Grande River. In the intervening time the explorations of Francisco de Ibarra and many others made it clear both that there were enough Indians in the northwest to make it worthwhile for the missionaries to go among them and also that there was enough silver (if nothing much else in the way of natural resources) to make it worth the while of some adventurers and non-ecclesiastical persons. From Zacatecas, since the discovery of silver there in 1546, missionaries and miners moved out and settled in the Indian country. From Compostela and Culiacán, missionaries and soldiers moved slowly up the west coast, establishing presidios and missions as they progressed from tribe to tribe. The Jesuit order of missionaries arrived in Mexico in the 1570's and began to carve out for itself the region of northwestern New Spain as its special field of mission work. In twenty-five years Jesuits became well established among Indians of the southern Sierra Madre Mountains

Tribal Name

as known in historical writing	*as used by members of tribe*
TARAHUMARA	RARÁMURI
MAYO	YOREME
YAQUI	YOEME
OPATA	TEWIMA, HEVE
SERI	KUNKAAK
PIMA	O-OTAM
PAPAGO	TOHONO O-OTAM
NAVAJO	DINÉH
APACHE	NDE
ZUNI	ÁSHIWI
MOQUI, HOPI	HOPITUH
HAVASUPAI	PAI
HUALAPAI	PAI
YAVAPAI	YAWEPE, TOLKEPAYA
MARICOPA	PIPAI
MOHAVE	HAMAKAVA
YUMA	KWATSHAN
PUEBLOS	(No corresponding general term)

Pueblo Village Name

TAOS	TEOTHO
PICURIS	PICURIA
SANDIA	NAFIAT
ISLETA	TUEI
SAN JUAN	OKEH
SANTA CLARA	XAPOGEH
SAN ILDEFONSO	POXWOGEH
NAMBÉ	NAMBE'E
TESUQUE	TETSUGEH
JEMEZ	WALATOWA
COCHITI	KOCHITI
SANTA DOMINGO	KIUA
SAN FELIPE	KATISHTYA
SANTA ANA	TANAYA
ZIA	TSEYA
LAGUNA	KAWAIK
ACOMA	AKÓME

as far north as the border of the present state of Chihuahua. This region was christened New Biscay, the northernmost province of Spain in the New World. A whole line of silver lodes was discovered on the eastern side of the Sierra Madres, extending from Zacatecas through a dozen smaller mines to Durango and finally to Santa Barbara.

The Indian tribes between had been defeated or frightened into subjection and were steadily being placed under missionary tutelage. The Jesuits established themselves solidly, as they believed, among the Tepehuanes and were beginning to plan their movement into the country of the Tarahumaras whose land bordered the Tepehuanes on the north. This was their farthest advance by 1600 in the mountain country of New Biscay. On the coast an able military man, Captain Diego de Hurdaide, made his way with firmness and the sword northward to the Sinaloa River, and built there a Spanish capital town. His plan was to work out among the usually initially hostile Indians of the region from this headquarters, paving the way for the missionaries who were avid for new missions. Hurdaide as protector of the Jesuits was regarded with immense esteem by them; his zeal matched their own as he pursued a vigorous campaign for the continued advance of sword and cross into the territory that was beginning to be called Sonora. Thus the Jesuits, well-provided with military protection, were pushing on beyond their mountain missions west of Durango into the dimly known areas of northern New Biscay and Sonora.

Meanwhile, in 1598, in contrast with the Jesuit advance from tribe to tribe, a leap was made over the unknown territory and undominated peoples between Durango and "Tiguex," the site of Coronado's winter encampment in 1540-41. Juan de Oñate and three hundred colonists, adequately protected with soldiers and accompanied by a few Franciscan missionaries, set out to establish themselves on the Rio Grande in what soon became known as New Mexico. Thus, two frontiers were in process of development at about the same time, one in the south where the missionary side of the Spanish advance was under the direction of the Jesuits, and one in the north where the Franciscans commanded the missions.

CHAPTER ONE

Tarahumaras

AFTER A PEACEFUL MEETING with eight hundred Indians in a valley of the Sierra Madre Mountains in what is now southwestern Chihuahua, the first missionary to make real working contact with the Tarahumaras said: "I am in a happy and enthusiastic state of mind, seeing the door now opened to us for numerous conversions, especially since these developments can go forward without the aid of captain and soldiers." The name of the young missionary was Juan Fonte. The meeting which so inspired him took place in 1607.

Fonte was enthusiastic at the prospect his own initiative had opened out before the Jesuits advancing northward from Durango — the peaceful conversion of a tribe later determined to consist of more than twenty thousand persons. Tarahumara leaders had invited him to come, evidently sincerely interested in Jesuit teaching and practice. Fonte responded with great vigor and went to work in accordance with the Indian vision of peaceful unfoldment of a new way of life. Yet this idyllic beginning gave way to something quite different. The next hundred years were interspersed with some of the bloodiest native revolts and Spanish reprisals ever to take place on the northwestern border of New Spain. It was not for a century that Spaniards could proclaim the Tarahumara country effectively subjected to their political control. And a bare ten years after he had laid the foundations for the Jesuit advance Father Fonte himself was killed by Indians thought to have been well Christianized.

The place where Fonte met with the group of Tarahumaras was a valley the Spaniards had named the San Pablo, some thirty miles west from the mining town of Santa Barbara. It was here between 1608 and 1616 that Fonte with a co-worker steadily built up a number of Indian communities centering about a church which was christened San Pablo Ballesa. The area had been a sort of no man's land between two tribes — the Tepehuanes on the south and the Tarahumaras on the north. Traditional hostility had resulted in fighting here to the extent of interfering with settled community life. Fonte came as a peacemaker with some ten years of experience in the Tepehuan missions and sponsorship by leaders of both tribes. As the intertribal warfare subsided, his efforts resulted in colonization of the valley by both tribes and the growth of a prosperous mission.

With Fonte's venture the mission frontier was advanced to correspond with the mining frontier of the Spaniards. Forty years before his arrival in the San Pablo Valley, silver lodes were discovered at a place named Santa Barbara. Miners promptly pushed into the area some five hundred miles beyond Durango; but the mission frontier advanced more slowly. The Jesuits did not begin to work until the 1590's among the Tepehuan Indians, who occupied an extensive area of the Sierra Madre Mountains northwest of Durango. They did not complete their missionization of the Tepehuanes until about the time of Fonte's entrance among the Tarahumaras. At the same time Franciscan missionaries were at work east of the mountains, extending their missions into the country of the Conchos north of Santa Barbara. Some Conchos, as well as Tepehuanes and Tarahumaras, were attracted to the Jesuit mission and villages of the San Pablo Valley, thus making the area much mixed tribally.

The efforts of the missionaries here, as elsewhere in New Spain, were directed toward the "reduction" of the Indians, that is, their concentration into compact settlements centered about mission churches. The Tarahumaras, like the Tepehuanes, were not accustomed to living in compact communities. They raised corn, beans, and squash and relied heavily on their cultivated foods, but their dwellings were widely scattered, houses of the same community sometimes being as much as a half mile apart. Moreover, many groups of Tarahumaras moved their settlements seasonally from field areas on high ground in summer to protected canyon sites in winter. Their basic community pattern which the Spaniards called "ranchería" therefore offered a great obstacle to the missionaries focused on reduction. If the Tarahumaras were fully to accept missionary leadership, it meant not only a replacement of beliefs about the spiritual world but also a thoroughgoing reorganization of family, neighborhood, and community life. The initial success of Fonte's activity seems to have been related to the fact that he was working in an area where traditional ways had been upset as a result of intertribal warfare. It appears that hundreds of Indians of the three neighboring tribes welcomed the opportunity to settle peacefully where they could farm more intensively, learn the new art of raising sheep and cattle, and listen to the preachers of a different way of life.

However, in 1616 the steady growth of the San Pablo settlements was interrupted. There had been some signs of discontent before. These were reported by Fonte as the sort of hostility which the missionaries very commonly encountered, namely, the opposition of "witches." The missionaries, whose belief in black magic was often as strong as that of the Indians, consistently referred to all types of Indian religious leaders as witches. This was probably a result of the belief that religious practices other than Christian had their source in the Devil and were therefore to be regarded as black magic. Thus, at San Pablo there were several instances of opposition to the work of Fonte and his assistant which were reported as "witch"–inspired. The mildness of this opposition was no adequate warning of the storm which broke in 1616. This was the great Tepehuan rebellion. For two years fighting raged in Tepehuan territory, resulting in the killing of several hundred Spaniards and at least a thousand Indians. Among those who lost their

3. TARAHUMARA COUNTRY ABOUT 1700

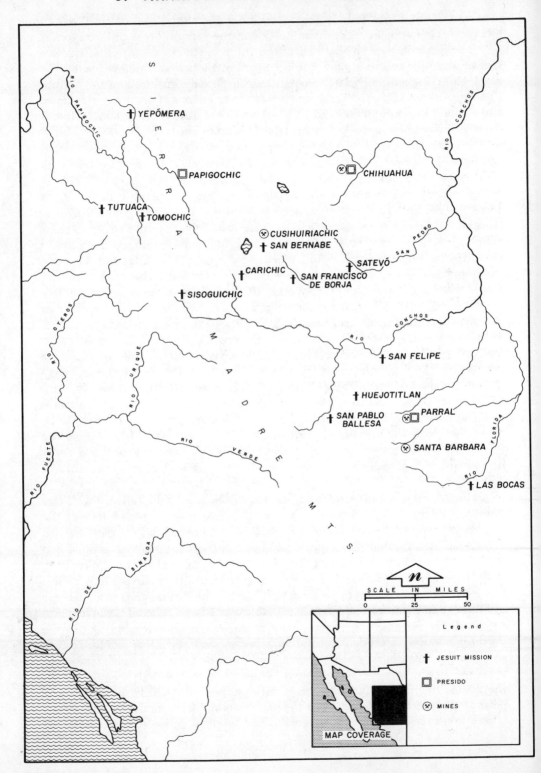

YEPÓMERA

PAPIGOCHIC

CHIHUAHUA

TUTUACA
TOMOCHIC

CUSIHUIRIACHIC
SAN BERNABE

SATEVÓ

CARICHIC
SAN FRANCISCO
DE BORJA

SISOGUICHIC

SAN FELIPE

HUEJOTITLAN

SAN PABLO
BALLESA   PARRAL

SANTA BARBARA

LAS BOCAS

SIERRA

MADRE

MTS

RIO PAPIGOCHIC
RIO CONCHOS
SAN PEDRO
RIO CONCHOS
RIO OTEROS
RIO URIQUE
RIO FUERTE
RIO VERDE
RIO FLORIDA
RIO
RIO DE SINALOA

SCALE IN MILES
0   25   50

Legend

JESUIT MISSION

PRESIDIO

MINES

MAP COVERAGE

lives were Juan Fonte and his able aide Father Moranta, killed on their way to a church celebration at a Tepehuan mission at the very outbreak of the revolt.

The Tepehuan revolt was one of the three bloodiest and most destructive Indian attempts to throw off Spanish control in northwestern New Spain. The other two occurred much later among the Rio Grande Pueblos and the Yaquis. The Tepehuan revolt gave Tarahumaras direct experience of organized resistance and probably strongly influenced later events in the Tarahumara country. It was essentially a religious crusade, in which the Tepehuan leaders tried, unsuccessfully, to enlist the other tribes throughout the Sierra Madres and on the west coast. The major leader was a Tepehuan named Quautlatas. He sponsored a stone figure which spoke as a prophet of hope. The voice proclaimed that the people should not accept the missionaries' gods, but should return to a belief in the old gods and drive all Spaniards out of Tepehuan territory. The voice guaranteed that there would be no return of the Spaniards for it had the power to wreck all ships which might attempt to bring more. The stone figure also promised that anyone who died fighting Spaniards would come to life again. Quautlatas and the stone image inspired Tepehuanes over the whole range of their territory. An uprising was planned and carried out in November, 1616, resulting in the almost immediate wiping out of the four hundred or more Spaniards resident among the Tepehuanes at mission and mining centers including all but one of seven Jesuit missionaries. A well-known image of the Virgin Mary in the mission church of Zape was broken and disfigured. The Spanish reprisal was immediate but not fully effective for two years. Three expeditions of Spanish soldiers from Durango were necessary before Quautlatas, the religious leader, and Cogoxito, the last of the military leaders, were killed and no one was left to organize resistance. Even though military resistance ended by 1618 as a result of ruthless executions by the Spaniards, it was not until 1623 that the situation resembled what it had been before the revolt. By that time seven Jesuits had re-established themselves among the Tepehuanes and in that year the repaired image of the Virgin Mary was reinstalled at Zape.

Meanwhile missionary work had lapsed in the San Pablo Valley. Two Tarahumara leaders there had taken advantage of the unsettled conditions of the Tepehuan revolt to raid Spaniards at Santa Barbara. Beyond this the rebellion had not spread into Tarahumara country, and apparently the settlements around San Pablo Ballesa remained occupied. The situation began to change profoundly in 1631 when a new vast silver strike was made at Parral, thus moving the Spanish mining frontier northward beyond Santa Barbara. The Parral mines rivalled those of Durango in richness. The immediate result was a large influx of Spaniards into this southern margin of the Tarahumara country. With the development of the Parral mines arose a sudden demand for labor to work the mines and for food to support the steadily increasing population. Indians from everywhere adjacent were recruited, since the Negroes and Whites imported to Parral could not fill the needs. Forcible recruitment, or enslavement, of non-Christian Indians was permitted under Spanish law. Thus the unchristianized Tarahumaras, at this time a very great majority since Fonte's work had affected only a tiny proportion of the tribe, as well as the nomadic Tobosos and others to the east were fair game for the slavers. As haciendas and ranches began to grow up in the vicinity of Parral, "wild" Tarahumaras were hunted down in the mountains as laborers. The peaceful conditions which had dominated the period of growth of San Pablo Ballesa near the relatively sleepy Santa Barbara gave way to troublous times. Many Tarahumaras came voluntarily to work with other Christianized Indians from the West Coast in the mines of Parral, but at the same time Spaniards raided communities and sometimes under the pretense of taking them to mission schools kidnapped Tarahumara children to be brought up as servants. There were also abuses by the mine owners, who often required Indians to work for two months without pay, then to work for two more months to get the back pay.

The pressures on the Indians to adjust to the invaders' institutions steadily mounted. The Jesuits renewed their mission program in the 1630's, shortly after the Parral silver strike, and intensified it over the next two decades under the vigorous leadership of Fathers Pascual and Figueroa. The missionaries often stood as intermediaries between wronged Indians and the increasing Spanish population of the region; they generally took the part of the Indians in matters of forced labor, kidnapping, and mistreatment at the hands of the Spaniards. Yet, spokesmen for the Indians though they were, they too exerted their pressures for change and a new kind of work discipline. Figueroa became very active in developing the irrigation systems of the valleys in which the old and the new missions were established. The Jesuits extended the missions farther north to the Conchos River and beyond, outstripping in fact the mining frontier. By the middle of the 1640's they had set up four new and prosperous missions reaching fifty miles beyond San Pablo — Las Bocas, Huejotitlan, San Felipe, and Satevó. Hundreds of Tarahumaras were gathered around the missions and put to work digging the ditches and building the dams of the new irrigation systems and tending the herds of livestock. Almost four thousand Tarahumaras had been baptized. This extension of missions was confined to the lowland area of the Tarahumara territory paralleling the Sierra Madre Mountains. The missions with their associated villages were formally established as a new mission unit in the Jesuit chain and became known as Tarahumara Baja, or Lower Tarahumara. By 1646 there were five Jesuit missionaries at work in the new unit. At the same time mining activity was steadily expanding at Parral, where hundreds of Indians not only from the immediately surrounding area but also from Sinaloa were employed.

Tensions were building up to a climax and a new rebellion. The missionaries protested in vain against the forced labor in the mines and in the Spanish settlements. The population of the newly missionized region began to decline, in some part as a result of disease, in far greater part as a result of Indian desire to escape the working conditions imposed by the Spaniards — missionaries and secular employers alike. Dissatisfied Tarahumaras left the settlements of the Lower Tarahumara and returned, or went as new residents, to the mountain country. Indians who had been converted turned anti-Christian and anti-Spanish. The problems of "apostate" Tarahumaras bitterly opposed to everything the Spaniards had introduced became serious. Apostates gave leadership among the still isolated Indians for resistance to the establishment of both mines and missions in their territory. The Tobosos to the east, who had not been successfully missionized by the Franciscans, raided and harassed the hitherto prospering missions and ranches. Accusations by missionaries on the one hand and settlers on the other increased against the governor of New Biscay for his abetting and condoning mistreatment of Indians in the mines, and for his ineffective efforts to control the Toboso raiders.

In 1648 Indians of various tribes, including reportedly one hundred from Sinaloa, organized a rebellion in the little Tarahumara community of Fariagic southwest of Parral. Under the leadership of four men, probably of several different tribes, hundreds of Indians, including principally Tarahumaras, moved northward apparently with the objective of attacking the new line of missions. Except for the destruction of San Francisco de Borja, the westernmost of the Jesuit establishments, little else was accomplished by the Indians. Soldiers from Durango immediately entered the field, captured two of the four leaders, executed them, and finally dispersed the rebels. Apparently the rebellion was poorly organized without general support among the Tarahumaras. Its major immediate effects were the extension of the line of Spanish presidios northward from Durango to Cerro Gordo, about fifty miles south of Parral, and the replacement of the vicious Valdés as governor of New Biscay.

The new governor Fajardo was intent on extending the province of New Biscay northward as a functioning political unit and apparently unaware of the dissatisfactions and hostility which had been building up among the Tarahumaras. Immediately after his quieting of the 1648 uprising, he provided for the establishment of a new villa, or Spanish town, almost in the heart of the still unmissionized highland portion of the Tarahumara country. At a place which he named Villa de Aguilar on one of the headwaters of the Yaqui River, which here reaches deep into Tarahumara territory, he set up a small garrison of soldiers and a number of Spanish settlers. The expectation was that this would grow as an important northern outpost of New Biscay. The secular frontier had now again outstripped the missionaries, but they were quick to respond and immediately made provision for the establishment of a missionary at a place called Papigochic, not far from Villa de Aguilar. There was probably no realization on the part of the governor or of Father Pascual, head of the Lower Tarahumara mission unit, that they had now moved into the midst of a hotbed of anti-Spanish feeling. Yet the founding of Villa de Aguilar almost immediately touched off another revolt.

The nature of the leadership of this revolt indicates much concerning the strains which had been set up among Tarahumaras. The Spaniards identified three men as the leaders of the early outbreaks—Don Diego, Yagunaque, and Tepórame. Not much is given concerning Don Diego, but it is clear that he was a product of the mission communities; he in fact had been given the surname of the Spanish captain who took the field against the Tarahumaras at the beginning of the revolt, namely, Juan de Barrasa. Yagunaque was well known to the Spaniards, but, at this point in his career, very unfavorably as an apostate. He had been a devout Christian, but had come to hate the missionaries and was known to have vowed death to the Jesuits and renounced the Christian God. He was representative of an increasing group among the Indians, those who had been drawn into the missions of Lower Tarahumara, but who had for a variety of reasons become bitterly antagonistic. Sometimes the cause was discipline for failure to attend Mass or the breaking of some other rule. Sometimes it was a serious injustice suffered at the hands of an employer. Quite often, it was the pull of relatives who withdrew from mission contact. Such apostates had been moving out of reach of Spanish control from the lowland to the highland country. The third reputed leader of the revolt was named Tepórame, or Tepóraca (there was disagreement among Jesuits and civil authorities concerning his name). He had acquired a Christian name, Gabriel, and was well known to the Spaniards with whom he had dealt on many friendly occasions. He was not described as an apostate, which probably means that in contrast with Yagunaque he had never publicly declared himself as opposed to Christian belief and the missionaries. The Spanish civil authorities had developed considerable respect for him as a reasonable man influential among highland Tarahumaras. The Jesuits were well aware of his exceptional oratorical abilities and the high regard in which these were held by Tarahumaras. It came as a surprise to the Spaniards to find him leading the revolt. Yet it was clear as the fighting intensified that he was the major leader.

The leadership, then, was not that of embattled tribal elders ignorant of what the Spaniards offered. The effective leadership consisted of men who knew in detail both the mission and secular sides of Spanish life. Tepórame had some degree of literacy. It should not be concluded, however, that men turned hostile to the Spaniards were the only leaders among the Tarahumaras. On the contrary, there were in the mission communities many who refused to support Tepórame and others like him. Thus, for example, the two communities of the missions of San Gerónimo (Huejotitlan) and San Felipe stood solidly against rebellious leaders and refused at any time to join the revolts. On the other hand, there was an influential man, Don Pablo, at the oldest of the Tarahumara missions — Ballesa — who did work for the revolt. There was another Don Pablo, however, who lived near Papigochic who helped the missionaries.

In short, one of the common results of the spread of Spanish civilization was fully apparent among the Tarahumaras less than fifty years after first contact. Factionalism within the tribe was well developed. A considerable portion of the people felt Spanish domination to be an issue and could be persuaded to fight for or against it. It is also clear, however, that anti-Spanish leadership was, and remained, quite unable to bring about more than a short-lived unity among Tarahumaras. All anti-Spanish leaders were constantly confronted by division of feeling among the Indians, and sooner or later faced betrayal by some of their own followers under the military pressure of the Spaniards.

Within a year after the founding of Villa de Aguilar relationships between the Spanish settlers and soldiers and the Tarahumaras in the vicinity were fraught with conflict. The Spaniards appropriated farming sites, assumed domineering attitudes over the Indians, and attempted to force Indians to work for them. The establishment of the Jesuit mission increased rather than eased tensions. The new missionary was identified, probably against his will, with the other Spaniards as he was embroiled in the local disputes, and equally with the settlers became an object of hostility and distrust to the Indians. A soldier lived with him for the purpose of protecting him. In 1650 the outbreak came. The missionary and his soldier protector were crucified, their bodies mutilated, and the church burned. Spaniards wherever they could be found were killed. The extreme mutilation of the body of the Jesuit was a good indication of the intensity of feeling which had been generated by this farthest intrusion into Tarahumara territory.

Soldiers from Parral under the command of the new governor halted the fighting in a matter of months, but only after they had pursued bands of Tarahumaras westward, fought bitterly with some, and laid waste to scores of rancherías. The governor of New Biscay made with some Tarahumaras what he understood as a treaty of peace. Villa de Aguilar was reoccupied and a new missionary was assigned to rebuild the mission of Papigochic.

However, the fighting had fanned hostility and the military invasion of Tarahumara territory had stimulated rather than broken resistance to Spanish control. As the Spaniards settled down in Villa de Aguilar again, anti-Spanish feeling smoldered among the Indians. The ablest leader — Tepórame — had not been captured and he set about organizing another attempt to eliminate Spaniards from Tarahumara territory.

There can be no doubt that the spearhead of the Spanish intrusion — Villa de Aguilar and its associated mission of Papigochic — had focused anti-Spanish feeling among the Tarahumaras. No longer diffuse and uncertain in their objectives, the followers of Tepórame saw Aguilar with its soldiers and land-appropriating settlers as a threat to their independence and way of life. They began to see a possibility of wiping out the Spanish settlement there and proceeding to the destruction of the Lower Tarahumara chain of missions. In 1652, barely a year after the re-establishment of the missionary at Papigochic the attempt was made. Again, the new missionary was immediately killed and the new chapel razed. Moreover, all those Christian converts who had settled at Papigochic were killed. This time the Indians were better organized and moved on to kill or chase away all the Spanish settlers around Villa de Aguilar. They continued their campaign eastward, attacking Satevó and trying desperately to persuade the Tarahumaras in the southern missions to join them. They were entirely unsuccessful in gaining this support, so that the hope of eliminating the Lower Tarahumara missions was not fulfilled. Nevertheless, a fighting contingent under Tepórame moved eastward and succeeded in laying waste seven Franciscan establishments among the Conchos, before Governor Fajardo in Parral was able to give battle. Then for nearly a year fighting continued as the Spanish soldiers and Indian allies pursued the rebels westward. Eventually the reported two thousand fighting men who supported Tepórame were whittled down and Fajardo's terms for peace, namely, the surrender of Tepórame for execution, were met. The third Tarahumara revolt was over and shorn of that part of its leadership known to the Spaniards. The Spaniards were again in control of the area, but their plan for a town in the heart of Tarahumara country was permanently given up. Villa de Aguilar was not resettled and the mission of Papigochic was abandoned.

The revolt of 1652 slowed down the missionary, as well as the civil, advance into Tarahumara territory. For twenty years the Jesuits contented themselves largely with the continued building up of the Lower Tarahumara missions. The herds of sheep, goats, cattle, and horses increased, and the surpluses produced were sold to the growing population of Parral and the other mining communities. The population of the five missions did not, however, increase. In 1666 and 1668 there were epidemics. Some damage was done by continuing raids from nomadic Indians to the east. While Franciscans entrenched themselves north of the Tarahumara country, as at Casas Grandes, the Jesuits undertook little but the exploration of the still unmissionized highland Tarahumara country.

It was not until 1673 that vigorous new action was taken. In that year a conference of Jesuits, Christian Tarahumaras, and the highest civil authorities at Parral considered the accomplishments to date and laid plans for advancing the Jesuit program further. Within a year two new missionaries had been secured and had established a new mission in the eastern margin'of the Upper Tarahumara country — the mission of San Bernabé near the ranchería of Cusihuiriachic. During the 1670's more Jesuits entered the field. By 1681 there were seven at work in the new highland Tarahumara mission unit. As the missionaries ranged more deeply westward into Tarahumara territory beyond Cusihuiriachic they encountered opposition. Especially at Carichic and Papigochic, where the last two rebellions had centered, they were met with deep hostility. Since they continued to talk with people and to preach, and since they proceeded to travel widely, as Fathers Tardá and Guadalajara did, without soldier escorts, they steadily gained acceptance. They also made use of a Tarahumara guide and interpreter, Don Pablo, who had been prominent as a supporter of the Jesuits in the 1673 conference at Parral. Fathers Tardá and Guadalajara explored the whole breadth of the Tarahumara country finding themselves received with friendly ceremony by Indians as remote as the ranchería of Tutuaca on the western margin of Tarahumara territory, where they were able to perform baptisms in 1676. There began to be requests for the Jesuits to come into the Jova country bordering the Tarahumaras on the west, and eventually a trail was established cutting east and west across the Sierra Madres and linking Lower Tarahumara with Sonora where missionaries were at work among the Opatas. Within less than fifteen years eight churches had been set up and some fourteen thousand Indians baptized in the Upper Tarahumara country. It had become a far larger and more active area of missionary accomplishment than Lower Tarahumara.

An era of peace prevailed from 1652 when Tepórame, the leader of the second and third rebellions, was executed to 1690 — a period of more than thirty years comparable to that between the Tepehuan revolt and the first Tarahumara rebellion. But now the full cycle was to repeat itself. Already in the 1670's at the time of the inauguration of the new Jesuit advance, disaffected Tarahumaras had begun to gather in the northern — as yet unmissionized — part of Tarahumara territory. This was in rugged country constituting the headwaters of the Yaqui River. Tarahumara apostates and other anti-Spanish leaders and families were here joined by Conchos and Indians from farther north who were in like manner opposed to the Spaniards as a result of their contacts in the Franciscan missions. Despite the Jesuit success in re-establishing themselves, in the early 1680's there were rumors of rebellion. Then in 1685 the Spanish miner-settler frontier again moved into the area of the new missions. Silver was discovered at Cusihuiriachic and the old phenomenon of the mining rush was repeated. Again conflicts between settlers and Indians arose as Spaniards moved into the Upper Tarahumara country. Anti-Spanish feeling began to center in the northern Tarahumara mission at Yepómera, and in 1690 a new rebellion was in full swing. It began, as usual, with the killing of the Jesuits stationed there and spread rapidly, as the Jova Indians joined, with the prompt killing of the missionary at Tutuaca. As in the days of the Tepehuan revolt, a belief was widespread among the Indians that one of their leaders had the power to make the Spanish guns useless in that any Indian killed by one would rise again in three days. Within the year troops to the number of two hundred arrived from Parral, met the Indians in open battle, killed their most prominent leader, and quieted the rebellion.

The next few years were peaceful on the surface, but the battles of 1690 were merely prelude to the most serious of all Tarahumara rebellions. The missions were re-established everywhere, even eventually at Tutuaca where hostility was persistent. A vigorous superior in the person of Father Neumann took charge of the Upper Tarahumara missions, and was himself stationed at Sisoguichic. The decade of the 1690's was destined to be a period of unrest. The eastern Indians, usually called Tobosos, raided the Tarahumara missions and the vicinity of Parral almost continuously. Epidemics of measles and smallpox broke out in 1693 and 1695. The stirrings of rebellion began to be definite after the last epidemic of smallpox. In Yepómera again and in Cocomórachic, not far to the southwest, where Lower Pimas, Tarahumaras, and Jovas bordered on one another, there began to develop open opposition to the missionaries and their teachings. Tara-humaras who had adopted the mission life began to revive old ceremonies. The belief was current that the church bells spread measles and smallpox. Various old men, as usual called witches by the Jesuits, began to preach open opposition to the missionaries. They advocated leaving the missions and returning to the old way of life in the scattered rancherías. A strong nativisitic movement had been stimulated, evidently closely connected with the hundreds of deaths resulting from the European diseases. The greatest strength of the movement seemed centered in the farthest northern extension of the missions, namely, at Cocomóra-chic and Yepómera. There were especially two brothers in the latter settlement whose anti-missionary teachings were very influential. Nevertheless, the move-ment was by no means confined to this northern area. It was also strong in the vicinity of Sisoguichic and Papigochic, in other words, over almost the whole length of the newly missionized area.

In 1696 the missionaries learned of what they regarded as preparation for war on the part of Indians at Sirupa west of Yepómera — the storing of corn and poisoned arrows on a cliff where also people were gathering. The Spanish commander, Captain Retana, was sent for from Parral and provoked battle.

The Indians of the area did not want to fight, but Retana was convinced that he must head off a revolt. Consequently he rounded up at least sixty in the general vicinity of the cliff interpreted as fortified, killed all of these, cut off the heads of thirty, put the heads on sticks and set them up along the road from Cocomórachic to Yepómera. Instead of putting the fear of God into the Indians, Retana's action now precipitated a general revolt embracing the whole of the Upper Tarahumara country from Sisoguichic in the south to Yepómera in the north. For two years the fighting went on with exhibitions of great savagery on both sides, especially in the actions of Retana who graced the vicinity of Sisoguichic as he had Cocomórachic, with thirty Tarahumara heads. One feature of the fighting in this last rebellion was the refusal of many whole bands to surrender, choosing death in battle instead. Resistance to the Spaniards had become for many a definite way of life, although it was indicated most clearly in the acceptance of death.

The Spanish exhibition of military power in the hands of Captain Retana was effective at last. The rebellion ending in 1698 was the last show of real military resistance on the part of the Tarahumaras (although two hundred years later in this same area centering at Tomochic there was fighting again). The Spanish military conquest was at last completed; it had taken almost one hundred years. From this point on, although a new silver rush took place in 1709, resulting in the founding of the city of Chihuahua, and settlers pressed with continuing insistence all along the eastern borders of the Tarahumara country, organized Indian resistance was at an end. The dominant reaction now of Tarahumaras who would not allow themselves to be assimilated into Spanish society was retreat — westward into the highlands of the Sierra Madres and southward in the deep and rugged canyons of the headwaters of the Mayo and Fuerte rivers.

The fifty years following the establishment of peaceful conditions saw two definite trends in the Upper Tarahumara region. One of these was a steady increase in the numbers of livestock in the mission communities and among Tarahumaras outside the missions. While horses and cattle had been well established in Tarahumara mission life before 1725, apparently sheep and goats were of importance only after that date and they increased rapidly once the Jesuits introduced them. This trend was indicative of a new economic dimension in Tarahumara life. The incorporation of cattle into their subsistence activities meant an important new element in food supply, as had no other of the Jesuit introductions (for Tarahumaras had not really permitted any European introductions to replace the corn, beans, and squash with which they had long since worked out their adaptation to their environment). In addition the sheep provided wool for the weaving of clothes, blankets, and belts. The latter occupation was an important one among the Tarahumaras, and the raising of their own wool supply assured their independence, so long as they cared to maintain it, from the Spanish economic system. There was then a trend toward integration of elements from the Spanish — livestock and weaving of wool — into the native economy.

The other discernible trend during this half century was the crystallization of anti-Spanish feeling among the highland Tarahumaras accompanied by a

pattern of withdrawal as defense against the various forms of Spanish encroachment. This developed at the same time that the trend toward assimilation into
Spanish culture proceeded in the communities of the Lower Tarahumara region.
The crystallization of hostility and withdrawal among the highland Tarahumaras
constituted the response to continued efforts by the Spaniards to force the Indians
to fill their needs for labor. The city of Chihuahua grew rapidly after its founding
in 1709, in fact steadily assuming a position as the metropolis of the north. The
mines were more extensive than those of Durango. Haciendas and ranches grew
up around the city. Spaniards constantly raided the Tarahumara settlements for
laborers and servants. By their law they were permitted to force four percent of
the Indians of any Christianized community to work for them provided they
observed the regulations regarding payment, the provision of food during travel
to the place of work, and humane working conditions. The four percent quota
was regularly so far exceeded, and the standards of humane treatment were so
frequently ignored that even the governor of New Biscay was dismayed and
sought help from the viceroy in Mexico City. Conditions were never substantially
altered, however, despite the governor's concern. The impressment of labor continued throughout the 1700's, and Tarahumaras simply had to learn how to live
with, that is, to avoid, this feature of Spanish civilization. Mission communities
where Indians settled in response to missionary efforts and persuasion were
constantly depleted of population, as a result either of successful Spanish raiding
parties who carried men, women, and children away or of successful flight on the
part of Christianized Indians who learned in time of the approach of labor
recruiters. The Jesuits protested in vain, although at times some were successful
in reclaiming a few Indians from their forced labor in the mines or haciendas to
the east. The situation resulted in implantation of deep distrust of Spaniards and
rendered the mission communities places of temporary and uncertain residence.
In general, there was a slow decline in the population of the communities from
1700 on, especially after 1725. The total Tarahumara population in 1759 was
reported as over eighteen thousand, probably a conservative estimate.

Nevertheless, missionary activities continued with considerable vigor. The
whole of the Upper Tarahumara region was steadily covered with mission
churches. By 1763 there were nineteen missionaries at work. Even though the
temporary or permanent withdrawal of Indians from the mission communities
was chronic, there was in general an acceptance of the Jesuits themselves as
friendly. Many were devoted and industrious and achieved good working relations. One of these was so capable and energetic that he became something of
a legend in his own time. This was Father Hermann Glandorff, who was reputed
to have accomplished such feats of travel on foot in the rugged country and
such successful ministration to the sick and dying that he came to be looked on
as having special supernatural power by Tarahumaras, and caused his Jesuit
colleagues also to wonder whether he had some unusual divine aid. Glandorff
was stationed at Tomochic and for more than forty years worked indefatigably
among the Indians. There were difficulties with small-scale nativistic movements
and, for the decade of the 1730's, with Tarahumaras joining Apaches on their

raids in northern Chihuahua. There were also clashes between Tarahumaras and missionaries over the latter appropriating Indian fields for grazing. But for the most part conditions were calm, and the missionaries went about the business, with the aid of their converts, of making the many churches as large and handsome as possible.

Meanwhile the churches of the Lower Tarahumara mission unit were secularized, that is, turned over from the missionary order to the management of the regular priests as parish churches. This process was completed by about 1753. It meant that it was the judgment of the church and of the civil authorities that the Indians of this area had become full-fledged Christians, no longer requiring missionary effort, and should be merged in their religious life with the Spaniards.

In 1767 the Jesuits were expelled, on the order of the King of Spain, from the whole New World. The hundreds of mission establishments, schools, and colleges such as those founded in Parral and Chihuahua were to be turned over to other missionary orders or converted to other purposes. In the Upper Tarahumara country there was no regular clergy to continue the management of the missions. The Franciscans were without the resources or inclination to do so. The expulsion of the Jesuits here, then, meant simply disappearance of a mission program. The nineteen mission churches were suddenly in the hands of those Tarahumaras who had constituted the Jesuits' working staffs — the men and women to whom they had taught the Christian ritual and the care of the church furnishings. For 130 years many of the churches continued to serve as community centers for Indians and for Spaniards, and later for Mexicans, who moved into the area. Sometimes some were served by regular priests from the eastern margin of Tarahumara territory, but for the most part the Indians were free to integrate them into their life according to their own lights.

The expulsion of the Jesuits marked the end of an era. The Tarahumaras had for 160 years been the object of organized Spanish effort to change their way of life. Changes had been wrought. A certain pattern had developed in Indian-Spanish relations here which was not to be precisely repeated anywhere else in northwestern New Spain. We may glance back over this period of Tarahumara history to see the main lines of this pattern so that we may better compare it with others which developed elsewhere.

In the first place, in large degree the Tarahumaras and their country remained peripheral to the Spaniards and their developing interests. To be sure, silver and gold were discovered in Tarahumara country, but the great silver strikes were on the margin. The deepest penetration was at Cusihuiriachic, but the mines there turned out to be much less rich than those of Durango, Santa Barbara, Parral, and Chihuahua. Although there were mines and miners in Upper Tarahumara territory, they were relatively few and scattered. We may be sure that if a strike as great as that at Parral had been found at Papigochic, the Indians would have been promptly overwhelmed in their own land. This did in fact happen with the minority of Tarahumaras who lived in the Lower Tarahumara area close to Santa Barbara, Parral, and Chihuahua. But the majority were able to hold out at a distance from the Spaniards.

What the Spaniards were interested in was Indian manpower. The Indians had few resources of value and were too poor to yield tribute, but they had arms and legs. Spaniards needed these for the mines, the haciendas, the ranches. This interest was of decisive importance in the relations between Spaniards and Indians. It was a major factor in bringing about bad working relations between the two — a hundred years of serious conflict leading ultimately into a period of distrust and withdrawal on the part of thousands of Indians. The Tarahumaras were near enough to the centers of Spanish activity to be profoundly affected by the forced labor program, even if they were not close enough to be wholly absorbed into the Spanish society at their border.

To a large extent the missionaries were left free to deal in their own way with the Indians and bring them into the Spanish sphere of influence. To be sure, this freedom for the missionaries was intermittent. We have described three revolutions of a recurrent cycle characterized by the three phases of peaceful missionary activity, miner-settler conflict, military action. But nevertheless, within Tarahumara country during the first hundred years there were two periods of more than thirty years each during which the missionary-neophyte relation tended to be dominant.

The missionary objectives were by no means realized. The reasons for this are not to be found merely in the "interference" with their activity by settlers and soldiers. That played a part obviously, but there were other at least equally important factors. One would seem to have been the piecemeal advance of the conquest. Throughout the whole of the Jesuit period there were two different social environments between which the Indians could choose. The whole tribal territory was never completely under Spanish control. From the beginning Indians could move out of the Spanish sphere, at first from Lower to Upper Tarahumara country, ultimately from the scattered mission centers to the relatively inaccessible canyons and highlands. The missionaries were thus constantly facing a hinterland of unsubjected people. They were well aware of the situation and suffered great frustration in their awareness of the always-present outer ring of "pagan darkness" surrounding their missions.

This outer ring against which the missionaries tried to prevail must be visualized as a distinctive feature of the Tarahumara situation. Something resembling it developed elsewhere among a few tribes, but the pattern which became established in Tarahumara country was nearly unique. It was not only the step by step advance of the missionaries which contributed to it, but also the direct opposition between the missionary objective of "reduction" and the traditional scattered settlement plan of the Tarahumaras. The community type which the Jesuits introduced became well established in the Lower Tarahumara area, but never in the upper region. There the compact settlement around the church was the unstable community type. The Jesuits tried desperately to stabilize it, but the Spanish raiders and the cultural conservatism of the Tarahumaras were too much for them. Movement of individuals and families between the missions and the rancherías was constant. The wideflung kinship ties of converted Indians drew them back repeatedly into the "outer ring" for a variety of reasons. By the time the Jesuits were expelled, most of the missions functioned as ceremonial centers for groups of families who lived there during important ceremonial seasons, or perhaps for as much as a year or two at a time, but whose ties were usually strong with Tarahumaras who appeared only occasionally at the mission center. In short, the missionaries' view of what was a proper community in which to live had not been established by 1767 over the greater part of the Tarahumara territory. The Tarahumaras in the upper region had adapted the Jesuits' idea of a mission-centered community to their own kind of community life.

It was this process of re-adaptation of what they had learned of Christianity, of Spanish colonial government, and of Spanish technology which then proceeded in the Upper Tarahumara country after the Jesuits were forced out. The process went on in a general atmosphere of withdrawal from the Spanish settlers, based in deep-rooted distrust. For Spanish settlers and miners continued their slow advance into Tarahumara territory.

As Spanish military power declined, and Apache raids increased in number and intensity, the Tarahumaras continued to receive less and less attention from the government. It was not until well after the Revolution of 1810 that official interest turned once more to the Tarahumaras.

As the state of Chihuahua took form under the Mexican government in the 1820's, the new officials were more deeply concerned with Indians in the north than with the Tarahumaras. The Conchos, the Tobosos, and the Jumanos of the lowlands and river valleys had either been wiped out or fairly thoroughly absorbed culturally by 1800. The Apaches, on the other hand, had harassed northern Chihuahua continuously throughout the 1700's. They were doing so with increasing intensity during the first half of the 1800's, raiding as far south as the city of Chihuahua and even beyond into Durango. Government bounties were offered for Apache scalps. Effort was poured into retaliatory raids on Apaches — to little avail. The northern part of the state remained uninhabitable for Mexican settlers. Meanwhile some attention was directed by the new state government to the promotion of colonization in the south and this included the country of the Tarahumaras.

In 1825 a Law of Colonization was promulgated designed to encourage the settlement of the state. It provided, among other matters, that cultivated land around the "depopulated towns" be distributed in individual parcels to the Indians resident there without payment for title. This applied to portions of Lower Tarahumara country, but also to the mission towns in the Upper Tarahumara region from which Indians had been steadily moving away. Few Tarahumaras were interested in taking advantage of the new law. The law also provided for the sale of lands which Indians did not claim, the proceeds to go to common community funds. A further provision of the Law of Colonization was that all uncultivated public lands be opened up to colonization by whoever cared to settle on them. This provision had a dual purpose, first, to stimulate the economic development of the state and, second, as stated in the law, to bring about the "instruction and civilization of the Indians." It assumed that Mexican neighbors would carry out the civilizing of the Indians, for which purpose there were now no missionaries. The net effect of the Law of Colonization was to encourage Mexicans to move deeper into Tarahumara country, to push the Indians further west and south into the mountains, and to intensify the old settler-Indian conflict.

By 1833 it was apparent that the expanding Mexican population was steadily absorbing in one way or another what land had been acquired by the Indians. It was thought necessary by the state government, in a law passed in that year, to reiterate the rights of Indians to their land and to affirm that their holdings should be respected. Nevertheless the same law provided for the distribution of land in parcels to families, whether Indians or not, the heads of which had been born in the towns where the land lay. The result was the legalization of all titles to land which had been forcibly taken from Indians, and the consolidation of the position of Mexican settlers wherever they had taken up residence in Tarahumara country. From this point on through the 1800's the process of voluntary isolation from Mexicans on the part of the great majority of Tarahumaras was intensified. Some Indians left the rancherías and became absorbed in the population of the Mexican towns, but the majority withdrew to the extent that they could.

As the Chihuahua state government became stabilized, under Governors Terrazas and Creel, during the last decades of the national administration of Porfirio Díaz, a new interest developed in Tarahumara affairs at the official level. After a lapse of considerably more than a century two new programs for changing the Tarahumaras' ways took form. On the one hand the Jesuit Order and on the other the state government laid plans for reducing the isolation of the Indians and bringing them into the sphere of Mexican cultural influence. The state's activities slightly preceded those of the church. During the 1890's the governor of Chihuahua talked of setting up six schools among the Tarahumaras. In 1899 one school was established in Tonachic; four years later two schools were set up in Rochiachic. The influence of, or the Tarahumara reaction to, these schools has not been recorded. But it is clear that they represented a growing concern at the highest official level over what was regarded as the shockingly backward condition of the Indians.

The advance of the Mexican frontier of settlement into Tarahumara territory had been steady, particularly in connection with mining. A railroad had been built deep into the mountains connecting the city of Chihuahua with Yepómera and was being extended southward to the vicinity of Sisoguichic. This resulted in an increasing awareness on the part of Mexicans of the situation of the Tarahumaras. In 1906 Enrique C. Creel, a banker and economist who had become governor of the state, said: *Scarcely a month, week, or day passes but that there comes to this government a deputation of Indians complaining of dispossession of their small and deteriorating lands . . . which are being occupied by the superior race . . . and at present they possess land of only insignificant value situated on the highest of the peaks or the deepest of the canyons.* Thus the problem of being crowded off their land was central to the Indians' view of their relations with the Whites, and they were hopeful that a friendly government would help them. Governor Creel recognized the land problem as basic, but saw the situation in much broader terms and from the particular viewpoint of reshaping Indian life to conform with that of the encroaching settlers.

In 1906 the governor proposed a "Law for the Betterment and Cultivation (Cultura)" of the Tarahumaras. This proposed the establishment in the capital of a board for the protection of Indian interests, and the setting up of committees in each of the seven municipalities where Indian population was heaviest. The work of the board was to focus on clearing and dividing the common lands of the Indian communities, congregating the Indians on these, distributing seeds, building schools, developing community government, and diffusing "among the Indians feelings of friendship and gratitude toward the white race" so that they would send their children to school. The point of view from which the governor worked is indicated in the following statement: "It is gratifying to see how this race, denied advantage by the weight of ignorance, begins to emerge from its lethargy of so many centuries and takes the first steps on the road of civilization." He may have been expressing the hopes which he had for a transformation of Tarahumara life in connection with the establishment of a "colony" at Creel, a new settlement at the south end of the railroad near Sisoguichic. This was a planned settlement of Indians and Mexicans, an agricultural colony, in line with general thinking by Mexicans concerning the best means for raising Indian standards of living and bringing about cultural assimilation. The colony of Creel was to consist of 75 percent Tarahumaras and 25 percent Mexicans, each family to be settled on ten hectares of land. By 1907 it had not attained expectations. It consisted of 30 Tarahumara and 21 Mexican families, a total of 191 persons. It was, nevertheless, the most concrete of Governor Creel's achievements on behalf of the Indians. His law for the betterment of the Indians remained a paper program and all other plans were unrealized when the Revolution of 1910 broke out.

Meanwhile the Jesuits carried through plans for reinstituting their work among the Tarahumaras. In 1903 they prepared a catechism in the Tarahumara language and made preparations for further activity. The following year the Institute of the Servants of the Sacred Heart of Jesus and of the Poor established a house for the care of orphans. In 1905 the Jesuits established four boarding schools in the area of their last intensive missionary work nearly a century and a half before — at Sisoguichic, Nonoava, Tonachi, and Carichic. Their work, primarily with orphans and other children, continued with little disruption through the revolutionary period.

The rise of interest in the Tarahumaras on the part of church and state and the renewal of efforts to change the Indians continued after the Revolution of 1910. Efforts by the Mexican government did not come to a focus for twenty years after the close of the fighting, but it was clear that during the 1920's the interest was there. The Tarahumaras appeared to the new officials in charge of education as culturally backward people at a disadvantage because of the ruthless cruelty of the Spanish conquest, the unenlightened viewpoint of the early missionaries, and the uncontrolled exploitation by settlers. It was believed that their capacity for civilization was equal to that of any of the Indians who had contributed the majority of the modern population of Mexico. The problem as seen by these officials was to bring to the Indians for voluntary adoption the advantages of

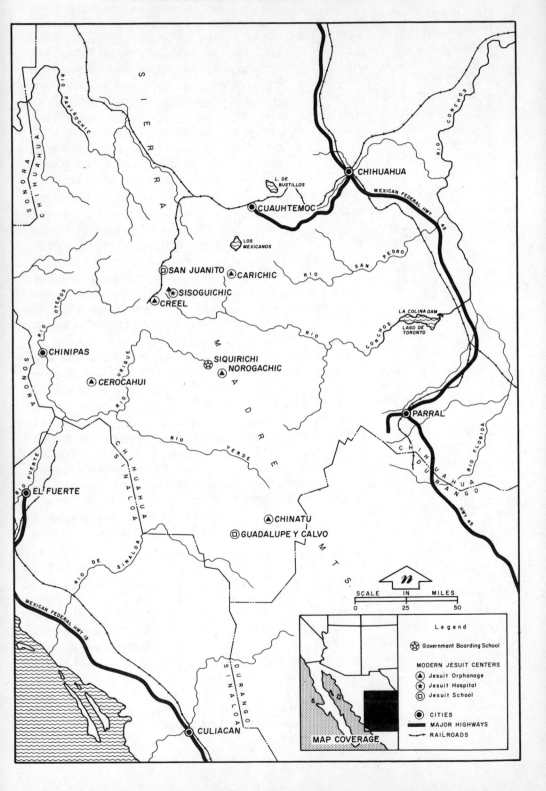

the urban culture of the Mexican nation, namely, writing and books, modern medical practice, modern agricultural knowledge, cooperative forms of economic organization, and a sense of being participating citizens in the Mexican Republic. To this end the Cultural Mission program was extended to the Tarahumaras. The missions were teams of a half dozen men and women trained in specialties such as agriculture, medicine and public health, the teaching of reading and writing, management of cooperatives, and so on. Three such teams entered the Tarahumara country in 1926 and lived for a time in Sisoguichic and two other Tarahumara communities. Two cultural missions came again in 1937. Their effect has never been adequately assessed. In 1936 the Federal Department of Labor made a study of the economic basis of Tarahumara life. These efforts probably affected the Mexicans more than the Tarahumaras, and resulted chiefly in the diffusion of some knowledge among government officials of the profound differences between the ways of life of the Tarahumaras and the Mexicans of the region. The new contacts also acquainted the Mexican officials with the hostility existing between Tarahumaras and the "Chabochis" (as the Tarahumaras designated the Mexican settlers in their territory). For example, a meeting in Creel in 1934, in which representatives of the federal government met with the elected headmen of Tarahumara communities (called "little governors" by the Mexicans), raised again the basic and never-settled problem of the land. It was encroachment on their land which the "little governors" saw as the fundamental issue in their relations with non-Tarahumaras. It was this, rather than schools or better health, that they proposed as the point of primary discussion between themselves and what purported to be a government friendly to their interests. It was clear, however, that what Tarahumara leadership regarded as most important did not coincide with the Mexican view. For the latter, education was the major concern. It was true that Tarahumara leaders also saw importance in what could be learned in schools, but for them control of the land was basic. The Mexican officials also realized, as they had since Governor Creel, the significance of the land question, but their approach placed major emphasis on teaching Tarahumaras to behave like Mexicans so that they could defend themselves against the encroachment of the Chabochis.

The Mexican program came to a focus in the last years of the Cárdenas administration. There were two major developments. On the one hand the newly created Department of Indian Affairs set up a normal school in Guachochi and immediately followed this with the establishment of four boarding schools in the southern part of the Tarahumara territory. The educational emphasis of the federal government in its approach to Indian problems was now clear. This approach contained, however, a new element which indicated a difference of viewpoint from that actuating the state and federal rural schools which had been provided to the number of twelve or more since the 1920's. The new program called for the teaching of reading and writing in the Tarahumara language, an effort which even the Jesuits with their emphasis on knowing the Indian language had not carried so far. Not only were a dictionary and grammars prepared, but also a great deal of effort went into the making of primers and other materials for teaching Tarahumara as a written language to young and old. This was part of a general federal program in Mexico for establishing the Indian languages as written ones.

Another major development which took form at the end of the Cárdenas regime was the inauguration of the Tarahumara Congresses. These were conferences in the Tarahumara country designed to bring together Indian and Mexican representatives for the discussion of common problems and the formulation of programs for their solution. The first was held in 1939, the second in 1942, the third in 1945. All had wide attendance and resulted in some broader acquaintance between Indians and others, but little in the way of concrete action. Possibly the major result was the stimulation of the participation of Tarahumaras in the municipal governments heretofore completely dominated by Mexicans. In 1939 for the first time two Tarahumara representatives took places in the town council of Batopilas, a municipality in which Tarahumaras constituted a majority of the residents.

With the establishment of a Coordinating Center of the National Indian Institute at Guachochi in 1952, a new factor entered Mexican-Tarahumara relations. Focused on the stimulation of economic and community organization designed to deal effectively with the problems of land encroachment and with economic development of the forest and other resources which remained in Tarahumara hands, the Center began the introduction of a new government-sponsored approach. Although the new governmental approach emphasized technical training for Tarahumaras, it aimed at something broader than schools and formal education. It sought to stimulate the mature Indians to readapt their community organization to the inescapable conditions of integration into Mexican national life.

Tarahumara population had increased, if we can trust the counts and estimates recorded, from over eighteen thousand at about the end of the colonial period to thirty-five thousand in 1930 to fifty thousand in 1950.

In general, the Mexican phase of Tarahumara history was characterized by a re-isolation of the Indians. The organized contacts of the Spanish phase were suddenly broken off. As the mission program and the political conquest ceased to be active, they left at the border of Spanish settlement on the east side of the Sierra Madre Mountains some twenty thousand Indians whose orientation had become sharply antagonistic towards Europeans. What they had learned and accepted from the Spaniards — such as domestic animals, fruit trees, elements of town and military organization, an additional ceremonial calendar, new concepts of supernatural power — they clung to and proceeded for several generations to rework and adapt into new creations of their own. Disengaged from the organized pressures to change of the Spanish period, the majority of Tarahumaras in their isolated rancherías nevertheless changed considerably during the next century. As a result of the new networks of communication and acquaintance which the church fiestas and the attempts at resistance to Spaniards had stimulated among them, there was probably a new level of integration in Tarahumara life. However, the Mexicans during the 1800's knew Tarahumaras so superficially that we shall probably never know very much about the new alignments, the conflicts and cooperations of leadership, and the internal crises in Tarahumara life during this phase.

The nature of the contact shifted from the centrally controlled Spanish program to the intermittent, individual-by-individual contact between Mexican settler and Indian. At no time following the retirement of the Jesuits was the Tarahumara country without miners and settlers. These had no concerted plan. They moved into Tarahumara areas of settlement and adapted themselves as best they could. Although male settlers often took Indian wives, a deep gulf grew up and became fixed between the two groups. In general, relations were non-cooperative and in general the advancing Mexicans maintained in one way or another dominance over the Indians. It was the old story of European advance in the nineteenth century — small-scale border warfare and the creation of a hate-filled subordinated native people.

When after a century, organized and centrally controlled contacts were renewed they lacked the unity of the Spanish program. They seemed, in fact, to be competing and their spokesmen in the 1950's said as much during a food shortage in the Tarahumara country. Mexican interest in the Tarahumaras took the form of a state program for education, national rural schools with "Socialist"-oriented curricula, a Department of Indian Affairs teacher-training and educational program, the National Indian Institute program, and the Jesuit program. By the time these were well established in the 1950's they had gone through numerous metamorphoses as a result of clash between church and state, uncertainty of direction regarding Indian education on the part of the government before and after the Revolution of 1910, shifting emphasis before and after the Cárdenas administration, and so on. In short, there were numerous false starts resulting in discontinuity and by 1960 there was great variety in those organized programs which were established. In this there was great contrast with the Spanish period, and there was an expectable reflection in all its heterogeneity of the nature of Mexican civilization.

The missionaries of the 1600's had been zealous workers for the replacement of religious concepts and practice and for agricultural improvement. The government workers for secular education in the 1950's, whether in the Department of Indian Affairs or the National Indian Institute, were often as dedicated as had ever been the earlier or the later Jesuits. The values of science, political democracy, nationalism, and cooperative economic organization dominated their teaching. Running through the variety of organizations and activities, there was a dominating theme of progress through schools. Progress had one meaning in the Jesuit orphanages, another in the federally sponsored schools, but in both there was the common faith in the professional teacher from outside the family imparting the key of literacy for participation in the vast miscellany of the published word.

CHAPTER TWO

Mayos and Yaquis

ON THE OTHER SIDE of the Sierra Madre Mountains from the Tarahumaras the Spanish conquest proceeded in a sharply contrasting
manner. Two of the major tribes who maintained their identities
throughout the conquest and into the twentieth century were the
Cahitan-speaking Mayos and Yaquis. They were of nearly identical
language and cultural background, but their reactions to the
Spaniards who first encountered them were very different. The Mayos consistently
sought friendly alliance with the Spaniards for the first two hundred years of
contact. The Yaquis, on the other hand, resisted armed intrusion in their territory
from the first, and were so successful that they were able to set their own terms
for the entrance of missionaries.

The first important contacts took place in 1533. In that year, ranging up the
west coast of New Spain on slave raids, Diego de Guzmán fought a brief battle
with Yaquis on the banks of the Yaqui River. His force dispersed the Indians,
according to his account, but he nevertheless seems to have lost heart for further
conquest and did not follow up his victory. He was greatly impressed with the
fighting ability of the Yaquis who opposed him. A soldier in his party laid the
foundations for the Yaqui reputation as great warriors by writing that nowhere
in New Spain had he seen such bravery on the field of battle.

When Francisco de Ibarra set out from Zacatecas on his major prospecting
expedition through the Sierra Madre Mountains in the hope of finding new silver
mines, he ended up in the Yaqui country. Received in friendly fashion, he spent
part of the year 1564 in a Yaqui settlement and repaid Yaqui kindness by helping
them in a battle with the Mayos, with whom the Yaquis seem to have been
sporadically at war.

Thus, the earliest contacts of Mayos and Yaquis with the Spaniards were
both hostile and friendly. By 1583 the city which was to become the major center
of Spanish operations in the northwest was founded on the Sinaloa River nearly
two hundred miles south of the Yaqui River. It was here in San Felipe y Santiago,
on the site of modern Sinaloa, that Captain Hurdaide made his headquarters in
1599; from here also he waged the vigorous military campaign which resulted
in the complete subjection of the Indians of the Fuerte River—the Sinaloas,

Tehuecos, Zuaques, and Ahomes. By a time shortly after 1600 these Indians, numbering some twenty thousand, were under Spanish domination, and Jesuits were at work among them. All except the Ahomes had resisted strongly and Hurdaide had had to exhibit his great ability as a military commander in order to bring them under Spanish control. They were all Cahita-speaking and were in close contact with the Mayos and Yaquis, also Cahita-speaking, to the north. As the Jesuit work developed among them, the Mayos sent delegations to inspect the new churches and to get an idea of what the missionaries were offering. The Mayo leaders were so favorably impressed that large groups of Mayos numbering a hundred or more also made visits and became acquainted with Jesuit activities. About 1601 the Mayos asked that missionaries be sent to them, and Hurdaide went to Mexico City to ask for an increase in the number of Jesuits. The additional Jesuits were not immediately available, but meanwhile relations between the Spaniards and the Mayos continued very friendly, and in 1609 Hurdaide made a treaty for both offense and defense with the Mayos.

Hurdaide, with characteristic vigor and aggressiveness, was carrying his operations northward. In 1609 he was engaged in pacifying the Ocoronis, another Cahita-speaking group of northern Sinaloa. In pursuit of a band of Ocoronis he came to the Yaqui River, where Yaquis under the leadership of a man named Anabaletei, or Ania-bailutek, refused to allow him to pass into their territory. The vigor of their defiance was enough to cause him to try a peaceful settlement. He persuaded them to agree to give up the two refugee Ocoroni leaders. However, according to the Spanish accounts, the Yaquis did not live up to their bargain to turn over the two men, Lautaro and Babilomo. Instead they killed Christian Indians who were sent to receive the two leaders.

Hurdaide was not prepared for a real battle and so returned to raise a larger force. When he did come back with two thousand Indians and forty Spanish soldiers, he was soundly defeated. He then put together all his resources and raised the largest army which had so far been put into the field in northwestern Mexico — four thousand Indian foot soldiers and fifty mounted Spaniards. Again, after a bloody battle, which lasted for a whole day and night, he was badly routed and was himself wounded and nearly captured. The Yaquis were reported to have put into the field seven thousand men who fought with great bravery and tenacity. They completely dispersed Hurdaide's army, and the captain barely got away in the company of a few of his men. For nearly a year the situation stood with Spaniards unable to renew the fighting. The Yaquis made no effort to carry the attack further.

Then suddenly, to the surprise of the Spaniards, the Yaquis asked for peace. This was an event which the Spanish in their chronicles spoke of as unprecedented in military history. The reasons for the Yaqui action remain uncertain; there were two versions current. One held that Hurdaide circulated stories about the arrival of reinforcements by sea. Another version was that the Yaquis were so impressed by the Spanish military ability and Hurdaide's miraculous escape that they thought it would be safest to ally themselves with the Spaniards rather than keep on fighting.

Subsequent events indicated that the Yaquis were sincerely anxious for peace with Spaniards and neighboring Indians, and that above all they wanted Jesuit missionaries to come and work among them. Probably they were influenced by the reports with which the Mayos had returned from their inspections of the missionary work in the Ahome and Tehueco country. The Jesuits evidently had worked in a manner that gave them great prestige with the Indians. At any rate the Yaquis began to negotiate with Hurdaide through two Mayo leaders — Osameai and Bothisuame. The Yaqui leader who carried through negotiations was not Ania-bailutek, who had initiated the resistance against Hurdaide, but another man named Conibomeai, who seems to have been influential through the subsequent period of missionary entrance into the Yaqui country. Conibomeai had to overcome the resistance of young men among the Yaquis in bringing about a peace treaty.

The Spanish accounts describe the treaty as an offensive and defensive alliance, which also required the Yaquis to give up the refugees Babilomo and Lautaro and all the arms and horses which they had captured from the Spaniards, and to agree to remain at peace with the Mayos and other Indians in the area. Hurdaide invited a group of Yaqui leaders to come to San Felipe y Santiago to complete the negotiations, where he arranged an elaborate ceremony. The Spanish accounts do not indicate that the Spaniards had to agree to anything, but it is a fact that they made no effort to establish any military or civil personnel in the Yaqui country for more than ten years afterwards, and that when they finally sent missionaries the latter entered the Yaqui communities with no military escort whatsoever. The Yaquis seem, in other words, to have successfully made the point that they regarded themselves as remaining autonomous and not under the sort of military domination which the other tribes of the region had accepted.

It was seven years before enough missionaries were on hand to fulfill the Yaqui requests for them. Meanwhile, in 1614, the Jesuits began work among the Mayos. A single missionary, Pedro Méndez, in company with Hurdaide and a number of soldiers went to Camoa where the long-expectant Mayos awaited them. The entrance was triumphal. In two weeks as Méndez moved down the river from ranchería to ranchería, more than thirty-six hundred children and adults presented themselves for baptism. Within four years sixteen thousand had been baptized and the Mayos had worked hard to build churches in seven places where Méndez set about concentrating the Indians in seven towns. Two years later in 1620 the Jesuit records indicated that thirty thousand had been baptized. Three missionaries were at work, and the Mayo country was organized into three *partidos,* or mission districts, with missions at Camoa, Navojoa, and Etchojoa. In addition, the two small Cahita-speaking groups upriver on the Mayo, the Tepahues and Conicaris — numbering twenty-five hundred — had also been brought under mission discipline. The Mayo acceptance of the mission system was thus complete within six years and the reduction to town life was well underway.

The Yaqui acceptance of the mission system was even more rapid. In 1617 Pérez de Ribas and Tomás Basilio, Jesuit missionaries, escorted by two Yaqui leaders and with no soldiers or other Spaniards, went to the eastern edge of Yaqui territory. Besides the Yaqui escort there were with them only some Christian Tehuecos to serve as godparents in the expected baptismal ceremonies. They were received by thousands of Yaquis carrying small crosses of wood in their hands. Arches of cane had been erected, through which the missionaries passed leading processions of Yaquis. On the first day they baptized two hundred. Within the first six months they had baptized four thousand, including a number of the head-men, who had also submitted to marriage ceremonies. Simple buildings were constructed for the holding of church services. Throughout the length of the lower Yaqui River all the way to the sea, Yaquis came for baptism and to help with the construction of churches. Within the next two years, by 1619, nearly thirty thousand Yaquis were baptized. Seven missionaries were now at work persuading the Yaquis, who were scattered in eighty rancherías along the lower course of the Yaqui River, to come and live in eight town concentrations where churches had been built. By 1623, six years after the beginning of missionary work, a stone chapel stood in the most central of the new towns — Torim — and the Yaquis had allowed Captain Hurdaide to pay them a visit and ride with a few soldiers from Los Hornos to Belem, the full length of the Yaqui territory. In 1623 they also allowed Hurdaide to appoint officials — governors, judges, and sheriffs — for the new towns. All the officials were Indians. Torim became the seat of the rectorate for a new mission unit for Sonora; and a 120-year period of peaceful economic and religious development set in on the lower Yaqui River.

The next sixty years were ones of unusual tranquility for any northwestern outpost of Spanish civilization. No Spanish settlers came into Ostimuri, as the area of the Yaqui and Mayo rivers had been named. No towns grew up closer than the Fuerte River, where the Fort of Montesclaros was built in 1610, and this was more than a hundred miles south of the Yaqui. There were no mines in the river-bottom lands of the Yaquis and Mayos, and no mines were opened until later in the mountain country bordering them. Both the Yaquis and Mayos took to church attendance and cultivation of the Catholic ritual with an interest that the missionaries wrote of as exceptional in any Jesuit experience. There was apparently no tendency to rebel and only an occasional difficulty with what the Jesuits called witches. The new religion was undergoing a most thorough and peaceful integration with the native beliefs and practices. Missionaries like Andrés Egidiano, who was posted at Bacum, learned the language thoroughly and preached and taught in it. Egidiano himself spent twenty-seven years continuously at Bacum and came to be deeply venerated by the Yaquis. Government of the towns, except for the very top office of the captain-general, was in the hands of the Indians themselves. They worked with practically no friction with the missionaries, not only building up the churches and the religious life centered in them, but also increasing their agricultural production. Seven mission towns on the Mayo River and eight on the Yaqui became thriving communities. The only serious troubles were the appearance of epidemics, especially a widespread one in 1641, which killed many Indians. The Mayo River villages lost half their population in the fifty years following the conversion, but apparently the Yaqui towns were not hit so hard and relatively few Indians died. Thus, for two

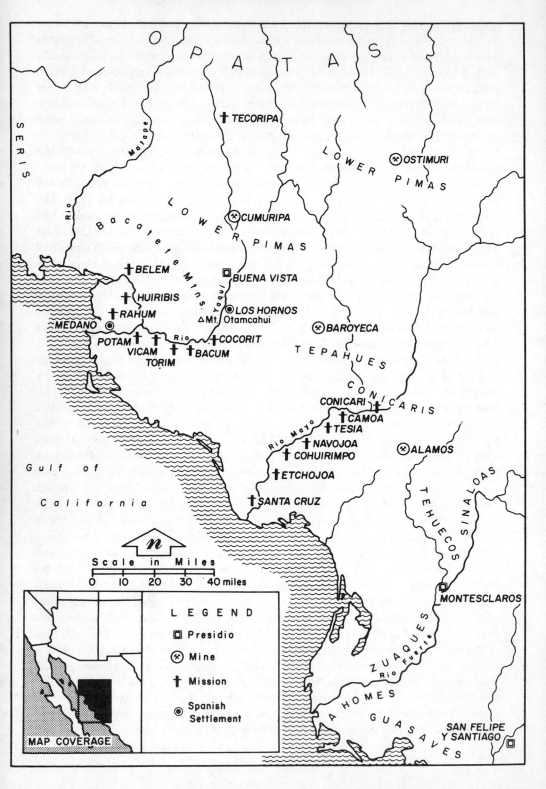

5. YAQUI-MAYO COUNTRY ABOUT 1740

O P A T A S

SERIS

LOWER PIMAS

Rio Matape

✝ TECORIPA

⊗ OSTIMURI

⊗ CUMURIPA

Bacatete Mtns.

LOWER PIMAS

✝ BELEM

▢ BUENA VISTA

✝ HUIRIBIS

✝ RAHUM

Rio Yaqui

⊙ LOS HORNOS

MEDANO ⊙

△ Mt. Otamcahui

✝ POTAM

✝ VICAM

Rio

✝ COCORIT

⊗ BAROYECA

✝ ✝ BACUM

TORIM

T E P A H U E S

C O N I C A R I S

CONICARI

✝ CAMOA

✝ TESIA

Rio Mayo

✝ NAVOJOA

⊗ ALAMOS

✝ COHUIRIMPO

Gulf of

✝ ETCHOJOA

California

✝ SANTA CRUZ

T E H U E C O S

S I N A L O A S

▲
n

Scale in Miles

0   10   20   30   40 miles

▢ MONTESCLAROS

Z U A Q U E S

Rio Fuerte

L E G E N D

▢ Presidio

⊗ Mine

✝ Mission

⊙ Spanish
  Settlement

A H O M E S

G U A S A V E S

SAN FELIPE
Y SANTIAGO ▢

MAP COVERAGE

generations there was peaceful integration of Spanish and Cahita culture.

In 1684 the situation began to change. One of the richest silver mines of northwest Mexico was discovered at Alamos at the edge of the mountains thirty miles from Navojoa. This brought Spaniards into the area and attracted some Indians away from the mission settlements. In those Mayo areas that had been depopulated by disease, Spaniards began to take up land and build haciendas. The encroachment, however, proceeded slowly. The Yaqui River lands were relatively far from Alamos, the center of Spanish settlement, and Yaqui population was still too dense to permit easy appropriation of land there. The Yaqui towns continued as thriving agricultural communities. The missionaries introduced wheat, cattle, and horses. A port was established at Medano at the mouth of the Yaqui River. Granaries were built at Bacum, Torim, and Huirivis. The people of Huirivis especially began to build up herds of cattle. From 1680 on the Jesuits were accustomed to provide wheat and livestock from the Yaqui surplus for the continuing missionary work in Lower California and to the north in Sonora. Tribute was still not required from the Indians and hence the missions were sources of real prosperity for the Yaquis and for the Mayos who still survived.

By the 1730's, however, the usual Spanish frontier difficulties began to develop. As mining increased at Alamos and northward in Sonora, Spanish settlers came into the region. With the coming of the settlers, encroachment on Indian lands took place, and the frictions between Indians and Spaniards began. Haciendas were established near Navojoa and southward along the Mayo River in the rich bottom lands, and it was apparent to the Spanish ranchers that the combination of missionary and Indian labor had developed highly desirable farm and pasture lands on both rivers. Resentment of missionary control of so much valuable land steadily grew. Friction came to a head in 1734 when Colonel Huidobro was named governor of the province of Sinaloa. He became increasingly antagonistic to the missionary program and allied himself with hacendados established in the vicinity of Etchojoa on the Mayo River. Signs of serious discontent among the Indians increased during the 1730's, culminating in 1740 in the first Yaqui-Mayo revolt.

The precise causes of the revolt remain obscure. It is obvious that the general cause was hostility between Spanish civil and religious authorities, but the nature of the situation among the Indians themselves can only be guessed at. As usual the Jesuits had one version, the civil authorities another. Some of the facts seem to be that a Yaqui named Juan Ignacio Muni became antagonistic to the missionary in Huirivis — probably as the result of an unjust whipping of a relative by the Yaqui governor of the town at the command of the missionary. Muni sought the backing of Governor Huidobro, who supported him against the missionaries. The small difficulty grew to large proportions when Huidobro failed to take action against anyone. Muni seems to have had wide influence with, and support from, both Yaquis and Mayos, but the issues remain unclear, for it also appears that Huidobro was generally disliked. Huidobro, in fact, seems to have been a very poor administrator in whom no one had much confidence — either missionaries or Indians. This is indicated by the fact that Muni with another leader, Bernabé, in 1738 felt it necessary to go to Mexico City to lodge his complaints. He was gone for two years and the rumor spread that he had been killed or imprisoned there.

As the rumors spread, an Indian named Juan Calixto instituted a revolt. Fighting began in 1740 with the killing of a governor of one of the Mayo towns, which suggests that a focus of friction lay in the appointment of the Indian governors, a matter with which the missionaries had much to do. The revolt was carried with the battle cries of "Long live the King, Long live the Blessed Mary, Down with bad government!" Calixto raised an army of six thousand and in a short time had complete possession of all the towns on the Mayo and Yaqui rivers. The Spaniards fled the country southward, a few remaining briefly with the frightened Huidobro in Alamos, whence all fled to a point outside the Mayo country.

With Huidobro offering no resistance, the fighting shifted to the Lower Pima country at Tecoripa, where Huidobro's lieutenant Vildósola was in command. Lower Pimas, Yaquis, and Mayos all united against the Spaniards, but the majority of the fighting force were Yaquis. Led by a Yaqui named Baltazar, a furious attack on Tecoripa was repulsed by Vildósola, and another force of Indians was defeated not far away. Vildósola followed up his advantage with continuous attack, fighting southward down the Yaqui River. He defeated a large force of Indians at Cerro del Tambor at the edge of the Yaqui country and then, pushing his way to the Yaqui River, he engaged the whole Yaqui army at Otamcahui (Hill of the Bones). Vildósola reported that five thousand Indians were killed in the course of the two battles. This broke the Indian resistance. Meanwhile, Muni and Bernabé had returned from Mexico City. Muni began peace overtures, and by the end of the year 1740 fighting was over. Huidobro appointed Muni captain-general of the Yaqui and Mayo area.

The revolt was a costly one for both Spaniards and Indians. Over a thousand Spaniards were killed and more than five thousand Indians. Every mine and hacienda in the Lower Pima, Yaqui, and Mayo territories was abandoned, except Alamos itself. All the missionaries had been forced to leave. Large numbers of cattle and horses had been killed or driven off. And a new atmosphere of suspicion and distrust had been created. Huidobro was immediately replaced as governor by Vildósola and the latter began an attempt to rule with an iron hand. He accused Muni, together with his Yaqui associates Bernabé and Calixto, and a Mayo of Etchojoa named Esteban, of plotting to exterminate or drive out all Spaniards from the region and make Muni "king" of the Yaquis and Mayos. Whether this accusation was true or not seems never to have been satisfactorily determined. The four leaders were executed and all suspects were deported.

Vildósola also instituted a series of restrictive measures, requiring that no Indian be permitted to leave any pueblo without the permission of missionaries, impressing Indians for forced labor on mines and haciendas, and requiring that there be daily recitation of prayers by all Indians in the mission communities. A presidio was built at Buenavista, on the border of the Lower Pima and Yaqui territories, and a force of soldiers was sent to man it. After 120 years the typical

Spanish frontier situation had finally developed in the Yaqui-Mayo country. Also typically, Vildósola was removed from office six years later for mishandling of government funds.

After the revolt, the missionaries returned to their missions and, for the twenty-six years that intervened until the expulsion of the Jesuits, busied themselves with recovering lost ground. The missions had not been destroyed, but the spirit of the Indians was different, and the old level of prosperity was not regained. The Mayo population continued to decline, so that even before the expulsion in 1767, it was reported at about one-fourth to one-fifth of its original, or less than six thousand. The Yaqui population at this time also showed a decline, being put at about twenty-three thousand. However, much of this decline may have been more apparent than real, since both Yaquis and Mayos had begun to migrate widely. The ecclesiastical Visitor and inspector reported in 1760 that "thousands" of Yaquis were living temporarily or permanently away from the lower Yaqui River pueblos. Two thousand Yaquis, who were highly valued miners, were said to be working farther to the north on the middle Yaqui River at mines around Soyopa. Many more were scattered through other mining areas in Sonora, Sinaloa, and even in Durango and Chihuahua. Also as haciendas had developed in Chihuahua and Durango, some Yaquis had crossed the mountains to work in the irrigated areas. Parral, Santa Barbara, and other towns of the plateau reported sizable colonies of Sonora Indians. This emigration dismayed the missionaries and gave the civil authorities the feeling that an era of declne had set in in the formerly thriving Sonoran missions.

The Jesuit reaction was to intensify their work among the Yaquis and Mayos who remained. In addition to continuing their encouragement of agricultural development, they also instituted schools—one in Navojoa on the Mayo River and one in Rahum on the Yaqui River. To these each year they brought two children from each pueblo, dressed them in red and blue uniforms, and gave them instruction in Christian doctrine and in reading and writing.

The civil authorities, aware of economic decline or stagnation in the area, concerned themselves with ways and means of increasing economic activity. Reports were made, the burden of which was that sea trade needed to be stimulated because of the bad roads and the consequent isolation from the rest of New Spain, that an increase in circulating money was needed, and finally that two forms of colonization should be stimulated. The failure up to this point to stimulate Spanish settlement was regarded as a major cause of the poor economic condition. It was proposed that more Spaniards should be brought to settle in the vicinity of presidios to provide increased protection from Indians in the form of "living walls" and also to offer more example of industry to the Indians. Along the same line, it was also proposed that carefully selected Spaniards be introduced into the Indian pueblos themselves. The civil authorities were aware that Spaniards "of a certain character" would have to be selected, meaning not the sort who had tended to drift thus far in the wake of the Spanish advance, but just what kind was not specified. Nothing was done about these recommendations immediately, but they were a basis for later efforts to develop the region.

At the time the Jesuits were expelled, there were ten missionaries at work in the Yaqui-Mayo territory, one-fifth of those employed in the whole of Sonora, Ostimuri, and Sinaloa. Their enforced departure resulted in an immediate disintegration of the Yaqui and Mayo mission communities. Although four Franciscan missionaries came almost immediately, in 1768, to the Yaqui-Mayo country, they seemed unable to take hold. The Royal Commissioners set up to handle the Jesuit property did a poor job. Much of the Jesuit resources on the Yaqui River went into outfitting a campaign against the Seri Indians to the north, and all the mission property fell into a state of nonproductivity. Poor local management, probably due to the Indians' lack of confidence in the new missionaries, together with spoilation at the hands of the civil authorities, resulted in real disorganization. Many Indian families left the pueblos and scattered. Town government was reported to be lax. This state of decline was increased as a result of great floods on the Mayo River in 1770.

The continued decline of the missions and the growing interest of the lay population of Spaniards in the Indian lands and resources led in 1771 to a program of secularization of the missions. The new personnel was, in general, inadequate both in numbers and training. The secular priests were shifted about with great frequency, so that in fact there was no stable program to take the place of that of the Jesuits. Steadily it became apparent that the new regime was designed to serve the interests of the civil arm of government. The program was inefficiently administered, and a whole new climate of relations between Indians and Spaniards was created — one which grew naturally out of the era of friction and distrust which had been initiated by Huidobro and Vildósola. The key ideas in the new program were taxation and land allotment. The first meant support for government officials at Indian expense, and the opportunity for exploitation of Indian labor under official protection. The second meant opportunity for Spaniards to obtain Indian lands either through purchase or through assignment after all Indians had been assigned.

Tribute, that is, taxes, had never been required of the Yaquis or Mayos; this had been on the basis of their being regarded as not yet ready for citizenship. Now in 1772 the governor of the province was ordered to allot land and work out a plan for getting Indians to pay tribute. The civil authorities believed that it would be dangerous to force payment. They were afraid of Yaqui military strength. Accordingly, only persuasion was used and it was not effective. Apparently neither Yaquis nor Mayos ever had paid tribute at any time to the Spanish king. Nor did the wavering government carry through division of the land among the Indians, although elaborate plans were worked out and a beginning was made. There seems to have been sufficiently strong Indian resistance to make the local officials fearful of carrying out the program. Land allotment was ordered again in 1778 and more land was surveyed and assigned, but apparently only a small proportion of the total holdings was ever thus dealt with.

The Yaquis were fortunate in one of the secular curates who was assigned to the church at Torim — Don Francisco Joaquín Valdez. He spent twenty-three years at his base in Torim, becoming widely influential among Yaquis. He was a man of unusually high education, holding a university degree. His major interest lay in developing crafts and manufacturing as a balance to the agricultural subsistence economy which the Yaquis had developed. He instituted a program of technical assistance and set up a school in Potam. He encouraged sheep raising and cotton and indigo production. In 1774 he secured looms and a technician who knew textile manufacture and was successful in getting Yaquis to weave for commercial production. A stocking factory was set up in Potam and hatmaking was introduced. He also is reported to have trained Indians in carpentry, masonry, and metal-founding. How much further he carried this than the Jesuits had done earlier is not recorded, but it does appear that craft industry received a considerable impetus among the Yaquis as a result of his efforts.

Nevertheless, after Valdez' departure from Torim to take another church, the tendency toward economic decline reasserted itself. Reports on the conditions of the Yaquis indicated a lessening respect for authority, a decline of industriousness, and much leaving of the towns to live in the hills and rural areas. Spaniards were convinced that the Indians were reverting to their pre-mission state. Quarrels over Spanish encroachment on land took place in the eastern part of the Yaqui country at Los Hornos. Disputes arose between the town officials and the government-appointed captain-general. How much Spanish infiltration of the Indian communities there was at this time is not recorded, but some was going on steadily. The frictions and discontents to which this gave rise caused the governor to order the dissolution of the Yaqui Bow Company which had been a feature of the military organization of the area for some time. The fearfulness of the civil authorities was indicated, as earlier in the case of land allotment and tribute payment, in that this move was ordered to be undertaken with persuasion rather than force, so as not to antagonize the Yaquis. What the outcome was is not recorded.

The Yaqui-Mayo contacts with the Spaniards present a number of sharp contrasts with those between the Tarahumaras and the Spaniards. Outstanding is lack of rebellion and armed conflict during the first hundred years. The causes and the effects of this condition of peace among the Yaquis-Mayos are worth some analysis as a basis for understanding subsequent events.

Certainly as a major cause we can point to the absence of conflict among Spaniards within the Yaqui-Mayo country during the first century of contact. The conflicts of interest between mine labor-recruiters and missionaries were a feature of Tarahumara life from the beginning of contact, but such conflicts did not develop in the Yaqui-Mayo country until the 1730's. Thus, the Indians were required at first to make their adjustment only to the stable mission program. Eventually, the conflicting interests of the Spanish missionaries and the Spanish civil population did upset the mission system, but this took place only after the long period of mission discipline and reduction had altered the native life.

Both the Yaquis and the Mayos, unlike the Tarahumaras, were concentrated in relatively small areas at the time the Spaniards came on the scene. Each tribe had a population of about thirty thousand (according to the Jesuit records) which lived along the lower courses of the Mayo and Yaqui rivers. The area within which they lived was in each case about sixty miles long and from ten to fifteen miles wide. The Yaquis, in 1617, were reported by de Ribas to live in eighty rancherías. This meant that possibly the average population of each ranchería was between 350 and 400. Furthermore, the Yaqui and Mayo rancherías were of a different type from those of the Tarahumaras. While each Tarahumara household was some distance from its neighbors, as much as a half mile and in some instances even farther apart, the Yaqui and Mayo rancherías were more compact, with houses from a few yards to a hundred yards apart. How long it took to reduce the population into the eight more compact local centers with the corresponding local group loyalties which were apparent by the end of the Jesuit period is unknown. It would seem, however, to have been accomplished fairly quickly on the basis of devotion to a particular group of Catholic images which the missionaries supplied for each of the eight churches. The point to be made, however, is that the Yaquis and Mayos were already a relatively concentrated population when Jesuits began to work. Thus, the reduction program of the missionaries was not in conflict with a developed way of life, as among the Tarahumaras, but rather was in harmony with cultural developments already well under way.

Both the Yaqui and the Mayo populations moreover already had a high degree of tribal consciousness, stimulated by the population concentration in their portions of river valley. The warfare between Yaquis and Mayos, which was recurrent before the arrival of the Spaniards, had undoubtedly also stimulated this condition. The missionaries spoke of both groups as being somewhat isolated from neighboring groups during the first years of contact. What they meant by this cannot have been wholly a geographical matter, for a number of other groups bordered on both their territories. The missionaries probably were referring to tribal exclusiveness which separated the Yaquis and Mayos from other Cahita- and Pima-speaking peoples in their vicinity.

Evidently this tribal consciousness carried with it a considerable degree of organization which linked the rancherías into tribal units capable of making war or peace with other groups. This is indicated not only in the first contacts but also throughout Yaqui history and, up to a point, also in Mayo history. One indication was the treaty which Hurdaide made with the Mayos. It is evident in this, as well as in the later Mayo reaction to missionary entrance, that the Spaniards were dealing with an organized tribe. The Mayos made and kept their treaty as a unit and there is no indication that any one village or group of villages became disaffected. The same is true for the Yaquis, as indicated at the very first in their unity in opposing Hurdaide. They seem to have fought as a unit seeking to protect the whole of the territory through which their eighty rancherías were scattered. Then even in the face of recorded resistance within the tribe (on the part of "young men") it was possible for the Yaquis under a unified leadership to make a treaty and keep it. There is no indication that the Yaquis were split, moreover, even after the missionaries came in. What trouble the Jesuit Basilio had seems to have been with individuals who never gained followings, so far as is recorded. The kind of factionalism that was almost immediately apparent in the Tarahumara country and which increased in bitterness was a late phenomenon among the Yaquis, not yet even apparent in the revolt of 1740, although of course there is some evidence for factionalism at that time. This occurred, however, well after the first century of contact.

It was fortunate for the Jesuit program that this relatively high degree of organization existed among the two river peoples. Among the Tarahumaras they had to work at conversion almost individual by individual. In addition, working in from the edges of the Tarahumara country they created schisms among the people by establishing mission communities in the marginal areas, while completely conservative communities continued to function in the interior without any real Spanish contact. In contrast, on the Mayo and Yaqui rivers each tribe was brought under the mission system as a whole, so that there was no division into Christian and non-Christian communities even at the very beginning. The program was accepted in each case by the whole tribe. It is true that there were individuals and families who resisted baptism and close contact with the missionaries. Possibly there were whole rancherías here and there which continued to live outside the mission system for some time, or even possibly during the whole of the Jesuit period. But these were obviously a very small minority, not important enough to concern the missionaries after the first five or six years of work. The tried leadership, which was responsible for the treaties with the Spaniards and the invitations to the missionaries, must have been very stable indeed, and capable of working together effectively from community to community. There is considerable suggestion in the data that this leadership was never dependent on particular personality characteristics, but rather that it rested on a democratic foundation through which popular desire expressed itself effectively. Despite the intimate knowledge of Indian life which the missionaries gained, they did not often mention particular leaders. Hence, it seems unlikely that the organization that was obviously there was a result of particular individual qualities in leaders.

That there was considerable compatibility between what the Indians had or were aiming at in the form of leadership and what the missionaries, in combination with the civil Spanish government, wanted is indicated in the readiness with which they took to church organization, village government, and the system of instruction introduced by the Spaniards. One of the striking features of Jesuit comment on Yaqui and Mayo reactions is their frequent statement that no Indians took more readily than the Mayos and Yaquis to both the carrying out of church activities and instruction in Christian doctrine. The missionaries spoke of the zeal with which the Indians followed the Jesuit ceremonial calendar. They were also amazed at the rapidity with which Yaquis and Mayos learned the required prayers and hymns, and at the vigor with which those who learned immediately began to teach others. It is unfortunate that more of the details of the processes of religious teaching and learning have not been preserved. As it is, we have little solid information on which to build an understanding of the points of harmony and conflict in the two systems of religious thought. We can only infer that some points of congruity must have been quickly found and that the techniques employed by the missionaries encouraged rather than interfered with the harmonious blending of the two.

It is also unfortunate that we can reconstruct nothing reliable in regard to the conditions that led the Indians to be so avid for new rituals and beliefs as to invite the Jesuits in. It is clear that the Jesuits enjoyed extremely high prestige in the general region. It is equally clear that the Mayos, after their first inspection visits to the Fuerte region, knew a great deal about the missionary work and highly approved it. But just what it was that impressed them we do not know. There is no suggestion of any current revolution in religious belief into which the arrival of the missionaries fitted, nor any special need of the time such as techniques of curing. This lack of data forces us to fall back on the hypothesis of high compatibility between what the Indians had and what the Spaniards offered.

There is, of course, the possibility that the high prestige of the Jesuits rested less upon their religious than their economic offerings. Every Jesuit was an agricultural extension worker, with new crops and new agricultural techniques to offer, and the mission was a center for the diffusion of agricultural improvements. We know that the Jesuits were unusually successful in their work in developing agriculture on the Mayo and Yaqui rivers, especially on the latter. We know also that they introduced cattle, sheep and goats, chickens, wheat, fruits and vegetables, as well as plows and carts, donkeys, and hoes. The advantages of all these for increasing and regularizing the food supply must have been even more quickly apparent to the Yaquis and Mayos than to the Tarahumaras, for the former were already intensive agriculturalists. Their habitat lent itself to large-scale agricultural production and to the development of herds of animals. The large expanses of tillable land with a fairly regular water supply from the river floods were quickly turned to account by the stimulus of the Jesuits and their new agricultural resources. The Jesuit records indicate that their work stabilized the food supply quickly, and within the first sixty years their efforts began to result in real surpluses which the Indians did not object to seeing exported. The significance of this economic revolution cannot be overemphasized. Unquestionably, the missionary enterprise raised the standard of living, and this was regarded as desirable by the Indians, especially because the efforts along this line were well integrated with the new social and religious life which the missionaries introduced. Once the mission discipline was generally accepted by all members of the tribe, agricultural development went along with it. Two distinct ways of life were not set up as a result of the mission system here, as occurred in the Tarahumara country.

The revolt of 1740 brought the Indians face to face with the deep-seated conflict between the Jesuit mission system and Spanish political and economic interests. It is significant that at times during the growth of the armed conflict the missionaries seemed to be lined up with the Indians against other Spaniards. It is also significant, however, that there were some Indians who understood the nature of the power centers in Spanish culture and who accordingly tried to employ Spanish political power in seeking their own ends. Juan Ignacio Muni seems to have been such a Yaqui. By this time enough migration out of the Indian country into the mines and haciendas near or distant had taken place so that both Yaquis and Mayos were aware of other aspects of Spanish culture than those which the missionaries had introduced. There was a good deal of literacy, knowledge of the use and value of money, understanding of Spanish political organization, and awareness of the Spanish cultural conflicts as concrete phenomena in the actions of different Spaniards. The full impact of Spanish civilization would seem to have dated from this set of events.

Interestingly enough, the meager record of this important period in Yaqui-Mayo history does not indicate any clear eruption into factions of the Indian population of either river. Muni definitely used Spanish political power in an effort to increase his own power in relation to the missionaries; up to a point he was successful. But the records do not indicate that there was a split within either tribe — one faction backing the missionaries and one backing Muni. On the contrary, the denouement was that both tribes in unified fashion opposed all Spaniards — missionaries and political officials alike. It is true that the missionaries were treated as personal friends and there was no indication of any general or particular animus against them. They were still popular, but they were nevertheless regarded as Spaniards and were not, with one exception, asked to stay and side with the Indians. It was accepted that in the ultimate showdown they would have to go over to join the other Spaniards, and so they were given food and helped to leave their missions when the fighting turned against all Spaniards in the region.

At this point, it was clear that the Yaquis and Mayos had been brought on the path toward acquaintance with Western civilization as tribal units. They were not split asunder even at this time of heavy impact, as the Tarahumaras repeatedly were. Their society as well as their culture remained an integrated whole, and they united against the Spaniards. Muni, the leader who knew how to make use of the clerical-political split in Spanish society, remained a leader of his people.

The disintegration of Spanish organization on the northwestern frontier by the early 1800's must have been fairly clear to the Indians. Missionary activities, aimed at making the Indians feel the impact of a new and wonderful view of life, had been reduced to almost nothing. All the Indians of Sonora, even including the Seris, had now lived with the Christian teachings for one hundred years or more, and had seen them in a setting of economic exploitation, land appropriation, warfare, and political conflict. Most of the Indians, excluding the majority of Apaches and a considerable number of Seris, had accepted some Christian ideas and ritual as an adjunct to living, tying them in in various ways with their daily lives. But the missionary, as a man with great new promises and hopes, was no longer present. The mission communities no longer existed as outposts of the new way of life where new material and spiritual benefits were constantly being offered. They existed rather as made-over communities where the true and right way of life had been discovered and was now practiced. The transformation of the river rancherías in the skilled hands of the Jesuits was an accomplished fact. The blending of Spanish-Catholic theocracy and Indian democracy resulted in very stable and tightly organized communities. These communities were not, however, conceived by the Indians as units in a European nation. Rather the Yaquis and Mayos, for example, still conceived themselves as independent tribal units holding their land from immemorial times and not by fiat of the Spaniards. It was growing clear that the Spaniards were fearful of challenging that view.

Conflict over these disparate viewpoints was postponed, however, by the War for Independence from which the Indians of the river pueblos remained aloof. It was not until the Mexican government attempted to integrate the Mayos and Yaquis into the dominant cultural pattern that actual hostilities broke out.

The weakness of the Spaniards in the face of Apache attack and their vulnerability before such a small group as the Seris were widely known by the Indians of Sonora. The fact that the Spaniards had begun fighting among themselves, as revealed when the War for Independence finally spread into the Sonora-Sinaloa theater, indicated that perhaps they were no more to be feared than any of the other neighboring tribes. From 1810 to the early 1820's, while Spaniard fought Spaniard south, east, and north of the Mayo-Yaqui area, the Indians of the river pueblos stood by and watched. This was a fight which they apparently regarded as concerning them but little. They waited until it was over, one of the clearest evidences that the issues of national independence and gachupin-criollo struggle for power meant nothing to them. It was not until independence was won and the necessity of dealing with the new Occidente State became a fact that Yaquis and Mayos ceased their passivity. When they did it was apparent that at least some Indian leaders had been aware of events during the War for Independence, that they were in sufficient communication to have learned even the nature of the symbols which the Mexicans employed.

Sonora, at first set up as an independent state with capital at Ures in 1823, was united with Sinaloa in the state of Occidente when a constitution was drafted in 1824. A provisional government was established at Fuerte in northern Sinaloa and the constitution of the state of Occidente was promulgated in 1825. The drafters of the constitution were well aware of a major problem which had been considered and reconsidered for a century on the northwestern frontier. This was the question of how to bring the large Indian population of the region into the economic, political, and social life that the Spaniards had introduced. The prevailing view was that which stemmed from the later Laws of the Indies, namely, that Indians should be full-fledged citizens and participate in political affairs like all others. The constitution of the state of Occidente was explicit in this matter. In the first place it included an article which prohibited "commerce in or sale of Indians of the barbarous nations" and provided for "setting free those slaves who at present exist in servitude as a result of that unjust traffic." This applied in Sonora primarily to the Apaches, although from time to time various other groups had also been dealt with in the same way, but it established also the foundation for full citizenship of the "less barbarous" people. Thus, the constitution stated that citizens were "all those born and resident in the state who have reached the age of twenty-one years, or eighteen years if married." This was in line with the Plan of Iguala which in 1821 declared citizens of the monarchy "all inhabitants of New Spain, without any distinction between Europeans, Africans, or Indians."

This meant, of course, in the eyes of the Mexicans that Indians, as citizens, were taxable. Accordingly, the struggling new Occidente government made tax assessments on Mayos and Yaquis along with other citizens. In 1825, when it was found that Yaquis refused to pay taxes on the ground that they had never done so, soldiers were sent to enforce the law. At Rahum in the western Yaqui country the people fought the soldiers. A priest, Pedro Leyva of Cocorit, urged the Yaquis to resist further and within a short time there was general rebellion. A priest was killed at Torim. Other Mexicans besides Father Pedro Leyva, including a man named Casillas from Tepic, participated in the organization of troops to resist the government. A force of two thousand fighting men was raised, most of whom were armed with bows and arrows, and a Yaqui called Juan Banderas took command.

Banderas and his White advisers worked out a clear-cut program. They adopted as their symbol the Virgin of Guadalupe, as had the original rebels against Spain. The symbol was that of Indian independence of Spain, and, according to the accounts of the period, this idea was carried by Banderas to the point of planning a whole independent Indian state in northern Mexico. As fighting continued throughout the Yaqui country, Banderas sought to enlist the Opatas and Pimas on the north and the Mayos on the south. He was successful and within the year the White settlers who had come into the Yaqui and Mayo territory during the preceding fifty years were driven out. Some two hundred Yaquis joined with Mexicans to fight against Banderas' forces, but for the most part the Indians were united behind him. By early 1826 he controlled all the settlements of the lower Yaqui and Mayo valleys and began organizing his new confederacy. Fearfully, the Mexicans moved the new Occidente state capital southward to Cosala from Fuerte, but Banderas apparently was not interested in expanding his control beyond the area of Yaqui and Mayo claims and into the country of his Lower Pima and Opata allies. Once he had done this, he ceased to attack.

The Occidente government, weak as it was, made an effort to assert itself. It raised a fighting force, small but far better armed than Banderas' men, and engaged them south of Hermosillo. Banderas' force was badly defeated, but the Mexicans were not strong enough to invade Yaqui territory or to force Banderas to submit. He continued consolidating his influence in the area which he already controlled and then, as he saw that Occidente would continue to wage war, he offered to arrange peace. In 1827 he agreed to submit to the superior power of the Mexican state, apparently in the belief that Yaqui local government would remain autonomous. He was pardoned, along with other leaders, by Occidente. At the same time he was recognized as captain-general of the Yaqui towns and received pay from the state.

In 1828 the Occidente government, still deeply concerned with the problem of "integrating the Indians" into the state, enacted three laws having to do with Indian affairs. One of these set up the eight towns of the Yaqui River and the military post of Buenavista on the eastern boundary between Yaqui and Lower Pima territories as a separate political district. This act also made Buenavista the head town of the district and gave it certain jurisdiction over the Mayo towns. This put local government in the Yaqui and Mayo areas into the hands of non-

Indians who made up the population of Buenavista. Thus, foundations were laid for the extension of the municipality-state system of organization into the Indian communities.

A second decree set up regulations for government in Indian towns. Besides affirming the privileges of citizenship for the Indians, it also required them to elect local officials and serve in public offices, to serve in the militia, and to carry out the administration of schools and the public lands. It made school attendance compulsory. It suspended the usual colonial offices of captain-general and lieutenant-general in the towns, although providing that any individuals holding such offices at that time would continue to draw their stipends from the state for life. A third decree had to do with the administration of land. It provided that the towns should administer their own public lands, and required each town to assign all subjugated land to individuals and give them titles for it. Boards consisting of three Indians were to be set up for the handling of these matters in each town. Land allocated could not be alienated within six years, and various provisions sought to insure fair distribution. This was an effort to make effective the individual apportionment of land which had been ordered by the viceroy in 1769, after the Jesuit expulsion, and which had been gingerly proposed for the Yaquis and Mayos even before that.

The three decrees made very clear the nature of state policy on Indian integration. They had special relevance to the Yaquis, who had never been taxed, had consistently resisted efforts to divide their land for individual ownership, and had maintained their own local government largely distinct from provincial or state governments. At the same time they struck directly at Juan Banderas in his office of captain-general. The land distribution decree went into effect a year after its promulgation, in September, 1829.

Banderas began to make preparations for resistance. He manufactured gunpowder, acquired arms, and consolidated the alliance with the Opatas through an Opata leader named Dolores Guttiérrez. In 1832 Banderas and Guttiérrez at the head of several hundred men again established control over the Yaqui towns and sought to extend their domination into central Sonora in the Opata country. After a year Banderas' force of one thousand Yaquis, Opatas, and Pimas was defeated near Buenavista; Banderas and Guttiérrez were captured and executed in 1833 at Arispe.

A contemporary of Banderas, Ignacio Zuñiga, commandant of Mexican forces at Pitic, in 1835 wrote of him as follows: *The chief of these last two [uprisings] has been the Indian Banderas, General of the nation, a man of genius for directing and enthusing his followers, gifted with a spirited imagination, with eloquence and with a rare talent, with which he could have accomplished many more evils if his plans had been favored. . . . He conceived the plan of crowning himself king and of bringing about a general reconciliation among all the tribes for establishing his monarchy and sustaining the cause of the Indians against the whites. To this end he sent envoys to the other tribes, charging them with artful and flattering messages to invite them to join cause with him. He reminded all of them of that which should move them most, that is to say, the question of the lands: he painted our race as ambitious and dominating, and made use of the [existing] hatreds, grudges, and [desire for] vengeance, passions common to all the Indians, to excite them to agree to the consolidation of his military movements. . . . This caudillo [chieftain], courageous and ambitious, was shot at Arispe, leaving a memory among his people which perhaps will contribute strongly to the development of his doctrines, which can one day be regrettable. They have been planted; if they are left to germinate, propagate, and grow, will they not produce their fruit? . . . the doctrines of this bandit, and the great riches of all kinds which he distributed to the Indians will be for a long time the food of frequent rebellions and raids; since he succeeded in convincing them that they are the legitimate proprietors of whatever there is; and he taught them to live by robbing, something they will not forget easily, if punishment be not exemplary and prompt, following immediately the crime.*

Zuñiga also described something of the results of the campaigns of Banderas: *Before the rebellion of the year 1825 there was considerable population de razon scattered in the interior of all the towns of the Yaqui and Mayo and a much larger number who populated a multitude of ranches and haciendas in the immediate vicinities. The greater part of this population emigrated, leaving deserted and in fearful desolation many leagues round about which had been cleared and the goods of the fields transported to swamps and islands of the Yaqui. It should be noted that such fear has been inspired and so little security for peace and good faith of the Indians exists that a new uprising is feared each day. For this reason the fields remain deserted, the Mexicans who had them before in the same towns of one river or the other, wandering and deprived of their property and all the State alarmed and in expectation of more calamity, which may come to make worse the public evils now so heavy and unsupportable.*

Zuñiga saw the situation, as no doubt did his other Mexican contemporaries, starting from the premise that the Yaquis had in all respects submitted to the power of the Mexican government. To him Banderas was a bandit, albeit a very capable one, because he had dispossessed Mexicans of land on which they had settled and goods which they had produced. He was a rebel, as Zuñiga saw it, because he had set up his own government within the state of what was now Sonora and had fought against the state troops. Thinking in terms of the *caudillismo* which had already developed strongly in Sonora, he saw Banderas purely as an ambitious man trying to gain power for himself and make himself a "king." The Spaniards had previously interpreted the actions of the Yaqui leader Muni of 1740 in similar terms. Such an interpretation was entirely in accordance with the behavior of Spanish and Mexican political figures in New Spain.

In view of later developments in the century, it appears, however, that Banderas and most other Yaquis started from a different premise, namely, that they had never submitted completely to Spain or now to Mexico. They had preserved their land largely intact through the Spanish period, and had maintained a very considerable degree of autonomy in their village government. The new government of the state of Sonora, clearly in view of the decrees of 1828, proposed to establish a new regime which did not take into account either the long-existing political or land situations. Yaquis were trying to maintain that status quo and, under the leadership of Banderas, to build an organization that would insure them against the encroachments on land and political autonomy which had increased rapidly under the Occidente government. To them the Mexican settlers in their territory were bandits, taking land contrary to the law which Yaquis recognized. To them the Mexican soldiers were invaders. To them had diffused the symbol of the Virgin of Guadalupe in the name of whom the Mexicans had achieved their autonomy. Unfortunately, the available records do not give us the Yaqui point of view as clearly as Zuñiga expresses the Mexican, but it seems safe to assume, especially in view of later developments, that Banderas' activities were not simply those of an ambitious chieftain looking toward personal power. His ambitions were closely linked with the aims of the majority of Yaquis, nourished for two centuries by the politico-religious system of the colonial period and based in the sacred beliefs of the tribe. The military weakness of the Mexicans at the time when they forced the issues of land ownership and local government had given an opportunity for unified political expression of the tribal sentiments. Zuñiga's presentiments of the effects of Banderas' leadership were well founded.

Within a year of Banderas' execution, in 1834, there was fighting again. Yaquis rose at Torim in an attempt to oust Mexicans who had resettled there. It was now clear, however, that the demonstrations of Mexican power and Banderas' leadership had definitely split the Yaquis. Juan Ignacio Jusacamea of Torim, who had on occasion opposed Banderas and had been made alcalde mayor of the Yaqui district, fought against the rebellious Yaquis and, asking that the Mexicans send no soldiers, forced them into peace. Jusacamea, apparently accepting the fact of Mexican dominance and in favor of the land distribution program, continued for the next six years, until he was killed in an uprising of Indians near Horcasitas, to be an important leader and to work for peaceful solution of Yaqui differences with the Mexicans. Factionalism thus clearly became established among the Yaquis, as it had not been before.

However, there was little in the way of clear-cut issue in Sonora politics for the factions among the Yaquis to take hold of during the next thirty-five or forty years. Reflecting the political disorganization of Mexico generally, the state of Sonora became the scene of operation of competing political chieftains. Political principles became subordinated to personal loyalties as different caudillos vied for power. The plans for agricultural development in the Yaqui and Mayo and other Indian areas of the state, which had been set forth in the Decrees of 1828, fell into eclipse as the state government passed from hand to hand. The compulsory school program found no funds for its support. Even land distribution ceased to be carried out, except on an unsystematic and usually illegal basis. The Yaqui and Mayo towns were left practically to themselves, with only an occasional secular priest in residence, and with Mexican administrators too busy with shifting political alliances to follow up the provisions of the Decrees of 1828. What issues developed during the 1830's and 1840's were those of federalism versus centralism in the national organization and the Laws of the Reform during the 1850's. From the 1830's until 1860 one figure moved prominently and continuously in the politics of the state. This was Manuel Gándara whose political principles are difficult to determine. He clearly sought political power and achieved it at different times by more or less legitimate election to the governorship, by appointment from the central government, or by simple usurpation. He struggled for power with rival caudillos until one of these, Pesqueira, finally eliminated him from the political scene in 1859.

Throughout Gándara's political and military machinations he found support from some groups of Yaquis, but it is difficult to know whether they supported him because of any policies for which he stood, or simply because they wished to help keep the state stirred up. It is certain that whenever it suited his political purposes, Gándara was able to stir Yaquis into battle. In his struggle for possession of the governorship with Urrea during the 1830's and 1840's, Gándara armed the Yaquis and incited them against state forces three times, in 1838, 1840, and 1842. The first of these outbreaks resulted in Urrea's invading the Yaqui country, waging vicious warfare, and taking over for state and personal revenue the salt deposits on the coast which Yaquis had used. There is no record in regard to Gándara's policies with respect to the Yaqui and Mayo interests. We may infer that he tried to let them alone except when he felt they would be useful to himself at times of election or attempted revolution. This, of course, may have been sufficient inducement for Yaquis to give him what aid they could. That Gándara was aware of need for some sort of program which would bring the Yaquis more fully into participation in Mexican life is indicated in the fact that during one of his administrations (1853) he and Santa Ana, who was president of Mexico and a supporter of Gándara, planned to send six thousand colonists to Sonora to settle among the Indians and help build up the northwestern state.

From 1857 until 1862 the Yaquis were in an almost constant state of rebellion against the state government. This was a period of bitter struggle on the part of Gándara to remain in power, after being forced out of the governor's office in 1857 by General Ignacio Pesqueira. Gándara's revolution lasted from 1857 through 1859 during which period he was strongly supported by the Yaqui leader Mateo Marquin (or José Maria Barquin). Fighting centered on the western margins of the Yaqui territory in the Guaymas Valley, but by 1858 extended to Cocorit on the eastern margin. In the same year, as Gándara's revolution failed elsewhere in the state, the Mayos joined forces with the Yaquis. While the Yaquis attacked and laid waste the Guaymas Valley, the Mayos attacked the lower Mayo River town of Santa Cruz and sacked it. By the end of 1858 General Pesqueira, whose troops had been busy elsewhere, turned his attention to the Yaqui and Mayo country. The fighting factions of both tribes were dealt defeats in 1859, but continued to fight. Beaten in their own territory in the following year, they nevertheless organized a joint expedition to Hermosillo, the state capital, where they were defeated by Pesqueira's forces and retreated back to their own lands. In 1862 Pesqueira found it necessary to invade both Yaqui and Mayo territory, defeating the Mayos at Santa Cruz and accepting peace offers from the Yaquis at Torim. Pesqueira established a military post at Agua Caliente in the Yaqui country, after giving pardon to the Indian leaders for their part in the revolution.

The nineteen years of the Pesqueira family's control of the Sonora state government were marked first by the vigorous attempt to establish peace by force of arms in the Mayo and Yaqui areas and second by the French invasion of Sonora. The several invasions of the river valleys by forces directed by Pesqueira and his able assistant Colonel García Morales during the Gándara revolution and its aftermath established Pesqueira, and hence the existing state government, as the enemy of the Yaqui and Mayo towns. Their hostility to Pesqueira continued throughout his regime and came to vigorous expression during the French invasion. In 1865 the French invaders defeated Pesqueira at Guaymas and began to consolidate their plans for taking over the state. This plan included capitalizing on the Mayo-Yaqui hostility to the Sonora government. Immediately after the defeat of Pesqueira, the Yaqui leader who had supported Gándara, Mateo Marquin, declared his support for the French Imperialists and carried a considerable number of Yaquis, although not all, with him. Supporters of the French had already been at work in the Mayo country and found a majority of Mayos ready to join them in an attack on Alamos. Meanwhile, in the center of the state, an able Opata military leader, Refugio Tanori, announced his support of the French and organized an army of several thousand Opatas and Lower Pimas. Alamos was quickly taken in the south; and Tanori's force, which included some Yaquis, ousted Pesqueira from his headquarters in Ures. Through 1865 and 1866 fighting continued, with the Indian allies of the French giving them strong assistance. However, the French were finally defeated and driven out of Sonora in 1866. Pesqueira then began again the pacification of the Mayos and Yaquis.

After campaigning into the Indian towns and accepting peace offers, Pesqueira appointed members of the peace-seeking factions to maintain order and administer local affairs. Two of these were promptly killed, at Bacum by the Yaquis and at Santa Cruz by the Mayos, and Pesqueira found it necessary to campaign systematically again against the Indians. The rebellious Mayos quickly capitulated in 1867, but immediately proceeded to attack the towns of Santa Cruz, Etchojoa, and San Pedro on the lower Mayo River in the following year. After this outburst, Pesqueira's troops were able to force the Mayos to accept peace again in early 1868.

The pacification of the Yaquis proved more difficult. Pesqueira placed General García Morales in charge of a determined campaign. The Mexican troops after establishing posts at various points around the whole margin of the Yaqui country, penetrated into the center where they established headquarters at the port of Medano. From here they carried on a war without quarter. They shot dozens of captured leaders, confiscated cattle and food, laid waste fields, took women and children prisoners. In 1868 an incident occurred which has gone into the Sonora history books and has become a symbol of Mexican cruelty to Yaquis. One of García Morales' colonels at Cocorit accepted the plea for peace of a group of six hundred men, women, and children. He asked them to turn over their arms and when a few were given up, he let 150 of the prisoners go and imprisoned the remaining 450 in the church at Bacum. He held ten leaders as hostages, saying that if there were any attempts at escape he would shoot all ten. During

the night he trained his artillery on the door of the church. There was a disturbance during the night. The colonel ordered the ten leaders shot and, as a fire broke
out within the church, the artillery shelled the doorway. The result was that
some 120 Indians were massacred.

By such relentless means García Morales obtained peace in the Yaqui towns.
He then proceeded to order the systematic distribution of the Yaqui lands again,
and arranged for establishment of three colonies of Mexicans to be protected
by the troops in their pursuit of agriculture. In October the most serious flood
ever reported engulfed the Mayo towns, destroying Navojoa, Etchojoa, Tesia,
Cuirimpo, and Camoa. It was eight years before fighting broke out again on the
rivers, but the continuous disturbances in southern Sonora, together with Apache
raids in the central part of the state had resulted in the emigration of thousands
of people. The Yaquis and Mayos, especially the former, were spoken of as the
major obstacle to civilization in the state.

Pesqueira's effective methods of force had brought a short peace in southern
Sonora which the Mexicans welcomed. It had also intensified the resistance of
both the Mayos and Yaquis to the Mexican program for civilizing them, although
the Sonorans did not become aware of this until a few years later. The Mexicans
were nevertheless well aware that the program for integrating the Yaqui and Mayo
towns into Sonora life had never been carried out as it had been envisioned in
the decrees of the state legislature of 1828. When, during Pesqueira's regime, a
new constitution was written to conform with the Laws of the Reform promulgated by Juárez and Porfirio Díaz, notice was taken of this condition. The new
state constitution, which went into effect in September, 1873, contained the following provision:

*Article IV. — To deprive the Yaqui and Mayo tribes of the rights of citizenship
while they maintain the anomalous organization that they have in their towns
and rancherías, but allowing the enjoyment [of those rights] to individuals of the
same tribes who reside in the organized pueblos of the state.*

In 1874, as peace continued, Governor Pesqueira appointed a Yaqui named
José Maria Leyva, usually called Cajeme (He Who Does not Drink) by Yaquis,
alcalde mayor of the Yaqui and Mayo towns. Cajeme had fought with General
Pesqueira against the French. The following year was election year and opposition to the long period of successive elections of Pesqueira as governor had developed. Rebellion against the family dictatorship was brewing and when the
governor's son, José J. Pesqueira, was announced as the successor of his aged
father, a revolution broke out under the leadership of Serna. This seemed also to be
the signal for disturbances on the Yaqui and Mayo rivers, as had elections in the
old days of Gándara. Yaquis burned the town of Cocorit and Mayos burned Santa
Cruz. Whites who had settled on the lower Yaqui River during the recent peaceful
years of Pesqueira's administrations began to flee, as rumors of a general uprising
increased. The new alcalde mayor, Cajeme, was seen to make frequent trips to
the Mayo towns, where long conferences were held. The fact that his appointment
also included responsibility for the Mayo towns was not regarded as sufficient

reason for these meetings. It was also rumored that Cajeme had ordered shot Mayo leaders whom he did not like. Whatever the plans, it was apparent that two towns had been attacked and steps must be taken. Accordingly Governor Pesqueira, ignoring the revolution of Serna for the time being, marched into the heart of the Yaqui country, defeating Cajeme and a troop of fifteen hundred Yaquis at Pitahaya on the way. Repeating his father's procedure, he established headquarters at Medano and began to pacify the Yaquis in relentless fashion. Pesqueira's soldiers killed indiscriminately, raided the Yaqui cattle ranches, and pillaged the towns, evidently believing that the same methods used by the earlier Pesqueira would bring the same results of peace. A fort for a permanent garrison was begun at Medano, but before it was finished, the Serna revolution gained such serious proportions under the military leadership of Colonel Lorenzo Torres that Pesqueira was forced to retire from the Yaqui country and seek to attend to it.

During 1876 the Pesqueira-Torres forces reached a stalemate and President Díaz was forced to send an intermediary to settle Sonora affairs. There were no more Yaqui outbreaks, but in the following year of 1877, two Mayo leaders, Felipe Valenzuela and Miguel Totolitogui, working from San Pedro, organized an attack on places near Navojoa. They were promptly beaten by Mexican troops, but meanwhile the fears of the Whites settled on the Mayo River below Navojoa were so great that nearly all of them fled the area.

While the Mayo-Yaqui area remained in a state of expectation of a new and devastating war under the leadership of Cajeme and his Mayo lieutenants, the Sonora state government settled its affairs in favor of the Torres family as against the Pesqueira family. In 1879 General Luís E. Torres, who had for some time held land and been interested in developing the Yaqui country agriculturally, was elected governor and began a political dynasty which lasted for thirty years, until the Revolution of 1910 ousted his family and friends along with President Porfirio Díaz.

The first administration of Governor Luís E. Torres, from 1879 through 1881, was a period of continuing rumors and alarms that the Yaquis and Mayos were on the point of a grand uprising. Settlers in the Indian country were convinced that Alcalde Mayor Cajeme was planning war. It was known that he had led Yaquis against General Pesqueira at Pitahaya when the latter had invaded Yaqui territory in 1875. Yet no steps were taken to remove him from office, so far as the records reveal. The costs of a vigorous campaign were beyond the resources of the state of Sonora, and besides there was strong feeling on the part of the state leaders that campaigns such as Pesqueira had waged did not solve the problem. Instead, the old program of colonization seemed to hold out more prospect for a permanent solution of the Mayo-Yaqui situation.

In 1880 the state legislature, Governor Torres, and General Bernardo Reyes, military commander of federal forces in the state, formulated a plan and asked the aid of the federal government for carrying it out. The legislature prepared a full statement of the problem as they saw it. After recounting how the Papagos, Opatas, and even the Seris had become peaceful and industrious citizens, the legislators went on to say: *Thus, little by little, and with the passage of time, the dominions of such tribes as populate Sonora have been narrowed, to give place to civilization and to form a people which if it is not the most learned in the Republic, is at least not the last.*

Only the Yaquis and Mayos have been able to remain obstinate in their savage life, occupying a great extent of land on both the best rivers which the state possesses, masters of the most fertile lands, without any organization, without obedience to either authority or laws, completely removed from obedience to all government, and what is more, constantly making collection of war materials, as though preparing for an armed struggle, and committing continuous robberies and assassinations against the interests and persons of those who get within their reach.

The legislators explained that "war without quarter" such as had been waged in the past did not work and that a "war of the castes" would not settle the problem. They discussed the "horrible anomaly" of the Indian-controlled governments of the Yaqui and Mayo towns and pointed out that some of the Mayo towns, namely, the upriver ones of Macoyaqui, Conicorit, Camoa, Tesia, and Navojoa, had "liberated themselves from the dominion of the savages" and were living in conformity with the laws of the state under the prescribed municipal organization. They closed by throwing the gauntlet to the federal government: "Is it perhaps that the Mexican government is so weak that it cannot reduce these savages to order, requiring them to live like the other inhabitants, and making them begin the life of civilization?"

They then went on to outline their plan. They asked the federal government for one thousand soldiers to be permanently stationed in the Yaqui and Mayo country. The soldiers themselves could take up land to their own advantage and set examples to the Indians as farmers. At the same time the soldiers would constantly act as protectors of civilian colonists who could steadily penetrate the fertile river lands. Gradually the Indians would come to understand the futility of resistance and would see the benefits of civilized life as desirable for themselves. Such a plan would be the least costly that could be devised and would bring peace and economic development almost immediately. Governor Torres, emphasizing that the Mayo and Yaqui land was the most fertile in the state and could become the base for the sound development of Sonora if it were placed in the hands of civilized men, approved the legislature's report. The plan was also strongly endorsed by General Reyes, the military commander, and sent on to the national Secretary of War and Navy. General Reyes pointed out that Cajeme could raise probably not more than two thousand fighting men out of the current fourteen thousand population of the lower river valleys and that a permanent force of one thousand national soldiers, aided when necessary by National Guard and state troops, could keep the situation well in hand.

The Secretary of War replied that one thousand soldiers were not available, but that he would be glad to help in case of emergency. Governor Torres, with foreboding, then turned to an effort to distribute the land around the Yaqui and Mayo towns and began preparations for building a large irrigation canal to improve the agricultural situation in the Yaqui area. At the same time he attempted to organize the Indian towns as agricultural colonies under state law. It was soon evident that the Indians were as resistant as ever to such measures and little was accomplished during Torres' administration.

His successor, Carlos Ortiz, was the holder of a large hacienda in the vicinity of Navojoa on the Mayo River. Immediately upon assuming office, apparently in response to the many rumors that the Mayos were preparing an uprising, he appointed his brother Agustín commander of state troops and established a large garrison at Navojoa. This action had two immediate results. One was the rousing of great hostility against him throughout the state, on the ground that he was using the state to protect his private interests. The other was the outbreak of war on the Mayo River.

Agustín Ortiz, hearing that Cajeme had come from the Yaqui towns to the Mayo to plan an uprising, gathered a force and attacked the rumored place of meeting of Cajeme with the Mayo leaders — Capetemaya. The battle of Capetemaya resulted in the rout of Ortiz' soldiers, as well as the dispersal of the meeting and the wounding of Cajeme. This took place in 1882. For two years following the Mayo towns were in a state of rebellion, and raiding of Mexican holdings around Navojoa continued intermittently. A small force of national troops came in to help. Mexicans in Navojoa and Alamos organized to protect themselves. The reputed "Chief of the Mayo Tribe," José Zarapero, was picked up and shot. Various Mayo leaders were dealt with in the same way. Cajeme named a successor to Zarapero in the person of Jesús Moroyoqui but did not himself bring any military aid from the Yaqui towns to the support of the roused Mayos. Fighting continued intermittently until 1884, but no effective organization developed among the Mayos. There was a good deal of evidence of disunity among them, and finally the small forces which were carrying out the raids asked for peace and agreed to recognize Mexican authority.

Meanwhile Carlos Ortiz was forced out of the governor's office and one of the Torres family was made interim governor. In the Yaqui country there were also signs of dissatisfaction with the existing leadership. Cajeme had made efforts, in his capacity as alcalde, to institute a more centralized control of government than the Yaqui towns were accustomed to. He represented himself as captain-general, the title which Sonora law had abolished, but which Yaquis had long recognized and regarded as necessary in case of war. Cajeme also set himself up as judge over all the Yaqui towns, and undertook to make himself in this capacity the highest judicial authority. Accepting the town organization pretty much as he found it and encouraging the town councils to act in the form of democratic bodies as they customarily had done, he nevertheless regarded himself as wielding an over-all authority, based upon but ultimately higher than the power of the eight governors who served as chairmen of the eight town councils.

In the course of attempting to bring about this concentration of power in his own hands, Cajeme encountered both strong support and opposition. Insofar as relations with non-Yaquis went, Cajeme apparently was permitted to exercise the power he wished. Thus in preparations for war with Mexicans to protect land encroachments, he found Yaquis generally willing to accept his leadership, for example, in carrying out the work of fortification of a place called Añil between Potam and Vicam, and in the training of cavalry and other troops. As a former captain in the Mexican Army fighting against the French and on the side of the Liberals, he was recognized by Yaquis generally as a tribal military chief. Also, he had instituted a tax on shipments of goods to and from the Yaqui port of Medano and this seems to have generally been regarded as a proper means of raising funds for military preparation by Yaquis generally. However, when he assumed judicial authority, making decisions in regard to land use and interfamily disputes, Cajeme incurred the hostility of many Yaquis. His actions began to be spoken of as arbitrary and his position of judge as an usurpation. During 1884, when he remained inactive in the Mayo uprisings, much opposition developed against him. For the most part, the opposition took the form of the departure of Yaqui families who objected to his activities. Many of these families bitterly opposed Cajeme because of his exercise of judicial power, as they thought, against them specifically. Others were opposed to what they regarded as a policy sure to increase the hostility of Mexicans, with consequent war. Among the latter seems to have been a man named Loreto Molina, who had been Cajeme's lieutenant, or teniente-general. Cajeme had deposed Molina and forced him to get out of the Yaqui country, for reasons which are not recorded. Molina then began to cooperate with the Mexicans and early in 1885, probably with full knowledge of responsible officials in Guaymas, devised a plan for ridding Sonora of Cajeme.

Molina sailed from Guaymas with a few other Yaquis to Medano near which was Cajeme's home. Here he burned the house, in an effort to kill Cajeme, maltreated his family, and returned to Guaymas with one of Cajeme's generals and several others as prisoners. Cajeme was in the Mayo country at the time, and when he came back immediately demanded of the Guaymas municipal authorities that they punish whoever committed the crime. His approach to the matter, according to Mexican accounts, was highhanded and antagonized the officials concerned. In the first place, Cajeme, without waiting for a reply to his demands, held some Mexican boats in the Medano port for ransom. When his demand for the extradition of Molina was ignored, instead of going through channels as Governor Torres suggested, he announced that he would carry out reprisals. Immediately, at both the eastern and western margins of Yaqui country, raids were carried out on haciendas. At the same time some ranches were burned on the Mayo River.

The Mexican reply was war. General Carbo, the military commander of Sonora, organized twenty-two hundred soldiers into two columns which proceeded to march from both the east and the west into Yaqui country. The western column reached the heart of the Yaqui country at Medano with only minor skirmishes; the eastern column, after reaching Torim without encountering serious resistance, engaged in battle with Yaquis at the fortified point of Añil. Here General Topete was badly defeated by a very small force of Yaquis, who utilized the Cajeme-inspired fortification of Añil to very good advantage. More fighting resulted for the most part in Yaqui defeats, especially at Omteme near Torim. Cajeme then offered peace, on condition that all troops leave the Yaqui country, a condition which he repeated again in later months, and which the Mexicans of course would not accept. Again in December of 1885, after many Yaqui families had fled the impending warfare and the Mayos appeared very divided in regard to carrying on any hostilities, peace negotiations were initiated at Potam. During the conference, Cajeme remained in the background, actually retiring outside the town. The upshot of the talks was that all the governors of the eight towns declared that they wanted peace, no conditions being stated, and the Mexican negotiators called for signatures on a peace pact. When Cajeme was called in to sign the pact, he said that if it was the will of the eight pueblos to have peace, he would obey it. He then said, however: "My word has as much value as my signature, and they [the eight towns] have always had peace without signing the least paper." The pact remained unsigned and both sides prepared for war.

The year 1886 opened with a determined campaign by the Mexicans. They met no resistance in the Mayo country, where the people were suffering from a serious smallpox epidemic. In the Yaqui country Mexican troops occupied point after point and finally defeated the Yaquis at Añil. Meanwhile Cajeme had persuaded most of the remaining families on the river to retire to another fortified point in the mountains — Buatachive north of Torim. Here with a reputed force of four thousand he proposed to withstand the Mexican attack. The battle of Buatachive was bitterly fought on both sides and the slaughter of Yaqui men, women, and children was great. At least two hundred Yaquis were killed, two thousand were taken prisoner, and the rest, Cajeme among them, fled with their wounded to escape without food into the mountains.

The defeat of the Yaquis seemed complete. Smallpox raged. The governors of five pueblos were prisoners. The families in the mountains, starving and without clothing, began to give up in small groups. The remaining governors gave themselves up and peace was arranged with all of them at Torim. Colonel Lorenzo Torres was commissioned to reorganize and administer the Yaqui towns. Three detachments of soldiers were stationed at Cocorit, Medano, and Torim, with headquarters under Torres' administration at the last point.

But the fighting was far from over. Some eight hundred Yaquis who had not submitted remained in the vicinity of Bacum and raided and resisted Mexican troops whenever they were encountered. Cajeme was still at large, and Yaqui parties harassed troops from one end of the Yaqui country to the other. While the Mexican forces were still trying to mop up in the Yaqui country, the Mayos put forces in the field, attacked Santa Cruz and were not pacified for some time. In the fall of 1886, a note from Cajeme reached the Mexican commander. In it Cajeme wrote that he and all "my people" were willing to give obedience to the government, providing that within fifteen days all military forces left the Yaqui country. But he added that if this was not done he regarded it as a sacred duty to defend the Yaqui lands to the last. Branding the note as arrogant, the Mexican commander replied that the Yaqui River was not independent of the Mexican Republic and that the mopping up would continue.

Cajeme was now completely isolated from a majority of the Yaquis. Thousands had fled the Yaqui country entirely to seek work on the haciendas of the state. Other hundreds had been shipped out involuntarily to work on the haciendas. From a population of fourteen thousand on both rivers, about four thousand Yaquis had formally submitted and put themselves in the hands of the Mexican authorities, while some sixteen hundred Mayos had done the same. The submitted Yaquis were utterly destitute, dependent on what the Mexican administration could raise for them. Ten centavos per day per person were allocated for their support until they could again plant crops. Seeds were given them, and Colonel Torres began to make Torim the center for administrative care of the Indians. As telegraph communications were established for the first time across the Yaqui country, finally linking the northern and southern parts of the state, Mexicans began to move in, taking up farm land and entering into trade with the troops established there. A later Mexican commentator wrote of this period: ". . . and now this was the beginning of a great and humanitarian work: the civilizing and incorporating [of the Yaquis] into the common mass of citizens of the Republic."

The chief obstacle to lasting peace seemed to the Mexicans to be Cajeme's leadership. None of the military forays was able to locate or capture him. Early in 1887 he left the Yaqui country and tried to hide in San José de Guaymas. Here he was captured, and several leading Sonorans became acquainted with him while he was being held. Among these was Ramón Corral, a high state official later to be elected governor alternately with General Luís Torres as a working member of the Torres dynasty, and still later to become Porfirio Díaz' right hand man as vice-president of Mexico. Corral, expecting to find Cajeme a taciturn and fearsome savage, was surprised to encounter a good-natured, suave, talkative man of fifty, proud of his Mexican nationality and of his having fought for the Liberal Revolution. In illustrating his Mexican patriotism, he once told Corral how he had refused an American permission to cut wood for charcoal in the Yaqui country, saying to the American, "We Mexicans do not need to have foreigners come and hold our hand to make the sign of the cross." Cajeme claimed that "the eight pueblos" had done everything voluntarily in the matter of resistance to the Mexicans, and that he had merely carried out their will, which was to keep their own land for themselves. Corral claimed that Cajeme said that now "he understood the necessity for a new existence for the Indians, based on submission to the Government."

Cajeme was executed at Cocorit in April, 1887, and Mexicans looked forward to an end to the Yaqui problem. Ramón Corral said, "The sacrifice of Cajeme has been very sad; but it will give as a result the guarantee of peace on the Rivers, the base and beginning of a period of civilization for the tribes."

The death of Cajeme, contrary to expectations, had no effect whatever on the last-ditch guerrilla fighting in the Yaqui country. In June, the moment troops retired from Cocorit, Yaquis burned the town, killed what Mexicans they could lay hands on, and sacked the ranches. On the Mayo River some Mayos rose and were not pacified until their leader Jesús Moroyoqui was killed. Anastasio Cuca, one of Cajeme's lieutenants was in Tucson, Arizona, seeking aid for the Yaqui cause. An estimated four hundred well-armed guerrillas were raiding from hiding places in the Bacatete Mountains, north of the river. It was reported that they were working under the leadership of Juan Maldonado, called Tetabiate by the Yaquis. In the midst of continued sporadic fighting at various points in the Yaqui country, General Torres set out once again to carry through the distribution of the Yaqui lands, to both the thirty-five hundred Yaquis still remaining along the river and the many Mexicans, including the Torres family itself, which had moved into the territory.

In 1887 the Scientific Commission of the state of Sonora, working under military guard, proceeded with the survey of lands and the planning of irrigation canals to water the land on both sides of the Yaqui River. A colony of Mexicans was established between Torim and Potam on the north side of the river (later to become Vicam station), and in 1889 a canal was opened to irrigate their fields. The three to four hundred Yaqui guerrillas working from bases in the Bacatete Mountains continued to harass settlements within and at the western margin of the Yaqui country. Military detachments were in constant operation meeting their attacks and pursuing them into the nearby mountains. Every week a few Yaquis were killed and a few families were captured. By 1890 the Scientific Commission finally completed the division and distribution of all the arable land in the Yaqui Valley. At the same time they continued, in the midst of guerrilla harassment, the work on two large canals, completing one on the north side of the river, opposite Bacum, called the Bataconsica Canal. The commission also worked at laying out the Yaqui towns on the grid pattern with central plazas and streets at right angles. The military authorities made an effort in 1890 to get Yaquis who had settled elsewhere in Sonora to come back and take advantage of the new irrigation works, sending emissaries from among the Yaquis who had remained on the river. No one came back, and the rumors grew that Yaquis outside the Yaqui country were helping the guerrillas with provisions and ammunition. Finally General Carillos threatened to force Yaquis to come back and resettle on the river. A few came, but the situation continued very much as it had been for the previous three years, with no appreciable weakening of the guerrilla forces, who were still reported to number about four hundred under the leadership of Tetabiate.

The Yaqui spirit of resistance continued to be expressed in armed aggression, and thousands of Yaquis refused to surrender by simply remaining outside the Yaqui country. At the same time the latter gave some help to the Yaqui guerrillas in the Bacatete Mountains. Meanwhile, the Mayos showed an entirely different sort of reaction. Their country, like that of the Yaquis, had been occupied by Mexican armed forces. Guerrilla resistance by small groups had continued into 1887, but after that year it disappeared entirely. The Mexicans had killed the major leaders, apparently leaving none who was capable of or willing to continue armed resistance. Between 1887 and 1890 the majority of Mayos had gone to work on the Mexican ranches and haciendas which occupied the greater part of the river valley from Navojoa northward. The Indian villages downriver from Navojoa had been largely depopulated either by smallpox, flood, or warfare. Not more than sixteen hundred Mayos were reported by the Mexican military commander to have formally surrendered in the towns of Etchojoa, San Pedro, and Santa Cruz. There were, however, hundreds of other Mayos scattered in small rancherías, or working on Mexican haciendas elsewhere in the Mayo country.

In 1890 the Mexican military became aware of activities among the Indians which they regarded as threatening peace. In the words of a military historian of the period: *It should be noted that since 1888 the Mayo Indians had remained peaceful and that, better advised or less inclined to war [than the Yaquis], they devoted themselves to their planting, coming down from the mountains to their villages, even though with the distrust common to these Indians. In the month of September [1890] almost all the people stopped their labors to join together to listen to the prophecies and teachings of men and women whom they called, and were recognized as, holy people among the said Indians. Because, preceding other uprisings, this kind of meeting had been held, Colonel Rincón, military chief of the Mayo, dissolved the big gatherings and brought various of the holy men and women to the towns in which they could be under his vigilance.*

The Mexicans apparently first became aware of the religious meetings in the southern part of the Mayo country near Masiaca at a place called Jambiobampo. Investigation revealed that some twelve hundred Mayos were gathered at Jambiobampo to listen to the preaching of a sixteen-year-old boy, whom they called "santo," or holy one. The boy, Damian Quijano, was the son of a Mayo general who had fought with Cajeme. He spoke no Spanish, only Mayo and carried on his preaching in conjunction with the traditional ceremonial organization and officials of the Mayos. He was representing not a wholly new cult, but a religious movement which remained within the framework of existing Mayo religion. His preaching was based on the teaching of the "Saint of Cabora," a Mayo girl, Teresa Urrea, who lived and had been preaching at the ranchería of Cabora in the northern Mayo country on the Cocoraqui Wash, the boundary line between the Mayo and Yaqui country. The message of the Saint of Cabora was that Mayos must pay special attention to right relations with God, for a tremendous flood was coming soon. If they listened to the teaching of the Saint, she could tell them the points of land which would not be flooded and where they would accordingly be saved. One such point was near the ranchería of Jambiobampo, and Mayos had come by the hundreds to this point to be saved.

It was not only here, however, that the Mexican officials found Mayos gathered in September, 1890. At six other places, besides Cabora, there were "santos" preaching the new doctrine. These were in the heart of the Mayo country, in the lands which the Mayos regarded as sacred for the tribe, between the coast and Navojoa. Three of the other preachers were women, three were men: Santa Camila, Santa Isabel, Santa Agustina, San Juan, San Luís (also called La Luz), and San Irineo. Each of these places was investigated by military parties and in each the Mexicans found that those who gathered had no arms, except for bows which they set up on altars along with flowers. The Mexican military men concluded that the meetings were merely an example of Mayo "fanaticism," but that nevertheless steps should be taken to prevent them from becoming more dangerous. Besides, many haciendas and ranches of the Mexicans had been left destitute of workers and, as Colonel Rincón put it, the Mayos showed no inclination to save their employers, only themselves. Accordingly, San Damian along with fifteen apparent leading adults at Jambiobampo were taken into custody by the Mexican authorities in Masiaca. Eventually most of the other saints, together with leading men and their families, numbering forty all told, were taken to Torim and sentenced to work in the mine of Santa Rosalia in Lower California at $1.25 a day. The Mayo country appeared to go back to normal, but the Saint of Cabora had not been included in the roundup.

The Mexican officials followed this up by establishing a school for Indians in Santa Cruz on the Mayo River. On the Yaqui River the program of peaceful colonization continued with some fifty families being set up at Bacum with irrigated land and agricultural implements. Similar groups of peaceful Yaquis were also established at Torim and Potam. Railroad connections were completed through the Yaqui country in 1891. Schools were opened in the same year in the lower Mayo country at Etchojoa, San Pedro, and Huatabampo. Nevertheless Yaqui guerrilla fighting, after a lull, increased, the Valley of Guaymas was harrassed again, and Mexican detachments were kept busy chasing Yaquis in the Bacatete Mountains. In May of 1892, two hundred Mayos suddenly attacked Navojoa and killed the municipal officials there. All through the lower Mayo country the Indians were in arms again, attacking Mexican settlers with the battle cry of "Long Live God and the Saint of Cabora." As groups of Indians were dispersed they fled to Cabora to be blessed by the Saint. An unidentified group swept down from the mountains of Chihuahua and attacked Cabora. Most of the Mayos who were picked up were armed with bows and arrows. The fighting was quickly put down and Teresa Urrea of Cabora, along with her father, Tomás, was taken in custody and transported out of the Indian country to Guaymas. From there Teresa went to Arizona, and the Mayo country was again quiet.

For the next five years guerrilla fighting continued in the Bacatete Mountains and on the eastern margins of the Yaqui country. In 1893 there was a notable increase in the number of Yaquis engaged in the warfare. Attempts had been made ever since 1891 to enforce the now-required registration of Yaqui workers in the haciendas of the state of Sonora. It was apparent to the Mexicans that many Yaquis, after supplying themselves with food and weapons during a period of work on the haciendas, either returned themselves to join the guerrillas or sent their provisions to aid them. It was not until 1897 that any important change took place, although the work of digging canals and encouraging peaceful Yaquis and Mexican colonists to farm went on.

In 1896 and early 1897 Colonel Peinado of the Mexican military forces entered into correspondence with Tetabiate, leader of the Yaqui guerrillas. He did this through a Yaqui family named Buitimea whom he had captured in one of the raids into the Bacatete Mountains. The Peinado-Tetabiate correspondence lasted several months. In the course of the correspondence, it became clear what Tetabiate was fighting for. He wanted, like Cajeme before him, the retirement of all troops from the Yaqui country and continued possession of arms by his troops, as he said he had heard the Apaches had been treated in the United States. Peinado appeared in one of his letters to promise the retirement of troops: "I order the detachments not to go out, but rather remain in headquarters, and when peace is arranged we will retire them little by little and we will not return to pursue you." In the light of later developments it would appear that Tetabiate and his lieutenants took this to apply not merely to the period of peace-making, but rather as a promise for general retirement of troops immediately after peace was made. In one letter Tetabiate wrote to Peinado, "I have taken your holy oaths; in the name of the Holy Trinity." He said that he had made his own promises on the same basis. Tetabiate wrote frequently of the "Holy Peace" which he hoped would be established.

The result of the correspondence was the eventual appearance of the whole force of Tetabiate—about four hundred men, women, and children—at the station of Ortiz on the new railroad which cut through the Yaqui country. They came for the signing of a peace treaty with Governor Ramón Corral and General Torres, military commander of the state of Sonora. The Mexicans arranged an elaborate ceremony in which the Yaqui drummers joined in martial music with the Mexican military band, and Yaqui and Mexican soldiers exchanged hatbands. The Mexicans dealt with Tetabiate as "Chief of the Yaqui Tribe" and so designated him in the peace treaty, a title which of course was not recognized by any of the eight Yaqui town governments. The peace treaty, which it seems doubtful that Tetabiate understood fully, said simply that the "Chief of the Yaqui Tribe recognizes the sovereignty of the supreme Government of the Nation and State" and that he "should submit to obedience." It also provided that the government would give two months' provisions for the surrendered Yaquis and their families, and that they would be given land from that not yet occupied and which had been set aside for Yaqui use. The treaty said nothing whatever about the withdrawal of troops or Mexican settlers, or the political organization of the towns. Yet Tetabiate, along with his chief lieutenant Loreta Villa and his interpreter Julian Espinosa, signed it. No other representatives of the Yaquis were called to the meeting.

The Mexican government then set about living up to the agreement and doing all that it could to win over Yaquis and establish peace on a firm footing. Tetabiate and his men, together with other Yaquis, were put on the payroll as auxiliaries to regular Mexican troops. Tetabiate was placed in command of the auxiliaries. Lands were distributed to Tetabiate's followers and all other Yaquis who would take them. Six thousand land titles were given out within ensuing months, but how many Yaquis received them is not recorded. Food, seeds, and agricultural implements were given out not merely for two months but for two years following the treaty. Thousands of Yaquis came back to live peacefully. Letters were sent from the Apostolic Visitor and President Díaz congratulating Tetabiate on his peaceful course. General Torres, through the authority of President Díaz, gave out grazing lands when Yaquis asked for them in addition to their farms, and even decreed that the salt beds were to be exploited by Yaquis alone. Loreto Villa, Tetabiate's ablest aide, and another Yaqui named Hilario Amarillas were sent to Mexico City for a month to gain a better understanding of the benefits of peace and the futility of uprising. President Díaz wrote to General Torres that "we should not be tranquil until we see each Indian with his plow in his hand, behind a team of oxen, cultivating the fields." A Mexican writer said: "In short, whatever resource it was humanly possible to use to move and convince the Indians, such was exerted to the utmost to domesticate the wild beast."

General Luís Torres, as military commander of the state with headquarters in Torim, became the patriarch of the Yaqui country, dispensing land and justice. His approach is well exemplified in the following statement to the Yaquis: *Don't believe that the parcels of land which now have been delivered to you are all that the Supreme Government will give you. Should one of you come and say to me: "Sir, I have sons. We lack land to cultivate"—you shall have what you need; but now, seeing that scarcely a tenth part of that which you possess is cultivated, you must agree that you have more than enough to cover your necessities.* Torres felt that a just peace had been arranged and that what was necessary to maintain it was a firm hand and the clear demonstration that the power of the nation, backing him in his administration of the towns, would be used to dispense land and agricultural aids under his guidance. This power was to be the ultimate authority and each individual should have access to him directly and not through any intermediary of the outworn system of town government.

General Torres proceeded to arrange for the spiritual needs of the people as well. He invited a group of the Sisters of Josephine to come and establish themselves at Bacum. With the help of a vigorous priest, Father Juan N. Beltrán, the sisters embarked on a program of reclothing the somewhat ragged images in the Yaqui churches and they together with Father Beltrán preached indefatigably of the benefits of industry and peace.

General Torres nevertheless had forebodings that everything was not working out. He deeply distrusted the Yaquis. Already after barely a year of the new regime, a careful reporter of Yaqui affairs, Colonel Manuel Gil, wrote: *A curious phenomenon: of the Indians who returned to occupy the river, ninety per cent had spent years practicing the civilized life in the towns of the state. Arriving in the Yaqui, they replaced, with pleasure, their delicious coffee with pinole; their shoes with sandals; and the women, keeping in the bottoms of their trunks, silks, laces, and stockings, returned joyously to bare feet and primitive clothes. The clothing of the children was reduced to its simplest expression.* Gil reported that at Bacum where the Sisters of Josephine energetically and constantly talked with the Yaqui women, the latter were unhappy. Instead of responding promptly to the urgings to change their personal and religious customs, they looked fearful and held that, if what the sisters said about the old ways were true, then a terrible punishment must be in preparation for Yaquis. Father Beltrán also found in his own experience that he was not welcome. The temastis (religious leaders) at Bacum told him that they got along perfectly well before without a priest, except when they wanted to take their children somewhere to be baptized, and that they saw no need for a priest now. Old men kept telling Father Beltrán that there had been no Mexicans in the Yaqui country when they were young. When a group of old men met with General Torres in the regular sessions which he held for the correction of complaints, they would say there were no complaints. Then suddenly some old man would say: "But when will the Mexicans leave?" To General Torres they appeared to be fanatics on this point.

Tetabiate's former lieutenant, Loreto Villa, who had been working hard to smooth relations with the Mexicans after his government-sponsored visit to Mexico City, and whose loyalty had been rewarded by General Torres with the command of the Yaqui auxiliaries, reported that he had made many efforts to explain to the old men the need for submitting to the Sonora government and trying to work out a peaceful life. Villa said that there was a recurrent response to his statement that all was changed from the old days. "The old man said to me: 'Nothing is changed. We cross ourselves now with the same hand that we have always crossed ourselves.'"

In 1899, two years after the Peace of Ortiz, Yaqui leaders at Bacum, where Father Beltrán and the Sisters of Josephine had been at work, appeared to be restless. El Jopo and Pluma Blanca were reported hostile to the Torres regime. General Torres did not hesitate. Putting Tetabiate temporarily in command of the Yaqui auxiliaries, carefully refraining from sending any Mexican troops, he ordered Tetabiate to disarm the Bacum dissidents. Tetabiate, along with his old lieutenants, Loreto Villa and Julian Espinosa, went to Bacum and executed the order. The next day the auxiliaries rebelled and with Tetabiate fled to Cocorit, leaving Villa to report the incident to General Torres. The general then received a letter from Cocorit, signed, "The eight Yaqui towns." It said, in effect, "What are you going to do about what happened?" Then it continued: "We don't want to fight the Federals, but we had to because Espinosa was with them." Espinosa and Villa, as supporters of the Mexican administration, were regarded as traitors.

The note concluded: *What we want is that all whites and troops get out. If they go for good, then there will be peace; if not we declare war. Because the peace which we signed in Ortiz was on the condition that troops and whites would leave and this they have still not done; on the contrary, in place of complying they have taken away [our] arms. Certainly now you are behind all the business, and we have no blame for all the misfortunes that there are.*

Meanwhile the rebels had killed Hilario Amarillas, who had accompanied Loreto Villa to Mexico City, but Villa had escaped to resume his command of those Yaqui auxiliaries who had not rebelled. General Torres replied:

You are not the eight towns of the Yaqui, but can be considered only as a gang of evil-doers, which, not desiring peace or honorable work and not recognizing the benefits you have received from the Government, have got together to commit robberies and assassinations.

The war was on once more. Bitter fighting against the rebels around Bacum resulted in the Mexicans taking that town. Cocorit also fell quickly into Mexican hands. The whole south bank of the river, however, where General Torres had made a large grant to the Conant Development Company, was promptly in the control of Yaquis. Fighting centered between Potam and Vicam and only slowly were the Yaquis who maintained the fighting driven back into the Bacatete Mountain strongholds. To Mexicans it now seemed that they were victims of a long-standing plot to which Tetabiate was a party. They felt that he had proved himself a traitor, incapable of living up to his word in the Peace of Ortiz, and that he had been secretly planning a general uprising during the two years of peace. It is clear that what happened indicated a widespread readiness on the part of Yaquis resettled on the river to resort to arms to put all Mexicans out of what they still firmly regarded as their territory. How much of this action was planned and fanned as a conspiracy, and how much Tetabiate was a party to it will never be known precisely. It seems likely that the Yaqui leadership, which was out of Tetabiate's hands from 1897 to 1899, was merely behaving in accordance with the old patterns which had developed through the whole of the nineteenth century. In maintaining an organization which enabled them to rise quickly against the Mexicans, they were merely continuing the old town organization which General Torres refused to recognize and which consequently continued to operate without his knowledge. The Mexican misconception of Tetabiate's role, their treatment of him as a supreme chief of the tribe, constituted an interpretation of Yaqui affairs in terms of their own culture which inevitably led again to hostilities.

The Mexicans now planned a campaign to end the fighting once and for all. The policy makers in the state had long since abandoned any idea of extermination of all Yaquis. For many years the reports on Yaqui affairs emphasized that Yaquis were the best workmen in the state and that they constituted some 15 percent of the population of the state. They were heavily relied on for labor in the haciendas and the mines. Proposals for extermination, which came up from time to time, were repeatedly met with these facts and the reply that the state would be crippled economically if that method were resorted to. Colonization of the Yaqui country with military occupation for the protection of colonists seemed still the best method. The military occupation was now to be preceded by an effective surrounding of the Bacatete Mountains. In addition to this measure there was to be instituted a program of "espionage," that is, of constant reporting on the movements and attitudes of Yaquis working in the state outside of the Yaqui country, together with constant checks on the Yaqui settlements on the river. In addition, rebellious Yaquis were to be deported from their country to the haciendas of the state. It was believed that this would be beneficial particularly since it would help breed the good Yaqui qualities into a mixed population. It was also held that Yaquis who were deported elsewhere in the state could be educated properly and their Mexican hostility bred out of them.

In 1900 these measures were undertaken. There were at this time already about half as many Mexican and American colonists in the Yaqui country as there were Yaquis. One report enumerated 7,606 Yaquis and 3,639 colonists. Torim had become a Mexican town of some importance, both as military headquarters and seat of the patronage of the Torres family. It had an intellectual life and a growing commercial and trades class. As the organized campaign began, Colonel Penna, who had been in charge of much of the development work in the Yaqui country, voiced the viewpoint of the Mexican officials:

Convinced that it should not concern itself with the question of justice in giving pieces of land to the Indians, that matter having been well debated and perfectly demonstrated that that is not what the Indians wanted, since they have abandoned their lands to follow rebellion and their titles have served as wadding for their guns, it is clear to be seen that their sole desire is but to drive out the

Mexicans; the land in the form in which they have received it does not interest them. Their reasoning in this particular is the following: "God gave the river to all the Yaquis, not one piece to each."

In 1900 Yaquis suffered a severe defeat in the heart of the Bacatete Mountains at Mazocoba. They left four hundred dead and many captives. Captured Yaquis in some numbers were shipped out of the Yaqui country to work for wages, it was maintained, at various places in the state. As the Mexican campaign tightened, with Loreto Villa now serving as a major and fighting against Yaquis, a letter came out of the mountains to the Mexican commander. It was signed by "The Eight Towns of Yaqui" and said that all Yaquis were willing to submit to the superior authorities of the state and federal government, providing that all Mexican settlers and all troops immediately left the Yaqui territory.

The fighting in the Bacatete Mountains and the Guaymas Valley went on. In 1901 Major Loreto Villa's detachment ran across Tetabiate escorting a group of women and children into hiding. They killed Tetabiate but the fighting continued. The surrounding of the Bacatete Mountains became increasingly effective, so that groups of Yaquis attempting to come back to join in the fight were prevented from entering the Yaqui country. Gradually all Yaquis were cleaned out of the Bacatetes and fighting flared up from San Marcial, thirty miles north of the Bacatetes, to the vicinity of Ures in the central part of the state. The Yaquis who had gone out to work, prevented by troops from fighting on their own ground, were fighting wherever they found themselves. Their resistance had been fired by a new series of regulations issued by General Torres, who was again governor of the state. The new regulations provided that Yaquis might settle only in prescribed areas of the state, that they must be kept together in their own settlements on the haciendas, that they be reviewed once a month by officials wherever they settled, that any Yaqui without registration papers must be jailed, and that constant observation be made in all Yaqui settlements. In 1903 Rafael Izábal, one of General Torres' friends, became governor and began a campaign of raiding the haciendas to pick up Yaquis, and other Indians. Those picked up were jailed in wholesale lots. At the same time large allotments of land in the Yaqui Valley were given to the Torres family and to various development companies. Near Ures one group of Yaquis fighting against Mexican troops from a mountain area sent word that they would be willing to stop fighting, providing that all troops leave the Yaqui country, that the land be given to the tribe, that they be permitted to maintain their own government, and that the state government prohibit Whites from crossing their territory.

The raids on the haciendas continued. Yaqui raids were reported as far north as Magadalena, fifty miles below the United States border. Rural police picked up Yaquis wherever they found them. The campaign outside the Yaqui country had been stepped up by Governor Izábal as a result of a new program which had taken form, namely, the deportation of Yaquis to other parts of the Mexican Republic, outside of Sonora. A regular traffic in Yaquis grew up which reached its greatest proportions about 1907. Extermination, military occupation, and colonization had not solved the problem. The new program consisted of sale of Yaquis, both men and women, at sixty pesos a head to henequen plantation owners in Yucatan and the sugar cane fields of the Valle Nacional in Oaxaca. The federal government and the state government worked together. Yaquis who had been jailed in Hermosillo and elsewhere were shipped by boat down the west coast and then marched across Mexico to be shipped again to Yucatan by boat. Up to 1908, five thousand Yaquis were reported dealt with in this manner. Families were broken up. Mayos, Papagos, and Opatas also fell into the net. The Yaquis, "obstacle to civilization" as they were called, no longer were able to fight. Thousands hid themselves, avoiding identification as Yaquis, and merged with the Mexican population of Sonora in cities and on haciendas. Hundreds fled across the border into the United States and settled permanently there.

By 1909 the Mexican hacendados of Sonora felt that the deportation had hurt their labor supply. They protested and General Torres who was again governor slowed the traffic down. A peace was again made with a Yaqui named Bule representing the Yaquis. When the 1910 revolution against Díaz broke out, Yaquis who were settled on the Yaqui River fought against the Maderistas at first and, as Obregón's revolutionary troops gained control of the state, also against Obregón. The Yaqui leaders, however, offered to make peace, providing that they were given full sovereignty over their land and the right to expel all non-Yaquis. To Obregón this demand seemed "atavistic" and calculated to "perpetuate barbarism" among the Yaquis. He accordingly sent General Lázaro Cárdenas to force the Yaquis into submission. After a vigorous campaign, lasting until 1917 and during which the Yaquis who had settled in Arizona made an unsuccessful effort to send arms and men to support the struggle against Cárdenas, the resisting Yaquis were beaten. Many Yaquis, believing that Obregón had made some sort of promise to restore to them lands which had been allotted to Mexicans and North Americans, agreed to join his forces in support of Obregón's wing of the revolution. Hundreds marched with his troops into Mexico City at the time of his final triumph.

In 1919, with the revolution accomplished, Adolfo de la Huerta became governor of Sonora and began again the task of rebuilding the Yaqui country. By this time Cocorit and Bacum had become Mexican towns, after the fashion of Navojoa in the Mayo country fifty years before. Belem, Rahum, and Huirivis on the west had become uninhabitable due to failing water supply as a result of changes in the river course in the delta. This left only three of the original Yaqui towns — Torim which had fallen into ruins after its flourishing period as the Torres center of government, Vicam which was overshadowed in size by the colony of Mexicans at Vicam station, and Potam. The conservative Yaquis nevertheless spoke of themselves still as the "eight towns" and sought government aid in rebuilding the lost villages. De la Huerta, with small resources, began plans for putting some of the privately owned land under government administration, and gave aid in rebuilding the ruined churches. He won much cooperation from Yaquis who began to return from the various areas of their dispersal, but became involved in a counterrevolution and left the state. As the federal government bought out the land of the Richardson Development Company on the south bank of the river and began its apportionment to non-Yaquis, the old Yaqui resistance began again to assert itself. In 1926, during his second campaign for the Presidency, Obregón, while passing through the Yaqui country by train, was detained by General Luís Matus, a Yaqui who had fought with Obregón, for talks about the Yaqui land problem. Word went out that Obregón had been "captured by the Yaquis" and troops came in to "liberate" him. Fighting took place between Vicam, where Obregón was held, and Potam. Yaquis settled in the towns began to flee into the mountains. A military campaign, designed to get the Yaquis down out of the mountains, lasted for nearly a year, and prominent Yaquis fled seeking political asylum in the United States. Captive Yaquis, including some important leaders, were impressed into the Mexican army and sent to far-away posts in Vera Cruz, Yucatan, and central Mexico. Military occupation of the Yaqui country was ordered and posts were set up in the principal towns and at all the important water holes in the Bacatete Mountains. More Yaquis fled to the United States in the half dozen settlements which had grown up in southern Arizona. At the same time various companies of Yaquis who had fought with the Mexican troops during the 1926-27 disturbance were allotted lands and settled as part of the occupation Army on the river. "The Yaqui problem" was still not settled. Slowly, however, more Yaquis who had spent periods in other parts of Mexico as a result of the Army impressment policy came back to resettle. During the 1930's the Yaqui population steadily increased, but it was confined almost wholly to the north bank of the river. The vast fertile farmlands of the south bank, having at last been brought under an effective irrigation system, were permanently in the hands of Mexicans and North Americans. A large city, Ciudad Obregón, rivalling Hermosillo in size, was booming in the midst of the extensive agricultural developments on the south bank on the site of the former hamlet of Cajeme.

In 1936 President Lázaro Cárdenas, who had beaten the Yaquis in 1917, sought, in line with his policy of government aid for Indians all through Mexico, to do something about the "Yaqui problem." His government under the auspices of the Department of Indian Affairs set up a school near Vicam for the agricultural training of young Yaqui men. Cárdenas himself entered into correspondence with the governor of Vicam, which, like the other Yaqui towns, still maintained its own colonial-period system of organization apart from the municipal state organization. In response to complaints over land encroachment, especially on the north bank of the river and to various types of exploitation of Yaqui resources by Mexicans, Cárdenas set forth a plan. It included the building of a large dam on the Yaqui River, the water of which was to go first to irrigate the north bank of the river where Yaquis were concentrated. It also set aside by presidential decree the whole north bank, a small portion of the south bank, and the Bacatete Mountain area exclusively for Yaqui control. Cárdenas also promised to help with the establishment of the lost towns within the north-bank territory and to give government aid in agricultural development. He refused a Yaqui request for help in rebuilding the churches on the ground of separation of church and state in Mexico. He refused to do anything about land already lost on the basis that he could do nothing about commitments of previous governments. These promises were made at a meeting with town governors in Potam in 1939, in which there

6. YAQUI-MAYO COUNTRY ABOUT 1960

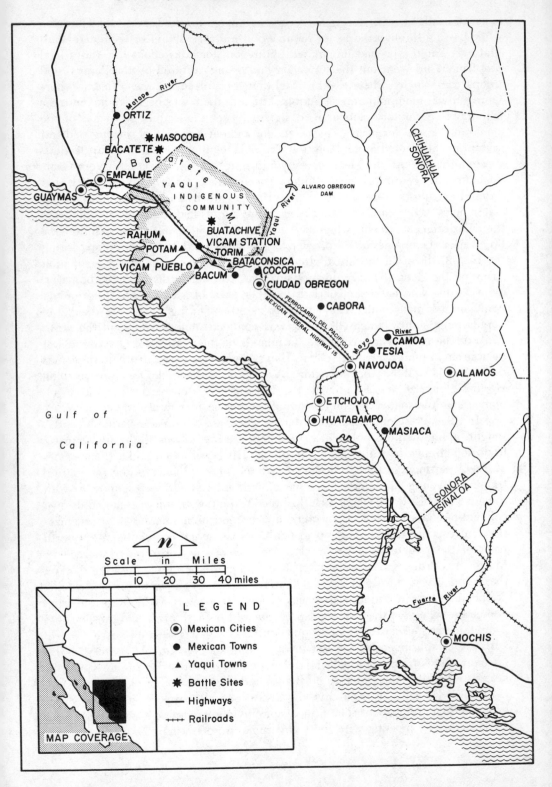

Matope River

ORTIZ

MASOCOBA
BACATETE

Bacatete

EMPALME

GUAYMAS

YAQUI
INDIGENOUS
COMMUNITY

Alvaro Obregon Dam

Yaqui River

CHIHUAHUA
SONORA

BUATACHIVE
VICAM STATION
RAHUM
POTAM
TORIM
VICAM PUEBLO
BATACONSICA
BACUM
COCORIT
CIUDAD OBREGON

CABORA

FERROCARRIL DEL PACIFICO
MEXICAN FEDERAL HIGHWAY 15

Mayo River
CAMOA
TESIA
NAVOJOA

ALAMOS

ETCHOJOA
HUATABAMPO
MASIACA

Gulf of

California

SONORA
SINALOA

Fuerte River

MOCHIS

Scale in Miles
0   10   20   30   40 miles

LEGEND
◉ Mexican Cities
● Mexican Towns
▲ Yaqui Towns
✸ Battle Sites
— Highways
+++ Railroads

MAP COVERAGE

was at least tacit recognition of the existing governmental system, and Cárdenas' letters and decree spoke of the "Yaqui Tribe." A system with some similarities to the reservation system in the United States was set up.

It was some fourteen years before the waters of the new dam began to be usable on the north bank. Meanwhile military occupation continued, Mexican land encroachment went on, and the Yaqui population increased to some ten thousand.

The Mayos had meanwhile pretty much disappeared from Sonora history as a distinct tribal group. While Yaqui armed aggression continued as late as 1927, no fighting took place in the Mayo country after 1893. The Mayos were pacified thirty-five years sooner than the Yaquis. Nevertheless, by 1950 Mayos in their own territory slightly outnumbered Yaquis in theirs. Forty percent of Mayos still spoke only the native Mayo language, while only an insignificant number of Yaquis spoke no Spanish. The widespread and long-standing dispersal of Yaquis throughout Mexico and the United States accounted for their greater use of Spanish. The Yaqui language continued, however, to be the language of home and village affairs as late as 1960. Mayo village government no longer functioned in the colonial-period manner, while every Yaqui town, including the ones in process of being rebuilt, such as Torocoba (replacing Cocorit on the north bank of the river), Bataconsica (replacing Bacum on the north bank), and Rahum and Huirivis (in new location), maintained the functioning colonial-type officials and the town governing council. Yaqui town ceremonial organizations had also been established in four Arizona settlements, although without the accompanying political organizations.

Mayo and Yaqui history during the Mexican period can be summed up as a struggle on the part of very much Hispanicized Indian communities to maintain control over their lands and local affairs in the face of a determined attempt to force them to change these patterns. The patterns which they sought to continue were those which they had developed under Jesuit tutelage during the two previous centuries. As Eduardo Villa, the Sonora historian has said: " . . . he [Cajeme] wanted to sign a peace more or less identical to that which in past centuries his elders had concluded with the Spanish Captain Martínez de Hurdaide. . . ." What Cajeme wanted to do, it is very certain from the record, was what Yaqui leaders generally through the 1950's have wanted to do; they have repeatedly shown that they want an independent local government, and jurisdiction through town management over lands which they believe were given them by supernatural fiat. The Mayos were only less determined than the Yaquis in these aims. To the Mexicans these objectives were not at first clearly seen, but, when it was realized what the source of Yaqui resistance was, they came to be regarded as signs of barbarism. The "horrible anomaly" of the colonial-type town government was not compatible with the nationalism identified by the Mexicans with civilization. A combination of circumstances, the most important of which was governmental disorganization among themselves, did not allow the Mexicans to force their land and political systems on the Yaquis for some eighty years. Even by the 1960's, despite dispersal and deportation, this had not been accomplished.

CHAPTER THREE

Lower Pimas and Opatas

WHEN THE SPANIARDS reached northwestern Mexico, the Indians of the central Sonora area seem to have been undergoing population shifts about which we know very little. Archaeology has not yet given us the story. However, there are indications from the distribution of Indian languages, and here and there in Spanish records appear some details about the relations of various groups which suggest unstable conditions. One of the most interesting and obscure facts about western Mexico is the peculiar distribution of the Piman-speaking peoples, who did and still do live in an area extending southwest from the Gila River for about one thousand miles. At the southern end of this area were the Tepecanos and north of them the Tepehuanes, whose revolt in 1616 shook the whole northwest frontier of New Spain.

The Tepehuan revolt was not a purely local uprising. It affected other tribes of the Sierra Madre Mountains, such as the Acaxee, the Chinipas, and, as we have seen, the Tarahumaras. The Tepehuan leaders — Quautlatas and Cogoxito — tried to enlist Indian support widely. In Sonora, Captain Hurdaide, who had just completed his campaigns of conquest against the Tehuecos, Zuaques, and Sinaloas, felt it necessary to carry his campaign into the mountains to prevent the revolt from spreading to the coast of the Gulf of California. It was apparent that envoys from the Tepehuanes had made contacts with Piman-speaking peoples in Sonora like the Nuris and the Yecoras. There was fear on the part of the Spaniards that the Yaquis would also join in the hostilities. Hurdaide's prompt measures prevented the uprising from spreading down from the mountain country, but actually there seems to have been no interest in rebellion at this time on the part of the Yaquis. The Tepehuan revolt nevertheless showed that there was widespread communication among the mountain tribes from Durango to southern Sonora.

LOWER PIMAS

One factor which facilitated such communication was a common language — the Piman. Tepecano and Tepehuan differed very little from the language of the Lower Pimas of southern Sonora, whom the Spaniards came to call the Nebomes. Moreover, up through central and into northwestern Sonora and what became southern Arizona, the Piman language was spoken by thousands more Indians. The long and sinuous distribution of these Piman-speaking peoples from the high mountains of the south to the desert valleys of the Gila River is a curious one. It seems probable that prior to 1600 the Pimas of Sonora were under some pressure from Opatas and that the Opatas had pushed into Sonora from the northeast. In southern and western Sonora Pima territory was being encroached on by the Opatas. Thus, there was bitter hostility between the Opatas of the upper Sonora and San Miguel valleys from Opodepe to Cucurpe and the Piman-speaking people of northwestern Sonora. Opatas also seem to have been advancing slowly down the Yaqui River, possibly pushing Pimas out of rancherías in the vicinity of Tonichi. There is some indication that the Lower Pimas of the middle Yaqui River area were, in turn, pushed against the Yaquis and that this stimulated Lower Pima and Yaqui warfare. At the time of Hurdaide's advances into Mayo territory at the beginning of the 1600's there seems to have been regular and persistent fighting between Lower Pimas and Yaquis, as well as between Yaquis and Mayos. There were certainly other causes for this warfare, but the tenacity with which Yaquis protected their tribal boundary suggests that they were already under some pressure and that this pressure must have come from their nearest northern neighbors — the Lower Pimas.

Yet the Lower Pimas do not seem to have been especially interested in warfare and fighting. The earliest Spanish accounts describe them as devoted farmers whose villages seemed well ordered, and whose inhabitants were inclined to peace. The hostility between them and the Yaquis suggests pressures on one another induced by pressures being exerted on the Lower Pimas by the Eudeve-Opatas on their immediate north.

The very earliest Lower Pima contacts with the Spaniards also suggest this pressure. In 1540 Cabeza de Vaca passed through Lower Pima country on the middle Yaqui River. A group of several hundred Lower Pimas were so attracted by his stories of the Spaniards that they went south with him to the Sinaloa River where they established themselves in a village called Bamoa. Such an exodus of families seems unlikely unless there had been dissatisfaction with their life in Sonora.

The group that settled two hundred miles to the south of their homeland were from rancherías along the Nuri River, a tributary of the Yaqui. They became famous in Spanish annals, prospered, and immediately accepted Christianity when the first Jesuits reached their area in 1591. They continued to maintain contact with those left behind on the Nuri River, and must have been a source of constant information to the Lower Pimas about the Spanish advance up the coast, and the advantages and disadvantages of mission life. The result seems to have been a generally favorable disposition towards the Spaniards.

In 1609 Lower Pimas, along with Mayos, were allied with Hurdaide and furnished soldiers in his attack on the Yaquis. About 1615 many rancherías of the middle Yaqui River asked for missionaries. This was a time when there were not enough Jesuits in the region to meet the demands of the Mayos, Yaquis, and other Indians who were asking for them. Some of the Lower Pimas decided they could not wait for missionaries to come to them. In 1615, therefore, about 350 Lower Pimas from various rancherías migrated southward to Bamoa and there, amid a great ceremony prepared for them by Hurdaide and the Jesuits, took up the mission life. Their reports must have been favorable for in the following year 230 more also went to Bamoa to live permanently.

By 1617 the Bamoa colony of Christian Pimas numbered more than a thousand. Father Pérez de Ribas, at work on the Yaqui River, was visited by a leader from some Lower Pima area who begged for missionaries and then went home, telling Pérez de Ribas that he would proceed immediately to build a church so that his people would be ready when missionaries should come. It was not, however, until 1619 that mission work began. In that year seventeen hundred Lower Pimas from unspecified areas were baptized by Father Guzmán. Following this a regular missionary, Father Burgencio, was assigned to those Pimas whom the Jesuits were calling the lower group, or Lower Nebomes, the missionaries having given the name Nebome, apparently, to all Piman-speaking people in the southern part of Sonora. Burgencio reached the rancherías in the vicinity of Buenavista (the southernmost area of settlement of the Pimas on the Yaqui River where over a hundred years later a presidio was established), Cumuripa, Tecoripa, and Suaqui Grande. Within about a year he claimed to have baptized some nine thousand. Thus, seven years before Pedro Méndez began systematic work among the Opatas, all of the Lower Nebomes had come under the mission system. There is no record of any but routine happenings in these missions for nearly 150 years.

Two years after the reduction of the Lower Nebomes the Jesuit Vanderzipe was assigned to the Upper Nebomes. These were the Pimans who lived in rancherías on the east side of the middle Yaqui River and extended up into the western slopes of the Sierra Madre Mountains. They included those Nuris who had not gone to Bamoa, and the people of Onavas, Movas, Yecora, and Maicoba. During 1622 the Pimas accepted Vanderzipe and built two churches in Onavas and Movas. In 1626 Hurdaide died and all the leading men of the Lower Pima rancherías went to San Felipe in Sinaloa for the funeral, along with other Indian leaders from Sonora. After the funeral, the new Governor Perea, who had heard a rumor that an uprising was being plotted in the mountains to the east of the Pima country, made prisoners of some of the Nebome headmen and held them at San Felipe. His idea was that they might have information which would be helpful to him, if they were not actually implicated in the plans. There were immediate repercussions at Movas among relatives of one of the detained men. Father Vanderzipe's house at Movas was burned and an attempt on his life resulted in his being wounded with a poisoned arrow. The missionary suffered the rest of his life from this wound which never healed satisfactorily. However, most of the inhabitants of Movas favored the missionary, and they quickly quieted the individuals who had tried to kill him.

For the next eight years, although new churches were built at Nuri and Tónichi, and a seminary set up at Nuri, Perea's hasty action made difficulties for the missionaries in the Lower Pima country east of the Yaqui River. There was resistance at Nuri about which we know little, except that medicine men opposed the missionary without success. In 1633 a revolt broke out with attempts to kill the missionary Father Olinano and a baptized headman. The leadership was in the hands of relatives of the men who had been imprisoned by Perea at San Felipe. A small expedition of Spanish soldiers came into the Upper Nebome country in 1634 and with the help of Nebomes themselves captured fourteen leaders of the revolt, who were immediately put to death. Father Olinano then went to work with redoubled effort and within a short time claimed 4,530 baptisms. There were now churches in four places — at Onavas, Movas, Tónichi, and Nuri — but it was not until forty years later that missions were established in the mountain area at Yecora and Maicoba.

In 1740 the Lower Pimas joined with the Yaquis and Mayos in their major revolt against Spanish rule. Some of the heaviest fighting was in the Pima country around Tecoripa among the Lower Nebomes. A few years later there were other signs of dissatisfaction among the Lower Pimas. A group known in the Spanish records as the Sibubapas, originally probably from the western Lower Nebome country, joined with the Seris in their revolt against the Spaniards. They surrendered and were brought to San Marcial about 1755, but were again reported to be fighting on the Seri side in 1768 and as late as 1770. A small rebellion that was quickly put down had also been instigated by a former governor of Tecoripa in 1766. He was reported to have become incensed against a missionary who had ordered him to be whipped, a common source of disaffection with the missionaries in this period.

In 1678 there were reported to be a little more than four thousand Lower Pimas living in the vicinity of the nine missions which had been established in their country as far east as Maicoba, the largest settlement being Onavas where there were reported to be 875 Indians. About a hundred years later, in 1769, the Lower Pimas were reported to number about three thousand. There were then eight missions in operation serving fifteen pueblos. Within the same area, where there were many small mines, there were reported to be 792 Spaniards, or *gente de razon.*

The story of the first 150 years of Spanish contacts for the Lower Pimas was largely one of peaceful reduction. It was characterized by an unusual eagerness for contacts at the beginning, even leading to migration out of Pima country. This suggests dissatisfaction with conditions in at least part of their country. The resistance which did develop before 1740 is easily traceable to the single event of the Spanish governor's unjust treatment of Pima leaders. Only a few families seem to have offered resistance, while in general the Pimas remained favorably disposed toward missionaries and Spaniards. Their country was penetrated by small groups of Spaniards very early and the Spanish population slowly increased, while the Indians slowly decreased in numbers. The proportion of Spaniards to Pimas within their country, however, never seems to have been so great as was the proportion of Spaniards to Opatas in the latter's country. When Lower Pimas did fight against Spaniards it was in conjunction with other Indians, first the Yaqui-Mayos and then the Seris. There is no evidence that they provided any

7. OPATA AND LOWER PIMA COUNTRY ABOUT 1750

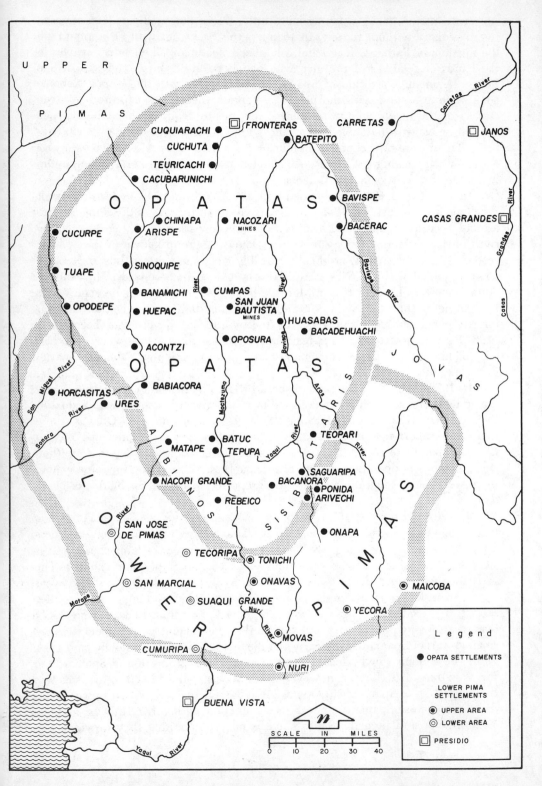

UPPER

PIMAS

OPATAS

CUQUIARACHI
CUCHUTA
TEURICACHI
CACUBARUNICHI
FRONTERAS
BATEPITO
CARRETAS
JANOS

CUCURPE
CHINAPA
ARISPE
NACOZARI
MINES
BAVISPE
BACERAC
CASAS GRANDES

TUAPE
SINOQUIPE
BANAMICHI
HUEPAC
CUMPAS
SAN JUAN
BAUTISTA
MINES
HUASABAS
BACADEHUACHI

OPODEPE
ACONTZI
OPOSURA

OPATAS

HORCASITAS
URES
BABIACORA

JOVAS

MATAPE
BATUC
TEPUPA
TEOPARI

NACORI GRANDE
REBEICO
BACANORA
SAGUARIPA
PONIDA
ARIVECHI

SAN JOSE
DE PIMAS
ONAPA

TECORIPA
TONICHI

SAN MARCIAL
ONAVAS
MAICOBA

SUAQUI GRANDE
YECORA

CUMURIPA
MOVAS

NURI

BUENA VISTA

LOWER PIMAS

San Miguel River
Sonora River
Matape River
Moctezuma River
Bavispe River
Aros River
Yaqui River
Carretas River
Grandes River
Casas Grandes River
Nuri River
Yaqui River

SISIB OTARIS

ALBINOS

Legend

- ● OPATA SETTLEMENTS

LOWER PIMA
SETTLEMENTS

- ◉ UPPER AREA
- ◎ LOWER AREA
- ☐ PRESIDIO

SCALE   IN   MILES

0   10   20   30   40

important leadership or that the Spaniards ever identified them as powerful enemies. They were followers of little importance in the wake of the Yaqui and Seri leadership. There is, moreover, a good deal of evidence that the Pima rancherías did not join with one another either as supporters of or antagonists to the Spaniards. Developments in the mountain country around Yecora seem to have had no connection with any farther west, and there is no indication that Tecoripa and Onavas, the important centers of the Lower and the Upper Nebomes respectively, were associated in any way with each other. There is a probably significant characterlessness about the Lower Pimas in the Spanish records. After initial approving references to their peaceful industriousness, there was little Spanish interest in them — in contrast with the very considerable preoccupation with, for example, the Yaquis and the Opatas. Part of this is undoubtedly due to the fact that the Lower Pimas were a relatively small group; part is also probably due to the fact that their territory was not so fruitful to Spaniards as either Opata or Yaqui.

OPATAS

The results of the Jesuit program among the people of central Sonora differed greatly from those obtained among the Tarahumaras or the Yaqui-Mayos. Neither the nature of the contacts with the Spanish nor the structure of the Indian societies was the same. The combination of these factors with the relatively constant factor of Jesuit program and techniques produced results that contrast with those which eventuated among the Tarahumaras and the Yaqui-Mayos. The Opata-speaking people moved much farther toward the Jesuit goal of complete assimilation into Spanish society during the more than 150 years of early contact than did either the Tarahumaras or Mayo-Yaquis. Cultural assimilation was not, however, by any means accomplished within the period.

The central Sonorans were not considered by the Jesuits in their first contacts with them to be a single tribal unit. The Jesuit appraisal was correct in that they were not tribal units in the sense that the Mayos or Yaquis were, and they never became such. They did, however, have fairly uniform behavior and beliefs, and the missionaries became well aware of this, once they had worked for a time among the different rancherías. There was not complete identity of language among them, as there was among the Mayos and among the Yaquis, nor even the degree of language similarity that there was among the scattered Tarahumaras. The Jesuits early became aware of language differences and made the distinction between the Opatas of the south and the Opatas of the north. Those of the south lived in the valleys of the Matape, Moctezuma, and middle Yaqui rivers, with centers near Saguaripa, Batuc, and Matape; but there was also a branch of this division which had settlements on the San Miguel River in the vicinity of Opodepe. The language of these southern and western groups came to be referred to more or less consistently by the Jesuits as Eudeve.

The Opatas of the north lived in many rancherías scattered along the whole length of the Bavispe, the upper Moctezuma, and the middle and upper Sonora River valleys. Their territory extended from the vicinity of the Huachuca Mountains in what is now southern Arizona well into central Sonora. The language of this much larger division was fairly uniform and came to be called Opata, or Teguima, by the missionaries. The fact that the missionaries called the different groups among the Eudeve and Opata by the names of their leading men, e.g. Sisibotari, or by the names of their principal settlements, e.g., Huazabas, Batuc, Huepac, or by village groupings, e.g. Aibino, Bacerac, indicates the lack of tribal unity among the Opatas. The missionaries were aware from the first that they were not dealing with people politically organized into a tribe.

The first contacts between the Opata-Eudeve-speaking peoples and the Spaniards were not friendly. There seems little doubt that the town which Coronado attempted to found on his way north in 1540 was in Opata territory. Called Corazones, it was established somewhere along the upper Sonora River. Two important facts are known about it. It lasted only a matter of months and was completely destroyed by Indians, probably Opatas of the Babiácora-Banámichi groups. The records agree in saying that Coronado's lieutenant, Alcaraz, was left behind to build up a small settlement in what appeared to be a very pleasant and productive place among well-organized and industrious peoples. Alcaraz, behaving like his superior, Coronado, forced the neighboring Indians to work for the Spaniards and went so far as to steal women for the pleasure of his soldier community. The Indians, as soon as they saw the character of the Spaniards, did not hesitate to attack and kill the whole settlement, except for two who managed to escape and tell the story. The actions of Alcaraz aroused the wrath of the once friendly Indians.

In 1564, in another part of Opata territory to the east in the vicinity of Saguaripa, there was another hostile encounter about which little is known. There, de Ibarra, who had been ordered to follow up Coronado's unsuccessful exploration of northwestern New Spain, encountered an armed force, probably of Opatas or Eudeves, with whom he fought. Although he reported a victory, he did not follow it up, but instead marched southwestward, leaving the country without discovering the mines in the vicinity, and eventually reached the Yaqui River. There is no record of the effects of this encounter on the Indians of the area, and no further contacts with Spaniards are mentioned until the early 1600's, when Hurdaide was actively pushing the missionary program in Sonora with the aid of Father Pérez de Ribas.

About the time the Jesuits began their work among the Mayos in 1614, Pérez de Ribas, who had heard of a very able leader among the Indians around Saguaripa, went to investigate. He met and talked at length with the headman, who was called Sisibotari, and came away with the impression that he had here met the finest of all the Indians among whom he had worked. He praised his dignity, ability, wisdom, and attitude toward the Jesuit teachings. The mutual admiration of the two men led to a visit on Sisibotari's part to San Felipe, where he became acquainted with Hurdaide and the Jesuits working in the area. He asked that missionaries be sent to his people near Saguaripa, who he claimed lived in seventy rancherías on the middle Yaqui River. However, since no missionaries were available at the time — indeed, there were not enough to meet the current Yaqui demand for them — Pérez de Ribas was unable to fulfill Sisibotari's request.

Meanwhile, Sisibotari kept in touch with the Spaniards. He brought eleven children from his rancherías to attend school in San Felipe at the Jesuit seminary. When Father Guzmán began work among the Lower Pimas in 1619, Sisibotari visited him and followed his progress, but in that same year he died and hence did not see the beginning of the Jesuit program among his own people. Nevertheless, it appears that knowledge of his interest in and high estimation of Jesuit work diffused among the seventy rancherías over which he had influence, for when Father Pedro Méndez visited Saguaripa briefly in 1621, he was welcomed and urged to build a church. However, it was not for six years more that the Opatas of Saguaripa were to have a missionary.

In 1627, Father Méndez, the veteran of the Sonora-Sinaloa missions who had carried out the triumphal large-scale conversion of the Mayos, came to live and work among the rancherías over which Sisibotari had been the headman. Méndez was received in the manner in which Sonora Indians now customarily received missionaries, that is, kneeling with crosses in their hands and forming processions which marched with the missionary through arches of green-leaved carrizo. All the Opata Indians of the area around Saguaripa were prepared to accept baptism. Within six months three churches were built — at Saguaripa, Arivechi, and Bacanora — and these remained peaceful missions for the duration of this Jesuit program. Méndez, although in his seventies, stayed for nine years and laid the foundations of mission work, being helped greatly by a headman of the Eudeves named Cruz Nesve. Except for an attempt on Méndez' life by a servant whom he had discharged earlier, no frictions seem to have developed. By 1678 there were over three thousand Eudeves and Opatas who had accepted mission life in six centers — Saguaripa, Teopari, Onapa, Bacanora, Arivechi, and Malzura. There had also come into these missions some Jova Indians, the mountain-dwelling neighbors of the Tarahumaras, who spoke a different language from the Opatas, and who were in process of being culturally and linguistically assimilated by the agricultural and well-organized Opatas.

In another part of the Opata territory, among people whose culture and language were almost the same as those of the people of Sisibotari, but who politically were entirely separate from them, missionary work began a few years after Sisibotari's death. Some of these people were called Aibinos and they were closely associated with the Eudebe-speaking people of the Matape Valley. The Aibinos in 1622 stirred up opposition to the missionaries who were working on the middle Yaqui River among the Lower Pimas. The trouble was serious enough to cause Captain Hurdaide to send an expedition of two thousand soldiers to the vicinity of Matape, where they defeated the Indians in a bloody battle. This was followed by the entrance of two Jesuits who baptized some four hundred children at Matape and Tepupa. No missionaries took up residence in the area, however, until 1629, when Fathers Azpilcueta and Cárdenas came to Matape.

Persistent resistance met the missionaries. Hurdaide's show of force in the area had stimulated opposition to the Spaniards, and, in the seven years since the first baptisms took place at Matape, local medicine men had talked against the Jesuits and opposed the occasional visits of those who were working among the

Lower Pimas. Instead of greeting the two new missionaries with crosses and arches, people stayed away from them. There were no large-scale baptisms, although some people presented themselves. At Batuc the people would not allow the missionaries to come among them at first, stimulated, say the Jesuit accounts, by a few persons who had been baptized but had then turned against Christian ideas.

In the face of this resistance, Azpilcueta took aggressive steps instead of calling for soldiers, according to his own account. First, he precipitated a crisis at an important shrine — the burial place of a headman who had been killed by lightning, to which people came for ceremonies which were designed to protect them from lightning. During a ceremony at the burial place, Azpilcueta launched into a sermon which denounced the ceremony as superstitious and urged the people to accept the Christian God. He followed this by systematically destroying both the shrine and the bones of the entombed headman. By this action, we are told, instead of rousing the people to action against him, he won their loyalty.

Another time Azpilcueta, with a few Indian supporters, stood off an armed party which threatened to destroy him and his church. The missionary took up an arquebus and fired at the hostile Indians which caused them to disperse. According to Azpilcueta's account, these bold measures on his part turned the people from hostility to acceptance of him, and his work proceeded without incident for eight years. The Indians built a church for him at resistant Batuc, and he was able to carry on the program, laying foundations also for work on the San Miguel River to the northwest where Eudeves lived. Before his death in 1637 he prepared a grammar and vocabulary of the language.

By 1638 there were more than forty-six hundred Eudeves living under the mission system at eleven centers in the Matape Valley, along the Moctezuma River in the vicinity of Batuc, and at the missions of Opodepe, Cucurpe, and vicinity on the San Miguel River. A school was set up at Matape which became a center of instruction in literacy and Christian doctrine for the Indians of central Sonora. Thus, by 1640 the southern and western part of the Opata territory, inhabited by Eudeve-speaking people, was missionized, and the Jesuit program continued to move peacefully in these areas until the expulsion in 1767.

Beginning in 1636 the missionaries proceeded to enter the valley of the Sonora River which had been the site of Coronado's settlement of Corazones nearly a century before. Here for some years an unusual man, a Portuguese Jesuit named Castaño, gained a great reputation among the Indians. He was very dark in color and for this reason came to be called the "Indian Father." He was an able linguist and a good musician. He begged food from the Indians and in general lived much as they did. He was popular and successful, apparently, in the area of Opata rancherías upriver on the Sonora from Ures (where Opata, Eudeve, and Pima territories came together). In 1639 Castaño and Pantoja, who worked with him, baptized large numbers of natives in the area of the old Corazones settlement. In a few months more than 4,346 persons among the Opatas were baptized, and the fathers proceeded to establish the missions of Babiácora, Acontzi, Banámichi, and Sinoquipe. Castaño's methods and style of life, however, gave his superiors some concern; they feared that his easy intimacy with the Indians would work against their developing respect for him, and he was removed, despite the fact that in 1640 the missions which he had established were reported to be in flourishing condition, and despite general praise for his mastery and use of the native language in his sermons.

During the early and middle 1640's, the Jesuit advance up the Sonora River was temporarily halted, when trouble developed between religious and civil authorities. Perea, as captain-general of Sinaloa-Sonora, proposed a separation of Sonora from the coastal province, the Sonora region to be called New Andalusia. At the same time Perea attempted to have northern Sonora turned over from Jesuit to Franciscan jurisdiction, the latter Order already having been established for some years in extreme northeastern Sonora. He brought five Franciscans to Banámichi and proposed to establish them in missions on the San Miguel, Sonora, Moctezuma, and Bavispe rivers. The Jesuits opposed the plan and Perea had to abandon it when the viceroy decided against him. Meanwhile, during the 1640's, Perea attempted several forceful reductions of Pimas (Hymeris) northwest of Ures and of Opatas and Sumas in northeastern Sonora in the Bavispe drainage area. These military campaigns were not successful in any way. With Perea's death in 1644, the Jesuit program once more expanded northward and eastward.

Father Jerónimo de la Canal (1648), who carried the mission program up the Sonora River from Sinoquipe to Arispe and beyond, met with resistance, even in Sinoquipe, where Castaño had worked. In none of the rancherías that he visited was he received with crosses and arches; but neither was he met with armed opposition. Resistance to him was passive and in at least one instance took the form of reasoned argument. In Sinoquipe the headman simply did not want to have anything to do with Canal, but the latter persisted in preaching, and after two weeks he persuaded most of the mothers to bring their children to him for baptism. At Arispe the resistance was similar, but two weeks of preaching plus the miraculous cure of a woman who had been accidentally shot with an arrow brought the people and the headman around. At Cacubarunichi farther up the river, the people scattered and hid and tried to scare the missionary away. When he persisted in staying, one of the influential men sat down with him and began to expound his own religion to the Jesuit. He pointed out that all this region had been created by another god, not the Christian God. He also, by mentioning cases, showed his conviction that baptism cured no one and that Christian ritual was not particularly efficacious for anything. So telling were the Opata man's arguments that this missionary became convinced that he was conversing with someone completely inspired by the Devil, and he departed without having converted anyone.

Later, however, Canal reported that in all these rancherías, and others between, the people came to be baptized and that shortly after 1648 three churches were built.

On the Moctezuma River to the east, by 1646 forty Opata rancherías were reduced by Father del Rio, who, after being invited by the Indians to work among them, had them build two churches at Oposura and Cumpas.

Between 1645 and 1651 there was similar peaceful construction of churches and acceptance of baptism among the Opatas of the Bavispe Valley, even among the Huazabas whom Perea had unsuccessfully tried to conquer by force in 1644. Thus, by the 1670's missions were established along the whole lengths of the Sonora, Moctezuma, and Bavispe rivers among the Opatas, and the mission system had been set up as far as the Suma, Apache, and Jumano frontiers. In 1688 there were twenty-two missions among the Opatas proper, and a population of some ten thousand Indians was listed as living around these missions.

Nothing that could be regarded as a revolt, or even a serious factional split among the Opatas was reported after 1696, until the nineteenth century. In 1696 the only Opata revolt under the Jesuit system occurred. In that year, an Indian leader named Pablo Quilme of Bacerac began to protest the effects on his community of the establishment of the presidios of Fronteras and Janos. He said that Spaniards had come in and appropriated land in his community of Bacerac and in others along the Bavispe River. He protested the taking of Indians for forced labor and the capture of children for servants. His viewpoint was influential among Opatas of Cuchuta, Teuricachi, and Cuquiarachi, and a plot was laid for an armed revolt. But it was discovered before the Indians could organize themselves effectively, ten leaders were hanged, and Quilme himself was killed at Janos in 1697.

Despite the wide extent of their territory and the difficult mountainous terrain the Opatas were missionized in the span of about twenty-four years. However, if we look at the various areas of settlement separately, we see that each one was missionized within a year or two after missionaries first entered it — even more rapidly than were the Mayos or Yaquis. The Saguaripa Eudeves were missionized in the year 1627, the Matape-Batuc Eudeves in 1629, the San Miguel River Eudeves probably in 1630, the middle Sonora River Opatas in 1639, the upper Sonora River Opatas in 1648, the upper Moctezuma Opatas in 1644-46, the Huazabas Opatas in 1651, and the other Bavispe River Opatas during 1646. Little direct force was employed, the only instance being Hurdaide's expedition against Matape. There was also fighting before the acceptance of missionaries at Huazabas, but the Indians were not beaten and did not come in as a result of Spanish military victory. The imposition of the mission system was nearly as peaceful as among the Mayo and Yaqui, but as we have seen, there were evidences of a rather mild opposition to the missionaries, which was eliminated or at least overcome by persuasion or idol-smashing techniques. Once established, the Jesuits experienced none of the rebellion against the missions that characterized mission history among the Tarahumaras. This was true in spite of the fact that Spanish settler intrusion into the missionized areas was even more intensive than it was among the Tarahumaras.

From the 1680's on there were two features of life in central and northern Sonora which profoundly affected the Opatas in the missions. One was the rapid growth of settlement by Spaniards, and the other was the steady increase in raids by Apache Indians from the northeast. Actually, miners had preceded the missionaries into the Opata country proper, mines having been opened at Cumpas and Nacozari on the upper Moctezuma River at about the time the missionaries were building churches in the Matape and Saguaripa valleys. As early as 1688 there were a few mining camps scattered through the areas surrounding the Arivechi and Saguaripa missions and also around Batuc. Small silver, gold, and lead mines continued to be opened in increasing numbers. In 1688 there were reported to be only one thousand Spaniards in all of Sonora and Ostimuri (which comprised the area of the lower Yaqui and Mayo rivers). This was just before the settlement of Alamos. By 1764, a little more than seventy-five years later, there were 4,266 Spaniards in central and northern Sonora alone, that is, only in the areas which the Eudeve and Opata missions served. There were 1,266 in the district of Oposura — more than in any other. This was because of the large mining developments at San Juan Bautista, which served as the capital of Sonora for many years. But there were additional hundreds of Spaniards, either mining or building up ranches and haciendas, in many other Opata areas. Thus, all of the following had Spanish populations of from fifty to over five hundred — Arivechi, Saguaripa, Fronteras, Chinipa, Sinoquipe, Opodepe, Tuape, Batuc, and Rebeico. The distribution of these places indicates that no important part of Eudeve or Opata territory was without Spanish inhabitants. Sonora north of the lower Yaqui River at this time was reported to have twenty-two Spanish towns inhabited and forty-eight which had been settled but were now depopulated, and 126 haciendas or ranchos depopulated, with two still inhabited. This indicates a shifting population as a result of both the working out of mines and the forced abandonment on account of Apache or Seri raiding of rural establishments. A few years later, in 1778, Arispe in the heart of the Opata country had become the capital of the province with a population of over fifteen hundred, one thousand of whom were Indians. In the century and a half since the introduction of missionary work among the Opatas, the Indian settlements were pretty thoroughly infiltrated by Spaniards, while hundreds of Indians had been drawn into the towns and mining camps to live.

At the same time the Opata-Eudeve population was declining. In 1688 shortly after the completion of the missionization of the Indians, 4,329 Eudeves and 10,045 Opatas were reported to be living under mission influence. It was also recognized that there were an uncounted number not living at the missions, but these were estimated to number only a few hundred. Forty-two years later, about 1730, both groups had declined to less than half — the Eudeves to 1,265, the Opatas to 4,901. In 1764 the situation was nearly the same — the Eudeve being listed as numbering 2,265 and the Opata 4,735. Thus, from a total of nearly fifteen thousand the Indian population of central and northern Sonora had declined in half a century to less than eight thousand. It was, in fact, less than twice the Spanish population in the same areas, and it must be remembered that there were additional Spaniards in the same areas immediately adjoining, such as at Alamos and in the Lower and Upper Pima country. This contrasted greatly with the relative isolation of both the Yaquis and Tarahumaras during their first hundred years of mission life, although, of course, large Spanish population centers developed at the southeast margin of the Tarahumaras.

The causes for the decline in the Opata population during this period are by no means adequately recorded. There were epidemics of European and native diseases mentioned by some of the missionaries. Also, part of the decline may have been more apparent than real, since the population records applied only to the mission centers. Indians were being drawn away from the missions to Spanish settlements to some extent, and undoubtedly many Indians, after the initial enthusiasm for mission life, simply moved to settlements of their own with which the missionaries were not in close touch. How many were so affected we have no way of knowing.

After 1700 warfare with Indians of the northeast and the Apaches also contributed to population decline. About 1686 Opata life began to be affected by the raiding of the northern Indians, and it continued to be so affected for more than a century and a half thereafter. The territory of the most populous division of the Opatas — the northern area — was a battleground during this whole period. Indian troubles in northern Chihuahua led to the establishment about 1685 of the presidios of Janos and Casas Grandes at the north end of the Sierra Madres. At about the same time, in 1686, Jocomes and probably Apaches from the vicinity east of Janos attacked Opata settlements north of Cuquiarachi. The Spaniards decided to establish another presidio west of Janos to deal with the Jocomes and Sumas, who had also been raiding to the south. In 1690 the Fronteras presidio was established, and the Opatas who had been settled at Corodequatzi at the northern bend of the Bavispe River were moved to the missions of Teuricachi and Cuquiarachi. From this point on warfare with the northern tribes was constant. In 1696 the Flying Company, with headquarters at San Juan Bautista near the Opata town of Oposura, was organized and campaigns were carried out in 1694, 1695, and 1696.

The Spaniards began immediately to make use of Opata warriors in these campaigns. In the 1694 campaign a combined force of Opatas and Pimas bore the brunt of an attack at Cuchuta, where the Opatas proved themselves extremely able in fighting off the Apaches. Opatas were impressed for service at the same time to the west against the Pimas, and it was Opata mission employees who were a major cause of the Upper Pima uprising in 1695. As the line of presidios was extended westward to include Terrenate, Tubac, and Altar, and as the Apaches extended their line of attack in the same direction, Opatas became a regular part of the fighting force on the side of the Spaniards. By 1756 there was a force of 140 Opata archers who engaged in pursuit of Apaches as far north as the Gila. From this time on there were three companies of Opatas who reinforced the regular presidio forces. They were enlisted in efforts to repel attacks of Conchos and Jovas east of the Bavispe Valley.

As allies of the Spaniards, the Opatas were protecting their own communities as well as those of Spaniards. Their communities bore the brunt of the endless raids, as the Spaniards themselves abandoned the mines in northern Sonora and the ranches and haciendas which had been established in central Sonora. We have no adequate record as yet of how many Opata settlements were abandoned, how many Opatas were killed either as soldiers or as civilians, nor to what extent the line of Opata settlements was driven southward and westward as a result of the intensifying Apache raiding during the 1700's. We may infer that there were losses and that settlements were abandoned and consequently that a good deal of disorganization and community breakup occurred among the Opatas.

This condition, together with the infiltration of Spaniards as miners and ranchers in the period just before the Apache raids began, led to a great deal of cultural assimilation. The missionary records speak of much intermarriage of Spaniards with Opata women. They indicate that the Opatas had learned to speak Spanish rather widely, and that there were many formal relations through the godparent sponsor system between Spanish and Opata families. The relations evidently differed from Spanish-Tarahumara relations in Chihuahua, where the Spaniards looked down on the Indians and refused to mingle with them on any basis approaching equality. Spanish writings repeatedly indicate that most Opatas were respected and regarded as "civilized."

The Jesuit program did not affect the Opatas in the same way it did the Yaquis. Among the latter, circumstances were such that an existing tribal unity was reinforced by the work of the missionaries and especially by the village and church organization they introduced. It is possible to isolate some of the factors that appear to have been effective in bringing about the quite different results among the Opatas.

In the first place, the density of population among the Opatas was far less than among the Mayos or Yaquis. The Opatas were spread over the greater part of the modern state of Sonora, inhabiting the central river valleys. Their areas of settlement were separated from one another by exceedingly rugged terrain, so that there was relatively little communication among the areas of more concentrated settlement. While their villages were of the ranchería type, like those of the Yaquis and other Indians of Sonora, it seems doubtful if, even in those areas where their villages were clustered, their rancherías were as large as those of the Yaquis or Mayos. Early mission records show church-centered communities of between two and four thousand for the Yaquis and Mayos. At the same time, after the Jesuit efforts to concentrate Opata rancherías into pueblos, records show no Opata pueblo larger than fifteen hundred persons, and practically all were between 150 and six hundred. Thus, it appears that Opata communities were relatively small, as compared with those of the Yaquis and Mayos, although they may have been more densely settled than those of the Tarahumaras.

All the Yaqui settlements constituted a single communicating area, as did those of the Mayo. The Opatas, on the other hand, were grouped in relatively isolated sections of river valleys, constituting some six or seven distinct geographical units. Sauer has estimated the Opata population at the time of contact as sixty thousand. To judge from the Jesuit records, however, this seems far too high. A more realistic estimate based on these records would seem to be about twenty-five thousand. If Sauer is right, then each of the geographical areas of Opata settlement would have had on an average about seven to ten thousand inhabitants. On the other basis, each area would have had a population of four thousand or less, which is what the Jesuit records indicate. With either estimate,

there is a great contrast with the lower Yaqui or Mayo valleys, where thirty
thousand people in each case were concentrated, even before missions were established, into areas of about the size of each of the seven Opata settlement areas.

Moreover, it is apparent from the fragmentary records that among the groupings of Opata rancherías there was frequently hostility and rivalry, rather than
close cooperation. Even the river valley units were sometimes split among themselves over such matters as rights to salt deposits. Thus, Sinoquipe and Banámichi
were allied against Huepac and Acontzí in the upper Sonora Valley, while Oposura
in the Moctezuma Valley was hostile to Banámichi in the Sonora. Opodepe on
the San Miguel was in its turn hostile to the various villages of the middle and
upper Sonora Valley.

These conditions influenced the missionary program. Instead of being baptized all at one time — within a short space of time by a single group of missionaries, and beginning under their direction immediately to organize for church
building and mission discipline — the Opata settlement groups were baptized at
different times, by different groups of missionaries. The long, friendly preparation
of the southeastern Opatas under Sisibotari contrasts with the hard-fought conquest of the southwestern Opatas (Aibinos). The Guazabas' resistance to Perea's
attempted conquest contrasts with the uneventful welcome of the missionaries
in the middle Sonora Valley and the San Miguel. The specific contacts of the
Opata groups with the Spaniards thus varied greatly.

Moreover, the missionaries behaved in quite different ways. Azpilcueta's
aggressive opposition to, and destruction of native ritual objects in the south
contrasts with Castaño's gentle and winning ways in the north. Méndez' skilled
and tolerant relations with the Sisibotaris were very different from Canal's argu-
mentative first contacts with the upper Sonora River Opatas. It would appear
that the Opatas were divided among themselves to begin with, and that the
Jesuit program did nothing to alter this fundamental division, so that the program
actually dealt in distinct fashion with separate small communities (none of over
four thousand). The process was different, however, from that in the Tarahumara
country, in that the Opatas were already to a much greater extent village-living
people, so that once missionary work began in a given area it proceeded rapidly
to affect the whole population of that area, and not to divide the people into
hostile pro-missionary and anti-missionary factions. If there had been greater
unity among all the Opatas, it seems likely that results might have been somewhat
like those among the Tarahumaras. There is a suggestion of this in the initially
hostile attitude of the Indians of the upper Sonora River rancherías when first
approached by Jesuits some twenty-five years after the southern Opatas had
fully accepted the mission system. However, as we have seen, the Tarahumara
type of factionalism did not develop on any comparable scale.

Another circumstance in which the Opata contacts contrast with those of
either Tarahumara or Yaqui-Mayo is in the nature of Spanish settlement in the
region. In this it more nearly resembles the Tarahumara than the Yaqui-Mayo
situation. Spanish settlements preceded or were contemporary with the missions
throughout the Opata region. As Opata population declined under the mission

system — as Indian population did nearly everywhere in New Spain — Spanish population increased greatly during the first hundred years. There were signs of missionary dissatisfaction with this situation, as in the Tarahumara country, but very little indicating that the Indians were made rebellious, certainly nothing to compare with the disruptive effects of Spanish population among the Tarahumaras. Either Spanish-Opata relations were very different from Spanish-Tarahumara relations or some other circumstances existed which prevented such results. The weight of evidence favors a different quality in the Opata-Spanish relations. Aside from the criticism of Spanish behavior by the Opata leader of the Bacerac plan for revolt in the 1690's, there is little mention of forced labor, land encroachment, or other sources of Indian dissatisfaction. Instead, there is frequent mention of the good relations that existed between Opatas and Spaniards. Unquestionably, the Spaniards found the Opatas of such habits and attitudes that they tended to accept them on a level of equality. The intermarriage, the extent of godparent relations, and the praise of Indian industriousness, bravery, and degree of "civilization" are all indications that the Spaniards did not so consistently regard the Opatas as their inferiors as they did the Tarahumaras. The tendency was toward intermingling and cooperation rather than toward separation and hostility.

This tendency may have been primarily a result of great compatibility between Spanish and Opata cultures, but it may also have been a result of the working alliance between Opatas and Spaniards against the Apaches. The two peoples, in the effort to protect their communities, found a common interest. It was to the interest of the Spaniards, once the Opatas showed their determination to fight against the Apaches, to maintain that situation. It was also to the Opata interest, in trying to preserve their communities, to keep the Spaniards well disposed toward them so that Spanish soldiers could be kept in the field against the Apaches. On this basis may have been built the special set of relations which contributed so much to the cultural assimilation of the Opatas.

Unlike that of the Yaquis, Mayos, and Seris, the adjustment of the Opatas and Lower Pimas to the Mexican regime which superceded the Spanish was relatively easy and uneventful. After an initial influence from the Yaquis, strong nationalism did not develop, nor did the Opatas show the deep resistance to Mexican culture demonstrated by the Seris.

The population of the Opatas at the beginning of the 1800's may have been a third that of the Yaquis, certainly under ten thousand. Because of the far greater degree of intermarriage with the Spaniards, their numbers were much more difficult to determine. The Opata population was also much more widely scattered than that of the concentrated Yaquis and Mayos.

Nevertheless, the Opatas were still a distinct group in the early 1800's. Some fought among the troops of Governor Conde against the revolutionaries in the War for Independence, and distinguished themselves in the Battle of Piaxtla in Sinaloa where Conde defeated the revolutionaries. In 1820 the presidio of Bavispe was partly manned by a company of Opatas. This company resented what they regarded as unjust treatment at the hands of the paymaster and rebelled. They were joined by other Opatas in Arivechi, Pónida, Saguaripa, and Tónichi. Fighting spread and troops had to be called in from Chihuahua. After demonstrating a fighting ability which gave rise to a reputation for bravery, they were defeated by a force much larger than the five hundred they had been able to muster. The heaviest battle occurred at Tónichi where the Mexicans were defeated. The disturbance was ended with the execution of the Opata leaders Dorame and Espiritu.

Unrest continued, however, among some Opatas and spread among the Lower Pimas who were scattered through the lower and eastern Opata country. In 1825 some Opatas and Lower Pimas joined with Juan Banderas, the Yaqui proponent of an independent Indian state. In 1829 the district of Moctezuma in upper Opata country became the scene of an incipient rebellion. A Spaniard, Antonio Archuleta, sought to enlist Opata support for a restoration of the Spanish monarchy. His plan called for a return of the colonial period missions to Opata possession. He aroused considerable interest among the Opatas and secured the support of several respected Opata leaders — Dolores Gutiérrez, Miguel and Bautista Sol, and Antonio Baiza. However, the plot was uncovered before it developed. Nevertheless, in 1832 when Banderas returned to his attempt to win independence from the Mexican government, Opatas were ready to listen to him with greater interest than they had shown in the 1820's.

Banderas' plan called for winning control of eastern Sonora so that Yaqui- and Opata-controlled areas would be in communication. This involved the Lower Pimas of the middle Yaqui River from Buenavista to Tónichi. Much of the fighting in the 1832 revolt centered in this corridor between the Opata and Yaqui country. Opatas joined with Banderas under the leadership of Dolores Gutiérrez, but the Mexicans were able to defeat the combined forces. From this time on Opata military activities followed the lead of Mexican commanders rather than Yaqui or other Indian, and no spirit of independence seems to have developed.

The Opatas were nevertheless much involved in the fighting which developed over various issues in Sonora. They were not a "naturally pacific" people, as later accounts often suggest. Opatas from Batuc, Tepupa, Matape, and Alamos fought alongside of Mexicans against invading North Americans at Guaymas in 1847. In the 1850's, like the Yaquis, Opatas and also Lower Pimas gave much military support to Gándara in his various schemes for maintaining political power. In Gándara's 1856 attempt to gain power, rebellion was initiated among the Opatas of Saguaripa. In the following year he was supported by Lower Pima troops from Onavas, and Opata and Pima troops from Tónichi. By 1859, when Gándara was finally driven from his role of rebel leader, he had enlisted wide support from Opatas and Lower Pimas, together with Yaquis and Mayos. In the course of the fighting in support of Gándara's *caudillismo*, two Opata leaders developed into capable military commanders. These were the two brothers Juan and Refugio Tanori. Gándara's defeat in 1859 did not remove them from the scene of Sonora's turbulent politics.

When the French attempt to gain control of Mexico took form in 1864, Refugio Tanori, at the head of several thousand Opatas and Lower Pimas of central Sonora, declared in favor of the Empire of Maximilian. In 1865 he attacked Ures successfully. For the next two years he fought as one of the important commanders of the Imperialist troops, gaining distinction for himself personally, and giving objective support to General Langberg and the other Imperialist commanders who fought in the Sonora theatre. One of his greatest triumphs was in the taking of Nacori Grande, within the Opata area, in 1866. In that same year the Imperialists were defeated by General Pesqueira. Tanori, after a flight to the Yaqui country for refuge and then an attempt to escape from Sonora by way of the Gulf of California, was captured and executed. His dying statement was to the effect that he had fought honorably for the Imperialist cause because he believed that it would, if it triumphed, regenerate Sonoran social life.

At the same time that Tanori's leadership had enlisted most Opatas on the side of the Empire, there were other Opatas who fought against it, most notably troops from Matape, who fought with Pesqueira.

Although for the most part Opatas lined up in these military conflicts on the side of the conservatives, or that is, of the old order, it would appear in general that Opata history, as recounted in these military annals, is hardly to be distinguished from Mexican history, at least insofar as the Mexican accounts go. It would seem that an Opata tribe, in the sense of a Yaqui, a Mayo, a Seri, and a Papago tribe, was less and less easy to distinguish after the defeat of Banderas and Dolores Gutiérrez in 1832. It is true that the books on Sonora history written by Mexicans never fail to mention that Refugio Tanori, whose courage and military ability are well attested, was an Opata. But it is obvious that he was a Mexican military commander and not a tribal chieftain. His dying words testify to his own conviction that he was a patriotic Mexican, who had fought for his nation.

From the time of Refugio Tanori's execution, historians of Sonora no longer mention the Opatas as a distinct group except to call attention to interesting folk customs or to make a favorable contrast between them and the other Sonoran Indians. Thus the Sonora state legislature, in 1880, in making its petition for federal troops to control the Yaquis, did not even mention the Opatas in its listing of Sonora Indian tribes and their history. So weak was Mexican consciousness of the Opatas by this time that the principal Opata communities were spoken of as Piman, and the word Opata nowhere occurs in the petition. A little later Governor Ramón Corral, in writing a resumé of the Sonora Indians on whom he had become a specialist, did mention the Opatas. He wrote: "[They] . . . are inclined to work, intelligent, docile, and obedient to the authorities and have very good customs: they are very little addicted to drunkenness, to robbery, and the other vices which unfortunately are so common in the other native tribes of the country; they live in honorable work and dedicate themselves to attend their families and educate their children." Building on Corral's summary, another historian of the Sonora Indians wrote in 1902 that the Opatas were "most distinguished for their peaceful tendencies and their love of work." They were the Indians, he said, who have "manifested greater sympathies for the white race, becoming mixed little by little with it." He continued: "Since the conquest until our days, all the governments have been able to utilize the services of these docile and devoted Indians sometimes in the war against the Apaches, at other times in foreign wars, and at still others, finally, in the local revolutions of the State." This student of Sonora Indian affairs concluded: . . . "in a short time this tribe, recognized as the most courageous of the Sonora tribes, will have lost its distinctive characteristics, mingling itself like the Pimas and Papagos with the rest of the population of the State."

Such statements are completely one-sided, reflecting the relatively good working relations between Mexicans and persons of Opata descent during the last half of the 1800's. They reveal a good deal about Mexican attitudes. However, they tell us nothing whatever about Opata consciousness of themselves as an ethnic group, or the real state of cultural assimilation. Such information must be derived from field study, since the historical studies do not provide it. Nevertheless, the contrast between Mexican writing about the Opatas and Lower Pimas with that about Yaquis, Mayos, and Seris is important evidence for the absence of overt conflict in the acculturative processes that were taking place during the 1800's in the Opata and Lower Pima country. Events there took a sharply different turn from those in all other parts of Sonora.

CHAPTER FOUR

Seris

ON THE WESTERN BORDER of the agricultural, ranchería-dwelling peoples of Sonora lived fishermen who roamed the coast. They were loosely organized in bands, some of which occupied the islands and coastal margin while others ranged farther inland.

How many of these people existed in the middle 1600's when Spaniards first began to encounter them is unknown. Nor is it known positively how many separate bands made up the population, nor even precisely what relations existed between them. Most disconcerting — for our purposes — even the earliest encounters with Spaniards are not clearly recorded, so that these first contacts must remain obscure.

After the reduction of the Yaquis, Lower Pimas, and Opatas in southern and central Sonora, parties of Spaniards ranged beyond to the west and northwest. Searching for mines and other resources, Spaniards encountered Indians on or near the coast of the Gulf of California, and such meetings were often fleeting. But, by about 1660, the Spaniards were sufficiently aware of these coast dwellers and their unsettled ways to have invented a name for them. They called them Seris — a collective term for the nonagricultural and, as the Spaniards said, "wild" peoples.

The earliest clearly recorded encounter with the coastal people was a hostile one. A party of Spaniards in 1662, at some point west of Ures, met and fought with a group of unknown size, but probably not over two or three hundred. The adults of this band fought to the last man and woman and, when all were killed, the Spaniards took the children and distributed them in the mission pueblos of the middle Sonora and San Miguel rivers. It is not definitely known to which of the bands — as the Spaniards later identified them — this group belonged. It seems likely that they were either of the Tastiateño band which ranged the coast south of Kino Bay or of the Tepocas north of Kino Bay. Later, in 1679, several hundred of the nomads, at the urging of the Jesuit missionary Fernández, came voluntarily to make a settlement at the mission of Santa María de Pópulo on the San Miguel River below Opodepe. For four years they lived at the mission and accepted the mission life, planting fields and building houses under the guidance of Fernández. But in 1683 Fernández was transferred elsewhere, an epidemic killed many, and the remaining families left the mission and began to wander about, ranging back and forth into and out of the San Miguel Valley settlements.

In 1685 Father Kino, after the failure of his mission in Lower California, visited some of the nomads on the coast near Tiburón Island. He was received in very friendly fashion, and they urged him to stay among them. Returning to Mexico City, Kino asked that he be sent as missionary to these nomadic peoples. However, he was assigned to the Upper Pimas instead. A German Jesuit, Adam Gilg, was sent to Pópulo to reinvigorate that mission. In 1688 Gilg arrived at Pópulo where he found the Indians who had been settled there under Father Fernández resistant to returning to the mission discipline. Nevertheless, he settled down and tried to win them back — with some success.

By this time the Spaniards were more or less aware of six different bands which roamed the coast and islands. Gilg concluded that these bands spoke mutually unintelligible dialects of a language that differed sharply from either Pima or Opata-Eudeve. Most of the Spanish contacts, however, had been with a group which they now called the Tepocas. This band ranged from the San Miguel River westward to the coast and from the lower Sonora River northward to the Magdalena River. Kino had made contact with these people on the coast and also probably with another band, centered on Tiburón Island, whom the Spaniards now sometimes referred to as the Tiburones. North of the Tepocas, ranging at least as far as the mouth of the Rio de la Concepción, was another group often called the Salineros. South of the Tepocas, below the Sonora River, and ranging inland from the coast, was a lesser-known group later called the Tastiateños; and between them and the western edge of the Yaqui country were the Guaymas. The last band seems to have been hostile to the others, and most of this group by this time had taken up mission life in the Yaqui pueblo of Belem where they were mixed with Yaquis and Lower Pimas.

Father Gilg began a systematic attempt to reduce the nomads north of the Guaymas to mission life. Because of the lack of agricultural land, it was considered hopeless to reduce them to settled life in their own territory. Hence the plan adopted was to bring them into settlements on the San Miguel River in missions occupied either by Eudeves or Pimas. In 1691 Gilg persuaded some Tepoca families to accompany him to Cucurpe and then to settle in a village which he called St. Thaddeus. He persuaded more families of Tepocas to begin the settlement of another village which he named St. Eustachius. The new settlements were somewhere in the area drained by the San Miguel River. However, they did not last very long. After being attacked by Indians whom Gilg called Cocomacaketz, the Tepocas dispersed. Probably many of their inhabitants came to Pópulo where in 1692 Gilg reported several hundred living a mission life. During the next ten years the program of reduction continued with mixed success.

In 1695 some "Seris" served as bodyguards for Captain Manje in a march from Pitic (Hermosillo of later times) to Caborca to punish Upper Pima rebels. These were probably Tepocas. In 1699 Tepocas who had not been reduced to mission life were molesting Tuape, Cucurpe, and Magdalena, stealing food and horses to be used for food. This resulted in an expedition by Captain Jironza into the country west of the San Miguel River. He captured 120 Tepocas and later another 112 who may have been Salineros, and brought them into the San Miguel missions. Some possibly were kept at Cucurpe, but the majority went to Pópulo under the care of Father Gilg. Either by force or persuasion the population of Pópulo grew, but how many of the nomads were there by 1700 is not recorded. It seems probable that most of them were Tepocas and Salineros, and that they were mixed to some extent with Piman-speaking people who were also being brought in from the west.

The nomads who had been persuaded to take up mission life still constituted only a small proportion of the whole. Gilg thought that the total of all the nomads may have been around three thousand when the reduction program began. In 1706 there were still an estimated fifteen hundred living in the area between the San Miguel and the coast north of the Sonora River. Kino made this estimate in the course of a trip through the area, recognizing, however, that some of the Indians were Pimas. He reported a fairly heavy population on the coast opposite Tiburón Island. There was some degree of intercourse between the nomadic peoples of this area and the missionized Indians on the San Miguel and along the Altar and Magdalena, for Kino recognized families who had made friendly visits to Caborca and Dolores.

During the next thirty years there was little change in the situation. It may be characterized as one in which the majority of the nomadic peoples remained undisturbed in their coastal and island territories, where also they were friendly to the missionaries, as indicated during Father Salvatierra's forced stay of two months when shipwrecked on the coast. By the 1730's, however, some were being attracted to the missions where they stole food from the mission settlements and where these forays and retaliatory raids resulted in some killings on both sides. In 1742 a presidio was established at Pitic to curb such activities. By 1748 considerably less than a third of all the Indians collectively called Seris by the Spaniards had accepted mission life. These were concentrated at Pópulo, Nacameri, and the pueblo of Los Angeles nearby on the San Miguel River. The total population of these settlements in the 1730's was 828, and many of these were Pimas. At least two thousand, chiefly Tiburones, Tastiateños, and Tepocas had remained uninterested in taking up the mission life, and forceful measures had not been continued to bring them in.

In 1748 action was taken by the Spaniards which completely upset the program of reduction for the nomadic bands. The Spanish presidio of Pitic was moved to Pópulo, where better farm land was available. The lands which the Seris had been farming with moderate success were distributed among the Spanish residents of the presidio. When the Seris protested, along with some Pimas who had been similarly treated, eighty families were arrested and the women of these families were summarily deported to Guatemala and elsewhere in New Spain. As might be expected, this was too much for the Seri men. They warned the missionaries, whom they did not wish to harm, and then attacked the Spanish settlers in the whole area from Pópulo to Pitic. The Spanish ranchers and miners who survived were forced to flee. An expedition of seventy-five Spanish soldiers and four hundred Upper Pimas, which set out to exterminate the Seris in 1750, traversed the whole Seri area and crossed to Tiburón Island, but failed completely — killing only a handful of Seris, mostly women.

Meanwhile the Seris and disaffected Pimas from Pópulo took refuge in the Cerro Prieto Mountains south of Pitic, and here they were joined by other nomads. The Spaniards were partly occupied at this time — in 1751 — with a revolt of the Upper Pimas in the north, and no effective measures were taken against the Seris, who continued to raid Spanish settlements from the Cerro Prieto. In 1753 the Seris offered to make peace if the Spaniards would return their women, give back the lands taken away at Pópulo and Los Angeles, return the presidio to Pitic, and give them the missionary of their choice. The Spanish governor, de Arce, was unable of course to meet the demand for restoration of the Seri women, and the Indians continued their raiding. They destroyed the Guaymas mission and kept the lower Sonora River area empty of Spaniards. In 1775 a Seri leader Becerro, as he himself was dying, killed Governor Mendoza who had led a campaign on the Cerro Prieto. In 1756, the Seri forces were augmented by a considerable number of apostate Pimas who had revolted against mission control in the north.

This combination of Seris and Pimas, with headquarters in the Cerro Prieto and also in the Bacoatzi Mountains north of Pitic, continued for twenty years to raid Spanish settlements and resist numerous punitive expeditions. In addition to the Upper Pimas, some Lower Pimas (the Sibubapas from Suaqui) joined them. They raided in the north around Magdalena and forced the building of a presidio at Altar. They kept the whole area from Pitic to Ures depopulated and forced the maintenance of a presidio at San Miguel de Horcasitas. Campaigns against them by Mendoza, de Anza, and Elizondo, in each of which a few Indians and Spaniards were killed, were complete failures. How many Indians actually engaged in the raiding and in the defensive fighting at Cerro Prieto remains unknown. In de Anza's attacks on the Cerro Prieto in 1757, he mentions no force larger than 170 Seris. In 1761 an attack resulted in the killing of 49 Seris, the capture of 70 women and children and 322 horses which the Seris had driven off from Spanish settlements and missions. When Elizondo attacked Cerro Prieto in 1768, he claimed that he was met by four hundred Seris. It would appear that this latter number of warriors was the largest engaged by the Spaniards. The figure may mean that as many as two thousand were finally concentrated in the Cerro Prieto, and this possibly constituted the great majority of all the Seris and their associates left at this time.

By 1769 the embattled Indians were beginning to fall apart as a group. Some had already separated from the main group and gone to live quietly in various missions, notably on the Altar River. In 1769 the Sibubapa Lower Pimas surrendered. During the next two years, one small party after another came down out of the Cerro Prieto or the Bacoatzis and went to Pitic to surrender. Food was running short and families were getting tired of the recurrent state of siege. The Seris who surrendered were held at a place on the Sonora River across from Pitic

8. SERI COUNTRY

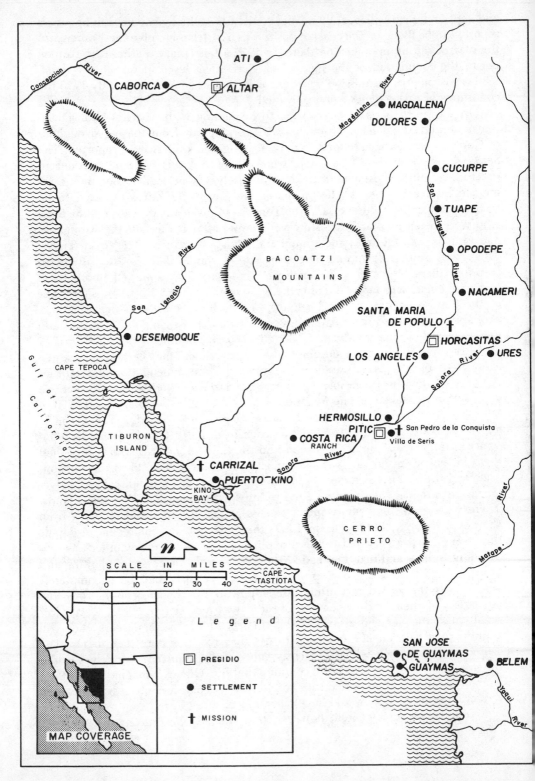

ATI •

CABORCA • ☐ ALTAR

Concepcion River

Magdalena River

• MAGDALENA
DOLORES •

• CUCURPE

San Miguel River

• TUAPE

• OPODEPE

BACOATZI
MOUNTAINS

San Ignacio River

• NACAMERI

SANTA MARIA
DE POPULO ✝

• DESEMBOQUE

CAPE TEPOCA

Gulf of California

TIBURON
ISLAND

☐ HORCASITAS

LOS ANGELES •

Sonora River

URES •

HERMOSILLO •

PITIC ☐ ✝ San Pedro de la Conquista

• COSTA RICA
RANCH

Villa de Seris

Sonora River

✝ CARRIZAL
• PUERTO KINO

KINO
BAY

CERRO
PRIETO

Matape River

CAPE
TASTIOTA

SCALE IN MILES

0   10   20   30   40

SAN JOSE
DE GUAYMAS •
• GUAYMAS

• BELEM

Yaqui River

Legend

☐ PRESIDIO

• SETTLEMENT

✝ MISSION

MAP COVERAGE

and kept under surveillance. By no means all of them had given up. Enough were reported to be living on the coast opposite Tiburón Island to give the Franciscans the idea of setting up a mission there. In 1772 a missionary, Father Chrysostom, began the foundation of the mission of Carrizal, a few miles from the coast. Within six months his mission was destroyed and he himself killed. By 1776 the conditions of earlier times again prevailed.

In the north Seris were reported to be joining with Apaches and "Piato" Pimas around Magdalena. Through 1777, working out from the old stronghold of Cerro Prieto, Indians robbed settlers, although no killings were reported. The Seris who were in the Cerro Prieto were evidently hungry· but not anxious to precipitate military campaigns against themselves. One leader, Boquinete, remained implacable against the Spaniards and during 1778 was reported to be trying to rouse the Tiburones and the Tepocas to make an effort to free the Seris who were being held at Pitic. However, family after family left the stronghold and also the coastal areas and, "nude and hungry," went to Pitic to surrender. There they settled down and agreed to attend church daily and to submit to learning Christian doctrine. A Franciscan missionary Jalisco worked among them and tried to acquire farm lands for them along the Sonora River. By 1786 most of the Seris were reported to be living peacefully across the river from Pitic. Probably no Spaniard really knew how many were still living on Tiburón Island and scattered in their usual haunts along the coast. Boquinete was killed in 1779 as the result of a Spanish expedition to the Cerro Prieto. Many certainly remained away from Pitic, as is indicated in the governor's recommendation of 1780 that the only solution for the problem of Seri depredations would be deportation. No such action was taken; yet depredations nearly ceased between 1780 and 1790.

The first hundred years of Seri contacts with the Spaniards may be seen as an unsuccessful attempt to carry out a program of reduction of a nomadic, non-agricultural people. The Seris were not hostile to the Spaniards who approached them in their own territory without force. They seem to have liked the missionaries and their ritual, as indicated in the experiences of Fernández, Kino, Salvatierra and others. They wanted Kino to stay with them in their coastal lands. There were even some who wanted to try a settled life in a mission away from their own country. Gilg says in the 1690's that under the mission regime at Pópulo they were about as devoted to the disciplines of the ritual as any other mission-dwelling Indians and that they had already learned the processes of planting and crop raising. That this group, probably chiefly Tepocas, had been completely won over to the settled agricultural life is indicated in their resentment over the alienation of their lands when the presidio was moved from Pitic. Even after rebellion at this act and a taste of the old freedom for several years, they still wanted their mission life and tried to get de Arce to restore their lands. The Tepocas of this nucleus had evidently successfully adjusted themselves under the mission system and wished to continue that life. One can imagine that if their women had not been deported they would have become a nucleus around which reduction of more Seris would have taken place.

It must be remembered, however, that the Pópulo Tepocas were a small minority of the Seris. It took more than a generation for their reduction. While they were adapting themselves to mission life, perhaps two thousand others were continuing to live the old life in the old haunts. These others were, however, visiting the missions, as Kino discovered, and learning about the life there. There probably would have been a slow drift into the missions, if the 1750 revolt had not occurred. That revolt cut short the Jesuit program.

After that, for a full generation, only a few devoted families continued under the mission system. Many of the others, who had never been in the missions, no doubt continued to live as they always had, particularly those who inhabited the islands. But the Spanish efforts to control the rebel group in Cerro Prieto influenced the life of all the bands. The accounts of the Spanish expeditions to the islands and through the band territories show that they made little or no distinction among Seris and classified all as enemies. Gradually the great majority joined forces with the rebels, absorbed their hatred of Spaniards and made what living they could from raiding the Spanish settlements. Undoubtedly this was a period, from 1750 to 1770, when a tradition of deep hostility to white men was built up among practically all Seris. Thus the friendly attitude to Spaniards with which contacts began was replaced with hatred. It seems doubtful however that much real tribal unity was born of this situation. The piecemeal surrender of the Seri groups, as the hostilities wore on, indicates otherwise. The concentration in the Cerro Prieto seems to have been an aggregation of not very highly organized family-band units forced by the circumstances of Spanish indiscriminate attack. It did not last long enough to forge a tribe with organization out of the various dialect and territorial groups.

One effect of the period of anti-Spanish action is difficult to estimate. This was the association with Piman-speaking people. The missionized Tepoca group had already been living in fairly close association with Pimas for a generation at Pópulo. After the revolt there must have been some intermarriage of Seri men with Pima women, as a result of the Seri men having lost their wives. Then the continued close cooperation with not only the few Pópulo Pimas, but also with the apostate Upper Pimas and with the Lower Pimas from Suaqui, must have influenced the Seris. What these influences were can only be told from careful ethnological analysis, but they must have been a factor in subsequent Seri cultural history.

We can surmise that by 1790 the Seris for the most part were a defeated and miserable group of Indians. Those who surrendered under pressure of hunger and want, and who went, family by family, to live under conditions prescribed for them, not by missionaries, but by the military commander of Pitic, must have been a very much broken people. They submitted to church discipline and a settled life out of necessity. They had lost heart and had become convinced of Spanish power. The Spaniards thought in 1790 that the great majority of all the Seris had surrendered and knuckled under to their control. Whether the capitulation was so complete as to include nearly all Seris is unknown. However, there were still some Seris who were not concentrated at Pitic and who had to some extent kept aloof from the events which had broken the spirit of the others.

The Spanish program for reducing the Seris to mission communities had failed completely. Aside from the few families who were absorbed into other Indian groups in the San Miguel and Altar River missions, the great majority of all Seris remained outside the mission communities throughout the Spanish period. The single Franciscan attempt to missionize the Seris in 1772 fared far worse than the Jesuit, despite the effort to bring the mission to the Seris rather than the Seris to the mission. Begun at a time when hostility to Whites was high, Father Chrysostom's program lasted only a matter of months. Further, the effort of the provincial government at what might be called a secular reduction program met with the same sort of result.

The Seri rebels and their associates of Cerro Prieto who surrendered during the 1760's and 1770's were concentrated on the south side of the Sonora River at Pitic. The new community was called Villa de Seris. Even though an irrigation canal was built especially for the Indians in 1772 and farm lands at least as good as those which had been taken away from them thirty-five years before at Pópulo were given them, the Seris would not settle down. They drifted away in steadily increasing numbers. By 1793 it was clear that the plan was a failure; the Seri lands at Villa de Seris were distributed among Spaniards who were ready enough to take them over. Most Seris had abandoned town life and rejoined those who had remained in the desert homeland on the coast and islands, especially Tiburón, of the Gulf of California. Gradually they renewed the old raiding habits. The Spanish ranches which had grown up in western Sonora, from Guaymas to Altar, were almost as much harried by Seris in the period from 1790 to 1810 as the ranches farther east had been by the Apaches prior to 1790. Although less destructive than the Apache, the Seri raids nevertheless kept the Spaniards of western Sonora in a constant state of fear and anxiety.

By 1807 the Sonora governor felt obliged to take steps, and carried a formal campaign to Tiburón Island for the purpose of rounding up and punishing Seris who had been stealing horses and cattle. Although he had one thousand troops, he killed very few Seris and obviously did not substantially alter the situation. The harassment of Spanish ranches and settlements continued through the period of the War for Independence, intensifying the disorganization of the Mexicans as the Apache raids broke out again from the northeast.

As the anarchy which marked the period of the War for Independence ended, the government of Sonora and individual citizens were able to devote more attention to the problem of the marauding Indians. By 1844 Mexican settlers began to stiffen their opposition to both Apaches and Seris. The Sonora governor sent Captain Victor Araiza to the coast opposite Tiburón for the purpose of rounding up hostile Seris and punishing them. His force killed eleven, mostly women and children, which struck the governor as inhumane conduct. Accordingly, a large expedition, designed merely to take all remaining Seris prisoner and bring them in to be civilized, was organized under the command of Colonel Andrade by land and Captain Spence by sea. This expedition, after many difficulties with water supply, eventually established a base on Tiburón Island and systematically traversed the island as well as the adjoining coast. This resulted in the burning of some 64 Seri shelters and 97 balsas, or cane rafts, and the capture of 104 family groups of Seris. In the course of the campaign, one war party of 70 Seris was defeated. The approximately five hundred Seri men, women, and children were brought to Hermosillo, where the children were all distributed among Mexican families in various parts of Sonora. An effort was made again to settle the adults in Villa de Seris across the river from Hermosillo. But within a matter of months most of the children had escaped from the families to whom they were farmed out, and the adults had also drifted away to their former life. The depredations against Mexican ranchers, who had been slowly extending their cattle operations toward the coast, continued as before.

A frequent activity of Seri groups was to attack parties traveling the road between Guaymas and Hermosillo, stealing horses and provisions and occasionally killing people. In one such attack in 1854 the daughter of a prominent Guaymas family, Dolores Cazanova, called "Lola," was captured. Her fate quickly became a legend in Sonora. This legend runs that Lola Cazanova was persuaded by the "Chief of the Seri tribe," Coyote-Iguana, who was a captured Pima raised as a Seri, to remain with him and become "Queen of the Seris." Lola bore three sons, two of whom succeeded to the "chieftainship" of the Seris, and she herself became thoroughly Seri in outlook and behavior. She and her husband and sons became a source of discord, according to the story, as a result of disputes over leadership. Yet she remained with her husband and died a member of the tribe. The Lola Cazanova legend has served as a vehicle for romanticizing the long-drawn-out struggle between Mexicans and Sonoran Indians.

The Seri depredations, now carried out by probably not more than five or six hundred Indians, became serious enough in 1880 to cause the governor of the state to organize another formal campaign. This expedition rounded up 150 Seris in the vicinity of Tiburón Island and brought them once again to Villa de Seris. This time a very determined effort was made to keep the Indians in the village. What Mexicans called a "kind of reservation" was established. Rations were issued regularly and federal funds were obtained to bring the Indians to "the civilized life." A "chief" was appointed to act as liaison between Seris and Mexicans. Seris believe that on at least one occasion Mexicans expressed their hatred for Seris by poisoning the rations; when some Indians became gravely ill and a few died, the rest managed to escape. Only a few remained behind to become absorbed into the Mexican population.

Meanwhile, a Mexican rancher named Encinas who had an interest in property near Bacoache, which had been a center of conflicts between Seris and Whites for a century, became involved in the "Seri problem." He was interested in extending the area of cattle raising farther westward into the desert country customarily roamed by the Seris and at the same time, as he said, "bettering relations with the Seris." He proposed to provide regular labor for Seris on a new large ranch which he built, called Costa Rica, between Hermosillo and the gulf coast. He also arranged for instruction in crafts and obtained the services of two priests. He achieved friendly relations with Seris who came to his ranch. He began the education of two boys, whom he proposed to train as catechists who could give Catholic religious instruction to other Seris. This program developed during the 1870's and 1880's, probably influencing in one way or another most of the remaining Indians.

However, the two boys who were trained did not turn out to function as he had hoped. One went to California after being educated, and the other returned to live among the Seris, but did not carry on any religious training among them. In addition, the establishment of the ranch of Costa Rica encouraged other Mexican ranchers to move into the area bordering the coast, and conflict steadily developed. The ranchers were in what had always been Seri territory; their cattle roamed the same country in which Seris hunted deer and rabbits. Seris killed cattle as well as deer. Encinas tried to check the conflicts, but soon found that his own cattle were as much the target of Seris as any other rancher's. Eventually he declared war on the Seris; the "Ten Years Encinas War" took place just before 1900. In one of the encounters between Encinas' cowboys and the Seris, seventy of the latter were killed. Small-scale fighting continued spasmodically, the general pattern of which was the following: A few Seri families would work for a time at one of the ranches, then disappear. One or more cattle would be reported killed. Ranchers would organize a war party. Seris would surrender to the angry ranchers, perhaps after one or two were killed. And the cycle would begin again.

For twenty-five years, until the 1920's, most Seris continued to live as hangers-on at the Costa Rica and other ranches, which steadily increased in numbers. As sporadic workers and occasional cattle-killers Seris incurred the hostility of the Mexican ranchers. Their numbers had been reduced to about three hundred. The school which was erected for them at Villa de Seris in 1890 was attended by the children of the Mexican families who had moved into and taken over the little settlement. The remnant of the Seris were still nomadic hunters and gatherers living at the edge of a still-advancing society, which, by means of wells and windmills, was finding a way to make the Seri country yield a living.

The continuing encroachment of the cattlemen on the Seri territory resulted in the steady reduction of the numbers of Seris, for the conflict between the Indians and ranchers was incessant, although on a very small scale. At the same time a new encroachment began, which was to have more constructive effects than the slow encirclement by land. As the cities of Sonora and Arizona developed during the 1920's following World War I, a market for the fish of the Gulf of California grew up. The little town of Kino Bay opposite the south end of Tiburón Island began to be a center for Mexican fishermen who supplied this market. During the 1920's most Seris moved into a permanent camp at the edge of this Mexican settlement. They shifted from being hangers-on at the cattle ranches to being hangers-on at Kino Bay. Some learned the fishing techniques of the Mexican fishermen; principally the use of wooden plank boats, metal fishhooks, nets, and dynamite. Gradually more Seris made boats and slowly they entered into the expanding fish trade. This constituted a renewal of intensive reliance on the sea, after an interlude of nearly fifty years; Seri fishing had been much curtailed in the interval since the last roundup in 1880. In the 1920's Roberto Thompson of Hermosillo became a champion of Seri interests and worked for years as go-between with often deeply hostile Sonorans, and as promoter of schools for Seris.

In 1930 a clubhouse was built at Kino Bay by sportsmen from the United States. The Seris added begging to their means of subsistence, as the North Americans amused themselves by giving out clothing, food, money, and knickknacks. The Seris in this period gave the appearance of being an almost completely dependent, poverty-stricken people. However, during the 1930's there was a change. A market for shark livers grew up, sponsored by manufacturers of vitamins. Sharks were abundant in the Gulf of California and enough Seris had learned the fishing trade so that cash income through the Mexican middlemen in the shark-liver, as well as fish trade became an important feature of Seri life. During the 1930's nearly every Seri family acquired boats. Food, clothing, and tools available through the stores maintained by the Mexican fish traders began to be more and more widely used. Essentially Seri life changed little. The old form of brush shelter continued to be used and the traditional forms of social life and religion were maintained. Although Kino Bay became a much-frequented base for the whole group, families still spent periods on Tiburón Island and along the coast north and south of Kino Bay, roaming in the old nomadic way. Their new mobility by means of the plank boats gave them, in fact, a somewhat wider range than before.

The Mexican government took a new interest in the Seris and in 1938 appointed a Mexican to help them organize a fishing cooperative. The government seemed at last to have decided to bring the Seris into the nation through economic activities adapted to their habitat rather than through removal, missionization, agriculture, or a reservation system. By 1941, however, the shark-liver market had declined to nothing, and the fishing cooperative slowly fell apart. The government efforts had included the establishment of a building at Desemboque fifty miles up the coast from Kino Bay to serve as a headquarters for the Seri cooperative. The objective was to remove the Seris from the demoralizing influences of the fishing town of Kino Bay and give them an opportunity to escape the friction and conflict with Mexicans which had developed in the Mexican town. By 1942 two changes had taken place in Seri life. The base camp had been shifted from Kino Bay to Desemboque. At the same time as the shark-liver market declined, Seris became increasingly nomadic, shifting residence between Desemboque and various places on the island and coast. However, the stores established by the Mexican fish merchants at Desemboque, where Seris sold their fish, remained a focal point in their lives.

During the 1940's the Seris continued to live basically as fishermen, dependent on markets of the Sonora and Arizona cities. The federal government established a short-lived school, but it, as well as the federal representative encouraging the cooperative organization, gave up by 1950. The nexus between Seris and the outside world again became the fish traders and their stores. The Seris by 1950 had been reduced to a group of about 230 individuals, living as fishing nomads, with no educational or religious institutions from the outside world established among them.

Seri history during the Mexican period is the record of a largely non-Hispanicized group resisting for a hundred years incorporation into Mexican society, and almost disappearing as a result, but finally, through mutual economic interests, moving slowly into the range of Mexican cultural influences. More than any other Indians of Mexico, the Seris escaped the impact of the powerful and pervasive mission system. By the time the Mexican period began, their life exhibited only the most minor and sketchy influences from Spanish culture in religious or social life. Due to the Spanish, and — at first — the Mexican lack of interest in the desert coasts they occupied, Seris rarely came into contact with settlers, except when they chose to visit settled areas, or when the recurrent, but infrequent military expeditions brought them as prisoners to the Sonora settlements. Their geographical location protected them from contact.

The Mexican government for over a hundred years conceived no different plan for "civilizing" the Seris than that which the Spaniards had attempted. The plan of removal to Mexican population centers, distribution of children to Mexican families, and forcible incorporation into Mexican community life was modified, up until 1938, only by a halfhearted attempt to impose the Apache system of rationing. When this failed no further policy was developed and private individuals like Pascual Encinas were permitted to try something akin to the old mission system. Encinas' effort foundered in the face of the growing interest of Mexicans in the resources for cattle raising which existed sparsely in the Seri country. It broke down as government programs had frequently broken down in both Mexico and the United States over the conflict between settlers and Indians in competition for the land and its resources. Border warfare and gradual decimation of the Indians took place with no government effort at control.

It was not until 1938 that a new conception began to actuate government policy. Undertaken by the Cárdenas administration and the Mexican Department of Indian Affairs, this was a radical departure from any previous policy. It called neither for removal nor for forcible imposition of religion. It proposed to encourage the Indians to organize as an economic unit, although, to be sure, in a form conceived by the Mexican government, to take advantage of the marine resources of the native habitat. The incorporation into the nation was to take place through economic means and, aside from the cooperative itself, the Indians were to be permitted to maintain their own forms of religious and social life. This program, in some degree, also failed. At least, it failed to work out as planned.

By the time this new economically-based program was put into effect, the Seri population was reduced to a tiny remnant of its former size. The two hundred remaining Indians were a concentration of the several original bands, which had never developed any tribal organization. They had a unity forged out of common customs and language as well as out of a common sense of deep hostility to Mexicans resulting from two centuries of armed conflict. They possessed a minimum of common cultural foundations with the Mexicans. The social distance between them and the Mexicans with whom they came in contact in their economic enterprises was very great and gave little promise for easy development of a common ground for cooperative relations.

In the decade from 1950 to 1960 a new series of heavy impacts from the dominant society rapidly followed one another. Most Seris now spent the greater part of the year concentrated at the new fish-trading center of Desemboque. This settlement became the target of different groups seeking to change Seri life. Regarded as a terribly poverty-stricken group by Mexicans and others who saw them, Seris became the recipients of blankets, clothing, food, and medicine on a charity basis. This kind of indiscriminate giving of material goods had taken place sporadically ever since the attempt of federal and state governments to relocate the Indians at Villa de Seris in 1880. But now it reached a new peak of intensity as a result of the great economic prosperity which affected especially the attitude of persons in the United States who became aware of the Seris.

An increasing number of visitors by automobile added to the outside awareness of the Seris, and there began a ten-year period of perhaps the most intensive cultural contacts which Seris had ever experienced. Through the efforts of a Protestant religious group a school was established which continued to be attended intermittently during the decade by Seri young people. At the same time a Protestant evangelist began the conversion of the Seris and met with remarkable success in a short time. By 1960 he had made nominal Christians of the great majority and had brought about the more or less effective prohibition of several old customs, such as face painting. Linguists took up residence at Desemboque and undertook for the first time the systematic study of the Seri language looking toward the translation of the New Testament. Several anthropological studies were made. In 1958 the National Indian Institute of Mexico revived the idea of a fishing cooperative and sent representatives with funds to bring this about. Thus the small band of survivors numbering little over two hundred became the focus of intensive efforts by the dominant society. The new phase was probably to be equated, in terms of cultural processes, with the late 1600's when the Jesuits began work, with the 1770's when the Sonoran provincial government dreamed of a thriving Seri town across from Hermosillo, and with the 1880's when the Encinas family had a vision of remaking Seri life.

CHAPTER FIVE

Upper Pimas

THERE WAS NO CONTINUITY in the Jesuit extension of their work from the Lower to the Upper Pimas. None of the missionaries with experience among the Piman-speaking peoples of southern Sonora went to work among the northern Pimas. This was because there was an interval of some seventy-five years between the establishmen of missions at Onavas, Nuri, and the other Lower Pima settlements and the beginning of missions in the north. During this interval, it is true, work was carried into the mountains at Yecora and Maicoba where Pimas of the lower group lived, but most of the energies of the Jesuits were concerned with the immensely successful reduction of the Opatas in central Sonora. It is also true that hostile contacts of Upper Pimas with the Spaniards developed before the intensive mission work began. The northwestern missions to the Opatas, at Cucurpe and on the upper Sonora, were visited by Pimas from the region of Imuris to the northwest. These same Pimas gained a name for hostility among the Spaniards as a result of an ill-planned military expedition which Governor Perea carried out against them. The expedition was repulsed and no steps were taken to make further contacts with the Pimans for another forty years.

At the time Father Eusebio Kino began his energetic work among the Upper Pimas in 1687, there was already a Spanish frontier of settlement bordering on the Pimas. The flourishing mining town of Bacanuche had been in existence for thirty years. Opodepe, on the San Miguel River among the Opatas, was a town of four hundred Spaniards and had been in existence for forty years. Since the 1630's the Opata missions, as far north as Cucurpe, had been flourishing peacefully and since the 1640's the Opata missions of the rich Sonora River Valley had been in operation. There was considerable knowledge, consisting of both information and misinformation, of the Upper Pimas on the part of the Spaniards, and of the Spaniards on the part of some Upper Pimas. It was in an atmosphere of fairly-well-developed attitudes on both sides of the frontier that Kino began to work. A hostile tone for Spanish attitudes had been set by the early contacts with the people of Imuris, and just before Kino's arrival a Piman leader — Cocagui — from the vicinity of Huachuca was hanged by the Spaniards for conspiracy to carry out an uprising on the northwestern frontier. Two years later in 1689 the southeasternmost ranchería of the Pimans, Mututicachi, suspected of confederation with hostile Indians to the east, was attacked and destroyed by the Spaniards — all of its men being killed and the women and children deported to the south.

In an area extending from Cucurpe on the upper San Miguel to the Gila River and from the San Pedro to the Colorado River there were possibly some thirty thousand Indians, as many as in the lower Yaqui Valley, but scattered through a region immensely larger and far more difficult to traverse than the Opata country of central Sonora. This mission field was undertaken at a time when financial support of the missionary program was considerably weaker than it had been at the beginning of the 1600's and consequently was slow in gaining momentum.

The Upper Pimas were, like the Opatas, a single tribe only in the sense that they spoke dialects of a single language. There were marked cultural differences among them; on the east, for example, Pimas lived in fairly concentrated rancherías sustained by irrigated agriculture, whereas in the extreme west Pimas were nomadic food-gatherers living on the meager foods of the poorest part of the Sonoran desert. Moreover, there was no permanent political organization linking more than a few rancherías in any part of the Pimería. Political coordination of rancherías for any purpose but warfare seems to have been unknown, although there were games and customs of ceremonial cooperation between rancherías. The widest political organization probably did not link more than fifteen hundred people, although Spaniards claimed that one "chief," Soba in the west, "ruled" four thousand. As we shall see, this view of Soba seems to have been more legend than fact.

Geographical factors were important determinants of Pima political separateness. The Spaniards, such as Kino and his associates, who first came to know the Pima country well, seemed to think of the Pimas in four major divisions. In the southeastern part of what they called Pimería Alta, bordering on the Opata-Eudeves of the upper San Miguel and upper Sonora rivers, were the people they called Pimas (without any qualifying adjectives). To the west they found that the Pimas made a distinction between themselves and people who were said to be under the influence of a single man named Soba. These inhabitants of the southwestern portion of Pimería Alta were at first, then, called Sobas, but the name was shortly seen rather inapplicable. Along the east and northeastern portions of Pimería were people who seemed to the Spaniards to constitute a distinct group — the Sobaipuris. The fourth division of the Pimas, as the Spaniards early saw them, remained somewhat vague as to geographical extent, as well as numbers. These gradually came to be called Papagos or Papabotas, a term used by the southern Pimas to refer vaguely to Piman-speakers to the north and northwest.

The early written history of these people revolves around the personality of the Jesuit missionary Eusebio Francisco Kino, an energetic Italian who was as much explorer as missionary. His exceptionally vigorous campaign to reduce the scattered ranchería people to pueblos lasted for twenty-five years, from 1686 till his death in 1711. Kino's efforts stirred the Spanish northwestern frontier, keeping at a high level of intensity the conflicts of interest between the Spanish settlers and the missionaries and even creating conflict within the Jesuit organization itself. Kino's activities, in short, profoundly influenced the whole early period of contact between Spaniards and Upper Pimas. It is necessary therefore to follow them in some detail.

Kino began his work at a time when Spanish interest in Indians as laborers on the northwestern frontier was well developed. Both mining and ranching had grown rapidly in central Sonora. Many Opatas had been absorbed into Spanish society as a result of these activities in their territory and Spaniards were looking for more labor — most naturally to the north of the Opata country where the Indians had not yet been reduced and where new mining opportunities were steadily opening up. The Pimas were generally regarded by both Spanish settlers and the missionized Opatas as extremely savage people who were, on the one hand, a threat to northward expansion, and on the other hand, fit for little except immediate impressment into the mines and ranches. An extended mission program placing the Indians under the care of the missionaries was looked on, not only as visionary, but also as an appropriation of resources, both land and labor, by the missionaries, which could be better used by the settlers and their civil government.

Apparently well aware of the growth of this attitude in the area, and familiar with it elsewhere in New Spain (as among the Tarahumaras), Kino made an effort before his assignment to the Pimería Alta to get some special backing for the mission program which he proposed. He secured from the viceroy a special cedula affirming the declared policy of no forced labor and exemption of Indians from tribute during the missionary program. He carried this cedula with him and before beginning work showed it to the governor of Sonora who vowed obedience to it. The result was that Kino did not encounter official direct opposition; rather the generally-felt antagonism to the missionary program was expressed in rumors and undercover gossip against the Pimas and the mission work among them. This indirect opposition existed throughout Kino's lifetime and played a great part in his activities.

The burden of the opposition charges was that the Pimas were involved in the growing border fighting with the Jocomes and Apaches to the east (there was some evidence for this in the Canito, or Ocagui, conspiracy trial of 1686), that the Pimas were generally wild and difficult people (which may have sprung from the early fighting with the Indians of the vicinity of Imuris, but seems to have had no other basis), and that there were so few Pimas that a missionary program would be a costly superfluity. Kino set out from the start to gather evidence against these charges and continued throughout his life to pile up such evidence. He demonstrated quickly that, whatever may have been the involvement of the massacred Mututicachi Pimas, elsewhere the Pimas were peaceful and quite ready either to ally themselves directly with Spaniards against the Jocome-Apache raiders or to live quietly under the mission system. Kino also during his first ten years of work steadily showed that there were enough Pimas to make a mission program well worthwhile. He himself never seems to have claimed that there were more than about sixteen thousand all told, but events even during his lifetime indicated the existence of considerably more than that. The existence of sixteen thousand Indians was of course sufficient to warrant a mission program in the eyes of the Spanish government. Kino for some five years worked singlehandedly, as the only missionary assigned to the Upper Pimas, but he had extremely able help and support from military and civil authorities — most notably Captain Juan Mateo Manje, who accompanied him on his early trips of exploration, and General Jironza, at first commander of the Flying Company set up against the Apaches-Jocomes and later alcalde mayor of Sonora at San Juan Bautista.

Kino began his work on the upper San Miguel River at the village of Cosari where Pima territory bordered on Opata. Cosari was some fifteen miles up the river from Cucurpe, at that time the northernmost of the Opata missions. Here Kino won friends immediately and established the mission of Dolores which became his headquarters during the subsequent twenty-four years of work among the Pimas. He had two able helpers with whom he worked closely during the early years — an interpreter named Francisco Cantor (apparently Kino did not know Pima when he began to work and was later accused of having an insufficient command of the language by his Jesuit superiors; he was in his early forties when he began work and may not have mastered the language), and a man named Coxi. Coxi seems to have had influence widely among the Pimas of the upper San Miguel and Magdalena River valleys. He accompanied Kino, sending ahead news of his coming to the various rancherías which he wished to visit. Cantor was also a trained catechist and with his knowledge of both Pima and Spanish assisted in organizing in various places the early nuclei of Pimas who listened to Kino's preaching and wished to form church groups.

Kino's method was not to establish himself at a single mission site and then work intensively there, limiting himself to a small area, while awaiting more missionaries. Rather he employed an extensive method — ranging widely in Pimería, creating a demand for missionaries among other scattered rancherías, maintaining the interest in them by subsequent rapid visits, and always hoping that he would be supplied with enough missionaries to meet the demand which he was constantly creating. He proceeded in this manner as soon as he had decided on the mission site of Dolores. He immediately visited rancherías farther up the San Miguel, then traveled westward into the Magdalena River Valley, meeting the Pimas of Imuris, of Caborcita (later San Ignacio), and what became Magdalena, and Cocóspera.

During his first year Kino interested the Indians in all these areas in churches and having missionaries. Everywhere he encountered friendliness, and nowhere did his soldier escort find it necessary to make any show of arms. Only at one point, though the Indians were otherwise friendly, did he find a lack of interest in the mission program. This was at the ranchería group which later became Remedios, twenty miles north of his home mission of Dolores. Here he found some definite opposition by people who were evidently familiar with the Spaniards' execution of Canito (Cocagui). They had observed also what had happened among the Opatas and presented some reasoned arguments against having a

9. UPPER PIMA COUNTRY ABOUT 1710

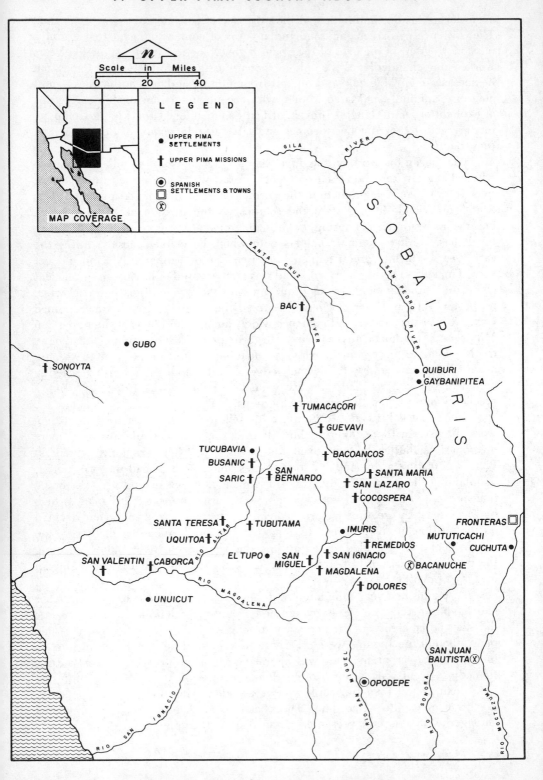

Scale in Miles
0   20   40

LEGEND

● UPPER PIMA SETTLEMENTS

✝ UPPER PIMA MISSIONS

⊙ SPANISH SETTLEMENTS & TOWNS

⊗

MAP COVERAGE

GILA RIVER

S O B A I P U R I S

SANTA CRUZ RIVER

SAN PEDRO RIVER

● GUBO

✝ SONOYTA

BAC ✝

● QUIBURI
● GAYBANIPITEA

✝ TUMACACORI

✝ GUEVAVI

TUCUBAVIA ●
BUSANIC ✝
SARIC ✝

✝ BACOANCOS

SAN BERNARDO ✝

✝ SANTA MARIA
✝ SAN LAZARO
✝ COCOSPERA

SANTA TERESA ✝
UQUITOA ✝

✝ TUBUTAMA

● IMURIS

FRONTERAS ▢
MUTUTICACHI ●
CUCHUTA ●

SAN VALENTIN ✝ CABORCA ✝

RIO ALTAR

EL TUPO ●

SAN MIGUEL ✝

✝ REMEDIOS
✝ SAN IGNACIO
✝ MAGDALENA
✝ DOLORES

⊗ BACANUCHE

● UNUICUT

RIO MAGDALENA

SAN JUAN BAUTISTA ⊗

RIO SAN IGNACIO

RIO SAN MIGUEL

⊙ OPODEPE

RIO SONORA

RIO MOCTEZUMA

mission. They said that the Spaniards hanged Indians, that they required too much work on mission lands to the detriment of the Indians' own farming, that too many cattle were pastured around the missions so that the water supply was seriously reduced, that people were killed by the holy oils of the missionaries, and that the missionaries were not able to keep their promises that they would protect the Indians from forced labor by the Spaniards. These, except the fourth, were telling arguments and ones which actually could not be denied. The Pimas of Remedios had critically watched the advance of the mission program in their part of Sonora. Nevertheless there were enough Pimas at Remedios who favored Kino so that eventually a mission was set up there, although there was still opposition as late as 1692.

While the Pimas went about building a church at Dolores, Kino extended his visits westward. By the end of 1689 he had established contacts, through the help of Coxi (who by Spanish appointment was now captain-general of "all the Pimas"), with some twelve hundred Pimas on the upper Altar at El Tupo, Tubutama, Saric, and Tucubavia. These were people of the same general group as those on the upper San Miguel and Magdalena rivers. Two years later, with the Dolores mission still under construction, he visited the rancherías of the lower Altar Valley where Caborca was later established and began visits to the relatively heavy Pima population of the upper Santa Cruz River at Tumacacori and Guevavi. At these places he gave out food, made talks about Christian belief, baptized a few children, and held assemblies of headmen for the purpose of discussing the mission program. In all these places his visits were preceded by requests for his presence. He made it clear, in his own mind as well as in Captain Manje's, that this whole large area north and west of Cucurpe was ready and waiting for missionaries. Except at Remedios, closest to the Spanish settlements, he encountered no opposition.

In 1687 Coxi of Cosari was baptized with the name of Carlos and was henceforth called Don Carlos. Other headmen of the vicinity had also been baptized and by 1689 Kino had a record of eight hundred baptisms — not the wholesale baptism of the Yaquis and Mayos or even the large-scale baptism of the Opatas, but a sizable beginning. (Kino's baptisms were always slower to get started than they had been farther south, because criticism of the former procedure had developed and Kino along with all the later missionaries was careful to precede baptism with fuller instruction). It was not until 1693, six years after the beginning, that the church at Dolores was completed. This was the occasion for a great assembly of Pimas from the whole area with which Kino had become acquainted. He invited headmen from the north and west and provided a great feast. There is no record of how many actually attended, but there were many more than had come for the previous occasion of the baptism of Don Carlos.

The attendance of headmen from the west led to Kino's immediately going to Caborca after the end of the ceremonies at Dolores. He asked General Jironza to go with him and appoint officers, and also had Coxi go along because there had been hostilities between the western, or Soba, Pimas and the eastern ones. Coxi was apparently successful in establishing peaceful relations. Kino's party carried holy pictures, distributed food to the groups which seemed poorest to them, and gave out canes of office. Captain Manje thought there may have been four thousand Indians in the general area of Caborca. They welcomed the Kino party in the now standard manner, with crosses and arches, and some asked for baptism. Kino preached at length. A year later he was able, at last, to provide a missionary for Caborca — Father Saeta.

Two other missionaries had already been placed in 1693 — Augustín Campos at San Ignacio in the Magdalena Valley west of Dolores and Daniel Januske at Tubutama west of San Ignacio. Now with Saeta at Caborca there were four missionaries in the field. Most of what is modern Sonora had been brought under the mission system. Cattle herds and fields and orchards were flourishing at Dolores, Cocóspera, San Ignacio, and Tubutama. Two hundred Pima soldiers had joined with Opatas in the defense of Cuchuta a few miles south of the presidio of Fronteras. Here in 1694 a force of Jocomes-Apaches had attacked this Opata mission pueblo, but the combined Pima-Opata force had beaten them and driven them off. It appeared that the new work among the Pimas had justified Kino's hopes. They were steadily accepting the missions, converts were being made by the hundreds, if not the thousands, and they were allying themselves with the Spaniards against the increasing threat of raids from the northeast.

In 1695, however, the complex forces which Spanish conquest had released on the northern frontier were swirling to a focus. Fifteen years before in New Mexico the Pueblo Rebellion had swept the Spaniards southward to El Paso. The pressure of conquest from the south had upset the balance of Indian relations in New Mexico, Chihuahua, and Arizona. Northeastern Sonora was increasingly beginning to feel the consequences of these reactions to conquest. The effects of the dislocations in 1695 reached as far west as Caborca, almost on the Gulf Coast, and set up a reaction which for a time changed the peaceful course of events in Pimería Alta. The ranches which had been set up by Spanish settlers in northern Sonora were suffering from raids by Indians in which they lost many horses and cattle; occasionally there were killings. At this time the Spaniards did not know enough about the tribes of the area to be sure who was responsible. Pimas had been implicated, as we have seen, earlier, and the idea persisted in Bacanuche and San Juan and the other Spanish border towns that the Pimas were as dangerous as the Jocomes, Janos, and Apaches of the east. In 1694 a lieutenant of the Fronteras force had unjustly and summarily killed three Sobaipuri men accused of horse stealing on the San Pedro River. The same lieutenant in that same year had forcibly quieted some Pima leaders at Tubutama who were said to be haranguing others against the Spaniards. Also at Tubutama, following usual custom, the Jesuit missionary Januske had employed already-Christianized Indians to oversee the operations of the mission herds and lands. In this case the overseer and his assistants were Opatas, who had long been accustomed to look down on Pimas as inferior savages. In 1695 feelings against Opatas came to a head; suddenly the peaceful Pimas of Tubutama killed the Opata overseer and two assistants.

This action released hostile feelings, of which the missionaries were apparently quite unaware. Undoubtedly the plan included the killing of Father Januske, but he escaped along with Father Campos from San Ignacio. The Tubutama Pimas who killed the Opata overseer seem to have been a faction, rather than a representative group of the mission pueblo. They made their way southwestward, enlisting confederates from other rancherías, including Oquitoa north of Caborca. They destroyed Altar and, entering Caborca, murdered Saeta, the young missionary who had barely been installed in his new post. They were not aided by the Pimas of Caborca, who, however, fled from the mission fearing reprisals by the Spaniards.

Spanish reprisal was prompt. General Jironza with Spanish soldiers and a few Seris marched immediately into the Pima country, but he and his lieutenants found few Pimas against whom to take action. They killed a few women and boys here and there, but there was no Pima force to meet them. They destroyed fields at Caborca, as a lesson to the Indians, and then decided that since there was no general uprising to combat by arms it would be best to work out a peaceful settlement.

In this Kino took the lead. It was arranged, largely through his efforts, that the Pima leaders who had not taken part in the killings would bring together their people, including the leaders of the rebellious group, with the Spaniards at El Tupo. There they would point out the rebel leaders, and the Spaniards could take them and do as they pleased with them. The meeting was arranged and the headman of El Tupo who had been prominent in the negotiations along with other peaceful headmen proceeded to point out the men responsible for the killing of the Opata overseer, the other Christian Indians, and Father Saeta. As soon as the first guilty man was pointed out, one of the Spanish officers in the midst of the assembly beheaded him with his sword. This produced consternation among the Pimas and many began to run away. The Spanish and Seri soldiers went wild and killed nearly fifty Pimas in a matter of minutes, including the peaceful headman of El Tupo and at least four or five others associated with him in the arrangements for the assembly. Most of those killed, Jironza and Kino both agreed, were innocent persons anxious to work out a settlement, and who had been promised immunity by Kino.

The result was the outbreak of real war. After the breakup of the peace assembly, the small force of Spaniards and Tepoca Seris went back southeast on other matters. No sooner were they out of the way than the Pima forces organized and destroyed Tubutama and Caborca and headed east. They moved on Imuris and San Ignacio and destroyed the churches there. By the time Jironza, who was at Dolores, heard of the outbreak, it was reported that the Pimas were threatening Cocóspera, Remedios, and Dolores. Attacks on these places, however, never materialized. The Spanish forces, augmented by troops from Fronteras, were mobilized to the number of some three hundred, which included many Pimas. They moved through the Pima country killing men and women here and there and destroying crops. But they did not find any force of Pimas ready to give battle. It was the same story as before. Once the attacks of revenge on San Ignacio and Imuris were accomplished the Pimas dispersed and the Spanish soldiers found no one to fight. Again the situation called for negotiations rather than settlement through battle. Again Kino took the lead in finding peaceful headmen — at Caborca, at Tucubavia, at El Tupo — who would negotiate.

There was no lack of headmen so inclined. Already some had made overtures to the Spanish military leaders. Now with Kino again promising immunity for those who had no part in the first uprising at Tubutama, a meeting of headmen was arranged again at El Tupo (which had come to be called The Slaughter). The Pimas had become convinced, if they were not before, that they could not successfully oppose Spanish military power. They agreed to turn over the Tubutamans who had engineered the killing of the Opatas, and the Spanish soldiers returned to their campaign against the Apaches.

The newly won territory was nearly devastated, only Dolores, Remedios, and Cocóspera having remained untouched, either at the hands of the Pimas or the Spanish soldiers. Spanish military might had been thoroughly demonstrated. Piman leaders had divided themselves into pro- and anti-Spanish. The Spaniards had demonstrated their inability to work together — soldier and missionary — and keep promises made. Force and distrust had been introduced into the situation and the Pimas, like the Tarahumaras before them, were divided among themselves. Yet, somehow the reputation of Father Kino as an honest man with great power for good survived among the Pimas. Jironza also was convinced that Kino, and Kino alone, was the best insurance against more Indian uprisings. He refused to allow Kino to leave on an expedition to Lower California.

While the mission program in the devastated area was being redeveloped Kino undertook, at the urging of his superiors, to carry his work to the northeast among the Sobaipuris. He had already made the acquaintance of Coro, a headman of the Sobaipuris of the upper San Pedro River rancherías, and had visited Quiburi, Coro's headquarters, on the San Pedro and Bac on the Santa Cruz where there was one of the densest settlements of Indians in the Pimería, numbering in the neighborhood of one thousand.

Now in 1696, Kino set out to bring these groups into the mission system. His methods may be noted. He drove cattle up to Bac and distributed them among the Indians of the Santa Cruz settlements, these cattle to be nuclei for mission herds which would furnish food to mission residents and also provide for Kino on his expeditions of exploration. Thus the mission cattle ranches, under Kino's management, preceded the missions themselves. Secondly Kino stopped briefly, set up altars in the open or under shades built by the Indians, said Mass, and then preached at great length on many aspects of Christian living both theoretical and practical. He thus brought spiritual as well as material gifts. Thirdly, and this was most characteristic of Kino, he organized a big delegation of Sobaipuri headmen and headmen from the upper Santa Cruz Valley to go to the Jesuit rector of the district at Bacerac and ask for missionaries. He made arrangements with the headmen on his visit to Bac in 1696. Then in 1697 they all assembled at Kino's mission of Dolores, feasted and talked, and then marched in a colorful pilgrimage through the northern Opata country from Dolores to Bacerac, a matter of one hundred miles. Impressed by the delegation, the father rector received them very favorably and promised to do what he could in response to their urgent demands for missionaries in their rancherías. None was available for many years, but Kino's method of creating demand for them was well demonstrated. He followed up the demonstration by taking a large party of military and civil authorities down the San Pedro Valley and into the country of the Gila River Sobaipuris. In the course of this relatively leisurely visit through Sobaipuri country some foundations for Spanish-Sobaipuri friendship were made. The officials had a chance to see the settled, industrious character of Sobaipuri life and to see for themselves that the Sobaipuris had not acquired the hundreds of horses which the Spanish ranches and presidios had been losing to Indian raiders. Moreover, welcomed by a big scalp dance at Quiburi, they could see that the Indians dancing under the scalps were implacable enemies of the Apaches whose scalps were on the poles. There was a great deal of speech-making on both sides, the appointment of officials including Coro as captain-general of the Sobaipuris of the San Pedro, and a general feeling of goodwill.

The Spanish conviction of Sobaipuri friendliness to them and hostility to the raiding Indians of the northeast was strengthened in the following year of 1698. In that year the upper San Pedro ranchería of Gaybanipitea was raided by a combined party of Jocomes-Apaches. The raiders were surprised by a force of Sobaipuris from Quiburi and the Santa Cruz Valley — some three hundred warriors. They offered to fight by challenging the ten best men Coro could present. The ten fighters, including their leader El Capotcari, presented by the Jocomes-Apaches were killed and the rest, in a terrible rout, were mostly killed by pursuing Sobaipuris. This victory of the Sobaipuris came at a time when Cocóspera mission had been burned by Apache raiders and a general drive westward into the Pima country was being carried out by the northeastern Indians.

The victory made Captain Coro famous along the frontier and Kino was careful to foster his reputation. Yet the military significance of the event was small, for Captain Coro with the five or six hundred upper San Pedro Sobaipuris who followed his leadership moved his whole population westward out of the San Pedro Valley to Los Reyes near the modern Patagonia. Here they stayed for seven years, leaving their rancherías on the San Pedro entirely deserted. The military situation improved sufficiently for them to feel able to return and rebuild Quiburi in 1705, but the Sobaipuris were never strongly backed by the Spaniards. They never had a resident missionary, although their requests for one were repeated regularly up through the 1720's, several years after Captain Coro's death in 1711. Although the presidio of Terrenate was built on the upper San Pedro River it was not in a position to give much protection to the Sobaipuri settlements. The ultimate result was the complete retirement of all the Sobaipuris from the San Pedro Valley. Captain Coro's people held out until 1762, when their remnants finally left to merge with people in Suamca, Bac, and Tucson. Already thirty or more years before — prior to 1732 — the Sobaipuris of the lower San Pedro River under the leadership of Humari had left to merge with the Sobaipuris of the Gila River to the northwest. It was not until after all the Sobaipuris were forced to leave the San Pedro Valley that the Spaniards built a presidio. This they did on the deserted site of Quiburi in 1772 and called it Santa Cruz de

Quiburi. The Sobaipuris of the San Pedro had not been encouraged or supported as Spanish allies, but had rather been allowed to bear heavily the Apache attacks and ultimately to suffer disintegration.

Meanwhile, having shown that the Sobaipuris wanted mission life and that they were potentially valuable allies of the Spaniards in their efforts to control the frontier against the Apaches-Jocomes-Janos, Kino continued with his work to the westward. This involved exploring and making known the locations and numbers of Pima rancherías in the desert area west of the Santa Cruz River, the area which is today the Papago Reservation, as well as vast tracts extending westward from it to the Colorado River. Slowly the previously missionized area from Caborca to San Ignacio was built up again under Fathers Campos and Minutuli, and Father Velarde came to help Kino at Dolores. By the time of Kino's death in 1711 the missions were barely built up to the level that they had attained before the uprising at Tubutama, and there was no important increase in the missionary force until 1732.

The Spanish settlers were by no means happy with the missionary program. Increasingly they felt that it conflicted with their interests, and early in the 1700's they found a spokesman in the person of Kino's old traveling companion, Juan Mateo Manje, who had become alcalde mayor of Sonora. In 1706 in a report, which was extremely laudatory of individual Jesuits and their work, he nevertheless proposed that the missionary phase should be regarded as over. In line with the feelings of the miners and hacendados of Sonora generally, he proposed that mission lands should be distributed among the Indians, that the missions be secularized, and that Indians be impressed for work on mines and ranches under the repartimiento system. Jesuit influence resulted in Manje's imprisonment in Parral for making such proposals, although he was ultimately released. The twenty years' exemption of Indians in missions from tribute and repartimiento which Kino's original cedula had affirmed was now up, however, and Spanish settlers in the area continued their pressure for breakup of the mission system. In 1722 citizens of San Juan Bautista petitioned for the complete removal of the Jesuits and the division of mission lands and cattle among the Indians.

These expressions of dissatisfaction with the missionary activities coincided with a twenty-five year decline in the missions in the Pimería. By 1730 there had been no increase in the number of missions over those established by Kino. The Sobaipuris, so well prepared by 1700 for missions, were still completely without missionaries. The populous upper Santa Cruz and Bac areas, even though cattle had been distributed and numerous demands had been made for missionaries, were still without even regular visiting missionaries. The Papago country of the western deserts, although rather well explored by Kino, also remained undeveloped. During the 1720's Indians who had gathered at Bac, Suamca, and Quiburi in expectation of the coming of missionaries began to disperse. Even the missionized areas centering around Dolores, San Ignacio, Tubutama, and Caborca had lost population and were, as compared with regions to the south, weak mission fields. In all these four areas together in 1730 there were fewer than fifteen hundred people living under the mission system. The least populous of the four was Kino's home area where only 135 Indians were reported in Dolores, Remedios, and Cocóspera. The most populous was the Caborca area, where 723 Pimas were reported in the mission pueblos. At the same time there were about three hundred Spaniards living in the district. Epidemics, Apache raiding, and declining vigor in the Jesuit program had all contributed to the loss of population. How many Indians there were in the area who had lost contact with the missions was not reported, but there would seem to have been a general withdrawal.

In 1732 came a new burst of activity by the Jesuits, as they found themselves supported against the citizen demands for their removal. Three new missionaries came into the field and work was taken up farther north on the upper and middle Santa Cruz River, at Suamca, Guevavi, and Bac. The focus of missionary activity now definitely shifted to the north again, as the area where Kino's activity had centered steadily became depopulated. The Pimas of the upper Santa Cruz and the Sobaipuris farther north around Bac received the new missionaries with eagerness and began again to gather around the missions in these areas, but the Jesuits never established themselves on the Gila and never built a church in the Papago country, although one was established at its edge at Sonoita.

By 1750 there were nine Jesuit missionaries among the Upper Pimas and work was proceeding as smoothly as it had in the early days in the Pimería. There were even attempts on the part of the Jesuits to extend themselves far into the north, as the result of a request made to them by the Hopis who were refusing to have anything to do with the Franciscan missionaries of New Mexico. These attempts failed, partly due to the barrier of hostile Apaches to the north, partly to the waning impetus of the Spaniards generally who seemed not to have the means or the spirit to establish a town and presidio as far north as the Gila River, and finally to the refusal of the Hopis themselves to deal with the Jesuits. The Pimería continued to be an area without any Spanish settlement of any size or importance. Apache raids into it from the east were frequent.

In 1751 occurred the second uprising of the Upper Pimas. This revolt definitely centered around one man, Luís Oacpicagigua whose home was in Saric. Oacpicagigua spoke Spanish and was friendly with Governor Parillas of Sonora. He served under the latter when the Seris of Pópulo rebelled against the distribution of their lands to the Spaniards of Pitic presidio. His service was so satisfactory to Parillas that he was made captain-general of the Pimas. The Jesuit accounts all depict Oacpicagigua as vain and anxious for personal power. His appointment, according to Jesuit accounts, gave him the idea of becoming chief of all the Pimas. It does appear that he planned a revolt which would oust all Spaniards from Pima territory and that he had very little support for his plan among the Pimas generally. His own account was that harsh and oppressive treatment by the missionaries inspired him to break their hold over his people — charges which did not stick in court against the accused missionaries.

The revolt began in the same area where rebellion had first occurred among the Pimas, namely, at Saric not far upstream from Tubutama. Captain Luís held many meetings there in 1751 at which he gained some allies — men from Sonoita and Caborca and a Papago headman named Javanino. What support he had seems

definitely to have been among western Pimas — the longer-missionized groups —
rather than among the Sobaipuris and the Pimas of the upper Santa Cruz. He
began the revolt by killing eighteen Spaniards whom he had invited to his house
at Saric. Then he attacked Tubutama. At Caborca and at Sonoita the missionaries,
Tello and Ruhen respectively, were killed and the fighting extended eastward
into the San Ignacio area. There was disaffection at Bac, but little destruction
and no other missionaries were killed. In the east there was only halfhearted
participation which quickly ceased when Captain Parillas brought a small force
into the field and killed forty Pimas, and the Papago Javanino deserted. Finally
after the killing of more than one hundred Spaniards, Luís made peace, Parillas
listened to his charges against the Jesuits, and had him jailed. The movement
does not seem to have been a general, popular one, but rather was dependent
on the ambitions of the one man Luís Oacpicagigua. Like the previous Pima
uprising it petered out quickly — to be settled by negotiation rather than by
desperate battle. One result was to bring about the establishment of one more
presidio on the northern frontier, namely the presidio of Tubac south of Bac on
the Santa Cruz River which was regarded as protection for the missions of San
Xavier del Bac and Guevavi.

Upper Pima history through the Jesuit period is a story of a people whose
interest in and demand for elements of Spanish culture was never fully satisfied.
It contrasts with the histories of the Opatas, Mayo-Yaquis, and Lower Pimas in
this. In the latter cases missionary work ultimately extended through their whole
territories and there was sufficient opportunity for all who wanted to accept the
mission way of life. It is similar to the histories of the Tarahumaras and the Seris
in that the missions never extended to the whole tribes. But there is a great
difference also between the Upper Pima situation and the last two. The missionaries among the Tarahumaras met periodic resistance for a hundred years, resistance which was not localized but rather widespread, influencing each time most
of the not yet missionized Tarahumaras. Fighting was desperate — last-ditch
fighting ultimately — and peace was possible only after real military defeats. The
history of conflict in the case of the Seris was very similar to that of the Tarahumaras. And in both cases considerable proportions of the tribes were able to
remain beyond mission influence. The Upper Pimas, on the other hand, did not
divide sharply into pro-mission and anti-mission groups. As far as we can tell
there was throughout the Jesuit period a genuine demand for missionaries all
through the Pima country. The fighting against the Spaniards was of a different
character from that of either Seri or Tarahumara. The 1695 uprising was very
sharply localized to Tubutama at the beginning and did not spread until the
slaughter at El Tupo threw people briefly into a frenzy of revenge. Even this
did not seem to have lasting repercussions resulting in the crystallization of
resistance, as among Seris and Tarahumaras. The 1751 revolt was more like a
Tarahumara uprising with its Hispanicized leader Luís and the more widespread fighting, but the Spaniards had difficulty in finding forces to battle with.
In general the Pimas did not want to fight and there was no hardening of
resistance after either outbreak.

Rather, the prevailing attitude of Pimas from east to west and south to north was one of desire for mission life. The Jesuits never kept pace with the demands for their offerings. Ultimately they left the Gila and San Pedro Sobaipuris wholly unsatisfied despite requests extending over two generations. Similarly they did not meet the repeated requests of the Papagos of the western desert. Here was a unique situation for the region. Certain elements of the mission system — chiefly cattle herds and rituals regarded as curing techniques — spread more widely than the missions themselves. These established desire for more among people who did not experience the rigorous discipline of mission life. The result was an increasing receptivity with no corresponding increase in resistance.

This situation was encouraged by relatively limited contact with other elements of Spanish culture, in contrast with the Tarahumaras and the early-missionized Seris. Spanish settlement remained confined to the extreme southern part of the Pima area. It was only here that Pimas experienced forced labor and the caste system of the Spaniards. Pimas migrated from this part of the area, but carried little if any hostile attitudes with them. At any rate what hostility was generated here was not sufficient to counterbalance the prevailing favorable attitude towards missions.

Like the Opatas, the Upper Pimas did not constitute a tribal unity. We have indicated the divisions among them and the considerable separateness of action of the different ranchería groups. We have seen the difficulty of the disaffected Tubutama-Saric rancherías in enlisting wide support of their opposition plans. The mission program, as a result of this as well as of the piecemeal development of Jesuit facilities, affected the Pimas consequently in very irregular fashion. The full program was nearly fifty years in reaching as far as Bac after work had begun with their neighbors to the south. As we have seen, the full program never did reach other thousands of Pimas on the east, north and west. This meant, as in the case of the Tarahumaras, a very uneven sort of acculturation, with some Pimas in intensive contact with the missionary aspects of Spanish culture from 1687 throughout the Jesuit period, many others with practically no contact at all, and still others with little more than a generation of contact in an intensive way. The contrast with the sudden and complete incorporation into mission life of the Yaquis and Mayos, and of the various geographical divisions of the Opatas, was very great.

One of the factors that contributed to the very uneven acculturation of the Upper Pimas was the considerable shifting of population within the area during the Jesuit period of contact. We have seen that there was a general movement of Pimas northward away from the Spanish frontier, resulting in the depopulation of the Dolores district by the end of the period, and there was a decrease in population in the Tubutama and Caborca districts. There was also movement westward from the San Pedro Valley, so that there came to be some concentration of population in what had been the central part of Pima territory, along the Santa Cruz and westward from there. At the same time, even by the end of the Jesuit period, some Papagos from the poorer desert area were drawn, not because of

Spanish or Apache pressures, but for better living, into the missions of the center. There had begun before the end of the Jesuit period a shifting in and out of missions on the part of the western Pimas. This situation was analogous to what had been going on in the Tarahumara missions. Yet it did not generate similar conflicts.

By the time missions were introduced to the Pimas the conflicting interests of Spaniards were well developed at their southern border. The very first contacts were made in the milieu of this conflict, with Spanish military men pushing one set of interests and missionaries another. Kino, like the Jesuits elsewhere, in many ways identified mission interests with the Indians and fought desperately to shield them from the results of these internal conflicts in Spanish culture. He had more success in this than did the Jesuits of the Tarahumara region and was fortunate in that there were not successive large silver or gold rushes throughout the Pima country.

For nearly fifty years preceding Mexican independence in 1821, the contacts of the Upper Pimas with Spaniards on the northwestern frontier had decreased in intensity. The Pima revolt in 1751 constituted a shock from which the Jesuit missions had not recovered by the time of the expulsion in 1767. The succeeding Franciscan efforts were relatively weak, although characterized by some strong individual work on the part of the energetic Father Garcés. Franciscan attention to the missions was largely confined to the Santa Cruz River missions of San Xavier and Tumacacori with some work on the Magdalena at San Ignacio. The missions of Tubutama, Oquitoa, Cocóspera, and Caborca remained in existence, along with San Ignacio, San Xavier and Tumacacori, but the reports indicated that all but the last two were in a state of decline. In the early 1800's a concerted effort was made by Franciscans to bring Pimas into the Santa Cruz River missions, and there are indications that a number of new converts were made at that time at, for example, Tumacacori. Outside of the three still somewhat active missions there was no contact between the Piman-speaking peoples and the missionaries. The vigorous mission communities of the early 1700's were a thing of the past.

Contacts were with prospectors, miners, and ranchers, and there were few of these in what is now northwestern Sonora and southern Arizona. Settlement was sparse in the Altar Valley and along the Magdalena, but some ranches existed. At times a little mining took place here and there through the area. Essentially, as report after report indicated, the Upper Pimas had returned to their "ancient barbarism."

An important factor in the increasing isolation was the intensification of the Apache raids after about 1810. During the late 1700's Piman-speaking people had steadily retired westward from their border position on the San Pedro River. By 1800 there were no Pimans east of a line between San Ignacio near Magdalena and San Xavier. Many had been killed, and a few had been absorbed into the central Sonoran communities of Opatas and Spaniards. The remaining Pimans, who were not at the mission sites along the Santa Cruz and Magdalena, were living in desert villages in the present area of the Papagos or the river villages along the Gila. The Apache raiding affected them profoundly. The raids became more frequent during the 1830's and 1840's. In 1848, as the war between the Anglo-Americans and the Mexicans over Texas was ending, the presidio of Tubac was abandoned. The 1850's were a period of widespread Apache raiding extending through the whole southern Upper Pima country past the Altar Valley to the coast of the Gulf of California. Occasional harassment of settlements in what is now northern Sonora continued until the 1870's.

At the same time two different kinds of relationships with Mexicans developed in northern Sonora. In the first place, a certain dependency of the desert Pimans on the Mexican farmers and ranchers grew up. They often came southward into the Altar Valley especially to work in the harvest, taking goods and sometimes money back with them from these seasonal expeditions, but maintaining their homes far removed from their employers. On the other hand, Mexican settlers steadily encroached on Indian lands, and hostile relations also developed. These were most intense for the scattered rancherías in the northern Sonora valleys and at the margins of these valleys, where Mexican cattle raising became more and more important. They often involved small wars over water holes. Indians and, occasionally, Mexicans were killed. Fighting of this sort was especially intense in the early 1830's and continued sporadically through the century. The hostilities were similar to those that took place between Seris and Mexican cattlemen. Slowly the Indians were killed off or, after the Gadsden Purchase in 1853, withdrew to the United States' side of the new international boundary.

Pimans also took part as soldiers in the various military conflicts in Sonora, fighting at first for Gándara, who held property in the Papago country in what is now southern Arizona, and later fighting on various sides. They took an important part in campaigns against the Seris. Other than this acceptance as soldiers, the Sonora government took little notice of the Pimans. There were very few, perhaps not over a thousand in the whole of their territory included in Sonora after the Gadsden Purchase. They were nowhere united in their resistance to the progressive land encroachment by Mexicans. They did occasionally harass cattlemen by killing cattle, but also periodically worked for them at times when their services were much valued. Their ability as fighters when fighting under the direction of Mexican commanders was recognized, but otherwise Mexicans showed little consciousness of them as a people.

Gradually crowded out of the Altar and Magdalena valleys into the desert, many emigrated northward into the Papago villages in the United States. By 1950 there remained in Sonora only some ten small villages with an over-all population of less than five hundred. The Pimans who remained in the Mexican towns in northern Sonora were nearly assimilated to Mexican ways.

The Gadsden Purchase in 1853 caused immediate important consequences for the Upper Pimas. In the first place it resulted in placing the great majority under the domination of a different political regime. The new international boundary, surveyed in 1858, traversed the region of the headwaters of the San Pedro and Santa Cruz rivers and ran through the middle of the desert lands to the west. This automatically placed at least three-quarters of the remaining Upper Pimas as residents of the United States. As much as sixty years later there were still Pimas in the desert rancherías, under the leadership of a headman named Pia Machita, who seemed unaware of the change and still professed allegiance to Mexico. Nevertheless, the invading Anglo-Americans regarded the Upper Pima territory north of the new line as part of the United States and proceeded to act accordingly.

PAPAGOS

The incoming Anglo-Americans almost immediately began to make a distinction between the Indians who lived on the Gila River, whom they often called "Pimos," and those who lived farther south in the vicinity of Tucson and westward. For the latter they took over the term which had come into use among Spaniards for the desert dwellers north of the line of Altar River missions, namely, Papagos. As more Anglo-Americans entered the area this distinction became solidly established, so that the term "Pima" was applied exclusively to the residents of the Gila Valley, while the term "Papago" came into use for all Piman-speaking peoples south of them.

At the time that Anglo-Americans took over political control of Papago territory, the Indians were ripe for a military alliance. During the Mexican period Apache raids had increased in frequency and intensity, and Mexicans, despite the maintenance of a garrison at Tubac on the eastern frontier, had furnished little or no protection to Papago communities. The first Anglo-Americans moved directly into the customary Apache raiding corridor. A cattleman named Pete Kitchen established a ranch south of the Santa Rita Mountains near Nogales in 1854; two years later four companies of U.S. dragoons moved into Tucson to replace the small Mexican garrison and troops were also posted at Calabasas; in 1856 Fort Buchanan was established near Sonoita east of Tubac; and in 1857 the large Canoa Ranch was taken over by Anglo-Americans near Tumacacori. These settlements provided something of a buffer between Papagos and Apaches. They also gave Papagos an opportunity to join with the United States forces as scouts.

During the twenty years following the Gadsden Purchase, the Apache raids nevertheless continued. Small parties of Apaches continued to swing deeply into Papago territory. The small eastern outpost of less than two hundred Papagos at San Xavier del Bac continued to suffer occasional losses of young men or captured women and children. Horses and cattle of both Papagos and the new Anglo-American ranchers were the focus of the Apache raids. Animals were driven off every year during the 1850's and 60's. The increasingly successful efforts of the Anglos to contain the Apaches north of the Gila and in the Chiricauhua Mountains, however, slowly decreased the danger, but the necessity for cooperation between Papagos and Anglos for survival continued strong. Meanwhile the habit of working together had grown. In 1865 the Papagos of San Xavier agreed formally to maintain a "standing army" of 150 mounted warriors to join with the Anglo-Americans in any effort to repulse Apache raids or to seek retaliation. This Papago help was greatly appreciated and publicly acknowledged by the new-

10. PIMA AND PAPAGO COUNTRY ABOUT 1960

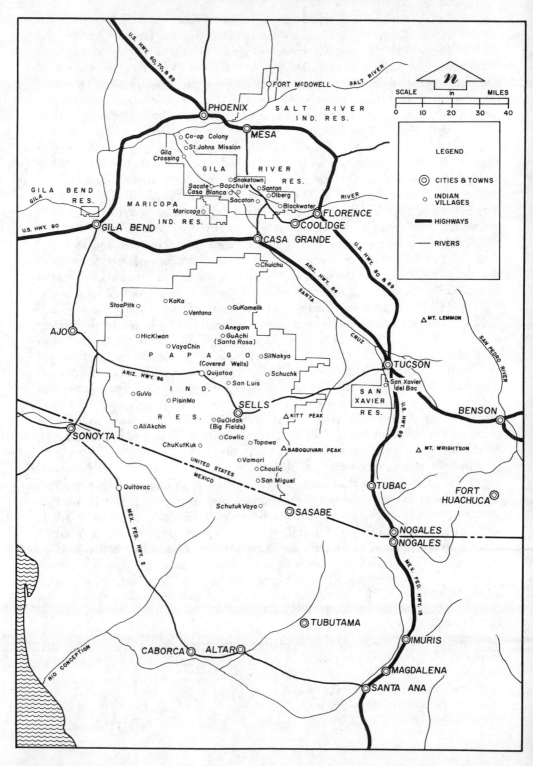

comers. In 1871 it was a party of Papagos and Tucson settlers together who carried out the Camp Grant massacre against the Aravaipa band of Apaches on the San Pedro River. It was not, however, until 1875 that a Papago recorder of tribal history at San Xavier was able to report the last of the Apache menace. It was not only the San Xavier Papagos who were involved in the ultimately success-ful working alliance. Even though there was no tribal-wide intervillage organiza-tion either for war or peace among Papagos, Indians in the desert area west of Tucson were brought into the coalition against the Apaches.

Well before the diminution of the Apache raids some fruits of the Anglo-Papago alliance began to appear. In 1863 an Indian agent was appointed for the Papagos and began his responsibility by giving out hoes, shovels, and picks — chiefly to the Papagos at San Xavier. In 1865 with the Civil War over and Anglos coming back into the Tucson area, the agent began more systematic efforts to become acquainted with the Papagos. A survey was made which led to the conclusion that there were in the neighborhood of sixty-three hundred Papagos. A distinction was made between the two hundred Indians at San Xavier and the "nomadic" Papagos of the west. The agent proposed that all should be collected at San Xavier, but this was never actually attempted. Also, a proposal for cement-ing the military alliance was made by arranging to pay the Papago "head chief" $500 a year and four sub-chiefs each $350. The head chief selected by the Whites was a man named Many Dresses of Atchi village. The following year Anglo-American interest in Papagos was affirmed by another issue of metal tools and the establishment of a school at San Xavier for a few months. The government interest in schooling for the Papagos of San Xavier continued for another ten years, resulting in an arrangement with the Sisters of St. Joseph to run a school at the village financed by government funds. By 1874 there were eighty-nine students enrolled, but in the following year the Pima agency took over Papago affairs and the school at San Xavier was discontinued.

In 1874 an executive order established a reservation of 69,200 acres surround-ing the mission of San Xavier, and in 1884 another small area near Gila Bend on the Gila River was set aside as a reservation for the few Papagos living there. This left the greater part of Papago territory between the Santa Cruz River and Gila Bend open to settlement by non-Indians. The Papagos were thus in a situation unique among Indians in Arizona and New Mexico. Elsewhere, relatively large portions of the territory ranged over by the Indians were set aside as reservations exclusively for Indian use. The Papagos, lacking any treaty with the United States since they had fought on the side of the Anglo-Americans, were given no formal protection against settler encroachment, except for the relatively minute areas at San Xavier and Gila Bend.

During this half century the population of the Papagos was usually estimated in the neighborhood of five thousand persons, only some four or five hundred at most being resident in the two small reservations. The majority were scattered over three million acres from the Santa Cruz River to the Gulf of California. They were by no means isolated from the expanding Anglo population. On the con-trary, much of their land became the focus of interest of both cattlemen and miners. Some Spanish and Mexican mining activity had extended on a small scale into Papago territory with the development of gold placers in the Altar Valley and a few silver mines such as the Arizonac. With the completion of the Gadsden Purchase, Anglo-Americans began prospecting, resulting in the discovery of what turned out to be one of the most productive copper mines in the world at Ajo in the western Papago territory, the Mowry silver mines in the Santa Rita Mountains east of Tumacacori, and in 1857 silver mines at Arivaca. Mining was largely discontinued during the Civil War, but became vigorous again in the 1870's. From the late 1870's through the 1890's dozens of mines small and large came into operation scattered widely over the Papago country. A few were in the vicinity of San Xavier, but the areas of most intensive development were in the very heart of the Papago territory — at Comobabi and Quijotoa. Quijotoa in 1884 was a town of ten thousand with the usual quota of blacksmiths' shops, stores, and saloons of the typical United States mining boom town. Within a few years it was a ghost town. In the Comobabi Mountains smaller camps grew up and disappeared as the small veins of silver, copper, and lead were worked out.

Papagos watched the growth of these communities, saw wells dug and water pumped. A few went to work as laborers and miners, earned wages, and learned some English words. How many actually lived in the evanescent camps we do not know, nor do we know how many learned any of the skills. They at least became aware of the Anglos throughout their range and saw the variety of their culture. Apparently the vast majority of Papagos had little intensive contact with the miners; they tended to remain secluded in their villages raising cattle and farming when there was sufficient rain. In bad years they ranged more widely for work at wages — to the Mexican towns in the Altar Valley, to Tucson which had become a town of three thousand as early as 1871, or to the villages of the Gila Pimas.

The efforts of Anglo cattlemen to utilize the usually sparse range of the Papagos resulted in contacts of more lasting effect. The old southeastern frontier of the Papagos where contacts with the larger world of Western civilization had begun — the upper Santa Cruz Valley — was one of the most attractive areas in Arizona to the incoming white men. It was here that cattle were brought in to supply the government-established Indian reservations with beef rations, and from those original herds larger ones developed. The Kitchen Ranch, the Canoa Ranch, and others in the Santa Cruz Valley flourished through the 1880's. New cattlemen appeared driving herds from Texas and seeking range for them. Most of the Papago country was not well adapted, but a considerable portion of the eastern and central parts had good grass cover in the 1870's. Ranchers moved steadily into these parts. In some instances they found water holes which they appropriated, driving off Papagos who customarily used the water. In other cases the new ranchers developed their own wells and water supply, excluding Papagos from what they developed. Small battles were fought. By 1892 the yield in cattle shipped from Pima County was 121,000 head. Only a small percentage of these were raised in the Papago territory, but the number had steadily increased over the preceding twenty years. Friction between cattlemen and Papagos had also increased since 1885 when the first battle over a water hole was recorded. But as the 1890's wore on the cattle market took a drop and ranching on the Papago lands declined. Moreover Papagos had begun to steal cattle, and damages resulting from such activities were reported by Anglo-Americans in three years during the 1890's as amounting to $300,000 and forcing out of business of at least one large cattle outfit.

The cattle ranching of the Anglo-Americans had several important effects on Papago life. In the first place, it resulted in the growth of hostility between Papagos and white men. The forcible appropriation of water supply and range land resulted in no general warfare, but it produced deep hatred on the part of Papagos and distrust that affected the families most injured. The attitudes of cooperation and mutual respect stimulated by the alliance against the Apaches were thus balanced by antagonism and hostility during the twenty years following the end of the Apache raids.

In the second place, some Anglo-Americans managed to survive the decline in the cattle business during the early 1890's and established themselves permanently in the central part of Papago territory. This area which was known as "the strip" became a source of friction between Whites and Indians. It was claimed by Whites as having been sold to them by a headman of Santa Rosa. The dispute, which eventually went into the Anglo courts, was not settled until 1929.

There was, thirdly, a constructive result of the ranchers' encroachments. Some Papagos worked as cowboys and learned a great deal about cattle raising. On the west side of the Baboquivari Mountains some Papagos began the transition from subsistence cattle raising, involving a few cattle on unfenced range to be slaughtered when food was needed, to the planned raising of cattle for the national beef market. Beginning in the 1890's, family groups in this favorable area which included villages such as San Miguel, Chukut Kuk, Topawa, and Vamori began to improve water holes and to appropriate for their own use, in the manner of the White cattlemen, these water sources. Slowly they began to build up cattle herds which brought them into the cash economy of the region.

During this period when there was no government supervision among the main body of Papagos, important new developments in the distribution of population began to take place. The banding together of Papago villages for defense was no longer necessary because of the cessation of Apache raids. Consequently small village units began to separate out from the confederated village groups throughout Papago country, increasing the number of separate settlements.

At the same time there was an augmentation of Papago population by migration of Piman-speaking people from Sonora. This was stimulated in part by friction with Mexican cattlemen, in part by job opportunities and better living conditions. In 1898 a battle broke out in a dispute between Papagos near the mine of El Plomo in Sonora and Mexican ranchers. So serious was the conflict that the Papagos involved fled for their lives to the United States. This was followed by other flights, so that the villages on the west side of the Baboquivaris increased in population. Many Sonoran Papagos also came to Tucson and took up permanent residence there. At the same time there was some movement of others from

Sonora into the Papago country. Several hundred Yaqui Indians in flight from the deportation program of the Mexican government crossed the international line and settled in Papago villages on the west side of the Baboquivari Mountains and among Papagos who were living in Tucson. At the same time, the traditional visits to the Altar Valley by Papagos from the north were slowly cut off as extensive opportunities for work for wages in bad years began to appear with the coming of the railroad through Tucson, the growth of irrigation in central Arizona, and many other opportunities of which the Papagos took immediate advantage.

Another Mexican influence which may have intensified with the movement of Sonoran Papagos northward, was the cult of Saint Francis. The mission traditions were strong among Sonoran Papagos of the Altar Valley area and the church of Saint Francis Xavier near Tucson was an important influence among Arizona Papagos. There was also an annual celebration at Magdalena, Sonora, which through the 1800's drew Indians from a wide area. This took place on the day of Saint Francis of Assisi on October 4, but utilized an image of Saint Francis Xavier, thus combining in a single event the two Saint Francises who had been important in Papago contacts with Catholicism, the patrons of the Franciscans and the Jesuits respectively. Certain images from Tumacacori, San Xavier, and perhaps other churches had been carefully preserved at San Xavier during the period of mission abandonment and Apache warfare. Out of these various influences an independent cult among the Papagos had developed — by what time is not clear. In little buildings in many villages pictures or images of Saint Francis Xavier were worshipped regularly. Papago families managed the services and the whole cult, like the church ceremonials of the Yaquis, went on quite independently of the Catholic Church. The San Francisco cult spread widely among Papagos during the 1890's and the next twenty years, so that all major village groups had at least one local chapel.

Other religious influences began to affect Papagos after 1900, and even before. As early as 1891 two Mormons were reported as resident at Gunsight in the western Papago country. They had missionary objectives, but it is not apparent that they influenced more than a few Papagos. During the early 1890's also, a boarding school was established by the Presbyterian Home Mission Board, which was designed to give a general elementary education plus religious instruction and some vocational, chiefly agricultural, training. About 1906 there were three hundred Papagos living more or less permanently on the southern outskirts of Tucson. They became much interested in a disciple of the "Prophet Dowie," a Protestant evangelist who preached in Phoenix and sent a Negro preacher and faith healer to the southeastern Papago villages. The followers of the Negro preacher called themselves "Israelites" and for a time there were Papagos in Topawa and other villages on the western side of the Baboquivari Mountains as well as in Tucson who were affected by the cult. One outgrowth seems to have been the organization of a group of families from the village of San Miguel primarily to prepare themselves for the end of the world. This group of some thirty to forty people took cattle and moved to a spot in the Cobabi Mountains where they remained to await the end. After several months' stay without any

indication of the end of the world they disbanded and returned to their village of
San Miguel. Perhaps the very unusual earthquake of 1887 which was felt throughout the Papago country had some part in the growth of this religious movement.

As indicative of the miscellany of influences that were altering Papago life
at this time it should be noted that a calendar-stick keeper of San Xavier recorded
that in 1910 at the village of Saddle Hanging occurred the first Anglo-American
style couple dance with drum and violin music — a hoe-down type of dance. By
1912, when a new era in Papago affairs began, the Indians had had some sixty
years' experience, most of it rather intensive, with Anglo-American warfare, mining, cattle raising, recreation, and religion.

In contrast with the first, the second fifty-year period of contacts between
Papagos and Anglo-Americans was strongly affected by government action. Yet
even so, it was probably less important as a factor in Papago lives than it was in
the lives of other Indian groups in Arizona. Government efforts to aid Papagos
developed unusually slowly. Not until 1917 was a reservation proposed for Papagos to embrace the area between Tucson and Ajo and south to the Mexican
border. In 1918 the reservation was established by executive order to include two
million acres, the disputed strip of territory through the center being excluded
from the reservation. The reservation areas now covered practically the whole
territory in which Papagos had established villages or over which they were
accustomed to range. In order to get the approval of the area as a reservation it
had been necessary for rights to the minerals that might be on the land to be
excluded from Papago possession, thus again putting them in a unique category
as compared with any other Indians in the United States.

The establishment of the reservation was the foundation for a general government program. An Indian agency was established at a location named Sells in the
central part of the large reservation and a superintendent took up residence. The
irrigation division of the Indian Bureau had already been at work on surveys of
the water resources, and throughout the 1920's government funds were used
either for the drilling or the purchase of wells which had previously been drilled
by White settlers. By 1933 thirty-two deep wells had thus been provided for the
Papagos. Some of these were meant for provision of domestic water supply near
the villages, some were designed for stock watering to enable Papagos to go
ahead with the cattle raising which had begun in the southeastern part of what
was now the reservation. Often resistance was met to the digging of wells in close
proximity to villages. There was a fear, based on very important parts of the
Papago mythology, of what might issue from the ground — evil winds or a flood.
Nevertheless the well drilling proceeded either by changing a proposed location
to a village-approved site farther away, or by gaining the support of a group within
the village which lacked the traditional viewpoint.

The creation of the reservation and the institution of the superintendency
fomented some factionalism, the bases of which were several and went back earlier.
On the one hand, the government, since the closing of the San Xavier school, had
been encouraging young Papagos to go to the Sacaton boarding school on the
Gila Pima reservation and had also been picking up children with or without

parents' consent to be sent to government boarding schools. For example, in 1902 fifty-three Papago children were sent to the Santa Fe Boarding School. By 1920 there were as many as fifty Papagos who had been away to school — at least to the Tucson Presbyterian Training School — and returned to settle down on the reservation. Many of these hailed the creation of an agency as a progressive step and sought immediately to work closely with the superintendent. On the other hand, there were members of families in each village from which village leaders were traditionally chosen who had not been away to boarding school and who opposed for various reasons the more assimilated leadership which had suddenly appeared, especially in the southeastern part of the reservation. By 1928 there were two organized groups with their leadership centered in the villages immediately west of the Baboquivari Mountains. The group which had a predominance of persons with boarding-school background called itself the Good Government League — reputed to have been organized in 1908. It tended to go along with the superintendent in most of his plans. The opposing group founded in 1925 called itself the League of Papago Chiefs and tended to hold out for traditional ways and a minimum of interference in village affairs by the superintendent and his assistants. One of the issues that gave rise to this organization had been the pushing ahead in some instances by government well drillers of wells in locations that traditionally-minded persons in various villages opposed. Supporters of the League of Papago Chiefs also held that traditional authority in various villages was being usurped by boarding-school graduates who properly should not have assumed prominence. Another source of support for the League of Papago Chiefs lay in those conservatives sometimes called "Montezumas" who had listened with approval to Dr. Carlos Montezuma in his speeches at Sacaton denouncing the Bureau of Indian Affairs and advocating its elimination.

Another factor which entered into the factionalism consisted of religious differences. Almost simultaneously with the inauguration of an active government program for economic improvement, there appeared two other programs of directed change on the reservation. A Catholic mission was started about 1900 at Sacaton and in 1908 one of the fathers visited the Papago country to survey the missionary field. In 1915 a Franciscan priest took up residence at Cobabi and in 1923 moved to Topawa. This then became a center of Franciscan missionary work which increased in scope as the years went by. In 1912 Presbyterians, following up their extremely successful work among the Gila Pimas, began to extend their program to the Papagos. Like the Franciscans, they concentrated in the southeastern part of what became the Sells reservation, setting up in 1912 a small school as well as a church at San Miguel. By 1920 they had churches also in Topawa and Choulic. By the middle 1920's a sharp sectarian division had developed in the villages west of the Baboquivari Mountains. Each of the villages was split internally into Catholics and Presbyterians, and often the feeling between the sects ran high. This played some part in the political factionalism. The League of Papago Chiefs tended to be Catholic while the members of the Good Government League tended to be Presbyterians.

The League of Papago Chiefs had the advice and help of a vigorous young

Franciscan missionary, Father Bonaventura Oblasser who for many years continued active in guiding relations between Papagos and persons in the federal government. Partly as a result of efforts of the League of Papago Chiefs, "The Strip" was restored in 1931. It was also partly as a result of this organization and perhaps the newly educated members of the leadership of the Good Government League that a superintendent who had shown himself not well disposed towards Papagos and somewhat incompetent was removed. This sort of active political interest characterized only the villages in the southeast. Beyond, in the greater part of the large reservation through the 1930's, there was little contact with the agency or either of the two new missionary programs. It was even true that in the northwestern part of the reservation contacts with Anglo-Americans were so slight that village leaders believed themselves to be under the political control of Mexico rather than the United States. Here neither government nor missionary program had yet penetrated, nor had the migration of Papagos from Mexico affected the area.

The new agency town increased slowly in size, drawing Papagos for work in the government program, but it lagged behind Tucson as a place of intensive contacts. By 1930 Tucson had grown to a city of twenty-four thousand, one-half of whose population was Spanish-speaking, deriving from migrants from Mexico as well as families whose residence in the city had spanned the Mexican and Anglo-American periods. In 1939 it was estimated that one-third of all Papago income was now derived from wage work off the reservations. It was to Tucson and to a lesser extent Phoenix that Papagos came to work. Many of the workers were women, particularly young women, who secured jobs as house servants. In 1915 even before the creation of the Sells reservation, the Bureau of Indian Affairs had decided that Papagos in Tucson needed help in adjusting to the off-reservation life. Janet Woodruff was placed in Tucson as a "matron," that is, social worker, to help Papago women meet the problems that arose. For fourteen years she served in this capacity and was followed by others, who injected an Anglo-American viewpoint at the level of sympathetic personal interest into the lives of dozens of Papago men and women who moved into the urban milieu.

A second and quite distinct phase of government effort to guide Papago economic and political life got under way in 1934. This was the year of the change of policy of the Bureau of Indian Affairs under the Indian Reorganization Act. It was also the period of general economic depression in the United States, and Arizona was affected by a decline in employment which led Indians who had begun to work regularly off the reservation to return to their villages. The immediate focus of attention of the Bureau of Indian Affairs officials was the political organization of the Papagos, the development of the reservation economic resources, and the provision of employment, and all three of these programs were closely interrelated in what was planned.

The reservation superintendent under the new regime was instructed to persuade Papagos to organize a tribal council based on a constitution in the formulation of which Papagos were themselves to participate. Meetings were held, at which as many as twenty-five villages were represented; at the end of

1934 a referendum was held in which 1,443 Papagos voted to accept the Indian Reorganization Act and 188 voted against. A tribal organization was a new concept in Papago life, but organization proceeded, and in January, 1937, a constitution was adopted. The new organization rested on a division of the Papago reservations into eleven districts, from each of which two representatives were chosen to sit on the Tribal Council. The districts were worked out not only as political districts for representation but also as grazing districts for the cattle on the reservations. The leadership in the Tribal Council was immediately assumed by persons from the southeastern area in what now became known as the Baboquivari District.

As the political organization developed, plans for economic improvement were carried out concurrently. The Bureau of Indian Affairs went ahead with the drilling of wells for stock and domestic supply, and built reservoirs throughout the reservations for the storage of water. The large amount of new work to develop the fullest possible resources for stock raising was financed by government funds in the form of work projects such as the Civilian Conservation Corps. Some twelve hundred men were put to work on the improvements. For six years a whole new set of conditions thus prevailed among the Papagos.

A new level of tribal life, such as had not prevailed even in the time of Apache attacks, was stimulated. The Tribal Council brought chosen representatives together from every part of the Papago country, including San Xavier and Gila Bend. Moreover, the systematic activities of the BIA officials required them to visit all districts and sit down with the new district councils, which consisted of representatives from all the villages in a district. In addition, Papagos were newly concentrated on the reservation. There was steady work throughout the year, so that the customary migration far and wide for wages was curtailed. Men were concentrated in the CCC camps, thrown together more intimately than Papagos had ever been before, from the farthest villages. There was also the stimulation of a considerable sense of participation in the new developments, for the BIA officials from the start recognized that they could save time and effort if they sought advice from the village leaders with respect to the location of reservoirs, checkdams, and other features of the range improvements. An effort was made to acquaint all Papagos with developments by the publication at the agency of a newspaper every month, in both Papago and English, which recounted the current activities in political organization and range improvement. It was a period of a sense of accomplishment and cooperation, and to some extent of withdrawal from the world outside the reservation.

At the same time there were clearly counter forces set in motion. In the first place there was vigorous opposition to government supervision of the cattle business on the part of those families in the southeast who had been most successful in developing a water supply for their cattle and in the building of large and marketable herds. It was they who resisted successfully the effort of the Bureau of Indian Affairs officials to organize cattlemen's associations for cooperative production and marketing. The placement of district fences also antagonized these cattle owners, who preferred to manage their own range and herds without help or interference from outsiders. Through the years opposition to regulation of the cattle industry with reference to total tribal interests was maintained by these wealthiest large cattle owners among the Papagos. In addition, there was no immediate acceptance of tribal organization in the terms in which the government men saw it. There had never been a subordination of one village group's interests to another, nor was there now. Representatives were not regarded by their districts as empowered to enact legislation, but rather were thought of as "legs," to use the old Papago term; that is, messengers and communicators of news to their district councils. This was notably true of San Xavier, which regarded itself as quite distinct from the "desert people" of the Sells reservation.

Despite these sources of friction and misunderstanding the Tribal Council continued to exist as an organization, and foundations were laid for at least closer communication, if not solidarity, among all the sixty-three villages included in the three reservations. At the same time day schools were instituted in a considerable part of the reservation. In 1935 there were 1,100 Papago children in school, 500 in the ten mission schools (both Catholic and Presbyterian), 376 in six government day schools, 56 in public schools, and 124 in non-reservation boarding schools. Ten years later there were twice that number in school, but this was still only two-thirds of the school age children. The government program had by the early 1940's resulted in the establishment of a tribal herd of cattle, a grazing fee applicable over the whole reservation, a rodeo association, a tribal flag, and other tribal institutions. At the end of World War II, as the 250 Papagos who served in the armed forces came home, it appeared that tribal organization was well established. A young Papago from the central part of the reservation was elected chairman and assumed leadership for six years. He was a capable speaker of English as well as Papago and brought the Tribal Council into close touch with surrounding Anglo-American organizations.

The role of Thomas Segundo, the young Tribal Council chairman, was an important one. It was the policy of the Indian Bureau to encourage Indian tribes to work with county, state, and local organizations and pave the way for the withdrawal of federal responsibility. Segundo worked effectively as ambassador, explainer of his people, and functionary in intertribal organizations which appeared in Arizona after World War II. Segundo was an indication of the emergence of a Papago leadership tuned to work in the Anglo-American milieu in the interest of developing tribal economic cooperation, and to utilize the organizational instrument which had taken the form of the tribal council. But he, like other able young Indians of the period, found more scope off the reservation and left tribal government to older men less well equipped to work with Anglo-Americans.

Meanwhile, through the 1950's there were two important trends in Papago life. Perhaps the most influential was the steady growth of off-reservation wage work. The raising of cotton had become the major farm industry in southern Arizona following World War II. Papagos had made a secure place for themselves as farm laborers on the cotton ranches, establishing residence on certain ranches for both the cultivation and harvesting of cotton, going back each year in the same groups to the same ranches. The great majority of Papagos had by 1960 made this as a permanent adjustment, so that the overwhelming portion of Papago income was now derived from off-reservation sources. At the same time they maintained residence in their home villages and returned several times a year there for ceremonials or other matters. The other trend was the increasing attendance of Papago children in public schools off-reservation, connected of course with the off-reservation employment. In 1958 there were 894 Papago children — or one-third of all Papagos of school age — enrolled in public schools and for the first time in Papago history, nearly all Papago children of school age were enrolled in either public, government, or mission schools.

There had been a notable increase of sympathetic interest on the part of Anglo-Americans in Papago economic and health problems. A Pima County organization called the Association for Papago Affairs was organized in 1952 to bring Papagos and others in the county together. Also the American Friends Service Committee participated in stimulation of cooperation between Papagos and others. As this took place there was a noticeable trend toward, on the one hand, inaction on the part of the Bureau of Indian Affairs, as its national policy emphasized the withdrawal of federal responsibility. However, on the other hand, there was a marked trend toward tighter government control of any activity for which the Bureau did take responsibility on the reservations. This was most notable in connection with an effort to establish a farming project at Chiuchiu in the northern part of the Sells reservation, a project which failed to attract Papago interest and was indicative of a lack of coordination between Bureau policy and general economic development in southern Arizona. It appeared by 1960 that tribal enterprise and tribal organization under government aegis were developing at a pace which lagged very far behind that in the region generally. The major factor in Papago life was an increasing linkage, family by family, of Papagos in the economic and school systems of the surrounding Anglo-Americans. It was here that the more dynamic processes of adaptation were taking place. They did so nevertheless under the conditions of the maintenance of the Papago land base under the protective auspices of the Bureau of Indian Affairs.

During the period of Anglo-American contacts to 1960 the Papagos had undergone several important metamorphoses. With the establishment of inter-tribal peace, population had increased, perhaps trebled, to about eleven thousand and accompanying this a very wide distribution of the people had taken place. This expansion, first involving the re-establishment or new settlement of some sixty villages over the old territory, was in the 1950's marked by a new phase, namely, the permanent or seasonal residence of most of the population outside the limits of the old tribal territory. This had thrown Papagos into a wider range of contacts with Anglos and Mexican-Americans in southern Arizona and resulted in a shift in their economic base. Except for some six or seven large family lines who subsisted on cattle raising in the southeastern part of the Sells reservation, most Papagos were living under the new conditions. They were now in large part agricultural laborers integrated into the local economy and, as the schooling level increased, were moving slowly into the general occupational structure.

At the same time they were distinct from the people among whom they worked in having a tribally-owned land base. The special status of Indian with the federal government gave them a certain privileged position with respect to the receipt of government services. Nevertheless, there was no effective mechanism for the collective development or use of this land through tribal organization. The Tribal Council remained an institution out of step and functionally inconsistent with the other developments in Papago life.

The Papagos had escaped the sort of close government control which characterized the other Indians of the state, having come under government supervision relatively late and undergoing the brunt of such supervision only after the new policy of the Indian Reorganization Act was put into motion. While a certain small proportion of Papagos developed the characteristic attitudes of dependency apparent on other reservations, the majority continued as before the establishment of the reservation in 1917 to rely on their own efforts to supplement their small-scale farming and cattle raising on the reservation. As resources became increasingly insufficient at home, they increasingly sought work for wages among the surrounding people, so that their primary economic adjustment was by 1960 no longer on the reservation.

PIMAS OF THE GILA RIVER

The Upper Pima group which had the least contact with the Spaniards was that which lived along the Gila River at the very northern edge of the Spanish frontier. They had lived along the Gila River from prehistoric times where they had irrigated their fields with an elaborate canal system. They had been augmented in the 1700's by the migration from the San Pedro River Valley of the Sobaipuris who had lived near the junction of the San Pedro and the Gila rivers. The residents of the Gila Valley spoke dialects of the same language used by all the Piman-speaking people of northwestern Sonora. They differed from other Upper Pimas very little culturally, chiefly in the more intensive agriculture carried on by means of irrigation canals. In this they resembled the Santa Cruz River Pimas, but differed from the more westerly villages of Pimas who occupied the desert country west of the Santa Cruz. Spanish influence had extended very little to these Pimas by the time Anglo-Americans entered their country.

Nevertheless the Gila River Pimas had been visited by Kino and subsequent missionaries. They had been approached by Spanish and later Mexican officials for assurances of peace in connection with Apache raiding of Sonora. They had accepted canes of office, or at least official designations, from the Spaniards and had acquiesced in a nominal obedience to the King of Spain. The Spanish introduction of wheat had considerably added to their agriculture and they had become acquainted with Spanish metal tools. They regarded the Spaniards as allies against the Apaches but received no practical benefit from the nominal alliance. In short, they had indirectly absorbed some benefits from Spanish culture, particularly in agriculture, but had never experienced intensive influences from either missions or Spanish towns since there were none in their territory. They were fighting off Apache attacks at the time Anglo-Americans entered their area.

The first contacts of the Gila Pimas with Anglo-Americans were uniformly friendly ones. The Gila Trail of the fur trappers, which began to be frequented by Anglo-Americans in the 1820's, passed through the Pima territory. From 1826 through 1844 there were meetings with the various parties of trappers, beginning with the Patties in 1826. The Pimas supplied food for such parties. In 1846 General Kearny and the Mormon Battalion had contacts with the Pimas. Reports from these various parties went out to the effect that the Pimas of the Gila River were the "most civilized Indians in the United States."

They continued to enjoy this reputation after the Gold Rush to California began in 1849. It was reported that some sixty thousand Anglo travelers passed through their villages during the westward migration. The villages in fact became a major depot on the southern route, as it became well known that travelers there could count on a peaceful reception and plentiful food. The travelers reported finding the Pimas always anxious to trade for metal and other goods and always with wheat and other food in good supply. In fact, the Pimas became accustomed to look on the travelers as needy people seeking their charity. They gave freely of their food supplies, whenever it was not possible to trade.

In 1855 the Pima leaders, most notably a man named Antonio Azul, first learned that their territory had fallen into the hands of the Anglos as a result of the Mexican War and the Gadsden Purchase. Concerned over what would be the attitude of the Anglos towards their status and their land, Antonio Azul went to confer with Emory of the U.S. Boundary Commission. He was assured that the United States had friendly intentions, that the land rights under the Spaniards would be fully recognized, and also that the United States government had in mind giving the Pimas agricultural implements to assist them in the valuable service they were rendering providing food for parties of travelers.

In 1858 the stage line between El Paso and San Diego was routed through the Pima villages and the calls for food increased. Pima land devoted to agriculture had been steadily increasing since the Gold Rush period and now during the next ten years it increased to fifteen thousand acres. In 1859, somewhat tardily in the view of some Pimas, the U.S. government made good its promise to give aid — axes, shovels, knives, plows, and other tools to the value of several thousand dollars. This act consolidated friendly relations, but at the same time the federal government began to apply its usual Indian policy to the Pimas. Ten thousand dollars was appropriated in 1859, partly for the purpose of purchasing the tools to be distributed but also to cover the expense of a survey of the land on the Gila River for the purpose of setting aside not more than sixty-four thousand acres as a reservation. This intention displeased Antonio Azul and the Pimas, who claimed a far larger area — one hundred miles along the Gila River westward from a point near the modern town of Florence. The issue of land hung fire for another ten years while the various Anglos, such as Sylvester Mowry, supported the Pima claim for more land.

Meanwhile the Pimas became a bulwark against the Apaches in the Anglo conflict with those Indians. For a time in 1861 they were the only armed force in the Arizona region and when the California Volunteers came through in that year to take possession of New Mexico Territory, they armed the Pimas, more fully recognizing their potential as allies against the Apaches. They continued to serve until 1873 as organized companies in the Arizona Battalion and fought and scouted continually with Anglo troops. Antonio Azul served as sergeant in the Arizona Battalion. The military aid given to the Anglos by the Pimas was recognized as important. The Pima reputation as good soldiers as well as good farmers spread widely over the United States. In 1871 the Army prohibited further enlistment of Indian troops; Pima young men settled down on their farms along the river, although some continued to serve until 1873, when the Apaches were for the most part rounded up and placed on the San Carlos reservation.

Since 1859 the government had appointed agents for the Pimas from time to time, but these men engaged chiefly in trading, lived at a distance in Tucson, and did nothing in the way of developing schools or other services for the Pimas, although one built a flour mill at Casa Blanca in 1864. Their trading activities were notorious and contributed to the dispute between the Army and the Indian Bureau over jurisdiction of the Indians. In 1869, temporarily winning out in this dispute, the army sent Captain Grossman to act as agent for the Gila Pimas. This marked the first responsible effort to apply a program among the Pimas by the government. Grossman built an agency in Pima territory at Sacaton and began the licensing of traders. He also pushed the Pima claim for more land than that which the government had planned as their reservation in 1859. Antonio Azul had insisted that the 64,000 acres contemplated allowed nothing for the grazing in which Pimas were engaged. In 1869 the original surveyed area was increased by 81,000 acres to make a total of 145,000. This was still far less than the Pimas laid claim to, but it did indicate a willingness to listen to the Indians' requests.

In this same year of the increase in the reservation the first hostilities of the Pimas with settlers occurred. By 1869 farm land along the Gila east of the Pima villages, where modern Florence is situated, had been settled by both Anglos and Mexicans. Resentful of this encroachment, when their crops failed some Pimas moved into fields planted by Mexicans and harvested the crops, claiming that the crops were theirs. The push of settlers continued, although there were no more hostilities of this overt sort.

A dry period had set in beginning in 1869 and hard times continued. The encroachment of settlers from the east went on; the Pimas again appealed for some consideration of their problems. Azul and other Pimas went to Washington in 1873 to present their case and also, as U.S. officials thought of it, to learn of the power of the Washington government. It was proposed that the Pima problems could be solved by removal to Indian territory. Azul went to Oklahoma to look at the proposed land to be assigned there, was favorably impressed, but met implacable opposition to any removal from all the rest of the Pimas. Instead the Pimas adopted their own method of solving the problem of the failing water supply. Twelve hundred, more than a fourth of the tribe, moved north on the Salt River where they began to farm among the White settlers located there. The remaining Pimas spread out along the Gila River in three major areas of water seepage and continued rather precarious farming there.

The period of the thirty years from about 1870 to about 1900 was one of increasingly intensive contact with Anglos and of numerous changes in Pima life. The surrounding of their land by Anglo settlers became an established fact. The Southern Pacific Railroad traversed their territory in 1878. Florence on their eastern margin became an important territorial town with an increasing population. By 1887 the irrigation canal constructed to take water out of the Gila River for the White settlers utilized the whole flow. No water reached any of the Pima fields downstream. Settlers were pressing to the edge of the reservation from the south in the Casa Grande area. Protests and representations had no effect except to increase by small parcels the size of the reservation. The real need, however, was for water, not land, as most government reports recognized; yet no effort whatever was made to protect the Indian water rights. The government ignored the problem, although agents in rapid succession continued to push for the Indian rights.

The Indian Bureau turned its attention to matters which would not throw it into conflict with the settler interests. In 1881 it established a boarding school at Sacaton, a day school having already been established by Presbyterians in 1868. Also in 1881 a force of Indian police was instituted and a Court of Indian Offenses set up. An Indian Bureau farmer was brought to the reservation to give agricultural advice. At the same time that the Indian Bureau made these efforts to give some services to the Indians, activities of the Presbyterian Church were intensified.

A missionary named Cook had lived on the reservation as schoolteacher from 1868 to 1878. He gained wide acquaintance among the Pimas and won the confidence of many of them. In 1879 he began a vigorous missionary campaign which had as its object not only the baptism of Pimas but also the reorganization of their deteriorating communities. Poverty through lack of water with which to farm and replacement of functions formerly performed by village headmen through the government agency had resulted in some degree of demoralization of the Indians. In 1878, just before Cook began his intensive work, a pitched battle occurred between two Pima villages — Blackwater and Casa Blanca — an indication of the disorganization which had set in in the formerly peaceful and industrious Pima villages. Three distinct factions had developed as a result of the efforts to solve the water problems by shifts in residence on different parts of the reservation. Murders and fights were on the increase.

Cook, the Presbyterian missionary, worked vigorously through the 1880's and 1890's. He baptized nearly half the tribe before 1899 and established churches throughout the reservation. In each community he appointed an elder, assisted by deacons, whom he held responsible for law and order and general moral standards. The elders were usually former village headmen. Gradually a transformation in village life took place, centering around the new religious organization. Annual revival meetings took the place of old ceremonies. Christian mythology and theology replaced older beliefs and the strict morality of the Presbyterians tended to reintegrate the disintegrating villages. The church affairs were almost entirely in the hands of the local Pimas, and ministers were trained to do the preaching. The Presbyterian missionary, Cook, became the most inflential force from Anglo society among the Pimas, although at the same time the Sacaton Boarding School and the other boarding schools set up elsewhere by the Indian Bureau were well attended by Pimas and worked together with the missionary in the transformation of Pima society. Cook continued as a powerful influence in Pima life until 1911 when he turned over his mission to Dirk Lay.

Economic conditions continued to grow worse on the reservation. In 1895 the government had to issue rations, because of the extreme shortage of food. River water was being entirely absorbed by the Anglo settlements upstream. Pimas in considerable numbers went away to boarding schools and many stayed away working wherever they could find work, because of the difficulty of living on the reservation. One group of school-educated Pimas, however, attempted with some success for a time to found a community, called Cooperative Colony, based on modern agricultural techniques. The Indian Bureau attempted nothing that would involve it in the matter of water rights on the Gila. It did however begin a program for solution of the water problem — the digging of wells to be served by electric pumps — in the eastern and central part of the reservation. Some fifteen wells were put into operation between 1903 and 1910.

In 1911 an Indian Bureau agent in league with White settlers to the east of the reservation, but working within Indian Bureau policy, began to develop a plan for individual allotment of land. A proposal for allotments of ten-acre plots was finally put into effect in 1914 and Pimas began coming back to the reservation to take these up. It was proposed to put up for sale all land which was not allotted to Pimas. The allotment program was in line with that which had been undertaken among most of the other Indians of the United States. It was bitterly opposed by a Yavapai who had been educated as a medical doctor in Chicago—Dr. Carlos Montezuma. In 1918 he began to devote his time to the problems of Indians and came frequently to the Pima, as well as to other reservations in Arizona. He published a monthly magazine and espoused the view that the Indian Bureau had no right to allot land, it being the property of the Indians to dispose of as they saw fit. Pimas, called "Montezumas," listened to him and opposed the allotment program. Nevertheless allotment proceeded and had the effect of scattering Indians more widely over the reservation, again disrupting community life. Dr. Montezuma also held that ten acres was insufficient and that each Indian family should be granted forty acres if there was to be any allotment at all.

Meanwhile proposals had been made repeatedly by government and others for a solution to the water problem on the Gila River by constructing a reservoir. A dam site at San Carlos on one of the Apache reservations was proposed, and a long fight developed to have this program put through. Dirk Lay of the Presbyterian Church took a prominent part in this struggle until his removal from the Pima reservation in 1923. He brought national attention to focus on the crisis in which the Pimas had been involved as a result of the appropriation of the Gila River water. Eventually in 1924 the San Carlos Project Bill was passed and the government reclamation service went into action for construction of the dam near the old San Carlos Apache agency. Many Pimas hailed this as the salvation of the reservation and many who had been working away from the reservation began to come back in order to make their land ready for the water.

In 1926, in accordance with Indian Bureau policy, the reservation superintendent formed an advisory council of Pima men. This was primarily for the purpose of having some sort of tribal group with which to deal in legal matters pertaining to the whole tribe. It remained little used. In 1930 under Superintendent Kneale, after the completion of the Coolidge Dam and San Carlos Reservoir, the work began of preparing for the new supply of irrigation water. At the same time extensive road-building programs were instituted, there was a shift to day schools from boarding school, and agricultural extension service was put into operation. In 1934 under the Indian Reorganization Act the Pimas prepared a constitution and formed a tribal council. In 1937 District Farmers Associations were formed over the reservation, and in 1938 a high school was established at Sacaton.

Misunderstanding and dispute continued to center around the farm program. The Tribal Council was denied the right by the courts to appear in connection with San Carlos water rights hearings and lost prestige with the Pimas. It was consistently bypassed in all important matters by the superintendent of the reservation and was not regarded by Indians as an effective representative organization. In general the 1940's saw very little improvement in farming on the reservation. Farm family income declined, and eventually by 1950 there was a growing loss of interest on the part of Pima farmers. The Tribal Council began in 1951 to operate a tribal farm which became a paying proposition, but individual farming declined in importance. Ninety-four percent of all Pimas were literate and 98 percent spoke English. The Gila Pimas probably were the most nearly culturally assimilated of all Indians in New Mexico or Arizona. The Pima Tribal Council continued in operation but it did not function as a political institution for Pimas as a whole. The tribe as a unit of social organization or culture had ceased to exist in the Arizona milieu. The tribal organization existed as a rather specialized mechanism for managing some economic matters for Pima settlements nearest the agency.

CHAPTER SIX

Eastern Pueblos

 BECAUSE OF THE STORIES of the golden cities of Cibola, New Mexico became a strong focus of Spanish interest earlier than the Chihua-hua-Sonora region. As a result, Indians and Spaniards came to know one another sooner in the north than in the south. Coronado's violence fell on the Pueblo villages seventy years before the Span-ish soldiers from Durango put down the Tepehuan revolt. The missionary program was under way among the Pueblo Indians some ten years before the Jesuits went to work with the Tarahumaras, nearly twenty years before Pérez de Ribas baptized the Yaquis, and almost a hundred years before Father Kino established the Dolores mission among the Upper Pimas.

Marked differences characterized the Spanish approach to the northern as compared with the southern Indians. One important contrast lay in the planned program for colonizing the valley of the Rio Grande, in contrast with the unsyste-matic infiltration of Spanish settlers into New Biscay and Sonora. Another differ-ence which had important consequences was the attempt to institute political control at a single stroke over the whole of New Mexico in contrast with the century of slow, if steady, advance of political control in the south. A third differ-ence was the placing of the missionary program in the hands of the Franciscans rather than in those of the Jesuits, and the simultaneous institution of missionary and civil authority, in contrast with the southern plan of missionary advance before imposition of political control. These differences in the Spanish approach were so great and so important in their consequences that the north and the south must be considered to be two quite distinct contact areas.

Although the people of the two areas were in contact for trade before the 1680's, there was little direct contact after that. The decrease in such contact was a result of the growth of what might be called the Apache Corridor, which extended from the vicinity of Santa Fe to central Sonora. After the 1680's until the third quarter of the 1700's this strip of territory was not passable for Spaniards except with full military escort, and sometimes not even then.

The area of Spanish colonization and intensive missionary activity was the Rio Grande Valley from El Paso to Taos. This was a region which during some 350 years before the arrival of Spaniards had been the scene of considerable migration and shifting of peoples. In this respect, it did not differ from the southern region where population shifts also preceded the Spanish entry. In the north, however, the archaeological record has been much more fully worked out. We know definitely that settled agricultural peoples from large communities to the north and west moved into the Rio Grande Valley during the last half of the 1200's, that there were two successive migrations, and that thrusts of people from the west were still moving into the Rio Grande Valley in the early 1500's. Moreover, before the Spaniards came, the settled valley people were subject to attacks from nomadic people to the east — probably ancestors of the Apaches. In 1540 Coronado's party listened to accounts of the destruction of villages on the eastern side of the Rio Grande which had occurred about 1525. When the Spaniards came in they gave impetus in numerous ways to hostility between the eastern nomads and the settled people of the Rio Grande Valley.

What the Spaniards found in this 350-mile stretch of river valley was a large number of villages of very similar character. No village was large, the largest probably being less than two thousand inhabitants. Most of them were not over four hundred people. The villages were compactly built, often containing several two- or three-story houses. Well-developed agriculture, carried out by irrigation methods, was the mainstay of life. Here was a situation in which the familiar program of reduction could not apply, except as small villages might be persuaded to combine into larger villages. The obvious program for missionaries working in communities like the Sonoran rancherías where houses of the same community were strung out for miles along a stream course was not applicable here in the north. In the Rio Grande Valley the Indians were already reduced to compact communities.

These communities were autonomous. The Spaniards found no tribal political organization linking them into effective units larger than the individual villages. Moreover, there were four or five mutually unintelligible languages, each with several dialects, spoken among the sixty to seventy different villages. In the villages just north of El Paso the Spaniards heard a language spoken which bore no resemblance to the Indian languages of the south; this the Spaniards began to call Piro. It was in use in a half-dozen villages scattered through the valley for some hundred miles northward, to the vicinity of modern Socorro, New Mexico. Adjoining on the north were twenty villages in which the people spoke a language the Spaniards came to call Tiwa. This resembled Piro somewhat, but immediately to the north were another seven villages speaking a totally different language which had no similarity to Tiwa or Piro; these were the Keresan villages of which there were six in the Rio Grande Valley and another large one called Acoma fifty miles to the southwest. Still a fourth distinct language — Tano — was spoken by the people of four villages in the Galisteo Basin east of the river. North of these villages was an area in which were seven or more villages where the people spoke a language different from but intelligible to the Tanos; this language the Spaniards called Tewa. Bordering the Tanos on the east, at Pecos, were people whose language was quite unintelligible to Keresans, Tanos, and Tewas. This was the Towa language which was spoken also by people in eleven villages across the

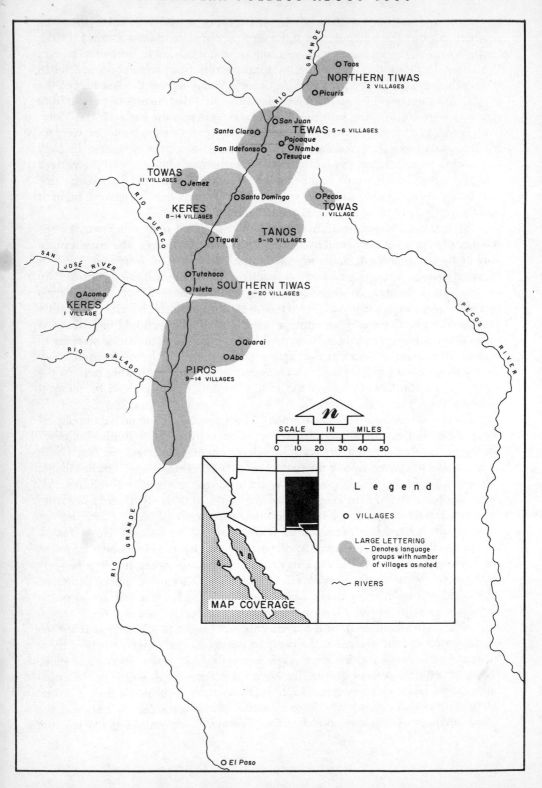

NORTHERN TIWAS
2 VILLAGES

○ Taos

○ Picuris

RIO GRANDE

○ San Juan

Santa Clara ○

TEWAS 5-6 VILLAGES

San Ildefonso ○

Pojoaque
○ Nambe
○ Tesuque

TOWAS
II VILLAGES

○ Jemez

RIO PUERCO

○ Santo Domingo

KERES
8-14 VILLAGES

○ Pecos

TOWAS
I VILLAGE

TANOS
5-10 VILLAGES

○ Tiguex

SAN JOSÉ RIVER

○ Tutahaco
○ Isleta

SOUTHERN TIWAS
8-20 VILLAGES

○ Acoma

KERES
I VILLAGE

PECOS RIVER

RIO SALADO

○ Quarai

○ Abo

PIROS
9-14 VILLAGES

SCALE   IN   MILES

0   10   20   30   40   50

RIO GRANDE

Legend

○ VILLAGES

LARGE LETTERING
— Denotes language
groups with number
of villages as noted

∼ RIVERS

MAP COVERAGE

○ El Paso

river to the west beyond the Keresans in the Jemez River Valley. Finally, beyond the Tewas in two or more villages as far north as Taos the Indians spoke a variety of the language of the southernmost villages, namely, Tiwa. Thus, there were more than sixty villages, not united in any way that would permit Spaniards to work through a few leaders. The situation, to anyone proposing political domination, must have appeared complex, but it is doubtful if the Spaniards fully understood it.

However, all the New Mexican villages together did not have a population as large as the fifty to sixty thousand of the lower Yaqui and Mayo valleys. It is doubtful if the whole Rio Grande Valley had a population of forty thousand at the time the Spaniards entered it. The Spaniards were dealing with a population no larger than that of the Opatas, but divided into a far greater number of separate political units and speaking many dialects of at least four distinct languages. Yet the Spaniards proposed to work with these people as if they composed a single unit. We shall see what the consequences of such a procedure were.

The first intensive contacts of any of the people of the Rio Grande Valley with the Spaniards came in 1540–41 with the arrival of the Coronado exploration party, which consisted of some three hundred soldiers with Christianized Mexican Indian servants. Coronado and his lieutenants dealt with Indians purely on the principle of force, but, unlike Cortez, they had no systematic plan for conquest. This approach by the Spaniards among the Opatas in Sonora had led earlier to the setting up of a plundering colony which was quickly wiped out by the Indians unable to endure atrocities committed by the soldiers. A somewhat similar series of events occurred in New Mexico after Coronado's arrival there. He established his men in a camp for the winter at Tiguex, probably one of the southern Tiwa villages near modern Albuquerque. Here the soldiers attempted to live by requiring the Tiwas to furnish them with food, clothing, and women for their use. As the Indians became aware of the aims of the soldiers, they resisted. Coronado's men retaliated by capturing two hundred Indians and executing them — mainly by burning them at the stake. The Tiwas were roused and fighting broke out in which the men of Tiguex, along with other Tiwas, were badly beaten by the Spanish soldiers. By the time Coronado decided to leave the country, disappointed by his failure to find treasure, the Spaniards were identified as ruthless — if wonderfully dressed and armed — plunderers, by at least the southern Tiwas and the Towa people of Pecos. Ten of the twelve Tiwa villages were abandoned as a result of the fighting with Coronado. The two villages in which the resisters settled to withstand Coronado's siege were ultimately completely conquered and hundreds of Indians killed.

By 1598 when Oñate introduced the full Spanish program of colonization and conversion into the Rio Grande region, four different Spanish expeditions had traveled the length and breadth of the Eastern Pueblo country—those of Coronado, Chamuscado-Rodríguez, Espejo, and Castaño de Sosa. The first and last of these were of a military character and engaged in plundering and fighting. In 1591 Castaño de Sosa's expedition of two hundred men found Pecos hostile and battled the village into submission. They found Taos also unfriendly but did not attack the village. The other two expeditions were non-military. The killing of the priest Rodríguez and his companions by the Tiwas presaged the difficulties ahead for a missionary program. On the other hand, the mineral-prospecting expedition of Espejo in 1582 experienced uniformly friendly contacts everywhere it went among the Pueblo villages. Espejo was given food and other provisions by the Piros, Keres, and Tanos.

By 1598 these expeditions had acquainted the Eastern Pueblos with Spanish horses, military equipment, and warlike qualities. The weakness of the villages in the face of any Spanish effort to conquer them was demonstrated clearly among the Tiwa and at Pecos. Willingness to accept peaceable Spaniards on a friendly basis had been shown in the general reception to Espejo's friendly procedures and in the Tano-Tewa acceptance of Castaño de Sosa's exaction of "submission." But nowhere had there appeared that demand for missionaries which was so characteristic of Indians of the south, and which there so frequently preceded other types of contacts with the Spaniards.

In 1598 Juan de Oñate was awarded a contract for the colonization of New Mexico, the extent and nature of which were now known in outline as a result of the four expeditions mentioned. The Oñate expedition was quite different from anything with which Indians of the south came into close contact. Oñate outfitted in southern Chihuahua, gathering about four hundred colonists, soldiers, Mexican Indians as servants, and Franciscan missionaries. It took three years to assemble the party. In 1598 Oñate himself with a party of soldiers, mounted and in armor, preceded the main cavalcade with its eighty carts and one thousand head of cattle. Wherever he went among the Rio Grande villages he obtained agreements of "obedience" or submission. For example, at the Keres villages of Santo Domingo, Oñate met with seven *caciques* or headmen, who were said to represent thirty-four villages. A general meeting was held in which Oñate told them of the King of Spain, offered protection from their enemies, and described the meaning and importance of baptism. At the conclusion, the seven caciques gave what the Spaniards understood as a pledge of allegiance to the king, and to Oñate as governor; then all knelt and kissed the hands of Oñate and Father Juan de Escalona who represented the Church. This ceremony was repeated elsewhere and thus, without bloodshed or overt resistance, Oñate began his program of colonization and missionization. There is no record of how the Indians interpreted the idea of obedience and submission, nor of their understanding of what Oñate proposed to carry out, but by the end of 1598 all the villages had made the pledge.

When his pack train, carts, and herds arrived, Oñate proceeded with them to the Tewa village of Okeh on the west bank of the Rio Grande and began to build a capital town. A mission church was built which the Spaniards named San Gabriel. The whole of New Mexico was divided into seven missionary districts; Spanish alcaldes were appointed for each, while Oñate set up a central government under his leadership. The headquarters of the church organization were eventually established at Santo Domingo where Oñate had obtained the pledges of allegiance of the representatives of the thirty-four villages upon his arrival. The new government extended its claim promptly from Taos to El Paso and from

Pecos to the Hopi villages 250 miles westward. It was a domain of eighty-seven thousand square miles, only spottily explored, but regarded by Oñate as properly subject to the King of Spain.

Oñate's own zeal, however, was not matched by that of his colonists, or even by the Franciscans who had come with him. Almost immediately the whole party seemed to lose heart and, after a number of quarrels between Oñate, the leaders, and the missionaries, almost the whole colony deserted and returned to Chihuahua while Oñate was off on an exploring trip to the northeast. The soldiers apparently were the most dissatisfied, but the missionaries were ready to listen to them. It was the lack of treasure, either in the form of gold or of quantities of human souls, which gave rise to the dissatisfaction. The scattered, small villages, in contrast with the relatively dense populations of the south, did not look attractive to the missionaries. The harvest of souls would be relatively small. Moreover, the Pueblos were lukewarm or definitely hostile in their reception of the Spaniards, although they remained at peace everywhere except at the far western village of Acoma. The Tewa village of Okeh — later to be called San Juan — where Oñate's headquarters were located, gradually moved across the Rio Grande to the east bank, revealing an increasing dislike of contacts with the Spaniards. The Indians thus left the mission church of San Gabriel isolated rather than concentrating themselves around it.

In 1598 the Keres village of Acoma, after formally vowing submission to Oñate, nevertheless showed signs of hostility. Zutucapan, one of the leading men of the village, was reported to have planned the killing of Oñate himself and later did kill Oñate's aide, Juan Zaldívar, after pretending friendliness and allowing Zaldívar's party to enter the village. The battle which ensued on top of the mesa resulted in the killing of the soldiers who had accompanied Zaldívar. In 1599 a punitive expedition of seventy soldiers was again met with defiance and another battle was fought. The Spaniards captured five hundred Acomans who were sentenced to have one foot chopped off and to twenty years at hard labor. The village was nearly destroyed by burning before the soldiers finally conquered it after a siege. As a result of the defeat, the villagers were split into two groups; under a leader named Chumpo, one group of six hundred, more friendly to the Spaniards, settled on the plain below the mesa; others rebuilt the village on the mesa and maintained an attitude of hostility to the Spaniards. Of the probable fifteen hundred inhabitants of Acoma, many had been killed.

The desertion of San Gabriel by most of the colonists in 1601 resulted in several years of delay in Oñate's program. By 1608, however, he re-established himself with the return of many of the colonists and the placing of nine missionaries in the field. About 1610 the capital was moved from San Gabriel to the site of the present Santa Fe, and the colonization and conversion program proceeded to operate from there. During the next twenty years, churches were built in all the pueblos, even at Taos in the far north, and in 1629 Father Juan Ramírez was even able, after winning prestige through curing a child, to build a church at Acoma. During the 1620's native secular and church officers were set up in all the villages — that is, governors, alcaldes, fiscales, and other officials. By 1630 there were fifty Franciscan missionaries working in twenty-five missions; and schools for instructing the Indians were in operation at each mission, where reading, writing, music, and trades were taught, as well as the Christian doctrine. In 1626, the missionaries reported that they had baptized thirty-four thousand and in 1630 claimed sixty thousand. The villages were peaceful and there was an increasing acceleration in the numbers accepting the mission way of life.

However, the next fifty years saw decline rather than progress in the extension of Spanish control and the mission system. As elsewhere on the Spanish frontier the seeds of difficulties lay in the relations between the church and the civil authorities. In New Mexico the conflict began as early as 1600 with friction between Oñate and the missionaries who accompanied him. In 1626 the Inquisition undertook to operate in New Mexico. Its investigations, while not much used as a tool of the clergy against the civil authorities, nevertheless made clear the incompetence and maladministration of various governors and their staffs. From 1637 to 1641 a long-drawn-out quarrel between Governor Rosas and the missionaries brought friction to a head and widened the breach. The quota of sixty-six missionaries for the whole area was rarely filled, so that many churches remained for extended periods without any priest. During the trouble over Rosas' administration the people of Taos killed their missionary and destroyed the church; the missionary at Jemez was also killed. The people of Jemez remained at odds with the Spaniards throughout the rest of the century and were involved in various plots for insurrection. The internal conflict among the Spaniards was reflected in unrest through the period from 1630 until 1680.

The essential point of trouble lay in conflicting interests between the mission system and the system of political control. The objectives of the missionaries were the building of agricultural communities consisting of peaceful persons actively engaged in the economic and spiritual affairs of church organizations built in their midst. Insofar as they promoted peace and industry among the Indians there was no conflict with the civil authorities. But the disposal of the products of industry became a major source of contention. The governors were required to collect tribute for the Crown. But in addition every governor had the privilege of engaging in trade and manufacture on his own account. There was, therefore, a fundamental competition between governor and church for the labor of the Indians.

The governors of New Mexico undertook their responsibilities not necessarily as government servants anxious to develop a peaceful and productive colony, but rather primarily because of the opportunities for personal gain. Each one built up a business in woven goods, hides, salt, and, to some extent, in agricultural products. What production could be stimulated over and above the tribute requirements for the King of Spain could be turned to the individual profit of the governor and the staff who worked with him. Thus, Governor López in the 1650's required large forces of Indians from the villages in the Piro and Tompiro areas to work for him in gathering supplies of salt, piñon nuts, and hides. The missionaries claimed that this resulted in taking Indians away from their agricultural activities around the missions and even from their own food production. Each mission maintained or tried to maintain herds of livestock as well as fields, the produce of which went to support the missionary and his staff, to improve the church and its furnishings, and to supply feasts for special occasions. The routine of mission life was interfered with by the recruiting of working parties to leave the mission village for extended periods on expeditions for the governor. Governors, seeking their own ends, were inclined to regard much of the mission activity as nonessential for the development of Christian life. To the extent that the missions made use of labor and natural resources, by so much were the governors' profits reduced. They saw the missionaries as building up little kingdoms of their own which robbed the civil authority of labor supply and at the same time created a rival power and authority.

It was not only the governors and their immediate staffs who came into conflict with the missionaries over these economic matters. In New Mexico a land-grant system had been introduced simultaneously with and as a part of the Oñate program of colonization. To encourage colonization, grants of land were made to soldiers who participated in the conquest. These grants, or *encomiendas*, carried with them the right of *repartimiento*, that is, the right to employ Indians living on the grants. The produce of Indian labor went in part to the king and in part to the proprietor of the land, the *encomendero*. Lands not in use by Pueblo Indians, some of them quite close to the villages, were parceled out to the Spaniards. By law the encomenderos were not permitted to live on the lands which they held as encomiendas, but in New Mexico this law was largely ignored. The result, recorded particularly well in connection with encomiendas in the vicinity of the Tewa villages of Nambé and Pojoaque, was persistent conflict between Spaniards living on their grants and the Indians, and between the settlers and the missionaries. This was an important cause of friction in the New Mexico region.

The major conflict at the base of the Spanish colonial system expressed itself in a variety of ways in New Mexico. The governors charged that the missionaries forced Indians to labor for them on their churches, in their fields, and with their herds. The missionaries countered with charges that the governors forced Indians to work for them without wages purely for the profit of the governors. By law, of course, Indian labor was supposed to be entirely voluntary, except for production of tribute to the king; and the labor was supposed to be paid for when volunteered. Thus both sides made charges which required investigation.

The civil authorities called attention to the missionary practice of whipping Indians who failed to follow the discipline of attending Mass and who were regarded as committing sexual offenses by the missionaries. Numerous cases of severe punishment of Indians by the missionaries were brought up in the various investigations which took place in New Mexico between 1626 and 1680. The civil authorities charged that this was a major cause of the growing unrest. Numerous instances of arbitrary and unjust treatment of Indians by missionaries were proven; in addition there were instances of sexual misconduct and other misbehavior on the part of the missionaries.

In their turn the missionaries charged, and in numerous instances produced substantiating evidence, that governors and their aides had not only physically abused Indians but had also been guilty of setting bad examples to the Indians by their own sexual license and immoral behavior. Investigators from Mexico City, sent up to examine the charges, were often greatly depressed at finding much evidence of blasphemous, licentious, superstitious, cruel, and unjust actions on the part of civil officials. Thus, there was corruption among both state and church officials.

Conflict raged between the two arms of the colonial government from the 1630's for the next fifty years. It was so bitter and so frequent that it became evident to the Indians that one group could be played off against the other. A government divided against itself began to appear less invincible than the government had at the beginning of Spanish rule.

There were still other sources of conflict. One major one grew in intensity from the 1650's on. This had its origin in the missionary attempt to stamp out Indian religion by forcible means. The first half of the 1600's seems to have been characterized by far less force than the latter half. The first gains of the missionaries, which were so rapid during the 1620's, seem to have been accomplished largely through constructive mission work, the development of churches and colorful ceremonies, care of the sick, and the introduction of new agricultural crops and techniques. But by 1630 the missionaries began to be aware of a contradiction in their program. They had baptized, they claimed, all the Pueblo Indians and all had become more or less regular participants in the ritual of the church. It was apparent, however, that the Indians had not given up their own ceremonies. The masked kachina dances were still given; there were still ceremonies in the kivas of the villages; prayer sticks were still offered; cornmeal was still strewn ritually. The native round of ceremonies seemed almost as strong as ever; there were instances of the civil authorities encouraging native religious ceremony, even on occasions for honoring the governor.

In the 1650's the missionaries' awareness of their failure to replace the old ways with Christian ways seemed to come to a focus. Their attitude was much influenced by the views of Governor López and some of his aides toward the native ceremonials. He stated publicly that he regarded the kachina ceremonials as merely "Indian foolishness," that he saw no harm in them. He gave official permission to the village of Tesuque and to other Indians to perform their ritual. He accepted the ceremonials as proper means for honoring his presence in a village. He even appeared to condone the participation of some Spaniards in the dances. All of this was taken by the missionaries as directly promoting opposition to their own program and, moreover, as a failure on the part of the governor in his duty to take measures against "idolatry," a duty required of all civil authorities in New Spain. Before the administration of Governor López, although missionaries had taken some positive measures to suppress Indian ceremonials, there had been a measure of toleration. Now, in 1661, the Franciscan custodian decreed an absolute prohibition of all kachina dances, and missionaries were instructed to seek out all materials of "idolatry," which included primarily kachina masks. Kivas, the Pueblo ceremonial rooms, were raided and in a short time sixteen hundred kachina masks were captured and destroyed, as well as prayer feathers and images of various kinds. Interestingly enough, the Franciscan custodian was not supported in these raids by the Audiencia in Mexico; it was held by that body that the burden of proof of the superstitious character of the kachina dances remained with the missionaries, and that Governor López was quite within his rights in allowing the public performance of the dances.

The continued internal conflict among the Spaniards in New Mexico was matched during the 1650's, the 1660's, and 1670's by external conflict. As already pointed out, nomads at least as early as 1525 had raided Pueblo villages east of the Rio Grande and on the Pecos River and had caused the abandonment of some villages. The Spanish occupation did not cause a cessation of such raids but rather, by the 1670's, resulted in a very considerable increase. When Oñate first came to Santo Domingo the Spaniards had promised the Pueblo Indians help against their enemies. They had attempted to live up to the promise and apparently during the first half of the 1600's had, together with forces of Pueblo Indians, kept raiders from the east out of the Rio Grande Valley. However, their efforts stimulated the eastern nomads to more intensive warfare.

This came about in several ways. In the first place, by providing a more firm defense on the eastern borders of the Pueblo country the Spaniards forced Apaches southward to some extent, in the face of the steady advance of the Comanches from the north. Thus, there were, by the end of the 1600's, two groups of raiding tribes to contend with on the east. In the second place, the growth of Spanish settlement — although there were still no more than twenty-five hundred settlers — and particularly of more productive Pueblo villages under Spanish stimulus, provided new and more attractive targets for raiding.

Probably the most important of the factors giving new impetus to raiding was the Spanish trade in slaves. Pecos and the Jumanos village east of Abo in the Tompiro country for many years had been centers where trade was carried on with the Apaches of the east. The Spaniards wanted slaves for household servants and laborers. The Apaches, and later the Comanches, found that they could sell captives from tribes farther east for such desirable things as horses, firearms, and knives. Every such trade rendered them more formidable as raiders. In addition, the Spaniards found that the slave supply was not sufficient for their needs; to increase the supply they provoked fights with the Apaches in these areas and then took captives as slaves. They went even further, making slave-hunting expeditions into the eastern plains. They thus supplied most of the settlers' houses with slave help and even developed some trade in slaves to the south. At the same time hostility between themselves and all the Apaches and Comanches to the east was stimulated.

In the 1670's warfare with the Apaches increased to the point where three southern Tiwa mountain villages had to be abandoned. The remnants of the villagers came in 1674 to live with the Tiwa in Isleta. Likewise, the Tompiro and Piro villages to the south were harassed constantly and became dangerous places to live. The Spaniards became increasingly concerned as the raiding intensified, but seemed unable to organize any concerted campaign, contenting themselves with brief punitive expeditions, which, if anything, merely stimulated the Apaches to more warfare. Finally, just before 1680 even Santa Fe was raided, indicating the extent to which the nomadic tribes had been emboldened.

During the five years of 1667–1672 there was extended drought and crop failure. This marked a low ebb in the affairs of New Mexico, but it did serve to bring church and state officials together on a somewhat more cooperative basis than at any time since the founding of the colony. Famine and attack from without were functioning to some extent to heal the breaches which had opened during the previous eighty years. In 1675, Governor Juan Francisco de Treviño even went so far as to cooperate with the missionaries in their efforts to combat the growing Indian interest in reviving the ceremonies of their native religion. Among other things, Treviño cooperated with the missionaries in whipping and imprisoning forty-seven Indian leaders from various villages who were accused of witchcraft, idolatry, or the promotion of idolatry. This unity, however, of the Spanish colonial administration came at a time when discontent among the Pueblos had reached a high degree of intensity. The whipping of the Indian leaders turned out to be a move which touched off the great Pueblo Revolt of 1680, a rebellion more extensive even than the Tepehuan revolt of 1616 and with more serious consequences for the spread of Spanish civilization on the northern frontier.

In 1680 there were probably between twenty-five and thirty thousand Indians in the villages of the Rio Grande drainage, including Acoma. There were 2,850 Spaniards. Most were concentrated in Santa Fe but some were living in the Tewa country to the north, in the vicinity of modern Bernalillo to the south, and also farther southward in the Rio Grande Valley. A few had taken up residence actually within Indian villages, as at San Juan, Pojoaque, Nambé, and other Tewa and Tano villages. There were thirty-three missionaries in residence at the villages — only one-half the quota which had been agreed on in 1631, and a good indication of the extent to which the missionary program had been allowed to lapse in New Mexico. The Spanish population was aware of discontent among the Indians, but probably was less prepared for a revolt than it would have been during any decade since the 1620's.

The rebellion obtained its chief leadership from the two original centers of Spanish administration — San Juan Pueblo and Santo Domingo. One of the most active leaders was Popé, a man from San Juan who, as a participant in the reinvigoration of the native religion which took place in the 1670's, was among those whipped at Governor Treviño's orders in 1675. Another leader was a man named Catiti of Santo Domingo. Both were officials in the native ceremonial organizations in their villages. Most vigorous in the early decisive fighting against the Spaniards were, first the Tanos from Galisteo Basin and second, the Tewas of the villages closest to Santa Fe on the north. It was people of these groups — Tewa-Tano — who had been thrown into closest contact with the Spaniards and knew most fully the character of their program. Popé, however, probably fearing pro-Spanish activity of his fellow villagers, directed the plans for the rebellion from the distant point of Taos. A San Juan Indian did reveal the plans to the Spaniards; however, this resulted merely in the revolt beginning a few days earlier.

A force of Tanos besieged Santa Fe, while Indians in all the villages except

Isleta and the Piro missions killed their resident missionaries and any other Spaniards whom they could lay hands on. The Tanos were reinforced after five days by Tewas and a force of northern Tiwas from Taos. Spanish resistance then quickly collapsed and the survivors (the great majority) were permitted to make their escape southward under Governor Otermín. Within a few days all the missions had been destroyed, 21 out of 33 missionaries had been killed, and 375 of the 2,350 colonists had been wiped out. The fact that the majority of the Spaniards were allowed to escape indicated that the major objectives of the revolt were, first to eliminate the mission system and, second, to drive all the Spaniards out of Pueblo country.

The surviving Spaniards took refuge for a short time at Isleta and then marched southward to El Paso. On the way they were accompanied by some southern Tiwas and by all the remaining people of the depopulated Piro villages in the vicinity of Socorro and southward. At El Paso the Spaniards remained for twelve years, unable to force their way back into the lost territory. Governor Otermín made a misguided effort to punish the rebels in 1681 by attacking Isleta (which had taken no part in the revolt), burning southern Tiwa villages, and taking 519 Tiwa captives. Again in 1688, the Spaniards marched as far north as the Keres villages, destroying and killing many people at Zia, but no effective effort at reconquest was carried out until 1692.

The Piros who had voluntarily accompanied Otermín, and those southern Tiwa captives who did not escape established a new pueblo at Isleta del Sur, south of El Paso, and remained there, never returning to their home country.

The unity displayed by the Rio Grande villages in carrying through the revolt was something new in the region. Every village north of Isleta had joined the rebellion, not only killing missionaries and other Spaniards in their vicinity, but also furnishing fighting men to aid in the siege of Santa Fe and to effect the exodus of the Spaniards southward. There had been a planned attack and campaign, led by a Tewa Indian working with headquarters in a Tiwa village and cooperating closely with Keres and Tano leaders. Tano, Tewa, northern Tiwa, and Keres fought effectively together in the siege of Santa Fe. This sort of concerted effort among Rio Grande Pueblos had not appeared before. It was an extreme reaction to an extreme situation. Spanish oppression and Spanish weakness had offered what seemed an unusual opportunity. The leadership had been created by the Spaniards themselves in their attempt to discipline the group of ceremonial officials. For the first time so far as we know in Pueblo history, a supra-village organization came into existence and focused all but the southern Tiwas and Piros on the single objective of getting rid of the Spaniards.

Once that objective was obtained, the unity of the Pueblos quickly disappeared. No confederacy was formed with a central council; no policy was formulated by the erstwhile leaders for meeting Spanish retaliation. In short, the organization of the Pueblos had been for a single, quickly accomplished purpose. Once done, the various villages returned to the old form of life. There was an abortive effort to turn the Spanish capital into an Indian capital, but lack of common purpose was most evident. The Keres and the Pecos people became

actively hostile to the Tewa and the Tanos. Apaches, instead of joining and working with the Pueblos to keep the Spaniards out, began renewed raids on the eastern
borderlands. The Tanos were forced to abandon the whole Galisteo Basin, as a
result of the Apache raids, and settle elsewhere, some in Santa Fe and some among
the Tewa in the former Spanish town of Santa Cruz. Various river valley villages
were abandoned for less accessible sites on the mesas, in anticipation of Spanish
punitive attacks. When Otermín did return in 1681 he found most of the pueblos
that he visited abandoned and was forced to content himself with burning kivas
and sacking the empty villages. At Zia, however, he found the people ready for a
defense and badly defeated them, killing many.

Otermín's quick forays probably had the effect of splitting the Pueblos apart
a little more on the issue of the advisability of holding out indefinitely against
Spanish attempts at reconquest. At any rate, when in 1692, the Spaniards under
de Vargas were finally ready for a strong campaign, the reception they got was
extremely varied. The Keres villages of Zia, Santa Ana, and San Felipe submitted
with no show of fight, while the other Keres villages of Cochiti and Santo Domingo
resisted. Cochiti people fought vigorously and were quickly defeated, while the
Santo Domingans left their village in ruins and joined the people of Jemez to the
west for further resistance.

The Tanos split similarly. Those who had settled in Santa Fe after leaving
the Galisteo Basin vowed obedience to de Vargas in perfectly peaceful fashion.
But the Tanos who had settled farther north among the Tewas did not submit
and joined with San Ildefonso, the most resistant of the Tewa villages in continued
defiance of de Vargas. The Black Mesa near San Ildefonso became a center for
Indians who refused to accept de Vargas' domination. Here the Tanos, San
Ildefonsans and other Tewas, and some from Cochiti, joined in a nine-months'
resistance during 1694. From this headquarters they raided Santa Fe and harassed
the Spaniards. Eventually all except some Tanos surrendered and again submitted to Spanish rule.

The lack of unity among the Pueblos was further demonstrated in the events
of the year 1694. By this time the new government of de Vargas had been established in Santa Fe and a new town built at Santa Cruz, forcing the Tanos in that
area to the east around modern Chimayo. Missionaries had taken up residence in
various villages, and it appeared that the Spaniards were again well established.
However, a new revolt broke out. The Jemez people killed their missionary and
with the aid of warriors from Acoma and Zuni fought the Spaniards bitterly. In
the expedition against Jemez the Spaniards were aided by men from Zia, Santa
Ana, and San Felipe, who, because of their new friendliness to the Spaniards, had
been suffering harassment by the Jemez people. The inhabitants of Jemez were
driven into the mountains and many joined with Navajos or went westward to
live with the Hopis.

In 1696, after the Jemez rebellion had been put down, still a new revolt
broke out. This time leadership came from the displaced Tanos of Chimayo and
from Taos. Six missionaries and twenty-one other Spaniards were killed. The
northern Tiwa of Taos and Picuris joined with the Tanos and with the still-

rebellious Santo Domingans and Cochitis. Zia, Santa Ana, and San Felipe remained loyal to and fought beside the Spaniards. The San Ildefonsans killed the two missionaries who had been placed at their village and again fled to the mesas. De Vargas finally killed or routed all the resisters, although at Acoma, which held his soldiers at bay, he had to content himself with merely destroying fields. There was after 1696 no further military resistance on the part of the Rio Grande Pueblos. Spanish control was again complete — after sixteen years — and the villages were thoroughly divided among themselves with the factions who favored submission as the best policy dominant in the remnants of the population.

The next twenty years were a period of factional strife and dispersion among the Pueblos. Every pueblo was affected, with the probable exception of the Keres villages of Zia, Santa Ana, and San Felipe, and some of the Tewas. The Tanos who had submitted to de Vargas were for the most part distributed as slaves among the Spanish colonists; those who were not so treated moved from Santa Fe out among the Tewa villages, particularly to Tesuque near Santa Fe. The resistant Tanos, after removal to Chimayo when they were forced from their lands at Santa Cruz and after participation in the 1694 and 1696 rebellions, migrated westward to take up residence among the Hopis. Some rebellious Tewas from San Ildefonso and other villages also went westward to the Hopi country. Rebel Cochitis had founded a village called La Cieneguilla near Cochiti along with some Santo Domingans after the 1680 revolt. Here they were attacked and captured by de Vargas in 1694. After 1696 the survivors, along with other Santo Domingans who had fought on the side of the Jemez, moved westward and founded a new village called Laguna not far from Acoma. Some Jemez people also migrated westward to the Hopi country. Thus during the early years of the 1700's several thousand Pueblos moved out of the Rio Grande Valley, rejecting Spanish control. They became known as the apostates and were regarded by the Spaniards as a menace in their influence on the Hopis.

Within the villages in the Rio Grande Valley there was dissension and discord. In 1700 at Pecos there was a strong anti-Spanish faction which was finally silenced by the pro-Spanish leader, Don Felipe, who executed five of their spokesmen. At San Ildefonso, lands which had belonged to rebel Indians were assigned to pro-Spanish people from the Tewa village of Santa Clara. Spaniards steadily infiltrated the other Tewa villages of San Juan, Pojoaque, and Nambé, and began to encroach on the lands of the northern Tiwa at Taos and Picuris.

In 1716 Governor Martínez decided to remove the threat of the "apostates" in the west and sent an expedition to bring them back. He was only partly successful, escorting back a party of 113 Jemez, some Tewa, and the few Santo Domingans who had been living in the area. He was entirely unsuccessful in getting the Tewa-speaking Tanos who had settled on the mesa near the Hopi village of Walpi to return. They defied him and remained.

Gradually the Pueblos settled down again under Spanish control. New churches were built. The number of missionaries by 1740 had increased to forty. The Spanish population steadily increased while the Pueblo population continued to decline. In 1630 the missionaries had claimed sixty thousand Christians, but at no time during the 1700's did they claim more than fifteen thousand. The Tano population had been almost entirely removed from the Rio Grande either by war, by absorption into the Spanish population, or by migration westward. Pecos declined to a handful of people. Taos declined from 700 in 1707 to 505 in 1765. Zia, from a village of two or three thousand inhabitants, decreased to 508 by 1765. San Ildefonso in 1765 had a population of 484, less than half the number of a century before. Similarly San Juan, Santo Domingo, and Cochiti lost population. Only Santa Ana and the new village of Laguna increased at all. Santa Ana, whose lands had become unfit for cultivation, purchased lands from Spaniards settled on the Rio Grande near Bernalillo and began a slow increase of population about the middle of the 1700's, but it was still a small village of little more than five hundred. Laguna also showed some measure of prosperity relative to the other villages. Between 1707 and 1765 its population doubled, augmented by refugees, but it was still only six hundred. In short, it may be said that the Spanish program to the middle of the 1700's resulted in cutting the Pueblo population by at least half, depopulation of a great majority of villages, a serious decline in economic prosperity, and generally hostile relations between Spaniards and Indians.

This trend was intensified over the remainder of the century. An important factor was the increase in Apache raiding, which affected the northeastern part of the area, now that the south was entirely depopulated by the migration of the Piro and many southern Tiwa to El Paso. In the 1760's and 1770's the Taos area was constantly harassed by Apaches, Utes, and Comanches. By the 1780's the Galisteo Basin, which the Spaniards had made an effort to resettle by gathering dispersed Tanos together at Galisteo, was finally abandoned, largely due to Comanche raids. The Comanches in this area had now replaced the Apaches. By the 1770's Apache raids on the west reached Zuni, and Pueblos campaigned with Spaniards and Navajos against the western Apaches.

A heavy smallpox epidemic hit the Rio Grande Valley in 1780-81 and also in 1788-89, contributing to the decline in population and general loss of prosperity. Meanwhile the Spanish population during the century rose from five to twenty thousand. Spaniards had infiltrated San Juan, where there were already in 1765 more than half as many Whites as Indians, into Taos where there were nearly one-fourth as many Whites as Indians, and into San Ildefonso where by 1793 after the smallpox epidemic had killed half the Indians there were two-thirds as many Whites as Indians. There were by the 1790's four Spanish towns in the Rio Grande Valley, each with a population of more than two thousand—Santa Fe, La Cañada (Santa Cruz), Albuquerque, and El Paso. In addition there were smaller Spanish towns — Belem, Tome, and Socorro.

The Spanish campaign against the native religion had been much modified, with no further raids for ceremonial paraphernalia and a much less rigorous discipline imposed on the Indians to attend Mass and other church activities. Schools had not been reinstituted after the revolts of 1680–1696. Although there were no more roundups of medicine men, the trials for witchcraft were continued. Such trials were prominent as late as 1799 in San Juan, San Ildefonso, Santa Ana, Isleta, and other villages. While there are many records of Spanish attendance at kachina and even kiva ceremonials prior to 1700, such accounts are rare for the next hundred years. It would appear that the Pueblos' experience of Spanish efforts to eliminate their rituals prior to 1680 had led them to become more secretive, so that they kept this side of their life hidden insofar as possible from the Spaniards. Further, the whole Spanish missionary program after 1680 was only an attenuated version of what it had been in the years before. The pressures which had been strong against the native religion earlier were very much lessened. In 1767 all missions adjoining Spanish settlements were secularized and the missionary program came practically to an end.

We see among the Eastern Pueblos during their first two hundred years of contact with Spaniards many of the familiar phenomena of the south — the conflicts within Spanish culture which resulted in effect in two programs being presented to the Indians rather than a single one, economic exploitation by the secular government and exploitation in a different manner by the missionaries, depopulation through war and disease introduced by the Europeans, initial friendliness of many but not all Indians, constructive agricultural introductions of the missionaries, Spanish stimulation of inter-Indian hostilities, Spanish infiltration of Indian communities, Indian reaction and resort to military resistance, Spanish military conquest finally subduing the Indians completely, and outward submission of the Indians. All of these phenomena were the stuff of the Spanish frontier. In the Pueblo country they almost all appeared in greater intensity than they did in the south as a whole. The Spanish program in New Mexico was much closer to what it had been in central Mexico than it ever was in Sonora and Chihuahua.

Spanish-Indian relations in New Mexico differed from those in the south chiefly in the following respects. The imposition at a single time of the whole program over all the various groups of villages contrasted with the tribe by tribe advance in the south. Within a few years after 1700, missions operating from a central administration in Santo Domingo had been set up over the whole of New Mexico. There was no preparation for missionary work with the different language groups, as the Jesuits had prepared themselves through preliminary explorations and the gathering of materials for language study. Without such preparation the contacts of the missionaries must have been superficial and forced during the early years. There was no period of native request for missionaries with a waiting interval during which Indian leaders could prepare their people for receiving the missionaries — something which characterized the Jesuit situation, whether intentional or not, in the south.

It must be remembered also that at precisely the same time that Pueblos were required to entertain missionaries in their villages they were also being required to pay tribute in the form of textiles, hides, and other goods to the civil governor. Taxation was just as new and strange to the villagers as the concept of Heaven and Hell, somewhat stranger than church ceremonial and a continent priest. The point is that to a greater extent than in the south the initial adjustment was to a larger array of aspects of Spanish life, including the family ways and morality of the Spanish colonists. It was not, as it usually was in the south, a matter of getting used to the missionaries first, then more intensive contact with civil officials, and finally after a considerable interval acquaintance with settlers. Moreover the forced labor program of the Spaniards was introduced immediately and was in direct conflict with the forced labor program of the missionaries. All of these initial contacts had a much more coercive character than they generally did in the south.

That militant reaction was not quite so immediate as among the Tarahumaras in a similar situation may be attributed to the stronger and more obvious nature of Spanish control to the Indians in New Mexico. It also may have been a result of the noncooperative character of relations among the Pueblo villages. Each village seems to have been trying to solve its problems of adjustment alone and so there was the outward appearance of peace through the first generation of the Spanish program — until the 1630's. The missionaries were by this time convinced that they had achieved great success with the Pueblos, as indicated in Benavides' 1630 report on the missions. It was undoubtedly this sense of triumph that stimulated the missionary efforts to wipe out all the vestiges of the native religion by simple force. They must have felt either that they were in a solid enough position of control to accomplish the forceful program without serious reaction or that what the Indians still preserved in the way of ceremonials was so little that a quick series of raids could wipe it out once and for all. Whichever view they had, it was obvious that they were ignorant of a great deal that was going on in the villages.

The intensified forceful suppression of the kachinas seems to have been the feature of the Spanish program which finally led to the one condition which could result in open conflict with the Spaniards — namely, intervillage organization. The Pueblo Rebellion of 1680 was the one instance of effective intertribal organization for the purpose of resisting the Spaniards. The Tepehuanes planned and organized well and fought fanatically under the influence of a revivified religion, but they had failed almost completely to organize other Indians. The Mayos, Yaquis, and Lower Pimas in 1740 almost carried out what the Pueblos accomplished in 1680 — the driving of the Spaniards out of their territory — and they did it through intertribal military organization; but they fell short finally, probably simply because of the superior military organization of the Spaniards under Vildósola. At any rate, no other organization of Indians in northwestern New Spain drove out the Spaniards and kept them out for twelve years. This result was due in part to the weakness of the Spaniards at the time on the northern frontier, but in part it was due to the organization of the Pueblos.

The 1680 rebellion resulted in something not known in the south, namely, complete freedom from Spanish control for a period of years after the experience of being under Spanish rule. The twelve to sixteen years of freedom from the yoke on the Rio Grande and the much longer experience of freedom on the part of the "apostate" Pueblos who went to the Hopi country was something not experienced in the south, where Spanish retaliation was immediate and effective.

In the respects that have been mentioned, Spanish policy in the north was harsher and less adapted or adaptable to the aims of the missionaries and administrators. It resulted in an ultimately more hostile reaction and a harsher settlement of conflict than occurred anywhere in the south. It is true that similar strong measures were taken by Spaniards against Tarahumaras and Seris, but these affected very few Indians. One of the results which contrasted greatly with the aftermaths of revolts in the south was the widespread dislocation and resettlement of the Pueblo population.

The disruption of the population, whether as a result of war or other causes, was greater among Pueblos than among the ranchería peoples of the south. The common Spanish frontier phenomenon of a declining Indian population was much more marked than in the south. By the time of the 1680 rebellion the Pueblo population had declined by about half what it was when the Spaniards came in. It declined by a half again during the 1700's. In the south the population also declined, but only the Mayos and Seris were reduced in comparable numbers. Most striking was the shift in population distribution in the north. Whole areas were completely depopulated — the Piros on the south and their neighbors the Tompiros, as well as the Pecos villages, and the Tanos of the Galisteo Basin. By the last quarter of the 1700's not a single Indian was living in these areas. In addition, of the sixty-six villages in the Rio Grande drainage when the Spaniards entered, only nineteen remained by the end of the 1700's; they had been reduced by two-thirds and only four at most were in the same places where they had been when the Spaniards arrived — Acoma, Isleta, Taos, and Picuris. The twenty southern Tiwa villages were reduced to one — Isleta — while the nine Piro and Tompiro villages were replaced by one — Isleta del Sur — which was completely out of their homeland area. The three valley and seven mountain villages of the Tanos of the Galisteo Basin disappeared and were replaced by a single village, Hano, far to the west in the Hopi country. The eleven villages of the Jemez declined to the one valley village. Only the Tewa and the Keres villages of the central Rio Grande Valley seem not to have been reduced in number, although they were moved about considerably and like all the others lost population. The Spanish program of reduction had worked in the Rio Grande area in a literal, if not intended, fashion; in the process the people were just as widely scattered as they had ever been — even a little more so — and the surviving communities were without exception smaller than the largest villages when the Spaniards came.

The Indian communities, and the Spanish settlements as well, were subjected to increased raiding by nomadic tribes as Spanish political and military control disintegrated. The ineffectiveness of the new Mexican government in controlling the far-flung area increased the boldness of the nomadic groups. For almost half a century after the Mexican War for Independence the New Mexico area was in a state of siege; raids by Navajos and Apaches were followed by retaliatory expeditions of Pueblo Indians and Mexicans. Not until some years after New Mexico was acquired by the United States were the raids brought under control and peace returned to the troubled land.

Peace did not come immediately for the Pueblos with Anglo-American assumption of control in New Mexico. When General Kearny marched into Santa Fe in 1846, he found that he had taken possession of a region which had become inured to unpredictable, periodic raiding by the Navajos and Apaches, and that

Mexicans and Pueblo Indians had begun cooperating with one another in raids against the Navajos. He found that the Pueblo villages regarded themselves as in a perpetual state of siege, prepared and organized to withstand the Navajo raiding. The taking of prisoners, especially children, to grow up as slaves among the Mexicans was an accepted practice. The hostilities between the Pueblos-Mexicans on one hand and the Navajos-Apaches on the other had become a regular part of New Mexican life during the previous hundred years, as Spanish political and military strength had disintegrated.

Even before the Treaty of Guadalupe Hidalgo bound the United States to pacify the Navajos and Apaches, General Kearny took steps to stop the sporadic warfare. He immediately sent a detachment of troops under Colonel Doniphan into the heart of the Navajo country with instructions to negotiate and secure peace agreements. For a time Navajo raiding stopped. Meanwhile, in the year following Kearny's taking possession of New Mexico the only armed resistance to the Anglo-American occupation occurred. Some Taos Indians, together with Mexicans from the vicinity of Taos, killed the newly appointed Governor Bent of New Mexico and began a march to attack Santa Fe. They were quickly routed and no further resistance by arms on the part of any Pueblos developed. Evidently Taos Pueblo as a whole was no more interested in armed resistance than was any of the others.

In 1847, the year that Governor Bent was killed, the New Mexico legislature, newly reorganized by him, passed a law defining each New Mexico Pueblo village as a unit of local government with perpetual right to its existing land holdings. This was a continuation of the status of the Pueblo villages that had obtained under Spanish and later under Mexican rule. It was a recognition of the land rights vested in the Pueblo Indians by virtue of grants of land to them by the Spanish Crown. It was also an indication of the attitudes which the new political authorities in New Mexico were adopting toward the Pueblos. From the first they drew a sharp distinction, viewing the Indians in two categories — the wild and lawless and the peaceful. General Kearny regarded the Navajos and Apaches as aggressors who would have to be dealt with by force. The first Indian agent for New Mexico, on the other hand, reported the Pueblos as peaceful and desirous of civilization, specifically schools and agricultural information. The approach to the Pueblos was totally different from that adopted for the Navajos and Apaches.

In 1849 the United States Indian agency farthest west was at Council Bluffs, Iowa. During that year it was transferred to Santa Fe and plans were begun for peaceful dealing with the Pueblos. They were to be given arms and ammunition to defend themselves against raids by the Navajos and the Jicarilla Apaches. Their peaceful tendencies were to be reinforced by sending "chiefs" from each village to Washington to learn the strength of the United States and the value of its civilization. They were to be given technical assistance with the placement of blacksmiths in the villages. A resident Indian agent was to be established in each village. At the same time all Pueblos were prohibited from making raids for any reason whatever on the "wild" Indians.

This program, formulated by James S. Calhoun, the first Indian agent and later governor at Santa Fe, was not realized for some twenty years and then not fully. Military campaigns against the Navajos and the Apaches occupied much government effort and funds and the Civil War interfered with the working out of an Indian program in the western states. It was not until 1864 that the Navajos were thoroughly defeated and the Bureau of Indian Affairs of the federal government could carry on a program with any consistency among the Pueblos.

Nevertheless, the threat of raids steadily decreased as United States troops conducted campaigns against Navajos during the 1850's and 1860's, and confined the Apaches to smaller and smaller areas during the 1870's and 1880's. The Eastern Pueblos experienced only a few raids — none of which were devastating — in the twenty years preceding the mid-1860's, and no raids after that time. Slowly they resumed a peaceful life such as they had not known since the early 1700's. Farming operations expanded and a new sense of security began to appear by the 1870's.

At the same time, however, that the peaceful conditions affected Pueblo life, they were also influencing the activities of others in New Mexico. People of Mexican descent, who came to be called Hispanos, also prospered and began to expand their farming and herding operations, with consequent small encroachments on the Pueblos and infiltration of some villages, such as Pojoaque and San Juan.

Anglo-Americans from the east began to come into New Mexico. By the 1880's there was a steady flow of new people, looking for land and for new opportunities. Cattle and sheep herds increased greatly in the years between 1875 and 1890. The new settlers acquired land everywhere, by purchase, by homestead, and by unlawful entry. The Hispano population was soon in desperate competition for the land with the newcomers, and unable to hold its own. In the relatively small areas of farm land along the streams which provided water, Hispanos pushed into the Pueblo lands little by little and the pressures on the Indians steadily increased. Some Indians acquired land by purchase, as Santa Ana village had earlier, and held on to it. Others slowly lost a little here and a little there. Flocks were pushed off grazing land to which Indians had no title but which they had long used. The pressures of war had lifted only to be replaced by the pressures for land acquisition.

In addition, the face of the earth was being rapidly changed. The English-speaking Americans from the east in less than a generation after 1865 populated almost every acre usable for grazing with sheep or cattle. With great swiftness thousands of acres, such as in the Rio Puerco Valley west of the Rio Grande, were overgrazed, and steadily the land was denuded. In the mountains where pine timber grew, logging companies began the cutting of the forests. The mountain watersheds thus also lost their cover. There were serious results for the Indian and other farmers in the valleys. The runoff from the rains became increasingly rapid and often devastating. Lands along the Rio Grande River and its tributaries which the Indians had farmed for centuries were washed away in floods. Nearly every Pueblo village lost old, long-cultivated fields bit by bit during the 1880's, and continuously for fifty years more until flood control and soil conservation measures were adopted in the 1900's. Crops were lost and food was sometimes scarce during this period; but most serious, the land itself was permanently lost.

Thus, the encroachment on the villages was not only by other farmers in competition for land, but also by the rivers themselves as the whole balance of nature was upset by the energetic newcomers.

Within the villages there was nevertheless a measure of prosperity even through the last years of the 1800's. The tracts of land surrounding their settlements granted by the Spanish Crown to the Pueblos were still recognized; they had been confirmed as Pueblo property legally in 1854 by the Territory of New Mexico and again by the United States Supreme Court in the 1890's. Hence there was security in each basic nucleus of village land. The intensive agricultural methods of the Indians yielded food at least sufficient for life in the village. Some land was lost and the pressures toward loss of more were constant. Floods resulted in periodic hardships for some villages in different years, but still by the early 1900's no village had lost more than small parts of its holdings.

It was not until toward the end of the first decade of the 1900's, when immigration into the state of New Mexico increased with great rapidity, that a most serious threat to the very existence of the villages developed. From 1910 to 1920, the population of New Mexico increased rapidly, from one hundred thousand to three hundred sixty thousand. Squatters on Pueblo lands multiplied; the pressure from cattle and sheep companies increased. By 1913, three thousand non-Indian families, a population almost as large as the total of the Pueblos, were living on Indian-grant lands. Taos village lost a large portion of land adjacent to the village center to the non-Indian town of Taos. The city of Espanola had taken over a large amount of Santa Clara village lands. Only two villages, Acoma far to the west, and Zia had lost no land at all. The old story of encroachment on Indian lands so familiar in other parts of the United States, in the Tarahumara country, and on the Mayo and Yaqui rivers in Sonora was being re-enacted.

Until 1913 the federal government stood aside from the Pueblos' land problems. The Pueblo Indians were legally in a different status from all other Indians who lived on reservations in the United States; their lands were not indeed classed as reservations. In 1854 the Territory of New Mexico, consistent with its recognition of Indian land claims as based — like those of other citizens of New Mexico — in Spanish land grants, had ordered the survey of all land into townships and the issuance of titles to Indians by the Land Office by the same procedure as applied to all others in the Territory. Also in common with other New Mexicans, the Indians were not restricted in regard to the sale of their land. Following the lead of New Mexico, the United States Supreme Court in 1876 ruled that Pueblos were not Indians under the law. This meant, despite the fact that the United States Congress had appropriated funds for Indian agents in the Pueblo villages and had provided schools for them in common with other Indians, that they were not legally entitled to any of the services or protective land measures which applied to other Indians.

Under the policy of the Bureau of Indian Affairs, Indians living on reservations held collective title to those lands which they had retained by treaty or which had been assigned to them by order of the President. These collective, or tribal titles, were held in trust by an official of the government, the Secretary of the Interior. No individual Indian thus could sell any piece of land or otherwise alienate it to any non-Indian (except in cases where after the Indian Allotment Act of 1887 the tribal land had been allotted). This all meant that the federal government, as trustee of Indian lands, recognized an obligation to protect Indian land ownership with all legal means at its disposal. The system had grown up as a result of the large-scale thefts and other means of dispossessing Indians which had been rampant during the frontier period in the United States. In New Mexico, however, the special legal status of Spanish land grants, the recognition of which was a provision of the Treaty of Guadalupe Hidalgo ending the Mexican War, had interfered with the application of the policy to Pueblo Indians.

Leaders in various Pueblo villages had been well aware ever since the late 1700's that their land rights were being disregarded through squatting and various other means. Some had begun to recognize that they could maintain their rights through the legal mechanisms which Anglo-Americans used. As early as 1880 suits were brought in the New Mexico courts by Pueblo Indians against those who encroached on their land. However, either the right to sue was denied or decisions went against them until 1913 when the Sandoval Case reached the United States Supreme Court. The decision handed down in the Sandoval Case reversed the Supreme Court decision of 1876. It held that Pueblos were Indians in the same sense as all those who lived on reservations in the United States. This ruling expressly provided that the federal government had the obligation to exercise the same protective measures over Pueblo land that it had for other Indians. The legal status of Pueblos was now the same as for other Indians, and the federal government began slowly to take steps to solve the land problems which had developed in New Mexico. In 1918 a government attorney was appointed for the Pueblos, and suit was opened in the courts to quiet titles to Pueblo lands.

The Sandoval Decision in 1913 opened a period of overt conflict in New Mexico of which the Pueblos were the center. Court battles and boundary disputes developed between Indians and the settlers who had moved onto their land. Influential New Mexican legislators took the position that Indians should not be maintained in any legal status different from citizens of New Mexico, although the state did not classify Pueblos as citizens except in regard to the right to alienate land. Federal legislation was proposed which would recognize the right of squatters established on Pueblo land and place the Pueblos directly under the jurisdiction of the United States District Court, eliminating their corporate existence. Public opinion over the United States was roused widely and various organizations of non-Indians were formed to lobby against this legislation. At the same time, with the encouragement of a few non-Indians, an organization of the villages sprang into existence — the first such over-all organization since the Pueblo Revolt of 1680 — for the purpose of fighting the proposed legislation. This All-Pueblo Council met at Santo Domingo in 1922 and through its efforts and those of the various non-Indian organizations, the measures were defeated in the national Congress. New legislation, called the Pueblo Lands Act, was then enacted by Congress in 1924; this provided for the restoration to the Pueblos of all grant lands lost or compensation in cases in which land could not be legally restored.

Thus the generation of Pueblo Indians which grew up in the period between 1880 and 1924 lived in an atmosphere free from military hostilities, but charged with threats to the very basis of village life — the land. It was a time of steadily intensifying awareness of the Anglo-American society which had begun to surround them. By 1869 Indian agents had been established for each Pueblo village, under the general jurisdiction of the Indian agency at Santa Fe. The Indian agent at each village was called a "farmer"; his duties consisted of giving the Indians help with their farming. During the 1870's government funds were used by the agents in building some dams and ditches for various villages, to improve their irrigation systems. In the early 1870's the Bureau of Indian Affairs got a school program under way, which moved slowly until the 1880's. A government schoolteacher took up residence in 1871 at Laguna and by 1885 two other day schools were established, at Jemez and near Santa Ana.

Meanwhile the federal government had conceived a program of boarding schools for Indians all over the United States. One was established at Carlisle, Pennsylvania, with the aim of educating children away from their parents so that the process of cultural assimilation would be more completely and quickly achieved. Pupils were recruited from the Pueblos and by 1889 a total of ninety-two Pueblo students were enrolled at Carlisle. Most of the villages, with the exception of Santo Domingo, sent a few students. Forced recruiting, as with some other tribes, was not necessary except at Santo Domingo. In the 1890's two more boarding schools were established, within the Pueblo area at Santa Fe and Albuquerque, and more children from the villages entered them for from one to three or four years of schooling. At the boarding schools the emphasis was on training the boys in various trades, such as carpentry and masonry, and the girls as homemakers in cooking and sewing.

By 1922 nearly all Pueblo children of school age were attending school, the great majority in government-operated schools at which no tuition was charged and toward the maintenance of which Indians did not pay taxes. At the Santa Fe, Albuquerque, and other boarding schools outside the Pueblo area there were 490 pupils. In thirteen day schools, six of which were at Laguna, two at Acoma, and one each at Isleta, San Felipe, Santo Domingo, Cochiti, and Jemez, there were 740 pupils. In Catholic mission boarding schools away from the Pueblo villages there were another 428 pupils. Thus, only 283 out of a total of 1,941 school-age children were not in school.

With the development of new machinery for farming, the Indian agents worked slowly at trying to improve Pueblo agriculture. During the 1890's threshers and harvesters were introduced in a few villages. There was resistance to them in some villages, as at Isleta and Acoma. Nevertheless, the machinery was slowly adopted and new ideas for the improvement of stock and crops filtered through the government agents and neighboring farmers to the Pueblos.

The government program of civilizing the Indians focused on economic changes and on cultural assimilation through schools. It replaced the Spanish focus of change through religious teaching. Nevertheless, some Anglos were interested in replacing Pueblo religion with Christian religion and efforts were begun as early as the 1850's. In 1851 a Baptist mission was set up at Laguna, but was received coldly and was quickly abandoned. More successful in its aims was a Presbyterian mission, established at Laguna in 1875. Many conversions resulted and the Presbyterian Church became an established institution at Laguna. A similar attempt was made by the Presbyterians at Isleta, but a mission school established there in the 1880's was abandoned by the mid-1890's. Nowhere else among the Eastern Pueblos did any Protestant church gain any foothold, although efforts were made from time to time, as at Jemez. Sometime during the 1890's the Native American Church, a religious organization which based its rites on the use of peyote, gained converts in Taos and continued to exist there with a small group of practitioners.

Meanwhile, in all the villages Catholic churches continued in existence and the vast majority of Pueblos continued to call themselves Catholics. They maintained their own ceremonies apart from or sometimes combined with Catholic practices. The Catholic churches in the villages were served by secular priests who visited them occasionally and who performed baptisms and marriages for the Indians. Usually a piece of land of the village was set aside for the maintenance of the church, but such land was not regarded by the Indians as the property of the Catholic Church. Its produce went for the payment of the priest and maintenance of the church, but the land itself was considered the property of the village. The only strong effort to revive the missionary work of the Catholic Church took place after 1900, when a mission was established by the Franciscans in Laguna territory; the mission was active from about 1913 till 1925, establishing several chapels in the Laguna settlements and gaining much influence among the Laguna Indians.

During the period of hostilities over land in the 1920's after the Sandoval Decision, the Bureau of Indian Affairs instituted an attack on Pueblo religion. Stimulated by the antagonisms roused in New Mexico on this issue, the Commissioner of Indian Affairs, who favored the New Mexican viewpoint that Pueblos should not have the federal protection of land enjoyed by other Indians, sought to turn public opinion in the United States against the Pueblos. One measure which he adopted was to send investigators to the Pueblos to gather information on their religious practices. The report of these investigators described rituals which required bodily exposure and sexual behavior which was contrary to the accepted Anglo traditions. On the basis of the report the Commissioner of Indian Affairs publicly denounced the people of Taos, with whose ritual the report dealt in detail, as "half animals." The Bureau then refused to release Pueblo children from boarding schools to take part in initiation ceremonies on the ground that the latter were depraved customs. The Indian Bureau had long maintained a set of regulations forbidding certain kinds of religious gatherings among the various Indians of the United States — the Religious Crimes Code. An attempt to enforce the code against the Pueblos was instituted, but received little support outside the Bureau and was abandoned with the appointment of a new Commissioner of Indian Affairs.

The pressure to change was thus constantly a part of Pueblo life from the 1880's on. Coupled with the land pressures, the Bureau of Indian Affairs program was a powerful influence on the Indians, even though direct coercive measures were employed only sporadically. Probably the major influence from the Anglo-American culture came through the enrollment of children in the government and church schools. But an almost equally strong influence was that of work for wages outside the villages. With occasional loss of crops due to floods, the necessity arose, especially after the 1880's, for finding additional means of support from time to time. Work on the railroad which was built through the Pueblo country in the 1880's became available and as the Anglo cities increased in population various kinds of jobs became available in Albuquerque, Santa Fe, Bernalillo, and the many new towns. In addition, the population of every village was slowly but steadily increasing, and there was less and less possibility of new families taking up new land, as a result of the Mexican and Anglo population expansion through the whole Pueblo area. Outside employment was more and more relied on as a way of making at least a portion of one's living. New skills were acquired and a closer acquaintance with Anglo-American culture steadily developed.

From shortly after 1900 on, the major addition to Pueblo income beyond their crops and herds began to come from a revival of their handicrafts. This took place as a result of two factors working in combination from the Anglo society. In the first place, the transcontinental railroad passing through the Pueblo country, together with the building of highways, resulted in a very considerable growth of tourist trade which opened a market for souvenirs and novelties of the Indian country. At the same time a great deal of scientific interest in the Indian way of life grew up in the United States after the 1880's, stimulated by attempts to reconstruct the history of human civilization. Anthropologists in the United States and Europe saw in the Pueblo culture a living example of one of the stages through which civilization had passed, and so many studies of both its past phases and its present began to be made. Archaeological excavations disclosed earlier phases of Pueblo crafts, particularly pottery, and archaeologists attempted to reconstruct the historical development of these phases from a simple early beginning through the "classic" period of high technical and artistic techniques to a present state of decline. In all the Pueblo villages, as a result of the introduction of tin and enamel containers in the 1880's and 1890's, pottery had come to be less used and its artistic quality had declined. Archaeologists working from the Museum of New Mexico about 1910 in an effort to learn more about the forgotten techniques tried to get potters at San Ildefonso pueblo to reproduce types of pottery which they were digging out of long-abandoned ruins.

As one potter took hold of this idea and, with the help of her husband, did reproduce some of the ancient types, it became apparent that there was an active market for the new-old pottery. The pottery was bought not only by the few students for their museums, as examples of an ancient handicraft art, but also by tourists and others who became aware of it. Nationwide interest in the revived craft was stimulated by taking the San Ildefonso potter to the World's Fairs in St. Louis and San Diego. Rapidly, the revived pottery art spread to other potters in San Ildefonso and neighboring villages. Not only were the old types reproduced with as much skill as that of the ancient potters, but new types were invented.

Within a few years after the first tentative efforts the sale of pottery had become a major source of income for families in San Ildefonso, and the market continued to grow. Potters from San Ildefonso, Santa Clara, and San Juan among the Tewa villages and from Santo Domingo and Acoma among the Keresan villages began to find sale for their pottery at the railroad stations, at their houses in the villages, and on the streets and in the stores in the growing cities. The revival of the ancient art quickly became a source of modern income of considerable importance, supplementing the traditional farming and working profound changes within the Pueblo villages. San Ildefonso was more affected than any other village, pottery eventually becoming the most important source of income.

The internal affairs of the Pueblo villages during the whole period of Anglo-American political domination were characterized by dissension and factionalism. The formal organization which combined aboriginal and Spanish features adopted under Spanish rule continued to operate without fundamental changes. Canes of office were in fact presented by the President of the United States in 1863 to Pueblo officials to signify the continued recognition of the Spanish system and the constitution of the villages as bodies politic by the New Mexico legislature in 1847. This system of community government was one worked out through centuries to meet the needs of communities in which there was a high degree of homogeneity in world view and in which government expressed the unanimity of feeling within the community on all important issues. Until 1934 the Indian Bureau made no serious effort to alter the system of government directly. Thus for nearly a hundred years the changes that were taking place in the outlook of individuals in the villages had to be accommodated to long-standing forms of community organization. Such accommodation was not easy, for it had to be done within the framework of a community organization which was based on unanimity of feeling in a homogeneous local group.

At Laguna the earliest dissension within the community of which there is record began in the 1870's. Laguna was less homogeneous than the other villages. It had been formed relatively late in Pueblo history, following the 1680 rebellion and was composed of people who had fled from Cochiti and Santo Domingo to escape the Spaniards. In 1851 a Baptist mission was set up but quickly ceased operation. In 1871 an Anglo-American named Walter G. Marmon was sent to Laguna as government schoolteacher. He was a militant Presbyterian and married a Laguna woman who was the daughter of a prominent Laguna man who had been converted to Presbyterianism by a missionary at Jemez during a short residence there. Previously, another Anglo-American had also married a Laguna woman and settled in the village. These two men gained considerable influence in the community and with the establishment of a Presbyterian mission in 1875 and the combined efforts of Marmon's brother, Robert, a considerable number of Lagunas became Presbyterians. The Marmons encouraged them to break away from old custom, including the establishment of a burial ground for Protestants separate from non-Protestants. The influence of the Marmons was strong enough that each was chosen at different times to be governor of the village. Their activities resulted in the solid establishment of the Presbyterian Church in Laguna and,

at the same time, the crystallization of far-reaching differences of feeling about
the old and the new customs. In 1879 friction ran high when Robert Marmon
became village governor. Two kivas were torn down and a group of about forty
Lagunans moved out of the village in protest, taking with them those sacred
objects to which their families held title. In the following year they went to Isleta
on the Rio Grande where the Isletans offered them land if they would stay. They
remained and established their own settlement, called Oraibi, at the edge of Isleta
where they constituted a conservative influence in that village. Meanwhile, although the Protestant faction remained dominant in community organization in
Laguna, the village never forsook entirely the old religion. Two factions remained,
with different degrees of conservatism toward the acceptance of new ways, but
still operating under the one Spanish-Pueblo type of community organization.

Friction was reported at Isleta as early as 1852, when troubles were discussed
with the New Mexico Territorial governor. During the 1880's and to a much
greater extent later, internal disputes continued to affect Isleta life. Isleta was the
only southern Tiwa village during the 1700's and was composed of the survivors of
the other Tiwa villages, after Coronado's conquest, as well as Piros and others
from the south after the Pueblo Revolt. Of all the Pueblo villages it was the closest
to an expanding Anglo-American city — Albuquerque. Although villagers took
sides on a variety of issues, such as the telling of sacred traditions to inquiring
Anglo-Americans, dissension centered primarily around the election of community
officers, the village governor and the war captain. Isleta was the only Pueblo village
to adopt the Spanish method of electing officers. After 1887, with the death of a
strong cacique, disputes over the election procedure became serious and continued as a source of factionalism. In 1949 Isleta adopted a constitution and tribal
council form of government.

In Taos in the 1890's a young man who had been away at boarding school
and come into contact with Plains and other Indians there brought back with
him a knowledge of and devotion to the beliefs and ritual of the Native American
Church. He instituted a church and gathered about him a group of men and
women who held regular peyote meetings. The leading men of the village opposed
the introduction and tried various measures to put a stop to it. They were often
led by Antonio Mirabal, who in regard to the acceptance of Anglo-American customs did not hold conservative attitudes (although much later in the 1930's he
bitterly opposed the appointment of a woman as superintendent of the Pueblo
Agency). The split over the Native American Church resulted in violence and
the creation of strong antagonism between the two opposing factions. It resulted
in the adoption of the new religion by only a few families, and even these families
did not wholly reject the Pueblo religion.

At San Ildefonso there was a longstanding tradition of a split, but not until
about 1910 did it become overt. Traditionally, the San Ildefonso people believed
that they had been tricked by witches (bad leaders) into changing the location of
their plaza a short distance north of its ancient and traditional location. About
1910 village leaders began to talk of moving the plaza back to the south; that is,
building new houses around the old location, in order to try to improve the fortunes

of the village which had been suffering like other Pueblos from floods and loss of land. Gradually some families moved back after the first new building took place in 1923. Other families refused to move and antagonism grew up between those living around what were called the North Plaza and the South Plaza. Dissension increased until in 1930 a fight occurred over possession of some sacred objects. This precipitated the split resulting in two separate organizations, one for the North and one for the South Plaza divisions. An important factor in the division at San Ildefonso was the growth of pottery-making as a new source of economic support. Women who had become independent of their husbands through this source of income were said to have taken positions which influenced their husbands and prevented them from compromising for the settlement of the various issues which had arisen.

At all the other villages, dissensions over one issue or another arose resulting in varying degrees of intra-village antagonism. It was obvious that no single cause in the form of religious dispute or progressive-conservative political views lay at the bottom of the factionalism. It arose over new religions, over old political mechanisms, over conceptions of village welfare within the framework of the old community organization. It was not a simple progressive-conservative differ-ence of feeling with reference to the acceptance of elements of Anglo-American custom, as, for example, it has been described for Acoma. It went deeper and rested on the multiplicity of influences on individuals from the engulfing culture. It was not a wholly new phenomenon, but had characterized Pueblo life even before Spanish influence.

In 1933 a new phase of contacts began for the Pueblos, chiefly as a result of the operation of the federal Indian program. As we have seen, prior to 1933 the federal Indian program of cultural assimilation touched the Pueblos at only a few important points. These were chiefly an effort to assist Indians in improving their agriculture, through providing money for developing their irrigation systems and persuading them to adopt improved seeds, agricultural machinery, and modern methods of stock raising, and through formal education. The latter feature of the program was far-reaching in scope, affecting habits of thought about the whole range of life for both males and females. It affected intimately nearly the whole Pueblo population, as the program gradually resulted in the enrollment of all Indian children in the federal or other schools. These services were free to the Indians and did not result in integrating them into the network of responsibilities in which citizens of the United States were enmeshed. The Pueblo communities remained largely separate enclaves in the political structure of the nation.

Beginning in the late 1920's and crystallizing into new and definite forms in the 1930's, Indian Bureau policy broadened in scope and for a time changed in fundamental approach. In the first place, the role of the federal government with respect to the land base of the Pueblos was clearly defined by 1924. The Indian Reorganization Act in 1934 further defined that role. The disputed titles to Pueblo Grant lands were finally, through government action, all cleared by 1938. In addition, with the aid of the federal government, the Pueblos bought additional land with the money given them in compensation for the land to which titles could not be secured. In this way the holdings of the villages were increased — in all except Cochiti, Picuris, Pojoaque, and San Juan — even beyond the extent of the original Spanish grants. No Pueblos, in 1950, were cultivating all the arable land which they possessed. The land pressure which they had experienced during the 1800's had been largely eliminated, despite some increase in population.

In the second place, the federal government began a program designed to adjust the community organization of all Indians in the country to changing economic and political factors. The Bureau of Indian Affairs proposed to all tribes that they adopt a form of government within their reservation territories like that of the United States, that is, a constitutional, representative system with officers elected by general suffrage. It offered aid in writing constitutions and setting up such local governments. There was to be no coercion; the adoption of a constitution would depend entirely on favorable majority vote by the Indians of any group. The tribal councils to be formed in this way would not have to conform in detail to any plan imposed by the Indian Bureau, but would be a result of the Indians' wishes. This system, accepted by most of the Indians of the United States, was rejected by all the Pueblos except the Tewa village of Santa Clara and later Isleta. The Indian Bureau assisted various villages who asked for help in writing out and clarifying some of the procedures already employed, but only Santa Clara and Isleta wrote constitutions and set up tribal councils. The old forms of the Spanish-Indian community governments, differing somewhat for each village, continued in operation. Nevertheless, a new discussion body was formed, with the encouragement of the Indian Agency. This was an over-all organization — the All-Pueblo Council — originating in the land troubles of the 1920's. Invested with no formal powers, it met irregularly and maintained a loose organization.

A third feature of the new government program considerably influenced Pueblo economics. This was the attempt by a government agency — the Indian Arts and Crafts Board — to build a nationwide market for Pueblo craft products. The Board stimulated outlets beyond the limits of the Pueblo country and attempted through its representatives to link the Indian work with certain aesthetic and craft values which obtained among Anglo-Americans in order to influence the Indian crafts. This fusion of traditions resulted in stimulating more pottery, silver, leather, and other craftwork for a number of years, until World War II virtually ended the Board's activities. This effort of the Arts and Crafts Board was supplemented, especially after 1933, by the activities of boarding schools under the Indian Bureau. In these schools, especially in one at Santa Fe, special efforts were made to encourage artistic talent among Indians. Students from various tribes responded, including Pueblos from most of the villages. From the 1930's on, there was widespread interest and activity in water color painting as well as in crafts in the various villages, most notably in San Ildefonso where the pottery revival had begun. The fusion of Indian and Western traditions in painting resulted in notable work which became an established minor tradition in American painting, continuing its existence on into the 1960's.

In all, the new influences which the Indian Bureau brought to bear on the Pueblos constituted pressures toward fusion of Pueblo and Anglo culture — not in the realm of supernatural belief as had the Spanish — but in other focal areas of Pueblo life. While the land program was one which stabilized Pueblo life, by relieving the land pressure, at least for the time being, the other Indian Bureau activities were of a different nature. In the Indian crafts program, the government encouraged a trend which had begun through other stimuli at San Ildefonso; it brought Indian aesthetic traditions into contact with those of Western culture. This had also occurred when archaeologists and traders had earlier bought the pottery of San Ildefonso; they took what suited museum canons or what they knew would be bought by tourists, thus applying standards quite outside of Pueblo culture. In this way there was a fusion of two traditions and the production of something new. At the same time the stimulation of an outside market was also conducive to participation in completely impersonal business operation, characteristic of Anglo-American culture. In these ways the Arts and Crafts Board became a factor of some importance in cultural change among the Pueblos.

The community organization proposals of the Indian Bureau were more far-reaching in their implications, although actually they had less immediate and less extensive effect perhaps than did the crafts program. Although villages were not required to adopt tribal constitutions and councils, the models were presented. The fact that two villages adopted them meant at least a small break in the old system. What was being held up was a model of a completely secular government system — such as the Spanish or Pueblo had never been — with mechanisms quite remote from existing Pueblo tradition, such as written tradition independent of the memories of particular older men, and voting by individual count. This proposed new form of government was in the air, its terminology on the lips of Indian Bureau people and of young people of the villages to some extent; the All-Pueblo Council adopted some of its procedures. There was now an alternative form of village government and many influences were working indirectly for its adoption.

The "educational" work of the Bureau representatives in regard to soil conservation and the relation of farm and grazing practice to the balance of nature was also a far-reaching partial introduction, since it set up also a system of ideas about nature competitive with that which prevailed in Pueblo religion. Like the tribal government system it was not imposed, but the strength of belief in the conservation ideas by Indian Bureau employees constituted in itself at least a mild pressure favoring this alternative set of beliefs.

The fundamental pattern of Pueblo life, as regards the physical basis of community life, had been rapidly altering since the 1880's; first with the elimination of the threat of raids from the Athapaskan tribes and then after the 1920's with the elimination of the land disputes. As farming expanded again in the 1880's, temporary shelters in fields some distance from the village began to appear. Gradually these were built into permanent residences by the families owning them, especially in the Keresan villages of Acoma, Laguna, and Santa Ana. But the building of outlying houses or small house clusters appeared also even in the smaller villages such as San Ildefonso, San Juan, Isleta, and Cochiti. The tendency of dispersion and separate family living units, with the old village site as a seasonal ceremonial center, intensified during the first fifty years of the 1900's. Laguna dispersed into six distinct villages, Acoma into three, Santa Ana into three, Isleta into four, and Cochiti into three. While no new villages could be said to have formed at Santa Clara, San Ildefonso, San Juan, Santo Domingo, Sandia, and Nambé, nevertheless the single-family unit a little distance from the village center had become an alternative pattern. Only Taos of all the Eastern Pueblos remained as compact a community as it had been at the beginning of the Anglo-American period.

The total population of the Eastern Pueblos in 1942 was 11,424, distributed as follows:

Acoma	1,322	San Felipe	697
Cochiti	346	San Ildefonso	147
Isleta	1,304	San Juan	702
Jemez	767	Santa Ana	273
Laguna	2,686	Santa Clara	528
Nambé	144	Santo Domingo	1,017
Picuris	115	Zia	235
Pojoaque	25	Taos	830
Sandia	139	Tesuque	147

The increase of population for the decade from 1932 to 1942 was 2,069 or about a 10 percent increase. This followed a trend of slower increase which had set in with the closing of military hostilities in the 1860's, and which continued thus for about one hundred years.

The last phase of the period of Anglo-American political domination was characterized by a rapid increase in inter-Pueblo contacts and in contacts between Pueblos and Indians of most other tribes in the United States. At no time in their known history had any Pueblo village been wholly isolated from others or from other tribes such as the Navajos. Contact with other Indians had been a regular feature of Pueblo life. In the 1850's Lt. Whipple of the U. S. Army found traders from Santo Domingo in Oklahoma exchanging goods with various Indian groups there. The tradition of traveling traders among the Santo Domingans was long-standing, and other Pueblos traded also among themselves and with neighboring tribes. The Taos fairs, bringing Plains Indians into the Pueblo country had been an institution at least since early Spanish times. This trade was stimulated as peaceful conditions grew under the Anglo-Americans. The Saint's Day fiestas, such as the one at Laguna, as well as many other ceremonial occasions drew Indians from all over the Southwest for trade and recreation, as well as for religious purposes.

To these long-standing contact institutions were added others. A major one consisted of the Indian Bureau boarding schools, which first began to attract Pueblo boys and girls in the late 1880's. Situated far from the Pueblos' homes in the eastern United States or in Oklahoma, the few Pueblos who first went to them were thrown into contact not only with Pueblos from other villages, but with Navajos, Pimas, Sioux, and all the tremendous variety of Indians living in the United States. The speaking of English was strictly enforced in the boarding

12. EASTERN PUEBLOS ABOUT 1960

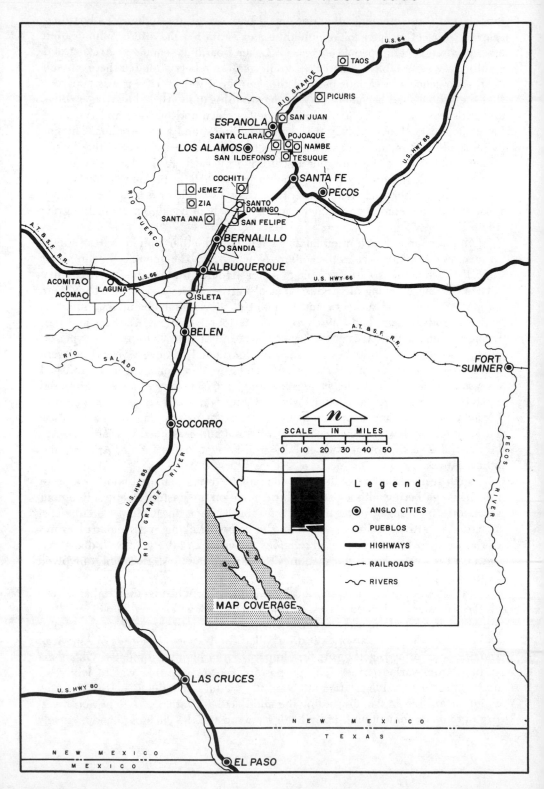

schools and thus communication developed between all the Indians. As boarding schools were set up later in Albuquerque and Santa Fe, the intercommunication among young Pueblo people increased. Other boarding schools in Arizona and California were established and Pueblos in small numbers attended these, as well as mission schools in various parts of the country. By the 1920's it was apparent that the schools had become a very strong stimulus to intertribal marriages. Boys and girls from different Pueblo villages fell in love and married and the same happened to Pueblos and Navajos, Apaches, Pimas, and all the others. This inevitably brought members of various tribes for permanent residence in the Pueblo villages, not many to be sure, but a scattering everywhere. It also meant correspondence and friendships linking Pueblo individuals in lifelong contacts with individuals of other villages and other tribes. A new world of intercommunicating persons with a common government or mission school background steadily grew up within the villages.

Another type of institution linking Pueblos with other United States Indians were annual festivals such as the Gallup, New Mexico, Ceremonials. Begun about 1926, the Ceremonials were designed to increase tourist trade in the Indian country through public showing of various types of native dances and music. They were an almost immediate success from the point of view of the commercial interests which founded them, and quickly became nationally famous. Dancers and performers from all the tribes of the country were invited to Gallup, their expenses paid. The Southwestern tribes generally predominated, but every year there were also strong representations of Plains Indians. Other ceremonials were established on a somewhat smaller scale, such as the Flagstaff Powwow, which also attracted Pueblo performers. At these affairs a sort of generalized American Indian culture began to develop and a premium was placed on maintaining Indian identity. Various Pueblo dances became nationally known and continued year after year to be danced in competition with equally well-known Plains Indian, Apache, and other dances.

Such festivals as the Gallup Ceremonials in turn stimulated another kind of intertribal gathering, although it had little effect on the Eastern Pueblos. Religious camp meetings began to be held at the same time as the Gallup Ceremonials, designed to attract Indians away from the heavy drinking and secular pleasures of the Ceremonials. They offered religious activities and drew a few Indians, but because they were Protestant meetings there were few Eastern Pueblos involved in them.

At the same time that such local gatherings brought together Indians from all the tribes of the United States, and in which the Pueblos from all villages took a prominent part, there was also the development of intertribal contacts on a political level. In the 1930's an organization called the National Congress of American Indians was formed, getting its first impetus from highly assimilated Oklahoma Indians from various tribes. The purpose of the organization was to lobby for and against national legislation affecting the welfare of Indians. It steadily grew in importance in Indian life and by the middle 1940's Indians from the Southwest began to be prominent in it. Individuals from most of the Pueblos joined it, purely as individuals, and slowly whole Pueblos, such as Tesuque in 1948, took up membership. In 1954 a man from Taos Pueblo served as executive secretary of the organization, and it became accepted procedure for a majority of the villages to send representatives to the annual meeting of the National Congress of American Indians. Like the boarding schools and the annual secular ceremonials, the Congress was contributing to the growth of a generalized American Indian "culture." In 1960 a San Carlos Apache was president of the organization.

Service in the armed forces in World War II also brought Pueblos into contact with one another, as well as with members of other tribes. The percentage of young men and women so serving was the highest for any ethnic group in the United States.

Another significant development in Pueblo life during the hundred years of Anglo-American domination was the growth of protective secrecy in regard to religious practices. Undoubtedly such measures as the exclusion of non-Indians from the most sacred ceremonies and those involving kachina dancers dated from the Franciscan missionary attack in the 1670's on the kachinas as heathen idols. In subsequent years, as some Hispanos moved into various Pueblos or into close proximity to them, it became accepted practice for the Hispanos to stay away from all ceremonies to which they were not expressly invited. In the 1880's there were numerous Spanish-descended residents on Pueblo lands who had never seen and did not know of the existence of the most sacred ceremonies in which Pueblo religion was expressed. This was an accepted accommodation principle between the two peoples.

The coming of the Anglos upset this arrangement. Government officials and others were curious and wanted to see what the Indian customs were like. There was at first little or no interest in suppressing or interfering with the ceremonies, but the Indian Bureau up until the 1890's had been accustomed to subsidize schools of religious denominations among the Indians, and at least two such schools were established among the Pueblos. Some of the government farmers and Indian Agents as well as the schoolteachers were shocked by some of the Indian ceremonies. There was some talk of suppression under the provisions of the Bureau's Religious Crimes Code. This resulted in reinforcing the wall of secrecy and the exclusion of Anglos as well as Mexicans from ceremonies. The appearance of scientific students — anthropologists — in the 1870's who began intensive study especially of Pueblo religion gave further strength to the tendencies toward secrecy. Despite the secrecy there were always individuals who would talk; books were published containing drawings, and later photographs, of sacred masks and paraphernalia. What had been completely unknown to even neighboring villages, now had currency all over the world. The Pueblo reaction was to attempt to throw up an even more complete wall of secrecy. Anthropologists, tourists, government officials, all were excluded from seeing all but a few public ceremonies. Protests were made regarding the use of costumes resembling Pueblo sacred costumes in Anglo secular celebrations. At the same time, the pressures created by such students as the anthropologists continued with increasing intensity. Through the 1940's nearly every year saw some attempted study and some new friction because of it. Breaches in the wall of secrecy came constantly as disaffected village residents gave out information for pay. The attempt to shield the religion became a source of mutual suspicion and antagonisms.

Eastern Pueblo history during the 110 years of Anglo-American political domination may be characterized in terms of three major phases. First, a period of some thirty-five years of growing peaceful relations with surrounding peoples during which the major influences for cultural change came through Mexican neighbors who moved into the villages and on to the village grant lands; second, a period of growing pressures from Anglo society chiefly through the enrollment of children in Anglo schools, a period which lasted from the 1870's through the 1920's; third, a period of intensifying pressures from Anglo culture through a many-sided government assimilation program and the growth of cities and towns in close proximity to the villages. The whole epoch was characterized by an absence of strong coercive measures, the increase of heterogeneity among the individuals living in the villages, the intensification of communication between Pueblo and other communities through the use of both Spanish and English, and the increasing economic linkage of the Pueblo communities with surrounding ones.

CHAPTER SEVEN

Western Pueblos

ZUNI CONTACTS with the Spaniards bore some resemblance to those of the Rio Grande Pueblos, but they differed in important respects. Two hundred miles from the center of Spanish administration at Santa Fe, the Zunis never experienced intensive contacts with either Spanish colonists or administrators. They remained after 1621 exempt from the payment of tribute. Like the Hopis to the northwest, they were regarded as a frontier margin of New Mexico and not actually as an integral part of the colony being built up on the Rio Grande. Accordingly, their contacts with the Spaniards resembled somewhat more those of the Hopis than of the Eastern Pueblos.

However, the first contacts of the Zunis with non-Indians were spectacularly unlike those of any other Indian group. Estevan, the dark-skinned Moorish slave who had been a member of Cabeza de Vaca's party, made the first direct contact. He came from the Sonoran region in 1539, preceding Father Marcos de Niza as the vanguard of the latter's expedition to find the Seven Cities of Cibola. An entourage of Indians from the Upper Pimería numbering some three hundred accompanied him. In some manner he offended the Zunis of Hawikuh and, after a conference, they killed him.

In 1540, Coronado's party came to the Zuni villages. There were at that time six villages, with a total population of three thousand to thirty-five hundred. The largest villages were Hawikuh and Matsakya, which were said by the Spaniards to have houses seven stories high — probably a use of seven as a magic number consistent with the belief in the Seven Cities of Cibola. The Zunis of Hawikuh who had killed Estevan were not friendly and Coronado engaged them in battle, capturing the village and taking the whole supply of food. The Zunis fled from Hawikuh as well as from the other villages and took refuge on top of a mesa called Corn Mountain. Coronado did not pursue them but continued on his way after taking the stores and spending a few weeks at Hawikuh. On the return trip Coronado's party left three Mexican Indians at the Zuni villages.

In 1583 Espejo's party was received in friendly fashion, the Zunis having adopted the policy of non-direct resistance to Spaniards after their experience with Coronado. Espejo found the Mexican Indians left by Coronado still there and living comfortably among the Zunis. He left a Franciscan missionary, Bernardino, at the villages, but the missionary stayed for only a short time. The Zunis nominally accepted the rule of Oñate in 1598 without show of resistance.

No contacts of Zunis took place with Spaniards during the early period of missionary work in the Eastern Pueblos. Missionaries were not sent to the villages until 1629. Between that year and 1633 four missionaries took up residence, built a mission church, and preached. They felt themselves to be well received but also noted opposition from "sorcerers" over a period of three years. In 1633 two of the missionaries were killed, along with their soldier escorts, and the Indians retired to their mesa stronghold again. Ten years later, having experienced no Spanish retaliation, they came down to two of the villages and helped missionaries build churches at Hawikuh and Halona. In 1670 one of the missionaries was killed by Apaches in a raid on Hawikuh and in 1680, in concert with the Eastern Pueblos, the Zunis killed the remaining missionary at Halona.

When de Vargas arrived in 1692 in his reconquest of New Mexico, he found the Zunis all on Corn Mountain. They permitted three hundred children to be baptized and promised submission to de Vargas. Nevertheless, in 1693 and 1694 they sent fighting men to help the Jemez in their continued resistance to the Spaniards. In 1699 they came down again from Corn Mountain and built a new village and a church on the east side of the Zuni River. During the first half of the 1700's the mission was only irregularly attended by missionaries and there seem never to have been more than two present. During the last half of the 1700's Apache raids on Zuni took place, and gradually missionary work, as well as contacts with Spaniards decreased, until finally the mission was wholly abandoned in 1821 as a result of Navajo raids.

Nevertheless the Hopis regarded the Zunis as Christianized as early as 1706 when Hopis attacked the village of Zuni in an effort to keep the Spanish mission program from extending to their own villages.

In general, the Zunis remained on the periphery of the Spanish domain in New Mexico. After their first encounter with Coronado, they avoided direct conflict and gave superficial acceptance to the not very vigorous mission program which the Spaniards imposed on them. Although they obviously felt as did the Eastern Pueblos about Spanish rule in 1680, they gave little support to the other Indians in the Revolt. At a distance, by sending some men to fight, they participated with the people of Jemez and Acoma in their attempted resistance to the reconquest. They nevertheless avoided any battles at their own villages and maintained only passive resistance when missionaries again came out to them. They remained in considerable isolation from the Spaniards during the whole of the 1700's and on into the early part of the 1800's.

The Hopis are probably the most famous "apostates" in the history of Spanish Christianity. The history of their contact with the Spaniards well illustrates the waning spirit and resources of Spain on her northern frontier in the New World. We can see most clearly in early Hopi history the nature of an Indian reassertion of their own values after a period of trial of the European way of life. We sense that the Hopis, chiefly because of increasing Spanish weakness, were able to

accomplish what most other tribes of the northwest would have wished to do
after initial contact with the Spaniards — namely, maintain freedom to pick and
choose from among Spanish ideas and artifacts with no compulsion to adopt any.
After initial contacts extending over nearly a century and a half, the Hopis
achieved an actual independence of Spain. They remained a deep concern of
Spanish administrators and missionaries, but the New Mexican governors were
never able to muster sufficient strength to cope with the determined and highly
conscious Hopi choice to live as Hopis rather than as Hispanicized Indians. In
this respect, the history of Hopi contacts with the Spaniards is unique; it is the
story of an Indian group who, after intensive experience with Spanish culture, was
able to fend off further contacts and go its own way.

The earliest contacts of the Hopis with the Spaniards were like those of the
Eastern Pueblo villagers. First in 1540 they experienced the ruthlessness and
arrogance of the Coronado party. While resting at the Zuni village of Hawikuh,
Coronado sent his lieutenant, de Tovar, northwest to explore the reports of cities.
De Tovar, with a party of seventeen horsemen, a few foot soldiers, and the
Franciscan missionary Father Juan Padilla marched to the easternmost villages of
the Hopis in what is now called the Jeddito Valley. At Kawaiokuh de Tovar was
received with a show of hostility and told not to cross a line drawn on the ground.
De Tovar, after some discussion with interpreters brought from Zuni, and on
advice of the priest, waived further peaceful conference and attacked. The Hopis
were quickly defeated and their village of Kawaiokuh was partially destroyed. The
inhabitants then submitted and gave de Tovar to understand that they were
speaking for all seven Hopi villages. De Tovar stayed a few days, visiting all the
villages, and then rejoined Coronado. Later another Coronado lieutenant,
Cárdenas, went to the Hopi villages with twelve men. This time there was no
show of resistance and the Hopis furnished guides to lead Cárdenas through their
country to the Grand Canyon.

The village of Kawaiokuh was abandoned from this time on, partly as a
result of the destruction of its houses by de Tovar and partly probably because of
the failing water supply which had been making life difficult in the Jeddito Valley
for many years before the Spaniards' arrival. Another village, Sikyatki a little
farther west, which de Tovar had visited, also was abandoned during this period.
Both were uninhabited at the time of the arrival of the Espejo expedition in 1583.
Espejo, with a party of a few soldiers and some Zunis, was intent on finding
mines. With the gift for winning the friendship of the Indians that he showed
throughout his travels in New Mexico he was able to overcome initial hostility to
his party. Convinced finally that he had no intention of fighting or forcing submission, Hopis in all five villages gave him an enthusiastic and hospitable welcome,
furnishing him with guides for his prospecting ventures in the area.

When Oñate came to New Mexico in 1598 he included the Hopi villages in
his program. He visited them before the end of 1598 and found the Hopis ready
to give formal submission to the King of Spain without any show of resistance.
He sent Captains Farfán and Quesada out to look for mines and later assigned
two Franciscan missionaries to the Hopi villages; however, the missionaries never

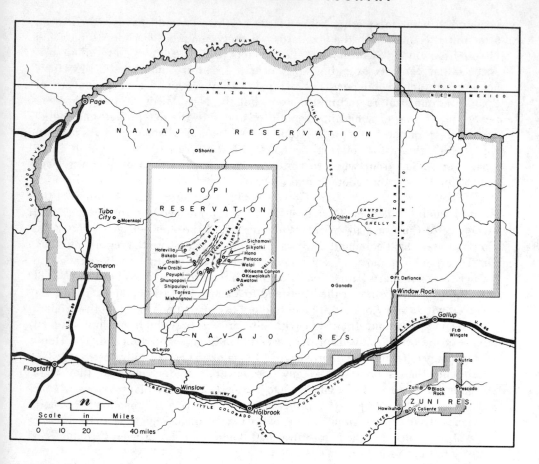

went to the Hopi country to take up their assignments. In 1599 two Hopis experienced Spanish brutality. In Oñate's battle at Acoma to punish the Acomans for their killing of Lieutenant Zaldívar, two Hopis were among the captives. They were sentenced to have their right hands cut off.

For thirty years after Oñate's securing of Hopi submission, there was no extension of the mission program to the Hopi villages. Oñate himself visited the villages, on his way to and from the west in an effort to find the Pacific Ocean. They were visited again in 1614 by Captain Márquez with twenty-five soldiers. Five villages were reported with a population of about three thousand, but no efforts were made at conversion. They and the Zunis were regarded as the frontiers of New Mexico and in 1621 were both exempted from the tribute payments exacted from the Eastern Pueblos for the maintenance of the garrison at Santa Fe.

The mission program was instituted in 1628 when one Franciscan visited the Hopi villages. In 1629 it began in earnest with the assignment of three missionaries. The Hopis were cooperative and proceeded to build three mission churches under Franciscan direction, providing all the necessary labor and materials. In the course of the next few years churches were completed at Awatovi, the easternmost village, at Shungopovi below modern Second Mesa, and at Oraibi, the westernmost village. The last two missions had visitas at Walpi (below First Mesa) and at Mishongnovi (below Second Mesa). The mission villages of Awatovi, Shungopovi, and Oraibi probably at this time also were provided with schools and village organization in the Spanish form. Two more missionaries came some time after. By 1630 Father Benavides claimed that there were ten thousand Hopis (probably a considerable exaggeration like his other population estimates) and that they were being "rapidly converted." The fact that he did not report that they were already converted is probably significant, for there were indications of troubles and resistance, and in 1633 Father Porras, the missionary at Awatovi, was poisoned. The poisoning of Porras did not deter the missionaries, however, and the program proceeded. That the Hopis were not too unhappy may be indicated by the fact that they refused, when asked, to join with the Taos people in a plan for revolt in 1650.

In 1655 in Santa Fe Hopis denounced the Franciscan Father Salvador de Guerra for his methods of enforcing discipline. They accused him specifically of being responsible for the death of a Hopi named Juan Cuna. Cuna had been accused by the priest of "an act of idolatry." For this Guerra gave him a bloody whipping in public and then took him into the church and beat him again. Finally the priest covered him with turpentine and set fire to it, as a result of which Cuna died. Father Guerra was convicted of this offense and of mistreating other Indians in similar fashion. He was removed from the Hopi country, although he continued to serve in New Mexico.

For the next twenty-five years the mission program was uneventful, so far as the record goes. Baptism proceeded and many Hopis were taught to read and write, most notably a leading man of Oraibi, who was baptized Francisco de Espeleta after one of the missionaries at Oraibi. In 1659 when crops failed food was sent from Santa Fe to Oraibi and Shongopovi. There is no report of the Hopi villages being included in the kiva raids by the missionaries in the 1670's. Nevertheless, when the Pueblo Revolt of 1680 broke out, it was obvious that the Hopis were wholeheartedly back of it. They immediately killed the four missionaries, two of whom were at Oraibi, and one each at Awatovi and Shungopovi. The fact that these priests had no military escorts at the time indicates that they must have regarded the Hopis as peacefully accepting the missionary work. Hopis do not seem to have contributed fighting men to the siege of Santa Fe or to have participated in the work of destruction outside their own area.

The Hopis, did, however, provide a direct service to the rebel Eastern Pueblos immediately following the revolt. People fled in fear of Spanish reprisal and as a result of Otermín's wanton burning of Tiwa and Keres villages in 1681. Tewa, Tiwa, Tano, and Keres families found their way to the Hopi country and took refuge there. There were so many that two new villages were built—Hano on First Mesa and Payupki on Second Mesa. The Hopis, too, had great fear of Spanish expeditions for new military subjection. They accordingly moved three villages which had been near springs at the base of the mesas up on top of the mesas where attack would be difficult. Thus, Walpi was moved to the tip of First Mesa, and Shungopovi and Mishongnovi were moved on top of Second Mesa. In addition, Shungopovi adopted an additional safeguard, establishing a new village of Shipaulovi on an even more inaccessible spot on top of Second Mesa. The new village was to be a place for ceremonial paraphernalia where it could be most securely kept from falling into Spanish hands.

The expected Spanish attack did not, however, materialize until twelve years later, after the refugees from the Rio Grande Valley had become well established. In 1692 de Vargas arrived before the Hopi villages and found them ready to resist. He offered not to fight, if the villages would swear allegiance. This the Hopi leaders decided to do, and de Vargas left without a battle and without even having gone as far west as Oraibi. During the late 1690's, following the 1694 uprising of Jemez and the 1696 uprising of the Tewas, Tanos, and Keres, still more refugees came to the Hopi country and the Hopis allowed them sanctuary in the new villages. The Hopis were nevertheless anxious to keep from real warfare with the Spaniards. In 1699, seeing the vigor and success with which the Spaniards had finally carried out their reconquest of the Rio Grande peoples, some Hopis, probably from Awatovi, offered to rebuild their mission. This was followed by a delegation of Hopis going to Santa Fe to ask for missionaries. We do not know which villages were represented in the delegation. In response, three missionaries came to Awatovi and preached for six hours. They reported that the Hopis were generally hostile and would not listen to them, but they also recommended that a garrison be posted in the Hopi country to protect the Christianized Hopis of Awatovi from other Hopis. It was evident that there was a difference of opinion among the Hopis in regard to the acceptance of Christian missionaries. Shortly after the preaching at Awatovi, Father Garaycoechea came up from Halona at Zuni, found a friendly reception at Awatovi, and even was able, so he claimed, to baptize seventy-three children. His visit apparently threw him into contact only with the Christian faction at Awatovi.

That the Hopis were by no means united on a desire for missionaries, but rather the contrary, is indicated by an event which occurred toward the end of this same year 1700. Hopis had evidently been vigorously discussing policy in regard to the Spaniards as a result of the request for missionaries by people from Awatovi. A policy which was finally offered as the Hopi policy was presented in Santa Fe by another group of Hopis who went there under the leadership of Francisco de Espeleta, the head man of Oraibi who had been baptized and taught to read and write by the missionaries prior to 1680. This group also wanted peace, but not at any cost. They were implacably opposed to the return of the mission program. They proposed a treaty of peace between themselves and the Spaniards, under the condition that each nation would keep its own religion and not try to convert the other. They proposed, in other words, a treaty recognizing religious freedom. Governor Cubero of New Mexico summarily rejected the proposal.

The Hopis under the Oraibi leadership made their visit to Santa Fe immediately following an attack on the village of Awatovi. After the missionary from

Zuni had come and baptized the seventy-three children at Awatovi, feeling against the village had arisen among the other Hopis. It was particularly strong at Oraibi, where Francisco de Espeleta raised a force of one hundred men and together with others, probably including Shungopovi and the anti-missionary faction at Awatovi, attacked Awatovi. The village was destroyed, all the men who resisted were killed, and the women and children were distributed among the other villages. Thus, probably nearly all Hopis who favored a return of the missionaries were wiped out at one stroke and the anti-missionary leaders were dominant everywhere. It was as the representatives of all the Hopis that Espeleta's delegation proposed the treaty of peace to Governor Cubero in Santa Fe.

In the year following these events, 1701, Governor Cubero made an effort to force the Hopis to agree to the Spanish terms and at the same time to punish them for the destruction of Awatovi. He marched into the Hopi country with a small force of soldiers, but found the Hopis unwilling to meet him in direct battle. He killed a few people and captured some others, but did not feel equipped to attack any of the mesa strongholds. Thus it appeared that the Hopi defensive measures taken after the Revolt of 1680 were effective. Their villages could not be attacked successfully except by a strong force, which Governor Cubero did not feel able to put into the field.

About this time the lands which had belonged to the people of Awatovi were distributed, going chiefly to the people of Walpi, although some were given to Shungopovi and people of Second Mesa. For some reason Oraibi did not share in the distribution, although Oraibians were convinced that they had some claim to the lands.

The Hopi policy now included efforts to unite Zuni with them in keeping the Spaniards out of their territory. In 1702 they tried to get the Zunis to revolt against the missionaries, but the Zunis refused. In 1706 Hopis attacked Christian Zunis, but the Zunis, instead of joining with the Hopis, allied themselves with a Spanish force sent to punish the Hopis. The Spanish-Zuni force attacked Payupki, the village of Eastern Pueblos, and was defeated. The Spaniards had to content themselves merely with destroying some fields before leaving.

For the next ten years the government at Santa Fe was much concerned about the Hopis and wavered in its policy. The governor was anxious to get the Tewa and Tano and other Eastern Pueblos back to the Rio Grande Valley. The New Mexico government was also anxious to see a mission program proceed in the Hopi country where it had flourished before. For five years from 1707-12 Governor Chacón tried to conciliate and persuade, using no military force, but he found no response from either the Hopis or the Eastern Pueblo refugees. A new governor, Flores, repeatedly considered military expeditions to force the Indians to do what the Spaniards wanted. His plans were interrupted by a group of Hopi traders who told the story, for their own protection, that the Hopis had agreed to accept missionaries. Eventually Spanish emissaries found that this was a pure fabrication. Governor Flores ended by doing nothing. When a new governor, Martínez, came into office in 1716, he decided to solve the problem forthwith by the application of force. He headed an expedition to the Hopi country prepared for battle. His immediate avowed object was to bring back to the Rio Grande Valley the apostate Tanos who had settled at the village of Hano on First Mesa. Martínez was able to engage in battle and defeat two different parties of First Mesa Hopis. But he found it impossible to get the Hopis of Walpi to cooperate with him in delivering the Tanos into his hands. Walpi leaders merely suggested that he storm the mesa and capture the Tanos. This appeared impracticable to Martínez who could find nothing better to do than lay waste many fields belonging to the Tanos. He then left, believing that he had given the Tanos a lesson. In 1718 he extended a peaceful invitation to the Tanos to return, but there was no response.

Meanwhile, rivalry had developed over the missionary jurisdiction of the Hopis. The 1680 rebellion had given rise to some criticism of the Franciscan policies and the question was raised especially as to their adaptation to the Hopi situation. In 1697 and again in 1699 Father Eusebio Kino, the Upper Pima Jesuit missionary, communicated with the Hopis. In 1716 after Kino's death, his associates Velarde and Campos, as a result of some Hopis having urged Campos to bring Jesuits to the Hopi country, proposed to the viceroy in Mexico City that the Hopi missionary field be turned over to the Jesuits in preference to the Franciscans. In 1719 the King of Spain in response to these urgings decreed that the Jesuits might add the Hopi province of Tusayan to Sonora. This was followed in 1725 by the viceroy's giving out a special cedula placing jurisdiction over the Hopis in the hands of the Jesuits. Because the Franciscans continued to work among the Hopis, two having gone to preach at Oraibi without success in 1724, the Jesuit Order instituted legal proceedings in 1730 to obtain the sole jurisdiction.

The major result of the jurisdictional dispute was to stimulate Franciscan activity in Tusayan. While the legal proceedings were getting under way, two Franciscans went again to the Hopi country to preach. They were completely unsuccessful in rousing Hopi interest and one was reported killed. In the following year, 1732, another Franciscan, Father Techungui, went to the Hopi country and persuaded five Tewas to come to Isleta in the Rio Grande Valley to live. In 1742 a Franciscan, Father Delgado, began a series of visits designed particularly to demonstrate that the Franciscans could be successful. In that year he and another friar went to the Hopi country, and although they did not receive a friendly reception from the Hopis, they were able to persuade 441 Indians to leave the Hopi country and take up residence at Isleta. Delgado claimed that these were Hopis, but it was evident that they were chiefly Tiwa and other Rio Grande Indians for they came from the post-1680 village of Payupki which was shortly abandoned.

Delgado followed this very considerable triumph in furthering the Spanish policy with another visit in 1743–44. This time he demonstrated further great ignorance of the Hopis in claiming that he had baptized five thousand out of the "10,846 Hopis." Actually, these turned out to be Navajos and the generally friendly reception he received was from Navajos rather than Hopis. Nevertheless, his report was received as indicating a great success for the Franciscans. In view of two failures on the part of the Jesuits during the years of Delgado's activities to reach the Hopis — Keller, who was stopped by Apache attacks in 1743, and Sedelmayr in 1744 — the King of Spain now changed his mind and supported the Franciscans as against the Jesuits for jurisdiction in Tusayan. In addition, the Jesuit provincial in Mexico City in this same year wrote a letter declining the Hopi missionary field. Interestingly enough, the Franciscan Delgado made still another trip to the Hopi country in 1745 and — in contrast with his usual announcements — reported complete lack of success in getting Hopis to listen to him.

The Hopis, who were now living in five villages with about eight thousand inhabitants, were more determined than ever to maintain their separate existence. In 1747, hearing of a Spanish expedition to enter their territory, they sent men to Zuni to intercept the party and prevent them from coming to Hopi country. In 1748 they allowed 350 Tiwa who were still among them to go back to the Rio Grande Valley and settle at Sandia. In 1754 they killed six Havasupai Indians who were on their way to Santa Fe to confer with the governor; their purpose was avowed to be to prevent any Whites coming back into the Tusayan region with the Indians. In 1755 Hopis allowed Father de la Torre to preach in the villages, but he reported that every time he seemed to be making anything like a favorable impression on anyone, older men would get up and talk against him, so that the net result of his proselytizing was failure. In 1755 Father Escalante visited in the Hopi villages for eight days. The people were friendly but they did not allow him to talk about religion. He came away and made a recommendation that the only progressive course with the Hopis would be to establish a presidio in their country, because all of the chiefs were hostile to Christianity and the Spaniards. In 1776 the great Franciscan missionary Garcés came up the Colorado with gifts and a desire to spread the gospel. The Hopis would not even accept his gifts and he left without having preached a word. Escalante came again in the same year and once more was accepted in friendly fashion but with absolute refusal to discuss Christianity. Again force was recommended as the only effective means of furthering Spanish policy.

In 1777 the situation changed somewhat. A series of very dry years with consequent crop failure left the Hopis in all villages in a precarious situation. They gradually depleted their stores, which were designed to last for three years. By 1779 many Hopis had gone to live at Zuni and some had joined Tiwa friends at Sandia. In 1780 Father Andrés Garcia took some two hundred Hopis to the Rio Grande Valley and distributed them in various villages. In the same year Governor Anza went to the Hopi country. He found that many were reported living with the Havasupai and that the population had declined in the preceding five years from 7,494 to 798 persons. Governor Anza offered the remaining Hopis a village site on the lower Rio Grande River and complete freedom from tribute or other forms of labor. It appeared to be a golden opportunity to solve the persistent "Hopi problem." A head man from Oraibi told Anza that so far as he himself was concerned he would stick to the Hopi religion and not move, but that he would not interfere with any others who might wish to go east or anywhere else. Governor Anza took another thirty families — 150 people — back with him to the Rio Grande. In 1781 a smallpox epidemic struck the Hopis, but in the same year the rains came, crops were good again, and Hopi prosperity began to return. By 1782 Father Juan Morfi wrote that the Hopis were far better off than any of the Rio Grande Pueblos, despite the fact that they had maintained their independence of Spanish rule.

Hopis were not disturbed by further Spanish contacts. However, beginning at least by 1812, Navajos began to harass them. By 1818 the Hopis had been so much harassed by marauding Navajos that they decided to turn to the Santa Fe government for help. They petitioned for soldiers to fight against the Navajos. Although it was recognized that here was another chance to end 139 years of apostasy, the Spaniards found it impossible to do anything. They were in the last throes of disintegration themselves.

In interpreting the fragments of information that come down as history, it is easy to jump to conclusions based on too little evidence. On a basis of the recorded fragments it is easy to build up a picture of the Hopis as a solidly unified group setting their minds and hearts firmly against the Spaniards and their culture. If such a conception were true, then it is clear that they would have been the only Indians of the northwest of New Spain who behaved in that way.

Actually, the record seems to yield some data which point strongly to the same sort of two-way pull in the face of Spanish contact which characterized all the other groups considered. The first and clearest evidence of the growth of factional difference with reference to the issue of the mission program was, of course, Hopi behavior in 1700 — some 160 years after the first contacts. It is obvious that at this time there were two well-developed points of view among the Hopis — not with reference to peace with the Spaniards but with reference to the acceptance of missionaries. The viewpoints were sufficiently well developed to have led to the sending of two different delegations to Santa Fe to present each of the views. The first delegation asked for missionaries. We can only conclude that they must have come from Awatovi, from the Christianized people of that mission village, because the missionaries who came in response to their request went immediately to Awatovi and later the missionary from Zuni was well received by Awatovians. Also it got into the record that Awatovi was later destroyed because the people of Awatovi had harbored the missionaries. Yet when the missionaries arrived, they found that they were received coldly in Awatovi. Did this mean that there was an anti-missionary faction in Awatovi itself which gained control after the delegation had been sent to Santa Fe? Or did it mean that Hopis from other villages with a hostile attitude towards the missionaries were in Awatovi when the missionaries arrived and influenced, perhaps forced, the Awatovians to give the cool reception? The first explanation seems less likely than the latter, because ultimately we are told that all the Awatovi men were massacred by the war party from Oraibi and the other villages.

Whatever the specific situation in Awatovi it seems fairly certain that there were two parties among the Hopis — split over acceptance of missions. Leadership for the pro-mission faction came from Awatovi certainly, and leadership for the anti-mission faction came from Oraibi certainly. How these villages were each divided or whether they were divided at all, and how the other villages thought, we do not know. It is only clear that there were Hopi leaders who wanted to continue the Christian program and Hopi leaders who wanted to maintain their own religion without any part of the mission program. The latter group became dominant very quickly, showing themselves quite willing to use force, during the twelve months of the year 1700. The Christian-inclined group was forcibly suppressed and probably completely wiped out in at least one village. The fate of Awatovi had the same effect on Hopis who might have leaned toward the missionaries that Spanish force had on the Eastern Pueblos. The Hopis after this did not remain split on the issue of missions, as did the Tarahumaras, but rather became united and were able to remain so for the next century and a half or more through lack of further effective pressure from the Spaniards. It is this that constitutes the real difference between the Hopi situation and that of each of the other tribes we have considered. As in the other cases, Spanish contact produced parties and issues with reference to the Spanish elements of culture, but as did not happen in the other cases, the Hopis for over a century were able to settle these issues among themselves without Spanish interference. The result was a clear choice of the Hopi way of life as against the Spanish.

We can only guess at the influence of refugee groups from the Rio Grande upon the Hopis. Of one thing we may be sure, namely, that such groups were able to tell the Hopis the details of what Spanish domination meant — details with which the Hopis had not had first-hand experience. For this reason it should not be assumed that Hopis were isolated from and ignorant of the Spanish world which had been created in the Rio Grande Valley.

It seems to be that the Hopis, in contrast with the Yaquis, developed what unity they achieved after, rather than during, their first period of intensive contact with the Spaniards. This period was shorter than that which the Yaquis experienced — 50 as compared with 125 years. Since nothing like the synthesis of Spanish and native cultures took place among the Hopis as among the Yaquis, we are forced to assume that the Franciscan missionaries worked in quite different ways from the Jesuits, for the Hopis, like the Yaquis, were shielded from contacts of any importance other than missionary.

Unlike the Eastern Pueblos, the Hopis and Zunis experienced relatively few contacts with Whites during the years that the American Southwest was a part of Mexico. Not only was there a vast distance between the villages of the Western Pueblos and the government at Santa Fe, but the widespread warfare which took place with increasing frequency during those years between the settled Pueblos and the far-ranging, marauding Navajos and Apaches — and which the Mexican troops were unable to prevent — virtually stopped all travel in the northern area. Neither Hopi nor Zunis felt the touch of Mexican political authority. Both groups were visited occasionally by Anglos — parties of trappers, and soldiers with early Anglo-American military expeditions — but it was well into the American period before Hopis and Zunis came into frequent contacts with Anglos and still later that they were brought under the full authority of the United States government.

Hopis and Zunis remained more isolated from white men than the Eastern Pueblos until the 1890's and as a result their contacts and history took a somewhat different course. Neither had had the close contact with Spaniards, or later with Mexicans, that characterized the Eastern Pueblos. Neither had a Catholic church in more or less continuous operation during the 1800's. The relations between Zunis and Hopis, especially after the drought of the 1860's, were probably closer through visiting and trading than were the relations between either of them and any other Pueblo villagers. All of these factors made for a certain similarity in their history as contrasted with the Eastern Pueblos. Nevertheless, when we compare Zuni with Hopi we are struck forcibly by the differences in the results of contact.

After the contacts with the Coronado expedition, probably following a tendency which had existed long before, the Zunis adopted a more compact settlement. What had been several settlements were steadily consolidated into one during the Spanish period and this tendency was accelerated during the years of raid and threatened raid from Navajos and Apaches during the late 1700's, and throughout the Mexican period. At the time of the Anglo-American invasion in the late 1840's, Zunis lived in a single compact community consisting of houses grouped closely together and rising as high as five terraces.

The Navajo raids had become severe enough so that the Catholic mission which existed at Zuni during the 1700's was completely abandoned during 1821. Although some Catholic priests probably visited Zuni occasionally later, the church fell into ruins and the Catholics did not return for a full hundred years. Zuni was further isolated from the Indian agency at Santa Fe by mere distance and lack of roads. Although it was included as part of the jurisdiction of the Eastern Pueblos, it was not until the late 1880's that any real contact was achieved between Indian Bureau representatives and the Zunis.

Meanwhile other types of contacts did develop, although Zuni remained far removed from any Anglo or Mexican towns, until Gallup grew up on the Santa Fe Railroad in the 1880's. The Anglo-American troops who entered the Navajo country in the 1840's had passing contacts at Zuni, and Colonel Doniphan's expedition in 1846 resulted in a treaty of peace between the Navajos and Zunis, which for a time checked Navajo raiding. The first intensive contacts with Anglo-Americans came in the early 1880's. Cattlemen were moving into western New Mexico and began to run cattle in the vicinity of Zuni. The usual conflict over springs and grazing land began. Senator Logan of New Mexico and others attempted to appropriate land which the Zunis claimed. Surveys were run and several of the important Zuni water sources were included in lands taken by Anglos. The controversy which developed generated antagonisms between the Zunis and the new settlers, but the efforts of the Indian Bureau and the War Department restrained the encroachments. Nevertheless, fairly serious hostilities did develop, as a result of Anglo theft of Zuni horses. In 1889 a fight occurred when Zuni protested one such theft and at least five Zunis were shot by Anglo ranchers. The Zunis called Army troops from Fort Wingate who besieged the rustlers and took them prisoner. Boundary and water hole disputes continued, but with no more bloodshed.

Meanwhile, another sort of contact with Anglos had developed which resulted in some Zunis making a wider acquaintance with Anglo culture. In 1879 a young ethnologist, Frank Hamilton Cushing, became interested in studying Zuni as a surviving primitive culture and came to live at the village. He was accepted hospitably and, as he and his wife continued residence at Zuni, he eventually was admitted to membership in the War Society of the village. After successfully balking a threat to his life, he was permitted to carry on intensive study of Zuni customs and before his death published many descriptions of ceremony, social organization, and daily life. Cushing's residence led to many other friendly contacts with Anglos for Zunis, including a visit to Washington and the eastern United States by a group of Zuni elders, some of whom came back with attitudes very favorable to acceptance of new influences from Anglo culture. One of the visitors to Washington, Pedro Pino, became a center of controversy in the village over acceptance of new ways, a controversy which during the 1880's developed into mild factionalism.

In 1889, after some preliminary contact which had extended over a dozen years, the Presbyterian Board of Missions established a school in Zuni in which more than one hundred Zuni children enrolled almost immediately. The Christian Reformed Church sent a missionary to Zuni in 1897. The Gospel of John was translated into the Zuni language and the church worked steadily down through 1955, converting an occasional Zuni to Protestantism. This missionary program was augmented in 1908 by the establishment by the Christian Reformed Church of a school which grew slowly until, by 1946, it had 150 pupils. In 1920 the Catholic missionary program was reinstituted, and a church, monastery, and school were built during the next few years.

About 1928 two more anthropologists took up residence at Zuni and made more intensive studies of ceremonial and other aspects of Zuni life. By 1930 attitudes of secrecy of the type long prevalent among the Eastern Pueblos concerning the religion had grown up among the Zunis. One anthropologist was ousted from Zuni in the early 1930's when he attempted to study methods of child training. On the other hand, by 1928 male ownership and inheritance of land had been taken over from Anglo culture and were well established.

The government program for the Zunis was also expanded as the years passed. In 1898–99 a smallpox epidemic struck Zuni, killing many people. Government efforts to vaccinate the people were resisted. The first government school at Zuni was established in 1896 when the Indian Bureau changed its policy of subsidizing mission schools among Indians and took over the Presbyterian school as a government day school.

A sub-agency of the Santa Fe Indian Bureau office was set up in the 1920's at Blackrock, three miles east of Zuni, where a hospital and agency buildings were established and where much later, in 1943, a junior high school was built. A sub-agent was in charge, who used government funds and Zuni labor to construct a reservoir and develop irrigation land.

By an act of the U.S. Congress in 1935, the Zuni land area was increased from the 17,635 acres of the old Spanish grant to 352,046 acres. The school programs of the Indian Bureau, the Catholic St. Anthony Mission school, and the Christian Reformed Church were all in operation by 1940, and all Zuni children were enrolled in one or another of these schools. This exposure to Anglo thought did not, however, bring an end to traditional Zuni life and religion. Following World War II, in which more than two hundred young Zuni men served, a serious controversy developed within the village over enforced participation in the village ceremonials. Some twenty Zuni war veterans were forced out of the village because of their refusal to participate.

In 1950 there were 2,563 Zunis living on the reservation and 547 living in Gallup and elsewhere off the reservation. The main village of Zuni was lived in by many throughout the year, but there were well-established permanent villages also at three other places on the reservation — Pescado, Nutria, and Ojo Caliente. About one hundred Anglos also lived on the reservation as teachers, missionaries, traders, or government employees of the federal Indian Bureau.

Zuni contacts thus differed somewhat from those of the Eastern Pueblos, being characterized by very little in the way of relationship with Mexicans during the Anglo period, by lesser contact with Catholic priests until after 1920, by more overt hostility in relations with Anglos, and by lesser contact with growing Anglo communities. There were also more than fifty years of close contact with a Protestant missionary group, comparable only with Laguna in this respect. Similar developments took place in regard to early land pressure with subsequent expansion of the land base as among the Eastern Pueblos. Factionalism, while present, was not disruptive until the late 1940's.

Although similar to Zuni in the lateness of development of intensive contacts, the history of the Hopis shows many important differences from Zuni. In the first place, at the beginning of Anglo contacts, the Hopis, while numbering about the same as the Zunis, were distributed in seven different villages. Instead of showing a tendency to concentrate there was rather a tendency, most marked especially after 1900, to separate and found new villages. Thus the early contacts with Anglos impinged in very different ways on the widely separated Hopi settlements, and the course of culture change varied considerably from one village, or at least one group of mesa villages, to the next.

The Hopis were even more isolated than the Zunis by geographical location from the town and city growth of the invading Anglos. They were not included along with Zuni under the administration of the Santa Fe Indian Agency and in fact cannot be said to have been administered by the Indian Bureau at all until about 1887. During the forty years between the beginning of the Anglo invasion and the establishment of a continuously operating agency at Keams Canyon, a few miles east of the easternmost Hopi village, Hopi contacts with Anglos were frequent, but largely with passing parties who did not return and who did not set up any form of continuing relationship. In this there was something of a continuation of the conditions of the Spanish period, but the passing contacts were nevertheless much more frequent.

Earliest contacts with Anglos were very fleeting and in general friendly. Parties of fur trappers visited the pueblos briefly in 1826–1828. In 1834, however, a party of Anglo trappers attempted to raid some Hopi gardens and were resisted by the Hopis. The trappers shot fifteen to twenty Hopis with no loss of life on their side. There was during this period continuous friction between Hopis and Navajos; the latter were steadily moving westward into what Hopis regarded as their land for some fifty miles surrounding the villages. In 1850 a delegation of Hopis went to Santa Fe to discuss the Navajo encroachments with the new government in the Territory of New Mexico. The Hopis were told of Anglo efforts to control the Navajos. Subsequently through the 1850's and 1860's various government surveyors and investigators visited the Hopi villages briefly to obtain information, and conducted themselves in ways that made for good relations, e.g., paying for rather than demanding goods and services. So that by the time an agency was set up at Keams Canyon there was a widespread favorable feeling toward the Anglos, in contrast with a generally unfavorable attitude toward Mexicans. In fact, a view had grown up that the Anglo-Americans were a race in Hopi myth called the Bahana who were to come out of the east and help the Hopis. Although one Indian Bureau agent offended Hopis in 1866 by trying to persuade them to move to better lands in the Tonto Basin in central Arizona, such actions of the U. S. troops as the restraining of the Utes and Navajos generally contributed to the growth of the favorable Bahana conception of the Anglos.

In 1858 the newly established Mormons in Utah, in the course of their explorations of the Southwest for favorable locations for agricultural colonies, became interested in the Hopis. The Mormon Jacob Hamblin tried for six or seven years to convert the Hopis to the Mormon religion. He came to know many village leaders intimately, learning something of the language, and held long conferences and discussions with them. He also took some Hopis to the Mormon area of settlement in Utah and made an effort to persuade the whole population to go there and settle. He was cordially received throughout his life and made a favorable impression on the Hopis with whom he came in contact, but his efforts at conversion failed completely; the major result of his activities was the founding of a small colony of Mormons near Moenkopi, the westernmost Hopi village.

In 1864, just as Navajo raiding was finally stopped, a severe drought struck the Hopi country, lasting long enough to deplete most of the food stores which Hopis always tried to keep for three years ahead. A delegation of Hopis went to the newly-established capital of the Territory of Arizona to see what help they could obtain. They were misunderstood in their requests and all were thrown in jail. They were promptly released, but the Territory had no means for helping the starving Hopis. As the drought continued, an epidemic of smallpox broke out in the Hopi villages and many Indians died. As a result of the almost impossible conditions in the villages, a considerable number of Hopi families left and took up residence at Zuni. They lived there for a year or more and when they returned they brought back with them three new cultural influences from Zuni — some knowledge of the Spanish language, a new style of pottery decoration, and some Zuni ceremonials.

In 1874 the Indian Bureau decided to establish an agency for the Hopis. Offices and a school, run by the Protestant Mission board, were set up at Keams Canyon, named for an Anglo trader established there. At this time there were eight villages. On First Mesa, nearest to the agency, were the Hopi communities of

Walpi and Sichomovi, and Hano — occupied by descendants of the Tewas who had settled in the Hopi country after the Pueblo Rebellion. On Second Mesa were Mishongnovi, Shungopovi, and Shipaulovi — all Hopi villages. On Third Mesa was Oraibi — the largest of all — with a population of one thousand. Still farther west was Moenkopi, a colony of Oraibi. The total population of the Hopi villages was estimated at 1,950 by the Bureau of Indian Affairs, a decrease of several hundred compared with the probable population during the Mexican period, undoubtedly due to the decimation of the population during the famine and epidemics of the 1860's.

In 1881 the transcontinental railroad — the Atlantic and Pacific — was built across northern Arizona about sixty miles to the south of the Hopi villages, not close to the villages as was the case in the Eastern Pueblos. This development, together with the continued efforts of the Mormons to convert the Hopis, led the government to take steps to protect the Hopi land. By executive order, a reservation was created surrounding the Hopi villages, extending to some fifty miles north and south of the immediate area of the villages and surrounded by the large reservation created in northern Arizona and New Mexico for the Navajo Indians. The Hopi Reservation was established in 1882, involved no treaty with the Indians, and, in the words of the order, was not exclusively for the Hopis, but rather "for whatever tribes the Secretary of the Interior may designate." Hopis shortly began to range through an area much larger than the reservation encompassed. By the 1890's a few Hopis who had acquired cattle ran their stock as far east as Ganado, as far northwest as Shonto, and as far south as Hopi Buttes.

Missionaries, working in the traditional evangelical style of the Protestants, rather than in the manner of the Mormons, had before this made an entry into the Hopi country. In 1870 a Moravian mission was established at Oraibi. In 1875 the Baptists established a mission on Second Mesa at Mishongnovi. A Mennonite missionary, H. R. Voth, was stationed at Oraibi in 1893. Voth learned the Hopi language and worked actively for more than a decade converting a number of Oraibi persons through his mission and school. He also made intensive observations of Hopi ceremonies and published careful reports on many of those which he saw. At that time Anglos and other outsiders were not barred from these ceremonies, but the publication of Voth's reports led to the growth of some secrecy.

In 1887 the Indian Bureau established its first school — at Keams Canyon — and asked the Hopis to send their children down from the mesa villages to be taught and boarded at the school. Hano, the village of Tewa-speaking people on First Mesa, immediately complied. From each village a child or two was sent but most people at Oraibi refused. Oraibi had also refused the government's request for a census in 1871.

The village headman at Oraibi was named Loloma. During the early 1880's he, with some other Hopi leaders, accompanied trader Keams, who spoke some Hopi, to Washington to ask for action against the encroachments by Navajos on the Hopi Reservation. While in Washington Loloma and the other leaders were advised to bring their villages down off the mesa tops and settle nearer their fields and grazing areas. It was urged that in this way they might better fend off the Navajo encroachments. Loloma and the others listened, but knew that Hopis could not be persuaded to move from the mesas where they had dug underground ceremonial chambers and become established during the three centuries since Utes, Navajos, and Spaniards had steadily driven them up out of the valleys. Loloma was nevertheless impressed with much of what he saw in the United States and came back with attitudes more favorable toward sending children to school. He was opposed, however, by another man at Oraibi who professed to believe that Loloma's leadership was in conflict with Hopi sacred traditions. There was dissent particularly from Loloma's inclination to regard Whites as the Bahana.

Over a ten-year period the people of Oraibi refused to meet the quotas for children to go to the new boarding school at Keams Canyon. The village slowly split into two determined factions. A precipitating incident was an attempt by the Indian Bureau to allot the Hopi lands into individual holdings, in accordance with the Land Allotment Act of 1887. In 1891 surveyors came to the Hopi country to begin work. All the villages opposed this. Walpi sent a petition to Washington to stop the action. Oraibi's leaders said that they would pull up the surveyors' stakes and burn the school. Troops sent to discipline the Oraibi leaders were resisted. This resistance resulted in five of the Oraibi leaders being held in custody for a time at Fort Wingate, and established Oraibi in the minds of the Indian agent as a recalcitrant and hostile village. Nevertheless, the Hopi protests against land allotment were successful and the program was not carried through on the Hopi Reservation.

Within Oraibi factionalism steadily developed, centering around disputes over the legitimate control of certain ceremonies and the clan lands. Loloma and his rival opposed one another on these religious matters, and the rival appeared to be questioning Loloma's legitimate claim to the village chieftainship. As the split widened, many new developments took place. Anglos began coming to see the annual Snake Dances, viewing them as spectacular primitive customs. At the same time anthropologists, like Stephen and Fewkes, took up residence in First Mesa villages and began studies of the Hopi culture. In 1894 a Baptist mission was established at the foot of First Mesa at a place called Polacca where a few Hopi-Tewa families from Hano had recently built houses. In the same year the Indian Bureau, now pushing its school program rapidly, set up day schools at Polacca and Oraibi. In 1897 a government day school was also established at Toreva just below Second Mesa.

The government efforts to get Hopis to adopt horse-drawn farm implements, such as plows and cultivators, began to meet with some success. Traders were now establishing themselves at the bottoms of the mesas where their stores were more convenient than Keam's old trading post at Keams Canyon — Lorenzo Hubbell below Third Mesa near Oraibi, and Tom Polacca, a Hopi-Tewa who was growing prosperous from cattle raising, at the foot of First Mesa at Polacca. At the World's Columbian Exposition in Chicago in 1893 some of the sacred Hopi ceremonial objects collected by the anthropologists and by trader Keams were exhibited. The Hopis reacted strongly against this sacrilege, and the tendency toward secrecy in connection with the ceremonials increased — a secrecy which had long been a

tradition among the Eastern Pueblos. In 1898–99 a smallpox epidemic again
struck the Hopi villages and some Hopis died as a result. Silversmithing, a craft
borrowed from the Zunis who, in turn, had borrowed it from the Navajos, was
introduced among the Hopi in 1890 and became a paying craft at Walpi. In the
acceptance of the new ways the people of First Mesa, and especially the Hopi-
Tewa there, were generally first. Here there was cooperation with the government
agents; here there was interest, especially on the part of the Tewas, in economic
enterprise and the amassing of wealth. A Tewa woman, Nampeyo, began to make
a living — like Maria of San Ildefonso many years later — by selling pottery whose
shapes and designs were based on prehistoric models dug up by archaeologists.

In Oraibi there were also tendencies toward the acceptance of some of the
new ways. Some Oraibians had later sent children to the government school after
the refusal in 1891. The people of Oraibi who inclined this way accepted the
leadership of the legitimate village chief, Loloma. He and his followers were
called the "friendlies" by the Hopis when they spoke English. But Loloma and
his supporters were bitterly opposed by his rival, Lomahongyoma, and his followers who were described as the "hostiles." The names were, however, misleading
since the basic issues involved seemed to be less the attitudes toward Anglos and
their culture than disputes over Hopi ceremonial propriety. By 1898 the trouble
had developed to the point where Lomahongyoma and his chief supporter Yokioma were defying the authority of Loloma in open meeting and even offering
threats of violence. In this year the leaders of the two factions began giving certain important ceremonies in dual fashion, that is, one giving the ceremony for
his faction of the village, the other for his faction. There was no cooperation ceremonially between the two groups and yet there was no precedent in Hopi tradition
for this fission of ceremonies within the same village.

In 1904, when Loloma was succeeded in the proper succession of the chieftainship by Tewaquaptewa, the hostiles invited a group of families from Shungopovi of similar attitudes to themselves to live at Oraibi. Tewaquaptewa, the village chief, opposed this on the ground that rain had been scant, crops short, and
there was not enough food to go around in Oraibi. His declaration was flouted by
Yokioma, now leader of the other faction, and the Shungopovi people stayed on.
More difficulties appeared during the year 1906 over the right to give certain
ceremonies and also over the rightful ownership of certain pieces of land. The
village was completely divided into hostile camps and finally Yokioma proposed
that there should be a bloodless battle to settle the matter. Since the hostility had
become too great for anyone to bear in the village, then each faction would try
to push the other out in a formal pushing contest. The defeated faction would
then have to abide by the result, move, and build houses elsewhere. The pushing
contest, in which Yokioma served as the object to be pushed across a line on the
ground, was held, and the "hostiles" under the leadership of Yokioma lost. The
hostiles, numbering about half the village of some twelve hundred moved to the
north on Third Mesa and built a new village called Hotevilla.

The immediate effects of this split were to bring the Indian agency into action
in a belated effort to "maintain peace." Behaving much as they had when the

"hostiles" threatened war with the government troops and death to Loloma in 1891, the superintendent from Keams Canyon appeared on the scene and arrested many "hostile" men including all their principal leaders and sent them to jail for a year. This left many of the families in the new village of Hotevilla without men and hence times were hard. At the same time the agent announced that the leaders of the "friendly" faction, Tewaquaptewa and one of his assistants, would have to go to school for a time to learn civilized ways. Hence the leader in the new crisis was shipped away to boarding school for four years at Riverside, California. When he came back he was strongly anti-Christian and refused to let anyone who had accepted or shown favorable inclinations toward Christianity live in Oraibi. Meanwhile, by letter he had refused permission for a slightly relenting group from Hotevilla to return to Oraibi, and this group had set up still a third village at Bakabi not far from Hotevilla.

Tewaquaptewa's new policy of excluding Christians from Oraibi after his return from Riverside in 1910 resulted in the stimulus to still another settlement — New or Lower Oraibi at the foot of Third Mesa. Here were established the big trading post of Lorenzo Hubbell and the Mennonite mission as well as a government day school. Steadily during the next decades New Oraibi grew and Old Oraibi declined in population, until in 1955 Old Oraibi had a population of less than one hundred and New Oraibi was larger than Oraibi had been before 1906, with a population of over fifteen hundred.

People had not relocated their villages intact on the low ground below the mesas as the Indian Bureau had suggested, but nevertheless new villages in the valley had sprung up, and the below-mesa villages became the location of the alien influences such as mission, school, and store, and the places of settlement for the disaffected and the acceptors of new ideas.

After 1907 the Indian Bureau again tried to carry through its program of individual distribution of land among the Hopi, but again failed to allot more than a few acres. Hopi livestock continued to increase and, at the same time, Navajo population and sheep flocks increased even more rapidly. The result was that the period 1910–1943 was one of border conflict between the two tribes. The much greater increase in the Navajos resulted in their occupying by 1940 nearly three-quarters of what had been set aside as the Hopi Reservation. In 1943, in an effort to settle the long-standing border conflict, the Indian Bureau decided that since the Navajos actually occupied the land, and since the executive order establishing the reservation had not limited it to Hopis, that the Hopis should be confined to the one-fourth of the reservation that they actually occupied, and that the Navajos should continue to live on the rest of the Hopi Reservation. The area assigned to the Hopis was, in fact, designated as District 6, one of the grazing districts of the very large Navajo Reservation. This occurred at a time when, under the encouragement of the Indian Bureau, both Navajos and Hopis had developed their livestock to a point where it had become necessary to reduce the stock if the land were to continue usable for grazing purposes at all. So, at the same time that the Hopis were restricted to District 6, they were also urged and pressed to reduce their stock, in accordance with studies made by Indian Bureau technicians

showing how many animals the land could be expected to carry without depletion. Hopis were advised to reduce stock by 24 percent in all, but the Third Mesa
people were told that they should make a 44 percent reduction. The villages of
First and Second Mesa acquiesced, accepted the technical recommendations, and
proceeded to sell the required number of stock while putting a set of grazing
regulations into operation. Third Mesa resisted for a time, with the encouragement
of Anglo stockraisers at the borders of the reservation, but eventually accepted a
plan and began to carry it through.

In 1935 the Indian Bureau presented its proposal for tribal organization to
the Hopis and sent a technical expert to the villages to work out a plan for a tribal
constitution and council. The Hopis in that year by a majority vote accepted the
plan and in 1936 adopted a constitution and set up a tribal court. In 1937 the
first Tribal Council meeting was held. This development increased the dissension
among the Hopis. Old Oraibi, for example, refused to recognize the new Tribal
Council, as did Shungopovi. The Council's active members were nearly all from
the First Mesa villages. Instead of a unifying factor it steadily became a bone of
contention and in general was regarded by a majority of Hopis as a rubber-stamp
organization for the Indian Bureau superintendent. It was nevertheless recognized
as the official body of the "Hopi Tribe" in 1953.

The Tribal Council continued to be opposed, through non-participation, by
Old Oraibi, Bakabi, and Hotevilla, as well as Lower Moenkopi which was closely
affiliated in leadership with Old Oraibi. In addition, there was a strong opposition
centering in Shungopovi. Thus, it was a council consisting chiefly of representatives from the First Mesa villages, factions of Second Mesa villages, and New
Oraibi. The procedures by which members were elected did not conform to those
established in the constitution. The Bureau of Indian Affairs, in officially declaring
it to be the tribal body, took the position that it should strive to make itself a truly
representative group. Nevertheless by 1955 there seemed to be no indication that
the non-participating groups were moving toward participation. They often sent
observers to the Tribal Council meetings, but in connection with issues in which
they felt themselves really concerned they held meetings of their own. In 1954 a
movement grew up on Third Mesa for bringing together old Oraibi, Hotevilla, and
Shungopovi "conservatives." Meetings were held with reference to several issues.

The issues which were involved were the building of a road with government
funds across Third Mesa and Second Mesa, the granting of leases to oil companies for drilling on the Hopi Reservation, and the bringing of suit against the
government for dispossession of Hopi lands, in accordance with the claims procedure established by the United States Congress. The position of the conservative groups was complex but might be briefly stated as follows: The land on which
Hopis lived and over which they had ranged customarily for generations was
sacred, having been laid out as Hopi land in the days of the supernaturals when
the ancestors of the present clans settled on the Hopi Mesas. The land could not
be lost to the Hopis because that would be contrary to sacred law. Thus the Hopis
could not sue the government for land which the government had taken away
because that would be the same as admitting that the government rightfully

possessed the land and had a right to give it away. Therefore land claims procedures could not be adopted because that would be denying the everlasting Hopi possession of the land. Similarly, leases to oil companies and the building of roads in places where the government engineers advised would be morally wrong. There could be no compromise on this basic point. But also it was advanced by the conservatives repeatedly that a road would bring merely fast automobiles and bad influences on young people and that money from oil leases would do the same. Such "advantages" as more money and quick transportation could not balance the breaking of the sacred relationship between Hopis and the land.

It was recognized by the conservatives that many Hopis had already broken this relationship. People living in New Oraibi had appropriated lands to which they had no clan right, but which the government had said they could use. Thus it was clear that Hopis were not all the same anymore. The conservatives, however, were clear on their position and said that they would not compromise on any of the issues that had a sacred base. It was similar considerations of sacredness that had been responsible through the years for the consistent refusal of Hopis in the mesa villages to have any wells drilled with government assistance to take the place of the springs at the base of the mesas from which Hopis obtained their domestic water supply.

In 1947 the Indian Bureau offered irrigated land to Hopi families on the Colorado River Indian Reservation, 250 miles southwest of the Hopi country, at Poston, Arizona. This was a measure designed to ease the land pressure resulting from the granting of most of the Hopi Reservation for Navajo use. Seventeen Hopi families took up residence there and slowly through the years a few more Hopis resettled as farmers on the government irrigation project at Poston, Arizona. To remain as permanent residents they had to renounce their rights in the Hopi country and become participants in the Council of the Colorado River Tribes, joining thus with Navajo and other Indians who had also resettled, as well as with the Mohave and Chemehuevi Indians already resident there. However, as a result of Mohave hostility and other factors, by 1955 no more Hopis migrated to the Colorado River Reservation.

By 1955 less than 2 percent of all Hopis had become practicing members of the various Christian sects which had been carrying on missionary work among them for seventy-five years. A Baptist church had been built at Walpi on First Mesa in addition to the other missions already mentioned. For the great majority of Hopis the native religion still functioned, but by no means in the manner in which it had before 1900. On Third Mesa particularly change was great; Old Oraibi had lost many of its ceremonies through fission, and New Oraibi people had reinstituted only a few of the old cycle. Nevertheless, the religious affiliation of the overwhelming majority of Hopis was still Hopi rather than Christian. The actions of some Anglos had confirmed the Hopi in the maintenance of their religion. During the 1920's particularly, when the Indian Bureau seemed to be determined to suppress much of Indian religion in New Mexico and Arizona, groups of Anglos took action. On the ground of religious liberty in the United States, Anglo organizations succeeded in eliminating the Indian Bureau Code of Religious

Offenses and in influencing public opinion generally in the direction of tolerance of the Indian religions. Tewaquaptewa, village chief of Old Oraibi, especially was in contact during the 1930's with Anglos taking this position. Certain Hopi ceremonies, such as the Snake Dances, were attended in large numbers by Anglos who began to accept them rather than work against them.

One feature of the Hopi viewpoint which Hopis said stemmed from the old religion was opposition to war. During World War II Hopi youths claimed exemption from military service on this ground, and the United States government recognized their position as conscientious objectors. Most Hopis who were drafted served in the armed forces, but a few were conscientious objectors. This position gained them the interest of some religious groups in the United States, such as the Society of Friends and the Fellowship of Reconciliation, who held that, in this respect, the Hopis were far advanced in civilization over the majority of Anglos.

As did the Zunis, the Hopis also gained recognition of their religion as being on a par with other religions in the United States through their protests against imitation and use of their sacred masks and costumes in secular contexts. In the 1940's and 1950's Hopis objected to the employment of copies of sacred paraphernalia in secular celebrations in New Mexico, Arizona, and Colorado, and obtained apologies from the persons and organizations involved.

From 1910 on Hopi population steadily increased. By 1955 it was double what it had been in the 1850's. Nine villages still existed on the tops of the three mesas, three on each. Below the mesas there were three villages — Polacca below First Mesa, Toreva below Second, and New Oraibi below Third. In addition, Upper and Lower Moenkopi existed at the far western edge of the Hopi country, and Hopis also lived at the agency town of Keams Canyon. In Winslow, a railroad town sixty miles south of the Hopi country, there were three to four hundred permanent Hopi residents. A considerable colony of Hopis were also living more or less permanently in Los Angeles. Furthermore, Hopis lived seasonally in most of the large cities and towns in Arizona, where many were well established as silversmiths and practitioners of other crafts.

Later Hopi history presents the picture of a tribe moving in the space of one hundred years from an aboriginal condition of homogeneous village communities to an enclaved heterogeneous collection of social segments. Until approximately the 1880's they had changed little — and only in unimportant ways — from what they had been when Coronado arrived; only perhaps more conscious of and more determined to hold on to their aboriginal way of life after having been able to compare it with what the Spaniards offered. During the hundred years of contact with the Anglos, with no very systematic attempt on the part of the Anglos to force their ways on the Hopis, the latter had changed profoundly. Most important of the indirect influences were the promotion of heterogeneity in outlook through schools and the growth of communication with Anglo communities. There is no question that the Hopi way had persisted into the 1960's, but it existed within a milieu of very great heterogeneity. Those who spoke of themselves as Hopis ranged from militant Baptists to rigid followers of the Old Oraibi "traditional" leadership. They ranged from college graduates aware of most of the elements of Anglo culture, to aged men and women who had the barest acquaintance with only a few material items of Anglo culture. They ranged from Hopi men married to vigorously progressive Tewa women, to Hopi girls married to Filipino migrants to the United States. They ranged from families still living on clan land and following through all the traditional ceremonies of their village, to families paying rent in Los Angeles on modern apartments and returning to their villages for an occasional Niman Kachina or Soyal ceremony. They ranged from men desperately wanting to obtain cash for land settlements or oil leases, to men convinced that the ancient sacred relationship to the land had nothing to do with cash.

This heterogeneity existed among Hopis in a way not duplicated among the Eastern Pueblos. Among the latter there was heterogeneity within the villages, to be sure, but each village remained a unit dominated by one faction or another and there was thus a restraint exercised over the growth of heterogeneity such as did not exist in the Hopi country. In the latter area it was possible with much greater ease for a Hopi to remove himself from the restraint of a given village atmosphere merely by moving a few hundred yards to an off-mesa village, and yet still feel strongly Hopi, since he still lived on the Hopi land and in the Hopi milieu. The dissident Eastern Pueblo, on the other hand, had to move into an Anglo-American community and thus move more definitely in the direction of renouncing his Indian heritage. The Hopi villages in their wide range of variation could harbor a much greater variety in political opinion and world view.

To say, as had become usual, that it was only a matter of time until Hopi culture would disintegrate and Hopis would become culturally assimilated was to miss the point of what was happening. The question was what form would the disintegration take and what forms of reintegration were taking place under the peculiar conditions of Hopi life. Formal education in Anglo schools did not inevitably have the result of rejection of the whole range of Hopi culture. Some of the most formally educated Hopi men and women were the most devoted to aspects of traditional Hopi religion and morality, and some were the most antagonistic to specific features of Anglo culture, particularly the religious and moral. Moreover Hopi "traditionalists" by the 1950's had the support of different sects, organizations, and individuals from among Anglos. Hopi and Anglo culture relations were not simple. The heterogeneity of the two different cultural systems insured more complex results of the contact than simple cultural assimilation.

Navajos

OF ALL THE TRIBES of the Southwest, the Athapaskan-speaking people who came to be called the Navajos and the Apaches by the Spaniards were the most radically changed by their contacts with European culture. The bases of change were established during the Spanish period of contact, although important processes set in motion then did not work themselves out fully until the Anglo-American period. It may seem something of a paradox, in view of these profound influences of the Spaniards on the Navajos, that contacts between the two peoples were less intimate and of shorter duration than those between Spaniards and any other Southwestern Indians except the Yuman-speaking peoples.

When Coronado entered New Mexico in 1540 there were small groups of nomadic people in the country west of the Rio Grande Pueblo villages. It seems probable that they were ancestors of the Navajos. Just how far these people extended northward and westward we do not know. There are two theories: one, that they were confined to tributaries of the San Juan River, such as Gobernador and Largo canyons, and another that they were fairly widely dispersed, as far southward as Acoma and as far westward as the Hopi villages. The latter seems more likely in view of the fairly wide distribution within this area that they had attained by about 1700. They were people of relatively simple culture as compared with the Pueblo villagers. They were probably in a state of transition from a nomadic hunting and gathering way of life, which they had pursued in a long southward migration into the Pueblo country. However, by the early 1600's they were a partially nomadic people who practiced agriculture. They relied much more heavily on hunting and wild foods than did the Pueblos, and their settlements were considerably smaller. They lacked the elaborately organized religious life of the Pueblos, although they were beginning to be influenced by it. Their ceremonial and social organizations were looser, generally simpler, and less definitely oriented. They may have been to some extent predatory on the Pueblos, but there is a good deal of evidence also that they lived peacefully in proximity to the latter. The most significant fact about them was that, at the time the Spaniards arrived, they were in a transitional state, ready to improve on what they had.

The Spaniards saw almost nothing of these people and were not sufficiently interested in them to give them a name until about 1626. Espejo and Oñate on their westward trips from the Rio Grande may have encountered some of them, calling them Querechos, or some other Spanish term for wanderer. But for the most part the Spaniards did not get into their territory until the early 1700's, and remained unconcerned about them as sources of tribute, subjects for conversion, or dangerous enemies. These western Athapaskans must have tread softly at first, showing no hostility to the Spaniards on the rare occasions when they met. On the other hand, it is probably true that the Spaniards did not know the difference between these people and the various bands of Apaches who came to the Taos and Pecos trading centers, and therefore did not distinguish between them in their accounts. Indeed, during the 1500's and early 1600's there may have been very little difference in fact between them. They were of the same language and general background.

However, by the end of the first quarter of the 1600's Spaniards had become conscious of at least one division of the Athapaskans. Father Zarate-Salmerón related in 1626 that the Jemez Pueblos spoke of people living north of them between the Chama and the San Juan rivers as Apaches of "Navaju." The latter, said the Jemez, lived between the Jemez and the Utes. In 1627 the Franciscans became sufficiently interested to provide a mission at Santa Clara, the Tewa village on the west side of the Rio Grande below San Juan, especially for work with the "Apaches of Navaju." This was founded by Father Alonso de Benavides, the Custodian of Missions of New Mexico. In describing the venture he indicated that the name "Navaju" was learned from the Tewa and meant "great planted fields." The fact that Benavides, as well as Zarate-Salmerón, used "Apaches" along with "Navaju" indicates that their affinity with other Indians to the east and west was known. It is a moot point whether Father Benavides' Tewa derivation of the word "Navaju" is correct or that of modern Tewas, who say it derives from words meaning "fields" and "to take from." However, Benavides' reference to the "Navajus" indicates that they were farming and that they seemed good prospects for a mission, although the mission he established did not produce any conversions. It was soon abandoned.

The Franciscans did not succeed in bringing any Navajos under the mission system during the 1600's. Perhaps too much concerned with the troubles that had arisen between them and the New Mexican governors in connection with the missions to the Pueblos, they were not in an expanding mood. Navajos of the western border of the Pueblo country, in touch with the Tewas and the Jemez, were undoubtedly considerably more conscious of the Spaniards than the latter were of them. They gradually acquired small numbers of sheep, horses, and even cattle.

As farmers they were subject to raids from Utes from the north and probably from other less settled Athapaskan-speaking people; this may have tended to push some groups eastward and southward into closer touch with the Pueblos. They remained quite marginal to the Spanish influences on the Rio Grande, however, until the 1680 rebellion of the Pueblos. They did not join with the Pueblos in the expulsion of the Spaniards, but the aftermath of the revolt had very important effects on the eastern Navajos. Pueblo people who left the villages after the revolt came in some numbers to hide in the canyon country where Navajos were settled

— in Gobernador and neighboring canyons. Many from different Pueblo villages
came about 1692 when news of de Vargas' coming to reconquer the Pueblos
brought fear to some villagers. After the unsuccessful attempt of the Jemez to
resist de Vargas in 1696, many Jemez people, along with the Tewas and Keres who
had joined with them, fled and settled among the Navajos. For the next thirty-five
or forty years — more than a generation — Navajos and Pueblos lived peacefully
side by side in the Jemez Plateau area.

This period was of profound influence on the eastern Navajos. There was
much intermarriage between them and the Pueblos; what became a major clan
was founded — the Coyote Pass Clan — composed of Jemez women and their descendants. The intermingling affected Navajo culture in many ways, chief of
which was the development of crafts such as weaving and pottery making and the
building of houses. The Navajo language remained dominant, however, so that
what took place was an absorption of the Pueblo people along with aspects of their
culture into Navajo society and culture, rather than the reverse. The situation also
resulted in the growth of hostilities between the northeastern Navajos and the
Spaniards. Thus during the ten years of 1706–1716 the reconstituted Navajos of
the east raided the newly re-established Spanish settlements on the Rio Grande.
Prisoners were taken on both sides and a tradition of hostility between Navajos
and Spaniards resulted.

At the same time, some Navajos developed friendly relations with the Spaniards. These were people who had moved south under the pressure of Ute depredations and settled in the vicinity of Laguna and Acoma near Mount Taylor. Here at
two places the Franciscans in 1745 began an attempt at missionization. They
established missions at Cebolleta and Encinal. The Navajos were friendly enough,
came to the missions, and listened to the missionaries for a time. They accepted
food which was obtainable at the missions, but when supplies ran short and it was
apparent that the missions were becoming poorer through lack of support by the
Franciscan organization, the Navajos lost interest. Their leaders told the missionaries that, although the Navajos had no enmity to the Spaniards, they had decided
that they could not accept Spanish ways and that Spanish gods were not their gods.
They ceased to listen to the missionaries, and after two years, the Franciscans gave
up the missions as a bad job. The Navajos of the Mount Taylor-Cebolleta area,
nevertheless, remained friendly with the Spaniards and continued trade relations
with the Laguna and Acoma villages. As a result of friendliness with the Spaniards
they came to be called "Enemy People" by the other Navajos.

During the 1700's the Navajos who had been settled in the Chama River-Go-
bernador area steadily drifted to the southwest. By the end of the 1700's there were
few, if any, left in the latter area. One leader of the Gobernador-Largo Navajos was
named Haske Lik'izhi. He was known to the Spaniards as Antonio el Pinto, or
Pintado, and was instrumental in keeping some groups at peace with the Spaniards.
The latter made him a "general" and kept him in their pay in an effort to control
the raiding of the Navajos. El Pinto persuaded many Navajos to move westward
from the Gobernador area. The gradual concentration of the Navajos westward
led to the establishment of important settlements, such as Bear Springs, or Ojo del

Oso, north of Zuni and others in the Chuska-Tunicha Mountains. At the same time, Navajos were settling in Canyon de Chelly, so that a considerable population developed in the region from Zuni northward to the San Juan River. By 1776 this region lying between the Rio Grande Pueblos and the Hopi villages became known to the Spaniards as the Province of the Navajo. It remained entirely without missions during the whole of the Spanish period and through the Mexican period.

Within the province the Navajos developed a new way of life. They farmed to an even greater extent than they had before, undoubtedly influenced by the Pueblos whom they had absorbed. But in addition they were working out a new basis of subsistence. They had acquired thousands of sheep and horses, to which they added periodically by raids on the Spanish and Pueblo settlements. The horses enabled them to become more mobile and carry out frequent raiding. At the same time the flocks of sheep contributed to a pattern of more or less settled life.

After 1800 when Antonio el Pinto died Navajos began to rely more and more on raiding the villages of New Mexico for their supply of sheep and horses and for captives whom they traded or kept. A "Mexican" clan developed among them, composed of descendants of Spanish women captives. They raided not only the Spanish but also the Pueblo settlements and came to be feared by both. The Spaniards maintained the hostilities with retaliatory raids as well as raids purely for the purpose of acquiring captives to serve them as laborers and household servants. The level of hostility against the Spaniards increased greatly in 1804–05 as a result of intensified Spanish slave raids, one of which resulted in the massacre by Lieutenant Narbona of hundreds of Navajo women and children in Canyon del Muerto. Hundreds of Navajo boys and girls by the early 1800's were growing up in Spanish homes as servants.

The twenty years after 1800 saw the development of the Navajos as raiders on a large scale. Their raiding extended to the Hopis. Even the Jemez became deadly enemies of the Navajos. The Hopis appealed to the Spaniards for help in 1818. Spaniards made a treaty with some Navajos whom they had defeated in a battle in 1819; the treaty was supposed to result in the Navajos staying west of Bluewater near Zuni but the treaty did not stick, since it applied, as the Spaniards did not understand, only to the small group whom they had beaten. In 1820 some Navajos attempted to make a peace with the Spaniards, working through Jemez, but the Jemez people so distrusted them that they killed the Navajo delegation and appealed to the Spaniards for help. Through the 1820's, especially after Mexican independence in 1824, the Navajos ran wild in northwestern New Mexico. In 1837, Navajos raided the Hopi village of Oraibi and killed or scattered almost the whole population. The Mexican government in Santa Fe remained unable to make even effective retaliatory raids, let alone control the now skilled raiders. Two young Navajos, Ganado Mucho (Many Horses) and Manuelito, began to gain fame among their people as fighting men. Warfare had definitely begun to rise to a place of great importance in Navajo culture.

The salient fact in the history of the contacts of the Navajos with the Spaniards was the maintenance of complete independence through the whole period of contact. No Navajos were ever subjected to the mission system; those at Cebolleta did not submit to mission discipline even for the two years that the Franciscans maintained the missions. Navajos were never reduced to concentrated settlements. Not even the outward forms of political controls were extended to the Navajos. The Spaniards, in fact, remained oblivious of the Navajos when Oñate began his colonization of New Mexico and they were not included in the reconquest of New Mexico by de Vargas. By the time the Navajos had become a definite tribal entity in the minds of the Spaniards — which would seem to have been about 1706 (the Apaches de Navaju of the 1620's were to them a rather vague group about whose distribution they were content to rely on other Indians' statements) — they were concerned merely about keeping them quiet by bribing leaders. The spirit of the Spanish conquest seemed to have spent itself.

This freedom from military, political, and ecclesiastical control did not carry with it a lack of opportunity for knowing about Spanish culture. Partly through direct contacts, of at least a small part of the Navajos in the vicinity of the Tewa pueblo of Santa Clara, and largely through indirect contacts by means of refugee Pueblos, the eastern Navajos over a period of some hundred years learned about and acquired domestic animals and other Spanish material culture. Those who chose to accepted and developed these in their own way and in the integration process had the help of the Pueblos whom they absorbed. Thus, there was a profound Spanish influence on the Navajo way of life — especially the economy. At the same time, there were some influences on Navajo social and religious life from the Pueblo refugees, but none from the Spaniards.

During the Mexican period the Navajos still remained free from all military, political, and ecclesiastical control. They continued to acquire items of Spanish material culture through their systematic harassment of the settled Mexican and Pueblo villages, but their social and political organization remained unchanged. Nor did they, during this period, have any contacts with Anglos which produced any lasting effect upon them. It was not until the United States undertook, as part of the terms of the Treaty of Guadalupe Hidalgo, to halt Navajo and Apache raiding, that the Navajos began to experience the contacts with Anglos which were to affect their culture so profoundly.

In the post-Spanish period the Navajos, like the Hopis, moved in the short space of one hundred years from a situation quite outside the pale of Western civilization to become an enclaved minority tightly surrounded by the dominant society and subject to a host of pressures for cultural assimilation. In this rapid change from political independence to domination by the Anglo-Americans they and the Hopis contrasted greatly with other tribes.

When the United States took over the government at Santa Fe, it faced the problem of making peace with the Navajos. In 1846, when General Kearny came to Santa Fe, the Navajos were well established in a symbiotic relationship with the Mexican and Pueblo villages of northwestern New Mexico. Raiding had become a way of life for the many independent Navajo groups scattered from the Rio Puerco to the Hopi villages. The seven thousand or more Athapaskan-speaking people, who by this time were differentiated from the Apaches, did not constitute an organized tribe. They lived as a great many different small communities — of from

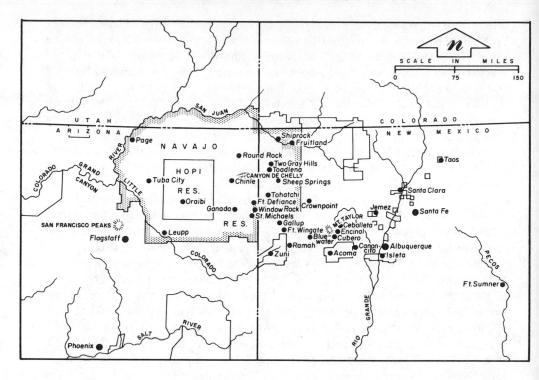

ten to forty families — each living within a defined area of agricultural and grazing land. Two or more of these sometimes united with one another for carrying out a raid, but the temporary associations resulted in no permanent wider organization. The raiding which they carried on against the Pueblo and Mexican villages was not a widely organized activity and rarely involved more than a few such groups on any occasion. The making of a raid depended on the food needs of the various communities. The objectives were food, material goods, and captives to sell or use as slaves. The killing of Pueblos or Mexicans, except in some instances of revenge, was entirely incidental to acquiring goods and animals. Raiding had become an established means of livelihood and the conduct of raids had become an institu-tionalized skill giving rise to "War Chiefs" who often paid little attention to the authority of the peacetime headmen.

When General Kearny set up headquarters at Santa Fe, he found the various Pueblos from Taos to Zuni as well as the Mexican population of northwestern New Mexico anxious to ally themselves with the Anglos for a vigorous war against the Navajos. He believed, however, that peace treaties could be made with the Navajos and that the sporadic raiding could be quickly stopped. He refused to organize a real military campaign until he had sounded out the Navajos and for that purpose sent Colonel Doniphan immediately with a company of Missouri volunteers into the Navajo country. Kearny and Doniphan were under the impression that they were dealing with a united tribe, and Doniphan proceeded to get the marks of

Navajo leaders on a treaty of peace; this took place at Bear Springs, near the present Fort Wingate on the extreme southern margin of Navajo territory. The leaders who signed included Zarcilla Largo and Narbona, headmen of groups living to the north of Bear Springs, who had authority over no more than a few hundred Navajos and who were not war leaders at all. Earlier treaties had been made with Ute Indians to the north of the Navajo country and these were kept, the Utes allying themselves with the Anglos. But the Navajo treaty had no force at all. Raids by various Navajos continued in precisely the same way as before the treaty.

During the next three years five military expeditions were launched into the Navajo country, expeditions which were often guided by "enemy" Navajos from the region of Cebolleta. Utes, Zunis, and other Pueblos helped the Anglos, but although they ranged the whole length and breadth of the Navajo country they were not engaged by any Navajos, who were uninterested in fighting for its own sake. In 1849 Colonel Washington took the field and eventually at Chinle, at the mouth of Canyon de Chelly, found three Navajo leaders again willing to talk peace. On the march, at Two Gray Hills Washington had found Narbona, signer of the Bear Springs Treaty, disposed to give up stolen animals, but in the course of the negotiations soldiers killed Narbona and incurred the enmity of his son-in-law, Manuelito (Man of Blackweed), an active and highly honored war chief of communities east of the Chuska Mountains. At Chinle a treaty was again signed by several leaders, including Zarcilla Largo, signer of the Bear Springs Treaty. Although this treaty was ratified by the United States Congress it, too, came to nothing. Raids continued as before, especially on the part of Navajos living in the eastern part of the Navajo country, often under the leadership of the widely famous Manuelito. In the four years of 1846–1850 nearly eight hundred thousand sheep and cattle and some twenty thousand horses and mules were reported stolen in northwestern New Mexico.

The War Department and the Territory of New Mexico decided that the problem of Navajo raids could not be settled with treaties and that direct forcible control of the Navajos would have to be undertaken. A military post with four companies of cavalry, one of artillery, and two of infantry was established. The site was at what later came to be called Fort Defiance in the heart of the Navajo country, but west of the area of the heaviest concentration of Navajos. The Navajos regarded this as an invasion of their country. Nevertheless, at first they offered no direct resistance to the companies of soldiers permanently stationed at the fort. In addition, an Indian agent was sent into the Navajo country by the Department of the Interior. The first worked from Jemez but the second in 1853 established himself at Sheep Spring, northeast of Fort Defiance, and set to work to persuade Navajo leaders to be peaceful. He had great success with Zarcilla Largo who continued to be a power among many Navajos. The Indian agent, Captain Henry Linn Dodge, also brought a blacksmith to his agency and began the instruction of Navajos in working metal. Dodge's personal efforts with Navajo leaders resulted in a period of relative peace, but in 1856 Dodge was killed by Apaches on a trip to the south, and trouble developed between the men of the Army post and Navajos in the area.

In 1858 the post commander set aside a large area of grazing land for the horses of the fort, excluding Navajo sheep from what had long been an important pasture. To enforce the regulation which the Navajos regarded as a ruthless appropriation of land, Navajo horses found on the pasture were shot. Feeling rose and a Negro slave belonging to the post commander was killed. Zarcilla Largo, who was regarded by the soldiers as "head chief" of the Navajos, was ordered to give up the murderer. He tried to settle the matter in accordance with Navajo custom by paying blood money, but this was refused, and the Navajos then dragged to death a Mexican slave and offered his body to the Anglos. This was not accepted and the post commander set out to punish the Navajos for not complying with his order. Three successive expeditions marched against Navajos with no results except the killing of a few peaceful Indians. Finally another treaty was prepared which was signed by a group headed by a man called Herrero (Iron-worker) who had learned blacksmithing from Dodge; Herrero was then appointed "head chief."

This treaty, like the others, had no effect, and the soldiers continued their campaign throughout the year 1859. The expeditions covered the whole territory lived in by Navajos, from Zuni northward to the San Juan River and from Mount Taylor westward to Marsh Pass. Although they acquainted the Navajos with the number of soldiers which the Anglos could muster, there was no appreciable effect on Navajo raiding, and no Navajos surrendered. The Navajos were impressed with the fact that the Anglos had enlisted the aid of all neighboring Indians; enemy Navajos, Utes, Zunis, Hopis, and other Pueblos were acting as scouts or troops with the Anglos.

Despite the show of Anglo strength, the reaction of the majority of the Navajos was not to sue for peace, but rather to try to drive the Anglos out of their country. The right of the Anglos to prevent them from the generations-long raiding of the New Mexicans had been questioned and resisted from the first. Invasion of the Navajo territory at Fort Defiance was resented, and trouble with, and the encroachment of, troops there fostered hatred. Now leaders who had tried for peace, like Herrero, and others who had never tried for anything but a continuance of the old life, like Manuelito and Barboncito, joined forces for an attack on the Anglos. Zarcilla Largo, who remained determined in his attempts to bring peace, and an important leader in the area close to Fort Defiance, Ganado Mucho, advised against war. But the war leaders went ahead and planned an attack on Fort Defiance itself. In April 1860 they carried it out with a force of more than two thousand warriors armed more with bows and arrows than with guns. The artillery of the soldiers was too much for them and after a two-hour battle they were badly routed with large numbers killed and wounded. The attempt to drive the Anglos out of their territory had failed, but the raids continued. After the attack on Fort Defiance the raiding extended as far east as Santa Fe and as far south as Zuni. The renewed vigor of the raids led New Mexicans to organize for retaliation; in a short time they took one hundred Navajo prisoners, mostly women and children who were disposed of according to custom as slaves. It was reported about this time that there were as many as five to six thousand Navajo slaves living with families in the New Mexican villages.

Although they were beaten at Fort Defiance, it began to appear to the Navajos that the Anglos were weakening. In 1861 the fort was abandoned and troops were withdrawn except for a small force at Fort Fauntleroy (later to become Fort Wingate). The United States Civil War was drawing the attention of the government elsewhere, and for two years it appeared to the Navajo war leaders that they were succeeding in their attempt to oust the Anglos. However, as Union troops gained control of New Mexico Territory a determined effort was launched to keep the lines of communication with the far west open. This resulted in an order to destroy at all costs the Navajo threat to white settlers. General Carleton, in charge of New Mexico Territorial affairs, assigned Colonel Kit Carson to carry out the order, instructing him to kill all Navajo men who offered resistance and to take the women and children prisoner. Carson undertook his assignment in 1863 at a time when probably a majority of Navajos had begun to believe that they were stronger than the Anglo-Americans who had interfered with them hardly at all since the defense of Fort Defiance.

Carson worked out a variation of the plan for killing off all the Navajo men, a task not possible with the seven hundred volunteers who came to him from the New Mexico settlements. He first occupied himself with the Mescalero Apaches in southern New Mexico, who surrendered to him four-hundred strong and agreed to remain on a reservation set aside for them at Bosque Redondo (Fort Sumner) on the Little Pecos River in eastern New Mexico. General Carleton then held a meeting with Navajo leaders at Cubero; he offered them land with the Mescaleros on the Pecos and rations until they could get well started in a farming life, if they would give up their raiding. The Enemy Navajos of Mount Taylor, under Sandoval, agreed and were immediately sent to Bosque Redondo. Barboncito of the Canyon de Chelly Navajos, who had been a major leader in the attack on Fort Defiance, affirmed that the Navajos were just as strong as the Anglos. Other Navajo leaders backed him up and said they would stay in their homeland. It was now up to Kit Carson to find a way to control the Navajos.

Carson with his seven hundred New Mexico volunteers marched into the heart of the Navajo country and re-established Fort Defiance which he adopted as his headquarters. In early 1863 before the meeting at Cubero, the Navajos had driven off cattle, sheep, and horses from Isleta, San Felipe, and Albuquerque. In June, an official declaration of war in the form of a General Order was made against the Navajos. General Carleton ordered Carson to force the Navajos to surrender to him at Fort Defiance where they would be shipped to Bosque Redondo. Carson began a systematic campaign of destroying all Navajo means of livelihood. His soldiers tore up cornfields wherever they found them and slaughtered sheep by the thousands, leaving them in piles to rot. They ranged through all the areas of heavy Navajo settlement. Navajos began to scatter to find food — some to southern New Mexico and southern Arizona, some westward to Navajo Mountain, some to join with Apaches in the White Mountains, many women to Jemez Pueblo. In the winter of 1863 Navajos began coming in to Fort Defiance to give up. Carson's decisive move was the invasion of Canyon de Chelly in early 1864. He marched a force to the west end of the canyon; another detachment entered from the east and marched through the canyon, destroying cornfields and cutting down peach trees as they went. They killed no one, but gave plenty of food to those they captured. A second detachment followed the same course, again dealing in kindly fashion with the Navajos who did not escape them. This demonstration of Carson's policy so impressed the Navajos of Canyon de Chelly that immediately more than two hundred followed him back to Fort Defiance — for food and security. Hearing that Carson was not slaughtering them, steadily more and more gathered there. Within a few weeks there were twenty-four hundred at the fort ready to go to Fort Sumner. Eventually eight thousand Navajos were taken in this manner and made the trip to Fort Sumner. Probably in the neighborhood of fifteen hundred to two thousand remained scattered over the Navajo country or outside it and never went to Bosque Redondo.

The Navajos who were sent into captivity underwent what became a focal experience in their contact with the Anglos. For four years they were thrown together into a single, closely supervised, and regulated group. Their way of life was completely altered from roving herders to thoroughly sedentary prisoners. They were expected to farm, but they never fully accepted the new dispensation. Disease and confinement reduced their numbers and gave them a sense of desperation. The memory of the "Long Walk" to and from Bosque Redondo and of the suffering there stood as an historical incident with as much significance for Navajos as the Civil War, for example, for Anglo-Americans. Events came to be dated from it, the sense of Navajo identity was heightened by it, and attitudes towards all Anglo-Americans were influenced by it.

At Bosque Redondo the eventual eight thousand Navajos were confined within a fort along with the four hundred Mescalero Apaches already rounded up. They were counted regularly and rations were issued to all. They had been allowed to bring some sheep with them on the three hundred-mile walk, but they were expected to farm the irrigated land along the river and become self-supporting as soon as possible. They were divided into twelve units within the fort, some six hundred in a unit, each with a head man. Soldiers were assigned to show them how to build rectangular adobe houses and to help them get started raising crops on the farmland which had already been prepared. The twelve leaders of the new tribal divisions were to constitute a "chief's council" for dealing with the Army officer in charge. The Navajos were thrown into close proximity to the four hundred New Mexican soldiers manning the fort, the four hundred surrendered Mescalero Apaches, and some four hundred Enemy Navajos from the Mount Taylor area. A Catholic school was started promptly, and General Carleton looked forward to a speedy progress toward civilization for the Indians.

The Navajos submitted to the daily counting and accepted the rations, but in little else did they show themselves willing to accept the routine planned for them. They dug round holes in the ground for houses and covered them with brush; they made no effort to learn the adobe construction. They tried to maintain their sheep, but there was not enough forage. The officer in charge steadily required them to get rid of their stock, so that they could get established as farmers. The work of planting the first crops, partly carried through by soldiers since the Navajos were not familiar with irrigation techniques, came to nothing for various reasons. Consequently, few Navajos paid much attention to the second planting. After all, they were receiving rations all the time. Quarrels broke out between Mescaleros and Navajos; early in 1865 the Mescaleros walked out and were not brought back. Navajos also began to sneak off. Finding that the Comanches were not far away, some sneaked out and raided them. They were brought back, but others crept away and never returned. A smallpox epidemic struck in 1865 and 2,321 Navajos were dead within a few months. Less and less of the cropland was planted. Corrupt agents in charge dealt in rations and blankets and the care of the Indians grew worse. In 1867 quarrels with the soldiers resulted in the killing of five soldiers. The Navajos steadily became more demoralized. Finally Barboncito, who had been recognized as "head chief," made a trip to Washington in 1868. The War Department was aware that General Carleton's plan for relocating all the Navajos was not working.

After an investigation by General Sherman, the decision was made to allow the Navajos to go back to a defined portion of their territory and to begin life again in their homeland. A treaty was drawn up and signed by all the leaders, including Barboncito of Canyon de Chelly, Manuelito of Tohatchi, Ganado Mucho of the Klagetoh area, Herrero, and others. They agreed to remain within a reservation which extended from Fort Defiance to a point on the San Juan River (at the mouth of Chaco Canyon) and from a point a few miles west of Chinle to a line running north and south through about Fruitland. This was hardly one-fourth of the territory through which they had formerly ranged. They also agreed to send their children to school and the government agreed to furnish a teacher and schoolhouse for every thirty children. Individual land allotments of as much as 160 acres would be given to individuals asking for them. The government would assist by giving agricultural implements and helping improve agricultural land. In small groups, in contrast with the great group migration of the Long Walk four years before, the Navajos walked back to their home country. The relocation program of General Carleton had not worked in the way he had hoped, but it did have a profound effect on the Navajos. They were a changed — and a much chastened — people.

Back too late to plant any crops and without any livestock, the Navajos relied through the first winter almost wholly on government rations, which were given out to them first at Fort Wingate and then at Fort Defiance. Some twenty-five hundred settled at Fort Defiance. The others scattered out through the newly-created reservation looking for their old homes. The government had promised to issue sheep and goats and in the following year fulfilled the promise. Fourteen thousand sheep and one thousand goats were distributed, two to a person, as far as they would go, to the ninety-five hundred Navajos who appeared for the distribution. Three years later another ten thousand sheep were given out. The Navajos were on the road to a new life as independent herdsmen.

Nevertheless, crops were poor through 1870 and rations had to be continued. It had been agreed in the treaty that the government would, if necessary, issue rations during a ten-year period — through 1878 — while Navajos were getting back on their feet. The ten-year "treaty period" was a difficult one for the Navajos, and seeds of antagonism between them and Anglo settlers were sowed during this time. Almost as soon as the sheep and goats were issued Navajos began to expand beyond the boundaries of the newly surveyed reservation. Many had lived far outside those boundaries before, and in simply returning to their homes broke the treaty provisions. Others found that the new boundaries had nothing to do with good forage, and followed their sheep and goats out into areas where there was feed. In the first years when crops failed and rations were irregular some of the young men went back to the old ways and made a few raids northward into the rich new Mormon settlements of Utah. The Mormons were forced in 1871 to send their famous apostle, Jacob Hamblin, to protest the raids.

In 1876 the surveys for the Atlantic and Pacific Railroad (later to be the Santa Fe) were carried through the southeastern part of the Navajo Reservation. The Navajos learned that sections of their land would be given up to the railroad and opened for Anglo settlement. These sections contained some of the finest of their winter range. Manuelito, who had been appointed "sub-chief" over the whole eastern part of the reservation, went to Washington to protest. He found that the land would be open to Navajos to homestead, as to the Anglos, and that it was planned that some lands north of the San Juan River would be given to Navajos in lieu of the lands relinquished to the railroad. By 1879 raids against Zuni and Mexican settlements south and east of the reservation were occurring once more. These reached such serious proportions that Manuelito and Ganado Mucho, who had been appointed "sub-chief" of the western part of the reservation, carried out a "purge" of some forty "witches" whom they regarded as responsible for the renewal of depredations. It was apparent to the agent for the Navajos that some six million acres of land (nearly twice the amount included in the reservation) was being occupied by the Indians outside the reservation boundaries. This was all land which they had used prior to the Long Walk.

Meanwhile, changes proceeded steadily. A school was set up at Fort Defiance in compliance with the treaty of 1868, but the first teachers who were assigned by the Board of Missions in accordance with Indian Bureau policy were driven out in 1873. The school continued, but with little effect, having a total of eleven pupils in 1879, and was generally condemned by those few Navajos who had any interest in it as a place where their children suffered from mistreatment. A settlement with a store slowly grew up around Fort Defiance and became a center for diffusion of Anglo ways. The Indian agent encouraged the production of wool and began shipping it out to the east. Navajo blankets had already become known widely in the United States and were traded as far as Utah and all through New Mexico. By 1873 they constituted a source of income of some importance, together with wool, and agents continued to work on the improvement of the weaving and the development of a market. In 1878 one agent organized a company of scouts in an effort to control the increasing raids outside the reservation. The scout organization lasted for a year and was finally reduced to a force of ten Navajo policemen who continued under the agent's direction to struggle with increasing problems of law and order. In the late 1870's some Navajos were recruited for the labor gangs which were working on the railroad in the southeastern part of the reservation. Whiskey, railroad ties for houses, and scrap iron began to be an influence on Navajo life. With the coming of the first train in 1881, a coal mine opened at Gallup south of Fort Defiance, and influences from Western culture intensified. In 1874 Lorenzo Hubbell had opened a trading post at Ganado Mucho's home south of Fort Defiance which also served to increase Navajo awareness of Anglo ways. By 1880 there were more than twelve thousand Navajos.

The 1880's and 1890's saw some intensive efforts on the part of the Indian Bureau to deal with the problem which the treaty reservation had created, and to live up to the provisions of the treaty in regard to schools. All the agents had been aware of the overflow of the Indians beyond the reservation. Not only had clashes developed between Indians and settlers in Utah and where Mormons had settled in the 1870's on the western edge of Navajo country, but conflict also began to increase during the 1880's on the southern boundary and eastern edges of Navajo country, and eventually on the southwest. The original land arrangement simply was not sufficient to support the increasing numbers of Navajos and livestock. In 1878 an addition of nearly a million acres was made to the reservation on the west, which carried it into the country claimed by the Hopis. In 1880 two more strips, almost equal in extent to the original reservation, were added along the southern and eastern boundaries of the reservation. In 1884 still more land was added — the Paiute strip which carried the reservation north of the Hopi country as far as the Colorado River, and an additional area which extended the northern boundary to the San Juan River.

Meanwhile, in 1882 the reservation for the Hopis was created, into which the Navajos continued to expand. The reservation area for Navajos was now three times as large as in 1868, and extended to the edges of land which Anglo settlers really wanted and found usable. A steady stream of homesteaders had moved into New Mexico and Arizona since the early 1880's. A focal point of clash between them and Navajos who were already settled with their herds developed at the southwestern corner of the reservation, where in 1897 Anglo ranchers attacked a community of sixteen families of Navajos and drove them northward across the Little Colorado River. Similar clashes occurred in the area on the southeast where the railroad lands checkerboarded the Navajo land and on the northeast where Mormons were developing the irrigation of the San Juan River. Navajos had never really recognized the treaty reservation and regarded the old haunts as their own. The government program to increase the reservation confirmed them in this, but at the same time intensified the antagonisms between the two expanding groups. Navajos had been granted the same rights as Anglos to homestead public domain, but Anglos continually refused to recognize as improvements the hogans which Navajos erected and pushed them off land which the settlers wished to homestead. There is no record of any Navajo homestead from 1875 to 1905.

The Indian Bureau school program also resulted in clashes. In 1882 a boarding school, managed by missionaries, was instituted at Fort Defiance and in 1890 a boarding school was set up at Grand Junction, Colorado, for all Indians of the Southwest. Meanwhile there had been recruiting for Carlisle. A few Navajos were sent, notably two of Manuelito's sons, but not more than a dozen all together. Navajos were either uninterested in or directly antagonistic to the boarding school at Fort Defiance. Its disciplinary methods were like those in force elsewhere in Indian Service boarding schools. Ankle chains and solitary confinement were common practices. Navajos of the period sent their slave children or weaker children and kept their healthy children home.

In 1887 the Indian Bureau passed a compulsory school regulation in an effort to counteract general Indian indifference to schools. On the Navajo Reservation this precipitated violence in several places — in the western part of the reservation and at Round Rock north of Fort Defiance. The superintendent, in an effort to fill quotas, found himself opposed and held prisoner at Round Rock. It was apparent, however, that the opposition came from a limited group and that a number of parents and children strongly favored schooling, despite the harsh and ineffective methods which characterized the Fort Defiance school at that time.

During the three decades following 1900 the Navajo population continued to increase, reaching more than forty thousand by 1930. Navajos also steadily increased the number of sheep, goats, and horses. The Indian Bureau continued its programs of land increase to take care of the expanding population and also its efforts to provide schools. Through 1908 additions were made to the Navajo Reservation on the west and south, but shortly after, in 1911, portions of land on the southeast of the reservation were returned to the public domain and the unsatisfactory conditions of Anglo encroachment and clash between Indians and Whites continued. The considerable increases in reservation land by executive order reduced the land conflict to some extent, but Anglo population was steadily increasing and the pressures on Navajos continued.

As early as the 1880's the Indian Bureau had adopted two approaches to increasing the productivity of the Navajo land. One was the improvement of the sheep raised and the finding of markets for wool and blankets. This proceeded slowly with special attempts to improve the sheep by introduction of Merino and Rambouillet rams. The other approach was the expansion of agricultural land. The areas around Fort Defiance, Chinle, Tuba City, and Shiprock were improved for irrigation with government funds, and this increased somewhat the amount of irrigated farmland on the reservation.

These measures by the Indian Bureau, strongly weighted on the side of encouraging herding, did not keep pace with the needs of the increasing population. The rangeland on the reservation was for the most part of relatively poor quality and as sheep and horses increased it was steadily depleted. A large proportion of Navajos had begun, with government encouragement, to devote themselves almost entirely to stock raising. The irregularity of rain and snow over the reservation resulted in great variation from year to year in the adequacy of range. Families developed a great mobility, shifting widely over the reservation as they sought good pasture. The nomadic character of life for a large number of Navajos increased greatly over what it had been before 1880. A few Navajos became established in areas where the range was consistently good in most years and these grew large herds and became well to do. But the vast majority were able merely to keep going by taking advantage of good range wherever they could find it from year to year. The per-family income began a gradual decline from 1900 to 1930; as late as 1913 it was still necessary for the government to issue rations to people in areas of the reservation suffering from drought and range depletion.

The Indian Bureau also pushed its program of providing schools, chiefly of the boarding variety. Between 1900 and 1913 boarding schools were built at Tohatchi, Tuba City, Shiprock, Leupp, Chinle, Crownpoint, and Toadlena in addition to the already operating Fort Defiance School. The few schools were spread widely over the large area of the Navajo Reservation and the schooling, as in government Indian schools everywhere, was free. After 1896 the teachers were no longer missionaries, but were required to pass a Civil Service examination for their appointments. The Navajo interest in sending their children to the schools was still at a low level, but increased up to 1930. At no time, however, were the schools sufficient to accommodate all Navajo children. They were crowded although only a small proportion of Navajo children of school age were ever in them. The development of Indian Bureau schooling coincided with the setting up of schools by missionary groups. The Franciscan missionaries instituted a mission at St. Michael's, in the vicinity of Ganado, in 1898 and four years later were operating a school. In 1904 Presbyterians also began a school in the same area. Both of these steadily developed into schools giving both elementary and secondary education and hundreds of Navajos passed through them in subsequent years.

From this time on, various religious groups entered the reservation setting up missions, hospitals, or schools in different areas. The area around Fort Defiance became the scene not only of the schools mentioned but also of hospitals sponsored by Episcopalians, Catholics, and Presbyterians. By 1955 seventeen different Christian sects were supporting missionary work among the Navajos in addition to the Catholics. These were the Seventh Day Adventists, the Church of the Nazarene, the American Baptists, the Southern Baptists, the Presbyterians USA, the Plymouth Brethren, the Christian Reformed, the Good News Mission, the Navajo Gospel Mission, the Navajo Bible School, the Home Missions Council of North America, the Episcopalians, the Free Methodists, the Methodists, the Brethren in Christ, the Wycliffe School of Bible Translators, and the Native American Church. Some maintained schools and various social services; others engaged merely in evangelical work. The two strong centers of missionary activity were in the northeastern part of the reservation near Fruitland and in the southern fringe south of Fort Defiance and eastward from there.

In 1915 the Indian Bureau divided the Navajo Reservation into five separate jurisdictions, with agencies at Tuba City, Leupp, Shiprock, Crownpoint, and Fort Defiance, each maintaining their own superintendents and staffs. In 1917 Navajos were encouraged to organize community councils, called chapters, for discussion of problems and as units with which the superintendents could deal. Six years later the Indian Bureau set up a group of advisers with whom they could discuss such matters as leases for oil, and the sale of timber and other common resources of the Navajos. Established by a special agent of the Bureau, Governor Hagerman of New Mexico, this group came to be called the Navajo Tribal Council. It consisted of two individuals from each of the five jurisdictions, usually selected by the superintendents of each. Its first chairman was Chee Dodge, a wealthy Navajo, who as the first Navajo able to speak English had long served as interpreter. He was a trader and sheepman and represented the shift from war chief to businessman as Navajo leader. This council of advisers was enlarged in 1936, after the five agencies were again consolidated into a single Indian Bureau agency at Window Rock in the Fort Defiance area; it was remodeled along the lines of a representative tribal council. It was never organized under the regulations of the Indian Reorganization Act, but began to function in a way almost identical with tribal councils instituted under the IRA. It worked under a constitution with elected representatives and played an increasingly important part up through the 1950's in relations with the Indian Bureau and in the management of the tribally-held resources of the Navajos. The development of an over-all organization among the Navajos had gone through the stages of (1) the appointment of former war chiefs by government agents to control raiding, (2) the complete breakdown with the death of Manuelito of any inter-community organization except the Bureau superintendents, (3) the functioning of a group of Anglo-chosen men as advisers to the government agents, and (4) an elected, representative group functioning under a constitution and, within the bounds of the reservation, assuming some responsibility for internal affairs. The process of integrating this last form of government with the Navajo local communities was under way in the 1950's.

Relations with Anglos other than government officials developed rapidly after 1900. In that year Fred Harvey instituted in Albuquerque what was called an Indian House, where Navajo and other Indian craftwork was exhibited and sold. The growing tourist trade in the Southwest gave this great impetus, and Navajo blankets and silverwork found an increasing market. Even by 1913 the Navajo income from weaving was more than half a million dollars. Navajo identity as Indians, as a cultural group distinct from Anglos, became increasingly a source of pride as well as income. Distinctive elements of Navajo culture, such as the blanket, the women's costume, the hogan, and even the rectilinear figures of the deities in the Navajo ceremonial dry paintings, began to appear in tourist brochures, in Anglo-American painting, and in serious literature. The Navajos became at least as well known in the general Anglo society as the Pueblos and even the Sioux Indians of the Plains. Studies of their religion and art and other aspects of culture were made with increasing frequency during the 1920's. They had become a recognized part of Anglo society, along with a few other well-known Indian tribes.

In 1893 Agent Plummer had thought it necessary to acquaint Navajos with Anglo culture by taking a group to the World's Fair in Chicago, a method which was employed with a great many different groups of Indians in the United States. Plummer said that he wanted to take a carload of Navajos "for the purpose of seeing something of the educational methods of Americans, and the power, extent and advantages of civilization." He thought it was less important to take the headmen, who were working fairly well with the Bureau agents, and more important to take the young men who were "rebelling" against reservation conditions. He took more than a dozen and felt that some good had been accomplished, but the government did not pay for the trip. The bill was finally paid by the Indian Rights Association, a type of organization which came to be of increasing importance in Indian affairs. The Indian Rights Association and other similar groups kept a critical eye on government policy and programs and became "spokesmen" for various Indian groups, such as in the Pueblo Indian land case·in the 1920's. By that time many people were coming to the Navajo country besides the government agents and were learning of conditions there for themselves. The Indian Rights Association type of organization, the various church groups with missionary interests, social scientists, and others focused heavily on the Navajos as representative of the American Indians. Their way of life was being explained over and over again in women's clubs, university classes, and other groups. It was such organizations and individuals as these that prevented the Indian Bureau policy of religious suppression from making much headway during the 1920's. The Bureau nevertheless continued to punish Navajos for maintaining such customs as polygamy and the execution of individuals for witchcraft, practices which were consistently condemned by Anglos. Now and then clashes with Navajos developed over the attempt to stamp out polygamy, such as the clash in 1915 at Beautiful Mountain.

In the early 1930's when Indian Bureau policy took a new direction and crystallized in the form of the Indian Reorganization Act, the Navajos were in a bad economic plight. Livestock had been developed to the point where the reservation range would not support the animals, and the Indian Bureau reported that rangeland was being washed away at an alarming rate. In 1934 the Bureau instituted a program of soil conservation which required the reduction of Navajo livestock by some 40 percent. It also required the division of the reservation into districts within which Navajos settled in the districts would have to keep their reduced herds. This meant a complete change of habits for Navajos who had been accustomed to aim for steadily increasing flocks and to unregulated wandering over the reservation wherever forage was available. They resisted the reduction; it was carried out largely at first by force, although Navajos were paid for stock which the government agents killed. Belatedly, the government instituted a program of education designed to acquaint the Indians with the seriousness of the situation, the reasons for stock reduction, and soil conservation measures. But on through the 1940's, after the government program of reduction had been accomplished, conflict and antagonism continued between government agents and Indians. Eventually, in 1952, the Navajo Tribal Council wrote and put into effect its own grazing regulations based on the technical knowledge supplied by the Indian Bureau.

In 1947 the Navajo Tribal Council passed a compulsory school law, thus adopting the measure which, when it came from the Bureau agents, had been opposed and caused armed conflict. School attendance steadily increased, but not until 1954 did the Indian Bureau, through arrangements with New Mexico and Arizona school districts, provide enough schools for all Navajo children of school age.

In World War II thirty-four hundred young Navajo men and women entered the armed services and returned to bring a still wider knowledge of the outside world to their families and neighbors. Also during World War II, thousands of Navajos began to work off the reservation in agriculture and industry through the western states. By 1955 the integration of this wider experience in the Anglo world with the reservation life was proceeding rapidly, much of it coming to expression and formulation in the deliberations of the Tribal Council to which a Navajo who had lived for many years in the Middle West was elected chairman in 1955.

Navajo culture was not being simply replaced through cultural assimilation. The language had been made a written language by efforts of the Indian Bureau over a period of some years. A newspaper, election regulations, and other literature were being printed in Navajo, although English was the language used in the schools. Navajo religion was still in existence as a practical and spiritual measure in Navajo life. Navajo cultural values were constantly being expressed and acted upon in the actions of the Tribal Council. A fusion of the Anglo and Navajo cultures was going on. Nevertheless, the dominant framework within which it took place was that set by the Anglos in schools, in the form of political organization, in the economy, and in the myriad pressures through wagework, missionary activities, the radio, and other means of communication on a mass scale. No Navajo community was as tightly organized around native cultural values as were the Pueblo communities. The structure of Navajo society having from the beginning of contact been looser, the individual Navajo communities had changed more completely, if in uneven fashion, than had those of the Pueblos.

Navajo history in the hundred years of Anglo contacts may be viewed as a series of profound changes in social type. At first, the Navajo communities were narrowly-ranging groups independent of any others, occasionally united for raiding purposes. They had been and still were focused on the struggle for food, interested in agriculture and hunting but increasingly, as the Anglos came on the scene, interested in sheep and horses which they had found could be obtained by raiding the New Mexico villages. This was the situation during the 1850's and 1860's, when the Anglos attempted to stop the raids. Considerable numbers of Navajos were more interested in farming and herding than in raiding, but the latter two went together and the younger men could not be controlled by those older and more inclined to peaceful ways. Since there was no organization that extended beyond the combinations of extended families, constituting two hundred to three hundred people, no formal cooperation was possible with the Anglos in their efforts to realize their program. The Anglo policy was consistently one of "offering peace"; it was not an approach of extermination. But the terms on which peace was offered eventually — the usual reservation policy terms — were completely unacceptable to autonomous roaming groups who knew nothing about the military strength of the Anglos. As soon as they learned it, they capitulated quickly and completely.

The second phase of Anglo contact was characterized by a sudden transformation of a society, as well as transplantation. The eight thousand Navajos — the great majority of the tribe — were together in the closest sort of proximity for four years, experiencing precisely the same miseries, both physical and spiritual. It was inconceivable that the kind of life they had been used to could have been replaced in three times this period even under the conditions at Fort Sumner. "Human nature" is not quite that plastic. But the effects nevertheless were tremendous. The awareness of Anglo military power and also Anglo mercy and generosity became intense. The whole set of inter-ethnic attitudes, from the Navajo side, was completely altered; there was general acceptance of being in the hands of "the government" or Washington, or in other words, a change from intertribal rivalry on a basis of equality to one of dependence. Also, some shift in social structure took place. Tribal organization was not suddenly created out of nothing. However, the idea which the Anglos held of dealing with Navajos as a single unit was impressed on them. Barboncito as "head chief" with his two "sub-chiefs," Manuelito and Ganado Mucho, was a fact at Fort Sumner and was transferred then on the return. The Anglos were making a tribal structure under conditions where almost all the Navajos could see it take form.

The third phase lasted from 1868 to perhaps 1924, some two generations. It was one of steady decentralization. It began with Navajo dependence on the government more fully impressed than ever, first through rationing and then through distribution of sheep and goats. But the 1870's were a period of dispersal and the winning back of independence to a large extent. There still existed a superstructure of tribal organization, but it broke down by the 1890's. By that time Manuelito had personally broken under the various impacts of Anglo culture. The "tribal organization" had steadily disintegrated as Navajos re-established themselves along the old lines of autonomous land-use groups. However, the new concentration on sheep herding plus the restrictions encountered on movement in certain directions made for a more fluid condition within the reservation area. There was wider contact, through searching out and using the variable good grazing areas, among Navajos. This, together with the pressures all around the edges of the reservation, probably made for a growth of tribal sense, and there was now in addition the foundation of tribal common experience in the memory of the Long Walk. The tendency to political separateness was stronger nevertheless than that toward tribal unity. Power was recognized as being in the hands of the government, not in the hands of Navajos, and this fact worked against a real tribal organization. The government recognized this by 1915 in creating the five separate jurisdictions.

Forces from outside the reservation were, however, working in a different direction — toward a tribal unity. This began to be definite by 1917 and in 1924 resulted again in the creation of a tribal superstructure in the form of a "tribal council" under the chairmanship of the trader and sheep-rancher Chee Dodge. Steadily, the tribal organization grew through chapter organization which became something of a channel of communication for the outside forces impinging on the reservation and as government policy in 1935 crystallized again in terms of a general Navajo welfare program. From 1924 through 1955 — a period of another generation — the growth was toward a functioning tribal government. The Indian Bureau recognized and encouraged this development by centralizing both its own and the Navajos' administration at Window Rock. The Navajos were finally restructured into a tribal unit through the remodeled Tribal Council. After a hundred years the tribal organization which Kearny had imagined to exist finally began to function as a reality, although it was still far from being regarded as their own institution by all Navajos.

CHAPTER NINE

Western Apaches

CONTACT WITH SPANIARDS more completely revolutionized the life of the Apaches than it did any other Southwestern people, even including the Navajos. The revolution, however, was of a kind which the Spaniards did not plan and did not want when it came. It was a revolution which resulted in the loss of control of parts of the northern frontier, as well as great destruction of life and property. The Spaniards unwittingly gave the Apaches the opportunity and the means for a warfare toward which they were already inclining before the Spaniards arrived on the scene.

The earliest Spanish expeditions did not even make contact with Apaches, although at certain points the Spaniards were informed of the existence of people who were probably Apaches. Thus, in passing through the area which later became the breeding ground of the most destructive Apache raids — southeastern Arizona — Coronado's party reported it as without population. Later Coronado was informed by Tano Indians in the Galisteo Basin just south of where Santa Fe was founded that since at least 1525 the people of that area had suffered from raids by warlike Indians from the east. Possibly the raiders were ancestors of people whom the Spaniards came to call the Jicarilla and Mescalero Apaches at a later time. It is possible also that some of the people whom Espejo's party in 1583 encountered in central Arizona were Apaches. Oñate in 1598 was aware of what probably were Jicarilla and other Apaches north of the Pueblos. It was not, however, until some twenty-five years later that the name "Apache" came into common use, and that the Spaniards became fully aware of a people quite distinct in language and way of life from the village and ranchería peoples.

Where and how these Indians lived before the middle of the 1600's we do not know. Our ignorance on the subject reflects the almost complete lack of contact between them and the Spaniards. We may infer with a good degree of probability that there were various bands of Athapaskan-speaking people scattered through New Mexico, both east and west of the Rio Grande River, and still more bands of similar people in what is now the whole length of eastern Arizona. It would be unsafe to guess, in the absence of fuller archeological work, as to where they ranged or what the divisions among them were during the 1500's while Spaniards were becoming acquainted with the rancherías of Sonora and Chihuahua and the villages of the Pueblos in New Mexico and Arizona. There were people who came to be called Navajos living in northwestern New Mexico and probably there were similar small groups nearly as far west as the Hopi country. There is indication that their numbers were added to during the last half of the 1500's by Athapaskan-speaking people who joined them from the south. Not much differentiated from other Athapaskan-speaking people during the 1500's, they became specialized as sheep raisers and weavers during the 1700's, after the Pueblo Revolt of 1680.

West and south of Zuni there must have been other Athapaskans, possibly during the 1500's and certainly during the 1600's. When they came into this region must be left for archeologists to discover. Not only their language, but also their whole way of life was different from that of the Pueblos or of the Pimans, Opatans, or Cahitans of the south. They practiced some agriculture, but they relied chiefly on hunting and wild-food gathering. They shifted residence a great deal within hunting and gathering territories, and their camp groups were much more loosely organized than the rancherías. Their population was relatively very small compared to that of any of the settled tribes.

These people of southwestern New Mexico and southeastern Arizona began to loom on the Spanish horizon in an important way after the Pueblo Revolt of 1680. Nevertheless, it is difficult to make out a case for the Pueblo Revolt being the cause of the Apache outbreaks. The Apaches who lived on the eastern border of the Rio Grande Pueblo country and who had continued their occasional raiding of Pueblo villages during the Spanish colonization did not join with the Pueblos in the rebellion. Both they and the Navajos stayed clear of any entangling alliances and let the situation alone. Later they began to raid with increasing intensity the re-established Spanish and Pueblo settlements — the Navajos from the west in the early 1700's and the Jicarillas from the east until, in the 1740's, they in turn were driven across the Rio Grande by the Comanches. Thus, the Apaches of the northeast (ancestors of Jicarillas and possibly Mescaleros) became an increasingly serious menace to the peaceful communities which Spaniards were trying to foster in the Rio Grande Valley simultaneously with the westward and southward advance of the Comanches. That the success of the Pueblo Revolt at first or its later consequences influenced the Apaches of the northeast seems very doubtful. They became more belligerent as they were wedged between the Spaniards and the advancing Comanches. They were battling for existence during the first half of the 1700's.

Farther south there were effects from the dislocations of peoples on the Plains margin of New Mexico. Very probably as the intensity of Apache-Comanche fighting increased in the northeast the ancestors of the Mescalero Apaches shifted their range southward and somewhat westward, so that they hunted and gathered along the Rio Grande in southern New Mexico and ranged into northern Chihuahua. The Mescaleros of later history were in part at least the Mimbreño Apaches of the early Spanish records.

The early focus of Apache raiding which most affected the Spaniards, however, lay neither along the Rio Grande among the Pueblos or in the south near

El Paso. It was farther west — in northeastern Sonora and northwestern Chihuahua. Here as early as the 1650's — well before the Pueblo Revolt — there were portents of the fighting and disruption that later developed. It was a region of borders. Here the northernmost of the Opata villages lay in the Bavispe and upper Moctezuma valleys surrounded by some of the most rugged mountains in all New Spain. Just east of the Opata outposts, separated by rough and nearly impassable ridges, were rancherías of the Conchos Indians — in the vicinity of modern Casas Grandes. These and the Opata communities were fairly prosperous, usually with stores of food, and became more prosperous during the first years of Spanish domination in the early 1600's.

Just north of this line of agricultural settlements in the 1650's was something of a no man's land. Concerning the groups of Indians who were here at that time little is known, although probably more can be discovered through both documentary and archeological research. It seems, however, that just north of the last Opata communities were Indians called the Sumas, who were described on first contacts by the Spaniards as "wild." These Sumans were probably not Athapaskan-speaking and were closely related to partially sedentary Indians living to the east, south of El Paso and ranging northward into the Plains, namely, those called "Jumanos." The Sumas were a more nomadic eastern branch of the Jumanos. They seem to have been interested in settling down to a farming life but were unable, as we shall see, to accept the mission discipline after they had tried it. The Sumas were in touch on the northwest with Indians who were called Jocomes by the Spaniards. These may have been an Athapaskan-speaking group, possibly a band of what later came to be called either Arivaipa or Chiricahua Apaches. On the northeast of the Sumas were people the Spaniards sometimes called Janos, who also probably were Apache-speaking and may have been a band of Chiricahua or Mimbreño Apaches. Still farther to the east were the "Chinarras" and "Mansos." The latter along with the Jumanos accepted mission discipline in the vicinity of El Paso before the 1700's, changing over from a completely nonagricultural existence. The Chinarras were possibly a band of nomadic people but similar to some of the Conchos.

Here, then, in this country of rugged mountains and not very productive desert in the north and fertile narrow river valleys in the south there were six or seven distinct groups at the time the Spaniards entered it. They ranged from the highly developed village Opatas to the completely nomadic Mansos. The Sumas, like the Jovas to the south, were in a state of transition from nomadism to settled farming life. It is not likely that the country north of the Opatas and the Conchos was divided into regularly recognized hunting territories. It seems more likely that its occupants were relatively new in the area and that Chinarras, Janos, Jocomes, and Sumas were in process of working out an adjustment among themselves as to territorial resources when the Spaniards came on the scene. There is some possibility that the Opatas had recently left the higher country for the valleys of central Sonora. Whether they had been driven out as a result of pressure from the less agricultural people is a question not now answerable. The Opatas seem to have been expanding southward at this time, but not at all northward. Anyway it is likely that this no man's land of borders between six or more tribes was in an unsettled state during the early 1600's. It was this fluid area of native life that became by the end of the 1600's the chief trouble spot on the northwestern frontier of New Spain.

It was also in the mid-1600's — like the Hopi country a century later — the scene of a minor conflict of missionary jurisdictions. It was a border between Franciscan and Jesuit mission efforts. The Franciscans had worked with the Conchos Indians in Chihuahua since the early 1600's and followed their settlements around the eastern margin of the Tarahumara country to establish an important mission at Casas Grandes. They had by the 1640's developed their mission work in this northwestern corner of Chihuahua and had expanded into the Bavispe Valley and the upper Moctezuma. This area was, however, Opata country and the Opatas to the south were a Jesuit field. Perea, a governor of Sonora, attempted to bring Franciscans into north-central Sonora in the 1640's but he was overruled by superiors, and the Franciscans he brought into the Sonora and San Miguel River missions were forced to leave. The field remained Jesuit, despite the fact that Jesuits were being criticized at this time for the Indian revolts which occurred in the areas where they had worked. There was thus some overlap during the middle 1600's of Franciscan and Jesuit activities, especially in this extreme northeastern part of Sonora, where the Franciscans had already made some contacts before the Jesuits reached the farthest outlying Opata rancherías.

It was the Franciscans who first felt the conflicts and unrest in the area. They complained of the "wild" Sumas and claimed that they annoyed them in the vicinity of the Opata mission of Teuricachi on the upper Moctezuma. This was in 1649. Two years later the Franciscan missionary was gone and Jesuit missionaries were working northward above Oputo on the upper Moctezuma River. The Jesuits found people whom they regarded as Sumas north of the Opata mission of Guasavas. They found them interested in establishing peaceful relations and encouraged a party of leaders, numbering one hundred, to visit the mission at Oputo where a "peace" was agreed on. Some Sumas came into the Teras mission above Oputo on the Moctezuma River and stayed awhile, but later revolted and left. During the next fifteen years or more many Sumas were reduced to mission life at Casas Grandes by the Franciscans, along with the Conchos resident there. Until 1684 the reduction of the various Indians in the vicinity of Casas Grandes and Janos in Chihuahua seems to have proceeded peacefully, as did the Jesuit work at the same time among the Opatas to the west.

In 1684, however, after the Spaniards who had been driven out of New Mexico by the Pueblos had established headquarters at El Paso, trouble broke out. Rebellion spread across northern Chihuahua from the sand hill area below El Paso to Casas Grandes. Involved were some Conchos, and according to Spanish accounts, five other groups. These were the Sumas, the Chinarras, the Mansos, and the probably Apachean Jocomes and Janos. The Sumas and Conchos of Casas Grandes plundered that settlement. The abandonment of Carretas, a settlement of Sumas, in the important mountain pass between Casas Grandes and Sonora was forced. Unrest continued into the following year, when Sumas were reported as planning another uprising in Casas Grandes. This rebellion was put down promptly and harshly by the Spaniards, with the execution of fifty-two Indians at Casas Grandes and twenty-five more in the Sonora mission area adjoining on the west. These events, in which Sumas seem to have been the leaders, appeared to the Spaniards as symptoms of serious trouble. They set up a presidio at Janos, north of Casas Grandes, to protect the frontier.

Nevertheless, from this point on the Spaniards lost rather than gained control of northeastern Sonora. Precisely where the Indians involved were centered cannot be determined from information at present available, nor what the relations among the groups were. For another fifteen years until the end of the century, the Sumas were mentioned prominently in the fighting and raiding that developed. Before 1690, however, they seem to have lost their leadership to the Janos and by the early 1700's the only group mentioned by the Spaniards as carrying out the raids are the Apaches. During the twenty years from about 1685 to 1705 the Sumas, Chinarras, Janos, and Jocomes either moved out of the area, died out, or lost their identity among the Apachean bands. An alternative interpretation of the meager facts is that as the Spaniards became increasingly aware of these groups, they recognized their basic similarity of language and custom and simply adopted a generic name which they applied to all raiders from the north. This theory would require, however, that the Uto-Aztecan-speaking Sumas were merged during this period with the other Athapaskan-speaking bands. Probably some were, but also probably other Sumas moved eastward, as we shall see, to join their more peaceful relatives, the Jumanos of the Rio Grande Valley.

The intensification of warfare on this border at this time does suggest a shift from tribal heterogeneity to the dominance of one group. If such a process was going on, it took place within a generation or less at the end of the 1600's. People whom the Spaniards called Apaches emerged as the dominant group north of the Opata villages as far as Zuni. The respective roles of migration, cultural absorption, biological extinction, and Spanish initial ignorance of the people in the area remain to be worked out by further research. It merely seems likely at the present writing that Apaches did absorb a number of other small groups who had been more or less insecurely established in the area at the time the Spaniards entered.

The establishment of the Janos presidio in 1685 seems almost to have been a signal for the beginning of a new and persistent type of warfare. In the following year conspiracy was reported involving Indians from the Pimas on the west to the Conchos on the east. Spaniards found evidence that the Janos, Sumas, and Jocomes were planning attacks on the Opata villages of the Bavispe Valley and farther west. They also satisfied themselves that Upper Pimas were implicated. They tried and convicted of conspiracy a Pima headman whom they called Canito, from the village of Mututicachi situated in the area of the headwaters of the Sonora River nearly 150 miles west of Janos. Canito was executed, but the aggressive plans of the Indians were not appreciably affected. About the time of Canito's trial Sumas and Jocomes raided the mining settlement of San Juan del Rio on the upper Moctezuma and the mission village of Teras in the same area. In 1688 a thrust against the Opatas began in earnest. Jocomes, Sumas, and Janos attacked the Opata ranchería of Santa Rosa near Cuquiarachi on the upper Moctezuma. They forced the Opatas to retire southward to the vicinity of where Fronteras later was founded. Here the Opatas were attacked again and the raiders, reported to be under the leadership primarily of the Janos now, ranged southward to the vicinity of the mines at Naco- zari, forcing Spaniards out of the area and Opatas along with them.

The situation was regarded as so serious by the Spaniards that fifteen soldiers were dispatched from Sinaloa, and in 1690 a decision was made to set up a presidio near the Opata village which had been moved from Santa Rosa on the upper Moc- tezuma. This was called Fronteras and was regarded as a supplementary military establishment to Janos for the purpose of stopping the depredations of the hostile tribes.

The raids, however, increased in intensity and frequency during the next ten years. In the same year that the presidio at Fronteras was established, the abandon- ment of Teras, forty miles southeast of Fronteras on the Bavispe River, was forced and the Opata villages of the northern bend of the Bavispe were repeatedly raided. Spanish settlements northeast of Fronteras along the San Bernardino River were raided and abandoned, and Batepito in the same area was attacked.

The Spaniards were not only losing control of the very area which they had tried to fortify, but they were also completely out of touch with the Indians north of the line from Fronteras to Janos. They spoke vaguely of Apaches, but still con- sidered the Janos, Jocomes, and Sumas as their chief enemies. At the same time the commander at Janos was convinced, probably as a result of the trial of Canito of Mututicachi, that the Upper Pimas and the Sobaipuris of the San Pedro River were all involved. Rumors grew of widespread confederation among the tribes for a general revolt — probably inspired by what all the Spaniards knew of the Pueblo Revolt and the confederation of Indians which had engineered it in 1680.

The frontier continued in turmoil, with the Spaniards unable to stop the raid- ing. The major corridor of the Indians for these raids was precisely the area between the two presidios of Fronteras and Janos — the Bavispe Valley of the west and the upper Moctezuma. In 1692 peace negotiations were initiated, but in the midst of these the Janos and Jocome leaders lost confidence in the Spaniards and fled to the north. In 1693 a Flying Company with headquarters at Fronteras was set up under the command of General Jironza, who had been governor of New Mexico at El Paso after the revolt. It consisted of mounted Spanish soldiers ready to pursue quickly any raiders reported anywhere in northeastern Sonora. In 1694 the Flying Company conducted four campaigns against the Indians, but with no important results. While it was in the field, horses were driven off from several missions and the Opata settlement of Cuchuta less than twenty miles south of Fronteras was raided. A party of soldiers under Lieutenant Solis marched into the San Pedro Sobaipuri country, under the impression that Sobaipuris had stolen the horses. Here they killed three Sobaipuri merely on the supposition that they were horse raiders. When Coro, the leader of the Sobaipuris, demonstrated that the men were innocent and that what the soldiers thought was horse meat was actually venison, the lieutenant admitted he was wrong. Nevertheless, the idea persisted that the Sobaipuris were involved. In spite of such provocation they remained friendly to the Spaniards. Solis' action was symptomatic of the Spanish lack of understanding of the situation of the tribes in the area at the time.

In 1695 the forces of the two presidios united in a campaign which resulted, according to their report, in the death of sixty Indians. But meanwhile Tonibavi, seventy-five miles south of Fronteras, was raided and other places along the now well-established southward corridor were molested. It was now becoming clear to the Spaniards at the presidios that the bases of operation of the raiding groups were well to the north and that the raiders were making a practice of slipping around the presidios, down between the valleys of the Bavispe and Moctezuma rivers. However, no additional presidios or even forces were set up.

In 1696 the situation was temporarily complicated by an outbreak of the Conchos Indians, who attacked Nacori not far from the borders of the Tarahumara country a hundred miles south of Janos. Lieutenant Solis marched from Fronteras against the Conchos and captured three of their leaders, whom he executed. No more hostilities were reported from the Conchos. But meanwhile raiders again attacked Tonibavi. General Jironza pursued the raiding party with his Flying Company and finally localized their starting point south of the Gila River. He pursued them to the Gila but was unable to engage them in battle.

In 1697 the Opata villages along the eastern Bavispe River were the scene of unrest. The Opata leader, Quilme, had become very much dissatisfied with the Spanish efforts to control the raiding of the Indians from the north. He was convinced that the friendship of the Opatas of the north with the Spaniards was gaining them nothing — no protection from Jocomes and other raiders — and that moreover it was resulting in the loss of lands to Spaniards who moved in to the presidios, opened mines, or settled near the mission villages. He was said to be urging revolts, but his plan was never put into operation. It was discovered and those implicated as leaders were executed, Quilme himself finally meeting death at Janos. Bacerac and the other Opata communities remained peaceful toward the Spaniards but continued to suffer from raids by Indians from the north.

By 1698 the Sumas decided that they had enough of warfare. They had established themselves in the Florida Mountains northwest of Janos and now found themselves the prisoners of their allies. They sent word that they wanted to make peace with the Spaniards, but they were prevented from doing so by "Indians on horseback" who kept them from communicating with the Spaniards. They asked for Spanish assistance. From this time on, no more was heard of the Sumas. We may speculate that their men were killed by their allies because of their defection, survivors among them being absorbed. Or they may have turned eastward to join their relatives, the Jumanos, and with the latter entered the El Paso missions where, like the Jumanos, they were eventually absorbed into the Spanish and Indian population of that area.

The disappearance of the Sumas from the alliance against the Spaniards did not result in any decrease of raiding. In the same year of 1698 in which the Sumas tried to make peace, the Jocomes and Janos and others now spoken of by Spaniards as Apaches extended their operations westward. Turning from their southward thrusts into the Opata country along the margin of the Sierra Madre Mountains, they now carried their attacks into the Upper Pima country 150 miles west of Janos and nearly seventy miles west of Fronteras. They attacked and burned the newly inaugurated mission of Cocóspera, where they killed some Pimas. In addition, Jocomes who had been given land to farm by the San Pedro Sobaipuris joined with Apaches and laid waste the Sobaipuri village of Gaybanipitea. Here, however, an interesting contest developed, as the Sobaipuris of the area were reinforced by others from the Santa Cruz Valley. A battle of champions was arranged, ten on a side. The ten Jocome-Apache champions were killed, including their war leader, and as their followers fled, many were killed. This became the most famous victory of the period over the Apaches, and the San Pedro Sobaipuri headman, Coro, was given credit.

However, the Sobaipuri victory had no appreciable effect on the raiding tribes. The raids continued, especially to the westward into Upper Pima country. In 1701 the raiding reached as far southwestward as Saracachi, fifty miles below Cocóspera on the San Miguel River. And in the same year, just to demonstrate that the frontier extended as far eastward as it ever had, the pueblo of Janos itself was sacked. Cocóspera and Remedios, the mission to the south, continued to be the targets of the raiders in the following years.

It was evident by about 1710 that forces had been unleashed in this part of the northern frontier which the Spaniards were unable to control. The line of Spanish settlement on the west had been stopped at the frontier of the Janos-Fronteras outposts, just south of what is the present boundary between Mexico and the United States. The few Spanish ranches and mining settlements which had existed north of this line were abandoned. Other ranches and mines south of the line, as at Nacozari, also had to be abandoned. The line of Spanish northward advance had been checked and was even receding somewhat. On the west, the advance had continued into the 1690's in the Pimería but now even the Upper Pima country was under attack and the advance was greatly slowed down.

A strip of territory nearly 250 miles wide, roughly from Casas Grandes to Zuni, now separated the Sonora-Chihuahua part of the frontier from the New Mexico part — an area in which there were no Spanish settlements and no semblance of Spanish domination and control. In this area during the next century the Apache culture developed with which the Anglo-Americans came into contact in the nineteenth century. Its western limits were at this time not known to the Spaniards. Its eastern limits were set along the Pecos River during the next few years by the southward advance of the Comanche Indians of the Plains.

This separation of the two northernmost provinces by a formidable Indian military power was not accompanied by vigorous action on the part of the Spaniards. Although the source of the raiders and a great deal about their methods were now known, no decisive measures were undertaken during the first half of the 1700's. There was awareness of the threat as indicated in the reports of Visitors, such as Almanza's in 1724; there was a slow, but steady depopulation of the whole northeastern corner of Sonora; but neither Spanish military or missionary activity was augmented to deal with the threat. Spanish affairs went on very much as they had during the first fifteen years of the raiding.

15. THE APACHE CORRIDOR, 1700-1886

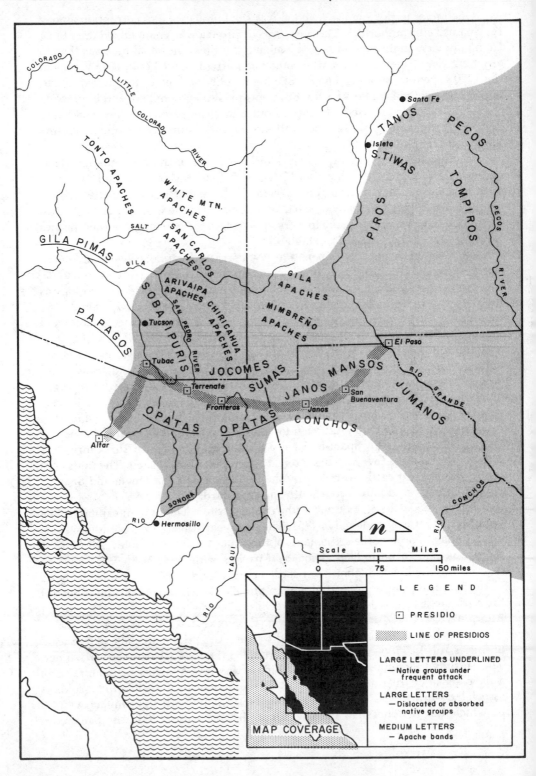

COLORADO

LITTLE COLORADO RIVER

TONTO APACHES

WHITE MTN. APACHES

GILA PIMAS

SALT

GILA

SAN CARLOS APACHES

• Santa Fe

TANOS

PECOS

• Isleta
S. TIWAS

PIROS

TOMPIROS

PECOS RIVER

ARIVAIPA APACHES

CHIRICAHUA APACHES

SOBAIPURIS

PAPAGOS

• Tucson

SAN PEDRO RIVER

GILA APACHES

MIMBREÑO APACHES

☒ El Paso

□ Tubac

JOCOMES

SUMAS

JANOS

MANSOS

RIO GRANDE

JUMANOS

□ Terrenate

□ Fronteras

OPATAS

□ Janos

☒ San Buenaventura

OPATAS

CONCHOS

□ Altar

SONORA

RIO

• Hermosillo

RIO YAQUI

RIO CONCHOS

↑ *n*

Scale in Miles

0   75   150 miles

MAP COVERAGE

LEGEND

⊡ PRESIDIO

⠿ LINE OF PRESIDIOS

LARGE LETTERS UNDERLINED
— Native groups under frequent attack

LARGE LETTERS
— Dislocated or absorbed native groups

MEDIUM LETTERS
— Apache bands

One factor in the Spanish inaction was the familiar one of corruption among the Spanish civil authorities. The successors of Jironza who commanded the Flying Company were more interested in advancing their own personal interests than in anything else. Tunon y Quiroz who commanded from about 1712 till some time in the 1720's spent most of his time developing ranches and mines for his own profit, letting the quota of soldiers for the Fronteras presidio go unfilled, and impressing soldiers to work for himself. He carried out a few campaigns against what were now generally called Apaches, but with no results of importance other than the killing of a few Indians.

Another factor apparently was lack of knowledge of the real situation. Thus the viceroy issued an order that after 1724 only defensive warfare was to be carried out. This meant that no expeditions were to be undertaken into the Apache country. The Flying Company was to take action only at the specific points of raids, a program which was calculated to work very well to the advantage of the Apaches as they pursued their hit and run tactics.

As a result the Apaches opened a new corridor for raids down the Sonora River Valley, while at the same time keeping up their attacks in the west and along the old corridor between the Bavispe and Moctezuma rivers. The new corridor was the pathway to the rich communities of central Sonora. Between 1730 and 1751 the raiding extended to ranches on the Sonora River south of Arispe, to mines and ranches on the middle Moctezuma south of Cumpas, and to the vicinity of Saguaripa on the upper Yaqui River. Cocóspera on the west was burned again and the mining country around Nacozari became uninhabitable. A new presidio was established at Terrenate, seventy miles northwest of Fronteras, and united campaigns involving Janos, Fronteras, and Terrenate forces were planned and partially executed, but it was evident that the presidio line was a sieve through which the Apaches penetrated at will. Although forces of as many as five hundred Pimas and Opatas augmented the Spanish garrisons and penetrated into the Chiricahua Mountains, killing a few Apaches, no real control was established. The raids continued, horses and cattle were lost by the hundreds, and the Opata and Spanish population was gradually forced south and westward.

In the 1750's the raids came with renewed force. The Sonora capital of San Juan Bautista was abandoned in 1751. The next year still another presidio was set up at Tubac to protect the settlements of the Santa Cruz River valley. About 1754 there was said to be unified action by Apaches with Seris as they engaged in devastating the lower Sonora River settlements in raids around Ures in the heart of the hitherto prospering central Sonora area. Meanwhile, in 1751, the Pimas of the Saric area revolted and still another presidio was set up on the far west at Altar, in 1754. In the same year, however, Fronteras itself was raided.

Spanish attempts at retaliation and to trace the raiders to their source were unsuccessful. In 1756–57–58 four expeditions to the Gila River were carried out. They resulted merely in the random killing of the few Apaches encountered and a deep sense of frustration on the part of the Spaniards and the Opata soldiers associated with them. They remained unable to cope with the running warfare at which the Apaches had become adept. By the early 1760's the San Pedro

Sobaipuris were finally forced to retreat westward, leaving the whole San Pedro Valley to the Apaches.

In the twenty years from 1765 to 1785 the situation grew even worse. It was evident that the Apaches had perfected a way of life which called for no increase in their own territory and no desire to defeat the Spaniards in what the latter called battles. The Apaches aimed merely at supplying their shifting camps in the mountains of southeastern Arizona and southwestern New Mexico by raids whenever they wished on the settlements of Spaniards, Opatas, and Pimas. They had come to desire the horses and cattle and other stock for food, as well as the grain and other products of the settled people. They maintained themselves by quick raids in which they drove off stock and plundered communities. They were not interested especially in killing people. Rather it was to their advantage that people continue to live in the Sonora settlements. They refused to meet Spanish forces in any extended engagements. This way of life was by 1785 well developed. Although Apaches had joined with Seris in the 1750's in central Sonora and again with Seris and Pimas (Piatos) around Magdalena in 1776, they were not formally confederated with any other Indians. Nor did they maintain anything resembling a tribal organization among themselves. They operated always as separate bands, stealing horses and other food whenever and wherever each saw the best opportunities.

In 1786, faced with the continuing desolation and depopulation of the northeastern quarters of Sonora, the Spaniards had to admit the failure of their hundred-year effort to bring the Apaches under control. Flying Companies, purely defensive warfare, the frontier line of presidios — all had failed to enable the Spaniards even to hold their own. The capital of Sonora had been moved to Arispe. The northwestern provinces of New Spain had been reorganized as the Internal Provinces. When Gálvez assumed their government he announced a new Indian policy with special reference to the Apaches. He admitted that "we have lost a large part of our old establishments." He took the ground that conversion to Christianity, for the present at least, was impossible. The civil authorities would have to take over the problem to the exclusion of the missionaries. He saw a policy of extermination as the only really effective one, but this could not be accomplished with the means at hand for military campaigns against the Apaches.

The new policy should be one of making peace treaties with each separate band of Indians. In making such treaties, Gálvez held, the Spaniards should keep them strictly, but it could not be expected that the Apaches would ever keep them in good faith. Instead they should be inveigled into keeping them by certain benefits which they would quickly recognize. They should be persuaded to make settlements near the presidios, where they would be given rations of food. Under these circumstances they would not take the trouble to do any raiding, so long as they remained well fed. In addition, they should be encouraged to use liquor as much as possible, so that they would increasingly want it. They should also be given firearms, of poor quality as compared with those of the soldiers, but nevertheless adequate for hunting wild game. They should also be encouraged to trade among themselves and with the Spaniards so that their desire for the things possessed by the Spaniards would increase. In this way they would become more and more dependent on the Spaniards and would gradually give up their hostility. However, whenever hostility developed between bands the Indians should be encouraged to fight among themselves. If at the same time, Gálvez maintained, Spaniards should be encouraged more than ever to settle among them and make new settlements in the depopulated area, peace would finally be won. It was a cynical policy for disorganization of the Indians. If it cost as much as thirty thousand dollars a year it would be worth it to have peace restored.

For nearly twenty-five years the new policy accomplished in some degree the results which Gálvez had predicted. Bands of Apaches did make peace and settled down in the vicinity of Spanish settlements, or at least made such places their bases of operation. Raids still took place, but they were occasional. Spanish mines and ranches began to appear again in depopulated Sonora and southern Arizona. Mimbreño and Chiricahua Apaches came in to Arispe to ask for peace treaties, and for the rations and other goods which went with them. By 1800 raiding had almost entirely stopped. A symbiotic relationship between Spaniards and Apaches slowly developed, with considerable disorganization among those Apaches of the southern part of the region who became involved. A group of Apaches living in the country between the San Pedro and the Santa Cruz came to be known as the Manso, or tame, Apaches. They lived in the vicinity of Tucson and Tubac, became more and more dependent on the Spanish settlements, and were regarded as enemies by Apaches farther north. Similar groups developed around Fronteras and Janos. How many began to live in this manner is not recorded, but it is clear that the bulk of the Apaches were ceasing their raids on the Sonora communities and a degree of peace had been achieved. Pacification by dependency might have been permanently successful if the Mexican War for Independence had not changed the situation.

After 1811 the policy began to break down. The disruption of government in Mexico was reflected from 1811 on in new outbreaks of Apaches on the northwestern frontier. The new Mexican government did not have funds with which to continue the rationing system, and steadily Apaches who had accepted it drifted away. The presidios themselves ceased to function as military establishments and whatever control had been achieved broke down. Between 1820 and 1835, five thousand Mexicans were killed by Indians on the northern frontier and four thousand others were forced to leave the area. Northern Sonora regressed again to the state it had been in before 1786. The raiding began again with some intensity in 1831. By 1833 the old pattern was already re-established. Raids extended as far south as Ures and the vicinity of Hermosillo in central Sonora. The Apaches were equipped with good firearms and again began to make use of the formerly well-worn raiding routes in northeastern Sonora.

The Sonoran Mexicans decided on a war of extermination, resisting new proposals from their governor for peace treaties. A volunteer army was raised and began to have some success. One important Apache leader was captured and executed in 1834. Bounties of one hundred dollars were offered for each Apache scalp. The Mexican campaign continued with great vigor through 1836, although it became impossible to pay for all the scalps that were brought in. A treacherous attack on Apaches at the Santa Rita mines in southwestern New Mexico resulted in embittering an Apache leader of the Mimbreños, Mangas Coloradas, who had been friendly with the Mexicans. A new and vicious war was on and northern Sonora began to be like the Sonora of the 1770's.

In 1847 Ures was raided and in the following year of 1848 Tubac had to be abandoned. Fronteras was in the hands of the Apaches, and the Mexicans were desperately proposing a series of military colonies to replace the old presidios. The latter plan was never realized although the Mexicans gained control of Fronteras again in 1850. During the 1850's the Apache raiding extended more widely than it ever had before. Not only was central Sonora raided repeatedly along with eastern Sonora, but now the raids extended to Tucson and even west of the Santa Cruz River well into the country of the Papagos. The Mexicans seemed powerless, as had the Spanish before them, to devise any lasting means for bringing about peace on the margins of the Apache territory. This was the situation when the Anglo-Americans took over control of southern Arizona in 1853.

It is instructive to compare briefly the nature of Apache and of Navajo contacts with the Spaniards. In the first place it must be pointed out that the Navajos were fundamentally similar to the Apaches before the Spaniards came in, with the same language and general way of life. The Navajos were early deeply influenced by circumstances attributable to the Spaniards, namely, the absorption of Jemez and other Pueblo peoples after the Pueblo Revolt of 1680. The Pueblos whom they assimilated linguistically and culturally also influenced them in such matters as agriculture, weaving, and other crafts. In these respects there may have been some parallels among the Apaches. The latter showed a similar readiness and capacity for absorption of other peoples, such as the Sumas and other people in the vicinity of Janos. However, these people were very different culturally from the Pueblos absorbed by the Navajos. They were marginal rather than intensive farmers, and they had nothing important in the way of crafts to contribute to Apache culture. Thus the absorption of other peoples by the Apaches was not so important for their future development.

Like the Navajos, the Apaches remained throughout the Spanish period quite marginal to the Spanish administrative-missionary system. Their country never became the scene of actual settlements of Spaniards. Such settlements begun at the margin of their territories were attacked and pushed out. Thus, as in the case of the Navajos, there was never any acceptance of Spanish political domination. There was nevertheless, in both cases, contact through two major channels. The most important was undoubtedly through active hostilities, that is, mutual raiding. Through these, of course, acquaintance with Spanish material culture, especially war accoutrements and the use of horses and stock, were gained by the Apaches. But the contact was rendered more intimate than a mere seeing and taking of artifacts would have been, by the taking of slaves on both sides. There are no figures on the number of captive Spaniards taken by Apaches, or vice versa, but the practice was common, as it was farther north in New Mexico. Women and children were taken by both Spaniards and Apaches and kept as servants. This important

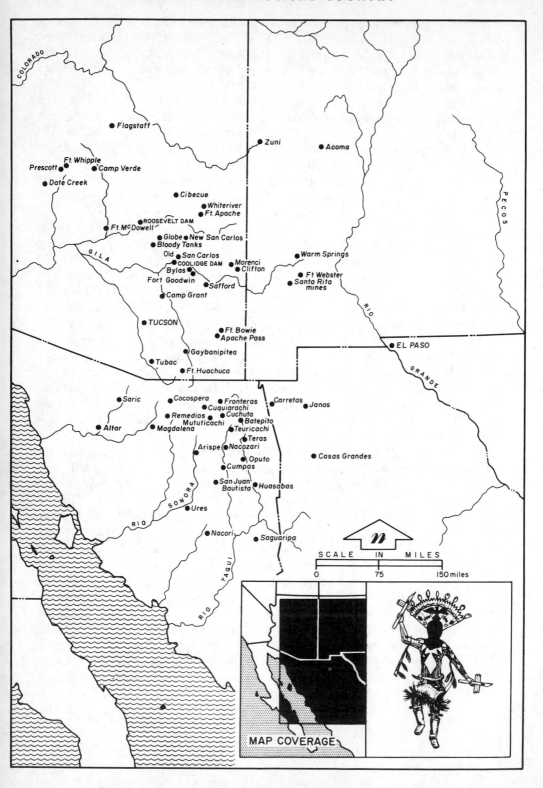

COLORADO

• Flagstaff

• Zuni

• Acoma

Ft. Whipple
Prescott •
• Camp Verde

• Date Creek

• Cibecue

Whiteriver
• Ft. Apache

ROOSEVELT DAM
• Ft. McDowell

• Globe • New San Carlos
• Bloody Tanks

Old • San Carlos
• COOLIDGE DAM
Bylas •
Fort Goodwin
• Safford

• Camp Grant

• Warm Springs

Morenci
• Clifton

• Ft Webster
Santa Rita
mines

GILA

• TUCSON

• Ft. Bowie
Apache Pass

• Gaybanipitea

• Tubac
• Ft. Huachuca

PECOS

RIO

EL PASO

GRANDE

• Saric

• Altar

• Cocospera

• Fronteras
• Cuquiarachi
Remedios •
Mututicachi
Magdalena •

• Cuchuta
• Batepito
Teuricachi •
• Teras

Arispe • • Nacozari
• Oputo
• Cumpas
San Juan
Bautista • • Huasabas

• Carretas
• Janos

• Casas Grandes

SONORA

RIO
• Ures

• Nacori

• Saguaripa

RIO
YAQUI

SCALE IN MILES

0   75   150 miles

MAP COVERAGE

source of contact applied in both the Apache and Navajo cases.

There were, however, also peaceful contacts in both cases. During the 1700's the Navajos lived for over a generation more or less at peace with the Spaniards of New Mexico. It will be remembered also that the Navajos around Mount Taylor sampled mission life for two years before giving it up as undesirable. Contacts of this sort gave an acquaintance on a broader and more balanced basis with Spanish culture. Similarly, the Apaches had peaceful contacts. However, these were confined almost entirely to the "Treaty Period" a hundred years after the beginning of intensive raiding. The peaceful contacts for Apaches came very late rather than early in the period of hostilities. Moreover, the Apache contacts during the treaty period were of a very special sort. They were in the first place exclusively with the soldiers and Spanish settlers who gathered around presidios. They were not with missionaries under the mission system. The contacts were debauching, through the Spanish determination to make drinking as popular as possible, and demoralizing, through the deliberate peace-through-dependency policy of the Spaniards. No Spanish official or citizen was engaged in promoting any constructive activity among Apaches. Even the discipline of forced labor was not included in the situation. Thus, the largely idle Apaches, both men and women, who gathered around presidios, not only became debauched but also to a great extent objects of scorn on the part of the Spaniards. There was nothing similar in Navajo experience during the Spanish period.

The basic situation of freedom from Spanish domination was the same for Navajos and Apaches. This led to the selection of elements from Spanish and from Pueblo cultures on the part of the Navajos which enriched and developed their own culture. The Apaches also selected, but what interested them was different. They chose horses instead of sheep, but they never raised and bred the horses. Habitat undoubtedly influenced them, but more important was the readily available supply in the vulnerable Sonora communities. The Apaches chose warfare as a way of life, somewhat as did the Plains Indians. The Navajos did not make such a choice, although warfare by raiding played a prominent part in their lives during the last part of the Spanish period. Over a period of 150 years the Apaches made warfare an integral part of their lives. It was this choice of warfare that constituted the revolution in Apache life stimulated by the contact with the Spaniards.

The Apaches remained isolated, in a way that the Navajos were not, from surrounding sedentary native peoples. It is true that the Navajos began before 1800 to raid and plunder the villages of the Pueblo Indians, but this was after a period of long and close contacts with much cultural interchange, both before and after the Spaniards entered the area. The Apaches, on the other hand, from the beginning, classed all the sedentary Indians to the south of them — Pimas and Opatas — as fair game and raided them equally with the Spaniards. Thus, they isolated themselves by high walls of hostility from all neighboring Indians. It is true that they maintained trading relations with Pueblo Indians of the northeast, such as Zuni and Isleta, but these were occasional and not very influential contacts. With their closest neighbors they were not on a basis of friendly interchange. Thus they were much less influenced by native sedentary peoples than were the Navajos.

There were probably about the same number of Athapaskan-speaking Indians south and west as there were north of Zuni at the time the Anglo-Americans took over political control of the Territory of New Mexico (which included modern Arizona). The Athapaskans north of Zuni who had come to be called the Navajos numbered probably around seven to eight thousand in the 1840's; south of them, between the Rio Grande and the Verde rivers and extending from the White Mountains to south of the Gila River there were also possibly seven thousand Atha-paskans. They were more widely dispersed than the Navajos and had even less tribal unity. In customs and language they were considerably more like the Navajos than they were like the other Athapaskans who roamed eastern and northern New Mexico. The Spaniards and Mexicans had come to call them Apaches, the same term that was applied to the Plains Indian-like Athapaskans of northern and eastern New Mexico. However, they lacked the cultural influences from the Plains Indians which characterized the other groups of Apaches and they also lacked the Pueblo Indian influences which had affected the Navajos. Like the Navajos, they farmed, but less regularly and less intensively, and during the previous two hundred years had come to rely heavily on the supplementation of their food supply by raids into Sonora and Chihuahua.

As hostilities intensified during the 1700's, the Spaniards and Mexicans slowly came to distinguish several sub-groups among these southwestern Apaches. On the east were bands which ranged the headwaters of the Gila River and southward along the Mimbres River; the Spaniards came to know these groups especially well after the first important mining in New Mexico developed in 1804 at Santa Rita del Cobre (near modern Silver City). The Apaches encountered here were often called the Mimbreños and this became a collective term for bands which recognized a man called Juan José as an influential leader. Southwest of the Mimbreños, ranging from about the present Arizona-New Mexico boundary to the valley of the San Pedro River, were groups who commanded the main corridors of Apache raiding into Sonora; they came to be called the Chiricahuas. North of the Chiricahuas, ranging the middle Gila River and its northern tributary the San Carlos, were a number of different groups under no unified leadership who were called the Pina-leños. North of the Pinaleños, from Black River through the headwaters of the Salt River to the edge of the Mogollon Rim, lived what may have been the largest of the groups, distinguished by the Spaniards as the Coyoteros. Northwest of the Coyo-teros, ranging the Tonto Basin and the Mogollon Rim as far north as modern Flag-staff, lived the fifth group which came to be known as the Tontos. The last three of these were the least known to the Spaniards and those who made the greatest use of agriculture; they constituted the greater part of the western Apaches and re-mained the most isolated from the Anglo-Americans during the early part of the Anglo invasion. Each of the groups was well established in the locations mentioned before 1800 and remained so localized until after the Anglos began to interfere in their ranges in the 1860's.

The contacts of the western Apaches with Anglos began well before the arrival of General Kearny in Santa Fe, and they were both friendly and hostile. By the 1820's trappers and traders had begun to come regularly from the northeast to

Santa Fe and had established something of a headquarters at Taos on the upper Rio Grande River. About one hundred Anglo trappers obtained licenses from Santa Fe Mexican officials in 1826 to trap along the Gila River; in pursuing their trapping they came into contact with Apaches along the river and twenty men in one party were killed at the western margin of Apache territory. At the same time Anglos leased the Santa Rita del Cobre mines and here made agreements for peace with the Mimbreños under the leadership of Juan José. Apache raiding had broken out again in Chihuahua and Sonora due to the Mexican government's failure to continue the Spanish policy of gathering and giving rations to Apaches around presidios. In an effort to control the Apaches, the states of Chihuahua and Sonora offered bounties on Apache scalps. Some Anglos entered into this trade along with Mexicans. The immediate result, during the 1830's, was a fierce renewal of Apache fighting. One American (or Englishman) named Johnson made himself infamous in 1837 among both Apaches and Anglos by a treacherous violation of friendship with Juan José, the influential Mimbreño. In an effort to acquire scalps, Johnson fired a howitzer into a group of peaceful Apaches near Janos, killing many including Juan José. This action turned Mangas Coloradas, a relative of Juan José, into an enemy of white men. Under his leadership the Mimbreños forced the abandonment of the Santa Rita mines and eliminated Mexicans from southwest New Mexico. By 1837 the beavers had been trapped out of the Gila, the fur trade was in decline, and Anglo contacts with Apaches ceased.

The United States government after taking possession of New Mexico and making it a Territory of the nation slowly moved toward consideration of the relationship of the Indians in the region to the country as a whole. The precedent followed was that of making peace treaties with the Indians as independent nations, or rather in the words of Chief Justice of the Supreme Court John Marshall, "dependent domestic nations." In 1847 when an Indian agent was appointed for New Mexico, the national Congress appropriated five thousand dollars for the purpose of gathering information as a basis for treaties with the Indians. In 1850, at the same time that a commission was set up for surveying the boundary established between Mexico and the United States as a result of the Treaty of Guadalupe Hidalgo, thirty thousand dollars were appropriated for making treaties with Indians along the border. Meanwhile, General Kearny and Colonel Kit Carson in following the "Gila Trail" between the Rio Grande and the Colorado rivers had passed through the territory of the Mimbreño, Chiricahua, and Pinaleño Apaches. They found all the groups wary, apparently feeling out the nature of the Anglos, but, upon proffers of friendship, ready to trade and not inclined to fight. It was apparent that Mangas Coloradas, the Mimbreño leader, and other Apaches were making a distinction between Anglo-Americans and Mexicans. Kearny and Carson informed them that the Anglos had conquered New Mexico, and the Indians were inclined therefore to look on the Anglos as their allies against the Mexicans, with whom they considered themselves in a continuing state of war. By 1850, however, after discussion in the vicinity of Santa Rita with the treaty-making officials accompanying the Boundary Commission, Apache leaders found themselves faced with a policy which they could not accept.

In the first place the Anglos insisted, as a result of the pacification provision of the Treaty of Guadalupe Hidalgo, that Apaches make treaties with them which would deny the right to continue their raids into Mexico. This would have meant giving up a way of life of long standing and moreover it did not make much sense to Apaches, who considered that, since both Anglos and themselves were obviously enemies of the Mexicans, the Anglos should encourage their warfare on the Mexicans. In fact, the Boundary Commission reported, the Apaches held that their Mexican raiding was legitimized as a result of their becoming peaceful with the Anglos. It also became apparent to the Apaches that the Anglos had adopted a position which was totally without reason, namely, that the Anglos, by virtue of having conquered the Mexicans, in some way became proprietors of Apache territory. The Mexicans had never conquered the Apaches and hence how could the Anglos as a result of conquering the Mexicans lay claim to Apache land? As one student put it, the Apaches could not understand by what legerdemain the Anglos claimed control of their territory.

As they became aware of the Anglo viewpoint, the Apaches grew increasingly wary of their new invaders. Moreover, the situation among the Mimbreños became touchy when gold was found near Santa Rita del Cobre in 1850 and Anglo prospectors who moved into the area beat up Mangas Coloradas when he tried to persuade them to leave by telling stories of more gold farther south. Nevertheless, progress in treaty making proceeded. In 1852 an agreement for peace was made at Acoma Pueblo with some Apaches who were probably Coyoteros from the White Mountain region. In 1853 and 1854 an effort was made to set up a reservation for the Mimbreños in the vicinity of Santa Rita del Cobre. These Apaches, often called the "Southern Apaches" by the Anglos, were placed under the jurisdiction of an Indian Bureau agent named Dr. Steck. An army post, Fort Webster, was established near Santa Rita del Cobre, and Mimbreños were persuaded to gather there upon the promise of food. The food did not come; the Indians left and carried out a few raids to the south, but in 1854 agreed to gather again and, under the direction of Dr. Steck, settled down to farm and accept some government aid. They continued under these peaceful conditions for another three years, despite the death of more than half of them through disease on the "reservation."

In 1857 Apaches from the west, as well as a few who had settled at Fort Webster, raided deep into Sonora, some settlers in Arizona were molested, and Agent Dodge of the Navajos was killed by Apaches. These events led to efforts on the part of Agent Steck to seek more peace agreements, at the same time that the army sent out a foray of four hundred soldiers to punish the killers of Dodge. Steck conferred with Cochise, a strong leader of the Chiricahuas, and got him to agree to permit the Overland Mail unmolested passage through his territory, an agreement which the Chiricahuas kept until 1861. Steck also extended his peace conferences to the Pinaleños, three thousand of whom promised to remain at peace with the Anglos, and to the Coyoteros whom he met at Safford and obtained the promise of what he reported as twenty-five hundred to keep peace with Anglos. These conferences indicated a desire for peace with the Anglos, but not the Mexicans. The continued peaceful farming activities of the Mimbreños under Steck's management and the supplementation of their produce with government rations suggested a means for maintaining peace. Apaches were apparently ready to grant permission for Anglos to pass through their territory, but they were not ready to accept prohibition of raids into Mexico nor unregulated settlement in their territory by incoming Anglos.

They were, however, willing to allow settlement providing settlers paid them for the privilege of mining or ranching on their land. Some Anglo ranchers had begun to do this, but the trend toward peaceful arrangements between Apaches and Anglos was suddenly upset in 1861. In that year a young cavalry lieutenant named Bascom stationed in Chiricahua territory sought to recover a Mexican captive from the Chiricahuas by taking Cochise and other leaders as hostages during a peace conference. Cochise escaped, the lieutenant murdered the other leaders, Cochise retaliated by murdering an Anglo trader, and war was on. The agreement which had been maintained for four years not to molest the Overland Mail was broken, and raids on Anglos in southern Arizona by various Apache groups broke out. In the same year the American Civil War began, Confederate troops entered Arizona, the cavalry detachments left, and Apache raids occurred in many places, so that practically all of the small Anglo population which had filtered into Arizona moved out. A turning point in Apache-Anglo relations had been reached. Lieutenant Bascom's action, together with the internal conflict among Anglos, ended the trend toward peace.

The new era in Apache-Anglo relations opened with the recovery of New Mexico by Union forces and the declaration of a war of extermination against the Apaches by General Carleton from his headquarters in Santa Fe. He had been ordered to keep the east-west communication lines open at all costs. His officers had been forced to fight as they came through southern Arizona at Apache Pass, fending off with some difficulty a coalition of Apaches under Mangas Coloradas and Cochise. Carleton's reply was the establishment of Fort Bowie inside Chiricahua territory and the increase of troops at Fort Webster. He was determined to keep the Mimbreños and Chiricahuas under control in order to maintain the Overland Mail. Within a few months after the regarrisoning of Fort Webster the troops killed Mangas Coloradas — in 1862 — and during the next two years, through disease and harassment by the cavalry, the Mimbreños were reduced to a state of weakness. Nevertheless, in company with the vigorous Chiricahuas, they continued to raid into Mexico and to harass Anglos wherever they found them in southern Arizona and New Mexico.

In 1863 gold was discovered at Prescott and immediately the Apache border warfare extended to central Arizona. Fort Whipple was established at Prescott and, although the Indian policy of the government now called for peace agreements rather than extermination, neither the military men nor the settlers appeared to believe in such policy. Despite an agreement with a band of three hundred Tontos in the vicinity of Fort Whipple, soldiers ranging the area killed twenty Indians, and hostilities between Tontos and the gold-seekers became bitter with sporadic killings on both sides. Farther south, in the vicinity of modern Miami at Bloody Tanks, Anglo settlers treacherously arranged for a peace talk at which they fed the Indians poisoned food and killed twenty-four. Raids continued back and forth between settlers and Indians, typified by bloody massacres led by the same Anglo who had engineered the poisoning at the "Pinole Treaty" incident in the Tonto Basin. This man had been commissioned as a colonel and, when the Territory of Arizona was created in 1863, the legislature backed his type of activity by calling for a war of extermination. In 1865 the troops from Fort Whipple killed another influential Tonto leader and a drunken Anglo killed a third. The retaliatory murders and massacres multiplied until it appeared that central Arizona might have to be abandoned by the Anglos. Coalitions of Tonto Apaches and Yavapais, who had also been victims of the ruthless feuding, cut off all communication between the Colorado River and the Verde.

At the same time fighting increased in southeastern Arizona. Fort Goodwin was established in the Pinaleño territory on the Gila River and soldiers campaigned in unsystematic fashion in its vicinity, killing those Apaches they came across. The troops from Bowie also campaigned here and there in Chiricahua territory. Fort Buchanan south of Tucson was captured by Chiricahuas in 1865. Conferences became impossible because truces were violated by one side or the other and neither soldiers nor Indians trusted one another. An effort to set up a reservation at Fort Goodwin with the offer of food and protection to whoever would settle there was ignored by the Indians. As fighting intensified in 1865 at the southwestern margin of Apache territory and threatened the Pimas on the Gila River, still another fort was established, Fort McDowell at the southern margin of Tonto-Yavapai territory. For the first time in history there was now a line of forts within Apache territory — Fort Whipple, Fort McDowell, Fort Goodwin, Fort Bowie, and Fort Webster, with other lesser posts between, such as Camp Grant. Designed to constitute a ring of protection from the Apaches for the slowly filling southern Arizona area, as well to contain the Apaches in their own territory to prevent raids into Mexico, the forts were far from successful. It was apparent that the forts could not keep the small Apache raiding parties from entering Mexico and that they were not effective even in providing protection for the settlers now pushing into the Apache country itself.

From 1865 to 1871 different arms of the War Department, the Department of the Interior, and the Territorial Legislature were at odds with one another on methods to be pursued to bring about peace with the Apaches. The Territorial Legislature, strongly backed by Arizona settlers who had precipitated the bitter warfare in central Arizona, wanted extermination or unconditional surrender of all Indians, but the Territory had no means for carrying out a war of extermination, the total of armed men it could muster being fifteen hundred. It was therefore dependent on the federal government, and the federal government was divided within itself. The Army, insofar as it could be said to have had a consistent policy, seemed to take the position that all that could be done was to punish Indians who committed violence and to let the peaceful Indians go their way. The various generals in command during this period seemed to waver between conducting vigorous cavalry raids on Indian settlements, trying to persuade Indians to settle around forts by offers of rations, and attempting to resettle groups out of areas where they customarily ranged. The variations in the views of commanders added up to no policy at all. The Department of the Interior showed a similar lack of clear policy, but nevertheless, first through Poston and then through Leihy, its general Indian agents in Arizona, showed a heavy leaning toward a policy of peaceful negotiation. The prevailing idea seemed to be the removal of Indians to areas where they could farm or learn to farm among already peaceful Indians. Thus eight hundred Yavapais were persuaded to move out of the embattled central Arizona area to the Colorado River; the remaining Mimbreños were urged to move from the Santa Rita del Cobre area to Bosque Redondo in eastern New Mexico. Neither plan worked, but both indicated the general drift of the Indian Bureau program.

In 1869 awareness of the seriousness of the issues involved in the Indian problems became strong throughout the nation. President Grant appointed a Board of Indian Commissioners to work out a humane and practicable policy to guide the Indian Bureau in its work throughout the whole United States. As the Commission began consideration of Indian policy, General Sherman announced, as the War Department's view of the Apache problem, that the best thing to do would be to have the Army and the settlers withdraw and turn the country back to the Indians. Probably a major precipitating incident for the crystallization of something that could be called a policy was the Camp Grant massacre in 1871.

This massacre typified Anglo-Apache relations in the early 1870's. Several of the many bands of Apaches had become convinced, often through capable and far-sighted leaders like Eskiminzin of the Arivaipa band of the Pinaleños, that a peaceful attempt at settled farm life under protection of soldiers was the only course for survival. Other bands who had suffered murder at the hands of Anglos were determined to fight against Whites in their territory to the bitter end. There were Army post commanders who had no conception of long-range policy and who merely shot Apaches wherever they found them. There were others who viewed the situation in the larger perspective and who tried to encourage good working relations between Indians and themselves and other Whites. Thus all over the Apache country there were different situations of contact. The Coyoteros had remained so far fairly isolated from the Anglo advance, valuable minerals not yet having been discovered in their territory. For the most part they spent their time in farming and hunting and took no part in the warfare that raged in central or southeastern Arizona, where feud and massacre had determined the course of Anglo-Apache relations. The Pinaleños were drawn now into the Chiricahua and now into the Tonto realm of hostilities, and they were still moderately interested in raiding Sonora, but many of them were inclined toward working something out with the Whites. They had been less involved in reprisal warfare than either Tontos or Chiricahuas, and they had not yet suffered the disorganization and disease which had weakened the Mimbreños in their closer contact with civilization.

One group of Pinaleños, the Arivaipas of the San Pedro Valley, new settlers themselves (for a century) in Sobaipuri territory, had decided, under the leadership of a man named Eskiminzin and the encouragement of the post commander at Camp Grant in the Arivaipa Valley, to settle peacefully and devote themselves to farming. This they were doing at Camp Grant in the spring of 1871. But other Pinaleños and Chiricahuas had been raiding in southern Arizona — the Pima villages and the settlements along the Santa Cruz River and the vicinity of Tucson.

People in Tucson were roused against Apaches; filled with the race hatred of the period and disrespect for the Army, a party of Tucsonans with a group of Papago Indians, who had long been enemies of the Apaches, set out for Camp Grant under the belief that Indians living there had raided the Santa Cruz Valley. Attacking early in the morning they killed at least seventy-seven women and children, seven men, and took prisoner twenty-nine children who were sold as slaves. The fighting men of the village at Camp Grant, including Eskiminzin, happened to be away at the time of the attack. This massacre was somewhat more extensive than most of the others carried out by Anglos and was widely reported over the United States. The fact that it had been carried out against obviously peaceful women and children roused Anglos outside the west and gave impetus to a federal Indian policy which the new Board of Indian Commissioners had been working out. Known as Grant's "Peace Policy," it was designed to replace the fumbling and frustration of the War and Interior Departments' handling of Indian problems.

The executor of the Peace Policy as now set up in 1871 was Vincent Colyer, secretary of the Board of Indian Commissioners. Congress gave him seventy thousand dollars "to collect the Apache Indians of Arizona and New Mexico upon reservations . . . and to promote peace and civilization among them." The program was one which was being applied throughout the western United States, confining Indians to portions of the land over which they had formerly ranged, giving them military protection from the invading Whites and providing food while they were encouraged to become self-supporting through agriculture or stock-raising. It was a policy already put into effect for the Navajos and the Mescalero Apaches of the east. Colyer worked hurriedly, over a period of several months, calling conferences with various Apache groups and designating areas for each as reservations. Colyer's plan called for creating reservations, wherever possible, in areas "remote from white settlement" where retaliatory border warfare could be most easily avoided. Colyer, after conferences with Apaches and military men and very little discussion with the Anglo settlers, designated four areas as Apache reservations – a large area around the army post of Camp Apache (later Fort Apache) where Coyoteros were to be gathered, the Tularosa Valley in southwestern New Mexico where the remnants of the Mimbreños were to be sent, an area around Camp Grant where Eskiminzin's Arivaipas and other Pinaleños were to live, and Camp Verde in central Arizona for Tontos and Yavapais. In addition a temporary reserve was set up at Date Creek west of Prescott.

Meanwhile the War Department, skeptical of permanent results from the Peace Policy, proceeded with its plans to control the Apaches. General George W. Crook, who had been engaged in confining Indians to reservations in the Plains country, was assigned to pursue the same policy among the Apaches just before Colyer had made his visit to Arizona. After an attack on a stagecoach near Wickenburg in which Anglos were killed by Indians from the temporary reservation at Date Creek, General Crook ordered that all Apaches would be required to be on the assigned reservations by February, 1872, and announced that after that date he would hunt down all found off the reservations. At the same time he instituted rigid control of Indians in the reservation areas with a daily roll call and count, as a measure for keeping them confined to the reservation areas. Many Indians came in to the reservations but many also remained away. Trouble developed at Camp Grant and for various reasons it was abandoned; in its place a reservation was set up adjoining the Camp Apache one on the south, with headquarters at San Carlos on the Gila River. In all the reservation areas the Indians were in a state of unrest and uncertainty. Fearful of white men's diseases, expectant of treachery and massacre from the Whites, resistant to the daily military muster, and often with insufficient food as dishonesty or inefficiency in administration interfered with rationing, the Indians, although generally anxious for peace, were in a far from happy condition. Only the Fort Apache Reservation could be called moderately peaceful.

Toward the end of 1872, as Indians ran away from the reservations and raided White settlements, especially in the Prescott region, General Crook began his campaign of rounding up all who were not on the reservations. Using Apaches as scouts, especially from the Fort Apache Coyoteros, Crook organized nine columns of troops to converge on the Tonto Basin from all directions, picking up and killing if necessary all Apaches encountered. In three months, by April, 1873, the campaign was finished. Three hundred Apache fighting men had been killed; several hundred families had been rounded up and placed on one or another of the reservations. Crook now instituted complete military control over all the Indians and instructed his post commanders at each reservation to help the Indian Bureau agents in their program of agricultural development and schooling. In his view the Apaches were to be treated "as children in ignorance, not in innocence." The Indians were now all placed on five reservations, for in 1872 another reservation had been created for the Chiricahuas in southeastern Arizona bordering on Mexico.

Immediately difficulties began, which were reminiscent of the troubles of the Spaniards in their early efforts to "civilize" the Indians of New Mexico, Chihuahua, and Sonora. Like the Spanish missionaries and civil authorities, the Anglo military and civil authorities came into conflict over policy and jurisdiction. Like the Spanish civil authorities, Anglo Indian agents sought to enrich themselves at the expense of the Indians (by corrupt practices in the rationing system). For more than ten years post commanders on the reservations and agents of the Indian Bureau maneuvered and opposed one another for control of the administration of the reservations; they fought over management of the roll call, the issue of rations, maintenance of law and order, and the management of agricultural improvements. Essentially the conflict was over the issue of the strictness of military control. Usually, but not always, the Indian agents stood for less strictness of control of the Indians; but on the other hand Crook's policy called for trial by Indian juries for Indian offenders, which Indian agents opposed. Often the conflict could be interpreted only as over authority, with no principles consistently involved. Apaches on the reservations inevitably became aware of the conflict in some degree and leaders were often resentful at finding their affairs tossed from one group of administrators to the other.

Within the Department of the Interior the idea grew that all the Apaches of the west should be concentrated on one reservation. The Arivaipa and other

Indians of Camp Grant had been moved in 1873 to San Carlos. In 1875 just after the mixed Tontos and Yavapais had begun work on a large irrigation ditch at Camp Verde, the fourteen hundred Indians were also ordered removed to San Carlos, a removal which was quickly accomplished but with a very serious factional fight among the Indians on the way. In the same year, after conflict between military and civil officials at Fort Apache, the Coyoteros were ordered removed to San Carlos and eventually sixteen hundred were reported to have been sent. In 1876, after a factional fight among the Indians and fighting between them and Whites around the reservation, about half the Chiricahuas were removed, 325 to San Carlos and 140 to Hot Springs where since 1874 the remnants of the Mimbreños had lived in New Mexico; 400 Chiricahuas remained at large but eventually came to San Carlos. In 1877, under the leader Victorio, 453 Mimbreños, together with the Chiricahuas who had gathered at Hot Springs, were removed to San Carlos. Thus by 1878, except for some groups which remained scattered through the old Coyotero and Tonto territories, all the western Apaches had been concentrated at San Carlos on the Gila River. There were more than five thousand Apaches now under the combined civil-military control on the San Carlos Reservation. They consisted of Indians who had never formerly been associated at all, such as Tontos and Mimbreños, Arivaipas and Coyoteros, Yavapais and Pinaleños. They included groups implacably hostile to Whites, such as the Chiricahua faction who recognized Geronimo and Juh as leaders, and groups consistently friendly to the Whites, such as the Coyoteros under Miguel and the Arivaipas under Eskiminzin. The majority wanted peace and were willing to settle down, but there were restive groups who could adjust neither to the reservation discipline or Anglo authority. Few of the groups had experienced precisely the same kind of administration on the reservations where they had lived. The Chiricahuas especially had lived with a very loose administration under Jeffords, the friend of Cochise; they had also experienced a great deal of freedom of movement between the Chiricahua and the Hot Springs reservations.

At San Carlos the administration took definite form under Agent John P. Clum, a man recommended, in accordance with federal policy, by the religious denomination which had been given the Apache field for missionary work — the Dutch Reformed Church. His administration lasted for three years, from 1874 to 1877. Clum was successful in ousting the military authorities from positions of administrative control and took over management of the daily roll as well as passes on and off reservation or to parts of the reservation away from the agency; he conceived the idea, and was successful in having it made a reality, that the Army serve merely as patrol at the edges of the reservation and as pursuers of groups who escaped. Clum installed a basis of self-government among the Indians by instituting an Indian police system. His system required that the various groups of Apaches and Yavapais elect from among their own number several individuals to serve as police. These men then became responsible for law and order and for representing the group to the agent. The police thus served as an advisory group and complaint channel as well as officers of the peace. Clum also maintained courts in which he with Indians chosen as judges passed sentences on offenders.

Clum believed that the giving out of rations should be stopped as soon as enough was being produced to feed all the Indians. He put as many Indians as possible, a majority of the able-bodied, to work on irrigation improvement, building, and road making, paying wages in the form of scrip cashable for goods at the agency store of the value of fifty cents a day. During Clum's administration foundations were laid for agricultural development and much work was performed by the Indians. But rations continued to be distributed for many years following.

In 1877 Clum resigned as a result of continued squabbles with the military over the handling of administration. This was after he had completed almost singlehandedly the concentration of all the Apaches on the San Carlos Reservation. The Mimbreños under Victorio and Loco had escaped from the San Carlos Reservation. They had for the most part, with the exception of Victorio himself who had escaped with a small band after being held elsewhere, been brought back and with them the dissident, anti-Anglo group of Chiricahuas under Geronimo's leadership. In 1878, after Clum's resignation, Anglos were hopeful that the Apaches were finally reduced to a state in which they could no longer oppose the invasion of their territory. About five thousand were now settled in the vicinity of the junction of the San Carlos and Gila rivers; a short distance up the Gila some five hundred Coyoteros were settled in the vicinity of modern Bylas. Irrigation canals had been constructed with Apache labor and government funds; there had been good harvests. Geronimo, as leader of the dissident Chiricahua group, had organized his followers for peaceful farm life. Anglo observers thought that the Apaches at San Carlos appeared to be on the road to self-sufficiency. In 1879 officials in charge decided that decentralization of the Apaches might be carried out. The large numbers living in close proximity around the agency bred some discontent, and there were many Coyoteros who wanted to move back northward to the mountain country around Fort Apache. Accordingly, some five hundred were allowed to go back and take up their old life there.

But meanwhile the Anglo invasion pressed on into the Apache reservation. On the east, copper deposits of great extent had been discovered and mine developers proceeded to disregard the reservation, beginning the working of what later became the rich Clifton-Morenci copper mines. On the west, silver, gold, and copper were found in the vicinity of modern Globe and Miami. Large pieces of what had been the reservation were sliced off for Anglo use and mines went into operation. The federal government did nothing to interfere with the encroachments. Miners pressed on from the west into the reservation and built the silver-mining town of McMillenville at the headwaters of the San Carlos River. At the same time, the expansion of the Mormon settlements into Arizona was taking place. West of Fort Apache, Mormon farmers pushed into the reservation, and on the southeast Mormons began the development of the rich Safford agricultural district on the Gila River, appropriating the water of the Gila to the extent that the Indian Bureau irrigation developments were seriously interfered with at San Carlos. What had appeared a scant ten years before to be an area sufficiently remote from White settlement to provide an isolated retreat for the Apaches now became an important focus of Anglo development. On the west miners and farmers were pressing into the reservation itself, and to the east the water which had been regarded as the basis for peaceful Apache life was being appropriated by Anglo farmers.

Moreover, the Indian Bureau agents themselves took an active part in the spoliation. The agent at San Carlos and the Commissioner of Indian Affairs in Washington not only permitted the encroachments and allowed the boundaries of the reservation to be surveyed in favor of the mining and agricultural interest, but they themselves even invested in the new mines. Graft in the purchase of ration supplies for the Indians also grew rapidly during 1878. The mismanagement of Indian affairs developed to such a point that in 1879 the San Carlos agent and even the Commissioner of Indian Affairs were removed from office, and a military officer was temporarily placed in charge of the Apaches. The shift in authority brought temporary improvement in administration of the agency, but as soon as a new Indian Bureau agent, recommended by the Dutch Reformed Church, was appointed, the graft and corruption continued anew.

The disorganization among Anglo officials was felt by the Indians, among whom dissatisfaction and factionalism again broke out. The policy of decentralization of the San Carlos agency had continued under the new agents, and many Coyoteros (of the Cibecue bands) had moved back into the very region where Anglos were pushing into the reservation from the west. In 1881 a religious movement began among them which had some features in common with the Ghost Dance messianic movement of the Plains Indians, which at the same time was being taken up by the Walapais to the north. A Cibecue shaman, Nocadelklinny, became convinced that he could bring back to life two Apache leaders who had died. Around his promises religious excitement developed. When his efforts failed to bring the men back to life, Nocadelklinny maintained that it would be necessary to destroy all the Whites before his power would work. Continued ceremonials with this purpose produced a high state of excitement among the Indians and Nocadelklinny was ordered arrested. A battle resulted in which Nocadelklinny was killed. The Indians then attacked Fort Apache and raided westward into the Tonto Basin. The uprising was put down only with the aid of troops from New Mexico.

Meanwhile, when the Cibecue rebels planned an attack on San Carlos, the Chiricahua faction under Geronimo's leadership became stirred up and fled the reservation. Geronimo and Juh joined Victorio, the Mimbreño leader, in Mexico. Later Loco and a portion of the Mimbreños at San Carlos also fled the reservation. Raids and depredations followed in southeastern Arizona, while a leader of the Cibecue Apaches, Nantiatish, attacked San Carlos and killed the chief of police. Nantiatish tried to promote a general uprising, but failed to gain more than a few hundred followers. His small force attacked McMillenville and was defeated. The reservation Indians refused to follow his lead and remained peaceful, but it was almost two years before the nearly one thousand Indians under Geronimo, Loco, and other anti-Anglo leaders were defeated and returned to the reservation. Their raids were stopped only after General Crook was brought back to Arizona and conducted a campaign which extended across the border into Mexico.

By 1884 peace was once again restored. The Nocadelklinny movement had been suppressed by the hanging of three leaders at Camp Grant. The raiding Mimbreños under Loco were back on the reservation and Geronimo, with his Chiricahuas, was established on the Fort Apache Reservation at Turkey Creek. The Army took complete charge of the San Carlos and Fort Apache reservations. Strict roll call and military discipline were once again introduced. Some seven hundred cattle were issued, and the Apaches were encouraged to raise stock in addition to continuing the farming which had meanwhile been proceeding as well as the reduced amounts of irrigation water, caused by the farming upstream on the Gila by Mormon settlers, would permit. The corrupt Indian agent, Tiffany, had resigned in 1882 and the slicing of the reservation by mining and other interests had been stopped in 1883. Crook's policy was one of "paternalism and justice." He had always been against the removal of Indians completely from their accustomed territory. He therefore encouraged the movement of Coyoteros to the Fort Apache Reservation, and nine hundred went back immediately after he took charge. He also continued the policy of native police and of trial by Indian juries. He believed that land should be assigned to individuals for their own use and that individual ownership be encouraged. During 1884 there was more intensive development of farming than ever before. Some twenty new dams were built by the Indians and on both reservations the Indians moved steadily toward self-sufficiency. Geronimo and his followers at Turkey Creek were among the most industrious farmers. Fifty-two Apache children, including the sons of Loco and Bonito, were sent to Carlisle boarding school in Pennsylvania. Again observers reported that civilization was steadily growing on the Apache reservations.

However, the old conflict between military and civil authorities broke out again. One issue was the trial by Indian juries, the civil authorities finding themselves shocked by such methods of execution as stoning and clubbing which the Apaches employed, rather than hanging or shooting. More important was a jurisdictional conflict over the management of the farming. The Army officials wanted to control it and particularly to have charge of land assignment. The Indian agent preferred that he assign the land. Eventually the decision went against the Army and the Indian Bureau took charge. There were now three thousand Indians, Apache and Yavapai, at San Carlos and two thousand Apaches at Fort Apache.

Then suddenly trouble developed again among Geronimo's Chiricahuas. General Crook believed that the drinking of homemade intoxicants, such as tulapai, was a major cause of disturbance on the reservation, and he had therefore ordered prohibition. Apaches settled at Fort Apache took the stand that he had no right to prohibit their use of homemade liquor. A number made tulapai and proceeded to drink it with the idea of making a test case. Tension was created by a delay in orders between Crook and his subordinate at Fort Apache; the 130 Chiricahuas under Geronimo's leadership became frightened and ran away from the reservation. The chase that was organized to bring them back lasted for four months. In the course of it Crook was replaced by General Nelson A. Miles. Eventually, after pursuit deep into Sonora in the Sierra Madre Mountains, Geronimo agreed to surrender and he and his followers together with other Chiricahuas who had remained at Fort Apache were sent to Florida, whence eventually, in 1913, the majority were sent to the Mescalero Reservation in New Mexico and a few were held as prisoners of war at Fort Sill, Oklahoma. Thus ended, after some fifteen years of effort on the part of the United States, the program to place the western Apaches on reservations and stop the conflict between them and the Anglo invaders of their territory. No further armed conflict between Apaches and Whites took place, except for isolated instances such as in the case of the Apache Kid, the lone raider.

Reservation life for Apaches settled down to peaceful acceptance of rations and constant effort to develop the reservation as a sufficient means of support. The agents discouraged quite successfully the old habits of hunting and food gathering which required scattering out over the reservation. To replace this means of support, Apaches worked at the irrigation projects on the reservation at San Carlos. By 1890 two thousand Coyoteros (later distinguished by ethnologists as White Mountain and Cibecue bands of the Western Apaches) had returned to the northern reservation and taken up pretty much their old life, namely, hunting, gathering, and intensive small-scale agriculture. They remained peaceful and were self-supporting, as they had been before the removal to San Carlos. At San Carlos it was a different matter. The land that could be irrigated for farming was far from sufficient for the support of the Indians and hence rations were necessary. A whole generation of Apaches grew up in this period accustomed to going regularly to the agency and there receiving the rations of beef, flour, beans, sugar, and coffee.

Meanwhile, agricultural development proceeded. The government farmers, assigned to carry it out with Apache labor did not always understand the technology necessary; flumes washed out or did not work; land was flooded out. As peace continued some Apaches moved northward up the San Carlos River and began their own farming development or continued the improvement of old dams which Pinaleños had used before the Anglos came into the country. The acreage under cultivation steadily increased and crops became more abundant. But outside events began to interfere. One long ditch at Dewey Flats, which had been the water-supply source for the Coyoteros settled upriver from the agency, had to be abandoned as the river level lowered in response to the unregulated taking of irrigation water by the Anglo farmers in the vicinity of Safford. During the 1890's more than half the Apaches at San Carlos had to have rations in order to exist.

Nevertheless, Apaches continued to develop and use the farm land and were consistently praised by Indian agents for their devotion to farming. Moreover a new source of living had grown up — work off the reservation for wages. The Territory of Arizona was growing rapidly; its population had doubled during the 1880's. Much of the new activity centered around mining and much of this, as we have seen, bordered the Apache reservation. Apaches during the 1880's worked at Globe and McMillenville, and still more were employed in Globe in the following decade. During the 1880's cattle ranching grew up rapidly in all the areas bordering the reservation and Apaches increasingly worked on the ranches. When a recession in the cattle business came in 1892, many Apaches had already become accustomed to wage work, so that when railroads called for laborers in the 1890's, many Apaches responded. The branch of the railroad from Globe to Bylas that later became a part of the Southern Pacific employed mostly Apaches during its construction in 1898. By 1901 so many Apaches were supplementing the reservation farming with off-reservation wage work that the agent contemplated discontinuing rations. In 1902 the last rations were issued — thirty years after the first issue when the San Carlos Reservation was formed in 1872.

In 1893 the Evangelical Lutherans established a school at Peridot some twenty miles north of the San Carlos agency. At nearby Rice the government set up a boarding school after 1896 and the usual methods of forced attendance were instituted. A large proportion of Apache children attended it during the next twenty years, learning to speak English, to read and write, to farm, to do housework, and the rudiments of various Anglo crafts. At the same time they learned harsh discipline and separation of the sexes. The school regime called for separation of boys and girls in all activities, the exclusive use of the English language, and the employment of punishments such as whipping, the carrying of a ball and chain, and solitary confinement on bread and water. Runaways were common. Many Apaches developed a hatred for Anglo ways as a result of the schooling, but many others also became devout Christians and devoted pursuers of the Anglo way of living. Many went from the school to other Indian Bureau boarding schools in Albuquerque and Phoenix as the latter came into operation.

Farming operations became less productive and less able to support the slowly increasing San Carlos population in the years following 1900, although the government continued their development and built a flour mill for the grinding of the wheat produced. Further attempts were made at encouraging Apaches to raise cattle, but with little success. Although the Apaches kept all the available acreage of farm land in operation from year to year, they did little with cattle. Instead the Indian Bureau began a program of leasing the large and excellent tracts of grazing land to white ranchers. Large cattle companies were formed and took over under lease almost the whole of the reservation. Proceeds from the leases were used in efforts to develop more farm land, by digging wells to supply water in place of the Gila River water which was being used in increasing quantities by Anglos upstream. The majority of Apaches were now making a living either off the reservation or through employment with the cattle companies which ran cattle on the reservation. Through about 1920, Apaches were largely excluded from mine work because of union opposition to their being hired. Nevertheless, other types of work were rapidly developing, particularly work on the large irrigation project of Roosevelt Dam, which was built during 1906–1911, and on highway construction. Roosevelt Dam lay in the former Tonto Apache and Pinaleño territory and was therefore readily accessible.

The trend was toward work for wages outside the reservation through the 1920's. The power of the mine unions was broken during World War I and this permitted more Apaches to go into mining. Many Yavapais drifted away altogether, taking up residence permanently away from the reservation, some going back to the Verde Valley. The Indian Bureau named an employment officer to take care of the considerable demand for Apache wage workers. Meanwhile, the Indian Bureau had determined to encourage Apaches to take advantage of the rich possibilities for cattle raising on the reservation and began to eliminate the Anglo ranchers, slowly discontinuing their leases during the 1920's. At the same time, the attempt to bring more farm land under cultivation, by drilling wells for irrigation water, was continued. In 1925 a new large irrigation project was begun with federal funds, designed to stabilize the Gila River water supply and to make it available for farmers farther down the river. This took the form of Coolidge Dam, situated very close to the site of the San Carlos agency. During 1925–1930, most Apaches of the San Carlos Reservation were employed in the construction of the dam and the other operations in connection with it.

When the dam was finished, however, in 1930 it meant that all the Apaches settled in the vicinity of the agency, as well as the agency itself, had to be relocated. The new site was near the Rice school on the San Carlos River, twenty miles north of the old agency. Here all the Apaches not settled at Bylas, which constituted practically all those who were not Coyoteros, were forced to move their homes and take up land which the Indian Bureau meanwhile developed for them. It meant a greater concentration of people and, moreover, as it turned out, it meant a practical end to farming. A considerable new acreage in addition to the small plots already being farmed was made available to the relocated Apaches. The work of preparation was, however, done entirely by the irrigation technicians of the Indian Bureau, and the land was entirely assigned by the superintendent of the agency. The idea of the superintendent was to make the Apaches self-sufficient with garden homesteads on a subsistence basis. The new and old land together was therefore, after it was prepared for planting, reassigned in two-acre plots to all families wishing to farm. The Apaches had become doubtful, so completely had they been left out of the planning and preparation, whether the land was really theirs any longer. Most had, moreover, become accustomed to outside work for wages. They showed little interest in the Indian Bureau's efforts to get them to take up subsistence farming on the new basis. For the next twenty years after 1930 they let most of the land lie idle or be farmed by the Indian Service farmer.

Meanwhile, the business depression of 1929 resulted in the curtailment of jobs anywhere off the reservation and Apaches who had settled elsewhere began coming back. The Indian Bureau, with the new policies of the Indian Reorganization Act as a guide, began intensive efforts to lay foundations for a cattle industry. Technical advisers were employed, good breeding bulls were bought, associations of Apache cattlemen were organized, and steadily during the 1930's a cattle industry developed. It was stimulated by the various types of federal funds which became available for use on the reservation. Civilian Conservation Corps crews of Apaches were put to work for wages improving the range and developing the water supply. As farming declined to almost zero, the cattle industry boomed, and by the 1940's San Carlos Apache cattle were in high demand in the market. By the mid-1940's the major source of San Carlos Apache income was from cattle, with off-reservation wage work on farms, mines, and construction running second. The annual income of the reservation in 1951 was $2,100,000, declining in 1953 by more than 50 percent to $900,000.

The growth of the cattle business among the San Carlos Apaches was accompanied and aided by a development of tribal government under the IRA. The beginnings of tribal government took place under Clum in 1874 when he organized "police" who were responsible for law order among the groups by whom they were elected. As Army and Indian Bureau control grew firmer all semblance at self-government disappeared, the agent seldom recognizing any actual leaders, but assuming sole responsibility himself for reservation affairs. This system of superintendent management was modified slightly in the 1920's, when the Commissioner of Indian Affairs asked all superintendents of Indian reservations to form some sort of group with which Anglos could deal as representatives of the tribes. On the San Carlos Apache Reservation, the superintendents of the 1920's gathered about themselves Apaches or Yavapais who could speak English fairly well and who were disposed to cooperate with the superintendent and his plans. This was called the Business Committee and was constituted as a formal body for the purpose of having some group to deal with in connection with the water rights and other aspects of the Coolidge Dam Irrigation Project. The superintendent did not actually know whether he had in his Business Committee a representative group; he knew only that he could fulfill the law by dealing with some group which could sign agreements with the tribal name.

As the San Carlos Business Committee became more active, an opposition to it developed, which was thought of by the superintendent merely as a group of chronic dissenters motivated purely by anti-Anglo sentiment. In 1935 when, in accordance with orders from the Indian Bureau, the superintendent of the San Carlos Reservation set out to invite the tribe to form a constitutional government and a tribal council, it was the Business Committee then existing who wrote a constitution which was submitted to the tribe for vote and which was adopted. A tribal council was set up in 1936 and immediately embarked on a number of activities, such as the reassignment of the farm land, the division of the reservation into grazing districts, the regulation of grazing and the reduction of stock to an operating maximum, and the organization of other tribal enterprises. The Tribal Council continued as an active element in San Carlos Apache life, organizing and managing from 1946 on two tribal stores, as well as the expanding cattle business, and arranging leases with Anglo miners for the operation of asbestos mines on the reservation. It also in 1954 took over the operation of a farm enterprise which brought the long-unused tribal agricultural land into production again. A chairman of the Tribal Council became an active leader nationally in Indian affairs through the National Congress of American Indians and the Arizona Inter-Tribal Council. By 1953 the Apache Tribal Council had hired an Anglo general manager to organize its business enterprises, but in 1955 replaced him with an Apache. The San Carlos Apaches had become a business corporation, producing by far the largest part of all Apache income and expanding steadily.

In 1918 influenza struck the reservation and two hundred Apaches died. This was also a period of depressed income when the copper mines shut down immediately following World War I. At this time about 1920 a man appeared in the Fort Apache area whose name was Silas John. He claimed to have magical power of a special kind for curing various diseases. His influence spread and a cult developed around him, extending over the two Apache reservations, to the Yavapais at Camp Verde and Fort McDowell reservations, and to the Pimas and the Mohaves. It became known as the Holy Ground movement and developed a ritual combining Christian and native Apache features. "Holy Grounds" were established at Bylas and at Rice. In 1920 Apache leaders petitioned the superintendent to permit these activities to continue unmolested, since there had been some overt opposition by missionaries on the reservation. At that time there were two active missionary groups, the Lutherans who had been on the reservation since the 1890's, and the Catholics who came in later. The leaders interested in the Holy Ground activity asked for religious freedom and maintained that their movement was devoted to the best beliefs in both Christian and native Apache religion; they held that missionaries from Christian sects were not making adequate progress. The movement was allowed to continue without molestation and grew through the 1920's, as Silas John became an accepted curing practitioner. He was, however, convicted in 1933 on a charge of murdering his wife and sentenced to life imprisonment. His cult continued, becoming a regular part of reservation religious life during his incarceration. Many leaders, especially from Bylas, kept in touch with him while he was in jail. He was released from prison in 1954 and returned to assume his place as head of the cult.

The majority of Apaches had come strongly under the influence of the Evangelical Lutherans, who sent a vigorous missionary to the reservation after 1900. Maintaining missions and a school continuously, the missionary studied the Apache language and translated hymns and doctrine into the language. The Catholic mission under the Franciscans also developed, so that by 1940 nearly all Apaches had been influenced either by the Lutherans or the Catholics. However, in the 1930's a group of Apaches who had been Lutheran, in protest against the lack of Apache participation in the church management, split off and organized the Independent Apache church which continued as one of the most important Christian influences in Apache life. It was affiliated with no other church, but maintained liaison with other independent Indian churches which had split off from Christian parent organizations on other reservations, such as the Yavapais of Camp Verde, the Hopis of Third Mesa, the Pimas, and the Mohaves. They held summer camp meetings jointly and there was an interchange of speakers and revivalists. The Assembly of God and the Pentecostal sects entered the reservation in the 1940's; the former was extremely active in welfare work and organizational activities, maintaining during the early 1950's the most active, if not the largest, congregation of any church on the reservation.

Apache history during the Anglo period was the record of a conquest. It takes us back again to the situation of the Pueblos, the Tarahumaras, the Mayos, and Yaquis as they came under the domination of the Spaniards in the 1600's. The Apaches did not suffer conquest until two hundred years after the southern and eastern Indians. Yet the process showed many similarities to what happened under the Spaniards — a heavy reliance on force of arms by the invaders; a division of the Indians into the resigned acceptors of domination and the implacably resistant;

sporadic religious movements hopeful of White destruction; intense conflict among the invaders over policy; and persistent but never wholly successful efforts to replace the Indian way of life with that of the conquerors. But there was also an important difference in the behavior of the Anglos as compared with the Spaniards. The essence of the Anglo approach was to wall off and isolate the Indians from their own society, in contrast with the Spanish assumption that the Indians were to assume full status in the society of New Spain. The Anglo program, it is true, shifted in various directions with respect to this point; there was no unity of view on the part of military and civil officials charged with carrying out the government program. These shifts had notable effect on the Indians. But in general the early pattern of Indian-White relations in the United States conditioned all subsequent developments and this pattern was one of isolation rather than direct incorporation.

The Apaches, contrary to Anglo tradition, were not fiercely resistant to friendly relations with Anglos. They began with friendly approaches, and many Apaches throughout were anxious to continue these. But the uncontrolled advance of Anglos quickly resulted in conflicts over land and resources, and hostilities developed. It required some twenty years of contacts before a majority of Apaches became convinced that they would have to give up their old way of life and submit to conditions laid down by the Anglos. But by the 1870's a majority did so decide and leadership for that course grew up promptly, as for example in the case of Eskiminzin, despite great provocation to behave otherwise. The Anglo handling of this majority however was very uncertain. The conflicts over authority among Anglos, the policy of concentration of all the Apaches, many of them far from their customary range, and the corrupt handling of Indian affairs all contributed to instability. The rationing system constituted a demoralizing influence, as it had around the Spanish presidios. The basis on which the rapid economic development of the Apaches grew during the 1930's and 1940's lay in Indian Bureau management rather than Apache initiative.

CHAPTER TEN

Yumans

ALTHOUGH THE SPANIARDS made some contact with all the Yuman-speaking Indians of the Colorado River Valley and those who ranged east of the Colorado, these contacts had relatively small influence on either Indians or Europeans. The Yumans, with two exceptions, remained outside the pale of direct Spanish influences.

The first Spanish contacts with the Yumans coincided with a period of marked migration and shifting of territorial base among these small tribes. There were movements taking place, apparently during the 1500's and the 1600's, which brought tribes from the west down into the Colorado River Valley (such as part of the Cocopas), which resulted in migration up the Colorado (as for instance the Mohaves), and which led to eastward migration toward the Pimans out of the Colorado River Valley (the Kavelchadom and Coco-Maricopa). The Spanish records are so spotty with reference to the Yumans that we have no way of knowing just how many tribes there were at first Spanish contact or where they lived. Alarcón as the marine arm of Coronado's expedition made the first contacts with Yumans; however, he mentioned only two of the several groups who were probably at that time in the vicinity of the mouth of the Colorado River. In 1540 Alarcón sailed up into the lower Colorado River, how far is uncertain, but probably not past the mouth of the Gila River. He encountered quite a few Indians and mentioned two names which may have been tribal — Quicama and Coana. His relations with the Indians were very friendly and he in some way without interpreters obtained stories of bearded white men and other marvels — very probably much influenced by his own preconceptions. He built a chapel somewhere near the mouth of the Colorado River and left a cross there.

No other Spanish expedition reached the Colorado River Yuman tribes until 1605 when Oñate's party in search of the South Sea came to the river and visited tribes on it in the vicinity of the delta and for some distance above the mouth of the Gila River. Oñate's party spoke of five tribes, two of which were mentioned in slightly different form by Alarcón. These were the Kohuana and Halyikwamai, corresponding to Alarcón's Coana and Quicama. The other three identified by Oñate's party were the Cocopa, near the mouth of the river, the Halchidoma farther north, and the Amacavas still farther north in the present Parker Valley.

The Halchidomas have since become extinct, while Amacava was the term applied to themselves by the group that came later to be known as the Mohaves. Oñate's relations with all of these were friendly.

For nearly a century there was no direct contact with Yumans on the Colorado River, although Kino in the 1690's made some acquaintance with "Opas and Coco-Maricopas" living among Pimas on the Gila River. It was Kino who was responsible for the first intensive contacts with Yumans of the Colorado in 1698. In that year his party, in an effort to determine the nature of California as island or peninsula, crossed the great desert of what is now southwestern Arizona and reached the Gila River not far from where it empties into the Colorado. Here they encountered Yuma Indians, and an interpreter who knew Pima and Yuma enabled Kino to converse with them. The Yumas were friendly, bringing food, and Captain Manje distributed canes of office among the headmen. As had other Yumans, they told remarkable stories to Oñate's party, including accounts of white men in buckskin to the east, and the Woman in Blue. The latter was a white woman dressed in blue who had preached in an unknown tongue some years before. She was veiled and carried a cross. She was shot twice and left for dead by the Indians, but came to life and eventually flew away. Manje connected this story, versions of which he had heard from Upper Pimas, with the Spanish woman María de Jesús de Agreda who believed herself miraculously transported to North America in 1630 where she claimed to have preached among the Indians. On the way back from this visit Kino's party traveled through villages on the Gila River — west of the Gila Pimas — which were inhabited by Opas and Coco-Maricopas. They were friendly and allowed Kino to preach and urge peace between them and the Yumas on the Colorado River.

In 1700 Kino made another trip to the mouth of the Gila and again encountered Yuma Indians in considerable numbers. They were anxious to see him again and at least fifteen hundred assembled for mutual speechmaking. The Yumas asked Kino to stay for a while, and announced that other Yuman-speaking peoples were planning to come and listen to him and to talk. They mentioned the Halchidomas who lived up the river, and the Kikimas, Hagiopas, and Hoabonomos from downriver. Kino did not stay, however. He baptized two sick adults by request, gave out more canes of office, and then returned to the Pimería. But he went back later in the year, in a final effort to determine the nature of California's relation to the mainland of North America.

This time, as before, he came first to the Yumas at the junction of the Gila and Colorado rivers, and then went south to enter the Kikima country. As he traveled, he had a retinue of three hundred Yuma and Pima Indians from the villages on the Gila, one of which he named San Dionysio. Kino had promised to barter for food with the Kikimas and turn over what he received to the Yumas, whose crops were short. There was no military escort with him on this trip and he was received with the greatest hospitality and interest. In the Kikima villages Kino gave out canes of office and stayed for two days talking and listening. Some of Kino's cowboys from Dolores gave a demonstration of horseback racing which greatly impressed the Indians, who apparently had never seen horses before.

Kikimas joined his party as he proceeded in his explorations, so that some five hundred Indians now accompanied him. Kino crossed the Colorado River with his Kikima escort and encountered representatives of the "Cutgan" tribe on the west side, who brought him blue shells from the Pacific Ocean. Kino was also introduced to a Hagiopa (Cocopa?) from the south to give him further information. His whole visit was marked by the most friendly relations.

In 1702 Kino again went west for final confirmation of his discovery that California was a peninsula. He visited the Yumas again in their chief village at the confluence of the Gila and Colorado rivers and then went downstream to reach the point where the Colorado River emptied into the Gulf of California. He was accompanied by Kikimas, Cutgans, and Cocopas. He preached and gave out canes of office as he gathered information about the delta country. After seeing the sun rise on the far side of the gulf, proving that he was in California without having crossed a sea, Kino returned again to his work in Pimería.

But the Kikima Indians kept petitioning him to come or send other missionaries to them. They were especially insistent in 1706, sending messengers as far as the Papago village of Sonoita. Although Kino decided to visit them again himself, he never did, and no missionaries reached the Colorado River peoples again until 1748. In that year Father Sedelmayr went to the Colorado and made some contact with the Yumas — who behaved, however, very differently from what they had with Kino's parties. The Yumas at the mouth of the Gila threatened Sedelmayr with hostilities and stole some of his horses. There was no further contact until after the Jesuit expulsion.

In the 1770's the Franciscan Garcés and General de Anza made several expeditions which acquainted them especially with the Yumas and, to a lesser extent, with other Yuman-speaking peoples. Garcés was vigorously exploring the possibilities of expansion of the mission field and attempting to find a feasible passage to the Hopi country for work there. Anza was opening the westward land route to Upper California. In 1771, 1774, 1775, and 1776 these expeditions went through the Yuma country. Garcés went up the Colorado River as well, making some contact with Mohaves and Havasupais. The Spaniards came to know two headmen of the Yumas, whom they named Palma and Pablo, and received hospitality in the two principal Yuma villages. Relations were generally friendly for both the missionary and the Anza expeditions.

In 1779 the Franciscans decided that the Yumas were ripe for mission work and Garcés who had visited them so frequently was selected as the man for the job. A new policy, in which the missionaries did not concur, was to be tried. This was to have a small garrison of soldiers resident with the missionary, rather than to have a large presidio in the general vicinity of the mission. With misgivings, Garcés and another Franciscan took up residence on the west side of the Colorado River just downstream from the Gila junction. They began the building of two mission churches. In 1781, less than two years after the beginning, the Yumas rose up against the little group of Spaniards — soldiers and missionaries — killed all of them and destroyed the mission churches. The mission effort was never revived during the Spanish period. A punitive expedition under Fages in 1781-82 killed a number of Yumas. In 1799 Cortez reported that there were three thousand Yumas. There were no other Spanish contacts with the Colorado River tribes.

Meanwhile, movements and fighting continued among them much as it had in pre-Spanish times. During the 1700's the Coco-Maricopas moved eastward to join the Opas already on the middle Gila River. In the process of this shift of residence they probably absorbed Halchidomas, Kavelchadom, and other Yumans who had formerly been resident along the lower Colorado River and the lower Gila. There remained on the lower Colorado River the Cocopa and Kikima around the mouth of the river, the Yuma above them around the mouth of the Gila, and the Mohave above the Yumas in the Parker Valley and farther north. The Coco-Maricopas, Yumas, Cocopas, and Mohaves were all hostile to one another. Their intertribal warfare and the accompanying tribal migrations were at least indirectly affected by Spanish activities in the Colorado River region and farther east.

The upland Yumans were even less well known to the Spaniards than were the river Yumans. Spaniards had begun by the end of the 1700's to make distinction among the "Yabipais" and "Coninas" and Walapais. But contacts remained very fleeting and before the middle of the 1700's they were so little known that they were classed as "wanderers" or "mountain people" under the vague Spanish terms for nomads in general, such as Nixoras (applied to the southeastern Yavapai bordering on the Gila Pima country in southern Arizona), or Querechos (applied to the northeastern or middle Verde Yavapais), or Serranos (also applied to the middle Verde Yavapais), or Jumanas (applied to the Havasupais).

Espejo's expedition in search of mines into central Arizona first brought the Yavapais into Spanish ken. He called them Querechos and noted that those he saw near the site of modern Jerome in the upper Verde Valley wore small crosses dangling over their foreheads suspended from their hair. He saw this in 1582 and it was noted as a characteristic for more than a hundred years after, giving rise to the names "Cruzados" and "Cruciferos" applied by Spaniards of the Farfán mine-hunting expedition in 1598 and members of the Oñate South Sea expedition of 1604–1605, both of which passed through Yavapai territory. After the 1690's the Yavapais were increasingly confused with Apaches on maps and records, but actual Spanish contact with them was negligible, and no contacts even as intimate as Espejo's in 1682 developed. Father Garcés seems to have been the first Spaniard to hear and apply more or less properly the name they used for themselves. Coming through their country in 1776 he recorded their name as "Yabipai."

Although there was probably a greater consciousness of the Havasupais among the Spaniards, relationships can hardly be said to have been any more intimate than with the Yavapais. Cárdenas of the Coronado expedition heard of Indians downstream who were possibly Havasupais, when he discovered the Grand Canyon in 1540. Again, the Hopis who prepared to fight when they heard of the coming of the Espejo expedition in 1583 asked aid from mountain dwellers to the west, possibly the Havasupais. The Hopis finally decided not to fight Espejo and their allies were told to go away, with Espejo's party only having heard them mentioned. Farfán, looking for mines for Oñate in 1598, also heard of wandering tribes, whom he called Jumanas, in the vicinity of the Havasupai territory. In the 1660's Governor

Peñalosa of New Mexico claimed that he had reduced to missions both the Coninas and the Cruzados. The Hopi term for the Havasupai is Cohonino; evidently Peña-losa was referring to the Havasupais and the Yavapais respectively. However, there is no record whatever that either group was missionized by this time; the presumption therefore is that Peñalosa, in an effort to present himself in a good light at his trial for malfeasance in office, was exaggerating greatly his encouragement of missionary activity.

In 1672 two Franciscan missionaries were assigned to the field of the Coco-ninos, but they seem to have remained in the Hopi country and never reached them. After the Pueblo Revolt of 1680 until the late 1700's no missionary effort on the part of the Franciscans extended that far west, or even as far as the Hopis. Father Garcés in 1776 was guided by Walapais to Havasupai Canyon where he became acquainted with the Indians and noted thirty-four families. Although the Spaniards thus knew something about, and had begun to use the Hopi term or some variation of it for the Havasupais, such as Cosnina, Conina, Cohonino, etc., no mis-sionary or administrative contact of other than passing nature was ever established. Relations, so far as is known, were all friendly.

There had been friendly relations between the Hopis and the Havasupais before the Spaniards arrived, and Havasupai-Hopi trade relations, and possibly a military alliance, continued during the Spanish period. Thus the Havasupais came to know something of the Spaniards at least indirectly. But it is also true that the Havasupais were interested in establishing direct contact with the Spaniards in the 1700's. Once, at the height of the Hopi efforts to keep the Spaniards out of their country in 1754, the Havasupais were reported to have sent ambassadors to the Spaniards to ask for missionaries. The Havasupais went through Hopi country and the Hopis, hearing of their intention, killed all the Havasupais, in order to prevent their making contact with the Spaniards. If this event actually occurred it is clear that it did not cause lasting hostility between Havasupais and Hopis. At the time of the great drought in the Hopi country, about 1780, it was reported to Governor Anza that hundreds of Hopis had taken refuge with the Havasupais, where they were received kindly and given food. There is no record of other contacts of the Havasupais during the Spanish period.

In general, the attitudes of the Yumans towards the Spaniards were favorable and friendly. The treatment dealt Garcés' mission was hardly to be expected. The explanation probably lies in the fact that the soldier garrison lived in such close proximity with the priests and also in the very great distance separating the Yuma country from the nearest presidio.

In the interval between the destruction of the Franciscan mission by the Yumas and the finding of gold in California the Yuman-speaking peoples of western Arizona and the Colorado River Valley had almost no contacts, and none of any more than passing effect, with white men of either Hispanic or Anglo background. They had become differentiated into some seven or eight groups by the early 1800's — three upland tribes, the Yavapai, Walapai. and Havasupai; and four or five river-valley tribes, the Mohave, the Maricopa, the Halchidoma, the Yuma and the Coco-pa. There were in addition other tribes of the same linguistic family living west of the Colorado River, such as the Kamia, the Paipai, and others; these were rather small in numbers and never came to be clearly distinguished from one another by the invading Whites.

During the seventy-five years following the killing of Father Garcés by the Yumas, the aboriginal ways of life along the Colorado River continued with little change. All the groups had for long been hostile to one another and carried on periodic warfare for the purpose of acquiring "scalps" or farm land. The scalps were an important source of supernatural power among the river tribes and constituted a strong impetus for intertribal warfare. Warfare was a major interest. It was carried out not only for different purposes from the warfare of the Navajos and Apaches, but also in totally different ways. The river Yuman tribes, in fact, despised the Apache mode of ambush, strike, and run. Their battles were announced, formal lines of warriors were drawn up, and direct hand-to-hand combat continued until one side was all dead or completely routed. This sort of warfare was common among them during the first half of the 1800's. There were no Mexican troops to interfere and intertribal hostilities continued in the traditional manner. It was not until the California gold rush that Yumans began to experience any contact with Anglos.

During the first half of the 1800's hostilities were recurrent between the Yumas and other Yumans both to the north and to the south. Halchidomas, Kohuanas, and Kavelchadom who had lived along the Colorado River north of the Yumas moved sometime during the late 1700's and early 1800's eastward along the Gila River. They were driven steadily eastward both by the Mohaves who were attacking them from the north and by the Yumas from the south. Battles occurred in 1842 and again in 1857 or 1858. But by the latter date the three tribes had merged with the group called Maricopas by the Anglo-Americans and had been given land along the Gila by the Pimas. The Pimas fought as allies of the Maricopas in the battle of 1857 and inflicted a severe defeat on the combined forces of the Yumas and Mohaves. Nevertheless, the retreat of the Maricopa group from the Colorado River left a large area of river bottom land vacant south of the present town of Parker, Arizona. Into this territory the Mohaves had expanded from the north, and a tribe of non-Yuman-speaking people, the Uto-Aztecan-speaking Chemehuevis, also moved into the area. This large area, which later became the Colorado River Reservation, remained in a state of disputed Indian ownership during the early days of Anglo contacts.

Meanwhile, beginning in the late 1840's, the Anglo-Americans moved into this region of intertribal hostility and shifting groups. Some parties of gold-seekers headed for California traveled the southern route, crossing the Colorado River in the Yuma country. Exploration parties sponsored by the United States Army and seeking a route for proposed railroads made brief contacts with Yavapais, Havasupais, and Walapais, as well as Mohaves. The Yuman country from the mouth of the Colorado to the Grand Canyon suddenly assumed importance in the westward expansion of the United States as transportation routes pushed westward to California. In 1852 a steamboat was brought and assembled in the Colorado River delta. Although it sank, further efforts to develop transportation on the Colorado

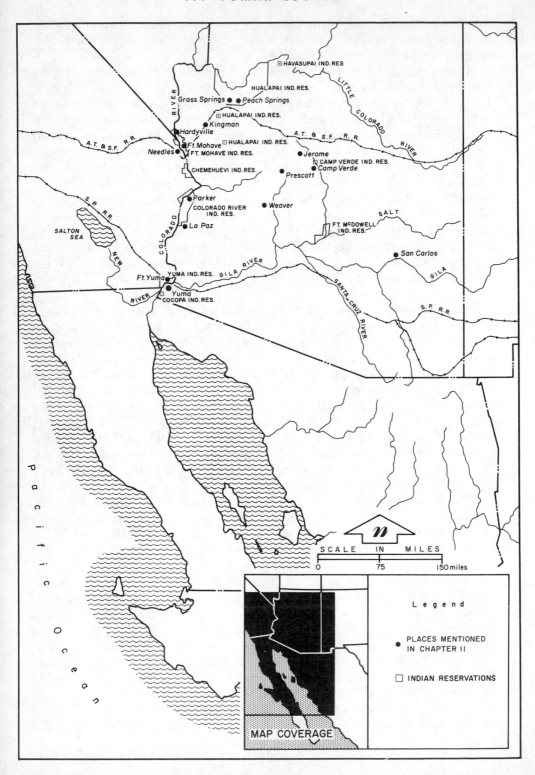

HAVASUPAI IND. RES

HUALAPAI IND. RES.

LITTLE

COLORADO

Grass Springs ● ● Peach Springs

HUALAPAI IND. RES.

● Kingman

A.T. & S.F. R.R.

RIVER

Hardyville

Ft. Mohave   HUALAPAI IND. RES.

Needles   FT. MOHAVE IND. RES.

● Jerome

CAMP VERDE IND. RES.

● Camp Verde

CHEMEHUEVI IND. RES.

● Prescott

A.T. & S.F. R.R.

RIVER

S.P. R.R.

SALTON
SEA

COLORADO

● Parker

COLORADO RIVER
IND. RES.

● Weaver

SALT

FT. MCDOWELL
IND. RES.

NEW

● La Paz

GILA RIVER

● San Carlos

GILA

Ft. Yuma ●   YUMA IND. RES.

RIVER

Yuma
COCOPA IND. RES.

SANTA CRUZ RIVER

S.P. R.R.

P
a
c
i
f
i
c

O
c
e
a
n

𝓃

SCALE   IN   MILES

0   75   150 miles

Legend

● PLACES MENTIONED
IN CHAPTER II

☐ INDIAN RESERVATIONS

MAP COVERAGE

River continued, so that during the 1850's, 1860's, and 1870's steamboats plied from the delta northward to Hardyville. It was apparent to the Anglo-Americans that the country of the Yumas must be controlled if the southern route to California was to be kept open. In 1853 some wagon trains were molested, and an Army detachment under Colonel Heintzelman was sent to establish a fort at the site of the destroyed Franciscan mission. The Yuma Indians offered some resistance, but were defeated by the troops, and the Army post was established. There were at this time between fifteen hundred and two thousand Yumas under the leadership of a man called Old Pascual by the Anglos.

In the north, immigrant trains had begun to travel the Beale Trail, crossing the Colorado in the territory of the Mohaves, near the present town of Needles, California, after passing through Walapai territory to the east. During the 1850's there were some small raids on such trains by the Walapais but no extensive fighting. A few Mohaves attacked a company of cavalry en route to Fort Yuma, but otherwise relations with Indians were friendly. The Mormons especially had made friends with the Mohaves, as part of their effort to win the Indians of the west, whom they called Lamanites, to their fold. By 1858 a few Mohaves had been baptized by Mormon missionaries, and some had listened to Mormon statements that the Army explorations and the railroad route through the Mohave territory would result in the Mohaves losing their land.

In 1858 a large number of Mohave warriors joined with the Yumas in an attack on the Maricopas. Badly defeated, the Mohaves fled back northward and found themselves taunted by Walapais who had learned of the defeat and who were not friendly with the Mohaves. Egged on by the Walapai jeers and anxious to win back their name as warriors, the Mohaves, according to their version of the incident, attacked a wagon train from Iowa which had crossed the Colorado River on the Beale Trail. The Mohaves killed eighteen Anglos and drove off six hundred head of cattle forcing the train to turn around and go back to Albuquerque.

An Army attempt to punish the Mohaves and to gain control of the area, as they had at Yuma, was immediate. A detachment of cavalry was dispatched promptly to the Mohave Valley to seek a site for a fort. Opposing the entrance of the soldiers into their territory, the Mohaves gave battle — with arrows and war clubs in their traditional manner of head-on combat. More than half the Mohave warriors were mowed down by the soldiers' guns before they retreated and let the Anglos have their way. In the following year, 1859, five hundred soldiers came to the surveyed site and set up Fort Mohave in the heart of what had been the Mohave river bottom lands. The post commander immediately called a meeting and told the Indians what the conditions of peace would be. They would have to give up men who had taken prominent parts in the raid on the wagon train and also give up leaders as hostages to be held in custody until it was clear that the rest of the Mohaves intended to live in peace. Probably without full understanding of what the hostage part of the bargain involved, the Mohave leaders agreed. The principal Mohave leader at the time, Cairook, himself, agreed to be a hostage and he with six other leaders was taken to Fort Yuma, along with three men given up as prisoners to atone for the raid. Here the hostages were kept under soldier guard but not in jail. According to a Mohave account, soldiers one day attacked the jailed men. According to the Anglo account, the prisoners and hostages tried to escape one hot day when they could no longer stand the confinement. The result was the killing of Cairook and four other Mohave leaders.

Yarateva, or Irataba as the Anglos called him, now became the most important leader among the Mohaves and from that time until his death was called the "head chief" of the Mohaves by the Anglos. He accompanied Anglos to Los Angeles and took the view that the Anglos were too strong to oppose and that the Mohaves must settle down and be peaceful.

The early 1860's saw a sudden influx of Anglos into the territory of the various Yuman tribes. In 1862 some gold-seekers discovered placers at La Paz on the Gila, which was in the country vacated by the Halchidoma and which Yarateva was interested in settling the Mohaves. In the following year, gold was discovered near Prescott, and brought a flood of prospectors into the country occupied by the Yavapais. In Cataract Canyon, where the Havasupais lived, lead was discovered in 1863 and a mine immediately opened. Cattlemen moved into the Walapai country and began to appropriate water holes at gunpoint.

War broke out first with the Yavapais. Two Indians accused by the Anglos of stealing were killed at the newly opened mine of Weaver. This happened almost at the time of first contacts after the Prescott gold discoveries in 1863. It opened a period of feuding and small massacres which lasted for eleven years and took a toll of four hundred Anglos and one thousand Yavapais.

With trouble brewing all through the Yuman country, Charles D. Poston, who had been appointed Indian agent for the Territory of Arizona, called a council meeting at La Paz in 1864. It was attended by representatives of the Yumas, Yavapais, Chemehuevis, and Mohaves. Other than a recommendation for a reservation, there were no results, but the meeting did establish Irataba in Anglo eyes as the major leader of the Mohaves and the most influential Yuman. The recurrent killings of and by Yavapais continued as the Anglos took control of their water holes, and drove mine shafts here and there in the hills. In the north, where Anglo cattlemen had moved into Walapai territory, some serious fighting broke out. The eight hundred or more Walapais had begun to resist. In 1865 Irataba tried to make peace between the Walapais and the Anglos, but the latter proceeded to kill an important Walapai leader, Wauba Yuma, and the peace efforts failed. The only peace negotiations that worked were an agreement made at Oraibi under Hopi auspices between Havasupais and Yavapais who agreed to remain at peace with each other.

In 1865 Poston decided to send Irataba to Washington in order to make sure that he would be impressed with the strength of the Anglos and influence his followers accordingly. Traveling by way of San Francisco, Irataba was received in Washington by President Lincoln, and was greatly lionized. He helped Poston present the needs of the Mohaves for a reservation and, so the story goes, came back with a promise, many medals and decorations, and a general's uniform. In the same year, in accordance with general Anglo policy for Indians, a large reservation, called the Colorado River Reservation, was set aside for the Mohaves. This included land in the river bottom around modern Parker — and presumably also included some seventy-five thousand acres surrounding Fort Mohave. The Colorado River Reservation was not only for the Mohaves but for all tribes of the Colorado River drainage.

Meanwhile, the resistance of the Walapais to the encroachments on their land had continued. The Army carried out a campaign against them in 1866–1867 and forced the surrender of the most hostile leader, Sherum, who was influential among the more northerly bands. Lleva Lleva, another leader in the south, also ceased fighting. By 1871 most of the Walapais were living on a military reservation in the vicinity of what is now Peach Springs, under the control of the Army.

In 1867 government funds were appropriated for the construction of a large irrigation canal in the northern part of the Colorado River Reservation. Work was begun and Irataba persuaded many of the Mohaves to move away from Fort Mohave and settle in the vicinity of the new canal. It was not ready for operation until 1870 and when it was opened was badly damaged by river flood waters. Nevertheless the Mohaves began to farm, making what use they could of the canal. Sporadic fighting continued between them and other Indians, but not with Anglos. There was fighting with Chemehuevis and also with Paiutes. In a battle with the latter, Irataba was captured and disgraced by being disrobed. From then until his death in 1874, he steadily lost prestige with Mohaves. The Army had also stimulated hostility between Paiutes and Walapais and occasional fights developed between them. In 1874 the agent for the Mohaves conceived the plan of bringing the Walapais to the Colorado River Reservation. They were brought to the river but were unhappy and ran away almost immediately. In 1875 they were rounded up and brought back to the southern part of the reservation near La Paz, whence they again escaped and went back to Peach Springs. They were allowed to remain and a reservation was created for them there eight years later, after some years of continuing border warfare with Anglo miners and cattlemen.

The Yavapais ranging the central part of Arizona from the Verde to the Colorado and from the Gila to the Plateau had been engaged in constant small-scale conflict with the Anglos. In 1872 some of them raided the Gila Pima villages. Army posts were set up near Prescott and on the Verde River, and southward to the borders of the Apache country. There was some mixture of northeastern Yavapais with Tonto Apaches; the Yavapais and mixed-bloods came to be called Mohave-Apaches, or sometimes Yuma-Apaches by the Anglos. By 1875 all had been rounded up and placed on a piece of land near the Army post at Camp Verde. After constructing a large irrigation ditch there, they were forced to move again — to the newly-created San Carlos Apache Reservation, where an attempt was being made to concentrate the Western Apaches.

In 1880 a reservation was created for the less than three hundred Havasupais at their summer territory in Cataract Canyon. Three years later some of the territory in which the Walapais had been living, bordering the Colorado River, was established by executive order as the Hualapai Reservation.

Thus, all the Yuman tribes were placed on reservations embracing parts of the land which they had occupied, with the exception of the Yavapais who were moved into Apache territory. The thirty years of settlement of the area by the Anglos had been characterized by sporadic fighting, but no concerted campaigns by the Indians. The Southern Pacific Railroad was completed through Yuma in 1877, and ten years later the Santa Fe Railroad was completed through Kingman in Walapai and Mohave territory. Anglo settlement was on the increase, particularly in the areas suitable for cattle raising, although the gold and other mines which had stimulated early settlement slowly ceased to produce. The brunt of the contact was now in the Walapai country. All Indians had been forced out of the Yavapai country; the Havasupais in their small canyon off the travel routes remained isolated; the Mohaves, Yumas, and Cocopas were in areas either not yet attractive to Anglos, or were effectively isolated by their reservations.

The Indian Bureau continued trying to build up the Mohave land into usable irrigated acres. Troubles continued with the irrigation system, but slowly Mohaves moved down from their land around Fort Mohave and worked at farming. A boarding school was established at Fort Mohave where Anglo children as well as children from various Yuman tribes attended. The Indian Bureau officials made efforts to stop the Yuman customs of cremating the dead and burning property at the death of an individual. They also made efforts to encourage the making of baskets as a means of income. Most of the Yumans in the period from about 1880 to after 1900 presented a sorry picture in the eyes of the Whites. The Anglo towns were growing, and on the outskirts of all those in Yuman territory groups of Indians established themselves, seeking odd-jobs and begging for food and clothing. Needles and Kingman on the Santa Fe Railroad developed little poverty-stricken colonies of Mohaves and Walapais respectively. Several bands of Walapais, driven out of their homes by the steady disappearance of game and food plants, camped habitually near Kingman. Much of the land on the Mohave reservation around Fort Mohave had become the property of the Santa Fe Railroad and although some dispossessed Mohaves moved south to Parker, many became hangers-on around Needles, living in ways that led the Anglos to despise them. At Yuma the Indians also became in part casual wage-workers and sellers of knickknacks to railroad passengers. The Yumas and Mohaves became well known to Indian Bureau employees and others living near them as a "depraved" group because of certain of their sexual customs. Epidemics of measles and other diseases struck the Walapais in 1886 and 1887 and killed some Indians.

In 1889 there was a revival among the Paiute Indians to the northwest in Nevada of a religious movement called the Ghost Dance. This spread widely among reservation Indians of the western United States. Paiute practitioners came among the Walapais in 1889 and explained the movement to them. The performance of a modified form of the traditional circle dance and the following of certain ritual rules, it was believed, would result in the disappearance of the white men, the return of game animals, and the repossession by the Indians of all their land. The Walapais immediately took up the new religion. At Grass Springs, seventy-five miles northeast of Kingman, some five hundred of the eight hundred Walapais prepared to dance and stay until the world should change. The immediate acceptance of the messianic ideas by the Walapais was based undoubtedly on recent events in their relations with Whites. They had been forced off land in dozens of places and excluded from the use of long-used springs, including sacred ones. Anglos had cohabited forcibly with Walapai women. Settlers around Kingman seriously considered poisoning the Indians by various means in order to rid the country of people they regarded merely as a nuisance. Immediately after the creation of the reservation in 1883, there had been conflict with Anglo squatters in the area, and with others who persisted in moving onto the reservation after its creation. Although the Indian agent attempted to protect the Indians, the latter found themselves up against men with pistols who were ready to use them without regard to any land or other rights, no such rights, of course, being recognized for the Indians. The disputes over the reservation had resulted in 1884 in the killing of both Anglos and Indians. The Walapais had reached such a state of poverty that rations had to be issued. It was in this atmosphere that the Paiute Ghost Dance was introduced.

For two years the Walapais participated in the cult. At least two bands of Walapais never joined — those of the southern Walapai country under the leader Lleva Lleva, and the followers of Walapai Charlie, both of which groups habitually camped around Kingman. But most of the tribe joined in. After the millennium failed to appear during 1889, they settled down to periodic five-night ceremonies. The first appearance of the Ghost Dance ritual brought fear to the Anglos around Kingman, as it did to Anglos elsewhere in the western United States where Indians embraced the cult. It was proposed to call troops, but when investigation revealed that the Walapais expected an end of the Whites through supernatural rather than military means, they were permitted to proceed. By 1891 various promised miracles had failed to take place, and the Indians gradually lost interest in the dance and ceased to perform it. But the Ghost Dance spread from the Walapais to the Havasupais. In 1891 Chief Navajo, the most influential leader among the Havasupais, visited a Walapai Ghost Dance and went home greatly interested in it. The Havasupais adopted the dance as a unit and danced it for a year, when it also died out among them as suddenly as it had been taken up.

During the 1890's the Havasupais received special attention from the Indian Bureau, in an effort to develop their farming. They had been excluded from land on the plateau from which they habitually derived part of their subsistence. A government farmer established himself in Cataract Canyon and built an irrigation system which brought more land under cultivation, but this was destroyed by flood in 1909 along with the agency buildings. In 1894 a school was set up in the canyon. Although there was resistance to any attendance at first, gradually all the children began to attend either there or at the boarding schools at Fort Mohave and Truxton Canyon. For some years after 1895 Agent Bauer carried on a campaign to eliminate cremation and the associated destruction of houses and property at death. The Havasupai population had dwindled since 1850 from about 300 to half that number, 166, in 1906. But a slow increase began at that time and by 1941 there were 250 living on the reservation and an unknown number off the reservation. An Episcopal missionary began to work among the Havasupais in the 1920's, but had made only a few converts by 1950. In 1941 the Havasupais organized a tribal council in accordance with the Indian Reorganization Act, and a shift in leadership from older to younger men began. For a generation or more before, the native office of headman had disintegrated as the government agency took over all the functions of leadership, such as irrigation, care of the aged, trail maintenance, education of the young, law enforcement, and the regulation of agricultural activities. The Indian Bureau in 1942 instituted a tribal herd of cattle with Indians in management positions.

After 1900 some Yavapais began to drift off the San Carlos Reservation where they had been placed with Western Apaches, many finding their way back to their old territory. As more settled around Camp Verde in central Arizona some land was set aside for them there in 1914 to be shared with Tonto Apaches, both being called Yavapai-Apache. Land had previously been set aside for "Mohave-Apaches" on the lower Verde River in 1903 at Fort McDowell. On both of these Yavapais gathered and remained under Indian Bureau jurisdiction. Several hundred Yava-pais, however, remained on the San Carlos Reservation and participated in the cattle raising industry which developed there among the Western Apaches.

After 1884 the Mohaves remained divided into two groups, the smaller stay-ing on the land around Fort Mohave and numbering around three hundred, while the larger took up residence on the reservation at Parker, where they numbered around eight hundred and shared the Colorado River Reservation with some two hundred Chemehuevis. There was far more than enough land for the one thousand Indians on the Parker reservation and the Indian Bureau steadily developed a large irrigation system. Anglo settlers moved onto the Fort Mohave Reservation and large ranches grew up, the Big Bend Ranch in 1910 and the Sota Ranch in 1915. In 1935 Hoover Dam was completed and the threat of flood from the Colo-rado River was removed, making the land more desirable to Anglos. As a result of Anglo pressure the reservation was opened in 1940 to White settlement and more Anglos moved in. Meanwhile, the irrigation developments of the Indian Bureau proceeded on the Colorado River Reservation. These were given impetus by the placing of twenty-five thousand Japanese-Americans on the reservation during World War II. When the latter were moved out the Indian Bureau asked the Mohaves and Chemehuevis to open the reservation to colonization by other Indians of the Colorado River drainage, principally Hopis and Navajos. In 1945 families of these tribes began to move in and establish themselves as farmers, rais-ing alfalfa. The Colorado River tribes organized a tribal council in 1937 under the Indian Reorganization Act. It was this council which gave permission for the colonization and which set up a land code in 1940 to regulate the use of the new land brought under irrigation by the Indian Bureau. As the Hopi and Navajo colonists increased in numbers, it began to appear to the Mohaves that they would be outnumbered in the Colorado River Tribal Council and they began to oppose the colonization, contending that the Indian Bureau program had been forced on them. In 1957 further colonization by Hopis and Navajos was stopped.

There were four religious denominations working on the Colorado River Reservation by 1950 — the Church of the Nazarene, the Assembly of God, the Presbyterians USA, and the independent Mojave Mission. After conversion to one or another Protestant sect, the Mohaves, together with some Yavapais, Walapais,

Chemehuevis, Gila Pimas, and Western Apaches organized an independent group of churches, in which the ministers were all Indians of one tribe or the other. They held joint camp meetings in the summer months and carried on religious work quite independently of any Anglo religious group.

Military force was required to bring all of the Yuman groups under United States political control with the exception of the Havasupais, who never carried on hostilities with the Anglos. Once brought under control and assigned to portions of their old lands or, like the Yavapais, transferred elsewhere, all the tribes submitted peacefully to the programs of the Indian Bureau. Only the Walapais continued in conflict for a considerable period as they struggled against encroaching Anglos to retain a hold on their land. The small numbers and the relative isolation of all the groups rendered them of no special concern to the Indian Bureau. All except the Mohaves escaped allotment of their lands, but all experienced, at least in mild forms, the religious suppression of the Indian Bureau. The Mohaves were unique among Southwestern Indians in having a large surplus of arable land on their reservation beyond their immediate needs.

PART II
THE FRAMEWORK OF CONTACT: PROGRAMS FOR CIVILIZATION

Introduction

THE EVENTS OF CONTACT which have been reviewed for each tribal group were in large part the result of purposeful programs put into operation by the conquerors of the Indians. Each of the three peoples who became dominant in the region — Spaniards, Mexicans, and Anglo-Americans — to a great extent worked in accordance with plans concerning what they wanted the Indians to become as well as in fulfillment of their own special interests. The plans which the dominant peoples formulated were rooted in their own cultural values and reflected their particular interests. In certain respects their objectives regarding the Indians were in conflict. On some important points the Spaniards, the Mexicans, and the Anglo-Americans held basically different conceptions of human nature, and these different views resulted in programs for remoulding the Indians which rested on opposing foundations.

In the part which follows we shall attempt to summarize some of the major features of successive Spanish, Mexican, and Anglo-American programs for civilizing the Indians. Of these the Spanish program was unquestionably the most carefully conceived and the most consistent within itself. By the early 1600's Spaniards had had a great deal of experience with attempting to make over Indian lives. Indian policy for northwestern New Spain rested on much trial and error in connection with the Chichimeca Wars and other Spanish-Indian conflicts and collaborations in New Spain. The 1600's opened as an era for the application of tested concepts. In contrast, the Mexican phase of Indian history, marked by dominance of the Mexicans as an independent nation, was unsettled and strife-ridden for more than a hundred years. Although an enlightened policy was early formulated which continued the best features of Spanish policy, the Mexicans were not united enough to apply the program effectively. It was not until the 1930's that a new working Indian policy began to take form. Built on awareness of weaknesses and strengths of both Spanish and Anglo-American programs, the National Indian Institute program began to be effective only in the 1950's. Meanwhile, the Anglo-Americans had for a hundred years, with characteristic vigor, moved in several different directions at once. They had developed an Indian policy which seemed at most points inconsistent with the means set up for realizing it. These inconsistencies were institutionalized in the reservation program, which had become well established and highly elaborated even by the 1890's.

Purposeful planning on the part of the dominant peoples constituted an important determinant of what happened to the Indians. The programs for civilization were perhaps the major factor in giving direction to the flow of events in Indian and White contacts. However, much of the planning was based on misconceptions of Indian ways and consequently did not turn out as the dominant people expected. Although the programs established a framework for interaction, much happened that neither Indians nor Whites foresaw or bargained for.

CHAPTER ELEVEN

The Spanish Program

THE INDIANS were less well prepared than the Spaniards for their first encounters. Unless the Indians had myths dealing with the coming of strange, perhaps bearded supernaturals — as a few did — there was no set of ideas into which they could fit the Spaniards; they were forced to learn by experience the nature of the newcomers and gradually build up a conception of them for better or for worse. The Spaniards, on the other hand, had a set of categories in terms of which they were prepared from the start to think about and deal with the Indians. They knew before they even met any members of a tribe that they could expect to encounter barbarians. The ancient distinction in Europe between civilized and barbarian peoples was ready-made for Spanish use. It is true that there was at first the expectation of finding people with great cities and wealth—Japanese, or Chinese, or other Asiatics—but this was quickly dispelled as expedition after expedition met only with the village and wandering people of the northwest. By the time missionary work began, it was generally accepted that throughout the region the Spaniards would be dealing with barbarians or savages. As a result of this prefabricated label, they probably learned less during the first hundred years about the Indians than the latter did about them.

The concept *barbarian* presupposed the concept *civilization*. It rested on the idea that the Spaniards enjoyed a way of life which was of a completely different quality from, and of course immeasurably superior to, that of the barbarians. Among the Spaniards, the idea also was tied closely with an obligation to civilize the barbarians. This sense of obligation to change the barbarians was strong at the upper levels of the Spanish civil hierarchy and was embodied in the laws and regulations set up to govern relations with the Indians. It was, of course, the ruling principle in the church organization. Although individual civilians, and some ecclesiastics, became convinced as they came into direct contact with Indians that various groups of natives could not be civilized, nevertheless it may be said that throughout the period of Spanish activity in North America general policy rested firmly on this sense of obligation to civilize. Such a program was never seriously questioned as the *raison d'etre* of the Spanish conquest.

Moreover, there was no uncertainty at high policy levels as to what it was that the Spaniards had to offer the Indians. Church and civil officials were in agreement from the start on what the Indians should be made to accept as fundamental elements of civilization. It was agreed that Spanish regal authority and law must be the framework of Indian life. It was also agreed that the setting for these primary elements of civilization must be town life. In addition, the Indians must be made to dress in the Spanish manner at least to the extent of trousers and shirts for men and skirts and upper garments for women. They must also practice monogamy and employ formal marriage ceremonies, and they ought to live in adobe or stone houses. It is doubtful that any Spaniard who thought about a program of civilization would have omitted any of these items, although there were certainly differences of opinion about precisely what features of each trait-complex were essential.

That the introduction of each of these basic elements involved any replacement of existing corresponding traits among the Indians was not generally accepted by the Spaniards. On the contrary, prevailing Spanish opinion, especially among officials at a distance from the Indians, was that the barbarians lacked law and real authority, that they had either no religion at all or a species of worship which was called idolatry and was wholly evil (usually being regarded as worship of the Devil), that their settlements were not organized communities, that their sexual lives were unregulated, that their forms of body covering were not clothing properly so called, and that they lacked houses worthy of human beings. Thus, the Spanish view in respect to the process of civilizing was not that they were replacing existing functional institutions and culture traits, but rather that they were giving the Indians things which the latter did not have. Lacking government, religion, and civilized decencies, the Indians were being given the opportunity to know these things and should be grateful for them.

The great effectiveness, up to a certain point, of the Spanish program in changing Indian lives undoubtedly lay in the unity achieved in the imposition of these fundamentals of Spanish culture. The energies of both civil and church officials were fairly well united in presenting and enforcing, for example, the nonmaterial aspects of the program, that is, political and social organization and Christian belief and ritual behavior. There were, however, other features of Spanish culture in regard to which there was not this same unity, although each of these was regarded by various groups of Spaniards as essential. The primary vehicle of Spanish culture, namely, the Spanish language, was not imposed consistently nor was it regarded by all the missionary Orders as a basic feature of civilization. Jesuits differed among themselves on this point and in general, after 1600, Jesuits differed from Franciscans. Moreover, it was obvious that civil authorities at either the national or local levels did not conceive the learning of the Spanish language as an essential in their program; they at any rate did nothing about it.

Another matter about which there was considerable divergence among Spaniards was that of economic labor. Certainly there was agreement among civil and church officials on the great importance of disciplined daily labor, as often indicated in their pronouncements on the laziness of Indians in general. But the differences in circumstances of work offered to the Indians were usually profound as between civil and church officials. This was, of course, related to the specific interests of missionaries and civil employers in the frontier situations. In general, the missionaries sought to build up gradually habits of regular work with some appeal on the basis of community benefit, not in terms of a wage system for individual gain. On the other hand, those mine contractors who conformed to the laws of voluntary labor employed the wage system with its strong basis in individual interest, while those who did not conform to the laws introduced forced labor with a basis in neither individual nor community interest. The enslavement of non-Christian Indians introduced still a different concept of work. The Indians must certainly have gained the idea that the Spaniards placed a high value on putting people to work, but they could not have had a unified idea of the meaning of work in Spanish life, for it was not presented with the unity of definition which characterized, for example, Christian ritual.

THE CULTURE OF THE CONQUEST

To assume that Spanish culture of the 1500's in all its European complexity was somehow transported to America and the Indians made aware of it is quite unjustified. The sixteenth-century culture of Spain exhibited great regional as well as class variation. What we know of cultural transformation in Mexico after the conquest indicates that only a small selection out of the multitude of forms of tools, organizations, rituals, and beliefs could possibly have been brought by Spaniards to the Americas. There was what has been called a "refinement," or distillation, of the culture of Spaniards in the process of its transfer to Indians, that is, a selection determined by the purposes which Spaniards had in mind.

The Spanish administrators and missionaries to Mexico came with blueprints constituting simplified outlines of various aspects of Spanish culture. For the colonial administrators there was the blueprint of regulations embodying the organization of towns and the relations between Indian communities and representatives of the king. These blueprints also described in outline the economic functions and relations of the native people and the Spaniards. But the administrators' blueprints were clearly not copies of Spanish institutions. The very physical form of communities in the grid pattern of street layout and central plaza prescribed for "congregations" and other communities in New Spain after 1590 was not an attempt to reproduce the plans of Spanish towns, very few of which were laid out in grids; it involved rather an attempt to use the experience of the Roman conquest and followed plans for Roman colonies in Spain. Similarly, the number and types of officials set up for Indian towns did not precisely duplicate the existing Spanish forms. Those prescribed were of course derived from Spanish town organization, but their functions were adapted to the military and missionary requirements of the New World situations. It cannot be said either that the church life and organization of old Spain was duplicated in New Spain. An outline of an imaginary ideal church community seemed often to be in the minds of the missionaries; and the organization and life of a mission adapted from this ideal were again adapted to the greatly varying situations, especially in the far frontier areas like northwestern New Spain. Only a portion of the rich variety of observances of a Spanish parish was brought by any missionary or secular priest, and for long years the missionaries concentrated only on what they regarded as the few minimum essentials of doctrine and ritual in teaching the Indians. This same condition obtained also for tools; it has been shown that of the large variety of plows developed in Spain only one of the simpler forms was introduced into Mexico, and in fact in all Latin America.

The Spanish culture brought by Spaniards to Mexico consisted of a number of elements believed by high state and Church officials to be essential for the civilizing process. These elements constituted a selection from the profusion of sixteenth-century Spanish culture, a selection based on the principles, first, of indispensability for the changing of people from barbarian to civilized or in other words essential to Indian welfare as conceived by Spaniards, and second, of workability in the developing American society. The first principle operated very strongly in Spanish policy during the first years of extension of the conquest to the northwest, that is, during the 1600's. The second principle, as we shall see, became considerably more important during the 1700's, its operation being determined by what had already been built or not built in the way of frontier institutions under the first principle.

Besides selected elements regarded by Spaniards as essentials in the Spanish way of life and constituting a sort of "refined" form of the culture, there were miscellaneous elements that came in through individuals of widely varied backgrounds. The form a tool took in one part of Mexico was influenced by the fact that a blacksmith who settled there came from Catalonia and made tools in such a form in his native region. In the same place a particular religious festival may have become part of the town life, because the first missionary knew about such a festival in his native Estremadura and encouraged the natives to have a similar one; elsewhere this festival did not appear in Indian life, because elsewhere the missionaries came from other Spanish provinces and even from other countries of Europe than Spain. In such ways ranging from handicrafts to religious practice additional elements of Spanish culture, not in the blueprints, were transferred and combined.

The term "Culture of the Conquest" rather than "Culture of Spain" fits, because what was presented was broader in base (especially through the Church) than Spain alone and because what gave the selected elements the unity they had was not so much their generally Spanish derivation, but rather the objective of conquest, which maintained a focus in the civilizing of the Indians. It was this program which knit the elements together into something, for all its tenuousness as compared with the ancestral cultures, resembling a way of life. Enough of European culture was presented to bring about the transformation, if it had been accepted, of the whole of Indian life. The selection covered the whole range of living. It was the Conquest, that is, the Spanish drive to change the Indians that gave the impetus which carried these culture elements deeply into the lives of the Indians. As the drive to remake the Indians weakened in the late 1700's, the spread of Western culture in its Spanish Conquest form slowed down and nearly ceased. What had been implanted was not Spanish culture but a European distillation made largely by Spaniards.

It cannot be too strongly emphasized that the outlines of the new culture which we have called the Culture of the Conquest would have to be filled out, if accepted, with many elements of Indian culture. Even if the Spaniards were successful in getting acceptance of every culture trait presented by them, the stuff of daily life still had to be largely Indian in origin. Especially in the northwest where colonization lagged and so much of Indian contact was at the level of the officials, civil and religious, was the limited character of the Spanish offerings apparent.

THE FRONTIER INSTITUTIONS

The high policy conferences in which Spain's program was conceived of course remained unknown to and unparticipated in by the Indians. No Indians ever reached the king for discussion of policy matters and only a few from the northwest (these being Yaquis and Yumans) in the whole colonial period ever reached the viceroy in Mexico City. Many came into contact with captains-general or governors in the frontier capitals, but at this level policy could not be fundamentally influenced. The framework of Indian-Spanish relations was determined unilaterally by the Spaniards. That it might or should have been determined in any other way did not occur to any Spaniard, so far as the historical record goes. Thus, although the plan of conquest and civilization with which the Spaniards started was modified in some ways in response to Spanish experience, it cannot be said that Indian experience was ever conceived as having any policy value. The Spanish program was an a priori, unilaterally conceived plan for improving, that is, civilizing, the barbarian Indians, who were not regarded as capable of participating in the formulation of any program for themselves.

The Spanish program, at the local level, where it impinged directly on the Indians, really consisted of two rather distinct programs, employing different means and having different immediate objectives. Let us take a brief look at the specific circumstances of the Indians' contact with Spaniards as it usually took place in areas of New Biscay or New Mexico. There were two characteristic types of contact, for example, for the Opatas of central Sonora. On the one hand, there were Indians in a village clustered around a mission church, in part living very much as they had before the arrival of the Spaniards and in part living, when they chose or were forced to, under the direction of the Jesuit missionary working on projects set up and managed by him. On the other hand, here and there among these mission communities and some distance from them there were mining towns like the capital of Sonora, San Juan Bautista. Here Opatas also lived and worked. They lived in or on the edges of a community such as had not existed before the Spaniards came in, under a police and legal system managed by Spaniards; they worked for wages (if they were actually paid) to produce ore with the use of which they had nothing to do. These two types of community represented not only two sharply distinct approaches on the part of Spaniards to the effort to change Indians into civilized people; they also represented different ways of life for those who lived in each. To be sure, the two approaches were recognized as complementary

18. SPANISH MILITARY FRONTIER, NORTHWESTERN NEW SPAIN
Showing Presidios, Important Mining Centers, and Spanish Towns

Legend

✕ MINES   □ PRESIDIO   ⊙ SPANISH TOWN   ▓ AREA OF MISSIONS AND SPANISH SETTLEMENT

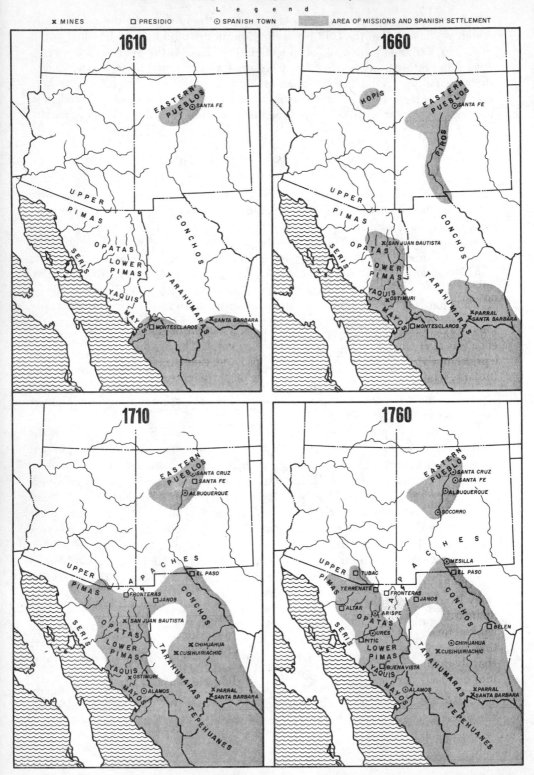

parts of the total Spanish program by the king, viceroys, and governors. Nevertheless they tended to function as rival institutional arrangements and steadily the conflict between the two kinds of program carried out in the two kinds of communities became more and more apparent. This conflict became a distinctive characteristic of the Spanish frontier communities and must be reckoned as in itself a major cultural influence on the Indians.

The mission system sought to bring Indians into participation in Spanish culture by forming them into largely self-sufficient communities under the direction of the missionaries. The missionary program of the Jesuits was less an effort to transfer individuals from an Indian-type community to a Spanish-type community than it was to remake Indian communities into tightly knit, church-centered social units, with Indian leadership (under one or a few Jesuits) still operative. The focus was very definitely on the maintenance of the modified Indian community as a political, social, and economic unit.

We may contrast this procedure in changing the Indians culturally with that which was adopted, however unconsciously, in the Spanish mining towns, presidio centers, or even haciendas, such as those which grew up in the Opata country. These were wholly Spanish-controlled social units; they were managed by Spanish governmental officials, in the selection of whom Indians had no voice, or they were controlled by Spanish employers as mining contractors or hacendados who unilaterally set up the conditions of work. An Indian in such a town was largely outside the network of kinship and local community relations which he knew in his home village or even in the mission village. He was forced into a new mould, working at tasks which had little significance for him except as they might bring certain amounts of money or goods. Thus, the Spanish towns and the mission communities were different social worlds. Individual Indians in each must have had sharply different experiences. One required a modification of old ways in the company of others who were like oneself; the other required a distinct break with old ways under the domination of foreigners. Thus two programs for changing Indian life, fostered respectively by missionaries and civil authorities, grew up side by side in Indian country, such as that of the Opatas.

Elsewhere in the northwest of New Spain it was similar. The Tarahumara situation differed chiefly in that the mission communities, at least in the south, were in themselves newly located and their populations were much more heterogeneous, so that they were far less like aboriginal communities than were those among the Opatas. The Yaqui and Mayo situation differed mainly in the absence, during early years, of Spanish settlements close to the Indian settlements, but Lower and Upper Pima conditions were very much the same as the Opata. In New Mexico the situation among the Eastern Pueblos was essentially the same as that for the Opatas, but some differences were important. In the first place the mission communities were rarely if ever centered around a church, as among the ranchería peoples, because original settlements were already concentrated and remained in their original locations. Instead, the church was built at the edge of the existing village and became more like an appendage than a major center of the community. In the second place, the encomienda system of forced labor was introduced on a small scale into the

Rio Grande Valley and in limited areas close to the Indian settlements created conditions like those of the Spanish towns.

THE MISSION COMMUNITY — It seems possible to give a generalized description of the mission communities which will apply in large part to all the missions, whether in the south among the Jesuits or in the north among the Franciscans. Even though the work of the Franciscans and Jesuits within their missions differed in some fundamentally important ways, the institutions which they created as mission communities derived from the same ideal conception, or blueprint. Differences, so important in the results of culture contact, which arose as between north and south stemmed in part from the differences in social structure and cultures of the Indians in the different areas or from relations between the missions and the Spanish settlers, but these factors operated in the contexts of mission communities which at least in plan were of the same type.

The conception held by both groups of missionaries of what they wished to create was a community of Indians obedient to the missionary priest and following his instruction in both secular and spiritual matters. In order to create such a congregation they regarded it as necessary that there be changes in the organization of existing communities, changes which they inclined to think of as creating order where none had existed before, rather than in terms of reorganization. The fundamental change which they proposed to introduce was summed up in the conception of "reduction." That is, they conceived the Indians as living under conditions of savagery, dispersed and unregulated, and as becoming susceptible to their ministration only if settled in compact villages. They accordingly sought first to persuade Indians to concentrate in villages, or pueblos, and immediately to construct some form of building to serve as a church which was designed to become the focus of activities in the new settlement. If the Indians, such as the Opatas, Eastern Pueblos, and Yaquis already lived in more or less compact settlements, they sought to shift the community to a focus around a church building nearby, or perhaps within, the existing settlement. In the cases of the most nomadic groups such as the Seris, the westernmost Pimas, and the Apaches, reduction involved a thoroughgoing reorganization of the native basis of living. In the cases of the Tarahumaras, most of the Upper Pimas, the Navajos, some of the Opatas, the Jovas, and the Lower Pimas a considerable amount of change in community type was required, for these people scattered their houses over considerable areas. The same was true of most of the Opatas, the Mayos, and the Yaquis, although all of these had existing communities which were considerably more compact than those of the Tarahumaras, Navajos, and Pimans. In the cases of the Eastern Pueblos, Zunis, and Hopis the existing communities were as compact in form as any European town. Thus the program of reduction involved different degrees of change in settlement pattern for the various Indian groups and did not affect them in a uniform manner.

Whatever the amount of change involved, the missionary proceeded to the construction of a church building and efforts to get the Indians to settle in its immediate vicinity. Usually before such a building was constructed some preaching was conducted and all children who were offered were baptized. These children with their families were regarded as the nucleus of the congregation. Perhaps the parents or perhaps other adults who expressed a desire for baptism were persuaded immediately to build some sort of structure as a provisional church. At the same time help was solicited in building a shelter for the missionary, who immediately began his work of instruction preparatory to making more baptisms. The community then grew on the basis of voluntary, if possible, labor in improving the church and the missionary's quarters, setting up corrals for animals, and planting fields for the use of the missionary and his converts.

No such community resting on these foundations has been fully described for us. What one seemed like to any Indian must remain purely conjectural; the descriptions by the missionaries are fragmentary and lacking in awareness of the details of life of the people among whom they were working. Some partial portraits of individual Indians emerge from missionary writings, but no community profile whatsoever appears, even though some missionaries who wrote made considerable effort to sketch outlines of various Indian cultures. We fall back, then, on a generalized picture of the mission community.

In early stages the Jesuit mission community in the south often contained merely a shade, or ramada, made of poles with a brush roof and one closed-in side which served as the background for any images, crucifixes, or other church furniture which the missionary possessed; this was the church. Near it, perhaps adjoining, were the quarters of the missionary, ordinarily at first a one-room adobe structure. Round about at various distances were the houses of those Indians of the area who were most interested in what the missionary was saying and doing. Usually there were also the houses of Indians who had previously accepted baptism. These might be from some adjoining tribe or a community of the same tribe where missionaries had worked, for the standard procedure of the Jesuits was to bring with them previously-Christianized Indians who preferably could understand and speak the language of the new group. It was also the procedure of the Franciscans who, it will be recalled, on their initial contacts with the Eastern Pueblos, took with them Tlaxcalan and other Christianized Indians from central Mexico. The Jesuits apparently attempted to have family groups of such Indians accompany them, the members of the families then serving not only as interpreters but also as all-around workers, preparing meals for the missionary, helping and supervising in the building and other work of setting up the mission center.

The first activities of the missionary made clear to the Indians what he valued most. The immediate construction of the church, the prompt beginning of regular prayers, and instruction in Christian doctrine must have left no doubt in the Indians' minds that the missionary was a ritual specialist and talker. This was reinforced by his immediate recruitment of individuals to memorize the catechismal questions and answers and to become teachers of the others. He also promptly appointed individuals to take care of the church. Within a matter of days or weeks a simple organization was established, consisting of a *temastian* and a *madore* who became the missionary's first assistants. The *temastian* served as catechist. He was taught the Spanish words necessary for this function as quickly as possible and served by helping the missionary translate the questions and answers into the

Indian language. The missionary taught him methods of instructing and the two gave such instruction daily to all who would gather at the church. The missionaries to the Mayos and Yaquis were explicit in saying that there was immediate and general interest in such instruction, that native catechists learned very quickly, and that they showed skill in carrying the work far beyond the number of people whom the missionary could have reached singlehandedly. Similar eagerness to serve in this manner, with ability for doing so, was apparently encountered among the Opatas. With other groups instruction went more slowly. The madore served as an administrator or governor of church affairs, perhaps calling people for meetings, maintaining order at such meetings, keeping up the church, overseeing work crews who made adobes and did other work in constructing the church and associated buildings. An alternative term for *madore* was *fiscal*.

This small organization was augmented as quickly as possible by the training of singers: the formation of a choir, ideally consisting of four men and four women, was a major objective. This required training of selected people whose interest in church affairs was steady, who had some musical ability, and who had become sufficiently acquainted with church services to perform properly. Eventually every mission community had such an organization of one or more catechists, one or more fiscales or madores, and a choir of singers, selected, trained, and officially appointed by the missionary. As permanent church buildings were constructed and the congregation increased, the group necessary for handling church affairs became larger and the duties became routinized and characterized by more and more definite responsibilities. The success of every missionary depended on his being able to build such a church organization around himself.

Training such a working organization constituted, however, only a relatively small part of the missionary's labors. He was also charged with making the beginnings of a secular organization of the community along Spanish lines. If the group was visited by the missionary first in the company of a Spanish military or civil official, the latter ordinarily appointed some man as governor at the same time that the missionary selected a catechist and fiscal. If the missionary were without such civil officials, he appointed a governor himself and arranged for him to receive a cane of office indicating his authority under the civil administration. Whether or not the original appointment was made by the missionary, the latter (certainly in all the Sonora villages) came to have a major part in the selection, the matter often being left entirely to his judgment. How the selection was made remains something of a mystery. It appears that missionaries attempted to find individuals who were already recognized as influential whenever they could, so that Spanish recognition reinforced the existing leadership. It is also true, however, that in many communities, as for instance among the Tarahumaras, the Lower and Upper Pimas, the Seris and others, the appearance of the missionary created an immediate division among the people. In such cases the appointee must have been someone from among the favorable faction who was especially aggressive in making contact with the missionary and whose personality appealed, and thus not necessarily one with influence or authority already established among the Indians. Often judges (*alcaldes*) were also appointed by the missionary to serve along with the governor in settling disputes and maintaining law and order. A duty which was of major importance for the governor, at least by the end of the 1600's, was the enforcement by means of whipping of the special discipline for church attendance and the observance of Christian ways. It is impossible to know how much new organization was involved in the establishment of these missionary-sanctioned appointees. That the situations varied greatly will become clear. There is no doubt that in the eyes of the Spanish civil government the missionary responsibility for developing the secular organization was considerable.

The missionaries also took vigorous interest in establishing an economic organization which involved a number of offices of a type wholly new to the Indians. Although the church organization took precedence and got underway most rapidly, there was also immediate need for getting the mission on an economic footing. Ordinarily the missionaries brought cattle, sheep, or goats, and some horses or burros with them or acquired them as soon as possible from other missions already established. They also began, where there was need and opportunity for it, to make improvements in the farming systems of the Indians, introducing irrigation, and instructing Indians in the care of new crops in the fields set aside for the mission. The usual organization for carrying on this work consisted of a group appointed by the missionary composed of a head herdsman, a head plowman, a general work overseer, perhaps a ditch manager, and crews of cowboys, herders, adobe-makers, and other laborers. This side of mission operation required at least as much training and supervision as did the church activities. Herds, plows, horses, adobe-and-timber building, and in some instances irrigation agriculture were new to the Indians. In addition, the crops introduced by the missionaries, especially wheat and the orchard crops, required new techniques. The missionary, who was aided only by other Christianized Indians sometimes not yet well versed in the new techniques, had to assume the responsibility for getting his neophytes as interested in these as in the novel practices of Christianity. He had to give instruction in handling cattle and in horsemanship, in times and methods of planting, and to select individuals who would take responsibility for instructing others and organizing their work efficiently. The success of a given mission would seem to have depended heavily on the missionary's ability as a farmer and builder, for the size of his congregation was often closely related to the benefits which he offered in the way of food and an impressive church building.

As a mission developed on a solid economic basis, the need arose for specialists in the various established European crafts. The plows, hoes, and gear for the horses broke and wore out and a blacksmith became indispensable. Accordingly most missions set up blacksmith shops and trained Indians as smiths. The demand for clothes under missionary pressure increased and so the native weaving was improved or weaving was introduced; sometimes weavers were imported to give instruction, and weaving shops were set up. As buildings were elaborated, masons and carpenters were trained from among the congregation to fill the need. To the extent that such craft specialties were developed the economic basis of life in the Indian communities came more and more to resemble that of Spanish communities.

Each missionary was ordinarily responsible not only for working out a church, secular, and economic organization for one village centered around the mission; he was also expected to develop two *visitas* in addition. These were other already established villages or new settlements which the missionary encouraged. They also were planned to center around church buildings, to which the mission- ary came whenever he was able, usually trying to meet a regular schedule of monthly visits. In each he tried to organize the church officials from among the natives in the same form as in the head, or mission village. Here he also appointed governors and frequently set up herds with local men responsible. Sometimes the visitas grew and flourished better than the mission, but usually the mission village, directly under the missionary's care, became the larger and more important. A mission community, then, was a group of three or more Indian villages transformed through the means of (1) resettlement into compact units, (2) improvement and increase in food and craft production, and (3) new community organization centering around a church and under the authority of the European missionary.

This mission community was a new phenomenon in Indian life, however- much of old customs and way of life was preserved in it. Under the direction of the missionary, the farms and herds were sources of supply not only for the village where they were located, but for all the villages of the area. Each aimed at producing a surplus which could be used by its missionary for furthering his work, that is, attracting more people, in his own area or for helping other missions to get started among other Indians. The improvement of agriculture and produc- tion of surplus was an integral part of at least the Jesuit mission program and in this aspect it brought about an important transformation in the economic life of most Sonora Indians.

The objective economically was to make a self-sufficient unit of each mission community. The introduction of herds, the improvement of crops, and the develop- ment of craft specialization indicated that the missionary conception was of com- munities developed to the point economically where they could continue indefi- nitely as independent economic units.

The mission communities were nevertheless a part of the Spanish Empire. The King of Spain had agreed that Indians among whom missionaries began work were to be exempt from taxation, which is to say from tribute payment, for ten years. It was believed that Indians must first be civilized and Christianized before they could be expected to become paying members of the Spanish Empire. At first it was thought that this process could be completed within ten years, and accordingly the missionaries began their work with the assurance that they would be free to develop their new communities without production for the king during this early period. The exemption obtained among all the Indians in Sonora and Chihuahua; Father Kino working among the Upper Pimas was able to obtain an extension to exempt the Indians for twenty years, which possibly indicated some recognition of difficulties in the civilizing process. Similarly in 1621 the king granted an indefinite extension of the exemption for Zunis and Hopis, on the theory that they still constituted "frontier areas" despite the fact that some missionary work had begun among them. The Eastern Pueblos, however, after the first ten-years' exemption came under the usual regulation for tribute payment to the crown, and tribute was exacted from them during the 1600's. In Sonora, however, tribute payment never was exacted, due at first to the pleading of the Jesuits and later to the inaction of the civil government.

In other ways all the Indians living under the mission system were part of the larger whole of the Empire. The Jesuit and Franciscan Orders were part of the Empire, insofar as they were responsible to the viceroy and king. The Jesuits, between 1591 when they began missionary work in northwestern Mexico and 1767 when they were expelled from the New World, developed an extensive bureaucracy. The Franciscans also, as a large organization of worldwide extent, constituted a similar intricate bureaucracy. Each mission community, it should not be forgotten, was affected more or less profoundly by being part of such organizations.

The Jesuit Order was an authoritarian, nondemocratic organization which pyramided up from missionaries to a single head of the order in Rome. In New Spain all the work of the Jesuits was under the direction of a Provincial who was changed every three years. The extensive educational institutions, universities and colleges, which provided most of what formal education there was in Mexico until 1767, as well as the missions were under the general supervision of the Provincial. Under the Mexican Provincial, between 1590 and 1767, there developed six provinces, or visitas, or missions. Three of the six were in the region with which this volume is concerned: Chinipas, Sonora, and Tarahumara. The other three were Nayarit, Sinaloa, and California. For each of these the Mexican Provincial maintained a Visitor, expected to make an annual tour of a province to render a report on activities within it, and to promote communication generally between the remote missionaries and the headquarters in Mexico City. The Visitors, like the Provincial himself, were changed every three years; they frequently were working missionaries stationed in the province which they visited. Each missionary province consisted of three or more rectorates, which were groups of mission communities under the supervision of a rector, who was always one of the working missionaries. The rectorship was also changed every three years, the missionaries of a rectorate district often rotating in office as appointed by the Provincial of Mexico. Under the supervision of each rector were three or more missionaries, each of whom was in charge of a mission community such as has been described.

By the time of the expulsion of the Jesuits in 1767 the missionary province of Sonora, for example, consisted of twenty-nine mission communities, divided into four rectorates. These were as follows: the Rectorate of St. Francis Borgia, consisting of six mission communities inhabited by Lower Pimas, Jovas, and Opatas of the south, extending from Onavas and Saguaripa westward to Matape; the Rectorate of the Three Holy Martyrs of Japan, consisting of seven mission communities of Opatas of the north; the Rectorate of St. Francis Xavier, consisting of seven mission communities of Opatas of the north and Eudeves extending from Cuquiarachi westward to Opodepe and Cucurpe; and the Rectorate of the "Pima Highlands," consisting of eight missions of Upper Pimas. The twenty-nine mission communities were composed of seventy-three villages and "several" ranches. One may hazard the guess that possibly one-third of all the villages of the Upper Pimas, three-quarters of those of the Opatas and Eudeves, and at least three-quarters of those of the Lower Pimas were part of mission communities, the other villages having more or less close contacts with missions as they desired, but not being definite parts of the organization.

The villages which were part of a mission community were not each visited annually by the official Visitors, but rather at irregular intervals although the head or mission villages were visited at least every two years. The visiting system brought an intensification of contacts among the Indians of an area, for each Visitor was accompanied by a larger or smaller retinue from his own mission village consisting of those Indians most devoted to the missionary and others curious to travel. Moreover, the rotating rectorships and visitorships within the missionary province stimulated a good deal of contact beyond the limits of a given mission community. The various missionaries, accompanied by Indian governors and others, went to discuss problems with the rectors of their districts or with the Visitor for the three-year period, and to seek help in increasing their livestock or mission equipment. This must have made for a good deal of interchange of ideas, as well as of tools and goods. The Jesuit governing system, in other words, brought about an intensification of contact on a friendly basis within and between the various tribal groups. It also introduced the Indians to a hierarchical type of organization with which they were not familiar and made those who were in close contact with the missionaries and trying to cooperate with them aware of a great world beyond the horizons of their own communities. They became aware of this world as a source of benefits to their own communities as well as a source of limiting influences, when, for instance, a missionary received an image for the church or some new equipment or learned that he had been denied such benefits by his superiors. In such ways each mission organization was a source of knowledge of the larger world.

Every mission community was a social unit organized for intensive efforts to change features of Indian behavior. The Sonora-Chihuahua missions of the Jesuits were established as cattle ranches or as extensive farms or as both. The livestock was something totally new to all of the Indians and, since the European background of the missionaries led them to emphasize wheat and other European crops, much of their farming was also new. The use of plows and draft animals, which was not universal in the missions but very common, was also something new for the Indians. Irrigation techniques were in some instances new. Building with moulded adobes, lime mortar, and the making of buildings with roof spans so wide as to require large tree trunks were all innovations, as in fact was the making of permanent houses, except among the Pueblos. As we have seen, work with such materials was begun immediately and each missionary had to spend much time demonstrating their use. If he himself did not do so, he nevertheless supervised the demonstration of their use by previously Christianized Indians who accompanied him. Thus culture transfer by demonstration was an important activity in all the mission communities and went on continuously.

Probably equally novel to the Indians, at least outside of the Pueblo area, was the daily routine of field and herd work and building insisted on by the missionary. Usually three days' work for the missionary was the rule, with some pressure from the latter to work equally regularly on the Indian fields. The work for the mission was strictly supervised by the missionary's appointees, such as the head herdsman and the head plowman, and the missionaries sanctioned whipping for the enforcement of the daily stint of labor. Grumbling and diatribes against Indian laziness are an almost constant theme of missionary writing, indicating a pervading feeling of failure to remould the Indian pattern of work in conformity with a European ideal. But it is also true that many missions flourished under missionary supervision and that production was immensely increased in some missions, most notably those of the Yaquis and, at first, the Tarahumaras. There seems, in fact, to have been less complaint in regard to Yaqui habits of work than for any other group and some praise, indicating a high degree of Yaqui conformity to European work habits. There is no way of knowing in detail how much increase in production actually came about, but it seems fairly certain that surpluses began to be produced which helped sustain neighboring Spanish towns as well as supply the needs of the expanding mission program as it moved from south to north.

Besides the demonstration of new tools and agricultural techniques and the enforcement for a part of the Indians of new work habits, the mission communities were, of course, also the scene of intensive instruction of a moral type. Most missionaries taught constantly by preaching, at least weekly in sermons, but probably much more often in brief exhortations to people gathered in the vicinity of the church. There are records of the preaching of some of the missionaries, such as Kino. They talked repeatedly of the existence of a God who was invisible and good. They went over and over the Ten Commandments as rules of life, the observance of which would ensure entry into Heaven and would deliver one from Hell. They described the glories of heavenly life and some spoke in great detail of the horrors of Hell. They told and retold the stories of the Bible, emphasizing Adam and Eve and the Flood and the Old Testament events which gave concreteness to the Christian conception of the Creation and early human history. The missionaries formulated in simple terms a minimum set of concepts which they regarded as essential for a Christian to know. The Opata missionary Castaño used a simple list of questions and answers as catechism which was widely adopted in Jesuit missionary work. With this outline the missionaries labored with their catechists to instruct all who would come to listen and repeat.

At the same time they employed demonstrations of the basic Christian ideas. They obtained images of the Virgin, various manifestations of Christ and the saints, and also paintings as large and as bright as possible and installed these in their churches. They also set Indians to work decorating churches with paintings. They made a great deal of use of dramatic presentation, one of their major activities being the dramatization of the Passion of Christ at Easter, in which they enlisted intensive participation of the Indians. They formed the Indians into companies representing the Pharisees and showed them how to enact the persecution of Christ, the Crucifixion, the Resurrection, and other events in the last days of

Jesus. They also organized Indians into groups to represent the struggle of the Christians against the Moors in Spain and encouraged them to give these dramas on regular feast days of the church. They introduced dances which had been developed in central Mexico for dramatizing the first conversion of Mexican Indians, in the story of Malinche, Montezuma, and Cortez.

The missionaries relied heavily on the repetitious acts of prayer, singing, and church-centered ritual. The Christian routine of worship in these forms was introduced immediately. Daily devotions were led at every mission by the missionary or by temastianes, fiscales, or madores appointed by the missionary. The Lord's Prayer, the Hail Mary, and the Credo were quickly translated into the Indian languages by the Jesuits. Those who learned them recited them together once or twice daily. Mass was said at least once a week by the missionary in the church, and people who had been baptized and those who were being instructed for baptism were required to attend this service as a minimum. The missionaries enforced the rule of attendance at Mass on Sundays by corporal punishment in the form of whipping, the missionary himself rarely doing the whipping but rather turning the job over to appointed civil officials.

It was a principle of Jesuit work that children should be the major focus of their doctrinal and ritual instruction. They baptized children without prior instruction, but once they had baptized a child they made it clear that they and the parents were obligated to instruct the child in Christian doctrine. They enforced continued attendance at catechismal instruction with corporal punishment whenever necessary. They set up schools at the church or near it and gathered baptized children for instruction. Here they taught reading, writing, and counting in Spanish, although not all Jesuits did so, but concentrated on the memorizing of doctrine, daily practice in the prayers, training of a few selected boys as acolytes, and singing of instrumental and sacred music. Many missions had schools; less frequently visitas did also. There was usually an effort to bring a few children in to these schools from all settlements close enough to make it practicable. In addition, higher instruction was promoted, as in seminaries at Navojoa, Torim, and Matape in Sonora and Parral in Chihuahua. To these were sent at least two children annually from the various villages within the neighboring rectorates.

Each mission became a place where people from that village and from all surrounding ones could come, see, and participate in the regular round of Catholic pageantry. Sunday service at Mass with a sermon, the dramatic representations of Holy Week and the processions of Lent, the enactment of dramas such as that of the Moors and Christians, and whatever other sacred ceremonies a particular missionary emphasized could be counted on for entertainment and instruction. The missionaries in Sonora and Chihuahua regarded it as an important part of their work to arrange large fiestas with beef or other meat to eat to which Indians could come and enjoy themselves at the same time that they attended the church ceremonies. It was also regarded by the missionaries as important that they make the churches, both inside and out, as striking and impressive as they could, to which end they secured the richest possible altar ornaments, paintings, and images. In this way they sought to make the mission communities centers of interest and activity for the whole area surrounding them. They tried also to bring in Spanish families settled nearby at ranches or mines and have them mingle with the Indians and, as they said, teach the Indians by example to behave as Christians. Often enough they were disappointed in these Spaniards whom they regarded as not living up to the Christian standards of behavior, but on the other hand some families became a major influence in changing Indian behavior.

There was constant pressure by the missionaries to alter certain features of daily life. They preached against plural wives and sexual relations outside of marriage; they preached the necessity of formal marriage ceremonies. They preached against drunkenness. They tried to introduce the confession and they carried out moral lectures whenever the opportunity offered. They also denounced forms of native ceremony which they regarded as in conflict with Christian belief and practice. Most of the Jesuit missionaries apparently behaved strictly in accord with their theory of sexual and other continences and thus also set examples in line with their preaching. It is clear that in a short time the effect of this constant preaching and practice was deep upon those who gathered around the missions. It was indicated, for example, in a conversation reported between Gilg and a Seri leader who was protesting the deportation of the Seri women from the mission at Pópulo. The latter's understanding of the missionary standard, even though he did not wholly agree with it, was reported as adequate from the missionary's point of view.

It is abundantly clear that the mission community in its ideal form, when handled by a well-trained and competent missionary, was a dynamic center for cultural change. There was a minimum of disturbing outsiders. The missionary in his isolation was required to adjust his personal behavior, in order to function at all, to what the Indians required for his continued acceptance. The missionary had many things to offer of immediate and obvious value, chiefly food and useful tools and striking and mysterious ritual objects. He had also a new system of magic which offered possibilities and cost little, except some discipline, to try out. At the same time the discipline under which the missionary labored and the techniques which he had learned in his training made him a constantly active force in the community life. In large measure in Sonora, although less so in Chihuahua and New Mexico, Indian acceptance of him and his offerings was a voluntary matter. Indians came first voluntarily. If then they found that he exacted too stern a discipline for them, it was perfectly possible to drift away. To be sure some of the missionaries sought out the drifters, but it was impossible to find them all or to exert much coercion when they were found. In the main, especially during the first years in Sonora, the acceptance of the mission system was a voluntary affair and accordingly had an abiding strength.

As a self-sufficient unit, somewhat isolated from Spanish towns, the mission community constituted a place where acculturative forces could be channeled in accordance with the given missionary's understanding of his immediate local situation. The tempo of change was largely guided by a single person who spoke the native language and had some understanding of the limitations of what he could and could not do. The mission communities as a result, for the most part, became the scene of peaceful, non-disorganizing culture change for long periods.

The picture of a mission community which has been presented here is, as has been emphasized, an ideal one. There were many missions, especially in Sonora, which conformed quite closely to the ideal. There were others which varied widely from the ideal. The history of the Tarahumaras indicates that a Jesuit mission community could have a very different character, especially when Spanish labor recruitment was intensive and when the Indian pattern of community life was strongly resistant to reduction. Moreover, our review of the history of Spanish contacts with the Eastern and Western Pueblos reveals a considerable divergence in the Franciscan mission communities.

In New Mexico the pattern which developed as the reality of the mission community had features which set it off sharply from that in the south. It was not an integral unit in the sense that the usual southern community was. The church was typically to one side of the Pueblo village and never became the center of religious life. It was a center, but not the focus. The church, moreover, was usually separated, and the missionary's quarters along with it, from the rest of the community by a wall of greater or lesser height. The missionary obviously lived in a situation of less intimacy than was characteristic in Sonora. This physical pattern was consistent with other features of the missionary-Indian relationship. The Franciscans in New Mexico generally lived with soldier escorts in the Pueblo villages. They rarely became proficient in the use of the Indian languages. They seem to have adopted a policy of much more rigorous prohibition of native ritual, including the use of sacred objects such as masks, and accordingly were involved in programs of destruction of the native religious objects. It appears also that their disciplinary actions, carried out by themselves or their military companions, were generally harsher than those applied in the south. It would seem clear from a listing only of these major differences that the northern and southern mission communities were very different theaters of culture contact.

THE SPANISH TOWN — The other important institution of the frontier through which European influences were exerted was the Spanish settlement, sometimes an ephemeral mining camp, sometimes a small agricultural establishment, sometimes an army garrison, occasionally a fully organized town modeled along the lines of a community in Old Spain. To class all of these together as the same sort of acculturating influence is justified on the ground that they were each dominated by Spanish settlers who wholly defined the institutional structure within which all inhabitants, whether Spanish or Indian, lived.

The Spanish town exerted by no means as uniform an influence on the Indians as did the mission community. There were not so many of them and their distribution was extremely irregular. They grew up only slowly in some parts of the frontier region so that various groups of Indians underwent no or almost no contact with them while they were experiencing their first generation or more of intensive contact with the mission community. In New Mexico the Spanish town was an influence from 1599 on, but there were no more than a half-dozen towns even by the late 1700's, while separate mining communities and military garrisons were absent. Nevertheless, the Spanish agricultural settlement in the form of the encomendero's establishment was an influence and there were some of these in the Rio Grande Valley from Socorro to San Juan. In Chihuahua, Spanish towns were an important influence at the edge of Tarahumara country in the form of large communities like Parral and Chihuahua during the 1600's and 1700's. There were also mining camps and numerous ranches along the eastern border of the Tarahumara country. In Sonora the Spanish towns were slow getting started, not being of importance until the late 1600's, but from about 1635 on they were many and widely spread among the haciendas, mining settlements, and ranches. Towns like Ures, Banámichi, San Juan Bautista, Arispe, Alamos, and Magdalena flourished. By the mid-1700's they began to be sharply reduced in numbers because of the raiding of Apaches, Seris, and other Indians.

Thus, the influence of the Spanish town exerted itself in irregular fashion, affecting some Indians like the Tarahumaras, the Mayos, and the Opatas in very profound ways, while other tribes like the Yaquis, Hopis, Zunis, Apaches, Navajos, and Yumans were far less affected and in rather different ways. In considering the effects of the Spanish town we are therefore dealing with a less uniform influence than that of the mission community. It was a force the effects of which are more difficult to assess than the latter. If accounts of the mission community are unsystematic and spotty and characterized by marked bias of the missionaries, the accounts of the Spanish towns and the life in them are still more lacking in completeness and adequacy. There were no observers with time to write living in such communities, and consequently we are forced to rely on accounts of court trials and a few scattered comments by missionaries who regarded the towns as bad influences on the Indians, both types of information tending to give a picture biased in the direction of the evils of town life.

As they advanced into northwestern New Spain, the Spaniards planned to build towns, or *villas*, which would be centers of Spanish culture. In such towns would be the center of government, including a military garrison, the palace of the governor as the seat of Spanish administration, the homes of officials, the homes and shops of settlers who were engaged in trade and manufacture, warehouses, and churches, seminaries, and all the other structures necessary for the usual activities of a center of Spanish civilization. On the east side of the Sierra Madre Mountains towns were founded in succession as mines were located, the number of settlers increased, and the Indians were reduced; Zacatecas in 1546, Durango in 1563, Santa Barbara in 1567 (although only a mining center rather than a political capital), Parral in 1631, and Chihuahua in 1709. Meanwhile, as a result of the Spanish thrust into New Mexico bypassing the steady advance in the south, Santa Fe had been set up about 1610, but its citizens were forced by the Pueblo Revolt in 1680 to move temporarily southward to El Paso. On the west a similar advance through Sinaloa took place, culminating in 1598 in the establishment of a presidio and the town of San Felipe y Santiago on the Sinaloa River, from which the reduction of Sonora proceeded. About 1720 San Juan Bautista became the capital town of Sonora and remained so until the seat of government was moved to Arispe in 1786.

Such towns were designed as places in which Spanish officials, civil and military, could live as fully as possible in the Spanish manner. From the late 1500's on, they were sometimes laid out, in accordance with royal directives, as grid-pattern towns with central plazas flanked by a large church, the governor's palace, and other governmental buildings, but often, as in the cases of Parral and San Juan Bautista where mining led to the founding of the town, the topography was such that streets could not be laid out at right angles, and the town followed the topography of the country, as was the case with most cities in Old Spain. None of the capitals grew to be larger than four or five thousand population during the Spanish period and most were smaller, including San Juan Bautista, Arispe, and Santa Fe. Unless they were the center of mining activities they did not draw much Indian population. Even if they were mining centers, like San Juan Bautista and Santa Barbara, the bulk of the Indian population was more or less transient. The Indians preferred to maintain their roots in their own villages, including the mission communities.

The capital towns thus became the places of residence of Spanish settlers, chiefly those employed in one way or another in governmental administration and others engaged in trade or mining. Indians went to them to purchase goods, but few Indian families settled there permanently. There was, nevertheless, a type of Indian town resident. In Santa Fe during the 1600's there was a whole barrio of several hundred people consisting of Indians brought by Oñate from Tlaxcala in central Mexico. In addition, the Spanish recruited Indians, by various means, as servants for their households and for common labor. Many of these in Santa Fe and Chihuahua and Sonora towns were Apaches, Navajos, Tobosos, or other non-missionized Indians captured in battles and indentured permanently. How many such servants, consisting chiefly of women and children, there were in any one town is not recorded, but over the whole region their number must have run into the thousands. In all of the towns there were also Indians from the reduced tribes who were serving sentence for crimes under the Spanish judicial system and who were put to work for the Spanish families for longer or shorter periods. There were probably also Indians who for various reasons left their home villages and took up residence voluntarily in the towns where they could get wages or find other means of support. Although many of the Spanish residents were regularly employed in trade or governmental activities, accounts also testify that each town had a considerable population of floating Spaniards who, after working in mines or at other occupations in various places in the frontier country, drifted to the towns to get work. Many of these were reported as mulattos and mestizos. They were most usually described as ignorant, superstitious, and lacking in industry. Efforts were made to control their movement in numbers into the frontier towns, but evidently with little success, despite the agreement of church and civil officials that they were undesirable and a bad influence on the Indians.

Under these circumstances the towns were composed of two groups: a heterogeneous and polyglot population of both Spanish and Indian derivation, and the families of the Spanish officials and the successful commercial men and mine contractors. The latter maintained a relatively high standard of living and occupied large and substantial houses. On the other hand, poverty-stricken Indians and Spaniards completely dependent on the wealthy group for their living and attached to them as servants or laborers lived apart in sharply contrasting circumstances. Many of the wealthier class were almost as transient, however, as the Indians, since officials appointed by the viceroy were frequently changed and, where mining existed, fortunes were made quickly or mines worked out, and those connected with them moved away. We must view the towns as very unstable communities, but in which there developed as the most permanent elements a poor class of racially-mixed people and impoverished Spanish families unable to move away.

The mining towns which did not serve as seats of government were for the most part very similar in character. A number of them, such as for example, Parral in Chihuahua and Alamos in Sonora, were situated in areas of minerals which were not quickly worked out and which consequently persisted throughout the Spanish period, growing into stable communities with considerable Spanish population. The towns of this character were few in number, but where they did develop they became the visible models of Spanish culture for the Indians. In them the Spanish class system with very great differences in living standards between rich and poor was strong. A sharp distinction was made between *gente de razon*, or upper class people of Spanish descent, and others of mixed blood, whether Indian and Spanish, Negro and Spanish, all three, or purely Indian. Only the gente de razon participated in the government and controlled the mines. Only the gente de razon had capital for the development of business enterprise. The intermarriage which took place between Indians and Spaniards involved only the poorer class of Spaniards, and except in the Opata country there was a very limited amount of this. What the Indians met with when they went to the towns was a Spanish way of life which excluded them except as servants and laborers. They encountered distinctions of dress and housing which left no doubt as to their not being encouraged to dress and live like the Spanish upper class. Moreover they encountered an attitude which held that the distinction between rich and poor was a permanent arrangement resting on the sacredness of "pure Spanish blood" and that therefore there was no expectation that Indians and mixed bloods would ever come to behave like wealthy Spaniards. They found an emphasis on rights by inheritance, on authoritarian government, and disrespect for labor with the hands. Very few Indians ever made any contact of course, with this aspect of Spanish culture, while thousands were directly influenced by the Spanish culture of the mission communities.

The mining towns were an especially important influence throughout Sonora. They existed widely through the Opata and Lower Pima country and were the scene of extensive and intensive contacts of those Indians with the Spaniards. We are told that contacts with Opatas were often on a basis of equality and that considerable intermarriage took place as a result.

Another type of Spanish settlement which became of increasing importance in Sonora during the Spanish period was the presidio. This was a military garrison of from thirty to fifty soldiers under a resident commander and subject to the direction of a civil authority. A presidio was composed of an adobe-walled fort, the houses of the soldiers and their families when they had any, and corrals for the horses which were an important part of the military equipment. Soldiers sometimes engaged in small ways in raising crops. Thus, a presidio was an outpost of Spanish culture, but an example of only a few selected aspects. In Sonora, companies of Opatas and Pimas sometimes lived for extended periods in the vicinity of the presidios, ready for campaigns against Apaches with the Spanish soldiers. There was probably a good deal of intermixture of the unattached soldiers with Indian women and some consequent marriages.

Outside of the mission communities, probably the most intimate contacts for the Indians were with Spanish settlers interested in farming or cattle raising. These took several different forms. In New Mexico along the upper Rio Grande Valley, where this kind of contact began immediately with the establishment of Oñate's colony in 1598, there were two types of settlement. Of greatest importance in the beginning were the encomienda grants to soldiers who had participated in the conquest of Mexico, who accompanied Oñate. These were sections of land given outright to individuals to exploit in any manner they could. The encomienda in the early 1600's included the right of repartimiento, that is to say, the right to employ (for compensation) Indians who were resident on the land granted. No encomiendas were granted in New Mexico which included the major pueblo settlements, but grants were made which did include some small settlements of Tewa Indians north of Santa Fe, some Tiwas south of Santa Fe, and many Piros and others north of El Paso on the lower Rio Grande. It was against the law for the person granted the encomienda to live on the land among the Indians, but this law was rather systematically ignored in New Mexico, especially in the Tewa country. New Mexican encomenderos forced Pueblo Indians to work for them, frequently with no, or very small, compensation and were reported to have disrupted the lives of villagers by interfering in their local affairs. Spanish employees of the encomenderos intermarried with Indians and gradually took over Indian lands. An early absorption of scattered Indian families took place up and down the Rio Grande Valley.

In addition, in New Mexico, another type of settlement by Spaniards influenced the Indians. This was the colony of settlers who were granted a piece of land as a village grant. Such settlements were frequently composed of ordinary soldiers who had served in the Mexican campaigns and were given a village grant in return for their service in assisting in the conquest. Some grants of this sort were made alongside existing Indian villages; others were made in uninhabited areas where irrigation was possible and there was land for grazing. At first there were some clashes with Indians over land rights and some Indians were driven away from their old settlements. But gradually peaceful relations prevailed and a great deal of intercourse and contact developed. Intermarriage took place, with Indian women going to live in the Spanish settlements and occasionally the reverse. In this way kinship relations developed between Spanish settlers and Indians and there was give and take on a basis quite different from anything that developed either in mission communities or Spanish towns. There was much cultural borrowing in craft techniques, food preparation, agriculture, language, curing, and many other aspects of culture, under conditions of equality. Here there was probably as much influence from the Indians on Spaniards as the reverse.

Similar situations developed in Sonora and Chihuahua. In these areas colonization took place more gradually than in New Mexico and at a time—the later 1600's

— when the encomienda system was no longer in full operation. It took the form of more or less isolated ranches and farms, or haciendas, scattered widely along the edges of the Tarahumara country and through central and northern Sonora in the Opata and Pima country. There was also considerable development of haciendas in the Mayo country. The ranchers and farmers employed Indian labor, to some extent captives, whom they bought, but also voluntary laborers especially at harvest and planting time whom they paid in kind. Living in isolated places, the proprietors were forced to a greater extent than were the mining contractors or residents of Spanish towns to adjust their behavior to a standard which the Indians would accept without rebellion. Hence their ranches and farms were often the scene of peaceful relations and considerable diffusion of Spanish ways to the Indians. Missionaries sought to incorporate into their mission communities such Spanish settlers whenever possible and urged that ranches and haciendas be set up near the missions. Nevertheless Spanish ranchers and hacendados also brought on conflict with the Indians since they frequently, as was the case in New Mexico, appropriated land which Indians had been accustomed to use, and their herds disturbed either the settlements or the water supplies of the Indians.

The authorities in the Spanish towns supported what amounted to a fourfold program for the incorporation of Indians into Spanish society. Their program stood in contrast with that of the missionaries although of course the king required them to recognize the missionary program as essential, and many were wholeheartedly convinced that it was essential. The missionary program might be summed up as an attempt to incorporate Indians into Spanish society through a gradual modification of Indian communities, through continuous teaching, demonstration, and instruction, through the acceptance of the missionary as a fatherly guide in the process, and through forcible imposition, when necessary, of church attendance and work routines. In contrast, the civil authorities urged incorporation through the organization of Indians into formal political units of Spain, the forcing of European work habits in mines and agricultural establishments run by Spaniards, the production of tribute, the distribution of tribal land to individual Indians, and the fusion of Spaniards and Indians through intermarriage and living together in the same communities. To say that all Spaniards who urged these measures were thinking in terms of a program of integration into the Spanish Empire, rather than in terms of their own private interests, would be absurd. Most civil authorities who urged the measures were thinking of their own personal interests or were responsive to the interested thinking of the mine contractors, settlers, and other Spanish inhabitants of the frontier. But the official justification of the measures, as expressed in reports of the viceroy's visitors, governors of provinces, and others who formulated official thinking, was that they were basic for the speedy and satisfactory incorporation of Indians as full Spanish citizens into the Empire.

The effort to organize all Indian villages into formal governments resembling the local governments of Spain was of course official policy from the first in northern New Spain. It involved the appointment by a governor of a province of civil and military officials among the Indians of each village. Canes of office were distributed to such individuals after they had been picked out. They were then held to be responsible for maintaining peace, for enforcing discipline by whipping or use of stocks as the missionary or other official might require, and serving as a communication channel with the Spanish civil authority. There was variation over the region, but the general pattern was the following. Each village was supposed to have a governor as general civil head, a captain as military and police head, and sometimes alcaldes who served as judges. These appointees derived their authority from the Spaniards and were responsible to them. In New Mexico village councilmen *(regidores)* were also required who constituted a governing council of the village. Various kinds of titled assistants were introduced in different areas. Terms were for one year and elections by the village were permitted, although Spanish approval was required.

We have seen that it was frequently the practice for civil authorities to rely on missionaries to select and appoint governors and other village officials and that it was regular practice for the missionary to appoint his own group of church officials. Apparently few provincial governors or even Spanish alcaldes were in close enough touch with the whole group of villages under their jurisdictions to make or check the appointments. Consequently it fell to the missionaries, under delegation from the civil authority, to do this, a situation which must have served to link civil and ecclesiastical government in the minds of the Indians even more closely than they were linked in ideal Spanish practice. It also served to place the missionary in an advantageous position for getting cooperation between civil and church arms of the native government in his mission community. The governor and his associated officials, once appointed (or elected), were, however, under the supervision of the Spanish alcaldes who were the administrative executives set up by a Spanish governor within his province. There is little indication that any but the most fragmentary communication systems were set up during the Spanish period between Spanish and Indian governors. However, channels did exist and were used and the village governorship came to be, if nothing else, an established means of communication outside missionary channels, when Indians wished, between their villages and the Spanish officials. In New Mexico where tribute was required from the Eastern Pueblos, the Spanish authorities made continual use of the native governors and the staffs in collecting taxes. Where tribute was not established in Sonora and Chihuahua, relations between the native governors and Spanish civil authorities were at a minimum. But we may say that generally some degree of political incorporation was achieved through the establishment of this formal organization among the Indians.

The second feature of the civil program consisted of putting Indians to work as soon as possible in Spanish-controlled enterprises, rather than on their own farms. In New Mexico this was quickly done through either the encomienda or tribute system, much as it had been in central Mexico. The same abuses developed as had developed in Mexico, namely, forcing Indians to work to the extent of injuring their own personal interests. The encomienda system had to be curbed by law in New Mexico as it was elsewhere and was eliminated only after the disruption of many Tewa villages and the creation of much hostility against the Spaniards. Tribute likewise became a source of exploitation, causing New Mexico missionaries to bring many charges against New Mexico governors who forced Indians not only to provide the required tribute for the king but also to produce textiles, pinyon nuts, salt, and other goods for the governor's own private commerce. In Sonora and Chihuahua the major form of production within the Spanish economic system was the mining chiefly of silver and gold. No tribute was exacted in the usual form. By 1725 the exaction of tribute was strongly urged by Spanish Alcalde Mayor Manje of Sonora and by other citizens, but the Jesuits were able to prevent these recommendations from being put into effect. Subsequent recommendations by other representatives of the viceroy in the late 1700's seem to have been ignored, chiefly because of fear of arousing the hostility of Yaquis and other Indians who still remained peaceful in Apache-ridden Sonora. Although tribute was not employed as a means to get Indians to work on the European basis in the south, the mines offered the opportunity to put them to work. Labor was at a premium from 1600 on in Chihuahua and from the 1680's (after the founding of Alamos) in Sonora. Spanish migrants could not fill the demand. Hence in the Chihuahua mines of Parral, Santa Barbara, and the later ones, Indians were brought in by whatever means was possible. Hundreds of Tarahumaras were forced into the mines and either not paid at all or paid inadequately. Indians from Sinaloa and later from Sonora also came by the hundreds to the Chihuahua mines. As the Sonora mines developed, as at Ostimuri, Soyopa, Alamos, San Juan Bautista, and dozens of other places during the late 1600's, Indians from all the Sonora tribes, except the Seris and Apaches, also went to work in the mines. Abuses arose as usual—forcing Indians to work, nonpayment of wages, underpayment, delayed payment, and so on. The only recourse which Indians had under the Spanish system was to tell the missionaries who could protest to the civil administration, to hide far away from any recruiting parties, or finally to revolt. All such methods were employed, with the result that abuses seem to have been considerably reduced by the mid-1700's, so that a more or less steady supply of voluntary Indian labor, to a large extent in the form of Yaqui migrants, was increasingly available, in both Chihuahua and Sonora. One is tempted to say that European work habits — a daily unit of labor for a fixed unit of pay — were successfully established only among Yaquis, and possibly the Opatas. The Spaniards spoke of Yaquis as consistent and able workmen in the mines in the early 1700's and had lesser praise for Opata work habits, but no reports by Spaniards (after a few early ones) indicate that the Tarahumaras or any other northern Indians satisfied their standards. The incorporation by work seems thus to have been only partially successful.

The third point in the civil authorities' program was the distribution of land to individual Indians. It had been generally assumed at first that this would be possible any time after the ten-year period of exemption from taxation. As we have seen, it never quite took place anywhere in northwestern New Spain. It began to be urged throughout Sonora, partly as a measure for breaking tribal solidarity of such groups as the Yaquis, as early as the 1760's. It was urged repeatedly thereafter at various times during the Spanish period, and steps were taken among the Yaquis and some others. However, very little Indian land was actually deeded by title to Indians, although a good deal was deeded to Spaniards. The pressures by Spaniards who wanted to acquire the rich lands surrounding Indian villages, such as those on the Mayo, Yaqui, and Sonora rivers was very great. But the process of acquiring the land was never fully legalized by a general land allotment during the Spanish period. Consequently the taking up of Indian lands by Spaniards had to proceed by squatting or illegal methods. Grants to whole Indian villages were made in New Mexico, and a few titles were given to individuals, but in the main this procedure for incorporation was blocked by a sort of passive resistance on the part of the various Indian groups, no doubt stimulated by the methods of corporate land management employed by the missionaries in the mission communities.

The fourth feature of the civil program of integration was also largely blocked —due partly to the difficult character of the environment in the northwest. Colonization was slow from the very start and consequently fusion of peoples either biologically or culturally was retarded. The first colonists to New Mexico turned around within two years and went back home; by the beginning of the 1800's there were only five Spanish towns of over 1000 population and the total non-Indian population was only about eighteen thousand. Towns grew rapidly in eastern Chihuahua where mines were rich, but these were outside the Tarahumara country and resulted in the incorporation of only a very small part of the tribe into an assimilated population. Settlement of Spaniards was slow in starting in Sonora and after fifty years it became so difficult to survive in the face of the Apache raids that the Spanish population began a steady shrinkage rather than increase. Throughout the 1700's reports of Visitors and others continued to urge that colonization by a "desirable type of Spaniard" be pushed. However, settlers could not be attracted to a country in which mines were petering out, Indians were raiding unrestrainedly, and most agricultural development was carried on against considerable odds.

THE CONFLICTS IN SPANISH CULTURE

The two major instruments of cultural change on the northwestern frontier — the mission community and the Spanish settlement — were deeply at odds with one another. Conceived as being complementary by the policy makers, they turned out to be increasingly in conflict. The heart of the conflict lay in the fact that the missionaries conceived of a transitional institution, the self-sufficient agricultural community, as a necessary vehicle for bringing Indians into Spanish civilization while the civil administrators wanted prompt and direct integration of Indians into Spanish-type communities.

Granting the need for a transitional phase, the king agreed at first to the ten-year period for missionary work. This turned out to be all too short from the missionary's point of view, although it is not precisely clear what standard of measurement missionaries were using when they urged extensions and held that even Indians who had been under the mission system for forty or fifty years were still not ready for taxation and other forms of participation in the Spanish program. The fact is that the ten-year period of grace did provide sufficient time in most cases for laying the foundations of the corporate communities which the missionaries had in mind. Such communities were created by the dozens in Sonora, and missionaries felt a great stake in maintaining them as they were. In them there was no individual ownership of land, there was no explicit taxation although Indians worked for the mission, there was no clear political integration with Spain, there was no development of Indians as individual wage laborers, there was no obliteration of the Indian as Indian through fusion with the Spaniard; there was, in short, not the sort of situation which made a Spanish alcalde feel that he could go to an Indian village, give an order, and have it understood in a way that would get action immediately to satisfy his superior, the provincial governor. The mission communities were not Spanish political units articulated effectively with the provincial government.

To non-clerical Spaniards generally in Sonora by the end of the 1600's, the practical isolation of the mission communities from Spanish economic life under control of the missionaries was insupportable. They wanted labor which could be employed according to whatever conditions the employers set up. Many wanted land, and Indians were living on the best farm and range land. These Spaniards didn't want to be bothered with what were, to them, alien communities of people with different ways of doing things. In their way stood the mission communities with the missionaries constituting a phalanx of defense, a phalanx whose leaders had the ear of the viceroy. So the two branches of the Spanish government moved into sharper and sharper competition for Indian labor, Indian land, Indian produce, Indian minds, and Indian loyalty.

The missionaries, on the other hand, had developed their interests effectively in the mission communities. Each lived in a little kingdom where he was the authority. He had the ear of the Indians. He had made progress in his teaching and in his building of churches. The life of the mission community, focused on God and spiritual things as defined by the missionary, was a thing apart physically and culturally from the Spanish town. The latter was full of undesirables, as missionaries never tired of pointing out, misfits and failures and drifters without moral foundations, family ties, or spiritual interests. Some Jesuit missionaries in Sonora hesitated to teach the Spanish language to their Indians, because as a later Jesuit historian put it, summing up their views, "If [knowledge of the Spanish language] favored public prosperity and the fusion of races, it was certainly also to the injury of the intellectual, moral, and religious interests of the poor Indians." He referred here to the detribalized and wandering Indians who began to appear in the 1700's as hangers-on around the Spanish mining settlements, poverty-stricken and often demoralized. To distribute the land to individuals, to permit the abuses of labor exploitation, to require regular tribute, to encourage Indians to mingle with the riffraff of the frontier settlements would indeed break up the little kingdoms of God, for in the missionary view the errors of lack of understanding rife in the mission populations were as nothing to the errors of commission to be learned from a disorganized Spanish lower class in a frontier town.

Thus the missionaries held on as long as they could against the breakup of their communities and looked toward secularization as the destruction of much of their work. Eventually, with the expulsion of the Jesuits, the entering wedge for the secular program was provided. The mission communities disintegrated; a new era for Indians began with the assumption of responsibility for the Spanish program by the civil authorities. The conflict in Spanish society between the values of the missionary Orders and those of the political hierarchy was apparently solved.

BEARERS OF SPANISH CULTURE

We have discussed the frontier institutions pretty much as though they operated and had certain effects independently of the individuals who manned them. It would be a great mistake to assume that this were actually the case and we do not do so here. They operated as limiting frameworks for action by individuals who often differed profoundly from one another. The fate of Indians of a given tribe often depended in large measure on the nature of the missionary who first began work with them, or on a particular succession of missionaries who carried on the work. Indeed, the fate of whole communities — whether they were wiped out or survived — often depended on the differences in the behavior of Spanish captains in Chihuahua and Sonora. Spanish governors and alcaldes executed royal policy in profoundly different ways in New Mexico and Sonora, and tribes were affected accordingly. The constellation of personalities in official positions for a period of years often had a deep-reaching influence on a whole generation of Indians and their relations with the Spanish world. We must, therefore, attempt to gain some conception of the range in behavior of different Spaniards, if we are to go on to an understanding of the processes through which Indian life was transformed.

It is not possible to present a representative sample of the attitudes and viewpoints of the bearers of the culture of the conquest who came into contact with the Indians at close range in the frontier institutions. The published data which are available have to do with missionaries to a far greater extent than with political and military officials, and there is almost nothing regarding ordinary civilians. Moreover, the accounts by missionaries or those describing them as persons are limited to the more articulate, or to those who, for various reasons, such as martyrdom, become more famous. We cannot assume that the more articulate missionaries were necessarily the more influential, and certainly they were a minute minority among all those missionaries who served in the missions. The best that we can do is to try to give some insights into the personalities and behavior of a small selection. These may indicate something of the range in types of behavior.

The sources of information about individual missionary attitudes and actions are chiefly their own letters and writings. Thus we have extensive material written by Andrés Pérez de Ribas, first missionary to the Yaquis and for three years Provincial of the Jesuit Order in Mexico City; by Adam Gilg, second missionary to the Seris with wide experience in Sonora missions; by Joseph Neumann who spent fifty-one years in the Upper Tarahumara missions; by Eusebio Kino, first missionary to the Upper Pimas and for twenty-five years active at the northern edge of the Spanish frontier; by Juan Nentuig, missionary among the Opatas and Upper Pimas; by Alonzo Benavides, Visitor of New Mexico and missionary among the Eastern Pueblos and Navajos; and by Ignaz Pfefferkorn also with wide experience among the Upper Pimas and Opatas. These men either wrote extensive descriptive and narrative accounts of missionary work and native life in the areas that they knew at firsthand, or happen to have had letters of theirs published.

In contrast, there are the missionaries whose experience and contacts were at least as extensive as those mentioned, but whose impressions and descriptions if they exist remain buried in the colonial archives, such as Father Figueroa whose long life was lived in the Tarahumara missions; Pedro Méndez, first missionary to the Mayos and Lower Pimas who worked among Indians for some sixty years; Augustín Campos whose period of mission work was the longest of any serving in the Upper Pima country; Father Parra who served equally long among the Opatas; and others in New Mexico. Most of those whose records we have available were of German or Italian origin rather than of Spanish, and hence the record is biased in terms of national origin. Yet there was considerable variety in the behavior and attitudes of these non-Spanish missionaries and there is not much reason to believe that the missionaries of Spanish origin were greatly different.

In considering the writings of the Jesuit missionaries one is struck with certain uniformities in their viewpoints. In the first place, they all exhibited a deep absorption in teaching and explaining Christian ideas to the Indians. Doing this and providing the means for furthering such activities was without question the dominant concern of these men. They were without exception focused on conversion of the Indians, on getting them to accept new ideas and behave in conformity with the new ideas. The missionaries obviously experienced an effective training which gave them a common objective seen in very much the same terms. Coupled with this was another common characteristic, namely, a lack of interest in or capacity to fathom the viewpoints of the Indians with whom they were working. Although some of them were capable of observing and noting fairly objectively the exterior behavior and characteristics of the Indians, none showed any evidence of having made close contact with the world view or moral standpoint of the Indians. This comes as something of a surprise when one discovers how intimate they became with individuals and how immersed they all were in the life which went on around them.

It is obvious that their training placed a barrier between them and the Indians. Puzzling, contradictory, and unexpected behavior they all noted at different times; explanations which were ventured were in terms of intercession of the Devil, childish inconstancy and nonrationality, or merely stupidity. The puzzling or stubborn behavior was not viewed as part of another moral system which could be understood and through understanding eliminated as a major obstacle in accepting the Jesuit moral system. Those missionaries who recorded their experiences were steeped in a particular world view to the extent that they were quite unable to make contact with any other. There is no evidence of a search for a common ground; there is a good deal of evidence of deep frustration in their work stemming out of ignorance of the people they worked with. The frustration that they expressed seems indeed to foreshadow the baffled frustration widely characteristic of United States Indian Bureau employees who were working with Indians in Arizona and New Mexico two hundred years later.

One of the earlier sufferers from this frustration was Father Joseph Neumann, missionary at Sisoguichic and Carichic in the Upper Tarahumara country in the years between 1681 and 1732. Neumann was born in Brussels of German parents and spent his early years in Vienna, entering the Jesuit Order in 1665 in Bohemia. He was posted at Sisigochic immediately, in the country of the headwaters of the upper Conchos River, where Jesuit work had been in progress for some twenty years. He spent most of the rest of his life there, but also served, under the Jesuit system of rotation, as rector and Visitor in the Tarahumara missionary province. He died after many years at Carichic with fifty-one years service as missionary. He came to be known in the Order as a capable, courageous missionary with a stern view of duty and some talent for administration.

Neumann, like most Jesuits, knew the varied demands of the missionary life. He served at his mission from the start as "cobbler, tailor, mason, carpenter, cook, nurse, and physician for the sick." At the beginning, as a result of the rule that missionaries were not permitted by the Order to set up a servant establishment with women to cook for them, he was required to cook for himself, except for tortillas which were made and sent to him once a week by a Tarahumara woman. He became closely associated with a lieutenant governor and captain-general, both Tarahumaras, of the district where he worked, and developed a warm friendship for them. Throughout his life he urged gentleness in dealing with Indians and emphasized the necessity for the exercise of deep Christian humility in all contacts. During his first years he wrote that the Tarahumaras were "simple of nature and unpolished" and, "naturally peace-loving, never quarrel among themselves," but "unwilling to work." He wrote that he found his work hard and often unrewarding, but apparently he never asked to be transferred, as did many who worked in the Tarahumara missions in the trying early 1700's.

He was extremely courageous, as indicated in one important event in his service at Sisigochic. After leaving his mission on a necessary trip, he unexpectedly turned back and found the Indians of the mission settlement beginning a dancing and drinking party, probably a "curing" ceremony of the usual kind in the native religion. Such ceremonies had been prohibited by Neumann and he was extremely angry. He went among the dancers and upset fourteen ollas of liquor (tesquino). The Indians, deeply incensed, nevertheless dispersed, but planned to hold the ceremony later. An attempt was made to get the missionary to leave on a pretext. He was also indirectly informed that he would be killed if he interfered again. On the night of the postponed ceremony, he disguised himself in blanket and headband and went to the dance. As the fiesta began he threw off his blanket and again upset all the ollas of tesquino and stood in the midst of the Indians to deliver a sermon on the evils of drinking. Instead of killing him, the headmen asked his forgiveness and promised to hold no more such ceremonies.

As the work went on and he lived through two Tarahumara rebellions, he became convinced of the necessity of force. In 1697 he approved the beheading of thirty-three rebel leaders and the posting of their heads on pikes in the vicinity of his mission. As Visitor he vigorously urged the placing of soldiers in the Tarahumara country.

In his mature years after long service he wrote the story of missionary work in the Tarahumara country, summing up his experience in his narrative.

These Indians are by nature and disposition a sly and crafty folk, from whom sincerity is not to be expected. They are accomplished hypocrites, and as a rule the ones who seem the most virtuous should be considered the most wicked of all. They say one thing to their people when in the presence of the missionaries and later in secret they say another directly contrary . . . . The missionaries were deceived by these men [the Indian governors], too, for they were addicted to the same vices . . . . Superficially the governors conformed to the wishes of the fathers, and their lives had the appearance of probity, but all the while they were secretly seeking the favour of their people by tolerating and cloaking their offenses . . . . In fact, I cannot deny that with these stony-hearted people the result does not repay the hard labor of the valuable seed. The seed of the gospel does not sprout, or if it sprouts, it is spoiled by the thorn of carnal desire . . . . For this reason we find little eagerness among our new converts who prepare for baptism. Indeed, some only pretend to believe, showing no inclination for spiritual things, such as prayers, divine services, and Christian doctrine. They show no aversion to sin, no anxiety about their eternal happiness, no eagerness to persuade their relatives to be baptized. They show rather a lazy indifference to everything good, unlimited sensual desire, an irresistible habit of getting drunk, and stubborn silence in regard to hidden pagans, and so we cannot find them and bring them into the fold of Christ.

One does not find a balancing statement about the Tarahumaras by Father Neumann; so we must conclude that this is an expression of his final feeling about the people and his experiences of working with them. It is presented in so unqualified a way as an indictment of a people that one cannot take it seriously as a careful characterization. Neumann worked for fifty years among the Tarahumaras. One would expect a more balanced appraisal, if he had really made contact with the Indians as human being to human being. What he wrote at the end of his long and devoted service seems to be less an appraisal of Tarahumara character than of the feelings produced in himself as a result of working under the Jesuit mission system.

Neumann does not actually claim that Tarahumara husbands and wives are sly and crafty in their relations with one another, or that mothers and children are so, or even that community officials are sly and crafty in their dealings with other Tarahumaras. There are no descriptions of the relations of Tarahumaras with one another. What Father Neumann characterized were the relations of the missionaries with those Tarahumaras with whom they came into contact. Very likely the description applies most fully to Neumann's own relations with Tarahumaras, for there is no evidence of a careful comparison of his own with other missionaries' experiences. What we have is a description of a situation in which frank and cooperative relations were not achieved. If Neumann was willing to write for all to read that the Tarahumaras whom he knew were all sly and crafty and did many things behind his back and were "stony-hearted," he cannot have had much, if any, real love or respect for them. One does not indict in such a way people for whom one has respect and warm kindly feeling. The fact that Tarahumaras, including persons such as governors in whom Neumann had placed some trust, went behind his back to work against him suggests that he kept them under some sort of pressure to behave in ways that were not compatible with their relations with other members of the community. He does not indicate that he had an understanding of the community pressures. Pushing his program vigorously, he did not learn about and gain respect for the problems which his program created for individuals who wished to be friendly with him and had some interest in his objectives. There is no indication that he sat down to discuss such problems from their, as well as his own, point of view. One is forced to conclude that he was working on a unilateral basis, so that he forced the Indians to hide from him their real difficulties in integrating him and his demands into their communities. He was isolated in his mission community, working largely in the dark; inevitably such social isolation led to intense feelings of distrust and lack of rapport. It is difficult to imagine how under such circumstances he could have felt anything but the deep sense of failure which he expresses. That he should blame this on inborn qualities of the Indians is to be expected, for he was conscious of having behaved in complete accordance with the Christian ideals which his Order set before him. To do otherwise would have forced him to question the soundness of the methods in which the Order had trained him.

The tragedy of Neumann must have been that of many other missionaries. He was working at a time of maturity in the development of the mission program among the Tarahumaras. He had not experienced the excitement and triumph of the first conversions, such as Father Fonte knew before he was murdered in the southern Tarahumara country or that Father de Ribas knew in the early days in Sonora. Neumann lived in mission communities torn by the conflicts in Spanish culture, among Indian factions created by one hundred years of being pulled and pushed by Spanish influences. His sense of failure and frustration was a reflection of the whole contact situation which had set Indian against Indian in the northwest of New Spain.

About the time that Neumann was beginning his work among the Tarahumaras, another Jesuit of German descent arrived in Sonora and took over the difficult job of reducing the wandering Seris to mission life. This was Adam Gilg, who was given the assignment of reorganizing the mission of Pópulo on the San Miguel River where Father Fernández had brought the first group of Seris and introduced them to farming. Pópulo had been without a missionary for several years and the Seris who had settled there had begun to drift away. Gilg found when he took over in 1688 that there were some families who wanted to continue the new way of life, but they were distrustful of him at first and opposed him in undescribed "offensive" ways. But gradually he re-established the mission and gathered more Seris about him. He made trips into the Tepoca country, became acquainted with more and more Seris, established some other short-lived communities of them, and brought those most interested in mission life to Pópulo. When he wrote a very informative letter back to Germany about his experiences, in 1692, he claimed to have learned the language, which he said had many words similar to German, and had evidently made many keen observations about Seri ways and character. On the whole, at this beginning period in his missionary life, Gilg felt more favorably inclined toward Indians than did Neumann. Yet a basic similarity in approach is apparent.

Gilg characterized the Seris with mixed feelings. *They live without God, with-*

out faith, without Princes, and without houses like cattle. Just as they have no religious worship, so too one finds not even the shadow of any idolatry among them, since they have never known nor adored either a true or a false deity. Still, they have known the word for devil in Spanish for some time. He describes at great length an appearance of the Devil, as a youth clothed in red, to a large gathering of Seris, about which he was unable to learn very much, however, because when he inquired into the event (which he himself did not see) he found the Seris "so changeable in their statements."

He continues: *Now just as my Seris . . . on the one hand are not serious and have no diligence, or stability, no muscles nor capacity to comprehend the Christian mysteries, thus on the other hand, they have none of those coarse vices which elsewhere have the upper hand among almost all heathen and which mightily deter them from Christianity; in the same way neither idolatry nor magic nor drunkenness nor avarice nor the abuse of having a number of wives at the same time, nor lewdness are in vogue among them. The whole time that I have been living among these otherwise half-bestial people, I have not heard that an unmarried woman has been seduced, although the silly thing (since almost everyone goes naked) must mightily incite them to it.* He goes on to speak of "the holy sacraments which they do not understand on account of their stupidity" and to say that the children as they grow up become "lazy and deceitful."

Gilg said that he found the Seris at Pópulo increasingly inclining toward the settled and Christian life, and that, for the most part, he found them attending church as regularly and with as much interest as newly established Christian congregations anywhere on the frontier. But at the same time this was far from what would actually be desirable and he felt constantly as though the return for his labors was far less in the way of Christian devotion than it should be. "The greatest and almost only sign that a missionary can work here at all times is his saintly way of life, guiltless in all things, together with an insatiable zeal for souls, generosity to the needy, a tender and pure paternal love for his Indians."

Gilg made extensive observations on the Seris' way of life. He showed himself capable of describing with some fullness their tools and clothing and weapons. He had studied the language diligently, and although a later Jesuit account says that he was removed from the Seri mission because he was unable to learn the language, his own account indicates that he had learned many words, including the profusion of terms by which relatives referred to one another. He had become aware of even a few features of social organization such as the taboo on speaking to each other between fathers-in-law and sons-in-law. In all of this he shows a real interest in the people and their ways and considerable freedom from preconceptions. He was indeed immersing himself in the Indian way of life with an unusual degree of curiosity, at least in these first years of work.

What we see in Gilg's account is a deeper interest in the people themselves than we find in Neumann and perhaps a greater readiness to regard them as ordinary mortals with both good and bad character traits. This was also characteristic of Neumann's early letters, before the frustrations of the missionary life hardened him to the problems which the mission system imposed on the Indians. But we also find in Gilg the seeds of the frustrations. We find the same tendency to take refuge in the solitary setting of an example in the missionary's personal behavior — a refuge from the problems of discovering why Christian ways were not adopted more readily and quickly by the Indians. We find the same frustration before the lack of "diligence" and "stability" in the Indians. We find the same tendency to attribute to "stupidity" the incomprehension of the Christian doctrines. In all of this, although Gilg shows a greater degree of concern to find out the nature of Seri ways, we see the basically unilateral approach of the missionaries, resting solidly in the belief that the Indians have no law, no faith, no deities, no leadership, in short, no organized way of life. Although Gilg says that the Seris are only "half-bestial" rather than wholly so, his conviction is apparent that they constitute a different order of humans from Europeans.

It would be interesting to know whether general frustration settled over Gilg as it did over Neumann as he became a veteran of the missions, for the letter we have quoted was written while he was still in his apprenticeship. In the case of another Jesuit, Eusebio Kino, we have an example of one who so far as we can tell never, in the course of his twenty-five years of missionary labor, became embittered or inclined to blame his failures on the inherent character defects of the Indians. Kino was a totally different sort of personality from Neumann, of an incurably optimistic approach to life and always interested in and delighted with other people, whether Indians or not. Strangely enough, despite his persisting interest in the Upper Pimas among whom he worked, he gave no evidence whatever of being able to make observations on the behavior or culture traits of the Indians at all comparable with Gilg's on the Seris. One can visualize little of Piman culture from the voluminous writings of Kino. With very abundant opportunity for observation in his dozens of trips to all parts of the Pima country and into the Yuman country at the mouth of the Colorado River, Kino set down almost nothing to indicate that he was interested in the Indians' ways of making a living, organizing their villages, or worshipping. In the course of recounting some events, inevitably some forms of behavior are recorded, but this is all incidental to Kino's description of his own relations with the people. One guesses that Kino was so completely wrapped up in his own purposes, which included exploration and map making as well as conversion and mission building, that he had no time for learning about the ways of the Indians among whom he worked and traveled. In part this may be due to the fact that everything he wrote was designed to inform the outside world of the great possibilities of the mission field in the Upper Pimería, but so consistently does he avoid setting down anything about Indian culture that one suspects the lack is primarily a reflection of his personality and interests. His abiding interest in Pimas was as they reflected Kino's plans, not in them as he might learn from them about themselves and the world view on which he sought to impose Christianity. In some degree this absorption in their own plans, to the exclusion of the Indians' plans, was characteristic of all the missionaries. Kino epitomizes the tendency in its best form.

Kino never departed from a view of the Upper Pimas as gentle, friendly, sincere people whom he could count on to live up to their word. This was a view in direct contrast to Neumann's view of the Tarahumaras. It is possible that there were fundamental differences in the character structure of the two peoples. But so consistently, from the beginning, and in the face of rebellion and rejection of himself, does Kino maintain this view that one suspects the bias of personality. Other contemporary accounts of the Pimas held just the opposite — that the Pimas were sly and crafty and ready to work against the Spaniards behind their backs, and a later missionary account held that the Upper Pimas had better all be exterminated or deported from Sonora. It would appear that Kino's bias in favor of the Pimas, while a part of his attempt to combat unfavorable views of them which hindered their development as a mission field, reflected his own relations with them, as Neumann's view of the Tarahumaras reflected relations between missionaries and Indians in the Chihuahua missions at his time. Kino began the work of missionization of the Upper Pimas and thus had the advantage of a long period of almost singlehanded building of social relationships between them and the Spaniards of the region. He built his own personality into these relationships.

Typical of Kino's finding of good will on the part of the Pimas wherever he went is the statement in a letter of 1687 describing his first tour of duty: "In all places they received with love the word of God for the sake of their eternal salvation." But this was not merely an expression of first enthusiasm in a new task, for in the following year he was even more enthusiastic: "God willing, hundreds, and later thousands will be gathered into the bosom of our sweet, most holy Mother Church, for about five thousand of the neighboring Indians have come asking at this time with most ardent pleading for holy baptism. They envy the happy lot of those in the three new settlements." And again five years after the first, of a visit to the Sobaipuris on the San Pedro River, he wrote "Captain Coro and the rest of them received me with all kindness." Two years later of a trip to the Gila Pimas, he wrote: "All were affable and docile people." In 1696 with nearly ten years of missionary work behind him and after previous visits to and work with the Sobaipuris of the Santa Cruz Valley, he wrote that at Bac he was "received with all love by the many inhabitants of the great ranchería and by many other principal men, who had gathered from various parts adjacent." In 1698 he again wrote after a trip through the whole Papago country that he was "grateful for the great affability and cheerfulness of everybody whom we met." And so it went throughout his life until he died in Pima country at Magdalena. Wherever he went, according to his accounts, among Pimas or Yumans, his reception was warm and hearty and he came away with feelings of great friendliness. He apparently was able to charm and to be charmed by all the Indians, whether on first visits or in the missions where they knew him well.

At the bottom of Kino's pleasant and easy relations with the Indians seems to have been a tolerant spirit. Not only has he left no record whatever of suppression of Indian ceremony, but in his writings there is no particular concern with Indian ways as evil. He does not inveigh against drunkenness, which was a common ceremonial practice among the Upper Pimas, as it was among the Tarahumaras. He spends no words on condemnation even of Pima witches. One would think that somehow he managed to remain blandly unaware of the existence of Indian ceremonial life away from the missions, if it were not for the fact that there are accounts of all-night dances and other ceremonies which took place at villages where he spent the night or visited for a period. Many such all-night gatherings with dances and music he evidently felt honored by, believing (probably correctly in some instances) that they were given in his honor.

Moreover, he gives a one-paragraph account of a scalp dance among the Sobaipuris, saying: *We found the Pima natives of Quiburi very jovial and friendly. They were dancing over the scalps and the spoils of fifteen enemies, Hocomes and Janos, whom they had killed a few days before. This was so pleasing to us that Captain . . . Bernal, the Alferez, the Sergeant and many others entered the circle and danced merrily in company with the natives.* This of course was a situation in which the Spaniards were delighted to celebrate a victory over mutual enemies, the eastern tribes associated with the Apaches, but it is also characteristic of the pleasant and noncritical way in which Kino took note of and sat in the midst of so many native ceremonials. He almost never permitted himself to be even mildly critical of native practices, if indeed it actually bothered him. Such tolerance must have made him welcome everywhere and caused him to be viewed only as a constructive bringer of new good tidings and never as one who was prepared to destroy what the people already had.

There was also a certain amount of give and take in his relations with the headmen of the many Pima villages which he visited. Repeatedly he describes how he sat and talked for hours in such villages. What he said must have had a great deal of interest; an example is the following — describing his visit to Bac in 1692 — which shows his teaching methods very clearly: *I spoke to them of the word of God, and on the map of the world I showed them the lands, the rivers, and the seas over which we fathers had come from afar to bring them the saving knowledge of our Holy Faith. I told them also how in ancient times the Spaniards were not Christian, how Santiago came to teach them the faith, and how the first fourteen years he was able to baptize only a few, because of which the Holy Apostle was discouraged, but that the Holy Virgin appeared to him and consoled him, promising that the Spaniards would convert the rest of the people of the world.*

And I showed them on the map of the world how the Spaniards and the Faith had come by sea to Vera Cruz and had gone into Puebla and to Mexico, Guadalaxara, Sinaloa, Sonora and now to . . . Dolores del Cosari, in the land of the Pimas . . . that they could go and see it all, and even ask at once their relatives, my servants, who were with me. They listened with pleasure to these and other talks concerning God, heaven, and hell, told me that they wished to be Christians, and gave me some infants to baptize.

This was, of course, the general method of teaching and preaching of the Jesuits. Certainly Kino was merely one of many capable missionary teachers who knew how to employ concrete demonstration, in this case maps and charts, and to spice the doctrine with history, and even to meet the skeptics with reference to Christianized Indians who could be questioned right there in their own tongue about it all. These merely show that Kino was capable in the missionary teaching tradition.

His special genius was his capacity to sit down immediately afterwards and listen to the Pima headmen. Over and over again in his accounts, he tells how he was invited to sit through a night or even two days and nights in which he must have done as much listening as talking. Thus in 1700 on one of his trips among the Yumas, he was persuaded to stay, even though he had wanted to push on, because people wished to hear him. He preached in his usual way. Then, he says, "These talks, ours and theirs, lasted almost the whole afternoon and afterward till midnight, with very great pleasure to all." He was not annoyed by having been put off schedule; rather he relaxed and enjoyed a day of mutual give and take. How much he understood, even though he always had interpreters with him, we shall never know, nor are we sure of his attitude about the content of the long talks of the Indian spokesmen. He never mentions the content unless it had some direct bearing on his mapping interests or the building of the mission chain. But at any rate he behaved in a way, at very great cost in time, which was regarded as courteous and must have made him a delightful guest. He behaved in this respect, in fact, in the way that any visiting headman among the Indians was expected to behave. Long talks by all parties were the rule, but they must not be one-sided — and this Kino seemed instinctively to understand.

Another of Kino's qualities, which was not by any means unique among the missionaries, but most abundantly developed in him, was that of organizing ability. He believed in gathering people together for particular and dramatic purposes. He showed his ability for this when Chief Coxi was baptized at Dolores shortly after the founding of that mission. Kino made it the occasion for inviting other Pima headmen from far to the west where he had made a beginning at contacts — and five attended. He also brought "Spanish gentlemen" from the mining town of Bacanuche to the ceremony. This sort of thing he continued to do on a grander scale as time went on. He brought hundreds of people from all over the Upper Pima country to the dedication of the church when it was finished at Dolores. He brought a large group of Pima headmen from the Santa Cruz and San Pedro valleys and elsewhere to Dolores and then had them go on a pilgrimage through the northern Opata country to have an audience with the Father Visitor at Bacerac and ask for missionaries to be sent to their villages. He called meetings at Bac and other Pima villages to discuss his interest in the problem of whether California was an island or not. His accounts indicate that he got great responses in such meetings and that he participated in the discussions rather than addressed the groups. He had some sort of genius for getting people to do things together and this must have been an important factor in establishing communication among Upper Pimas who had been isolated from one another before.

It would seem, however, that it was Kino's personal characteristics — his enthusiasm, his warmth of feeling for individuals such as Captain Coro, Coxi, and others with whom he became associated, his tolerance of ways not in accord with European, his delight in big and ceremonial gatherings — rather than any inclination or ability to understand other ways and reconcile them that lay at the bottom of his successes in the Pima country. There is no indication that he organized people on the basis of anything other than their devotion to him. He indicates no understanding of Piman social organization; in fact, in the few instances in which he mentioned having selected a governor and given out a cane of office, it was always

on the basis of the person's having helped Kino and his party. He does not indicate
that he knew anything about the existing place of such individuals in their native
communities, and when it does turn out that an individual such as Coxi had wide
influence this seems likely to have been post- rather than pre-Spanish. The basis of
Kino's operations, then, would seem to have been not a deep knowledge of the
Pimas specifically, but rather a good understanding of what we usually call
"human nature" in general.

There is a small incident which sheds much light on Kino's whole approach
and personality. On a visit to a small Papago community north of the present
Tucson, he found that the people had erected a cross to honor him. At the base
of this were placed seven carved wooden "daggers" painted blue, ceremonial
sticks such as the Pimans used in many different types of ceremonies. Kino was
delighted with the cross (and there were others erected in his honor), but most of
all he was intrigued with the blue "daggers." He picked them up and took them
home with him, telling Captain Manje his traveling companion that "they represented to him the Seven Sorrows of Holy Mary." The fact that they represented
something quite different to the Indians who made them either did not occur to
Kino or was ignored by him. Certainly he did not inquire into the matter. He took
what he found and incorporated it into his ideal world, ordered by Christian concepts and his hopes and plans for the future of the people of the little Papago
village. The cement of this imaginary world in terms of which Kino interpreted all
that happened in Upper Pimería was warm human affection. It governed the
actual human relationships which he built there.

Some insight is also given into the man's spirit from the following incident
of a trip with Father Salvatierra. In 1700 while Salvatierra and Kino and their party
were traveling through a section of the worst desert of North America in what
is now northern Sonora, he says, "Almost all day we were saying and chanting
various prayers and praises of Our Lady in different languages — in Castilian, in
Latin, in Italian [Kino was Italian, as was Salvatierra], and also in the Californian
tongue." Intoxicated with human fellowship and plans for the future, they saw no
difficulties in the Devil's Highway, over which they were riding.

Kino's personality probably had greater scope in a new mission field than
it could have had in a mature one such as the Tarahumara, where Neumann
worked. And probably many of the missionaries who spent long years in various
of the fields, after they had been more or less stabilized, lived and worked and
thought much like Kino, learning little or nothing about the people they worked
among as products of tradition and culture, but winning the devotion and loyalty
of individuals because of their sincerity and warmth and allowing that to serve as
the bridge on which Indians moved over to a new way of life.

In 1763, after eleven years as a missionary in Sonora among both Upper
Pimas and Opatas, Father Juan Nentuig made a very successful effort to let the
world know what life in general was like in Sonora. He wrote a book in which he
described the geology, fauna, flora, Indian tribes, mission work, etc. Like Kino's
works, it was in part inspired by an effort to get action from higher up the hierarchies, action to stem the scourge of Apache raids which by 1763 had resulted in

the depopulation of the whole northeastern part of the mission province. The book ended in recommendations for controlling the Seris, Upper Pimas, and Apaches, but in the course of setting forth his practical proposals, Nentuig showed himself a man of wide interests and very good powers of observation and organization. At the same time he reveals much of the spirit in which he carried on his own work among the Indians. He had served at Saric at the time of the 1751 Pima rebellion, where he came into firsthand contact with the rebel leader Luís of Saric and where he barely escaped with his life. Most of his time as a missionary, however, had been spent among the Opatas, chiefly at Guasavas on the Moctezuma River among Opatas of the north. He knew the Opata language with apparent thoroughness.

Like Gilg, and unlike Kino, Father Nentuig was capable of learning a great deal about the Indians, at least about the Opatas among whom he felt most at home. He gives us detailed descriptions of their ways of making a living and division of labor, their artifacts, some of their ceremonies and religious beliefs, and even, in that area in which Jesuit missionaries seemed least able to determine the existence of anything at all — social organization. He knew the terms in the Opata language for most of the culture elements which he described. In his writings he shows more insight into some of the psychological reactions of the Opatas than perhaps any other Sonora missionary who has left a record:

The Opatas and some of the Eudebes, though in a limited degree, are, in comparison to the other Indians, as the people of the towns are in comparison to the country people; for, although they do not cease to be Indians, yet in the end, reason prevails with them; among all of these they are the best Christians; they are the most loyal vassals of our Lord the King, never having rebelled against him or his ministers. They are the most inclined to work, to till their lands and to raise cattle; they are the truest and bravest in war, and many times have shown their courage, both by aiding the Royal troops, and, on their own account, in various campaigns at the expense of the Missions.

After describing in detail their technique of weaving and expressing high admiration for its products, he goes on to say: *Although this kind of handiwork is slow and tedious, the weavers would not think of employing looms with a great saving of time, patience and work; for the Indians are unwilling to adopt improvements which were unknown to them before. The same is true in regard to any other kind of work, such as cultivating the land and reaping. All the operations might be done with greater ease and better; but it is useless to struggle with them in order to make them give up their routine; their patience can tire the world.*

In this matter the Pimas, recently converted, have been more docile than the Opatas; for the latter are persuaded that they have nothing to learn no matter how primitive their ideas, while the Pimas, conscious of the scantiness of their knowledge of things necessary to their welfare, are more willing and docile.

He continues: *A favorable characteristic of all the nations which people the Province of Sonora, even including the Seris and Apaches, is that they neither have been nor are at present idolators; nor have they any inclination to become so. Thus far no trace has been found at all of such worship or adoration — no idols* or objects which would indicate that such a thing had existed up to the present time. The only devotion that has been observed is one to the Devil, and this is rather caused by fear and stupidity than by inclination. I am led to believe this because in all the ranches or villages there has always been one or more sorcerers; at least they are called so; and these have ever been suspected and feared on account of the belief that they can do evil.

The Indians, like all other simple people in the world, sometimes show signs of having superstitions and silly beliefs, inherited from their forefathers; but I cannot be persuaded that such foolishness has taken deep root in their minds, since, enlightened by the Missionary Fathers they give it up without much difficulty, at least apparently. . . . ¶ The Opatas had retained, until lately, among others a very curious custom. A number of girls, dressed in white or simply wearing a chemise, would come out at night to dance. . . . This ceremony was called "invoking the clouds," for they performed it in times of drought, fully believing that in consequence of this performance the clouds would stop and sprinkle their fields. With God's help, however, this incantation became known to the Missionary Fathers in spite of the secrecy with which it was held; and being shown their evident delusion, the abuse was stopped. . . . ¶ During thunderstorms, when sensible people are frightened by the noise of thunder and lightning, the natives begin to jump with pleasure, rejoicing and exulting; and although I have not seen it in all of those nations very often, I have not been able to find out the reason for such unseasonable jollification; and I am inclined to believe that rather than an expression of real pleasure, it is a kind of ceremony.

Drunkenness is not so bad among these nations as among others that we hear of; and among the Opatas and Eudebes, thanks to the assiduity and watchfulness of the Ministering Fathers, it has disappeared entirely. The Pimas, particularly those of the mountains, are still addicted to the habit, and the reason for that is, that, owing to their rising in 1751, and their not having been punished for it, they continue their heathen usages. The Missionary Fathers, to their great sorrow, were unable to remedy the evil, neither did they dare to attempt it; for by reason of false suspicions and evident slanders they were overpowered by hands armed against them instead of being armed against the true enemies of God, the King and the people. . . .

In their carousals and conventicles they follow their whims unrestrained; an old man usually sets himself as a preacher on the theme of his ancient exploits real or false; and the sermon lasts sometimes a whole night or until the panegyrist of hell, who generally is a war chief or a bully, claiming to be a sorcerer, becomes hoarse or loses his breath. Besides the sermon, in order to lend variety to the general monotony, there is no lack of dancing and singing, but it is as mournful and doleful as the sermon. And I may say from my own experience that never in my life have I spent sadder nights, than when on three or four occasions, although not in close proximity, I was an unwilling listener to their revels.

. . . The ceremonies of their heathenish weddings are not fit to be described in detail; I shall only mention the more decent. They gather together, old and young, and the young men and marriageable women are placed in two files. At a *given signal the latter begin to run, and at another signal the former follow them. When the young men overtake the young women each one must take his mate by the left nipple and the marriage is made and confirmed. After this preliminary ceremony they devote themselves to dancing, . . . Then all at once they take mats of palm tree leaves, which are prepared beforehand, and without further ceremony each couple is placed on a mat, and the rest of the people go on rejoicing. . . . These performances are carried on in the woods not far from the villages, and are practiced even by the Indians of the gangs working for the Spaniards . . . for I saw such a performance myself and took the participants by surprise, dancing in a wood, quite a distance from the habitations.*

In burying the dead, all these nations, the Apaches excepted, either heathen or newly converted, have had the custom of burying with them their furniture and clothes, their favorite dish, a basin of water, etc. Such is their fidelity to the dead that among the Pimas of the Sierras, the Missionary Father, in order to avoid this custom, has to remain by the grave until it is well filled up.

Observations such as these — and these are only a small sample — indicate that Nentuig had a keen sense of the differences among the Indians of Sonora. In other words, he was not thinking in terms of Indians in general, nor did he think of the various tribes in terms of a stereotype for each. Rather, he had observed and listened rather carefully, and out of this experience was capable of giving a fairly systematic account of the ways of each of the Sonoran tribes. His viewpoint toward the customs of which he has become aware is very definite. Thus, he condemns Opata resistance to improving their weaving techniques, indicating that he has reasoned and tried to persuade to this end but without success; he is pleased with the Pimas because of their comparative readiness to adopt new laborsaving devices. He praises all the Sonora Indians as non-idolators and expresses satisfaction over the apparent ease with which the Opatas, at least, have been persuaded to give up their superstitions. The ceremonies, such as those for rain, he regards merely as silly and indicative of a foolish childishness. His observations on the public gatherings at which native headmen exhorted and gave sermons seem to carry the most rancor; in these he saw no order or purpose and could conceive the Indian leaders only as spokesmen of the Devil. One may guess that efforts to break up such meetings had resulted for Nentuig in some personally unpleasant experience, and obviously the music, according to his own account, had a depressing effect on him. He is shocked at, although interested in, the unabashed sexuality of Opata weddings and disapproves the custom of putting a dead person's belongings in the grave. We can see from these vigorous expressions of opinion the direction that Nentuig's efforts at changing the Indians would take — for example, the improvement of technology, the giving up of all native ceremonies, the substitution of the missionary for native preachers and headmen, the suppressing of open expressions of sex. We can also see something of the very considerable knowledge possessed by Nentuig of the human material with which he was working.

He shows further his awareness of certain behavior characteristics of the Indians which were of prime importance in the mission program. Thus he says: *It seems incredible that many of the relatives, even husbands or wives, when they*

*have them, should not know anything about the runaway Indian, but it is a fact
that no notice is given, either to the magistrate or the ministering father, until they
are missing from the town, and then it is impossible, even by offering mines of
gold, and promising secrecy as to who told, to make anybody say what direction
the fugitive took. And here again we find a contradiction in their disposition; the
inviolability of secrecy in helping one another, notwithstanding their inconstancy
and fickleness.* Here Nentuig was certainly on the threshold of understanding the
conflicts which mission life set up in Indian society. He went on to say: *In view of
this and many other contradictions to be met with every day in their character we
must acknowledge that, not only in the hemisphere they inhabit but in their tem-
per, customs and inclinations these American Indians are the antipodes of all other
people. Notwithstanding their uncultured state, however, as has been said, they
have a reason withal; and thanks to incessant labor, the bad seed is being eradi-
cated, and a commonwealth may be formed, not only political as far as their disposition will allow, but even Christian.*

*This, — God be thanked — we have obtained, principally among the Opata
and Eudebe nations, which being more devoted to the tilling of the land and the
breeding of cattle, are more faithful to their villages, and consequently better instructed in the mysteries of our holy Faith. It is true that it costs infinite trouble
and anxiety to make them get rid of a phrase, which certainly must have been
invented by the enemy of the human race. It is this. To everything they hear (no
matter from whom), not having seen it with their own eyes, they say:* Sepore ma de
ni thui. *Perhaps thou speakest truth. Until the ministering Father is able to banish
this phrase from his neophytes they cannot have the faith required by the infallible
authority of God and Church.*

These paragraphs contain the essentials of Nentuig's approach to the Indians.
He is aware of specific behaviors of the Indians and has been sufficiently interested to learn and record in the Indian language such a phrase as the one quoted
in Opata. He is aware that it is a key to a basic resistance exhibited by the Indians
to accepting Christian doctrine. He may not have been aware that it was a part
of the basic world view of the Opatas, knitted into their culture through the structure of their language, but at least he was on the track. He knew that dogmatism
about the spiritual world was a difficult idea to get over to the Indians; he had
become aware that they had safeguarding features of language and culture against
such dogmatism. These insights of Nentuig, based on the soundest sort of observation of the behavior around him, perhaps made him a very effective missionary,
but they also gave him a general sense of frustration, probably not so complete as
Neumann's, and certainly coupled with a deeper and fuller understanding of the
situation within which he was working.

His frustration is summed up in a general characterization of the Sonora
Indians, with which he prefaced his penetrating comments on particular tribes.
*In regard to the character and disposition of the Indians in general, although so
various it seems impossible to define them, I shall report the judgment formed by
my constant intercourse of twelve years with different nations . . . the disposition
of the Indian rests on four foundations, each one worse than the other, and they*

*are: ignorance, ingratitude, inconstancy, and laziness. Such in truth is the pivot
on which the life of the Indian turns and moves.*

*Their ignorance causes them to consider themselves children, and to act as
such in spite of their gray hairs, which probably for this reason, appear seldom or
late. Their ingratitude is such that whoever wishes to do them good must arm
himself with the firm resolution of doing it for God; for, should he expect gratitude
from them, he is sure to loose capital and interest at the first shock of a refusal.*

*Their inconstancy compels their ministering priests, civil judges and military
officers to be constantly watching their movements, particularly of those recently
admitted into the Church; for one single malcontent, one puffed up, haughty man,
like a Luis del Saric, with the reputation of a sorcerer, is sufficient to cause the ruin
of a whole nation . . .*

*Their laziness and horror of all kinds of work is so great that neither exhorta-
tion, or prayers, nor indeed much less the threat of punishment by the authorities,
are sufficient to make them, by the sweat of their brows, procure the necessary
sustenance of life by tilling their own lands. This love of idleness keeps them poor
and needy, so that the ministering priest has to provide them during most of the
year with victuals and clothing, if he wishes them to attend the instructions in their
villages, and not rove about among the placer mines of gold and the mining settlements, where in a short time they forget the teachings and the Christianity which
for many years and with indescribable labor has been imparted to them, and
learn in a few days vices of which they had no knowledge in their villages.*

Nentuig's indictment is quite a different thing from Neumann's. He is not
accusing the Indians of being in general double-dealers and dishonest persons. He
reserves such criticisms for application to their behavior in particular types of
situations. But Nentuig, like Neumann, is describing, in terms of European values,
Indian behavior which arises out of the contact situation. The weaknesses of Indian behavior from his point of view are ignorance, which he goes on to say he
believes can be corrected since the Opatas have reason; ingratitude, which would
seem to indicate that the Opatas did not put the same valuation on the missionaries' behavior as did the latter themselves, or more likely that Nentuig merely
failed to understand the customary expressions of gratitude current among the
Opatas; inconstancy, which is a common complaint on both sides of the line in
cross-cultural situations; and laziness, which was the universal complaint of Europeans about the Indians, and was symptomatic of the deep and widely-ramified
differences between Western and Indian cultures at this time in regard to economic
labor. Nentuig's generalizations seem more broadly applicable than Neumann's,
but all are descriptions of clashing values in the contact scene rather than of Indian
character structure.

Nevertheless, Nentuig was convinced that the best policy for bringing peace
to Sonora would be the thoroughgoing elimination of the Seris and the Pimas.

These four sketches of the missionary as bearer of European culture are offered
primarily as examples of how white men may be viewed as working within the
frontier institutions and as part of the mechanism of cultural transmission. A representative sample of the bearers of Spanish culture would include Franciscan as

well as Jesuit missionaries, Spanish-derived missionaries such as Andrés Pérez de Ribas and Benavides, captains and alcaldes mayores, foot soldiers, governors' ladies, and on and on. A well-described gallery, chosen carefully with reference to representativeness, would greatly add to our understanding of the "contact of cultures" in northwestern New Spain.

TECHNIQUES OF CULTURE TRANSFER

In what has been said above, the methods by which the Spaniards expected the Culture of the Conquest to be transferred to the Indians are abundantly illustrated. The general concept of civilized ways presented to and accepted by the Indians, not as replacement of an existing way of life but as a gift filling a void, has been outlined. The various methods of getting Indians to accept the gift have been indicated in the descriptions of the frontier communities, and some of the Europeans who lived and worked in them. It will be well, however, to discuss a little more systematically the character of the methods employed, for on them depended ultimately the effectiveness of the Spanish program for civilization.

The general methods of changing the Indians' ways of life may be listed as (1) forcible imposition, (2) persuasion, and (3) demonstration. Each of these general methods was carried out through a variety of specific techniques which varied at different stages in the contact situation. At any given time, all three were being employed in the frontier communities, but in different forms by the different agents of contact. None of the agents, whether civil or religious authorities or ordinary settlers, used exclusively one method or the other, and the reactions on the part of Indians to specific techniques influenced the development of the approach.

Force, as we have seen, was universally employed in the form of simple military coercion for establishing the authority of Spaniards over Indians in the latter's communities. Wherever the authority of Spaniards was resisted after it had once been established by actual military defeat or by demonstrating Spanish ability to use force, military campaigns and the execution of leaders were re-employed to maintain Spanish authority. In such campaigns as reprisals for rebellion, the missionaries usually took part, associating themselves with the military commanders as advisers in the conduct of the campaign or as spokesmen in negotiations. This was true especially in the campaigns against rebel Indians among the Tarahumaras and the Upper Pimas, but it also occurred among the Eastern Pueblos, the Lower Pimas, and the Apaches. Everywhere the missionaries not only accepted military domination as the basis of their relations with Indians, but in areas such as the Tarahumara and Upper Pima they urged the posting of soldiers to insure their authority. In Chihuahua and New Mexico, among both Jesuits and Franciscans, it was accepted practice for the missionaries to have soldier escorts living with them in the mission communities. In Sonora this was the exception rather than the rule.

In the mission communities the discipline of church attendance and in some cases the work in the mission fields was enforced regularly by corporal punishment.

Where soldier escorts accompanied the missionaries, whipping of Indians who refused the discipline or flouted mission authority in any way was carried out by the soldier at the command of the missionary. In Sonora corporal punishment was usually carried out by other Indians — either Christianized Indians brought into the community to assist the missionary and hence from another tribe, or by village officials appointed by the missionary or Spanish civil authorities from among the native group. A whipping post was a frequent feature of the mission community, and generally stocks were also introduced, since a strong element of sanction in Spanish punishment was public display of the offender. Missionaries were also empowered to turn over offenders to the civil authorities in the Spanish towns where they might be jailed or indentured for a period to work for Spaniards. Everywhere on the frontier missionaries urged the full extension of Spanish law and its penalties into both Spanish towns and mission communities. There was persistent criticism by the missionaries of failure of the Spanish authorities to enforce the law adequately. At the same time, as we have seen, there was persistent criticism by both Spanish civil authorities and Indians of the harshness of the mission discipline.

How harsh the missionaries were in their enforcement of discipline remains a moot question. In all areas — particularly Tarahumara, Eastern Pueblo, Yaqui-Mayo, and Upper Pima — charges were leveled at them by both Spanish civil authorities and Indians to the effect that their discipline was so stern as to make the Indians rebellious and that in the cases of Tarahumaras, Upper Pimas, Yaquis, and Eastern Pueblos it was a major cause of Indian armed revolts. The missionaries were cleared in court trials of extreme harshness in all these instances, or at least the charges were not proven. Yet the fact remains that whipping by missionaries or their agents did take place in the events preceding many revolts, including the Mayo-Yaqui revolt of 1740, the Upper Pima revolt of 1695, the Lower Pima revolt of 1650, all the Tarahumara revolts, and the Eastern Pueblo Revolt of 1680. Missionary discipline by the whip was a factor in the resistance of Indians, and the missionary control which whipping sanctioned was resented by Indians.

The harshness of the punishment unquestionably varied greatly from place to place and time to time. Kino, who seems to have been the gentlest of missionaries, was nevertheless accused of whipping brutally. A Franciscan missionary among the Hopis in the 1650's was convicted, according to Spanish records, of applying hot turpentine to a Hopi accused of idolatry and causing the latter's death. The court of trial agreed that he was unnecessarily brutal and removed him from his mission. The important point for our purposes is simply to note that the Spaniards did generally introduce systematic and regulated corporal punishment, together with forced labor, as sanctions of their legal system and also of their religious training system.

Another element of force in the Spanish contacts besides military coercion and civil-missionary corporal punishment was applied in the technique of "idol-smashing." This term we may use to apply to all forms of destruction of ceremonial paraphernalia without permission of the owners or worshippers. There was definitely a difference in the extent to which this was employed as between the north and the south. Among the Eastern Pueblos the Franciscan missionaries, as we have seen, became extremely violent in the 1670's in their efforts to end the native religious ceremonies. They were especially horrified by the kachina masks, and organized raids which resulted in their securing and destroying thousands of these sacred objects, along with others. At various times before and after this major period of raiding the kivas they pursued the same technique in trying to eliminate the ceremonies. In the south, the Jesuit missionaries did not find, north of the Tepehuanes, religious objects which seemed to them to be "idols." The masks and effigy forms used by the Opatas and Pimans and the sacred wooden objects, often cross-like, of the Seris, Yaquis, Mayos, and Tarahumaras either escaped their notice or seemed harmless in the less highly organized, as compared with the Eastern Pueblos, cults of the southern Indians. At any rate, there were very few instances of destruction of sacred objects by the Jesuits. That the Jesuits were ready to employ forcible destruction, however, is clear enough. The destruction of a sacred shrine of the Opatas by Father Azpilcueta, the angry destruction of ollas of tesquino by Neumann and Pfefferkorn testify to the willingness of Jesuits to employ this technique. It merely happened that the forms of religious expression in the south did not go counter to their prejudices in regard to "idolatry." They consequently did not regard themselves as required to destroy anything, but merely to focus Indian interest in the sacred figures and pictures which they introduced in the mission churches.

Nevertheless, they did force the Indians into secrecy in such ceremonies as the Opata weddings, the Tarahumara and Pima drinking ceremonials, and probably many others of which they did not become aware. Nentuig testifies to the stern refusal to permit such things as burial of possessions with the dead and rain ceremonies, but leaves us in the dark as to how violent the Jesuits were in eliminating these customs.

We may say that the Spaniards employed force to get the Indians to live according to their legal and political system, to make them work regularly in their economic enterprises, to persuade them to follow the weekly plan of worship in the churches, and to give up aspects of their religion classed by the missionaries as idolatry or worship of the Devil. For other changes desired or pushed by Spanish agents, forcible coercion stood in the background, but meanwhile other techniques came into play.

Persuasion was a many-sided and multi-formed approach. We may speak of preaching and teaching as one form, of the giving of gifts and goods as another form, of the give and take of argument as another. We have discussed at some length the teaching and preaching activities of the missionaries. They were not alone, however, in employing the preaching technique. Captain Manje, for example, tells how he and associated civil-military officials spent hours telling Upper Pimas about the nature of the Spanish Empire and political system, and civic duty within it. However, most of the preaching and teaching was carried on by the missionaries and the Indians whom they trained directly for this work. The missionaries came into the northwest of New Spain with the concept of teaching "sons of caciques" in Christian ways. Such schools had been an important part of the

Spanish program in central Mexico. However, the cacique, or powerful headman, as known in central Mexico, was nonexistent in northern New Spain. Indian government everywhere was on a more democratic basis and hereditary power was not developed. Consequently, only one "school for sons of caciques" was established at Parral and it was such in name only. The many informal schools around the missions took all who would come and some selection was made from the most receptive of these for further instruction in the seminaries set up, as among the Mayo at Navojoa, among the Yaquis at Rahum, and among the Opatas at Matape. In general, it may be said that equal opportunity for schooling was extended to all the Indians of the north. Unfortunately, there are no good records indicating how many children were instructed at the seminaries and hence what proportion of the population received intensive schooling. But if two were taken annually from a Yaqui town, as reported, then one-half of one percent were so instructed.

It was recognized by the Jesuits that effective preaching and teaching depended not only on training children in Spanish and developing interpreters, but on the missionaries themselves learning the Indian languages. There is good evidence that the Jesuits sought to make all their missionaries proficient in whatever language was spoken by the people among whom they worked. They early required each missionary going into the field to learn Nahuatl, the language of central Mexico, but quickly found that this, while it helped in learning the languages of Sonora and Chihuahua, did not enable them to preach to the northern Indians. They then instituted short periods of training for missionaries to learn the language of the area to which they were going, and encouraged all missionaries to compile vocabularies and grammatical analyses which could be used by the newcomers. All of the major languages of Chihuahua and Sonora, except Seri, were thus reduced to formal writing by the Jesuits. However, it is evident, as for instance in the report of the Visitor Guendulain in 1725, that the Jesuits had not been able wholly to live up to their principles. He found that there were many instances among the Tarahumaras, as well as elsewhere, in which the missionary did not speak the native language and was therefore quite unable to preach to his mission community. He attributed this in part to the too frequent changes of missionaries from one post to another — one of the bureaucratic tendencies which had developed in the Jesuit organization. He reiterated the old Jesuit regulation that missionaries must know the language of their people.

In New Mexico the Franciscans never placed as much store in this technique as the basis for preaching and teaching. The Franciscans did not produce studies of the Eastern or Western Pueblo languages and obviously did not work in them as systematically as the Jesuits did in their areas. Moreover, in the early 1700's the dominant individuals in the Franciscan hierarchy had formulated a definite policy of eliminating the native languages as quickly as possible. It became the policy to have missionaries use exclusively the Spanish language and to prohibit Indians from using the native language in their presence. In other words, in order to gain an understanding of Christianity it was believed necessary that they gain an understanding of Spanish — a principle at complete odds with the Jesuit contention that Christianity could be taught in any language and was best learned in one's native language. The Franciscans in this manner increasingly set up barriers between themselves and the bulk of the Indian population. When the Jesuits were expelled, this left missionary work entirely in the hands of the Franciscans and hence the employment of native languages in teaching and preaching lapsed.

The extent to which the missionaries or civil authorities worked, or tried to work, through the native social structure remains very doubtful. It is clear that they did try to find Indian leaders who were influential and worked through them as much as possible. The expressions of pleasure and satisfaction in their writings over the baptism of "chiefs" or "caciques" are frequent and definite. Apparently all the Jesuits had the objective of influencing such men and when they thought they had found them making special efforts to convert them. It is also clear that much of the early missionary work in Sonora got its start through headmen becoming convinced that the Jesuits were desirable, such as Sisibotari of the Opatas of the south. However, it is not clear to what extent the men who helped the missionaries most at the beginning, or later, were actually influential men to begin with. They often appear to have been made into influential men through their contacts with the missionaries and the benefits which the latter had to offer. Examples of such individuals are Coxi (later Don Carlos) of the Upper Pimas who helped Kino, and Don Pablo of the Tarahumaras who became a leader of the pro-Spanish factions. There is very little indication that any of the missionaries, either Jesuit or Franciscan, possessed much real understanding of the village and social structures in which they worked. Both missionaries and civil authorities gave out canes of office on the most superficial contact and, although such individuals often became helpful, there were few instances in which the individuals they chose can be clearly recognized as previously prominent in village organization.

Persuasion through gifts and other benefits has been sufficiently indicated to require little more discussion. This technique was employed by all the missionaries and officials at the beginning of their contacts to show good will and secure friendship. The Jesuits provided themselves carefully with beads, gifts of food, and knickknacks of all kinds which they thought Indians would appreciate. Kino and other Jesuits developed such giving on a grand scale with the posting of herds of animals at villages long before the establishment of missions there. Also, of course, the missions themselves, once established, were sources of many very tangible benefits in the form of food and tools and other European objects useful to the Indians. It would often seem that Indians accepted the mission discipline primarily because of what the missionaries had to give in a material way and this was sadly recognized by the missionaries, who nevertheless regarded the situation as a basis for making some progress in spreading spiritual benefits. Medical aid and help in nursing the sick was also an important service rendered by all the missionaries.

The give and take of argument seems to have been little used by missionaries or civil authorities. They conceived persuasion more in terms of presenting the Spanish beliefs and customs, leaving no room for argument. We have seen how one Opata missionary has described his consternation at finding an Opata governor anxious to argue and discuss with him the plausibility of the Opata beliefs about creation and human destiny as against the Christian. To the missionary this was merely the Devil speaking through the old man. The long days and nights of alternate talking by Kino and Indian leaders whom he was visiting might seem to constitute an exception, but there is no record that Kino paid any attention to the contents of the talks to which he listened. Perhaps he and the Indians were both merely being courteous and neither side learned much from the other. The possession of reason as attributed by Nentuig to the Opatas seems to have rested, in Nentuig's belief, on the Indians' finally accepting his viewpoint on what he discussed with them. But it is unlikely, in view of his attitude that the Opatas were childlike, that he deigned really to discuss with them any pros and cons which he might have discussed with someone he regarded as an intellectual equal and whose premises were intelligible to him.

Demonstration was much employed by the missionaries and much advocated by the civil officials. Every mission village was an agricultural demonstration center where the missionaries and their assistants demonstrated daily the use of plows and other European agricultural implements, seeds and ways of planting, craft techniques and much of the material side of Spanish culture. They were also places of demonstration of the Christian life, through transplanted Indians previously Christianized elsewhere, and the neophytes gathered around the mission. The missionary himself was a demonstration also, and the importance of himself as an example in behavior and devotion was much emphasized, as we have seen, by all the missionaries. It seems to have been true that a greater proportion of Franciscan missionaries in the north than of Jesuits in the south failed to live up to their own moral precepts, thus setting bad examples for the Indians. But it is also true that among the Jesuits there were individuals who maintained unduly harsh mission regimes, who were lax in giving Mass and other ceremonies and who even disdained, as Visitor Guendulain reported in 1725, to enter the houses of the Indians. There was apparently a great deal of variation among the missionaries in regard to the intimacy of contact that they made and would accept with the Indians. In other words, there was variation with respect to the Christian fellowship demonstrated by them. The Visitor of 1725 mentions the refusal to enter Indian houses even for giving last sacraments. Such refusals may have rested partly on different standards in regard to cleanliness, since we find some missionaries very much concerned over the "bestial" conditions of Indian life. Neumann also regarded it as absurd that he should beg food from his Tarahumara congregations as part of his meeting the final requirements of ordination as a Jesuit. He felt that he must go to Parral, a Spanish town, to make this formal exercise of humility, a fact which can be interpreted as meaning that he hardly regarded the Indians as human. On the other hand, Father Castaño among the Opatas on the Sonora River ate and shared shelter with the Indians regularly and became so popular, being called the "Indian Wiseman" by them, that his superiors apparently feared that he would not maintain the Indians' respect and transferred him. In short, as demonstrators of Christian asceticism there was probably no great degree of variation among the Jesuit missionaries, but as demonstrators of Christian brotherhood there was evidently a great deal of variation. The Upper Pimas seem to have had an unusual effect on their missionaries, causing them to identify with the Pimas as even against their Order. In this connection we may well mention Father Kino, who dared calumny and strong criticism from even his father superior in defending the Upper Pimas. Father Campos who became the dean of the Upper Pima missionaries also identified himself so fully with his Upper Pimas that he was rebuked by his superiors and came into conflict with the Spanish military commander of his area; he was regarded as insane by fellow missionaries, which might or might not have been a sound interpretation of his behavior. Father Keller, too, defied his superiors and the civil authorities in an effort to keep a section of the Upper Pima field all to himself. All in all, the missionaries must have expressed to some extent the conflicts inherent in Spanish civilization, gradually giving the Indians some concrete demonstration of these.

One of the most important of demonstration programs, as conceived by the Spanish civil authorities, worked out in a way not very satisfactory to anyone on the frontier. This was the demonstration of the Christian way of life through Christian Spaniards living and working among Indians in their own country. To some extent this demonstration mechanism was utilized in the manner envisioned in New Mexico, where communities of the original Spanish colonists settled near Pueblo villages and the effect was much as hoped for, with a fusion of race and culture. But the Spanish culture did not always become dominant and where it did, a folk variety of it developed which was in the eyes of Spanish authorities an inferior version. Elsewhere, the greater number of Spaniards who demonstrated European culture in their own behavior were, by admission of religious and civil authorities alike, extremely inferior specimens. They encouraged the breaking of most of the rules that missionaries had instructed Indians in in the mission communities — so that missionaries were shocked.

Father Nentuig wrote as follows on the subject: . . . *in the first ranch of a mining settlement or Spanish town, where the day laborers live separately, the runaway Indians meet with teachers of such a character, that in a couple of hours they are led into errors which corrupt them and cause the ruin of both body and soul; and, although having lived in their own villages and enjoyed the ownership of their property, their liberty, and their own persons, subject only to the easy duties and ceremonies of the Christians, for the love of a licentious life, they stoop to slavery and condemn themselves to exile.* Such a statement was typical of the missionaries both north and south from the early 1600's on; they evidently did not regard the life of the Spanish towns as in any way a demonstration of Christian civilization. Nevertheless, they were good examples of what being a Spaniard was, and many Indians learned a great deal about the Spanish Christian culture from these condemned spots. By the middle 1700's, especially in Sonora, representatives of the viceroy were urging planned colonization programs, in which picked men and women would be selected to come and live in the frontier settlements, especially around the Sonora presidios. This was partially in response to a manpower problem that had to be solved, but it was also a recognition of the need for reconversion of the Spanish settlements into examples of communities approved by the policy makers rather than as demonstrations to the Indians of the worst, as the officials saw it, that European culture had developed.

Another aspect of demonstration important in missionary method must be mentioned. This was in the presentation of Christian mythology and concept through dramatization. Much time and effort must have been devoted to teaching the Indians the Passion, the struggle of the Christians and Moors, the Christianization of the Aztecs, etc., and these became major vehicles of demonstration of the Christian faith — consciously used to reach a generally nonliterate population.

CHANGES IN THE SPANISH PROGRAM

To a large extent, the major outlines of the Spanish program for civilizing the Indians remained the same from the early 1600's to the early 1800's. During this time the policies which became dominant as a result of the de las Casas agitation constituted the core of the program. Briefly, the program after 1600 placed prime importance on turning Indians into good Christians with the employment of as little force as possible. This was in contrast with the early policy which had resulted in the extermination of the West Indians and which had given priority to enrichment of Spaniards over conversion of Indians. The policy which prevailed during the two hundred years with which we are concerned here resulted in the killing of relatively few Indians, the giving of a fairly free hand to the missionaries (particularly in the Jesuit area), a constant effort to curb the abuses of forced labor in all the varied forms which it assumed on the frontier, and the progressive elimination of the encomienda system of incorporation of Indians into the Spanish Empire. A major effort of this policy was to encourage and bring finally into sharp relief the conflict between the missionary approach and the civil authority approach. The culmination of the conflict was the elimination of the Jesuits. Significant changes in Spanish policy took place only after the expulsion in 1767, and represented the new dominance of the secular authorities.

There were a few adjustments of program on the frontier nevertheless which took place before the expulsion of the Jesuits. A notable one was the modification of the reduction program among the Tarahumaras. By the 1690's both missionaries and civil authorities in the Tarahumara country had become convinced, although they did not put it in these terms, that they were encouraging resistance to Christian conversion by requiring the Tarahumaras to settle in compact communities around missions. The missionaries had discovered during the nearly one hundred years of mission work that the Tarahumaras had developed a type of community in which dwellings were widely scattered, but that they were not nomadic. The missionaries also found that Tarahumaras loved and clung to this traditional isolated farmstead type of life (which bore a certain resemblance to the North European settlement pattern). They tired of life at the missions, even though they became devoted Christians and left for less urban living conditions. Until the 1690's the missionaries and military authorities alike had thought that flight from the missions meant rejection of the Christian life. Slowly they began to realize that the two were not necessarily connected. As Neumann put it, *They*

*[the people who refuse to dwell in the mission communities] are quiet and peace-
able, and our brethren visit them frequently and in perfect safety, baptizing the
children and feeding the others with the food of the divine word.... Therefore they
show plainly what their feeling is toward us, and reveal their desire to preserve the
peace, which has been granted them.* In other words, the Tarahumara missionaries had decided, after somewhat bitter experience, that reduction to towns and
Christian conversion were not necessarily linked. It had taken a century to learn,
but they now proceeded to adapt their original program to the conditions of culture in the Tarahumara country.

   At the same time, in the Tarahumara country a procedure was adopted which
had long been in practice among the missions of Sonora. This was a result of
recognition that the enforcement of mission discipline by the soldier escorts of the
missionaries had been a sore spot in the Tarahumara program. It had been a source
of resentment against the missionaries, who were identified more readily with the
soldiers. Consequently the military commander of the Tarahumara region — General Retana — began about 1690 to give instruction to the Indian governors of
Tarahumara settlements in how to administer the usual whipping discipline of
the Spaniards. This, it was argued by the missionaries as well, would likely reduce
the resentment against Spaniards generally, and would result in the employment
of methods more acceptable to the Indians in fixing guilt; it might also build up
an Indian organization with powers as well as titles comparable to those in the
Spanish settlements. This was actually a policy of making something functional out
of the relatively functionless organization which the Spaniards had thus far imposed on Tarahumara communities. At the same time that it relieved the pressure
on Spaniards — both missionaries and military — it was a step toward building a
new organization of village life. It was the adoption of a system which had already
been employed in the Yaqui villages since 1617 and was in use in most places in
Sonora by the time the administrators of the Tarahumara area seem to have come
upon the idea.

   A third modification of policy which may be noted was that which took place
after the expulsion of the Jesuits and in regard to the Apaches in northern Sonora.
As Bancroft points out, there was underlying Gálvez' policy a cynical acceptance
of the desirability of extermination of the Apaches, but extermination could not
be an immediate objective — in part because Spanish policy in general could not
allow it, but largely because the Apaches were masters of fighting techniques which
the Spaniards could not match and the latter had begun to admit this. But the
policy which Gálvez instituted was one which bypassed the mission system as an
accepted step from barbarism to civilization. His policy proposed the bribing and
corruption of Apaches into accepting a peaceful life. It substituted the presidio,
with its fringe of Spanish undesirables, for the mission as the way-station into
Spanish civilization. It relied as much on the creation of a taste for liquor as on
any other feature. It was a frankly cynical policy based on the view that the
Apaches could never be civilized, and thus represented a very sharp alteration of
what had been the Spanish approach, namely, the belief that all Indians were
capable through moral suasion of changing from barbarians to civilized Christians.

The Gálvez kind of adjustment to frontier conditions, involving a loss of faith and hope, took place also in the viewpoints of some missionaries, like Juan Nentuig who came to the same conclusion about the Seris and the Upper Pimas that Gálvez and his associates did about the Apaches. Gálvez' program for the Apaches involved the idea of moral destruction, while Nentuig's seemed only to advocate physical destruction.

It is difficult to interpret any other events as adjustments on the part of the Spaniards to what they encountered in northwestern New Spain. There was surprisingly little indication of any feeling of need for adjustment, with the exception of the idea that the Western Pueblos should be turned over from Franciscan to Jesuit jurisdiction or that northern Sonora should be turned over from Jesuit to Franciscan. For the most part the failures and lacks of success felt by the Spaniards were blamed on one another — missionaries on civil authorities and vice versa — rather than on weaknesses in their programs which might be adjusted better to the realities of the situations. However, by the end of the 1700's the feeling that things were generally wrong became common, and a ferment of proposals as to what to do in the Apache situation, how to stimulate colonization, etc., began to be made. But the power to carry out adjustment, except on the cynical and short-sighted basis of the Gálvez policy, seemed to have been lost. The Spanish program slowly petered out.

CHAPTER TWELVE

The Mexican Program

THE CHAOTIC FIFTY YEARS in Mexico following the end of the War for Independence in 1821 saw the problem of Indian relationship to the new national unity emerge as a major concern for the new leaders. By the 1850's, however, it was apparent that the policies adopted had resulted in creating not a solution but a most serious threat to the very existence of Mexico as a unified nation. In Yucatan a "war of the castes" had broken out between the Maya Indians and the Spanish-derived Yucatecans. In the Isthmus of Tehuantepec, Zapotec Indians had to be put down by force by the state government under the leadership of the culturally assimilated Zapotec Indian, Benito Juárez. In the northeast, the Huaxtec and other Indians constituted a threat to national unity; and in the west, the Indians of the southern Sierra Madre Mountains in Nayarit were following a leadership at odds with the federal government. In the northwest, in Sonora the threat of the Apaches, as well as of the Yaquis and Mayos, was a constant concern of the state government. Throughout Mexico it was apparent that the problems of Indian adjustment had not been solved.

This situation had arisen despite immediate attention to the problems in the 1820's on the part of the successful leaders, such as Morelos, of the War for Independence. The difficulty lay in the nature of the measures which they adopted — measures conceived as eliminating "the Indian problem" in one stroke. The first of these consisted of the granting of full citizenship. Indians were to be treated precisely as any other citizen of the republic. The Plan of Iguala had insisted on no racial distinctions for citizenship, and the federal constitution adopted in 1821 pursued this course. The state constitutions of Sonora and Chihuahua followed suit. No status of "Indian" was recognized — only Mexican citizen — and government records were not to use the term Indian. If, as in Sonora, it was necessary to spell out laws concerned with the pre-existing entities of "Indian towns" and "Indian lands" and the institutional survivals of the mission communities, the term "indigene" was to be used. All Mexican-born persons were to be citizens, and all citizens were guaranteed equal participation in the political life. In Sonora and Chihuahua even the exclusion of "domestic servants" from citizenship, a discrimination which appeared in several states, was not written into the constitutions. All persons were to be equal under the law. Indians no longer existed politically.

The second measure, following logically from the first, consisted of the political incorporation of all citizens into the state. Thus, for example, the people of the Yaqui and Mayo River valleys in Sonora were required immediately to set up municipal government with a roster of local officials prescribed by law. The duties of these officials, in relation to state and federal authorities, were clearly set forth, and their authority was to derive from election by all the adult males of their communities. The idea of representative government with democratic election was to prevail, and the whole citizenry was to enjoy the basic political rights of man.

The third measure carried the concept of equality and individual responsibility into the realm of economic life. It consisted in the equitable distribution of land in parcels adequate for the support of families. Landholders were to have titles to their lots, and thus full freedom to use and dispose of their lands in their own best individual interest. The new laws required that this individual distribution take place as soon as possible, so that excesses of land beyond the individual needs could be handled in the best interest of the states and the nation as a whole. Lands belonging to inactive missions were to become state property and were to be available for distribution to indigenes if needed. Community lands were to be managed by local governments, but were also to be distributed in part where conditions required. In this way the states could lay a foundation which would permit the expansion of population into areas where large mission holdings and Indian communities with large traditionally-defined areas had constituted an obstacle to settlement. At the same time no one would suffer, for the basis would be the initial assignment of land in accordance with the need of each family. The distribution of the land, and the giving of deeds would also promote individual responsibility and initiative which would make it possible to develop a system of taxation for the local support of schools and the expenses of the state.

These measures appeared to the writers of the constitutions and the laws to be obvious steps to carry the Mexican people out of the system of bad government and economic stagnation which had characterized the final phase of Spanish rule. By making the Mexican people one, and by legalizing their human rights, both political and economic, the friction between "the castes," fostered by Spanish distinctions of race and birth, would disappear and open the way to vigorous nationhood and economic progress. The underlying assumptions were, of course, rooted in the equalitarian, democratic ideas of the French and American revolutionary movements of the epoch.

They nevertheless also had roots in the Spanish Culture of the Conquest. The concept of Indians as, ultimately, full citizens of the Spanish Empire was generally accepted as the basis of missionary work and had been a part of the working philosophy of those Spanish administrators who bothered with political thought, at least since the time of the agitation of las Casas. The attempt to incorporate Indians into the Spanish political structure was far from new, since nearly every initial contact with Indians had involved the selection of a native governor and usually a lecture on the nature of the Spanish Empire. Efforts to build the Indian communities more closely into the Empire were a constant feature of the Spanish program. Similarly, economic incorporation, through the individual assignment of land, was an old element in the Spanish program dating from the 1500's. In the north, however, in Sonora and Chihuahua the political and economic aspects of the Spanish program had been, as it were, suspended. Taxation and the distribution of land had indeed been ordered during the 1700's, but only the barest halfhearted attempts had been made to carry them through. Actually, neither those measures, nor the effective political incorporation of Indian communities, were ever carried out among the Mayos, Yaquis, Opatas, Pimas, Seris, or Tarahumaras. On the northern border of New Spain, they were not even fully in effect in New Mexico. So that although the laws of the revolutionary leaders did not embody wholly new views, they were nevertheless being applied to people who had never been required to conform to such ideas.

Having eliminated, in the new legal structure, the Indian problem by declaring it nonexistent, the writers of the new laws in Sonora and Chihuahua nevertheless recognized that care would have to be exercised in applying the laws if complete justice were to be done the Indians; they showed awareness of the fact that lands had been illegally taken from Indians in the past. They decreed measures which they thought would make the adoption of citizenship and land ownership easy and fair. They called for elections for the municipal offices immediately, so that a democratic base would be laid at the beginning. They provided for Indian officials as managers of the public lands. They called for commissions composed of the villagers themselves to sit on the problems of land distribution. They provided for disputes over land between Indians and non-Indians to be resolved in favor of Indians. In many such details, it was clear that there was a recognition of past injustices and that a spirit of fair play actuated the writing of the new laws. Based in the assumptions of individual rights, they were to be carried out with scrupulous regard for the interest of each individual, but with the scales slightly tipped to favor the Indians.

The effects of the efforts to put these well-defined policies into operation were unexpected. The policies were offered as liberation from oppressive Spanish policies and as an opportunity to abandon unenlightened primitive custom. They were, however, received as a new form of oppression and a threat to a well-established way of life. Throughout Sonora, wherever the program was attempted (the Upper Pimas were not presented with the new measures), there was a greater or lesser degree of resistance, ranging from flight on the part of Seris to armed revolt on the part of Yaquis. In Chihuahua, the predominant reaction of the Tarahumaras was rejection through withdrawal, but there was also scattered resistance by forcible means. The resistance was seen by the Mexicans, not as an indication that the means adopted were badly conceived, but rather as demonstrating the barbarism of the Indians. The Mexican reaction was not to modify the new laws, but rather to force their acceptance. The continued resistance was regarded at first as in large part the result of subversive activity on the part of royalists influencing primitive and ignorant minds.

However, what the Mexicans saw as the barbarism of the Indians was the product of something more than pro-royalist agitation. The resistance in Sonora persisted long after the last pro-royalist was rooted out. The causes of the resistance were complex, but not hard to reconstruct through a careful reading of history. To discover what lay behind the resistance it is necessary to look at the situation of tribes like the Yaquis and Mayos at the time just preceding the application of the new liberal laws.

Throughout their contact with Spaniards, the Yaquis and Mayos and other Sonorans had had the benefit of the concept of transitional communities. This was an idea and an institution for which the Jesuits had been strong proponents, although, to be sure, it was the foundation of the whole mission system, Jesuit or otherwise. According to this idea, it was necessary for the success of the Spanish program of civilization that the Indians be brought gradually into the orbit of Spanish culture. A mission was a place where Indians learned rudiments of civilization without certain pressures such as forced labor and taxation. Thus, they were supposed to learn the meaning of Christianity and improved agriculture, while being exempt from tribute and while working their land in the traditional communal manner. Whatever their own Order's special interest, the Jesuits had worked hard to maintain such mission communities, repeatedly in Sonora obtaining their continuance on the ground that the Indians were "not ready" for direct incorporation into Spanish society. The Indians were conceived of as being in a transitional state. Secular Spaniards had been protesting what they regarded as undue protective measures for more than a century in Sonora, at the time the new constitution makers finally legally abolished the whole apparatus of the transitional community.

The transitional community had in fact softened the pressures toward cultural assimilation, and the impact of political domination. Now, with the mission community completely disestablished by the new legislation, the pressures were suddenly applied in areas of Indian life which the missions had not only protected but had actually developed and fostered. For the Yaquis, local government managed by the Indians themselves, and the communal administration of land had hardly been altered in their essential features during the Jesuit regime. This was true only to a lesser extent for the Mayos, Opatas, Lower Pimas, and Tarahumaras. For the Yaquis particularly, town government, although now employing many new formal features of Spanish organization, had by 1800 crystallized into very definite patterns of political autonomy and corporate land control. The two features on which the Mexicans focused as necessary for bringing the Indians into the nation — individual land holding and political hierarchy — flew in the face of the previous two centuries of development. Political equality with Mexicans was meaningless in the limited context of the autonomous Yaqui River communities. It was not in any sense regarded by the Yaquis as a desirable privilege, particularly since the growth of tribal feeling and anti-Spanish attitudes after the revolt of 1740. The Spanish contacts had stimulated a vigorous Yaqui separation based on the colonial mission type of nearly autonomous communities. No matter how much participation in the new political and economic institutions the Sonora laws allowed, these laws were in fact planned as something quite antithetical to the existing institutions.

The Mexicans sensed the situation, as resistance took form. But they viewed it always from the standpoint of the idea of a Mexican nation which they were trying to build. They saw the Indian attitude as resistance to a loss of special privilege — the exemption from citizenship responsibilities. The pro-royalist agitators who did appear among the Opatas and Yaquis in the 1820's and again later tried, with some success, to stir up the Indians over the loss of the mission-period immunities. So long as they emphasized the continuance of freedom from interference in local affairs they found hearers, but the Yaqui leadership as exemplified in Juan Banderas was actually interested in an Indian nation, and not a return to the Spanish Empire. The Mexican leaders, seeing the resistance simply in terms of desire for special privilege under an outmoded political system, regarded the Indians merely as dupes of the royalists, and fought them with the vigor with which they fought any proponents of royalism. Forcing the Indians to accept the new regime was a part of the general struggle for setting up the independent Mexican nation. The use of force was justified by the ideal of a unified nation, and Indians could not be permitted to stand in the way.

Thus, wherever the Indian reaction took the form of determined resistance, the Mexican policy became one of simple force. The view developed that the Indian tendencies toward tribal separatism and the corporate community were a species of barbarism which had to be destroyed if Mexico was to become a functioning nation. The concept of individual ownership of plots of land became sacred in the Mexican program, and was pushed repeatedly whenever cessation of hostilities with Indians and among Mexicans themselves permitted. Steadily, this aspect of policy came to be regarded as the cornerstone of a solution of the Indian problems, and finally was embodied in its fullest expression in the Laws of the Reform in the 1850's.

It is true that some doubts prevailed as to the lack of need for compromise with the Indian viewpoint. There was some nostalgic looking back to the successes of the missionaries in their work with the Indians. During Santa Ana's regime there was even federal acceptance of a proposal for reinstituting the Jesuits as mediators in the process of civilization. A plan was worked out for bringing them back into the Indian field in the northern states, but neither the federal government nor the missionary Orders were sufficiently possessed of energy for putting the plan into effect. It collapsed for want of funds and missionaries willing to undertake the task.

Benito Júarez, the Mexicanized Zapotec Indian from Oaxaca, probably most clearly expressed the viewpoint of the Mexican policy makers. In justifying the land provisions of the Laws of the Reform and the action of the state of Oaxaca — when he was governor there before he assumed the presidency — in putting down the revolt of the Indians of Juchitan in the Isthmus of Tehuantepec, he held that the existence of Indian communities based in the colonial system constituted a threat to the nation. They must be broken up at all costs, so that individual initiative and modern forms of representative government could prevail. It was this viewpoint that underlay the vigorous, if sporadic, prosecution of the distribution of land to individuals through the system of survey and denunciation of community and state lands in Sonora. That the process resulted merely in a shift from a village system of communal land control to a collective control through the land companies was not recognized. As forcible suppression of the Indian resistance by the federal government became successful, the distribution of lands and the destruction of Indian communities continued through the late 1800's.

Meanwhile, in the various states where Indian resistance was not completely suppressed or the Indians were unable to withdraw from the continuing pressures, the state governments continued the simple policy of the forcible "civilizing" of the Indians. In Sonora forced assimilation took a great variety of forms. Military domination reached a first high point in the 1840's under Governor Pesqueira when he sought to employ the same methods used by the Spaniards earlier with the Tarahumaras. Fighting their way into the Yaqui country in 1849, his troops attempted to eliminate resistance by wholesale killing of Indians and destruction of crops. Perhaps Pesqueira would have been successful, if it had not been for revolution within the state which took his attention elsewhere.

Nevertheless, the Sonoran leaders came to look on this method as unworkable with the Yaquis and tried others. The one for which they held out the most hope was a sort of nondestructive military colonization. This consisted of posting military garrisons through the Indian country. The soldiers were to farm land and by example show the Indians the benefits of civilization at the same time that they provided protection for other Mexican colonists who would also demonstrate the values of civilized life. Such infiltration often merely stimulated resistance. Colonization took place from the 1820's on, but periodically it broke down. It steadily became clear that it, too, was not working.

Military domination and colonization were nevertheless carried out with increasing success among the Opatas and the Mayos in Sonora and eventually eliminated resistance among them, the Opatas being brought into line as early as the 1830's and the Mayos in the 1880's. For the Yaquis these policies did not seem to work, despite the fact that they were put into effect with additional means during the 1880's and 1890's. They were supplemented with efforts at reinstituting missionaries with the old persuasive techniques, and with attempts to improve agricultural resources at government expense, together with the distribution of agricultural implements and livestock. But still resistance was strong. Through an unusual combination of circumstances, Yaqui resistance was able to maintain itself.

The final policy was a tacit admission of complete failure of all the other policies. It was one which had been repeatedly proposed for other groups at various times in the past. During the 1700's, Spanish missionaries proposed it for Seris and for Upper Pimas who seemed to them hopelessly recalcitrant candidates for civilization. It had been adopted finally for Seris as the one workable policy, although it continued not to work. This was the policy of deportation. The Sonora government throughout the 1700's and 1800's worked with the idea that the Seris must be deported from the home country and established in one or more colonies within the midst of non-Indians. It resulted in the cultural assimilation of a small portion of Seris, but never accomplished the ends sought by Spaniards or Mexicans. With the Yaquis, when attempted on a grand scale after 1900, deportation similarly failed. The adoption of deportation as a policy amounted to the admission that Mexicans were unable to find any basis for cooperative adjustment between Indian and Mexican society.

In the course of the Sonoran efforts to civilize the Inidans one other method had been proposed, but had never really been put into effect. This consisted of schools and the method of education. Regarded as a fundamentally important technique by the legislators of the 1820's, it was proposed to establish schools in all the Indian towns and to make schooling compulsory. But for want of the means to establish such schools on the part of the state or federal government, nothing of importance was accomplished along these lines.

The Mexican period differed from the Spanish in that no special form of community was ever established in which Mexican-Indian contacts could take place in a framework of cooperative interaction. The Indian-dominated community of the mission in which Spanish representatives nevertheless had a prescribed sphere of action went out of existence before the end of the Spanish period. The Spanish town, of course, persisted, and Indian contacts in such towns continued, where Indians worked chiefly as laborers. The cultural influences of such contacts operated on Yaquis and other Sonoran Indians throughout the 1800's, and were, in fact, greatly intensified during the period. Thus Indian life continued to be modified, through the effects of individual cultural assimilation.

But the other aspect of contact was one calculated to foster inter-ethnic resistance rather than the flow of cultural influences. It consisted of a continuous border warfare, like that at the edges of reservations in the United States. The representatives of state government sought at all times, whenever conditions were peaceful enough, to impose elements of culture which were incompatible with the existing Indian community organization. The ordinary Mexican settlers exerted pressures in their competition for the land. The result was continued hostility and the growth of a sort of caste type of inter-ethnic relationship. Indians like the Tarahumaras and the Seris simply withdrew from this sort of contact, the Tarahumaras to the mountains where resources were not so desirable to Mexicans, and the Seris to the desert coast where Mexicans were for long unable to subsist at all. The other Indians, unable to withdraw, resisted to the extent that they were able. Only the Yaquis were able to maintain resistance throughout the 1800's.

At the same time, however, there was a steady forcing of Indians off their land and into the Mexican towns and haciendas as laborers. Hundreds of Indians moved in this way into the Mexican settlements and moved far toward cultural assimilation under Mexican domination there. Resistance continued only where Indian-controlled settlements were able to maintain their existence.

The rigidity of the Mexican program, focused around two features of culture fundamentally incompatible with Indian community life, resulted in an era of steadily intensifying conflict. Attitudes on both sides hardened. The local distinction between Indians and non-Indians became a part of Sonoran life — "gente de razon – Indio" in the Mexican terminology, "yori – yoreme" in Yaqui terminology. The latter crept into the literature and folklore of Sonora. Mexicans came to regard Yaqui women as the ultimate source of the hostility, because, as they said, Yaqui women trained their children from birth to "hate the Yoris." Atrocities were committed on both sides and the Yaquis came to think of the Mexicans as savages, just as the Mexicans came to regard the Yaquis. One peculiar feature of the situation was that the Mexican stereotype of the Yaqui did not include that of laziness, so common in other areas of Indian contact where hostility developed. On the contrary, the general Mexican view throughout the period was of the Yaquis as hardworking laborers, very necessary to the existence of the state. It was this aspect of Mexican attitude which worked against the acceptance of a policy of extermination and which ultimately put a curb on even the deportation policy, when that policy took the form of deportation outside the state of Sonora. The stereotype of the Yaquis and Opatas as brave fighters and courageous people also was well marked by the end of the century, so that there were mixed feelings in regard to the Indians, as there were contemporaneously in the United States.

The 1910 revolution saw a general modification of Indian policy in Mexico, based on agrarianism. Indians were not given any separate political status, but such arrangements as the ejido system were substituted for the Reform Laws which had required the individual assignment of land under individual control. The zeal of the republicans for land distribution during the 1800's, which had resulted in the growth of the hacienda system and a great rural proletariat, was now modified. The result was to some extent a lifting of the pressures which had been exerted on the Indians of the north. Both in Chihuahua and Sonora, Indian adjustment was recognized as a problem that the earlier Mexican legislation had not solved. A conception of need for special programs designed to deal with the problem slowly developed as soon as more urgent national problems were taken care of following the military phase of the revolution.

In the 1930's the Cárdenas government was ready to repudiate President Obregón's view that Yaquis must conform to the system of individual landholding. It went so far as to recognize "the Yaqui tribe" as at least a landholding unit, although it definitely refused to recognize it as a political entity. At the same time the early dream of secular education as a solution to the problems of Indian adjustment began to be realized — but through federal rural schools rather than local community means. A short-lived boarding school for technical education in agriculture was established in the Yaqui country, and federal rural schools were extended to the Indian country. As a development of the conception that Indian problems might be solved through federal recognition of special conditions existing locally, a National Indian Institute was organized in 1948. It adopted the view that it would be necessary to work through the community organizations then existing, regardless of their differences from the prescribed municipal organization. The belief was held that the existing organization among Indians must be brought into contact with national life through specially trained personnel, chiefly schoolteachers trained in normal schools of the federal school system, together with *promotores* trained in specially designed schools of the National Indian Institute. The techniques adopted were chiefly those formerly employed by the missionaries, namely, persuasion and demonstration. The Tarahumaras were the second of the Indian groups of Mexico to have a center of the National Indian Institute established among them. Although by 1960 the educational and community organization work of the Institute had not yet been extended to the Yaquis or any other Indians of Sonora, an effort was made to set up a fishing cooperative among the Seris. The new program, after an interval of some 150 years, somewhat resembled in its methods that of the Jesuits. It was focused again on building a type of community organization, although the values around which the community was to center were those of economic progress and national organization rather than the Kingdom of God.

The Mexican program had thus passed through one phase and entered another by 1960. It had proceeded from forcible imposition of democratic individualism to persuasive presentation of democratic community responsibility through educational techniques. For more than a century not considered a legitimate governmental problem, Indian adjustment had come to be recognized as a special problem calling for special techniques of solution based on the existing forms of Indian culture and social organization.

CHAPTER THIRTEEN

The Anglo-American Program

WHEN ANGLO-AMERICANS first came in contact with the Indians of New Mexico Territory in the 1840's they had had some two hundred years' experience with Indians. This experience strongly influenced their attitudes and their objectives as they tried to develop working relations with the Pueblos, Navajos, Apaches, Pimans, and Yumans. What had most strongly influenced them was, in the first place, the nature of the Indians with whom they had come into contact heretofore, and, in the second place, the Indian policy which they had inherited from Great Britain. The Indians whom they knew were those of the Great Lakes region, the southeastern United States, and the Great Plains region. They were all Indians who placed very considerable reliance on hunting and gathering of wild foods, although the eastern Indians were also farmers. Nevertheless, their farming was not carried on from permanently established villages with lasting house construction, as among the Pueblos. The Plains Indians had largely abandoned farming for hunting bison and raiding neighboring tribes by the time the Anglos encountered them. A stereotype of Indians as more or less wandering groups addicted to warfare existed in the minds of the Anglos as a result of these contacts and they were inclined to apply it when they came into the Southwest. The completely sedentary Pueblo Indians were something of a surprise to them and they were at first regarded by the Anglos as "civilized" people. The Gila Pimas also struck some Anglos as "the most civilized Indians in the United States." Accordingly, the first attempts to develop working relations were characterized by a distinction between "civilized" and "wild" Indians. The simple classification for all Indians with which the Spaniards had begun, based largely on religious behavior and belief, namely, that of "barbarians," was reserved for those who as time went on vigorously opposed the Anglo invasion, such as the various Apache tribes, the Navajos, and the Yavapais.

Another difference between the Anglos and the Spaniards at first consisted in the weak development among Anglos of a sense of mission to civilize the Indians. Spanish policy was based from the start on the conception of a duty to change the Indians from heathen barbarians to good Christians. Lacking this religious focus, the Anglos of the frontier conceived their civilizing mission, insofar as they conceived it at all, in terms of technological improvement of Indian farming and way of life. But even this sense of mission developed only slowly. For the most part the Anglo approach was dominated by the idea of pushing the Indians out of their way and keeping them apart from themselves. In general, the settlers thought in terms of extermination or forcible isolation, rather than Christian conversion.

HISTORICAL BASES OF ANGLO POLICY

Following the lead of England in her approach to Indian tribes during the days of American colonization, the United States government in the 1840's had no settled policy for "civilizing" the Indians. In contrast with Spain, England had conceived of the Indians of North America as continuing to exist as separate nations outside the political organization of Britain. The British government organized no campaign for conversion of the Indians to Christianity. It proposed to acquire land for colonization by purchase, by simple appropriation of unoccupied or sparsely settled areas, or by conquest and treaty where necessary. The basic approach was that of dealing with tribes as separate nations with whom treaties for coexistence were to be made. Even though the English settlers, as their desire for increasingly large amounts of land led them to disregard treaties made by the government, continually expanded and maintained a constant hostile frontier with the various Indian tribes, the British government persisted in trying to establish stable relations by negotiating treaties which guaranteed certain areas to the tribes. Throughout the period preceding the formation of the United States, the British failed to conceive of an empire which should include the Indians as an integral part of its citizenship. As the settlers pushed westward, the result was the growth of a territory inhabited almost entirely by Europeans with few persisting Indian communities. To be sure, some individuals and groups of Indians remained as a backwash of conquest within the borders of the British colonies, but where they existed there was no recognition of their land rights or local government and no systematic efforts were made to incorporate them as citizens. They existed merely as objects of charity with doubtful human status. At the shifting boundaries of European expansion the British government continued to try to settle the border warfare by negotiating new treaties and dealing with the tribes as foreign nations.

This approach was adopted by the United States in 1776. The basis was a concept of a wholly non-Indian nation which might grow by pushing Indians westward where they would be free to live in whatever way they cared to, providing they remained peaceful with the Whites settled at the borders of their territory. Eventually, however, in the early part of the 1800's it became apparent that the Anglo advance was outstripping the westward movement of the Indians, despite the fact that thousands of Indians had moved beyond the Appalachian Mountains. Certain large tribes, like the Iroquois and the Cherokee, had refused to move from their homelands, and others in the Great Lakes region were offering resistance. In the 1830's the concept appeared of enclaves of Indians within the American nation, or as Chief Justice of the Supreme Court John Marshall phrased it, of "dependent domestic nations." The Iroquois and the Cherokee were legally defined in these terms. Anglo settlement had expanded around these tribes, yet they remained not as disorganized individuals, but as politically organized communities, the Cherokees even having formulated and adopted a constitution of their own with a political capital and a form of representative government. As "dependent domestic nations" they were now regarded as having legal right to land which they occupied, but they were not political units formally integrated with the United States. There was no set of liaison officers linking them with the Whites, as in the Spanish alcalde system. The laws of the United States did not apply within their territories, and there was no government-sponsored program for systematically changing their beliefs or their customs. The missionaries among them worked as private citizens with no support, military or otherwise, from the United States government. Moreover, even officers of the government did not fully accept the "domestic nation" arrangement. President Jackson, for example, in the 1830's worked constantly in terms of the older idea of forcing the Indians out of White territory completely and turning their land over to settlers.

The proposal was made in 1832 to create an area west of the Mississippi River, the Indian Territory, to which all tribes which were being enclaved by the Whites should be sent. There it was expected that they could continue to live as Indians on the land set aside for them by the bounty of the Whites. Thousands of Indians were transported there, either with or without their consent, and proceeded to set up their own forms of local government without Anglo participation or interference. The concept underlying this approach to problems of Indian affairs was that the solution to conflicts over land and way of life lay in isolating the Indians as completely as possible from the Whites and letting them go their own way. The whole idea of incorporating Indians as citizens into the American nation, as the Spaniards and Mexicans had conceived it, seemed to be foreign to the Anglo viewpoint. It was this viewpoint which led to the reservation policy as the advancing Anglos encountered more and more Indians west of the Mississippi River and it became increasingly apparent that the Indian Territory could serve for only a small fraction of the tribes.

THE CONTENT OF ANGLO POLICY

It was the concept of the reservation (which had slowly developed out of the policy of isolation) that dominated Anglo thought about Indians at the time when the United States acquired by conquest and purchase from the Mexicans the vast Indian-inhabited area which included modern New Mexico and Arizona. In 1846 the first moves of General Kearny and the Indian agent Calhoun for New Mexico Territory were to negotiate treaties with all the Indians they could reach. The treaties were regarded as insuring peace for Anglo expansion and, less clearly at this early date, setting territorial limits within which the Indians were to remain. It was quite apparent that the content of policy at this point was extremely simple. Treaties made with the Navajos, with the Eastern Pueblos, and a little later with the Apaches were nothing more than agreements to remain at peace. They did not at first involve any definite statements in regard to territorial boundaries. They contained no promises even that the Whites would not settle in areas claimed by Indians. On the contrary, the assumption was that the United States had acquired the whole territory and that Anglos were free to settle where they wished and to pass through the territory, and hence that Indian land rights were not recognized. This curious paradox — recognition by the Anglos of the Indians as a political unit capable of making binding treaties but without rights in the land where they lived — provided no basis whatever for mutual adjustment of interests; it constituted a sort of reversal of the Spanish policy which recognized the land rights of the Indians but not their political independence of Spain.

It was true also, however, that there was indication of a growing conception among Anglo officials of some sort of plan for "civilizing the Indians." The management of Indian affairs was transferred in 1849 from the War Department to the Department of the Interior. Policy called for civilian officials known as Indian agents whose function was to promote peaceful relations between Indians and settlers. At this time the means for carrying out this function was not very clearly seen by those in charge of Indian affairs. Calhoun, the first agent for the Territory of New Mexico, wrote of the need for aid to the Pueblo Indians in their pursuit of agriculture. Agricultural and other tools were given out to the Pimas in the 1850's. Thus, it is apparent that there was some conception of technical assistance and hence of economic development with which the government proposed to aid the Indians in a peaceful life.

Events between 1850 and 1875 rapidly shaped Anglo policy into something more closely resembling the considered programs of the Spaniards and Mexicans. Characteristically, it was fast-moving events rather than theoretical principles which gave form to the Anglo program. The policy which did emerge maintained its base in the tradition of "dependent nation" which the controversy over Cherokee removal to Indian Territory had crystallized. Expansion into the territory west of the Mississippi River brought Anglos into immediate and sharp conflict with the various bison-hunting tribes. The conquest of those tribes required intensive military action. Although it was possible after conquest to transport a few of them to the Indian Territory, the majority could not be contained there, and so the reservation policy developed. This was an application of the peace-through-isolation program and consisted of forcing conquered Indians into those parts of their territory least desirable to White settlers and keeping them there through force. The basis for the concentration of the various Plains tribes was a treaty made with each one in which peace was agreed to by the Indians within the assigned territory; in turn, the Anglos promised protection from encroaching settlers and agreed to certain cash payments or payments in food, clothing, and other necessities. That is to say, the Indians were made dependent on land which usually could not support them on the basis of their hunting and gathering habits of life. The United States government undertook therefore to support them on a ration basis for agreed-on lengths of time. It steadily became clear that if the Indians were to become self-supporting after that, vigorous steps would have to be taken to set them up as cattle raisers or as farmers, and this also required government aid in the development of what natural resources existed. This meant that the officials of the Department of the Interior were forced to undertake measures for economic and educational development of the Indians forcibly assigned to the reservations. One after another, the tribes of the Plains were conquered by the United States Cavalry and placed on reservations scattered widely over the west, and slowly the Indian Bureau worked out a "program for civilization."

It was this policy of isolation on reservations applied to the Plains tribes which guided government action in the Territories of New Mexico and Arizona. Before 1880 the Navajos, the Mescalero and Jicarilla Apaches, the Pimas, the Yumas, Mohaves, and other Yumans were dealt with in this manner. Nominally, the Eastern and Western Pueblos were also similarly dealt with, but actually the Eastern Pueblos and Zunis were in a somewhat different situation since the United States had been forced to recognize their land rights by virtue of the old Spanish land grants, as a result of the Treaty of Guadalupe Hidalgo. In 1872, recognizing the anomalous situation of dealing with Indians as independent nations after conquest, the United States Congress prohibited the further making of treaties with any Indian tribes. This was a move in the direction of an explicit recognition of a problem involved in the political, economic, and social incorporation of the Indians into the American nation. The United States was slowly, by force of circumstance, moving to a position in which it was taking cognizance of the fact of envelopment of the Indians, and of the necessity for some sort of program for their integration into the nation. The program of isolating the Indians had proven to be shortsighted. Even the remote White Mountain Apache area was being sought by Mormon settlers and miners. No spot in the United States could any longer be thought of as a permanently isolated area. Isolation being patently impossible, there was nothing to do but consider ways and means of integration. During the 1880's, spurred by the Apache troubles and then by the Ghost Dance movement, citizens and officials steadily evolved a program of "civilization" which seemed logical and workable to nearly all who knew anything about Indian affairs.

Crystallized finally in the Dawes Act of 1887, many different interests in Anglo-American culture influenced the program of the Indian Bureau. Chief among these were the Protestant churches which had been engaged in missionary work among the Indians, organizations of United States citizens such as the Indian Rights Association who had been roused to advocate elementary human rights for Indians in the manner of Bartolomé de las Casas three hundred years before, and the liberal wing of the Republican Party under the leadership of such men as Carl Schurz. Indians themselves were not in a position at this time to take part in the policy formation, since no system whatever for representation in the government of the United States had been encouraged and Indians were not citizens.

The Anglos who conceived the policy which began to be put in operation came up with one major element of program which Mexicans had been attempting to apply since 1824. This was the idea of allotting land in individual assignments to Indian families. In the thinking that lay behind the policy this held the central place. It was thought that the Indians needed to be civilized and that the basis of civilization consisted in knowing how to handle individual property. Out of such experience, it was reasoned, would come responsibility and awareness of the obligations of citizenship. Hence, if the land which had been assigned as reservations to each tribe were now reassigned on an individual basis, there would appear stimulus to economic improvement. On such a basis would grow industriousness and desire to be like the Anglo-Americans. The tribal ties, which were believed to be conducive to lack of industry and lack of individual responsibility, would melt away and the Indians would become participants in the American nation.

It was believed also, however, that the Indian societies with their barbaric influences could be broken apart more quickly if all the Indian children were required to be educated in Anglo schools, whether they and their parents wished it or not. Therefore, a second basic feature of the program consisted in the establishment of boarding schools far from the reservations, in which there was to be compulsory education for the Indian children apart from the parents and the Indian communities of the reservations. These were thus conceived in somewhat the manner of the schools for caciques' children in New Spain.

A third feature of the policy consisted of the suppression of religious ceremonies which seemed especially offensive to the missionary groups, and the institution of some schools on reservations to be managed by missionaries who would inculcate their beliefs and moral codes in place of the Indian ones. The Indian Bureau worked out a Code of Religious Offenses and proceeded to try to enforce it. It also gave government funds to various church groups for the establishment of schools on reservations, assigning different reservations to different denominations.

This program with its threefold approach — individual landholding, compulsory education, and religious replacement — differed in two respects from the program which the Spaniards had developed during the later phases of their political domination of the Indians. One was its emphasis on education apart from the Indian community which contrasted with the mission school program of the Spanish missionaries, although actually this was only a matter of emphasis, since the Spaniards also had the idea of schools for sons of caciques away from the homeland, and of schools in the homeland administered by religious teachers. In another respect the difference was fundamental; this was in the matter of political participation. The Anglos had no program for developing political participation. Citizenship was conditional on proven ability to manage a piece of allotted land. No liaison institutions between tribal governments already existing and the national political organization were formed; the reservation communities remained in a limbo of political isolation. Moreover, when such tribal governments as existed on reservations opposed the land allotment feature of the new policy, they were ignored and the United States government proceeded with its land program. No substitute institutions were set up.

In place of political organization such as the Spaniards and later the Mexicans tried to develop, the Anglos instituted an administrative control over the Indians by agents of the Bureau who took up residence on the reservations. The agent behaved as a member of the government hierarchy, employing the funds assigned him by the Bureau for use on the reservation, managing the allotment of land and all the complexities to which this led, all entirely without any controls on his actions by the Indians themselves. The agent (later called a superintendent) gave orders to a group of employees, usually consisting of a government farmer and one or more teachers. The farmer carried on the program of technical assistance in developing farming, cattle raising, and other subsistence activities. What the farmer, the teachers, and the superintendent did was determined by the Indian Bureau officials who made policy in Washington. Besides the functions of maintaining technical assistance, carrying out land allotment, and securing pupils for the compulsory education, a major function of the superintendent was conceived as that of protecting the Indians from the ever-encroaching Anglo settlers in the vicinity of the reservations. Thus, each Indian reservation became a small department of the federal government within a state, no longer isolated geographically, but effectively isolated politically and socially. With no control over affairs on the reservations, the state populations became antagonistic to the reservation communities and no means existed for resolving locally the antagonisms which developed.

Only a part of the new policy of the Indian Bureau was ultimately applied to the reservations of the states of New Mexico and Arizona. What the Anglos regarded as the fundamental feature — land allotment — was never widely carried out. The complexities of the program as it developed elsewhere, growing chiefly out of Anglo efforts to acquire Indian land as soon as Indians were given individual titles, resulted in its gradual abandonment. Only small portions of the Navajo, Pima, Papago, and Colorado River reservations were allotted. Even in the cases where there was some allotment the program was not followed through, so that except for a small part of the Navajo Reservation these reservations were never opened to Anglo settlement. They remained intact as Indian-owned units.

The enforcement of the Code of Religious Offenses proved an impossible task and, although Indians on most reservations were made aware of Anglo disapproval of certain of their religious observances, the occasional attempts at suppression resulted merely in driving certain ceremonies under cover. The missionary schools resulted in some replacement of native religion, but the major effect where they operated was not complete replacement, but rather the creation of a diversity of cult practices and belief.

The application of the boarding-school program did extend widely through the Southwestern tribes, so that a fourth or more of the generation coming of school age from the 1890's to the 1930's did experience boarding-school life. The majority of these, however, came back to the reservations to participate in greater or less degree in the Indian cultures.

The most definite effects of Indian Bureau policy lay in the influence of the superintendent and his staff on the development of the reservation communities. In the absence of the application of allotment on the New Mexico-Arizona reservations, the superintendents concentrated their activities on the development of what resources existed on the reservations, chiefly the extension of farming and stock raising. Parallel with the vigorous efforts of the federal government in constructing irrigation systems for the Anglo settlers in the region, the Indian Bureau established its own staff of irrigation engineers and set out to increase the acreage of irrigated land on most of the reservations. At the same time it sought to improve the crops raised and to increase the grazing land on some reservations. The record of accomplishment was not great, in terms of acres as compared with the Anglo projects, but on every reservation some increase in acreage was accomplished, even despite the appropriation of water resources by the expanding Anglo population.

In this work the superintendents of each reservation gradually built little paternalistically managed groups of communities. The government technicians undertook to plan and carry out the improvements in irrigation. The superintendent chose Indians to work with him and his technicians, often paid for functions such as ditch boss which men had formerly carried out as community obligation. The superintendent also, as on the San Carlos Apache Reservation, made assignments of new land which his engineers brought into production and reassigned old land which had been improved. He appointed policemen and paid them from government funds for the enforcement of law and order. He acted as judge, or as ultimate appeal from Indian judges, in trying and meting out punishment for offenses within the reservation. Schools were planned, built, and managed, without any Indian participation in the form of school boards, by the government-paid officials. The system was one of government financing and management in which Indians had no voice, in which problems were defined by government officials far away, and means for solution came in the form of money appropriated by the national Congress. The only participation of Indians in what the superintendent carried out as "reservation development" was as wage laborers. Economic and educational aspects of life were the focus of effort.

The ruling goal during the whole period from the 1890's to the 1930's was usually conceived as the creation of a self-sufficient group of Indian communities on their respective reservations. This took the form for the Gila Pimas, for example, of a plan for making them into small farmers on ten-acre irrigated plots. It took the form of encouragement of sheep raising for the Navajos. On all the reservations the attempt was to make territory which had been more or less arbitrarily set aside into some sort of self-sufficient economic unit. This was in contrast with the course of economic development in the region, where larger and larger farm units were developing with more and more highly mechanized agriculture. The accidents of reservation formation and the paternal system of government bureau management resulted in the creation of economic arrangements on the reservations which were generally at odds with the trend of economic developments in the region.

The government program was not, however, static. It had, in fact, been characterized by much shift and change from the 1840's. Not only were there very frequent changes in the superintendents and other responsible officials, whose tenure averaged less than three years on a reservation, but there were also shifts in features of policy, depending on the viewpoint of each Commissioner of Indian Affairs and the interest of the national Congress. One sharp shift came in 1934 with the passage of the Indian Reorganization Act. This act not only completely stopped the land allotments as injurious to the Indians and shifted emphasis from the off-reservation boarding schools to on-reservation day schools, but it also instituted for the first time an effort to provide some sort of means for political integration of the Indians with the rest of the nation. An earlier move had been attempted in 1924, after the manner of the Mexican government just one hundred years before. In that year, the national Congress decreed that all Indians were citizens of the United States. No longer conditional on ability to manage an individual allotment of land, citizenship brought with it all the rights and obligations of the United States citizen, provided an Indian lived away from a reservation. If he lived on a reservation, there were differences. Thus, for example, he did not pay taxes on land which the federal government continued to hold in trust for him, and he did not have a local government in which he could participate. He was still subject to the paternal rule of the Indian Bureau superintendent. If he lived on a reservation outside of the states of Arizona and New Mexico, he could vote for state and national officials, but until 1949, in those two states Indians were prohibited, on different grounds, from voting.

The Indian Reorganization Act of 1934 proposed, for the first time in United States history, to make a beginning at political integration of Indian communities. In substance, what it proposed was a transitional community, something like the Jesuit mission community in which Indians maintained a form of Spanish local government but in which they were exempt for a specific period from paying tribute (taxes) and could continue to hold land as a corporate body. The IRA proposed and all New Mexico and Arizona tribes, with the exception of Navajos and Eastern Pueblos, accepted a plan for tribal representative government on the reservations. The form proposed was constitutional, the constitutions to be written with special reference to each tribe's social structure with the aid of technicians in government from the Indian Bureau. The tribal councils formed on this basis had jurisdiction within their reservations, except with respect to ten major crimes which since 1885 had been handled in federal courts. They had powers of taxation and many other powers over the tribal members, whose qualifications they defined. They had no formal working relations with local and state governments, their only channels of communication being through the Indian Bureau. They were thus a peculiar form of isolated institution, not actually a working part of the political structure of the United States. They nevertheless were considered a means for gaining experience in the type of constitutional, representative government which existed in the United States generally. Together with their powers as a managing body for the tribal resources in land, timber, minerals, etc., they constituted a school for learning to work together politically in the Anglo-American way. It had taken nearly one hundred years for the Indian Bureau to devise this transitional mechanism. It was applied only after Indians had lived for generations under the superintendent system, and moreover the latter was not abolished.

In providing this new form of organization for communities of Indians on the reservations, the IRA brought about a fundamental change in what had become the structure of those communities. As settlers had pressed around the reservations, the Indian Bureau had become aware of the necessity for some sort of political organization for the tribes. The need for agreements by tribes as wholes in regard to use of such reservation resources as oil and minerals by Anglo entrepreneurs had resulted in the Indian Bureau setting up groups of Indians to act as legal spokesman for the tribes. These were Indians, hand-picked by superintendents, who acted as their "advisers" in tribal matters and signed legal papers when necessary as in the case of oil exploration leases on the Navajo Reservation. They were in no sense representative bodies, but, consistent with the paternalistic regime of the superintendents, were groups selected by the latter to function in name as the tribe. They increased the hold of the superintendent over reservation affairs. The IRA plan in principle, and as it turned out to some extent in practice, instituted a more representative system which in some measure modified the control of the superintendents.

In addition, the IRA established new means for breaking down the social isolation of the reservation populations. The most important of such means consisted of the Johnson-O'Malley Act which enabled the Indian Bureau or the tribal councils to make contracts for services with state governments or with private corporations. Under this act it became possible to contract with state governments for the education of Indian children in state and county schools, thus throwing the Indian children in closer contact with non-Indians in their own localities. Similarly, health and other services were contracted for with state governments or private groups. Although still quite separate from the local governments of their areas, Indians on reservations came to participate more in the society surrounding them, and the virtual limitation of contact to federal bureau officials began to change.

The basic idea of the IRA policy was that the cultural assimilation of Indians, individual by individual, as conceived in the former policy of land allotment and boarding-school education, disorganized both Indian personality and communities, and that influences from Anglo culture could be best assimilated through the medium of the tribe as an organized entity set up to deal as a unit with the outside influences. It was in a sense a concept of transitional community such as underlay the Jesuit mission program. The day schools, which IRA emphasized and attempted to establish, were designed to keep children in touch with their parents and communities rather than to separate them. The tribal councils were to provide scope for leadership within the communities and to eliminate the paternal control of the superintendent. The shift in policy was an expression of a completely different viewpoint toward Indian affairs on the part of government officials. It took place at the same time that Mexico also was adopting a new view of Indian affairs. The fact that the Collier regime in the Indian Bureau was contemporaneous with the Cárdenas administration in Mexico was no accident. Views of Indian problems in the two countries were a result of activities extending through both American continents which resulted at the end of the 1930's in the formation of the Inter-American Indian Institute, with headquarters in Mexico City, which sought to find an approach to Indian problems in the Americas based on systematic appraisal of the effects of national programs on Indians up to that point.

Anglo-American policy may be characterized generally as having moved from indifference to Indian internal affairs to intensive concern with them. It moved from absence of program for changing Indian culture, to one of replacement of tribal landholding with individual landholding, replacement of native religion with various forms of Christian religion, replacement or improvement of Indian economies, and replacement of informal home education with formal secular schools. In terms of political aspects of culture, the program changed from regarding Indian tribes as independent nations, to considering them as enclaved dependent nations (that is, without control of their external relations but with control over their own internal affairs), to administrative communities under the control of a government bureau, to communities transitional toward representative government. By 1934 government policy had eliminated as a feature of its program any attempt to replace native religions with religions of Western culture. It concentrated its support chiefly on the development of natural resources, roads and other forms of communication, on subsidizing education in secular schools, and on subsidizing health services to Indians. It had finally instituted political organizations within the reservations, but had made little effort to integrate these formally with political organization outside the reservations. Nevertheless, both states and nation had incorporated Indians into the national organization in terms of suffrage and taxation, with the exception of taxes on land. The special status of Indian land and the special status of Indian local government with limited jurisdiction over the Indian residents on the land constituted what were regarded as anomalies by most Anglos; pressures were constant to alter these special conditions.

THE NATURE OF THE CONTACT COMMUNITIES

As in Mexico, the contacts of Indians with the invaders in their territories took place under two quite different sets of conditions. On the one hand, there were contacts within the Indian communities. These took place in a very special type of community which we may call the "reservation community." On the other hand, there were contacts within the invaders' communities established in Indian country — frontier settlements ranging from isolated ranches to mining towns and farming villages which grew into the towns and cities of the modern states of Arizona and New Mexico.

THE RESERVATION COMMUNITY — What we shall speak of as the reservation community was a form of social grouping which went through considerable change during the century of Anglo contact. Nevertheless, it is clear that important basic characteristics took form early and persisted throughout. Like the Spanish mission community, the reservation community constituted a very definite type of social and economic unit which had a profound effect on the cultural development of the Indians.

Among all the tribes of New Mexico and Arizona, with the exception of the Eastern Pueblos, the Indian Bureau, beginning as early as the 1850's, established agents and erected buildings in which they were to live and conduct business. At Sacaton on the Gila Pima Reservation, at Fort Defiance, Tuba City, Leupp, Shiprock, and later Window Rock among the Navajos, at San Carlos, Fort Apache, and Whiteriver among the Apaches, at Parker and Yuma on the Colorado River, at Peach Springs and Truxton among the Walapai, in Havasupai Canyon, at Black Rock on the Zuni Reservation, at San Xavier and Sells on the Papago Reservations, and at Keams Canyon on the Hopi Reservation the Indian Bureau established its agents. These eighteen settlements steadily grew during the century into communities which ranged in population from only a few dozen to several hundred inhabitants. These places became the focal points of Indian contacts with government officials and therefore of formal contact with Anglo-American culture. Indian families who obtained jobs at the agencies moved in permanently to live near the agency. Traders' stores usually grew up in their vicinity. The number of government offices steadily increased. After 1934 offices for tribal government were established. Hospitals and schools were built at the agencies. Various churches erected buildings and gathered congregations at them. They became the scene of visits by government and state officials, tourists, students of Indian culture, and a great variety of other persons having business or other interests with the Indians.

Like the Jesuit or Franciscan mission, the agency town was an arm of an organized hierarchy reaching directly into Indian communities. Like a Jesuit or Franciscan missionary a superintendent on a reservation was not responsible to the Indians among whom he lived; he was responsible only to his superiors in the hierarchy of the Indian Bureau. Superintendents differed greatly in regard to the sense of responsibility toward the Indians, and some felt such responsibility very deeply, but the fact remained that any such feelings had to be expressed within the framework of bureau organization. Thus, although superintendents differed very greatly, unquestionably to a greater extent than did the missionaries because they lacked the common intensive discipline which characterized the missionaries, every agency town resembled every other agency town as a symbol to Indians of lost political autonomy. Although Indians may have requested certain help or services from the federal government there is no evidence of any having asked for the establishment of agency towns within their territory. Political domination involved for the reservation Indians neither enforced attendance at Mass or other religious ceremonies (as it had under the Spaniards), nor taxation (as it had under the Mexicans), but it did involve the sufferance of the agency town.

Physically, an agency town began with a small building for an office for the agent and a house for himself and his family to live in. These buildings were in the architectural style of the period, usually very plain rectangular stone constructions, built by paid Indian laborers. Steadily in every agency town there was an accretion of such buildings—perhaps a school, quarters for schoolteachers (who were usually women), a house for the "farmer," and then more offices and more houses, as the government program of land improvement, road building, health services, and soil conservation steadily developed. By 1950 the typical agency town contained houses for thirty to forty Indian Bureau employees with their families and five or six offices, in Anglo style and furnished in the current Anglo manner. Smaller and less expensive houses, often in the native style of the Indians, grew up around these in which Indian employees paid by the Bureau lived with their families. Usually also two or more stores were built by individuals who obtained trading concessions for selling goods to the Indians.

The agency town, thus, was a community newly formed and patterned among the existing Indian communities, its character fundamentally determined by

Anglo purposes. In this sense it was similar to the Jesuit mission communities which grew up at the southeastern margin of Tarahumara country. It was in general, however, not like the other mission communities, in that the Anglos did not attempt to "reduce" the Indians to concentrated settlement around the agency (the San Carlos Apaches being the only clear exception to this). Reduction was not a part of the Anglo program, although in a very limited way some concentration did take place, as among Mohaves, Havasupais, and the Apache tribes.

The agency town, despite its Anglo patterning, however, was a very different sort of community from the mining and farming settlements which grew up at the margins of reservations and elsewhere in New Mexico and Arizona. Its functions were totally different, as the Anglos conceived them and as they worked out in respect to influence on the Indians. The agency town at first existed, in Anglo eyes, for the purpose of "supervising" the Indians in the interests of peace. This purpose gradually expanded to the wider one of "civilizing" the Indians as the Indian Bureau came to accept this function by the 1880's. These purposes called for the assumption of special roles by the Anglos living in the agency towns, roles nonexistent in the other Anglo settlements which in general tended to ignore the Indians.

Fundamental in the influence of the agency town on the Indians was the authority of the agent, or superintendent. During the first twenty or thirty years of Anglo control of the Indians the agents acted to a large extent merely as supervisors of the distribution of rations; enforcement officers for the regulations, such as the daily count, which the military had conceived; intermediaries in trade with the Whites; and dispensers of such benefits as agricultural and other implements which in some cases the Indian Bureau secured. They made beginnings at the organization and enforcement of law and order, especially among Navajos and Apaches, often by organizing forces of Indian policemen whom they armed. Gradually, as peace developed and restrictions were placed on trading activities because of the great amount of corruption which characterized the agents' participation in trade, and as rations were discontinued, the agents' function shifted to economic improvement of the reservations and to the carrying out of the educational program which the Indian Bureau adopted.

In these functions the authority of the superintendents was based on the assumption that the Indians had no governing bodies which should exercise control of their actions. Compulsory education, for example, was a measure conceived as for the good of the Indians regardless of what they might think of it. Similarly, the steps to increase irrigable land or to make individual assignments of land were measures to be executed by the superintendents on orders from their superiors. It was apparently not believed that the Indian communities as they existed could or should participate in the formulation of such programs or organize their execution once they were formulated. Both the objectives and their execution were matters which concerned only the authority of the employees of the Indian Bureau. In short, what Indian organization existed was treated as if it did not exist, except where it might be used to smooth the course of administrative management by the superintendents. The authority system was that of a government bureau integrated with Indian local organization only insofar as it suited the superintendent. The inevitable result was the breakdown of many aspects of Indian community organization, and a strong sense on the part of the Indians that what was being done was being imposed on them.

Since the superintendent's power was thus imposed, and there was no possibility of modifying his actions through any means except direct request to him, a strong sense of dependency on the superintendent also developed. The various aids which were available through the superintendent, food in hard times, medicine, tools, protection from encroaching Whites, etc., could be obtained not through the operation of any community organization, but only by going to the superintendent's office and making a personal appeal to him. He controlled the distribution of such benefits. He also acted as judge in matters of offense and punishment, so that his power extended to the social and political, as well as the economic, affairs of the Indian communities. His staff of employees was ordered by him, as in any functioning administrative organization, to carry out actions such as the construction of a new irrigation ditch or the building of a school, and if the Indians had other ideas the appeal could not be to the employees carrying on the work, but only back to the superintendent. Inevitably, the superintendent became a patriarchal power on all the reservations. The extent to which he consulted with Indians on any matters depended entirely on himself. If he had such tendencies, as part of a democratic ideal, or an element of personality, he became especially appreciated by Indians, but he still exercised the same kind of imposed authority.

Steadily, through the 1920's this system turned the agency town into a place where Indians who were isolated from their own communities came to live. They, by virtue of having lived for some years in a boarding school where they had adopted Anglo ways, or simply by personal inclination to accept White ways, were ready to accept the rule of the superintendent and found that advantages in the form of paying jobs or prestige among the Anglos accrued to them. Thus, there came to be a classification employed by the Indians on a reservation into "agency Indians" and others. The superintendent and his staff often regarded the agency Indians who clustered around them as "the progressives" and the others who stayed away from the agency as "conservatives." Actually, the Indians with whom the agent had his contacts were usually not the only ones who wished to accept various Anglo ways; there were others who did but who often shunned contact with the agency merely because they disliked and distrusted the socially-isolated Indians who, under the superintendent, dominated affairs there.

By the 1930's the Indian agency town had grown into a peculiar expression of Anglo culture, quite different from other types of communities elsewhere in the United States. It was a place where an enclave of Indian Bureau employees lived a life in large degree separate and distinct from the Indians about them. There were usually strong caste feelings which kept the Anglos and Indians from marrying or intermingling in ordinary intimate social life. Indian Bureau employees' children went to different schools from the Indians. Indians remained in the lower paying and lower prestige jobs at the agency. They did not participate in policy determination by the men who had control over them. Schools and school policy were imposed from above. The whole system of democratic community organization which existed elsewhere in the United States was suspended here.

The basis of the system was the belief that Indians were incapable of governing themselves. Their extreme dependency on the agency staff was frequently pointed to as evidence for this. It was also based, of course, on the legal framework which had been developed in Indian affairs, without provision for Indian self-government as a recognized institution on the reservation. There was no mechanism in the social structure for resolving the conflicts which had developed on the reservations as a result of the systematic imposition of agricultural programs, schools, etc., on the Indian communities. The result was the growth of a feeling of helplessness on the part of the Indians in the face of the uncontrollable bureaucratic authority: officials changed constantly, policy veered according to the thinking of men in power in Washington, contributing to a spirit of resignation and apathy. The effect on the Anglos who served on the reservations also was the creation of a sense of helplessness; they came in general to look upon the Indians as not capable of civilization. Frustrated by the situation of Indians antagonistic to them, and with no organizational means for entering into real contact with them, Indian Bureau employees gained little sense of progress in their work, except insofar as results of a material sort could be reported on paper to their superiors.

When not brought directly into the activities of the superintendent, many Indians, of course, continued to live in their own communities on the reservations relatively unaffected by the patriarchal agency town. In fact, the nature of developments in the agency towns often turned them away from a desire for contacts. Nevertheless their land, their children, and other interests were affected in some degree by the superintendent and his program. Although they regarded him as an interloper and sometimes became fiercely antagonistic, if he exercised his power in extreme ways, they did not remain completely isolated. Actually the agency town was a major nexus between them and the outside world. Thus, the contacts with Anglo culture for all the Indians of a reservation were strongly influenced by this authoritarian, caste-organized, imposed community.

THE ANGLO-AMERICAN TOWN — Indians in Arizona and New Mexico by no means confined their contacts to the paternalistic regime of the reservations. From the early 1900's on some worked and lived in the growing number of Anglo communities in the region. For the following fifty years a slow but steady movement off the reservations continued, a movement which took two forms. On the one hand, individuals and families moved permanently into Anglo towns and cities and adopted at least all the externals of Anglo life. No data exist as to the number of Indians from the various tribes who were thoroughly assimilated into Anglo culture. The number certainly must have run into the thousands. On the other hand, there was a great deal of temporary residence off the reservations; some of it was regularly seasonal in response to opportunities for agricultural work, some of it was in the form of residence for a few years away from the reservation with ultimate return.

It is difficult to generalize about the nature of the lives of those who took up permanent residence off the reservations. It is certain that many individuals attained the educational and economic levels of middle and upper-middle class Anglos. But it is also certain that a majority of those Indians living off reservation remained in the lower educational and economic levels of Anglo life. It appears that there was a trend toward wider distribution of such persons in the various levels of Anglo society.

The outstanding fact in regard to off-reservation life for Indians was, however, its temporary character, despite the very large number of individuals whom it influenced. The general tendency for Indians in Arizona and New Mexico was to continue to regard the reservations as their permanent homes, and to take up residence outside in response to temporary economic necessity or youthful motives of adventure and wider experience.

For the majority of temporary residents, off-reservation contacts were most intimate with Anglos and Mexican-Americans of lower economic and educational levels. They worked in railroad shops and with railroad section gangs. They worked in agricultural harvests. They worked as servants and menials. This was true to the extent that they became stereotyped generally by the Anglo population as capable only of the less responsible and less skilled kinds of work. They encountered caste and strong class attitudes which encouraged them to regard their off-reservation life as temporary and to seek the less exclusive attitudes of other Indians on the reservations. Off-reservation life often threw them into the poverty-stricken and disorganized areas of Anglo communities, and, by contrast, made the reservation appear secure and pleasant.

THE CONFLICTS IN ANGLO CULTURE

Like Spanish culture, Anglo culture was characterized by various inherent conflicts and functional inconsistencies. The mission community was a focus of the conflict between economic and religious interests in Spanish society. The agency towns of the Indian reservations in the United States were characterized by tensions which reflected conflicts in Anglo-American society.

The early conflict on the reservation between military and civil officials was, from one point of view, a minor maladjustment in administration. The control over Indian affairs was in process of transition at the time the first Southwestern reservations were formed and there was consequent confusion of authority. Nevertheless, this transition was an expression of the persistent conflict in Anglo culture over the sphere of the military. Military officials, such as General Crook, saw the strict discipline and authoritarian control of the Army as the effective means for bringing Indians forcibly into the orbit of Anglo civilization. The Department of Interior officials saw this process as requiring a different sort of control and, more or less consistently, championed more democratic conditions. Yet in the end the latter established what was, essentially, administrative structure of a military type, even if without the minute control over each individual Indian. However minor as a conflict in Anglo culture, the struggle between the military and civilian administrators was of very great effect on at least the Apache Indians during their first years of reservation life. It made clear to the Apaches the existence of uncertainty and insecurity involved in government control of their lives. Their first experience of Anglo government did not open up for them a view of a stable political authority with singleness of purpose through the years.

Nevertheless, all the Indians of the Southwest experienced something of the greater dependability of the federal government in its actions than that of the settler population in their country. Anglo-American colonization of North America, like that of the Spanish, was characterized by a constant conflict between government policy in regard to Indians and the interests of the settler population. Where each of the governments had stood for humaneness and recognition of Indian land rights, the colonists had in general stood for neither. The Anglo settlers proceeded on the assumption that Indians had no land rights, even after treaties were made. The federal government tried to protect land rights established by treaty, and later by executive orders. The consistent refusal of settlers to recognize such rights even forced the federal government to take military measures against their own citizens. The whole reservation policy was a compromise between what federal government officials regarded as justice and what settlers regarded as justice. The conflict between settler interests in establishing themselves, and government interest in broader justice gave the Indians profound experience of the persistent sectional-national conflicts in Anglo-American life. At first expressed in the lawless behavior of Anglos toward Indians both in regard to land appropriation and murder, this conflict was later expressed in the persisting conflict between states and federal government over Indian affairs. The result was distrust by Indians of state government, and greater trust in the federal government's power to protect Indian interests.

Another conflict which affected Indians was that between church and state. At first this was little apparent. The early efforts of the Department of the Interior to manage Indian affairs were to a large extent put in the hands of the churches, even schools being turned over to the various missionary churches. By 1896, however, popular protest resulted in the secularizing of the Indian schools and the promulgation of a policy of government management of the schools. Finally, by the 1930's, special church interests had been eliminated entirely from influence on government policy and a conscious policy of religious freedom, recognizing Indian forms of religious expression equally with Christian forms, was adopted. Also, the abandonment of the Code of Religious Offenses by the Indian Bureau marked the separation of church and state still further. Considerable adverse criticism by various churches of the government's handling of Indian affairs developed among missionaries on the reservations. Indians inevitably became aware of such criticisms, such as that the government schools were Godless.

Perhaps the most profound conflict in Anglo culture in regard to Indian Affairs centered around moral issues and civil rights. During the 1860's and 1870's, when corruption was quite common among Indian Bureau officials in their management of rationing and other programs, United States citizens from various parts of the country united into organizations, chiefly at first the Indian Rights Association and later the Association on American Indian Affairs, devoted to the securing of what they regarded as elementary human rights for the Indians. In a sense, their activity paralleled that of Bartolomé de las Casas, the Spanish champion of Indian citizenship rights.

In the view of such associations the Indians on reservations were being dealt with unilaterally and as such were in constant danger of being dealt with arbitrarily. The Indian Rights Association took upon itself the task of constantly criticizing Indian Bureau programs from the point of view of what it regarded as justice to the Indians. This required investigation of various Bureau policies to determine their results and to propose modifications of policy which would be more in the interests of the Indians. The Indian Rights Association and its point of view became increasingly influential in the making of Indian policy and played a large part in the fundamental changes in approach which were marked by the adoption of the Indian Reorganization Act as a guide for Indian Bureau programs.

The conflict involved here was primarily over the right of self-determination, although it was not always clearly recognized as such by the Indian Rights Association and similar organizations. Often spoken of as the issue of humanitarian treatment, it nevertheless rested on a view of political rights and the belief that these were being ignored by denial of citizenship to the Indians. Actually the Indian Rights Association itself assumed the role of representative of the Indians. In a sense its activities did not fundamentally attack the issue involved, so long as it undertook to assume this function for the Indians.

BEARERS OF ANGLO CULTURE

The range of persons with whom the Indians of Arizona and New Mexico came in contact during their hundred years of association with Anglos was far greater than that with whom Indians came in contact during the preceding Spanish period. The contacts were moreover more intensive and many-sided, consistent with the greater complexity of the Anglo society which took form in Indian country. While one might limit the type contacts with Spaniards to those of missionary, soldier, colonial governor, administrative aides, occasional trader, farmer-settler, and possibly one or two others, the list of type contacts with Anglos was far longer. Thus, the following might be listed as fundamental type contacts during the Anglo period: trapper-frontiersman, soldier, settler, early-type Indian agent, reservation superintendent, schoolteacher, missionary, reservation trader, IRA superintendent, agricultural engineer, Indian Bureau doctor, tourist, tribal lawyer, Indian rights organization representative, writer, scientific student, and some others. On the basis of contacts with these various types, which increased steadily in numbers and in intimacy especially during the latest phase, Indians learned the nature of Anglo behavior and formed their attitudes towards the way of life being offered them.

The individual personalities playing these particular roles in Anglo culture, of course, varied greatly. Nevertheless, it is perfectly possible to identify, in the abundant literature on Indian contacts for the Anglo period, recurrent behavior and attitudes indicating a limited number of roles which the diversity of personalities played in their contacts with the Indians. There tended, for example, to be a standard attitude which frontiersmen like Kit Carson, Bill Williams, and other Mountain Men maintained in their dealings with Indians. Similarly, once the agency town and the Bureau superintendency became institutionalized, it was apparent that superintendents, insofar as their attitudes and relations with Indians went, also conformed to a pattern. Their memoirs show a considerable consistency in their understanding of Indians and the conceptions they held towards their work with them. This was true also of the Indian Bureau technicians of various sorts and of such occasional visitors as representatives of Indian rights organizations and anthropological students. The Indians inevitably tended to form their stereotypes of Anglos on the basis of what they came to know of these recurrent roles.

To offer more than two or three sketches of characteristic bearers of Anglo-American culture would unduly expand the scope of this study. Reservation superintendents, schoolteachers, and missionaries were certainly among the most influential in Indian life. We shall present here, again as in the case of bearers of Spanish culture only as examples of what might be done, analytical sketches of two superintendents and two missionaries. The sources for further illumination of the contact situation along this line have recently become rich, especially with the publication of numerous memoirs of Bureau of Indian Affairs employees.

By the time the paternalistic community of the agency town became a well-established institution on the reservation, men had been found to play the role of superintendent in such communities. An example of one of these persons is Leo Crane who served during the 1920's and earlier as superintendent among the Pueblo Indians, the Navajos, and the Hopis. Crane's interest in the Indians whom he supervised was deep; he learned a great deal about their history and was keenly interested in what had happened to them from the beginning of contact. He was devoted to the protection of their interests against Anglos who sought to appropriate their land. He came to know a good deal about the workings of their communities, and showed great ability in establishing and running efficiently the schools which Indian Bureau funds permitted him to build. After he had spent nearly twenty years in the Indian Service he wrote two books of memoirs which reveal his attitudes towards the Indians and the work of the Indian Bureau.

The basis of Crane's relations with the Eastern Pueblo Indians is suggested in the following paragraph. *The thing that our tourists, and especially those who eulogize what is termed by them "Indian culture," are pleased to admire as a democratic and equitable form of tribal government among these Pueblo people is actually a barbaric despotism once necessary because of the need for irrigation water. This despotism sprang up to assure the feeding of communities, and amid a primitive people naturally made use of mysticism and a savage mythology, thus immeasurably strengthening the authority of those who found power necessary to existence.* To Crane the community organization of the Pueblos was consequently an evil to put up with, not an institution through which a superintendent could hope to influence cultural change in the Pueblo villages.

It seemed silly to Crane to attempt to work with and through such an organization. As he said: *The opera bouffe that has grown up around these native pueblo officials never did appeal to me, but up to a certain point it had to be recognized for reasons of diplomacy; and, to be plain about it, to avoid furnishing ammunition to those zealous friends of the Indian who every now and then arise to chant about liberty, democracy, and freedom and who, when on the ground, would seem to enjoy making obeisance to an unlettered native. An Indian Agent should be prepared to report, when necessary, two things: first, that he treated everyone courteously; and second, that he carried out the regulations. With how much inflexibility an Indian Agent carried out the regulations, and the interpretations that may be placed on some of them, depends on himself. Opera bouffe, in the theatre, is very amusing; but in real life it soon becomes boring.* This outburst was occasioned in Crane's telling of the story of a Pueblo official who defied Crane's authority to remove a body for a medical examination from the Pueblo graveyard.

Crane's somewhat cynical attitude concerning Pueblo religion is apparent in the following: *There may be those to despise and ridicule the thing I have termed a "compromise" between Franciscan dogma and pagan forms .... I have wondered why this compromise should not have been carried even further. If an Indian refuses to be baptized with water, why not humor him and baptize him with corn meal? It seems to me that several of the faiths, as well as the earnest padres, have overlooked this means of attacking native reticence.*

Crane's general approach to Indian affairs seems to have been one which was very common among superintendents of his era. He maintained a fatherly interest, touched with some sentimental feeling and sympathy for lost customs and past suffering of Indians — in general a fairly well-informed interest. He was conscious of, and derived considerable satisfaction from, being in an unusual and at that time often romantically-regarded profession. He saw Indians as children who needed much guidance and conceived of his own role of superintendent as that of fatherly counselor, working against the barbaric influence of their old village organization and religion. The values toward which he wished to steer the Indians were those of hardy, upstanding, enterprising individualism, of scientific reason, and of economic progress. The absence of these values in the Pueblo world view he deplored, but felt that sufficient training in the schools set up by the Indian Bureau would eventually inculcate them and replace the backward conservative Indian viewpoint.

Very similar to, but differing in important ways from Leo Crane was a contemporary Indian Service official, Albert H. Kneale, who served on many reservations. In later years he acted as superintendent at Shiprock on the northern Navajo Reservation and still later served for six years as superintendent of the Gila Pima Reservation. Kneale had chosen the Indian Service as a career and altogether served for thirty-six years in it. He had a capacity for seeing clearly and describing material aspects of life on the reservations. Kneale had been raised on a farm and looked at Indian problems primarily from the point of view of improving Indian agriculture. It was a recognition of this primary interest that led to his being given the very difficult assignment of working out the plan for agricultural improvement of the Pimas when water was restored to their reservation after the forty years of progressive destruction of Pima economy by the appropriation of water by Anglo settlers.

When he first came to the Navajo Reservation at Shiprock, after twenty-four years among Plains Indians, he realized that all Indians were not the same, and slowly groped toward some understanding of the Navajos and their culture. Impressed by the difficulties of life in the arid Navajo Reservation, he wrote of his first impressions: *It was in this area that 50,000 Navajo Indians made their homes. Made their homes? Well, not exactly! The Navajo had a dwelling but in his vocabulary there existed no word that could be interpreted "home." He had no mental concept of the idea civilization expresses by this term . . . . Here, isolated from the rest of mankind, they dwelt, assured in their own minds that here was the hub of the universe.*

I have seen ancient maps depicting the terrors that lay beyond the then known world. According to these maps, the land "beyond" was filled with dragons and other terrifying monsters. This was the conception held by the Navajo of the land beyond their ken. Of course, they knew that a portion of this terra incognita had been subdued by the whites . . . . They also knew that these whites were few, the Navajos numerous, and that, although the Navajos were in every respect superior to the whites, the whites possessed some strange medicine (magic) that rendered them immune to the power of these direful creatures . . . . Here they dwelt in peace and contentment, surrounded by their flocks and herds, even as Abraham of old, asking of the government but one thing: "Leave us alone."

Kneales' relations with his interpreter and other Navajos with whom he came into personal contact were intimate, kindly, and friendly. He was willing to listen to and learn about Navajo religion from them, and while he regarded their beliefs about the spiritual world as "superstitions" he nevertheless did gain some understanding of how these beliefs influenced their lives and their attitudes toward Anglo culture. He remained tolerant of Navajo custom and dealt with Navajo misunderstanding of his counsel, as reservation judge, tolerantly as one would of children.

After six years of hard work on the Pima Reservation supervising the subjugation of new land and the construction of an irrigation system for making use of the water now restored to the Pimas in part with the construction of Coolidge Dam, he regarded the problems of the Pimas as essentially solved: *As I saw the task nearing completion, as I saw the Pimas prosperous — good dwellings where formerly had been hovels; good roads where formerly had been trails; alfalfa, wheat and cotton-fields where formerly had been mesquite and sagebrush dunes and gullies — I realized that the mission had been accomplished. I was weary. I felt out of step with the administration.* In 1935 he resigned from the Indian Service. He had continued throughout his work to see the problems of the Indians in terms of economic resources. The cultural conflicts and the failures in social and political organization hardly crossed his vision. The Gila Pimas appeared to him as finally civilized, since he could detect little difference in their behavior from that of surrounding Whites: *The Pimas were neither picturesque nor colorful. Here was no blanket, no men with braided hair, no scalp lock, no buckskin, no paint, no moccasins, no pipe bag, no pipe, no tribal dances, no strange habitations, no wild or semiwild herds of ponies, no intriguing language to be studied, no interesting superstitions, no tribal customs.*

The Pimas differed little from the inhabitants of the typical back-country, white community. They were religious and liked to attend the church of their choice. . . . They had their church bazaars. . . . They slept in clean beds. . . . They were intensely interested in their schools and the children, clean and well clothed, attended with regularity. They had their P.T.A.'s ... Nostalgically he summed up his work among them: ... *every hour of every day was full of the joy of planning and accomplishment and if there is any keener joy it is the joy of being instrumental in the restoration and reestablishment of a deserving, appreciative people. And this joy was mine too.* The continuing poverty of the Pimas after Kneale's time, the continuing lack of integration between the economy for which Kneale had laid foundations for the Pimas and that of the world outside the reservation, would have surprised Kneale who had been working within the isolated world of the Indian Bureau and whose vision failed to penetrate, so preoccupied with his engineering problems was he, into the core of the disintegration of the people with whom he had worked.

More varied perhaps than even the Indian Service employees who worked among the Indians were the missionaries, who ranged from isolated individuals or couples with no very clear-cut sectarian identification, to directors of large missionary enterprises like the Ganado Presbyterian Mission and Hospital on the Navajo Reservation. One of the former type is described by Kneale about 1923. *There were three missionary groups operating on the Northern Navajo Reservation, two of which ran true to form, but the third was different. We had been at Shiprock but a short time when we made our first call upon the Holcombs who lived about fifty miles west of the agency. The family consisted of Miss Clara, her father and mother, and a trained nurse ...*

Where Miss Clara acquired her command of the Navajo tongue, I do not know; however, she possessed as complete an acquaintance with this language as did any white person with whom I have come in contact. This does not mean that her knowledge was comprehensive, but rather that she had gained from some source a working acquaintance with this most difficult of Indian languages.

When we knew them, they occupied two or three hogans which were rented from their Indian owners. Water was carried from a spring. For light, kerosene was used when available, otherwise candles. When both oil and candles were lacking, they were content to get along in the dark.

They had two saddle horses and Miss Clara and the nurse made regular trips covering the country surrounding their home for a radius of about twenty-five miles. Every family in this circle was known and known intimately to these two young women. They cared for the sick, endeavored to teach sanitation, hygiene, domestic science, but never for a moment forgot that the primary object of their existence was spreading the Gospel.

Indians were urged to visit them in their home, where they were introduced to washtubs, sewing machines, and many similar contrivances which the civilized women of the back country consider essential to their comfort and wellbeing. These contrivances were always available for the use of such visitors.

We both enjoyed being with the Holcombs and made it a rule to stop whenever we were in that part of the reservation. During one of these earlier visits, I asked Miss Clara what denomination she represented and was informed that she represented no denomination.

"Surely," I said, "you represent some denomination."

And the reply was the same, "We represent no organization."

"But," I insisted, "there must be someone backing you. From what source do you secure funds and supplies."

The reply was, "When we feel the need of anything, we take the matter to the Lord and leave it in His hands."

"And do you always receive the things you feel are essential?" I inquired.

"Not always," was the reply, "but when we fail to do so, we know that the things we have asked for are not necessary ..."

Small sect groups worked at conversion through more than half a century on various reservations. In 1897 the Christian Reformed Church sent Andrew Vander Wagen to Zuni as missionary. Of him another missionary of that church wrote: *Missionary Andrew Vander Wagen ... was a product of the Christian School in the Netherlands, and after coming to Grand Rapids, Michigan, he acquired further knowledge of the Christian faith . . . . The fact that his devoted helpmeet was a registered nurse, gave added reason for his appointment to the mission field . . . . He sacrificed this further training in order to go at once, as Philip, to the Desert . . . . Riding on to this Zuni of historical fame, Van, "that cowboy preacher," was deeply impressed by the missionary challenge and the manifold opportunities in this pueblo. What he saw of their religious life showed him how these Indians were sunk in paganism; but their compact community life seemed to offer a golden opportunity to contact large numbers of Indians with far less effort than was necessary to reach scattered Navajos on horseback ....Mr. Graham, the trader and storekeeper who later became Zuni's first Indian Agent, and Mrs. Matilda Coxe Stevenson, the ethnologist and writer, introduced the missionaries to the Zuni leaders. They explained how a carpenter such as the Rev. Fryling, or a farmer and stockman such as Mr. Vander Wagen, could be a great practical help to the Zuni people. Naochi, the Priest of the Bow, and chief among the leaders, listened gravely.*

"Your words have not alone entered our ears," spoke Naochi, "but they have entered our hearts. Come over and help us." Thus at last the door was open.

The Christian Reformed missionaries continued to work at Zuni and were still vigorously maintaining a school as well as mission in 1955. The Reverend C. Kuipers who worked there in the 1940's became a student of Zuni culture. He learned from the various studies made of Zuni and from his own direct and careful observation the most minute details of Zuni ceremonialism, social and economic life. He wrote in 1946 a running account of Zuni religious life during a year and described against this background the continuing work of the missionaries. His viewpoint was clearly described in this calendrical presentation of modern Zuni life. Summing up the missionary work to 1946 he wrote:

Zuni's pioneer missionary Vander Wagen, and every missionary who succeeded him, speak with conviction when they are asked about the fruits of the Gospel. Theirs is not a shallow optimism that mistakes external friendship for the transformation of men and women in Zuniland. They are convinced that God's Word never returns void because they have seen its power at work in Zuni. Admittedly, the converts were not as numerous as missionary reports elsewhere have shown; but those who withstood the tremendous pressure and resisted the diaboli-

cal cunning characteristic of a pagan pueblo, though they are few, stand out as heroes of faith. Passing these acid tests, they are the more precious jewels in the Master's crown.

At Zuni today there is no Macedonian call, "Come over and help us!" It is not like the parched land that drinks up the water of life eagerly. It is not like an empty glass which one can fill; to the contrary, it is filled already to the brim with every concoction the devil can contrive. Zuni is satisfied with its own religion. The Center of the Earth is self-centered; no missionary impulse radiates to the far reaches of the earth; nor is any religion from without, desired within.

Little wonder then that the early missionary enterprise of Catholicism was long withstood. Little wonder then that every spurt of missionary endeavor today is followed by gatherings of the council and of those who do not want the Christian way. As the Zuni ancients said they shut their blinking eyes to the radiance of the sun when they came back from the dark womb of the earth, so their children today in the clutches of the dark domain shut their eyes stubbornly to the Light of the World. In the thousands of years since the Dispersion, they have dimmed such revealed truth as they had, and interwoven it with human speculations and carnal desires into a baffling pattern of realities and distortions ...

With a full knowledge of Zuni mythology and ritual and beliefs, the Reverend Kuipers came to know precisely what his efforts to replace one religion with another were encountering. He knew the size of his task, but continued unshaken to carry it out. He gives the setting of missionary work as he understands it in the following account of a Christmas party given by one of the few Zuni converts, the Chavez family: *Mission workers for years had given the Christmas party; in 1943 the Chavez family determined to put on a party for the mission workers and friends. Christmas carols in the Zuni language never rang more joyfully.*

Of course, all the Zunis like Christmas. Before the eventful day, for weeks one hears "How many days Christmas?" After the program and the impressive services, one hears even more emphatic "Where's my Christmas?" Christmas is a time of great joy because it is present-getting time, just as the white man received the baby Jesus from the Father ...

In reality, however, Christmas for Zuni is the anti-climax of December's ceremonies. Shalako is the climax of the Zuni ceremonial year. Six masked impersonators, called the Shalako gods, come from the hills to dedicate new homes and bless the food and all native industry. Ten feet tall, wearing awesome bird-like masks with huge head-dresses, covered with conical mantles of white deerskin, these gods are the royal ambassadors between Zuni and the other gods ....

Thus Zuni prays. It prays to these gods who come from the sacred lake or other sacred shrines and thither return when their visit is concluded....It prays to the departed dead, who are now with the rainmakers....It prays to the Sun-Father, the Earth-Mother and the hosts of heaven. It prays to the idols made of wood, who are the Twin Gods of war. It prays to the Beast Gods....It prays to an untold array of fetishes, reeds, stones, concretions, effigies, masks and all that human ingenuity can contrive.

Indeed, the Zunis also pray. On the devil's loom, they have woven elaborate patterns of ceremonial expression with the warp of their own imagination and have all but covered the woof of dim revelation. But neither the outward beauty nor the pulsating rhythm can hide the void and the unrest within.

By way of summary, it may be pointed out that the programs of directed change conceived by the Anglo-Americans differed in fundamental ways from those worked out by either Spaniards or Mexicans. The important differences might be summed up by saying that the Spanish program was dynamic and geared to the changing character of a frontier area, while the Anglo-American program tended to be essentially static. There was never any real uncertainty among Spaniards, including the missionaries, that the mission communities were training grounds for Indians and would give way in due course to the usual Spanish town under ministration of the secular clergy. There were clashes between missionaries and civil authorities over the suitable moment for effecting the transition, but the transitional character of the total situation was not in doubt. The reservations in the United States, on the other hand, were set up without time limit. Each was provided with an administrative organization the length of life of which was never defined as a part of official policy. There were no built-in features of the reservation program which emphasized anything but permanency. The effect was the growth of a sense of permanence regarding the status of Indians in relation to the dominant people such as never developed under colonial Spain. In Mexico there was a strong tendency to pursue the course of dynamic integration defined by Spain, accompanied by refusal to establish any institution really the equivalent of the United States reservation. The Yaqui indigenous area appeared superficially to resemble the reservation, but its administrative organization and hence its integration into the national whole was totally different. The static character of the official Anglo-American program was an important source of conflict and insecurity for Indians as Anglo-American society continued to expand rapidly around and into the reservation.

PART III

THE RESULTS OF CONTACT:
THE COURSE OF CULTURAL CHANGE

CHAPTER FOURTEEN

Political Incorporation

EACH OF THE PROGRAMS for civilization — Spanish, Mexican, and Anglo-American — aimed eventually at making Indians a part of a modern nation. Each sought to bring Indians into the position of citizens with the same rights and obligations as other citizens of Spain, Mexico, or the United States. It is true that neither Spain nor the United States immediately conferred full citizenship status; Spain instead provided for a transitional period during which Indians were to learn the rudiments of "civilized" behavior; the United States began her program with no clear conception of moulding Indians to fit into American citizenship patterns. Nevertheless Spain had as her ultimate ideal the participation of all Indians equally with non-Indians as taxpayers, as soldiers, and as sharers in the benefits of heaven and of the peace on earth which she proposed to enforce. The United States only after some seventy years of administration in the Southwest evolved a policy of citizenship for Indians. Mexico, building on the Spanish experience, was the only one of the three nations which began with a program of immediate Indian citizenship. What Mexico wrote into her national and state constitutions in the 1820's in regard to full and equal participation of Indians in the national political life expressed what Spain had aimed at for three hundred years, and what the United States ultimately wrote into law in 1924.

In view of these aims it was a striking fact that four centuries after the beginning of the conquest the great majority of the Indians did not function as full citizens of the nations by whom they had been dominated. Two or three groups in Mexico lived in communities which were fully functioning parts of the state organization, but the others could not be said to have accepted modern Mexican forms of political organization. In the United States every one of the Indian groups, where they lived on reservations, existed in a special political status which set them apart from all the other United States citizens among whom they lived.

If Spain, Mexico, and the United States had such definite aims with regard to Indian citizenship, we may legitimately ask why they were not realized after so long a period. Why did Indians not quickly accept the proffered citizenship? Were they incapable, as Bancroft the historian and others have maintained, of civilization in this sense? Were they, in other words, inherent barbarians? If not, what characteristics of the conquerors or of their approach to the Indians resulted in the failure to transform Indian political life? What forces were generated in the societies of the conquerors which led them to suspend the processes of political assimilation brought to bear on thousands of immigrants who assumed citizenship in the United States and Mexico? With such questions as these in mind we may reconsider the political history of the Indians from the time of their first contacts with the Spaniards.

STARTING POINTS

The change that was demanded of the Indians was a tremendous one. It was the change which Sir Henry Maine regarded as the most crucial in the growth of civilization — the shift from a family and kinship dominated society to the impersonally organized state with its legions of kin-detached citizens. Of more fundamental importance, in Maine's eyes, than even the invention of writing, the transformation of the family-involved and family-oriented person into the nation-focused individual of immensely wider loyalties has been the foundation on which civilization has grown. The emergence of the citizen out of the kinsman has made possible the wide integrations of people on which the most complex developments in the division of social labor have depended.

As Maine knew, this shift in the basis of societies was nowhere accomplished as a sudden and single step. The nationalism of the countries of Europe at the time of the conquest of North America had been growing for centuries. It had evolved out of the priest-king irrigation empires of the eastern Mediterranean, the city-states of Greece and Ionia, the world-conquest state of Rome, the feudal baronies of western Europe. Slowly, as one type of organization succeeded another, a heritage of custom and law accumulated, aided by the use of writing, until it was possible by the time of Coronado and Bartolomé de las Casas to speak of the subjects of a king as citizens, with loyalty to a man personally unknown being recognized as more compelling than loyalty to one's own father or brother. The nations of Europe at the time of the conquest of Mexico were built, more or less solidly, on the idea of citizenship, which had evolved as far in Europe as anywhere else in the world. It was this idea and the kind of social organization which embodied it that the Spaniards proposed to introduce among the Indians.

What to the Spaniards seemed a simple, obvious, and right way of behaving was something totally new to the Indians of northwestern New Spain. It had no links with anything in their experience. Kingship, royal possession of great stretches of territory, absolute power to command any person, payment of tribute — such things were not known to the Indians even approximately from their own way of life or even from neighbors with whom they traded. Even with the help of the Tlaxcalans who accompanied the first Spanish colonists to New Mexico, it is doubtful that Pueblo Indians could imagine such conditions very clearly, let alone accept them for the orientation of their lives. The world in which they lived had no points of reference for such an arrangement of human relations. The fact of a bloody conquest, like Coronado's, by a captain of the king could indeed be understood and accepted, but the changes for which the captain asked presupposed a wholly different order of society.

As it turned out on the far frontier, that new order could not readily be imposed. Instead, the old order absorbed a few titles, a few phrases, and the commands to act in certain ways which the king's representatives required. The fundamentals of the old order persisted within the new framework. The old forms of government changed slowly and often in only superficial ways. Moreover, they did not change in the same way from tribe to tribe.

THE NATIVE POLITICAL SYSTEMS — At the time of the first *entradas*, this old order was by no means uniform throughout northwestern New Spain, but there was nevertheless a common viewpoint regarding government. Whether among the village, the ranchería, or the band peoples, government rested on a foundation of a few common principles. These principles, which the tribes shared, contrasted fundamentally with those on which Spanish governmental conceptions were founded. All tribes, for example, lacked anything approaching the idea or the actuality of an hereditary ruler; leadership roles were conferred by the community on individuals who demonstrated various kinds of abilities or who attained certain ages. The principles of inheritance and leadership were generally kept separate. Further, the idea of absolute power to command as vested in a European king, that is, in a single person, was absent from the Indian societies. The very idea of command itself was not well developed, since common action rested rather on spontaneous common feelings generated in the small communities. There had never been in the region any conquest, in the European sense, of one tribe by another. There had been competition for land and fights for possession, as in central and southern Sonora where Opatas, Yaquis, and Pimas developed conflicting interests, but the results of armed conflict in such cases never involved the political subjection of the defeated group; they merely fled. No political mechanisms for domination had been developed.

Even in cases in which the people of one tribe, such as the Maricopas, were driven from their territory and were able to persuade another tribe to let them use surplus lands, as the Maricopas persuaded the Gila Pimas, the relationship was not one of political domination. It was rather an alliance involving many cooperative activities, but the communities of the respective tribes maintained their customary political autonomy. For some, intertribal conflicts and expansion, as possibly among Cahitan tribes like the Mayos and Yaquis, may have been generating new political forms, but up to the arrival of the Spaniards military victory meant merely spoils, not the establishment of control over alien peoples. Northwestern New Spain was a region of atomic communities, separate and independent of one another even when their members spoke the same language, believed in the same gods, and maintained the same forms of government.

Despite such a basic and general likeness in the framework of government, there were important differences. It would not be easy to understand the effects of Spanish contacts on Indian political life without some knowledge of the range in

governmental forms which characterized the Indians at the beginning of the
Spanish conquest. There was a wide range in the degree of complexity and elaboration of the basic institutions, with the extremes represented in the Eastern Pueblo
villages and the Seri food-gathering bands. Most of the people with whom the
Spaniards had to deal represented an intermediate degree of complexity; they
were the ranchería-dwelling peoples of the desert riverlands and the high mountains, who numbered probably one hundred fifty thousand at the beginning of
their intensive contacts with the Spaniards. Among them were the Tarahumaras
of what is modern Chihuahua, the Cahitan-speaking Yaquis and Mayos of southern
Sonora, the Opatas of central Sonora, the Piman-speaking peoples ranging from the
mountains of Chihuahua to the desert lowlands along the Gila River, and the
Yuman-speaking peoples of the lower Colorado River.

Fundamental in the constitution of the rancherías was the recognition of peace
and war conditions as sharply distinct realms, and the organization for each as
necessarily separate. The peace organization of the ranchería ranged from an
extremely simple form among the Tarahumaras through a scarcely less simple
form among Upper Pimans and river Yumans to one of some complexity among
Opata's, Mayos, and Yaquis. The rapid fusion after contact with Spanish forms so
transformed the governments of all but Upper Pimas and river Yumans that we
know them only through ethnological reconstruction. Basic to ranchería organization was the recognition of one man as the moral leader of the group; it is possible
that some rancherías recognized a group rather than a single individual. Among
the Yumas they were called *kwoxot*, among the Tarahumaras *seligame*, among the
Upper Pimas *junjukshim*, and among the Yaquis probably *susuakame*. Such a man
gained recognition through stability of character and speaking ability. His status
as leader rested in part on his personal ability to command attention when he
spoke, but this was in turn based on his capacity for learning and repeating the
phrases which his people regarded as proper and wise and which constituted a
body of traditional knowledge of the truth. The office was not hereditary in principle, although sons or other relatives sometimes succeeded their fathers because
of their opportunities for learning the prescribed behavior. A man who achieved
the status held it for as long as the people would listen to him, normally from
perhaps the age of forty or older until his death, or until he became senile. A successor to a recognized leader assumed the title by general recognition, sometimes
by a more formal process of acclamation in a public meeting. Probably each ranchería had such a moral leader, but also there were men whose leadership was
recognized beyond their own rancherías and who, as among the Yumas, were
looked to for advice and wisdom by people over a wide area.

A moral leader was in no sense an executive or commander. He was a repository of wisdom and a source of the group's well-being. He was looked to in the
routine of living as one who ordered peoples' lives by constantly giving them,
sometimes in nightly meetings as among the Upper Pimas, the traditional words
confirming their family relationships and the morality of their interfamily relations.
In disputes over land use or personal injury he was a judge who pointed out what
was right but had no power to punish or penalize. If things went wrong he might

be looked to for advice as to the course of action, although his advice might merely point the way to the right appeal to the supernaturals, the actual ritual being prescribed by some specialist. Although he was sometimes possessed of special supernatural powers, he was not necessarily such a specialist. He was above all the recognized master of moral exhortation, the preacher who kept before people the right course of action.

Over and over again, in endless repetition, he told people how they should behave and stated for them the mythological sanctions for their behavior. In this sense he was a major source of the group's well-being, embodying the traditions by which they lived and from which they derived security. As such he was sometimes in himself a semi-sacred thing — among the Yumas, for example — and was protected from death or injury in time of war. He was surrounded by ritual and his discourses were sacred, even though outside of public meeting he dressed like everyone else and cultivated his fields and lived like the usual family man. Moreover, the moral exhortation at which he was the recognized adept was not his exclusive prerogative. Every father of a family also practiced it, at least at home in the evenings when his children were going to sleep, and many who spoke well joined in in public meetings with the community leader, echoing and adding to the group's wisdom.

As one among equals, the moral leader of the community thus had no authority in an executive sense. His authority as a spokesman of the right way of living depended on his saying what everyone knew was right, not on esoteric or special knowledge. Authority to force anyone to behave in accordance with the right was nonexistent. When people listened, they then knew what was right. It was, as modern Pima usage has it, then "up to them" to do what was right. The moral sanctions of community life, voiced and made applicable to the present instance, brought conformity; a command by the leader would have been meaningless. In a public meeting a course of action was stated and repeated, a way laid out, until all the men present, normally all the men of the ranchería, could see its wisdom. The rest depended on the cohesion and solidarity of the community; if it was strong the ranchería acted in unison. Thus the sense of well-being of the community depended not on power to command by the leader, but on unanimity of feeling in the group in the light of the leader's words.

The moral leader acted as one of a group in the community house of the ranchería. There was no such thing as an independent decision by him. He had officers to help him in his work of leadership. He had messengers, or "legs"; he had a "voice," that is, a town crier, who announced meetings and who sometimes repeated decisions of the community council; he had other formal helpers charged with special jobs, such as the organization of work on irrigation ditches or the keeping up of the community house. Probably these other officials were appointed by him, but his appointments were often not final until the people of the ranchería had approved by general acclaim. These groups of officials, where they existed in the large rancherías, did not constitute a ruling group. They were, like the headman, spokesmen and servants of the people. What they did was decided in general meetings to which the men, and sometimes women, of the ranchería came. The active participants in these gatherings were the older people, usually men over forty; each man of such age could speak in the meeting. The decisions of the community were formulated, in the light of the wisdom of the headman, in the meetings. When a meeting was over the formal business of government on the points considered was over. What organization was needed, as in public works, was traditional and each man's role was well known. Commands were not necessary, although smaller meetings on specific matters by the responsible groups might be held.

In such a form of government no individual emerged as a functioning part of it until he was an "elder," that is, a man of long experience in the community. No set age for participation existed, but it was probably rare for any individual under thirty-five to dare to say anything in the community council. Once he reached the age for such participation, he was well versed and strongly conditioned in the traditional ways. He had listened for years to the moral exhortations of the older members of his household and when he began to sit in the council he heard these again for years, in fuller form, from the headman and the elders, until he himself felt ready to voice them in the community house. Thus, an individual did not function as a subject loyal to the interest of a commander, working for those interests against competing ones, nor yet as a citizen feeling the right to speak for his own interests. He functioned rather as an interpreter to others of the unalterable right path which he had spent long years learning to follow and which he knew was laid out by the supernatural powers in whose hands the community's welfare lay.

One activity of community government which was of special importance in the larger rancherías, as among the Mayos, Yaquis, and Opatas, was that of managing the land. Disputes arose over boundaries, especially where river overflow obliterated boundaries from one year to the next as in most of the ranchería communities. There were formal ways to settle these, such as pushing contests. Sometimes the families involved simply went ahead and settled disputes in one or another of these traditional ways. Sometimes the whole community had to make a decision as to who was right, because the families were not satisfied. Land was a matter of great importance for the whole ranchería and as such was handled by the whole group. The community council, working as always in the light of the wisdom of the moral leader, settled disputes and assigned land when people asked for it. The principles involved were simple ones of family need and prior use. There was no ownership of land; if a family group did not work land continuously, it was assigned to someone who needed it. Long-continued use of a particular piece of land indicated family need for it; it could not be appropriated by another family. The general principle of land use was family proprietorship within the pattern of needs of all the families. The landholding unit was, first, the whole ranchería and, second, family groups within the ranchería; an individual was never regarded as a distinct entity apart from his family group.

Among ranchería people generally, back of these concepts of landholding, lay broader ones, which made some contribution to tribal feeling. The river Yumans had long myths, epic cycles, which told of the travels of Mastamxo and other supernatural beings through areas which the given tribe — Yuma, Mohave, Cocopa —

claimed as its own. The myths described in detail various landmarks and important mythological events which had occurred at these spots. The myth cycles thus defined a tribal territory, and the various groups of rancherías had myths also which told how their particular ancestors or supernatural descendants of the great gods established their territory within the tribal whole. The Pimas had long myths describing the very creation of their territory at the beginning of things and the adventures of various supernaturals at specific points within the territory; their mythology included a great flood, destruction of a succession of races, and the ultimate peopling of their territory by the Pimas. The Mayos and Yaquis similarly had a myth of a flood, and the saving of ancestral supernaturals on particular peaks in the Mayo and Yaqui River region. Like the Yumans, they also had myths describing the adventures of great supernatural beings who traveled about the country after the flood and performed miraculous deeds at specific places.

Such myths were one of the bases of the sense of tribal identity, but they were more than that. They defined a relationship between people and land. In their geographical details they showed how the tribe was rooted in a very specific locality. These roots were implanted and fixed by higher beings than men. They had existed from the beginning and could not be conceived as alterable by men, since gods had decreed them. Thus the people and the land were associated forever in an indissoluble sacred relationship. The councils of the rancherías were not thought of as making new legislation or planning for an unpredictable future; they were rather conceived as maintaining in the unchanging traditional way what had been decreed for eternity.

One important characteristic which marked most ranchería peoples was a strong sense of tribal identity. The Cahitan-speaking Yaquis and Mayos exhibited both the strongest and most widely extended tribal feeling. All the rancherías of the thirty thousand Yaquis and all those of the twenty-five thousand Mayos were capable of united action in war. From what is known of Yaqui history, it appears that threat to the tribal territory could most readily call forth the tribal feeling and mobilize it for common action. The Mayos had a word, *yoreme* or *yoremia,* which designated all those who felt the obligation to protect the tribal land; the Yaquis also had the concept expressed in a similar word, *yoeme.* These were actually tribal names, symbols of their unity and of their distinctiveness from all other peoples. Similarly, the Yuman-speaking people of the Colorado River Valley had a strong tribal sense; the Cocopas, the Yumas, the Maricopas, and the Mohaves had terms which included members of all their rancherías. Like the Cahitans, each of these tribes intermittently organized as a whole for defensive or offensive purposes against their neighbors. While the tribal sense was at least equally as strong as among Yaquis or Mayos, it was not so widely extended; none of the Yuman tribes consisted of more than three or four thousand people.

The other ranchería peoples were characterized by a considerably narrower tribal sense at the time of the entry of the Spaniards. The Opata-speaking peoples of central Sonora were often at war among themselves. Groups of rancherías, such as those under Sisibotari in the vicinity of Saguaripa or the Bacerac group in the Bavispe Valley, made common cause over the possession of salt beds and fought neighboring Opatas for possession, but the extent of any such emergency unions seems not to have gone beyond a few dozen rancherías. There were eight or nine such subtribal divisions among the Opatas during the early colonial period; there is considerably less indication in the Spanish records of tribal feeling and solidarity, even within these small groupings, than among the Yaquis, Mayos, or river Yuman tribes. Tribal feeling seems to have been of a similar nature among the Lower and the Upper Pimas. Although there were some influential leaders among them, such as the Upper Pima Coro, Soba, and others, the influence of such men extended only to a few hundred persons. It would appear that tribal feeling was of even narrower extent than among the Opatas, and it is doubtful that it should be spoken of as tribal identity at all. It was, rather, a locality feeling which often caused a division within the common language group. Such division within the tribe, or language group, seems to have been even more pronounced among the Tarahumaras, where only very small groups of rancherías seem usually to have felt common cause or shared a feeling of group identity.

Where tribal feeling was strongest and widest in scope — among the Mayos, Yaquis, and river Yumans — warfare was of fairly frequent occurrence at the time of the coming of the Spaniards. Warfare was by no means unknown to the Opatas, Pimas, and Tarahumaras, but there was less in the way of formal organization for fighting, and it appears to have been less of a focus of cultural interest. Probably the institutionalization of warfare had something to do with the different intensities of tribal feeling which existed.

It was chiefly in response to the needs of warfare that any wider organization than that of the single ranchería developed. There were recurring common enterprises, such as inter-ranchería games or ceremonies, in which neighboring settlements cooperated. These were managed in the same way as internal affairs, by common agreement among elders from two or more rancherías in the light of the wisdom of the headmen. It was for purposes of offense or defense, however, that the widest organizations of rancherías took place. In the organization for war, the peacetime government was normally without function, and even tended to be ignored entirely by those who organized the fighting. This was to be expected, for one did not go to war with people who lived in accordance with the moral order of one's own ranchería; one went to war with people who were strangers quite outside that order.

Few ranchería headmen were ever leaders in war. A person did not shift automatically from the role of peace leader to war leader when war broke out. In fact, for the moral leader to have assumed military command would have been regarded as endangering the well-being of the community. What happened was that a different leadership sprang up, usually of a younger age group. Those who took command were recognized war leaders who had proved themselves in battle as brave and capable, or shamans practiced in war magic. The latter were men who had demonstrated ability to predict favorable times for attack, or had shown that they were able to weaken the enemy through magical means. The best combination for a war leader was bravery and effective magic. Men who possessed these qualities did not need to be elected or specially chosen; they were known. They might live for months or years as ordinary persons without expressing themselves in council, but when they wanted to raise a war party or when an attack came, they assumed leadership promptly and, sometimes against the urgings of the headman, proceeded to lead the fighting men.

As leaders in activities that required speedily formulated plans and movements, they commanded. Thus they were leaders of a totally different type from the ranchería headman and his associated assistants and elders. In the smaller rancherías and among those in which fighting was an occasional activity, as for most of the Upper Pimas and most of the Tarahumaras, the war leader was a temporary official without special status except during actual crises of attack or defense. Among the river Yumans and probably the Opatas, the war leaders fought often enough to give them a continuing recognition in times of peace, but it is doubtful that they functioned as officials in the rancherías in any way. On the other hand, there is an indication that among the Mayos and Yaquis, and possibly some Opatas, the war leaders headed an organization of warriors, which existed with important ritual and other functions during peace times and which was integrated in some ways with the peace organization of the rancherías. There was thus for these large rancherías a military arm of government, whether war was in progress or not, which functioned jointly with the peacetime arm of government.

In summary, the ranchería system of government organized moral leadership in peace and executive leadership in war as separate functions. These functions were kept separate with distinct personnel assuming responsibility in each. The moral leadership included the judgment of right and wrong in disputes between family groups and in the management of land, but not the punishment of offenders against the moral law, such punishment being left to the supernaturals and the criticism of the community. Ranchería government included a wide range of formal variations from the simplicity of perhaps a single headman in Tarahumara and some of the Yuman communities, to the complexity of several official statuses in the large communities of the Opatas, Mayos, and Yaquis. Procedures in choice of officials, rules of deliberation, and methods of decision were democratic in the sense of giving at least all older men a voice. Decision by authority from above or by majority rule was unknown; unanimity of feeling as revealed in discussion was the only acceptable basis for action by a ranchería. Unanimity did not necessarily prevail, however, under conditions of war, when experienced military leaders took command.

In the north the compact villages of the Pueblos maintained forms of government which were basically like those of the ranchería peoples. They were, however, very much more complex than even those of the large rancherías of the Mayos and Yaquis. They exhibited such a degree of elaboration of governmental principles found in the rancherías that they may justifiably be considered as a distinct type. There was far greater uniformity in the northern villages compared with the wide range from simple to complex found in the rancherías. The total population of the northern villages was somewhere between forty and fifty thousand — barely one-third the number living in ranchería-type communities at the time of the entrance of the Spaniards.

The fundamental concept of the division of labor in government was the same in the Pueblo villages as in the rancherías. The peacetime yearly round of activities was regarded as part of a moral order, supernaturally decreed and sanctioned, and requiring for direction a single individual set apart from other people. Such village heads among the Eastern Pueblos came to be called by the Spaniards *caciques,* a term introduced into New Spain from a West Indian language. Each village had its own name in its own language for this official, although Spaniards never learned them. At the same time, whether war was going on or not, each village also had a military arm of government with a War Priest as its head. This branch, as in the larger rancherías, was closely interlocked in its functions with the other aspect of village organization. Like the rancherías also, the affairs of a village were subject to discussion in a community council where unanimity was developed and was the basis of any action. Villages rarely united with one another temporarily for purposes of war; aside from such occasional arrangements every village was an autonomous social unit. It is not indicated that a sense of tribal identity existed on the scale that characterized the rancherías of the Mayos and Yaquis; nor was there a unity of any linguistically-close groups of villages strong enough to lead them to conduct campaigns against other tribes as a unit in the manner of the river Yuman rancherías. The Eastern Pueblos seem in fact to have limited their feelings of common purpose solely to the village unit; the villages of the same language group seem often to have been at war with one another. On the other hand, the several villages using a common language among the Western Pueblos possessed a sense of tribal identity and were capable of united action, at least for defense; thus the Zunis and the Hopis, each numbering in the neighborhood of three to four thousand divided into six or more villages, were distinguished from the Eastern Pueblos by possession of a sense of tribal identity and more capability of unity of action among villages.

More is known about the nature of Pueblo government than about the ranchería organization because it has been more resistant to Spanish influence, preserving more of its aboriginal features into the present. It may be that the greater amount of information makes it appear more complex and more elaborately organized, but it seems likely that it actually did consist of offices and activities which were specialized and elaborated considerably beyond those of even the more complex ranchería type of government. At any rate, the data available reveal a high degree of formality and organization as compared with any ranchería government described by the Spaniards.

The peace leader among all the Pueblos, except the Zunis, was the dominant power in every village in the sense that he was regarded as maintaining the welfare of the whole community. He did this not by commanding people to follow a code of law, but by leading a life of more strict ritual observance than anyone else in the village. He rigorously prayed for the village; he fasted and observed other taboos on behalf of the village. He was, in fact, so devoted in his own life to the observance of the traditional rituals that he was somewhat removed from the routine of village life. Others worked his fields for him, at least in part, so that he could devote his time to retreat and prayer. His functions seem to have been far more concerned with the annual round of religious ceremony than were those of the headman of a ranchería, and consequently moral exhortation was a relatively minor activity. The cacique, as the Spaniards called this functionary, achieved office by general agreement of the village and after long service as first assistant to a predecessor cacique. The basis of selection was membership in a particular ceremonial society and extensive knowledge of the whole round of annual ceremony. A cacique held office for life. Other village officials held office by virtue of appointment by the cacique.

The cacique was the head of a village on the basis of being the person best able to manage the relations of the people and the supernaturals in whom they believed. The decisions in regard to when and precisely how to give the large number of ceremonies for rain, growth, and general welfare came from him. But he did not carry on this work as an individual with sole or absolute authority to decide ceremonial affairs. He was merely the most respected (and most specialized) one of a group of ceremonial leaders. The religious life of a village was carried on by a number of organized societies, each of which controlled, or possessed, particular supernatural powers. Some societies dealt with rain and weather power, others with curing of disease, others with fertility, and so on. The heads of these societies, either the oldest members or those with longest membership, constituted a council which, together with the cacique and his assistants, deliberated on and planned the whole religious life of the village. Since these activities were a major focus of interest and since they consumed a very large amount of time of the people, the council of ceremonial leaders was the most important governmental body in a village. The primary function of government seemed to the people to be the maintenance of proper ritual relations with the supernaturals. It was in the ordering of these relations, that is, in the maintaining of long-since-divinely-revealed ways of behavior, that the cacique served as the unifying symbol and focusing authority.

Like the headman of a ranchería, the cacique was never an executive, although orders to carry out ceremonies or to do various things were frequently spoken of as his judgment. Executive action came from another branch of government, well recognized in most of the Pueblo villages. The major figure here was a War Priest. Probably all the Pueblo villages had, in addition to the dozen or more ceremonial societies mentioned, a warrior society which controlled the supernatural powers necessary in making successful war and also powers for the ritual purification which war required. The War Priest, in various forms in different villages, headed such a society and participated in the religious councils along with other society leaders. At Zuni, which had no cacique, he was the dominant authority. Usually a village had two other functionaries, believed to embody the powers of the Twin War Gods, important figures in Pueblo mythology. These men, not always members of the warrior society, were the executive leaders of a village. Chosen by general acclaim and appointed by the cacique not for life, but for indefinite periods so long as their behavior suited the people, they had several functions. They probably carried out what few police duties were necessary, including the finding and execution of witches when such were believed to be working harm in the village; they executed the decisions of the council and cacique in regard to the carrying out of ceremonies; and probably they assumed whatever executive duties were required in organizing any communal work such as maintenance of irrigation works. These were their peacetime functions. In case of war, they commanded the military parties with the help of other members of the warrior society, usually having gained their status originally as successful warriors.

The two branches of government functioned together, with a large number of officers for carrying messages, making announcements, and performing special duties in regard to the ceremonial activities. They functioned as the organizational nucleus of general village councils which met whenever necessary to decide disputes between family groups, to deal with details of the management of the land, and to decide on general courses of action, outside of ceremony, for the village as a whole. The cacique's branch of government was thought of as an "inside" organization concerned with the continuing welfare of the village, the War Chief's branch as an "outside" organization concerned with relations of the village to other villages. It is clear however, that the "outside" functions were only a part of the latter's duties. They actually had much to do with internal affairs. In general village councils all older men, as in the rancherías, had a voice.

A major basis of village unity was the conception of divinely ordained relation to the land which the people of the village customarily used. The myths giving sanction to this relationship differed somewhat from those of the ranchería people. The usual Pueblo myth was one recounting an emergence from an underworld, with subsequent wandering by the people in a search for the middle place. Once found and recognized as the middle of the world, this became the proper place for the people to live and farm. Among the Hopis the land was established as belonging to the first clan group to arrive at the designated spot, later-arriving clans holding their land by virtue of assignment through the first clan. Among the Zuni and Eastern Pueblos it was the village, or group of villages, which was divinely ordained to hold and work the land. On the whole, with the exception of the Hopis and Zunis, the Pueblos' conception of their relation to the land was less fixed and unalterable than that of the ranchería peoples, involving as it did myth and legends recounting migrations and earlier settlement at different places.

The organization of the people living in bands of more roving character was surprisingly like that of the villages and rancherías in fundamental outline. It was, of course, much simpler and less formal, and differed in some important respects. One difference was in the smaller size of the groups involved. While the villages and rancherías rarely consisted of fewer than one hundred people at their smallest and ranged as high as two thousand, the bands ranged in size from fifty or even fewer to not more than two or three hundred persons. There is no way of knowing, unless archeology ultimately discloses it, how many inhabitants of the region of northwestern New Spain actually lived under band types of organization at the time the Spaniards appeared. The Spanish contacts with them were relatively slight, especially during the 1500's and early 1600's; many of them were probably in process of migration at the time into the region; and of course censuses or even good estimates such as the Spaniards carried out for the more settled people were not possible. It seems very probable that those who later came to be known as Navajos could not have numbered above a few thousand. The Athapaskans — Navajos as well as the various Apaches eastern and western — were in process of movement and probably of augmentation of their numbers by absorption of other peoples during the whole first three hundred years of their contacts with the Spaniards. Since they did not number above five or six thousand by the middle 1800's, it would seem highly improbable that they numbered more than that in the 1500's. The highland Yumans — Yavapais, Walapais, and Havasupais — must have been even fewer, possibly not over three thousand. The Seris have been estimated as high as three thousand during the Spanish colonial period. Recognizing all of these figures as pure guesses, they may nevertheless be taken as an indication of the maximum number of people organized in band fashion — no more than twelve thousand at the very most. The people of the bands, then, constituted less than a third of the number of those living in villages and made up less than one-tenth of all the inhabitants of the region of northwestern New Spain which we have under consideration.

The Navajo, Apache, and Yuman bands were all loosely organized, but not so loosely as the Seris. The Navajo band consisted of some ten to forty families who made use of the few and scattered patches of land in a given area which could be used for the rudimentary agriculture which they practiced. Each such band group was independent of others who occupied neighboring territory. There was no tribal organization whatsoever and it was rare for two or more bands to cooperate on any activity such as even a military raid. The leadership of these small independent bands was on the same twofold basis which we have noted for the villages and rancherías — a peace and a war leadership with separate personnel for each. The peace leader — the term *natani* was used for both peace and war leaders — was chosen in what amounted to a competitive manner. Any man or woman of the band membership was eligible, hereditary right to the office not being recognized. A candidate had to know at least one ceremony — the Blessing Way — but ordinarily had more of the traditional chants at his disposal. A meeting of the men and women of the band was sometimes held to choose a natani especially when there were two or more candidates. Any individual considered was already well known and a person who had demonstrated himself or herself as good, wise, and ceremonially capable in the traditional ways. If there were competition for the office, the decision was made on the basis of speeches by the candidates in the meeting. A peace leader held the office for life, or until unable to fulfill the duties of leadership.

Unlike those of village and ranchería, the peace leader of a band was less a symbol of the welfare of the group than an actual administrator and judge. He directed agricultural activities and judged in disputes between families. He had the responsibility of taking care of poor families, such as those of widows. He was also the representative of the band in any dealings with other bands. His powers in these activities were simply those of a person who commanded respect; he had no recognized power to force anyone to do anything that he advocated. No regular schedule of community meetings existed, but all older men and women had a voice in gatherings called for particular purposes.

Quite apart from the peace leadership of a band, and sometimes at complete odds with it, was the war leadership. A war leader was any member of the band who possessed recognized supernatural power for successful military enterprise.

Any man who knew the war ceremonials could become a war leader and organize
a raiding party. Such men organized war parties when they wanted to and when
they could persuade followers to join them. They were, in other words, self-ap-
pointed and although a successful war leader might attain strong influence within
his band and also with neighboring bands, he was not recognized as an official
in the routine band government.

The various Apache tribes had a similar simple form of band organization,
with the same separation of peace and war functions, as did also the upland Yumans. The Seris, on the other hand, possessed an even simpler form. It is doubtful
that they recognized so clearly a single person as band leader, or that they carried
on enough warfare to have had any specialists in war leadership. A Seri band
consisted of five to twenty or thirty families who habitually traveled over the same
area fishing and hunting together. Leadership depended on individual abilities,
as hunter, fisherman, or ritual specialist. Perhaps one or more individuals were
regarded as wiser or having stronger power than others and were listened to accordingly, but there is no evidence for formal recognition of the status of headman.

Tribal identity for all the band groups developed only under the stresses of
contacts with Europeans and with other Indians after the entry of the Spaniards.
It is difficult to say what the nature of it was in the 1500's when these contacts
began. It was probably little more than a generalized sense of common origins
with neighboring band groups who spoke the same dialects. The Navajos used
the word *Dineh* as a general designation for all who spoke the Navajo language,
but there is no early data to indicate how widely a given band of Navajos extended
a sense of common identity. They certainly extended it to all bands speaking
Navajo with whom they came in contact, but tribal feeling of the type that was
found among the river Yumans, the Mayos, the Yaquis, or even the Hopis with a
clear conception of geographical location and population limits, certainly did not
exist. Probably it was the same in the case of the different Apache groups — a
vague sense for each band of language and custom affinity with neighboring bands,
but no clear placement of all Apache-speaking bands in an actual world of intertribal relations. The upland Yumans had a clearer conception of territorial and
population limits, as did possibly also the Seris. They had names which were
tribally extended, across even dialect groups, and had lived for a longer time in
the territories where the Spaniards found them.

CONTRASTS WITH SPANISH GOVERNMENT — It was such an atomistic world of politically separate communities which the Spaniards proposed to incorporate into the
Spanish Empire. They undertook the task of linking into a single organization and
implanting a sense of unity and common loyalty in several thousand communities
of sharply different language and customs. In Europe the building of nations had
proceeded on centuries of common experience of Roman conquest institutions and
the feudal system of loyalty. In central and southern Mexico the Spanish conquest
institutions could be built on the foundations of the priest-king hierarchies of the
Mayas and Zapotecs and the tributary town organization of the Aztecs. But in the
north, although the numbers of people were vastly fewer, no such intermediate

forms of political organization had ever developed. The task of the Spaniards in accomplishing their aim was therefore of a very different order.

The Spaniards undertook the task with no study of the native institutions of government, and on the basis of assumptions that the Indians either had no such institutions at all, or that whatever they might have were simply primitive versions of their own. Both assumptions, of course, were wide of the mark, especially for the village and ranchería people who constituted the overwhelming majority of all the Indians in the region. What the Spaniards proposed was, from their point of view, simple enough. They wanted the Indians to recognize the King of Spain as proprietor of all the land in the region and the source of all authority there. They wanted the Indians to accept a simple form of local government in which Indian governors, sheriffs, captains, and judges would, with the help of similar, but higher ranked, officers of the king enforce Spanish law and order. They wanted the Indians to accept Catholic missionaries as their moral and spiritual leaders. This was the substance of the new order which the Spaniards tried to impose — a simple enough program when viewed from the standpoint of a Spaniard who knew no other way of organizing affairs and assumed that the absence of such an organization meant the absence of all organization.

However, when viewed from the standpoint of a person living in one of the atomistic communities of northwestern New Spain about 1600, the changes proposed involved a profound revolution not only in the relations among men, but also in their relations with their economic base, the land, and with the supernaturals who they believed controlled their lives. It is unlikely, of course, that any Indian saw clearly the implications of the changes proposed in all their revolutionary meaning. The habit of comparative analysis of institutions was no better developed among Indians than among Spaniards. Nevertheless, the story of Indian reactions to the changes shows clearly how impossible it was for any one of the communities to change with the rapidity which the Spaniards seemed to expect. The acceptance of a new framework for community life was not all that was involved; the Spanish form of government rested on a wholly different system of religious belief and human relations. The remaking of a way of life which was called for could not take place in ten or fifty years, unless the human communities were completely uprooted and torn apart — and this it was not in the interest of the Spaniards to do in the north as they had in the south of New Spain.

What the Spaniards were proposing was a complete shift in the basis of human relations. Even if the proposed political changes are considered alone, apart from the religious transformation of which the missionaries were dreaming, it is quite clear that a whole new world view would have been necessary as a foundation for the shift in human relations involved. Let us look more specifically at what the Spaniards were asking. In the first place, they asked that the Indians look at the familiar fields, mountains, and hunting grounds as somehow being the possession of a remote person who was spoken of by Spaniards as unique and powerful, but nevertheless a man. This was revolutionary to people who thought of their land as being possessed by themselves through an arrangement ordained by the highest supernatural power. To them the use of land was not so much a right as a duty in fulfilling obligations to this supernatural power. Against this background of belief the new Spanish dispensation might be regarded either as an unholy usurpation, or it might be interpreted as a new development in the supernatural world, the King of Spain being an important new supernatural of whom they had not heard until now; as we shall see both these interpretations were employed by different tribes at different times. Both sprang out of the concept of a sacred relationship between people and the particular locality which they inhabited, a relationship resulting in intricate and holy identification of men with locality and locality with men. What the Spanish asked in this connection in the way of overt behavior, such as permitting a Spanish capital to be built at San Juan on the Rio Grande, was readily submitted to under coercion, but submission was not accompanied by simple erasure of beliefs about the sacred land arrangements which had existed from the beginnings of creation.

In the second place, the Spaniards asked that the Indians recognize obligations to work and fight for a man whom they had never seen, who lived at a vast remove from their community, and who proposed to do nothing in return except "protect" the Indians from their neighbors. For the most part, at least among the band and ranchería Indians, military protection from neighbors was of no great interest. Fighting was generally carried on among them for purposes of acquiring supernatural power believed to be necessary for their community welfare or for the pleasure and excitement of the fighting. The village people, too, shared this view of the small-scale military activity which they carried on. There may have been a few hard-pressed groups, such as the Lower Pimas and some of the river Yumans, at the time the Spanish appeared, but military protection only became of real importance, as for the Hopis and Opatas, long after, when Spanish efforts at conquest had stimulated warfare among the Indians and the Spaniards were unable to furnish effective protection. The Spaniards were asking for an immense extension of loyalty and personal obligation from people whose horizons of mutual obligation had always been limited to a primary group whom they knew intimately face-to-face. The recognition of obligations depended heavily on training from infancy in the intimate life of family group and community. It rested on mutual gift-giving and tangible rewards for cooperative relations. Outside the autonomous village or ranchería, social relationships were sporadic, uncertain, and not to be depended on, except in the case of the supernaturals, and the supernaturals after all were, although relatively intangible, really a part of the community since they dwelt or visited there regularly in ways that could be depended on. The extension of loyalty to the king, or even to his representatives, was being required of people who had no precedents for such relationships, except possibly in their relations with supernaturals. It would have to be built on the growth of dependable relations with captains and officials in the Indian country, who had something to offer in return. It could grow on such a basis, as it did for some Indian communities who wanted protection, but the idea of loyalty to the king could not be suddenly implanted. Its development depended heavily on the behavior of the king's officials.

Thirdly, and here we see most clearly how an apparently simple change involved great complexity, the Spaniards asked for a complete shift in the division of labor in government. They proposed to introduce a set of community officials who would work for the interests of the Indian and insure order. Yet what they proposed involved completely new concepts of government, which, if they had been thoroughly accepted with the promptness expected, would have upset rather than guaranteed order. The Spaniards proposed to separate the moral-ritual leadership which was the heart and center of Indian communities from the administrative-executive leadership and to subordinate the former to the latter. This was a thorough turning upside down of the Indian systems. The separation and subordination of the moral leadership was to be accomplished in the following way. Moral leadership, in the Spanish view, was to be centered in the missionaries, who actually were not officially regarded as part of the government of a community. The effective community leadership was to consist of Indians, set up as governors, sheriffs, judges, and in some instances captains with their assistants, working under the command of the Spanish provincial governors, judges, and captains. What could the Indians, organized as they were, make of such an arrangement?

From the Indian viewpoint the change would have amounted to putting community government in the hands of war leaders, that is, officials with the power of command. War leaders in the Indian communities had always been either completely subordinate to the community government, or had functioned entirely outside. The change further proposed to replace the highest official of a community with an outsider, the Spanish missionary, and to remove him from any position of effective control over the war leaders. This, if it had been accepted, would have meant complete community breakdown, unless by some miracle the principles and ideas of Spanish government were quickly and completely revealed to and understood by all the people. The Spanish impersonal, written code of law administered by governor, sheriff, and judge functioned in Spanish communities as the actual person of the moral leader did in an Indian community. But the Indians had not developed written codes of law, and still essential in their concept of government was the human embodiment of the highest principles of conduct of the group, namely, the peace or moral leader. Moreover, moral conduct was not for the Indians separate from ritual behavior; the two were intricately interrelated, and the principles of both were combined in the exhortations and the behavior of their peace leaders. The Spanish system required a separation of moral and ritual behavior and, moreover, distinguished two types of morality, namely, the absolutely required rules expressed in the legal code, and the ideal Christian forms expressed by the ritual leader in the person of the missionary. The specialization, and consequent complexity, of the Spanish governmental system, was far beyond that of any of the northern Indian tribes. The Indians had not separated church and state, and this meant that the required behavior of every member of the community included ritual obligations to the supernaturals, as well as the minimum moral rules for the smooth functioning of daily life. The Indians had not, moreover, gone so far in the specialization of state functions as had the Spaniards; with them the judge was one with the moral and ritual leader. They had indeed separated the sheriff in the form of the war leader, and he to some extent had the functions of the general administrator, or governor, but rather than being the center and source of authority in government as in the Spanish system, he remained subsidiary. The Spanish system was therefore a topsy-turvy system from the Indian point of view.

To have accepted the Spanish system outright the Indians would have had to abandon their deep-rooted view of their relationship to the land, in fact their whole conception of the order of men and gods in the universe. What was involved in the Spaniards' attempt to widen the political horizon of the Indians was not merely a broader view of the possible extent of peaceful cooperation among human communities. The Indian world view was deeply involved in even the apparent small changes in community officials which the Spaniards demanded. It is not surprising therefore, since the Spaniards did not generally attempt to break the communities apart and remake them, that political integration on the wider basis of the nation, which the Spaniards had through centuries come to understand, took a devious and slow-moving course. Three centuries would probably have seemed to any of the Spanish colonial administrators or missionaries an impossibly long time to wait for successful "civilizing" of the Indians that they knew in the 1600's. Yet, at the end of that time, political integration was still not achieved. On the other hand, in any conception of social evolution, such as for example that of Sir Henry Maine, three hundred years must appear rather a short period for the transformation of the tribesman into the citizen.

FIRST STEPS IN POLITICAL ADAPTATION

However, the significant factor in cultural change is never merely time in itself; the time period for accomplishing any directed cultural change is always relative to the methods employed for bringing it about. The Spanish methods for accomplishing a wider political integration of the Indians of northwestern New Spain seem in some respects to have been well designed for bringing about a slow and gradual change rather than the rapid, revolutionary changes which they seem to have envisioned.

The first moves which the invading Spaniards made after the conquest, or the voluntary submission, of groups of rancherías or villages consisted of the holding of meetings with Indian leaders. Just what types of leaders the Indians sent to such meetings we do not know, but it would seem probable that they were chiefly war leaders, since such officers had the function in the Indian communities of dealing with outsiders. In these assemblies, as for example in the meetings which Captain Juan de Oñate held in 1598 at Santo Domingo where he spoke to representatives of thirty-four Pueblo villages, and those which Captain Hurdaide held in 1610 at San Felipe where several hundred Yaqui and Mayo leaders gathered, the representatives of the King of Spain described to the Indians the power of the king and the necessity for obedience to him, the vast extent of the king's territory and his possession of the newly conquered area, and the king's guarantee of protection to the Indians so long as they remained peaceful. Oñate and Hurdaide, like other captains in lesser assemblies of the same kind, were accompanied by Franciscan or Jesuit missionaries who described the supremacy of God, the importance of baptism, and the principles of Christian life. What sort of understanding of the Spanish system the Indians gained from these speeches we cannot know; among the Pueblos at the time of Oñate's Santo Domingo meeting there were no interpreters who could explain what he and his Franciscan associates were saying, although among the rancherías Hurdaide was well supplied with interpreters by the time he dealt with the Sonoran tribes. Certain features of the Spanish system must nevertheless have been clear enough, such as the military force which would be the basis of the new relationships, and the close cooperation of Spanish military and religious officials.

Promises of peace and obedience were exacted from the Indians in the meetings; there is no record of what the Indian leaders went back to their people and reported. In some cases immediately, as among the Eastern Pueblos, and in most cases within a few years, as among the Yaquis, the Spaniards next moved to establish missionaries. Thus, the first direct experience of Spanish organization for most of the people of the region was in connection with the mission system. But at the same time, the Spaniards also established a royal town where military and civil officials lived and the work of Spanish government was carried on. From these two sources, as contacts increased, emanated the Spanish conceptions of government, and in the two places Indians could see governmental practices in action. There is no evidence to indicate that the Spaniards forcibly deposed or eliminated Indian leaders at the start, or that they tried to force the Indians to break up the system under which they had been living. The Spaniards probably did not gain a good enough understanding of the latter to focus on it as an obstacle to adoption of the Spanish form of government.

What the Spaniards did was to focus their efforts along two lines. In the first place, they tried to get acceptance of the missions and, in the second place, they tried to institute the Spanish town organization in the Indian communities. They appeared to regard both the mission and the town organization as introductions filling voids in Indian society. When the missionaries encountered opposition from some of the ranchería or village officials, they looked on such persons as individual witches. They did not seem to conceive of their work as involving a process of replacement of one form of organization with another.

In addition to fostering the mission and town organization, they proclaimed the village lands of the Pueblos and the tribal lands of the rancherías as part of the territory of the King of Spain. This specifically meant in New Mexico the designation of boundaries for each of the villages, and the proclaiming of the land within such boundaries as a grant to the village from the king. In Sonora and Chihuahua only very vague tribal boundaries were designated, since colonization was not immediately instituted there, and these remained merely administrative demarcations for the functioning of missions and the never-very-clearly outlined provinces of the colonial administration. Within most of the land granted to the Pueblos, the Spanish administrators did not interfere, and hence the territorial concept underlying Spanish government did not become a practical reality. Among the ranchería peoples, such as the Yaquis and Opatas, the town boundaries were sanctioned by the erection of crosses marking the limits of a mission's jurisdiction, but here also no other changes in land administration were required by the Spaniards until late in the 1700's. The only feature of the Spanish invasion which actually brought to an issue the king's jurisdiction over the land was colonization. In New Mexico this was settled early by the grants to the Indians which gave them largely what they claimed. In Sonora, Chihuahua, and Arizona the unsystematic colonization on a small scale brought the land issue to a head only slowly. Thus, one of the fundamental and major oppositions between Spanish and Indian governmental systems was not forced to an issue at the start by the Spaniards.

Nor was another of the fundamental issues between the two systems pushed very far by the Spaniards. The Spanish system required tribute from the conquered settlements, but this requirement was suspended in what were called frontier areas where either the Indians were too unsettled and resistant, or were regarded as still in process of Christianization. The Hopis and Zunis were not required to pay tribute, nor were the Chihuahua and Sonora ranchería peoples. The Eastern Pueblos were required to pay tribute before the Rebellion of 1680, although not afterwards; at least tribute was not systematically collected afterwards. The Eastern Pueblos, therefore, did experience the taxation system of a modern state although only for a relatively short period — only, that is, for as long as the state was strong enough to exact tribute. They submitted to Spanish authority under repeated application of force, but never accepted taxation as a legitimate institution, with its underlying principle of payment for military protection.

The feature of their system which the Spaniards pushed most consistently and systematically among the northern Indians with whom they made close contact was that of town organization. The first contacts of both missionaries and military men with the Indians were characterized by the appointment of governors (*gobernadores*) or judges (*alcaldes*) or both, with some explanation of the duties required. Usually such appointments were made on the most meager knowledge of the groups. Indians who presented themselves as friendly and helpful to the Spaniards were given the appointments, often immediately with a cane as badge of office, and without any inquiry into the status of the individual in his group. Sometimes the appointment of officers was made only after their duties had been fully explained in community meetings and the whole community had an opportunity to act. In New Mexico, simultaneously with setting up his capital at San Juan, within one of the Pueblo villages, Oñate divided the whole province into six districts and set up a Spanish *alcalde mayor* over each district. As military officer and judge of a district each alcalde mayor was then charged with bringing the Pueblo villages, as well as the Spanish colonists, into his organization. Taking each Pueblo village as a municipal unit in a district, the Spanish official working with the missionary, where such were established, then proceeded to appoint Indian officials. Apparently the office of alcalde for Indians was not used in New Mexico. In each village the following officials were named: governor, lieutenant governor, sheriff (*alguacil*), and ditch boss (*mayordomo*). In addition there were probably *regidores* (councilmen) who were to constitute, as in all Spanish towns, a deliberative body to assist the governor in his work. These officials were charged with administering law and order under the direction of the Spanish alcalde, transmitting messages from the provincial governor, punishing offenders, and generally representing the higher officials' wishes to the community. The missionary also appointed caretakers for the church, called *fiscales*.

Similar sets of officials were instituted in the ranchería communities, where more often than not at the beginning they were appointed by Jesuit missionaries rather than by military or civil officials, since the latter were often too few and far away to make direct contacts with all the communities. In addition the missionary also appointed fiscales, who were charged with the management of the church and its monies, as well as other church officials. According to the Spanish system all of these officials were to be elected by the town council every year and were not supposed to hold office for two years in succession. In contrast with New Mexico, in Sonora an official called a captain, with powers to command all the fighting men of a tribal or smaller group of rancherías, was sometimes appointed and held an executive rank above the governors of the rancherías. He was probably to be equated with the Spanish official called *alcalde mayor*, who commanded a district in New Mexico, both with respect to civil and military affairs.

The system of town officials was introduced among all the Eastern Pueblos, the Zunis, all those Tarahumaras who came into the missions, the Mayos, Yaquis, Lower Pimas, Opatas, and the southern Upper Pimas. Although the Hopis, some of the Eastern Navajos, the Seris, and the Yumas had missions established among them there is no evidence showing the organization was introduced among those groups. The Yumas and Eastern Navajos had missions for such short periods that if the system was introduced it left no impression. The Seris and Hopis had missions for longer periods, but developed such hostility to Spaniards that the latter were unable to re-establish control after initial success. The Gila Pimas and river Yumans (other than Yumas) had no missions; although they had friendly contacts with Spanish missionaries, they were beyond the limits of effective operation of the colonial administration. The Apaches, the upland Yumans, and most of the Navajos remained outside the pale of the Spanish program completely, and today show no trace whatever of any contact with the governmental system. The most populous and the most highly organized tribes of Indians were the ones who experienced the most intensive efforts of the Spaniards to change their political organization.

Changes were wrought in the community organization of these populous groups, but by no means in the same way for each one. There were, in fact, three very different ways in which these groups accepted the Spanish introduction of town organization. The Eastern Pueblo Keres, the Yaquis, and the Upper Pima Papagos exemplify these three types of reaction. The Keres accepted the town organization simply as an adjunct to their existing village government, adding the set of officials but keeping them distinct in function as well as name from their other officials. The Yaquis accepted the organization, integrated it closely with their existing government, and redefined both the Spanish offices and their own. In the Upper Pima rancherías a slow process of replacement of the office of peace leader by the office of governor was still going on as late as the 1930's.

The Keres adaptation to Spanish pressure for political change seems simple and practical under the circumstances. The Spaniards insisted on giving canes of office to the men who were dealing with the alcaldes mayores in matters of tribute payment, contribution of men to the Spanish troops protecting the Pueblo villages, the management of the church and other affairs connected with the mission. The alcaldes mayores regarded such men as the heads of the villages. But in Pueblo conceptions of government the handling of such matters, obviously "outside" affairs concerning non-Pueblo people and often intimately connected with warfare, were not the sort of thing with which the peace leaders should deal. It is possible that at first the dealings with Spaniards were turned over to the War Priests, but at some point early in the Spanish contacts entirely separate officials were invested by the villages with the Spanish titles of governor, lieutenant governor, sheriff, and mayordomo. These men became the go-betweens with the Spaniards, receiving the Spanish officials to talk over matters when they came to the village, relaying orders and messages to and from Spanish officials, and attending to matters of law and order on which the Spaniards insisted. Under the Spanish system such officials were to be elected each year, but the Pueblo villages (with the exception of Isleta) never adopted this method of selection. Instead they were kept strictly under the control of the peace leader (cacique) by being appointed annually by him. They conformed to Spanish custom by undergoing official installation on the Day of the Kings on January 6 each year. They worked closely with the executive war arm of village government, but their roles were defined strictly as limited to dealings with the Spanish outsiders. The village government continued in its old form, with few if any changes.

Thus, the Keres villages did not accept Spanish concepts of government. They merely created a new department of government, a special foreign relations branch, as it were, and added it to their existing system. This new department did not, however, take over any of the functions of the old organization, not even those of war. The old war branch continued with its same functions of executive activities and ritual specialties, although, of course, it found itself frequently closely involved with the governor's branch. The Spaniards must have realized at least dimly what was taking place, for they understood that what they called caciques existed, but they remained content to deal with the governor and his helpers as though they constituted the government of the villages. The colonial administration made no attempts to suppress systematically the old organization, although the missionaries recognized it as an obstacle to their purposes, and tried at times to get civil authorities to take measures against it.

The other Eastern Pueblos made precisely the same adjustment to the Spanish demands, with only minor variations in the interrelations of the new external relations department and the existing branches of government. New activities being required in the new situation of Spanish domination, a new part of village organization was created to carry out these activities and these alone. The fundamentals of the old order were maintained.

The Yaquis, under considerably less pressure from Spanish civil and military authorities than the Pueblos, responded quite differently. As has been said, it is more difficult to know precisely what took place because we have less knowledge of Yaqui government at the time the Spaniards began their attempts to change it. The intimate influence of highly respected missionaries working from within the newly concentrated Yaqui towns probably was a major factor in the extensive changes which took place in Yaqui government. The Yaquis accepted more fully than the Pueblos, although not completely, the Spanish idea of separation of secular from religious functions of government; they also invested the Spanish-introduced secular offices with functions inside as well as external to the town. This resulted in a really new form of organization, but it remained one which combined much of the old with the Spanish introductions.

By the end of the first 125 years of contact the Yaquis had developed a town organization with three major branches of government — civil, military, and religious or ceremonial. In contrast with the Pueblos, the offices in all three branches bore Spanish names, indicating the greater penetration of Spanish conceptions. The civil branch of government consisted of four governors (the term lieutenant governor was not used) and a sheriff, all with assistants. The military branch consisted of a group of captains, with lieutenants, sergeants, and corporals as assistants. The religious branch consisted of a complex organization of church officials commanded at the top by *maestros* (readers of prayers and ritual), a head sacristan and church treasurer (called *temasti*), and a female ceremonial official. The relations among these officials preserved much of the older Yaqui concept of government.

In large degree the church organization maintained the central position of the old moral-ritual leader. Its leadership nominated men for the civil offices, and no action by the town as a whole could be taken without its concurrence and active support. The church leadership was also strongly charged with moral exhortation, and the church sponsored within itself a special ceremonial organization (the customs chieftainship) which assumed civil control of the town during Lent and Holy Week. This latter organization was required, like the old moral leader, to emphasize during its period of supremacy what were regarded as the most sacred and important customs of the people. The church organization was thus central in maintaining the ritual values of the town, and had a prominent and active part in the rest of the government. Civil order, including management of the land, had nevertheless been relinquished to the other two branches of government. This separation of powers gave responsibility for law and order and administration of punishment by means of the whipping post to the civil governors and sheriff. They also, rather than the church leadership, served as chairmen of the town meetings, acted in matters involving relations with the Spaniards and other outsiders, and had powers of command in carrying out communal work other than ceremonies. The governors and sheriff were assisted in the punishment of offenders by the military organization. The latter also, as had the war leaders formerly, carried out important ceremonial duties as leaders of a warrior organization and assumed command in time of war. The three branches of government acted as a single organization in matters concerning the whole town and had equal voice in deliberations and decisions. In the meetings of the town council, ordinary citizens under the leadership of a *mayor,* or old man, regularly took part, thus making the assembly fully democratic.

The Yaqui organization was by no means a simple civil government divorced from direct influence of the church, as proposed by the Spaniards, nor yet did it follow the old form with merely a limited adjunct for external relations, as among the Pueblos. It was a far more complex organization than the old Yaqui form, with a greater specialization in governmental labor and a deeper permeation of Spanish ideas in that division of labor. It was a new integration which had moved appreciably in the Spanish direction, but which had not discarded the fundamental native conceptions.

The Mayos reintegrated their government in very much the same way as the Yaquis. Probably the Opatas did the same, although we know little of the details of the form which their organization took. As a result of greater infiltration of Opata communities by the Spaniards during the 1700's, it is probable that their form of government more closely resembled that of a Spanish town. The Lower Pimas were subject to similar infiltration of Spaniards and probably developed a town organization similar to the Opatas. The Tarahumaras did not develop town organization so complex as that of the Yaquis and Mayos, but the simpler form which they did develop had much the same basic character as that of the Yaquis, showing similar influence of Spanish ideas and forms. A major difference was the continuing existence of many Tarahumara rancherías which maintained the older form of organization without important changes.

The third form of adjustment to the Spanish governmental system is represented by that of those Upper Pimas who came to be called Papagos. The northern Papagos, like the Gila Pimas, did not come under Spanish influence in this respect but those who lived along the Altar and Santa Cruz rivers did accept some Spanish ideas. As among the ranchería people farther south, these people were in contact with Spanish administrators and missionaries and in various rancherías accepted appointments and canes of office as governors. However, their contacts were relatively slight, tribute was never exacted, and the pressures to develop a full-fledged town organization were therefore minimal. Nevertheless many of the rancherías recognized the office of governor and some erected whipping posts. Their own organization had consisted of little in the way of permanent institutions beyond a group of moral-ritual leaders who acted informally in nightly meetings as counsellors and as a fountain of collective wisdom. Some of these peace leaders apparently accepted offices as governors. None seems to have built any further organization in accordance with Spanish patterns, but in some villages the term *kobanat* (the Papago form of gobernador) was adopted. By the end of the Spanish period the governor's functions had been defined as punisher of offenders and go-between with outsiders. By the time of the coming of the Anglo-Americans it was traditional in most villages to have a governor as well as a Keeper of the Smoke, or moral leader. The governor was a moral leader also, but his functions were secular ones not tied up with the traditional ritual, such as the tending of the sacred objects of the ranchería group. By the early twentieth century, governors, or village chiefs as they came to be called under the Anglo-American regime, were full-fledged secular officials with responsibility in land management, external relations, communal work, and moral exhortation (although the last was not essential). As new proselytizing religions gained influence, the Keeper of the Smoke became a ritual specialist with declining influence. He was being steadily replaced as the guiding voice in ranchería affairs by the kobanat, or secular governor.

Political changes during the Spanish period may be summarized in the following way. The most populous tribes accepted Spanish forms of organization at the local level of government. They fitted these to their own institutions in a way to preserve the fundamental values of the latter. They maintained moral-ritual leadership as an integral part of government and still believed in the sacred identification of people with a specific locality. At the same time they integrated the Spanish separation of civil and religious functions in different ways into their systems of government; this resulted in a wider division of labor. There is some evidence that the reality of a distant civil functionary with great power, namely the king, became established in the minds of the more populous groups. The Yaquis, for example, accepted the King of Spain as a reality, at least of the order of various supernaturals in whom they believed, and they attached some value to the placing of his sanction on their claims to tribal territory. Less a reality for the Pueblos, the king was nevertheless accepted also as confirming their land claims. It is doubtful, however, that the concept of loyalty to the king was established as an accepted value. Obedience to his orders through his representatives was regarded as an imposition, but practically necessary. The value of the king's armed forces as protectors of the peace had hardly been effectively demonstrated. However, up until the early 1700's a general peace had been established and the military branches of village and ranchería government had been influenced to modify their functions in the direction of ceremonial and civic activities.

The villages and rancherías remained discrete units, as they were before the conquest, except for tenuous connections with the central government of New Spain and temporary confederation under native "captains." Although they remained discrete organizationally, there was some growth in intensity of tribal feeling stimulated by opposition to the Spaniards. This was strong among the Eastern and Western Pueblos, the Mayos, and the Yaquis (as well as among the band-organized peoples), but among the Opatas and Pimas, with the exception of the Gila Pimas, there was less tribal feeling. Hundreds of individuals among Conchos, southern Pueblos, and Opatas lost a sense of tribal identity altogether and became assimilated into the Spanish settler population.

POLITICAL RESISTANCE AND ASSIMILATION
IN SONORA AND CHIHUAHUA

By the time of the formation of the Mexican Republic the Eastern Pueblos, the Mayos, the Yaquis, the Opatas, most Pimas, and some Tarahumaras had reorganized their communities according to one or another of the three patterns described. The new forms of organization were well established and the Indians had been living for generations under them, but significant new conditions had developed. Between 1767 and the 1820's both the village and the ranchería peoples had become accustomed to a growing local autonomy. The mission organization in their communities had largely disintegrated, and in the absence of priests, they had themselves begun to manage church affairs. The Spanish military had shown itself less and less able to give protection against the increasingly active Navajo and Apache raiding; Pueblo villages and Opata and Pima rancherías alike had been forced into a revival of their independently directed retaliatory actions against the raiders. The Spanish governors had ceased to exact tribute in the north and had shown themselves fearful of pushing either that or the land distribution program among the well-organized Yaquis, Mayos, and Opatas in the south. It was at a time when the growing sense of freedom from Spanish control had reached a high point that the Mexican government was formed and turned its attention to the Indians of the north.

Although weaker in a military way than Spain had become, the Mexican government had an even clearer and more definite Indian policy. It was a very simple one; in the new constitution, Indians were immediately declared citizens, whether or not they were currently in the status of slave or indentured servant. Moreover locally in the two new northern states of Sonora and Chihuahua some careful planning was carried out for the incorporation of Indians into the municipal-state organization. The constitutions of both states spelled out in detail how the incorporation was to be accomplished. Indian towns were to become participating units in municipalities. All adult males were given the voting privilege and Indians, like any others, were to hold office at any level in the political organization. Land boards composed of Indians in Indian areas were to supervise the distribution of land under individual title. Schools were to be established in Indian as well as other towns and schooling was to be secular and universal. These plans, which became law in the 1820's, reflected the egalitarian and positivist thought which was to become dominant in Mexican government as the nineteenth century wore on. In the north such thinking was already strong. In two important respects, land distribution and general taxation, the new program was a continuation of Spanish policy with, in addition, a careful administrative plan for execution of the former. To these individualistic features of the Spanish program were added others characteristic of the revolutionary political thought of the time, such as general male suffrage and the full separation of church and state.

There seems little doubt that the framers of the state constitutions expected immediate and happy acceptance of the new laws by all those Indians who had been organized into towns, although they foresaw a continuing need for transitional arrangements for such groups as the Seris and Upper Pimas and regarded military action as the only possible method for dealing with the Apaches. The state governments undertook immediately in Sonora and Chihuahua (in New Mexico the government was too weak to make any such attempt) to carry through the new program. The Opata, Lower Pima, Mayo, and Yaqui areas became the scene of efforts to make the new laws a reality; and the focus of interest of the state officials lay in the Yaqui country, for it had long been clear that the Yaqui lands were the most valuable in the region and that they could support more people than the approximately twenty thousand Indians who then lived there. Tax collectors and surveyors were sent into the communities; settlers, called "colonists," were encouraged to move into the Indian territory. Administrative centers, called *cabeceras,* were established in towns in which non-Indians were the dominant population. The Mexican officials apparently expected a quick shift from one institutional framework to another, but there was no such easy transition.

The Mexican actions constituted the final drawing of the issue in regard to land and to outside authority over the local community—the issues which the Spaniards had dealt with so gingerly for more than a century. From the Indian viewpoint, to accept individual title to land from a government outside the Indian country was not merely to flout the authority of the existing town organization which managed the land, but, far more serious, to attack the collective sacred relationship to the land, which the Spaniards had never seriously challenged. To pay taxes and to accept a Mexican town (the cabecera of the new municipal district) as superior in authority was to overturn the long-enjoyed autonomy of the church-centered communities. These were the issues which the Mexicans had now joined and of which they had little or no understanding. In their view they were merely completing in just and legal fashion the process of political integration over which the inefficient and corrupt Spanish government had so long dallied.

The Mexican attack on the autonomous status quo brought immediate resistance from Opatas, Yaquis, Mayos, and Lower Pimas (the program had not been extended to the Upper Pimas). The processes of civilization thus far had resulted in the creation of strongly knit towns capable of determined and united action to maintain themselves. The Mexicans had not foreseen the depth of the Indian devotion to the institutions which had developed out of the fusion of Spanish and native forms. Where they looked for pleased acceptance of citizenship equality, they found a determined and exclusive tribalism. Where they expected a welcoming of a secular government wholly freed from entanglement with the clergy, they found an Indian movement for independence inspired by a religious vision.

The effects on the Yaquis may be taken as the extreme example of resistance to the Mexican program of full citizenship. The Yaqui rancherías had been organized at a new level of integration as a result of the Jesuit work. For two hundred years, since the 1620's, Yaqui community life had been developing on a pattern of wider integration and increased complexity over the pre-Spanish form. The eighty rancherías encountered on the lower Yaqui River by the Jesuits had been consolidated into eight towns. The population of each new local group was in the neighborhood of three thousand, as compared with an average population of less than four hundred for the previously existing rancherías. As we have seen, this change in local group size was accompanied with an elaboration of governmental organization. Spanish forms of civil, church, and military organization had been accepted and integrated into a type of social unit which approximated, but by no means duplicated a Spanish pueblo. We do not know precisely how well organized and unified this new community type was by the end of the Spanish period. It is probable that, under the pressures from both civil and ecclesiastical authorities from

Spain, it remained in a fairly fluid form until the expulsion of the Jesuits. Through that period missionaries were a part of the organization and it may be presumed that they constantly exerted influence for continuing change.

It must be noted, however, that there was decreasing Spanish influence in the Yaqui towns after the expulsion of the Jesuits and the secularization of the missions. By the middle 1820's, after the definition of Mexican policy and after the first Banderas uprising, there were no regularly constituted officials other than Yaquis in the towns. Not until after the defeat of the Yaquis in the 1880's did the Mexican government institute administrative controls within the communities. Consequently Yaqui political organization during the nineteenth century, from the 1820's through the 1880's, developed in isolation from direct outside influences. The form which it had attained by the 1880's was a product of Yaqui thinking and leadership working with the Spanish forms which had been accepted up to 1767 and combining them in a new sort of governmental system with the surviving aboriginal elements.

The major stimulus to the growth of the close-knit town organization which Yaquis developed over the seventy years of conflict with Mexicans may be presumed to have been the threat to town autonomy which became apparent in the 1820's. The Mexican efforts to collect taxes, distribute land, and institute municipal government which took place with the formation of the Occidente state government were clearly such threats. Since the Mexicans were not able to maintain political control of the Yaqui towns, Yaquis were able over a period of more than two generations to mould their organization in their own fashion. In doing this they moved into a new phase of political development, but not the phase which the Mexicans sought to bring about.

The town organization very probably did not change insofar as its general pattern of division of labor went. A five-fold authority system which was well established by the 1880's probably existed in major outline during the Jesuit period, or at least during the years immediately following the expulsion. The church, the governors, and the military society, which constituted the formal departments of the town government took form during the time of intensive Spanish influence. While the church organization and the governors both in their formal characteristics and at least their general function were direct introductions by the missionaries, the military society was a native institution reinterpreted in form and function under Jesuit influence. It seems consistent with the leading role which the missionaries took in Yaqui life that the church should have been emphasized as the dominant authority, particularly since a missionary was the administrative head of the church. The civil authority under the governors may have been more of an independent entity than it became during the nineteenth century. Whatever the specific relationships of the three branches during the Jesuit period, it is clear that by the 1880's they had become co-equal arms of government. Moreover they shared their authority with two other organized branches — the fiesteros and the customs chieftainship.

The equality of these five departments was an expression of the strong democratic character of the town governments. No matter of general interest or concern to the town could be considered formally except in a meeting in which representatives of all five departments were present. While the first governor was chairman of such meetings, members of other hierarchies were just as free to speak or to bring up business as any of the governors. The governors were elected in a general meeting open to all annually, and it even seems that officials in the other hierarchies were subject to approval by the whole town populace. Moreover, a general town meeting required, as well as the officials of the departments, the presence of a group of older men without formal office who likewise had equal voice with the officials and who sponsored any other adult of the town who wished to express a view. The town was, therefore, a thoroughly democratic organization, despite a considerable complexity in the division of governmental labor. It seems unlikely that this degree of democratic procedure and decision had been encouraged by the missionaries, although it was not inconsistent with Spanish custom at the village level. The only remnant of church precedence in the organization lay in the custom of having the top church officials nominate the candidates for governors each year, and this could have been, as among the Pueblos, derived from native procedure.

The trend toward democratic management of town affairs was one major change in Yaqui political life during the 1800's. It resulted in an extremely close integration of all the organized aspects of town life. Since no one department, whether civil, military, or any other, could take action except in cooperation in open meeting with all the other departments, each town constituted a tightly unified whole. Since all the officials and those without office met frequently, especially in times of crisis, to discuss and decide on all important matters, there was the creation and maintenance of a solid community consensus. This probably became stronger as the towns became smaller in size during the nineteenth century, partly as a result of the migration out of the Yaqui country of those individuals who became more favorably disposed toward mingling with Mexicans. The unity of the towns as social units was emphasized repeatedly in connection with the making of agreements or treaties with Mexicans. The Yaqui conception was that their military leaders had no right to make treaties with Mexican commanders or officials in isolation from the rest of the town organization. Cajeme's behavior in the last phase of his leadership, when he insisted that Mexican leaders meet with the town officials while he withdrew, is an illustration of the operation of the Yaqui governmental concepts and a demonstration of the refusal of Yaquis to adopt the *caudillo* conception of leadership which prevailed among the Mexicans.

The democracy, the close integration of special departments of government, and the monolithic unity of a town were related to Yaqui religious beliefs. A major development of the nineteenth century was the growth of a concept of the sacredness of each town. This was less a new growth than an intensification of old views of the Yaqui relationship to the land. The form which this conception took during the period that Yaqui control of their land was under threat by the Mexicans seems clearly to have involved a combination of aboriginal and Christian myth. Precisely when it crystallized we do not know, but it appears to have existed at the time of the Banderas uprisings in the 1820's.

The ideas which underlay the town organization were based on a systematic mythology which possibly by the middle of the nineteenth century had been codified into forms in which the young men were regularly instructed. They rested on a conception of the whole tribal territory, as well as that of each town, as divinely ordained. It was believed that following a great flood a band of angels appeared in the Yaqui country and was joined by Yaqui prophets. This group of supernaturals and inspired men then proceeded to define the tribal territory. As they sang hymns of a Christian type, they traversed the whole boundary from a point between the Yaqui and Mayo territory on the south to a peak west of Guaymas on the north. Some time after this "singing of the boundary" Yaqui prophets in succession experienced visions at eight different points within the tribal territory. One had a vision of the Garden of Eden and at this spot it was ordained that the town of Potam should be founded. Another saw Santa Rosa in a vision and here Bacum was founded. Thus for each of the eight towns, a sacred location was determined and the eight towns became realities. Tradition apparently was bounded by the beginning of the Jesuit period, for there is no suggestion in the mythology that the towns were conceived as consolidations of smaller rancherías. This mythology gave supernatural sanction to the concept of both sacred tribal territory and eight sacred towns. Under this sanction it was inconceivable that human beings could in any way presume to change the tribal boundaries of the locations of the towns. Moreover, the land had been given by God to the Yaquis and therefore it would violate the sacred order if they shared it with anyone.

It was these sacred beliefs which underlay the reiterated demands of all Yaqui leaders from Banderas (and perhaps Muni) through Tetabiate that no settlement could be reached with the Mexicans unless they agreed to withdraw to the last man from Yaqui country. We may assume also that it was these beliefs which focused Yaqui resistance to the proposed individual parcelling of the land of the town territories. And finally the sacred land concept led to the intensive efforts, under almost impossible circumstances during the twentieth century, to reconstitute the Mexican-dominated towns of Cocorit and Bacum and to the refounding of the western towns of Rahum, Huirivis, and Belem.

The major effects then, of the Mexican program for equal citizenship were to lead the Yaquis to develop a tighter and more democratic town organization and to invest this with an intense sacredness. They were therefore moved in the opposite direction from wider political integration with the Mexicans, and thus toward rejection of outside linkages of even the tenuous administrative type such as had existed with the Spanish national structure.

It is probably also true that Yaqui tribal consciousness was intensified over what it had been during the previous two centuries, although this is difficult to measure on available evidence. It should be recalled in this connection that great unity in Yaqui tribal action had appeared in two major crises before the rise of Banderas, in 1533 at the time of Guzmán's attack and again in 1610 in opposing Captain Hurdaide. It further should not be forgotten that Yaqui tribal unity during the nineteenth century was maintained at the expense of losing many individuals who sought peaceful lives elsewhere in Sonora. Yaqui tribal unity was strong but it was always expressed in the phrase, "The Eight Pueblos," thus emphasizing that the autonomy of the separate towns was a basic part of the Yaqui conception of sacred common cause in the land.

Once crystallized, Yaqui devotion to tribal and town autonomy showed a rigidity which seemed to permit no compromise. Following dispersal and after the 1910 Mexican revolution, under conditions more permissive than those of the nineteenth century, Yaquis revived the sacred town organization in identical form to that which had existed before their dispersal. They did this in each of the river towns in which they resettled regardless of the fact that the Sonoran government maintained municipal officers as well. The terms in which Yaquis thought of their organization were the same as before; they held that all Yaquis in the towns should be loyal to and serve in the traditional government and that the municipal authorities had jurisdiction only over Mexicans. This uncompromising position showed no tendency toward change as late as 1958, when a plebiscite encouraged by the national government resulted in overwhelming majorities in the towns favoring retention of the old form of organization and rejecting a proposal to accept integration into the municipal-state framework. The political isolation of the Yaquis which had been created by war during the nineteenth century had continued under a de facto political and military domination.

The other ranchería peoples of Sonora who had also organized towns under the Jesuit plan reacted at first to the Mexican citizenship program in the same way as the Yaquis. The Mayos, the Lower Pimas, and the Opatas all joined Juan Banderas in the effort to maintain the kind of autonomy which their towns had enjoyed under the Jesuits. The Lower Pimas and Opatas discontinued their alliance with the Yaquis, after the execution of major Opata leaders in 1832. Nevertheless some Opatas showed strong interest afterwards in reinstituting mission type communities. It is probable that Opata military support of the French invasion of Sonora under Tanori was connected with a desire to maintain the colonial type of town organization, but from the 1840's on we have no indication either of the persistence of colonial forms of organization or of Opata efforts to restore them.

The Mayos were more persistent, maintaining their alliance and fighting intermittently with Yaquis or on their own until 1893. There is an indication that they maintained mission type institutions in some of their towns, possibly Santa Cruz and smaller settlements, until the 1920's. But the meager historical data so far put together suggest that a process of Spanish infiltration into Mayo communities began as early as the 1680's and that this resulted in quite different conditions among the Mayos as compared with the Yaquis. The situation among the Mayos more closely paralleled that among the Opatas. The important differences between Mayo and Yaqui conditions were the following: Mayo population was early reduced by epidemic while Yaqui population was not; Spanish haciendas on a large scale were therefore possible in Mayo country as early even as the middle 1600's while there were none in Yaqui country until the early 1800's; Mexican control of such native towns as Navojoa and others upriver had taken place perhaps before 1800 while in the Yaqui country it was not until the late nineteenth century that such replacement of Indians by Mexicans in the Indian towns began to take place;

the presence of the large Spanish and Mexican establishments in the heart of Mayo country set up divisive influences among the Indians. Despite such conditions, and probably as a result of the comparative isolation until the early nineteenth century of some downriver Mayo towns, there were enough Mayos with the Yaqui-type viewpoint to offer effective resistance to political incorporation on through the 1870's. It was obvious however that Mayo resistance needed Yaqui leadership to make it militant and that far more depended on the quality of specific leaders than was the case among Yaquis. In other words, the Mayo communities, insofar as there were any, were divided and under pressures from Mexicans. The kind of unified community which inspired and backed Yaqui resistance probably did not exist anywhere among Mayos by the middle of the nineteenth century.

Once the Spaniards had obtained sufficient foothold for the establishment of haciendas in Mayo country, moreover, a process of deculturization was set in motion. The labor for the haciendas came largely from the local Indian population. Under the peon system, this meant a disintegration of native community structure and a growth of dependence on the paternalistic hacienda owner. How extensive this system became among the Mayos, especially after the defeats of the late nineteenth century, is indicated in the accounts of the Saint Teresa cult of the 1890's. The Mexican accounts suggest that at that time nearly all Mayos had been impressed for service on the haciendas and ranches in their country. This would have meant the breakdown of organized town life, such as existed in some Mayo communities on into the early nineteenth century. It is possible then, to attribute the difference in Mayo and Yaqui reactions in the late nineteenth century in large part to the nature of community life among the two tribes. After defeat Mayos resorted to religious nativism; Yaquis continued militant. Yaqui behavior was based in the experience, right up to the time of defeat, of vigorous town organization controlled by themselves; Mayo behavior was a result of the progressive disintegration of their communities and their assumption of the role of dependent peon. This latter process was never complete for all Mayos perhaps until the 1890's or there could not have been as much militant resistance as there was.

The Chihuahua government made a similar effort to that of Sonora for incorporation of Tarahumaras into municipal organization. The pressures on the Indians which developed here never met with the kind of resistance that flared up so promptly in Sonora. We may infer that there were two major causes for this. First and most important was the absence of the kind of integrated town organization which Yaquis, Mayos, and Opatas had developed under missionary stimulus. The other factor was the possibility for Indians to retire into the mountains and thus escape the pressures while still remaining in Tarahumara homeland. Tarahumara town organization, built on relatively loose aboriginal local government and relatively erratic missionary influence, did not provide an effective basis for military resistance to the Mexicans. Moreover in the lowland Tarahumara country, where the pressures from settlers were the strongest, a considerable amount of peonization and disintegration of the never-very-unified mission communities had already taken place. With no basis of organization for expressing resistance, the most common Tarahumara reaction to the Mexican program was flight into areas where Mexican settlers had not yet penetrated. Yet wherever Tarahumaras went they maintained at least the outlines of the Spanish town organization with a roster of civil, church, and military officials.

There was another important aspect of the Mexican program for political integration besides the conferring of full citizenship. Like the latter this was also a development out of Spanish policy of the eighteenth century. It consisted in what Mexicans called "colonization," and was much urged throughout the nineteenth century. Colonization failed completely for some seventy years to provide the "civilizing" influences on Yaquis which Mexicans desired. No colony was in fact permanently established in the Yaqui country until the 1890's, after secure military control had finally been achieved by the Mexicans. The plan for systematic colonization of the Yaqui country which the state legislature urged in the 1880's was never put into effect; it called for a constant military guard. A few subsequent efforts at colonization of Mexicans or "tame" Yaquis appeared to promote, not intermingling and growth of cooperative relations, but rather hostility and separation.

Colonization elsewhere in Sonora and Chihuahua had different results, leading to political incorporation based on cultural assimilation. In brief the process operated as follows. Mexicans moved into Indian country and began stock raising, farming, or trading. Sometimes land was seized regardless of Indian rights, sometimes merely a source of water supply for cattle was seized and held, sometimes a legal title to the land was acquired either through assignment by the state government or by purchase from Indians. Usually during the expansion of the settlers into the Indian country a small-scale border warfare developed, with Indians attempting to oust settlers by force and settlers maintaining their positions by taking the law into their own hands and killing any who stood in their way. These small-scale conflicts proceeded in an atmosphere of intense group hatred, the Mexicans making a classification of the Indians as not quite human and therefore fair game, while the Indians with analogous feelings about the Mexicans were forced to accept their dominance. Since there was often little, if any, physical difference between the Mexicans and the Indians, the antagonisms did not involve concepts of racial inferiority but rather rested on different evaluations of customs and beliefs.

As Mexicans gained numerical superiority in an area, two developments ordinarily followed. In the first place, Mexicans formed their own political units, whether or not a given community consisted only of themselves or included Indians, which then became linked to the municipal-state system. In this way it was not Indian communities which became participant in the Mexican political organization, but rather governmental units which ignored Indian communities in their vicinity and developed participation in the larger political framework entirely on Mexican terms. No adaptation of Indian governmental forms was involved; rather they were isolated from wider relations and usually steadily disintegrated. In the second place, as Mexican political dominance became established and the Indian economic position deteriorated, Indians themselves began to accept the Mexican valuation of their customs and beliefs as inferior and moved steadily toward cultural assimilation. This process went on in Tarahumara, Mayo, Opata, and Pima territories with greater or less rapidity, depending on the relationship in numbers of Indians and Mexicans and on the intensity of their contacts.

This kind of political incorporation of Indians took place in one part of the Yaqui country during the late nineteenth century, namely, the eastern section which included the two sacred Yaqui towns of Cocorit and Bacum. It proceeded with little interruption in the Mayo region through the last half of the nineteenth century and was nearly complete by the 1950's. With considerably less of the usual group antagonisms, it had resulted in the full political integration and nearly complete cultural assimilation of the Opatas by the beginning of the twentieth century. In the 1950's it was still in process, with the usual complement of group antagonisms, among the few Upper Pimas in western Sonora, among the Lower Pimas of the highlands in the vicinity of Maicoba and Yecora, and among the highland Tarahumaras where Mexican settlement and competition for the land had become intense during the first half of the twentieth century. The same process had even before 1900 isolated the remnant band of two hundred Seris on the Sonora coastal margin and Tiburón Island. The beleaguered Seris had been affected less than the other groups by the process of cultural assimilation.

Before the 1910 Mexican revolution two other programs had been added to those of forced citizenship and colonization. One was of very minor importance, namely, the attempt to reinstitute missions. This was tried with the Yaquis in the interval just following the defeats of Cajeme and Tetabiate, when Mexicans in the Yaqui country continued to be harassed by guerrilla fighting. The establishment of a missionary and the Sisters of Josephine at Bacum had completely negative results. Yaquis generally regarded the religious functionaries as intruders as much as any other Mexicans and refused to relate their well-developed independent church organization to the mission activities. Too much inter-ethnic hatred and distrust had developed in the century since the breakdown of the first mission program. In the Tarahumara country the reinstitution of the Jesuit missions met with much greater success. Focused around improvement of health, formal schooling, and religious instruction, the missions did not, however, directly bring about important changes in political organization.

The other program adopted prior to the 1910 revolution consisted of deportation. It can hardly be said to have been aimed at political integration directly, but rather at social and economic integration. It was applied to the Seris and to the Yaquis and, incidentally to other Indians who happened to fall into the net spread for the Yaquis. Seris were deported twice from their native haunts during the Mexican period, in the expectation that they might be incorporated as a group into Sonoran life as a community in the Villa de Seris across the river from Hermosillo. In neither instance was any effort made to encourage their own community organization and in neither instance was there any positive result, from the Mexican viewpoint, other than the cultural assimilation of a few individuals. The colony of deportees gradually drifted away from the Villa de Seris to resume their wandering life again. The Yaqui deportation was a large-scale effort to break up any congregation of Yaquis and to absorb them into the hacienda life of Yucatan and Oaxaca. This, too, failed as a program for integration into Mexican life. Those who did not die under the harsh labor conditions escaped and, one by one, returned to Sonora or found refuge in Arizona, where they sought with as much vigor as before to indoctrinate their children against Mexicans and to support the revival of the old forms of Yaqui government on the old sacred town sites. Regarded as vicious persecution by Yaquis, deportation had the result of strengthening the devotion to the old institutions in those who survived. As in the case of the Jews the experience of deportation or the knowledge that it had happened to fellow Yaquis intensified the conviction of moral superiority over Mexicans and made more solid than ever the belief in the importance of maintaining the distinctive Yaqui way of life.

In the 1930's the influence of the kind of thinking about Indian affairs which in Mexico was called "indigenismo" came to have some practical effect on the three groups in northwestern Mexico who had managed to maintain most fully their identity — the Yaquis, the Seris, and the Tarahumaras. The Department of Indian Affairs initiated during the Cárdenas administration made a brief and unsuccessful effort to provide vocational education for Yaquis and economic organization for the Seris. No incentives were found for stimulating Yaqui interest in agricultural training and the Seri fishing cooperative fell apart after a brief existence. Both attempts were formulated on the foundation of respect for Indian cultures, but neither was carried out in the light of a clear understanding of the nature of the specific Indian cultures involved. Neither effort received any continuing government support once the programs began to run into difficulties of Indian non-acceptance.

It was not until the 1940's that a government program was organized which had both the viewpoint of "indigenismo" and well-organized government support. The National Indian Institute shied away from any Yaqui program, but in 1946 began work among the Tarahumaras. It was not clear by 1960 what direction Tarahumara adjustment to Mexican life had taken as a result of the stimulus of the new approach. However, the program began on the foundation of clear understanding of the complex of processes which Mexican encroachment and local hostility to Tarahumaras had set in motion. A strongly emphasized feature, along with formal education in both Spanish and the Tarahumara language, was the systematic stimulation of forms of community organization designed to enable Tarahumaras to work together as community groups in solving economic and political problems. The existing Tarahumara organization was recognized rather than ignored and Tarahumaras were brought together on a wider basis than had been customary for discussion of means of developing their economic resources. In 1957 the National Indian Institute also began encouraging Seris to start a new fishing cooperative.

In summary it may be said that the early Mexican attempts to bring about wider political integration of Indians either precipitated conflict which resulted in crystallizing opposition to any new forms of adaptation in political life or fell back on infiltration of Indian communities in a way that resulted not in the adaptation of the native institutions but rather in their disintegration. No systematic administrative links were developed with Indian communities; thus no Indians or Mexicans had experience in trying to adjust Indian forms to Mexican. These conditions prevailed for over a century despite a well-developed program, formalized in Mexican law, with both an ultimate objective of full citizenship and detailed planning of steps in the process of political integration.

PROTECTION AND DEPENDENCY IN ARIZONA
AND NEW MEXICO

The first serious efforts of the United States government to establish working relations with Indians in its newly acquired territory of New Mexico were directed toward those tribes who had remained outside the political control of Spain and Mexico. The Navajos and Apaches never considered themselves to have been conquered by Spaniards or Mexicans, although the latter had claimed as part of their nation the great expanses of land over which the Indians roamed. The United States worked on the assumption that it had acquired, as a result of the capitulation of the Mexicans, the whole vast area of Indian-ranged territory and proceeded to offer peace on that basis to the "wild" tribes. At first some simple agreements for mutual friendship were discussed with various Navajo and Apache headmen, without mention of specific territorial limits on either side. The Indians assumed that their territorial position would remain as it had been, while the Anglo-Americans assumed that the Indians understood modern national conquest. As Indians continued their customary raiding on Mexican communities, they found that representatives of the United States government objected vigorously. This was difficult to comprehend from the Indian viewpoint. They regarded Mexicans as the common enemy of themselves and of the Anglo-Americans. They could not recognize a right of Anglos either to restrain their raids on the common enemy or to assume control over themselves on their own territory.

The early agreements were therefore understood in quite different ways by the two parties to them. They moreover were made by individual war leaders, only occasionally by band headmen of the Navajos and Apaches who did not, contrary to Anglo belief about Indian chieftainship, have any but a narrow authority within one, or at most, a few bands. As a result of this mutual misunderstanding there was constant treaty-breaking with general warfare finally erupting between Anglos and both Navajos and Apaches, with feelings of betrayal and distrust on both sides.

The second step in working relations with these hitherto unconquered tribes was taken only after Anglo armed force had prevailed. This consisted in making treaties, and later simple agreements, with the United States recognized as conqueror and in a position to dictate the terms. These agreements amounted to a sort of enforced gift exchange from the point of view of the Indians. They agreed to give up large portions of their land to Anglo settlement, in return for which they received gifts of food, clothing, and other goods. From the Anglo point of view it was not a gift exchange, but a one-sided giving — of land which the Anglos now possessed by right of conquest and of food and goods to keep a conquered people from death and starvation — for the Anglos worked on the same theory as the Spaniards, namely, that the whole territory belonged to their government and was to be dispensed by the government for individual use. Besides the giving of land and rations, the United States affirmed the obligation of protection to the Indians, both of their right to the assigned land and from attack by settlers. It asked in return that the Indians remain within the assigned territory and stop fighting — important limitations of freedom from the Indian viewpoint.

19. EXPANSION OF THE NAVAJOS

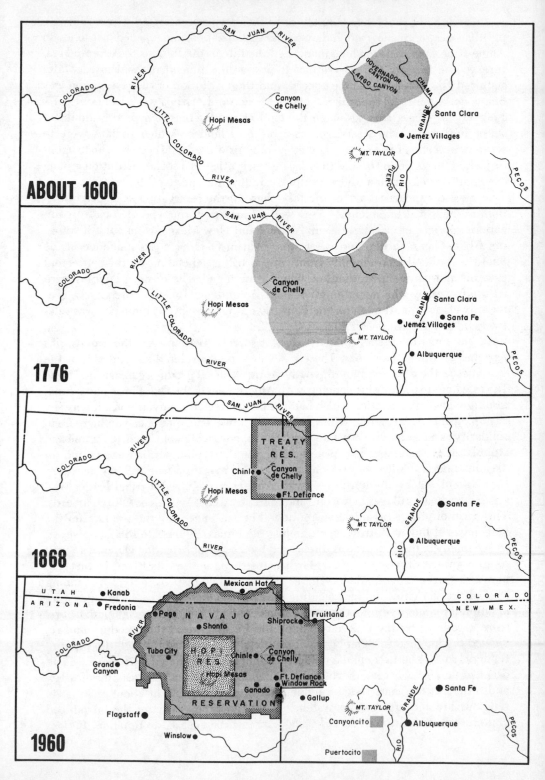

The idea of protection turned out to be a two-edged sword which fell with peculiar destructiveness on Indian social organization and opened breaches in Anglo-American society which influenced the fate of the Indians. Its essential feature was ultimately the reservation. It was at the time that the United States acquired New Mexico that the concept and the institution of the reservation was being worked out. All the Indians of New Mexico and Arizona were, by about 1875, assigned to reservations, although the land of the Pueblos remained in doubtful status until 1913. The reservation as a piece of land on which Indians were to receive protection from settlers and other Indians was established as an instrument of United States policy by the 1860's. The reservation as a social institution among the Southwestern Indians did not fully crystallize until perhaps the 1890's.

We have spoken above of the first phase of the reservation as a social institution as the "superintendency." This was a fairly uniform type of social organization, not different in essentials in Arizona and New Mexico from what it was in the Great Plains, in the Northwest, and even in Oklahoma. Its influence in the Southwest varied considerably from tribe to tribe, depending on the settlement patterns and native institutions on which it impinged. The Eastern Pueblos were least affected by the operation of the superintendency; all the others were profoundly affected, although for the Papagos and the Navajos its influence was relatively inhibited until the 1920's.

The superintendency had its deepest effects, perhaps, on the San Carlos Apaches and the Gila Pimas. These cases may be considered as examples of the extremes in the destruction of the native forms of local group organization. In the 1850's when their intensive contacts with Anglos began, the Gila Pimas had a functioning village organization which had not been affected in any important ways by the Spanish colonial system. The villages had, however, experienced an increase in solidarity as a result of the warfare with the Apaches which the Spanish regime had stimulated. The villages had peace leaders of the type described above and an organization of adult males which managed the irrigation works. They also, perhaps stimulated by the hostilities with Apaches, recognized a tribal leader who could coordinate villages in warfare and to some extent in relations with Spaniards. This form of village organization continued in existence until the 1880's after the placement of Indian Bureau agents among the Pimas. By the late 1880's, however, the economy of the Indians was threatened by the loss of irrigation water as a result of appropriation by Anglo settlers farther upstream on the Gila River. In this economic crisis the superintendents increasingly assumed responsibility, for planning agricultural activities and for executing the plans. Ditch bosses of the villages were appointed by the superintendent and some conflict of authority developed. Courts were organized by the superintendent and he supervised the procedure and reviewed the judgments. Relations with settlers were funneled through the superintendent, so that he became the official channel for outside relations. Warfare and organization for war ceased. The superintendent's staff took responsibility for law and order. At the same time an influential missionary brought about changes in religious life and organized a system of village elders as part of the introduced church system. Gradually the old village organization ceased to function. Indians participated in the new organization, but always under the direction and by appointment of the superintendent or the missionary.

In this way the Pimas were not without organization, as their old village form disintegrated, but the new organization was one which outsiders controlled. The policies of these outsiders were determined at the national level of life in the United States by the federal Indian Bureau and by the Presbyterian Church. Insofar as the Indian Bureau aspect of the organization was concerned, there was not democratic participation by the Pimas. The superintendent was responsible to his superiors in the government bureau, not to the Pimas. His decisions with reference to the all-important economic crisis were based on policy and information which came to him from outside sources. The school and agricultural services which he administered were extended to the Indians as gifts, for which the Pimas assumed no responsibility. School boards or agricultural advisory groups were not created. Consultation with Indians was limited to those individuals with whom the superintendent and his staff personally preferred to associate. The result was an administrative unit on the reservation which operated entirely in terms of the Anglo-American culture. No obligations in connection with it were required of the Indians, who increasingly lost any sense of control of their lives. There even began to be a feeling that the land itself was no longer theirs.

A similar kind of organization with similar consequences grew up on the San Carlos Apache Reservation. Here the initial phases established an even more extreme condition of dependency for the Indians. Unlike the Gila Pimas, the Apaches were forced immediately with the creation of the reservation into a new kind of life. Their raiding and their wide-ranging food gathering activities were stopped. The Indian Bureau had to issue food rations to keep them alive. Rations were issued during the first twenty-five years or more of the existence of the reservation. At the same time the Indian Bureau officials made an effort, with considerable success, to get the Apaches to develop more intensive agriculture than they had been accustomed to practice. These new activities were planned and supervised by the superintendents. The superintendents also managed a court for settling local difficulties and the Indians came under the jurisdiction of federal courts for major crimes. As Anglo-American appropriation of water upstream on the Gila River created difficulties similar to those among the Pimas, the superintendent increasingly assumed responsibility for planning the development of economic resources. Farming and cattle-raising enterprises were organized and supervised by the Indian Bureau staff. Land was assigned by the superintendent, and Indians lost the sense of ownership of farm land.

The San Carlos Apaches moreover were concentrated into settlements surrounding the agency, a form of community arrangement which contrasted strongly with the band settlements. Children were placed in a boarding school on the reservation where they underwent severe discipline which removed them from traditional parental relations. By the 1930's the result was an extreme breakdown in traditional forms of authority with the substitution of no authority except that of the superintendent and his staff. The only approximation to the encouragement of any community organization to supplement the superintendent's administrative unit was the appointment by him of a "business committee." This consisted of a small group of men selected at the personal preference of the superintendent to advise him on matters in which, under the Indian Bureau regulations, the "tribe" as a whole was concerned. This committee over which the Indians had no controls contributed to, rather than ameliorated, the growth of community disorganization. It may be said that, as in the case of the Gila Pimas, what local organization had existed among the San Carlos Apaches had been consistently ignored. The administrative organization which had grown up rested on no foundation of functioning local groups or other forms of organization and the growth of any such forms had been inhibited by the thoroughgoing control exercised by the superintendent. The superintendency, as in the case of other reservation systems, was related through no regularized and formal linkages with the county-state political organization.

In similar fashion the superintendencies on the Walapai, Havasupai, Yuma, Mohave-Chemehuevi, and Fort Apache reservations weakened or destroyed local organization and isolated the Indians from the dominant political organization. In each case the Indians found themselves constituting an administrative unit at the end of the line of command of a federal bureau. The superintendencies administered government plans and regulations for Indians on land controlled by the federal government and on which only the federal government had jurisdiction. The administration of the reservations was built on the idea that the Indians were being prepared for integration into the nation as a whole but up until the 1930's no institutions were being encouraged there by which this linkage could take place. Even the program for allotment of land to Indian individuals which was carried out elsewhere in the United States was not carried through on the reservations of Arizona and New Mexico. Thus in respect to land system and local government the reservations were anomalous phenomena within the nation as a whole, and a very special kind of dependence on the national government had been encouraged and continued to be sponsored.

Unlike the Pimas and Apaches, the Navajos until the 1930's to a great extent escaped the influence of the superintendency. Most Navajos, having scattered widely after returning from Fort Sumner, continued to live under conditions of the old band organization, that is, in social units composed of several extended families ranging over a defined territory within which they raised corn and herded their sheep. The undesirability of Navajo land to the Anglos kept it isolated from the settlers who had poured into New Mexico and Arizona after the coming of the railroad. Navajo isolation was so great that, after the death of Manuelito, Indian agents maintained contact with only a small minority. There was consequently, with the exception of the region in the vicinity of Fort Defiance and perhaps Shiprock, no pressure of importance for changes in political organization. There was, moreover, a minimum of control by the Indian agent; the superintendent-controlled community just described existed only in feeble outline among Navajos. Navajo life should be thought of rather as developing along a number of different lines with respect to local group organization.

While the band, or "outfit," type of organization was general among the thirty thousand Navajos in the 1920's, there were in different parts of the reservation newer groupings which strongly affected Navajo life. The isolated situation of the people encouraged Anglo traders to settle among them; one of the most character- istic integrations of Navajos had become the clientele of a trader, embracing a num- ber of bands. In a somewhat similar relationship were Navajo bands settled near new mission centers, such as St. Michaels of the Franciscans and Ganado of the Presbyterians. These and some other missions became communities with school and hospital and other Anglo type facilities, where Navajos settled and worked and to which Navajos scattered widely over the reservation sent their children for school and came to visit. Such growing institutions competed with one another and with the superintendency for Navajo interest and loyalties. But none recognized the reality of Navajo local group life. Thus, there was little actually going on between the 1880's and the 1920's in the way of political integration at the level of local group organization.

Nevertheless there was a development of some importance at the tribal level. Superintendents were instructed in 1922 to appoint advisory committees of Indians, so that tribes, which were legal entities, would have legal representatives in deal- ings that involved their land and other resources. The advisory committee ap- pointed for the Navajos by the superintendent consisted of nine men well known by the latter and regarded by him as "leaders." They included one of the wealthiest of Navajo sheep owners — Chee Dodge who was influential with many Navajos in the Ganado-Fort Defiance area. The advisers were in no manner elected or approved by a Navajo electorate. They worked as friends of the superintendent and existed as a formal body on his sufferance. Needless to say, there was little or noth- ing in the way of formal working relationship between this appointed group and the vast majority of Navajos.

Attempts to introduce Indian Bureau programs had twice precipitated Navajo resistance, but in general the Indian Bureau staff was faced with problems of organ- ization on the Navajo Reservation which were quite beyond the means which the national Congress provided; consequently there was no concerted development of a program as in the case of the smaller reservations where the Indian Bureau staff could come closer to maintaining contact of some sort with a majority of the Indians. The Papagos, likewise because of their geographical situation, escaped in large part the most destructive phase of Indian Bureau management. No reserva- tion was created for the great majority of Papagos until 1917; thus except for the few hundred at the village of San Xavier the four thousand or more Papagos lived outside of bureau supervision for a generation longer than any other tribe in Ari- zona. In addition, although there were considerably fewer Papagos than Navajos, there were more than sixty small rancherías scattered over an area almost as large as the Navajo Reservation. This meant limited contacts for the single superinten- dent with very small staff who was assigned to the administration of the Papago reservations.

Until the assignment of the reservation in 1917 Papagos had experienced at the hands of Anglo-Americans much the same kind of pressures which Pimas, Seris, Mayos, and Tarahumaras had undergone. The encroachment of Anglo cattlemen on Papago land and water holes, the appropriation of mines and land near mines had proceeded in unregulated fashion and created distrust among Indians. Almost immediately with the creation of the reservation a form of organization appeared among the Papagos which seems to have been unique for Southwestern reservations. By the time the Indian Bureau Agency was set up a number of Papagos had attended boarding schools in various parts of the United States. Among those who had returned to the reservation the idea was conceived of relating the ranchería organization to the superintendency. This resulted in the organization of the Good Government League and later its splitting into a progressive and conservative faction, the latter being called the League of Papago Chiefs. These groups which worked to some extent through regularly constituted ranchería headmen and "governors" exercised considerable influence on the operation of the superintendent during the 1920's, but had disintegrated by the early 1930's, as the superintendency began to assume the form taken elsewhere. Papago communities to an extent comparable to that for the more isolated Navajo bands maintained their organization as it had developed through the Spanish and Mexican periods. Papago local groups were still strongly functioning units at the time the next phase in reservation life got under way.

The Eastern Pueblos escaped the influence of the superintendency almost completely. This was largely a result of Anglo-American conviction at the beginning of their regime that the Pueblos needed little attention since they were not "wild." As Indian Bureau management was established for the Pueblos it took the form of a centralized superintendency for all Eastern Pueblos, rather than a superintendent for each village. Although "farmers" were placed at most villages, they were kept at arm's length, as the Franciscan missionaries had been, and were refused residence within the village. The result of these factors was that Indian Bureau officials were not able to involve themselves in any very important ways in Pueblo internal affairs. The family and village life, except for influences that came through boarding schools and contacts with neighboring communities, continued very much as it had throughout the later Spanish period. No changes in political organization developed until about the 1890's, and these will be considered below. The villages managed their own affairs, but like the superintendencies elsewhere they were just as completely isolated from state-national political participation.

In 1934 the Indian Reorganization Act was passed by the national Congress and for the first time the reservation began in some measure to be organized as a political unit rather than purely as an arm of federal administration. The Apache, Papago, Pima, and Yuman tribes promptly organized tribal councils and began to deliberate and take action on reservation affairs under the aegis of constitutions. These constitutions defined political subdivisions on the reservations, set up qualifications for tribal membership, provided for universal adult suffrage, defined the functions of a set of tribal officers, and in short set up a formal pattern for organization of the reservation populations. This pattern, like that proffered by the Spaniards to the village and ranchería Indians, was one in the image of the conquerors' nation. It was made designedly so by the new program makers in the Indian Bureau on the theory that participation in such institutions on the reservations would lay foundations for participation in the national political life. The framework within which the tribal councils operated was still, however, that of the Indian Bureau, not the state and national political organization.

The establishment of elective councils gave some voice in reservation affairs to what Indian leadership cared to participate. While superintendents still held ultimate power of decision in important reservation affairs, the existence of elected Indian spokesmen introduced a new factor. From 1934 until 1946 superintendents were, in fact, instructed to act primarily as advisers to the Indian leaders who emerged. The intent of the new policy was to develop Indian leadership, but it became clear that such leadership was not going to develop within a few years. The first phase, lasting for about ten years, consisted of the employment of the councils by the Indian Bureau staffs on the reservations as mechanisms for instructing a limited number of Indians in the details of agency administration. To some extent the members of tribal councils became a supplementary staff in the management of projects which were still conceived and administered by Bureau officials — such as tribally-owned cattle herds, for example. The councils in no way operated as independent political bodies as yet, although they sometimes criticized and advised on what the agency undertook in reservation resource development.

The second phase, beginning about 1945, consisted of efforts of the Indian Bureau to have the councils assume more management responsibility, particularly with respect to handling the reservation law and order problems. There were also efforts directed towards acquainting the elected Indian leaders more intimately with the operation of state and national politics and administration. Council chairmen and committee members accompanied Indian Bureau officials to Washington and to the state capitals, joined in conference with national and state officials, and slowly began to gain some experience with the political organization of the nation. As this happened a few Indian men and women emerged as spokesmen who began to speak and to be listened to in their own right as representatives of the reservation residents. An intertribal council of Indians in Arizona was formed for discussion of Indian affairs. Indian leaders began also to take some part in a national Indian organization — the National Congress of American Indians — which engaged in lobbying for Indian interests in general. Through such contacts the tribal councils had by 1955 begun to function in some degree in the adjustment of Indian interests on the reservations to those of Anglo-Americans in surrounding communities, even though the organization yet had no formal links with the state. Each reservation where councils existed could now indeed be said to have been organized into a transitional political unit, somewhat in the nature of the Spanish mission communities, where Indians were learning the political behavior of the conquerors.

The acceptance of the tribal council form of organization, unlike the Spanish town organization, had been made voluntary by the Indian Bureau. The Navajos refused to adopt it. Yet nevertheless between 1934 and 1960 they, too, built a tribal organization, on the nucleus of the superintendent's advisory committee, of precisely the form proposed by the Indian Reorganization Act, with a constitution, universal adult suffrage, and political subdistricts within the reservation. With a rapidity comparable to the Apaches, the Navajo Tribal Council undertook, with

Indian Bureau aid, the management of economic enterprises such as logging and range development. At first a vehicle for discussion of tribal affairs composed of Navajos in closest communication with Anglo-Americans, the Navajo Tribal Council by 1960 had broadened its base in the isolated communities of the reservation. Election regulations, for example, were printed in the Navajo language, and efforts were being made to encourage local group organizations called chapters.

These developments in internal organization on the reservations were accompanied in the late 1940's by the extension of voting privileges to all Indians by the states of New Mexico and Arizona. This took place despite the fact that the federal government's protective function, which did not permit jurisdiction of the states within the reservations, was maintained. The result was the participation of Indians in a dual political system — on the one hand in their own tribal organizations and on the other in the state and national political life. The Indians maintained their own courts, under tribal council jurisdiction, and within the Indian Bureau framework took a part in managing their internal affairs; yet at the same time they were taxable by state and nation and had a voice in state and national government. They still held their lands in accordance with the old domestic nation arrangement, however, and hence were not subject to a state land tax. To this right they clung desperately, with federal sanction, but the fear among them was intense that the state land tax would be imposed and that they would lose their land.

Taxation of Indian lands had in fact become a major issue, along with legal jurisdiction on the reservations, between Indians and the states in which their reservations were located. In much the manner of pressures on the ranchería and village Indians during the Spanish period, pressures were constant from the states to abolish the whole system of internal organization on the reservations and bring the Indians completely under state jurisdiction. The Indian Bureau stood as a buffer between the pressures for state control and the Indian fear of it. The dual political system under which the Indians lived was obviously not in a state of stable equilibrium; uncoordinated changes, both in the direction of strengthening the tribal organization and of extending state services to Indians, were going on constantly.

The contradictions in the Indian status affected all the tribes and, as well, the Indian Bureau officials and state officers concerned with Indian affairs. The situation bore more than a passing resemblance to that which generated conflict between missionaries and colonial administrators in Spanish New Mexico and Sonora. Indian affairs were in a constant state of flux and Indians had come to believe that the behavior of Bureau officials was unpredictable. The transitional nature of political relations in this period was indicated by their instability; the general trend appeared to be toward the elimination of the special status for Indians which had developed.

It was also fairly clear that the tribal council organization on each reservation was more an extension of the organization of the Indian Bureau than it was a representative body of Indians comparable to, let us say, a county within a state. While some learning of political and administrative ways of the Anglos had taken place among some few Indians elected to the councils, it was by no means clear that the councils had been related in a meaningful way to the life of the reservation residents in general. Councils were considered by most Indians, with justification, as tools of the Indian Bureau or as powerless groups of no significance in the basic problems of making a living. Hostilities which the dependency situation had generated toward the Indian Bureau were extended to the councils. A sense of participation in important political activity was largely limited to the few individuals regularly re-elected to the councils. There was, in short, little integration of the people generally on the reservations into the new political structure. Integration had developed in some degree at the top, but the councils remained relatively poorly or not at all integrated with Indians generally. The lack of relationship between tribal organization and local group was most clear on those reservations where strong superintendencies had most completely disintegrated Indian communities, namely, the Gila Pima, the Yuma, the Mohave-Chemehuevi, the Walapai, the Havasupai, and the San Carlos Apache.

Finding the Eastern Pueblos inclined to peace, the United States government at first paid little attention to their political status after acquiring New Mexico. In fact, no systematic steps were taken to change their community organization until 1934. Their land was treated at first by the state of New Mexico like all other land in the state, that is, as Spanish land grants, title to which was valid for the Indians and should be granted to them. Both the United States Supreme Court and the New Mexico courts agreed until 1913 that the Pueblo Indians had a different legal status from other Indians, as a result of their Spanish land grants, and that therefore the protective measures which the federal government took toward other Indian lands did not apply to them. This meant that the Eastern Pueblos were regarded as politically in the same status as other residents of New Mexico, and sporadic efforts were made by the state to bring them under its political and judicial jurisdiction. The federal government disputed this interpretation of status and was finally upheld by the Supreme Court of the United States in 1913, after which the Eastern Pueblos came under the provisions which applied to all reservation Indians in the United States.

On into the 1950's the cacique-controlled village organizations continued to function as the central theocratic government with the executive-ceremonial war leaders and the civil governor and his aides as appendages. Only one village, the Tewa village of Isleta, had ever adopted an elective system for governor and war leaders, and it continued to function badly, being a source of factionalism and disputes. Isleta and the Tewa village of Santa Clara chose in 1955 to adopt the tribal council-constitutional form of government prescribed by the Indian Reorganization Act. In only one village, the relatively recently founded and faction-ridden Laguna, was the cacique-ceremonial society system still not in operation by 1960.

In the other villages, during a hundred years without direct pressures to change, the major changes which took place were the following: The scope of the governor's activities had increased; he had become chairman of the general village council and had assumed the duties of judge in the case of interfamily land and other disputes. The governor had become the focus of all Indian Bureau business, which meant that he was concerned with matters pertaining to agricultural development, medical service, and schools. In general, then, there had been an expansion in the functions of the governor and consequently in the civil functions of government generally. At the same time, there had also been some expansion in the duties of the War Chief. He usually directed work on the irrigation systems and in most Pueblo villages was in charge of the horse herds; probably the water-supply functions had been part of his activity before the Spanish period, but they were now increasingly important in Pueblo life, and amounted to an increase in the civil duties of the War Chief. In general, it was indicated that Pueblo government was flexible enough to take care of new civil functions by assignment to either governor or War Chief. Within the framework of the governmental system originally adapted to Spanish requirements there was a continuing specialization of function, but since it was not a constitutional form of government it was apparent that conflict was developing between it and Anglo forms.

The increasing importance of civil aspects of government was also indicated in the formation of an All-Pueblo Council, in the early 1920's, to which the various villages sent delegates for the purpose of discussion of problems common to all the Pueblo villages. Without executive authority, the All-Pueblo Council functioned as a forum and means of intervillage communication. Like the tribal councils of the other Indians, the Pueblo village organization had no formal organizational relations with surrounding communities of Anglo-Americans.

In contrast with the other Pueblos, the Hopis became divided over the issue of accepting the tribal council-constitutional type of government. Without direct pressures to change their peace leader-war leader type of theocratic village organization after 1680, they had maintained it with no important changes during the following 250 years. Indian Bureau superintendents during the early 1900's instituted interference in the villages of Oraibi and Shongopovi when the two split over the issue of sending children to boarding school. The interference consisted of sending soldiers to the villages to pick up children for the purpose of taking them to school. Resistance by villagers resulted in the sending of the peace leader of Oraibi to a boarding school to "learn white man's ways." He returned deeply hostile to Anglo-Americans and especially to Christianity, whereas before he had favored cooperation with Indian Bureau officials. However, the Indian Bureau officials did nothing further by way of interfering in village affairs until after 1934. Then they worked with Hopi individuals who favored adopting a tribal-council form of government and helped them write a constitution. A vote was obtained which led the government officials to proceed with setting up a tribal council.

The Hopi Tribal Council, from 1936 to 1960, remained a bone of contention rather than a unifying influence in Hopi life. For the most part the First Mesa villages accepted it as an instrument for working with the superintendent, while the other villages either split or refused to recognize it at all as a proper means of organization. The superintendent persisted in recognizing it as the official political body of the tribe. Most of the villages refused to send representatives to it, although some sent "observers" to keep in touch with what it was trying to do.

The basic issues as seen by the villages or parts of villages which refused to accept it were the following: In the first place, they insisted on the autonomy of village deliberation and action which they had always enjoyed. In the second place, they recognized no legitimate right of the Indian Bureau to concern itself in their affairs, and Tribal Council activity was chiefly concerned with business originating from the superintendent. In the third place, and this was probably most important in their position, they regarded the sacred tradition of their identification with the land as being infringed upon by most Tribal Council actions or attempted actions; such actions involved tacit acceptance of the United States government's ruling that a portion of Hopi land belonged to Navajos who had long used it, efforts to lease drilling rights to oil companies within the Hopi reservation, approval of an Indian Bureau plan for a road connecting all the Hopi villages across the traditional site of Shongopovi on Second Mesa, and prosecution of a suit in the federal Indian Claims Commission for land claims against the United States government.

Like the Yaquis, the Hopis had developed a systematic body of sacred tradition concerning their land and the Hopi relation to it. This tradition functioned as a "Sacred Book" among these groups, such as the residents of Old Oraibi and Hotevilla who opposed the Tribal Council organization. It described divinely ordained and unchangeable boundaries for the Hopi land, which considerably exceeded those decreed by the United States government. It detailed the sacred sanctions for this territory in the form of ancient myths and described a sacred stone on which the boundaries were recorded and which would be understood by a savior or messiah — the *bahana* — who it was prophesied would appear and resolve the conflict between Hopis and Anglo-Americans. The stone itself was regarded by some conservative groups as in the possession of the Oraibi peace chief who had been sent to boarding school and returned opposed to cooperation with the Anglo-Americans. Any form of cooperation, such as recognization of the Tribal Council, was considered by this peace leader and his associates as contrary to the sacred body of tradition and therefore impossible. Even prosecution of the proposed suit for lost lands was regarded as amounting to tacit admission that land had been lost, and such a condition was contrary to the scripture; hence no suit for recovery of damages could be sanctioned. The conservative groups differed somewhat among themselves on details, but they were agreed on the impossibility of accepting the Indian Bureau-inspired form of tribal organization. Nevertheless there were younger leaders among them who by the 1950's were working desperately at forging some sort of formal cooperative organization among the conservative groups themselves.

Thus, there existed among the Hopis what amounted to a triple system of government. The so-called conservatives lived as village groups, or factions within villages, under the old Hopi form of village government, largely unchanged since the entry of white men. Other villages, and factions in some villages, lived under the new Tribal Council plan of government with its recognition of a distinct civil arm of government working under a constitution. At the same time federal law in regard to the ten major crimes, the administration of the Indian Bureau and state and national taxation (except for land), voting, and office-holding privileges all applied on the reservation. In these respects all Hopis were integrated into the United States state-national political organization. The situation was the most complicated, not excepting that of the Yaquis, of any among the Indians of the region. One of the most apparent overt conflicts between the systems was precipitated during World War II when the United States government applied its program of drafting men for war service among the Hopis. Hopis of the "conservative" groups refused to be drafted on the ground that their religion, or view of life, did not recognize warfare as a legitimate or morally acceptable activity. The United States government proceeded then to demonstrate that it regarded its jurisdiction as extending over the Hopis in this regard by treating Hopis who resisted as conscientious objectors and placing them in noncombatant war service.

By the 1950's the sense of tribal identity was strong among the Indians living on reservations. It rested on different conditions applying in different combinations and in varying degrees among the Indians. No reservation group was homogeneous. Individuals differed in regard to extent of formal education in Anglo schools, kinds of experience in Anglo communities, participation in Anglo churches and other organizations, extent of knowledge of their tribal traditions and history, and so on. Yet there were common experiences contributing to the sense of distinct identity. The continuing existence of well-defined tribal territories in the form of reservations for all the groups was a major basis. The practice of sharply distinct religious customs was especially influential among both Eastern and Western Pueblos and for large numbers of Navajos who had been little influenced by the various Christian sects. Among the Hopis and Pueblos and some Navajos the existence of and continuing indoctrination in a traditional mythical-legendary tribal lore played a great part. For Apaches and Navajos, and to a lesser extent for Papagos and Gila Pimas who had worked a great deal off the reservations among Anglos, experiences of discrimination in a variety of forms played an important role in maintaining a sense of difference. These factors operated in conjunction with the continuing separate jurisdiction maintained by the Indian Bureau over the Indians in regard to schooling and many different reservation services, such as medical attention and economic development. The literature of the Anglo-Americans also played a part. In its various forms, ranging from newspapers to novels and poetry, the distinctions among tribes and their differences in custom from Anglos were made much of and stimulated consciousness of tribal identity.

Developments in the political integration of the Indians under Anglo-American methods may be summarized in the following way. The traditional Anglo method of attempting to thrust the Indians aside after conquest, with no plan for making them a part of the nation, gave rise to the reservation system which still obtained in the Southwest in 1960. Under the reservation system Indians were isolated politically and socially from Anglo-Americans and learned to adjust themselves to living under a form of administrative dictatorship, in the course of which a strong attitude of dependency on the United States federal government developed — from the 1870's until the present. Meanwhile local organization of the Indian communities was not directly suppressed, although indirectly it was undermined, as the reservation superintendent took over many economic and political functions. Despite these conditions, Eastern Pueblo and Hopi village governments retained the same form that they had under the Spaniards. Beginning about 1934, an effort to institute a form of Anglo constitutional, representative government was quickly taken up by all the tribes except the Eastern Pueblos. Among all except the Hopis the result was a tribal organization for the first time in the whole history of the Indians. The Anglo governmental form was strictly limited in its jurisdiction to internal affairs on reservations and allowed only for informal relations with county and state organizations. Its forms were somewhat modified to adapt to existing Indian custom, as for instance in the modification among Papagos of majority rule to a species of unanimous decision, but for the most part the tribal councils functioned primarily as extensions of Indian Bureau administration rather than as independent political units. The effective range of acceptance by Indians of tribal councils widened only very slowly, if at all, from 1934 to 1960. The result was the growth of a dual system of government on all reservations, which stimulated pressures from the Anglos to eliminate the tribal councils and to bring Indians completely under state jurisdiction. Only a faction of the Hopis, however, accepted the tribal council form of government, so that a triple political system existed on the Hopi Reservation, and intense conflict grew up between the Tribal Council and certain of the persisting village organizations. Meanwhile, all but two of the Eastern Pueblo villages continued with only slight changes in governmental form, chiefly expansion of functions of the civil branch under the Spanish-introduced governors.

RESULTS OF POLITICAL INCORPORATION

The process of political incorporation involved two kinds of adjustment. On the one hand, there took place a progressive adoption by Indians of forms of political organization and conceptions of government like those of the invading and ultimately dominant peoples. On the other hand, new forms of organization grew up through which Indian communities and the invaders cooperated for common purposes. We may call the former political assimilation and the latter political adaptation.

In general Spain, Mexico, and the United States sought to bring about political assimilation. Nevertheless Spain was forced through her own weakness to accept Indian-adapted forms of her political institutions, most notably among the Eastern Pueblo villages and the reorganized rancherías of Yaquis and Mayos, while many remained completely outside the range of her political influence. Quite aware that the program for political assimilation had bogged down, the later frontier officials in northwestern New Spain nevertheless remained powerless.

The Mexicans required not only continued changes along the lines mapped by the Spaniards, but also some important additional ones which conflicted with adaptations already well established among the ranchería Indians. One such conflict was in connection with the complete separation of civil and ecclesiastical functions; another lay in the sharing of jurisdiction over land with a non-Indian cabecera, or municipal center of administration. The general resistance of ranchería

Indians, especially those who had moved farthest in the direction of adaptation of native to Spanish institutions, found the inexperienced Mexican state governments without any policy but force. No intermediaries comparable to either missionaries or even alcaldes were assigned systematically to deal with the problems of Indian adjustment. There emerged the concept of infiltration of the Indian country through colonization as an alternative policy to force. Force applied to the more widely dispersed and more infiltrated groups resulted ultimately over a period of twenty-five to fifty years in political incorporation. Applied to the more concentrated and best organized groups, such as the Yaquis, force had still not by the middle of the twentieth century resulted in assimilation. It had rather intensified the sense of difference from and hostility to Mexicans and had led to the political institutions of the Spanish period being regarded as sacred and necessary to religious life. This resulted in continued conflict.

Once military dominance was established over those tribes never brought under control by Spain or Mexico, Anglo-American policy showed that it derived from a fundamentally different cultural tradition than that of the Spanish-Mexican. Political assimilation was not clearly sought. Policy in regard to Southwestern Indians remained unclear and contradictory from decade to decade. In general, the trend of stated objective was for cultural assimilation, but the trend of administrative action veered for and against political assimilation. Only during one ten-year period did any clear policy emerge; this was for a sort of political adaptation embodied in the tribal council program. The effects of this uncertain policy by the 1950's were varied.

The uniform features of the Anglo-American program consisted of the formal isolation of Indians on reservations, insuring that their communities would not be infiltrated by non-Indians. This maintenance of a land base for even the smallest of tribes led to the development of strong feelings of tribal identity. It also led to the placing of Indians under the administration of a government bureau in which they had no representation or control. The effect on most of the tribes of Arizona and New Mexico was a general breakdown in local group organization and the growth of deep feelings of dependency on the bureau. The institution of tribal councils, aimed at encouraging political organization within the reservations, came at a time when community disintegration was well advanced. Those tribes, such as the Navajos and the Papagos, which were so widely scattered as to have avoided the intensive influence of the reservation agencies to some extent escaped the process of social disintegration. Also the tribes which had worked out an effective adaptation to the Spanish regime, the Eastern Pueblos, adapted further in the direction of greater specialization of governmental functions, but continued very much as they had since the time of Spanish contacts. An unstable political adaptation, rather than progressive assimilation, prevailed in New Mexico and Arizona, giving rise to conditions satisfactory to neither Indians nor Anglo-Americans.

Linguistic Unification

 THE UNEVEN political integration of Indians into the three nations which successively expanded into the Southwest was matched by an equally uneven adoption of the official languages of those states. Up to 1960 the process which was set in motion by the impact of the cultures could not be characterized as one of progressive disappearance of the Indian languages.

What had happened could be summed up in the following figures: (1) in 1950 in the states of Chihuahua, Sonora, Arizona, and New Mexico twenty-eight Indian languages were spoken; (2) the total number of Indian speakers was somewhere in the neighborhood of two hundred thousand, or about the same number as may be assumed were living in the region at the time of European discovery; and (3) after a long decline the number of speakers of Indian languages had been slowly but steadily increasing during the preceding half century. These figures in themselves give no clear answer to the question as to what had been the general trend of linguistic change over the previous four hundred years.

Superficially they seem to suggest the conclusion that, since there were as many speakers of Indian languages in 1950 as there had been in 1540, the use of Indian languages was little affected by the conquests. It would appear from these figures that Indian languages about held their own in the face of the introduction of Spanish and English. Thus it might be concluded that the dominant process was that of the persistence of the Indian languages and even that language was considerably more resistant to change than political organization.

Such conclusions are entirely unjustified, because the figures present only a single aspect of a complex cultural situation. They do testify to the persistence of the majority of the Indian languages throughout the four hundred years, but they do not indicate the altered role of the Indian languages in the lives of their speakers, nor do they indicate anything concerning the important changes which took place in those languages during the period. These aspects of the situation must be taken into account for a full understanding of how culture contact affected the linguistic behavior of the people involved. We may point out here that by 1950 the Indian languages for most Indians were only alternative means of communication; most such speakers were bilingual, using Spanish or English in addition to their native tongue. They used an Indian language, but only in some of their relationships with others. The Indian languages, in other words, although retaining in large degree their form, had been reduced to narrower functions in the lives of their speakers. They served for their speakers only a portion of their communication needs, in contrast with the totality which they had served before the coming of white men. An understanding of this shift in function gives the best clue to an answer to the question of whether the trend was consistently toward extinction of Indian languages.

But even when put in this way, the real situation is somewhat distorted. For what could be identified in 1950 as the Yaqui or the Navajo language was not precisely what it had been one hundred or four hundred years before. All languages change constantly. Some Indian languages were much influenced by the first impact with speakers of Spanish and continued to change throughout the following centuries. Others were little affected by Spanish, but experienced greater or less change after the entry of the Anglo-Americans into the region. Indian languages influenced one another under the new conditions and they were not without influence on the languages of the conquerors. Although some twenty-eight languages were identifiable in 1950 as non-European and as distinct from one another, these languages all reflected in greater or less degree the history of cultural change in the Southwest. They had all changed in response to a variety of influences, from the borrowing of words to programs for writing the Indian languages instituted by both the Mexican and the United States governments from the 1930's on. In the light of knowledge of these changes it becomes clear that language was no more static an aspect of culture than any other.

The story of the mutual influences of the Indian and the European languages on one another gives many insights into the changing relations of conquerors and conquered. Although this story has been insufficiently studied as yet, its outlines can be sketched. While up to 1900 the long-term trend had seemed to be toward the complete replacement of the Indian languages, one could not be sure of this in 1950. Toward the end of the nineteenth century certain counter-trends began to appear, and no student had adequately assessed these. On the other hand, one trend was clear — the steady growth of a kind of linguistic unity over the whole region. This consisted of the dominance of the two Indo-European languages — Spanish and English.

THE DIFFUSION OF SPANISH

In contrast with the aim of making all Indians citizens, it cannot be said that Spain had the clear objective of making all Indians speakers of Castilian — the standard language of Spain. On the contrary, the mastery of Castilian by all the Indians of New Spain was no more regarded as a prerequisite to citizenship than it was for citizenship in Spain itself. There the existence of many distinct languages, such as Catalán and Basque, was not seen as an obstacle to Spanish national strength, so long as there was in every province a ruling class who used the official language. In New Spain, emphasis on the importance of a common language did not become very strong until some 150 years after the conquest of Mexico.

In fact the earliest approach to the Indians seemed definitely to be based on the assumption that most of them would never learn Spanish. The first missionaries — notably the Franciscans — frequently set out to learn the Indian languages of the region around Mexico City. They wrote grammars and dictionaries, translated Indian chronicles into Spanish, translated Catholic prayers into Nahuatl and other Indian languages, and generally seemed to assume that the important thing for the purposes of conversion was that the missionaries get immediately into touch with the Indians through their own language. There were no official laws requiring Indians to learn Castilian and of course, nothing like public schools of a later period where Castilian was the official language. Instead, the concept was that "sons of chiefs" should be taken for special instruction into schools away from their homes where in the course of receiving instruction in the subjects of the day they would learn Spanish. This policy definitely did not look toward the learning of Spanish by the general Indian population. It was apparent that the use of interpreters in dealing with the Indians of the repartimientos was accepted as a permanent arrangement.

This general policy, based on the social structure of Spain and on the ethnic and linguistic diversity of that country, prevailed at the time colonization and conversion of the Northwest began. The Jesuits who pushed into Chihuahua and Sonora from the 1590's on worked in ways that were much in accord with the early work of the Franciscans and others in central Mexico immediately after the conquest of the Aztecs. They took as the foundation of their approach to the Indians real linguistic understanding. The learning of the Indian language was prerequisite to responsibility for a mission in Sonora. Thus there was a major emphasis in the Jesuit missions on the missionary's conversion of his teachings into the native language rather than on the Indians' learning of Spanish. The teaching of Spanish took the form of the Indians memorizing the catechism in that language, of the recitation of five or six Spanish prayers daily by all the children and adults who could be assembled, and of listening to the sermons which the missionary preached at least weekly. These were not formal classes in the Spanish language, but rather highly specialized instruction in the acquisition of specific formulas in a strange tongue. It is doubtful that any but the small corps of special assistants and choir boys to the missionary learned to use Spanish as a spoken language in the Jesuit missions, except where those missions were in close proximity to a Spanish settler population. While such nuclei of Spanish speakers in most of the missions became important groups for the dissemination of Spanish ideas, they remained specialists language-wise, somewhat apart from the general life of the community.

Slowly, however, this group was added to as a result of the schools which the Jesuits established. In these a selection of students was made, partly along the lines laid down in central Mexico. They were selected, we are told, from among the families of the "chiefs" but also according to demonstrated ability to learn. Some were sent from each "pueblo" to schools such as the one at Matape where they received more intensive instruction and, it may be presumed, gained a fair command of both spoken and written Spanish as they completed elementary school. The proportion of Indians educated to this degree among any of the tribes by the time of the expulsion of the Jesuits remains unknown. But such men existed and were scattered widely through the communities. As early as 1678 the Visitor Zapata reported that at Ures, a community of Pimas and Opatas in central Sonora, a majority could understand Spanish and "many" could speak it. The whole choir was literate in Spanish. This was not unrepresentative of the Sonora mission communities by 1700.

In New Mexico and where the Franciscans worked in Chihuahua there was at first an approach basically like that of Jesuits in Sonora and New Biscay. That is, the Franciscan missionaries did not set out to teach the Spanish language to the whole Indian population, but they did aim at teaching Spanish to some in all the mission communities. By the 1620's, during the period of first zealous activity, there were reputed to be twenty-five missions established in New Mexico. Also there was the objective, if not the realization, of a school at each mission. In these schools, taught by the resident missionaries, there was instruction in reading and writing Spanish, in music, trades, and of course Christian doctrine. It is not clear whether such schools existed in all twenty-five missions, but it is likely that the date of about 1630 marked the fullest development of a school program. After that time for the next 250 years there was a steady decline in mission activities. The ideal of a school in every mission in which *reading and writing* was taught to all who would come suggests a more extensive program of teaching Spanish than characterized the program of the Jesuits. But it is also unlikely that this aim was actually realized.

The Franciscan missionaries working among the Eastern Pueblos must have been less well prepared than the Jesuits of Sonora for any linguistic work. There is no indication that any but one or two missionaries successfully learned the Indian languages. In the period before the Revolt of 1680, not a single grammar or dictionary of a New Mexican language was prepared and there is record of only a single catechism (in Jemez). This was in great contrast with the Sonoran Jesuits and consistent with what we know of the Franciscan schooling for missionary work and their attitudes toward it in this period. The emphasis on reading and writing in the mission schools also suggests the trend in Franciscan opinion favoring the replacement of native languages with Spanish.

The results in terms of language learning of the Franciscan efforts to establish schools for the Indians are unknown. If they were effective in teaching a large number of Indians to speak and to read and write Spanish, the new knowledge was not permanent. The Pueblo Revolt of 1680 and the subsequent great decline in missionary activities must have resulted in considerable loss of knowledge of Spanish by the Indians, for in the late 1700's reports of observers generally agreed that few Pueblos spoke Spanish effectively. It seems more likely that the aim of a school for literacy in each mission was not realized even in the relatively flourishing periods of the 1620's and 1630's. Nevertheless it does appear from Benavides and later accounts at least that there were many Indians in every village who had the kind of knowledge of Spanish which characterized the Indians of Sonora generally, namely, ability to recite the standard prayers and the catechism.

Thus, by the beginning of the 1700's wherever missions were established, there was a knowledge of a specialized vocabulary — that pertaining to Christian doctrine — among a majority of the Indians. For such persons Spanish was a somewhat esoteric language associated with ritual. In the Jesuit missions it is clear also that there was an additional small percentage of the population of the mission communities who spoke and read Spanish, not only as an esoteric language but as a general means of communication. These were the core of *temastianes,* the choirs in Opata country, and special assistants to the missionaries as well as a few who had been selected for systematic study in the schools of the head missions of the districts. It is not at all clear, on the other hand, that the Franciscans in New Mexico were successful in building up permanent groups of mission assistants or that they had developed elementary schooling to the extent that the Jesuits had.

However, the missionaries did not constitute the only medium through which a knowledge of Spanish diffused. In Chihuahua the ranches and haciendas which grew up in the country east of the Sierra Madres to serve the mining communities such as Parral hired Tarahumaras, Conchos, and other Indians to work seasonally or sometimes through the year. To a lesser extent they forced Indians to work on the repartimiento system. Under these conditions a minority of Tarahumaras and most Conchos learned a practical spoken Spanish of limited vocabulary pertaining to work activities. It was also true that Indians from Sonora, probably chiefly Opatas prior to the 1730's and Mayos later, worked in the Parral and other mines and again, in association with Spanish foremen and town dwellers picked up knowledge of Spanish. Since they were segregated in their own quarters of the mining town, as at Parral, it is probable that their knowledge of Spanish remained limited and adapted only to particular activities.

In Sonora there were similar developments as mines were discovered after the middle 1600's along the western margins of the Sierra Madres as far north as Janos. The Opatas and Eudeves especially were affected by this growth of mining and cattle ranching. These Indians, as the missionaries were frequently at great pains to point out, often maintained closer contacts with the Spanish settlers than with the mission staff, and this sort of contact intensified on through the 1700's. The result was a steady growth in knowledge of Spanish as a spoken language in everyday affairs.

The situation in New Mexico with reference to secular Spanish was somewhat different, resulting in probably a less intimate contact for the Indians throughout the colonial period. The informality of the mining towns with their miscellaneous population which did not always draw sharp lines against association with Indians was absent. The Indian settlements were more tightly knit communities than were those of the Opatas and Eudeves, and there was somewhat less association with the Spaniards in the villas. Indians did work on haciendas, as in the Nambé-Pojoaque area, and some were forced or hired into gangs for various projects of New Mexican governors. Such work gangs were most characteristic of the Piro and Tompiro peoples, far less so of the northern Pueblos. But trade, forced labor as servants, and curiosity brought Indians to the towns where contact with Spanish speakers took place. From the early 1600's on there were many opportunities of this sort for hearing and learning a little Spanish in the settlements near the pueblos, and these increased through the 1700's as smaller Spanish villages grew up along the Rio Grande and unofficial and friendly relations developed between Indians and Spaniards.

It should be said, then, that there were two channels of diffusion for Spanish: on the one hand, through the specialized activities of the missionaries in connection with Christian doctrine; and on the other, through secular activities in association with the Spanish settlers. The first resulted in special vocabularies memorized by rote and employed within the Indian settlements as part of what became a segment of the Indian cultural heritage. The second resulted in practical knowledge of spoken Spanish, used during the colonial period chiefly outside the Indian settlements in connection with Spanish activities. In addition, some of those who became proficient in the ritual vocabulary also went on, under missionary encouragement, to gain a knowledge of reading and writing in Spanish. Individuals with this sort of knowledge who remained in the Indian country were found chiefly in the Sonoran communities, not in New Mexico.

How many speakers of Spanish there were or how many were literate in Spanish by the end of the colonial period can only be guessed at. There are no systematic records, merely impressions of various ecclesiastical visitors and others. The lack of such records is of course an indication of the lack of governmental concern about the state of literacy as well as about the extent of knowledge of spoken Spanish. (The modern records reflect a concern which developed only after about the middle of the 1700's.) In 1760 Pedro Tamarón y Romeral, Bishop of Durango, made an expedition of inspection through New Mexico and came to the conclusion that the Indians, with the exception of those of Isleta, did not speak Spanish or understand it. He wrote by way of summary of his inspection: *I soon observed that those Indians were not indoctrinated. They do recite the catechism in Spanish, following their fiscal, but since they do not know this language, they do not understand what they are saying. The missionaries do not know the languages of the Indians, and as a result the latter do not confess except at the point of death, and then with the aid of an interpreter. I remonstrated about this repeatedly, and I ordered the missionaries to learn the languages of the Indians.*

In 1779 Father Francisco Atanasio Domínguez visited all the Franciscan missions in New Mexico and made a report. His impression was that in all the pueblos the people spoke a kind of Spanish, but he wrote of Tesuque pueblo: *They also speak our Castilian, but not very well, for if we and they manage some mutual explanation and understanding, it is in such a disfigured fashion that it is easier for our people to adjust to their manner of speaking than for them to attempt ours, for if one speaks to them rapidly, even without artifice, they no longer understand.*

This estimate he said applied to all the Pueblos. It appears that his contacts were with relatively few Indians in each case and that those with whom he did have contact were those put forward as having the best knowledge of Spanish for dealing with him.

It would appear from these and other confirming accounts that in New

Mexico the missionaries still relied on interpreters for communication with people of the villages and that therefore very few Indians, perhaps only one or two in each village, could be said to have been using Spanish as a means of communication by the end of the 1700's. Yet familiarity with the language as an esoteric ritual medium was extensive throughout the villages.

In Sonora the situation was considerably different for some tribes. The intermingling of Opatas and Eudeves with Spaniards in mining towns and on ranches and haciendas had been intensive enough by the late 1700's so that the impression of Spaniards was that nearly all these Indians spoke Spanish with some degree of proficiency. Father Ignaz Pfefferkorn, one of the last of the Jesuits to work in Sonora, wrote after his expulsion in 1767: *The almost general and, so to speak, innate hatred and distrust of the Indians for Spaniards had been noticeably moderated among the Opatas and Eudeves. Frequent association with the Spaniards and a knowledge of the Spanish language thus gained, the customary barter of mutual necessities, but most important the teaching of Christian charity inculcated in them by the missionaries, all these gradually dispelled their ill feeling and made them friendly toward the Spaniards. . . . In short, these Indians were in every respect much more human and civilized than the other Sonorans.*

But of the Upper Pimas among whom he also worked he had this to say: *Sonorans do not at all like to speak the Spanish language even though they may have learned it quite well by constant association with Spaniards living among them. When they are questioned in Spanish, they reply in their own language. They may rarely be persuaded to give answer in Spanish, even though they know that the person who is speaking with them understands not a word of their language. On the other hand, those who are raised in the houses of the missionaries prefer Spanish to their own language. These are even proud of their eloquence, which they generally like to display by answering in Spanish if they are addressed in Sonoran.*

But even they seem to forget every Spanish word the moment they come into the confessional. They say that it is more difficult for them to confess in the Spanish language than in their own. They will, therefore, tell of their sins and answer the questions propounded them only in Sonoran. If, however, the father confessor tells them that he has been unable to understand clearly a word of an expression, they are able to repeat in Spanish what it is they have said.

This considerable acquaintance with Spanish on the part of Opatas, Eudeves, and some Upper Pimas was probably not matched for the Yaquis and Mayos, although there is little data to go on. The penetration of Spaniards into Yaqui country was checked by the rebellion of 1740. Consequently Yaquis were relatively isolated from the kind of opportunities which the Opatas had for learning Spanish. Nevertheless Yaquis began after the rebellion to go out from their river villages to work in mines and on haciendas. That they were moving in the same direction as the Opatas so far as knowledge of Spanish as a second language goes is fairly sure. The Mayos too since the early 1700's had suffered encroachment of Spanish hacendados into their territory and they had gone out to some extent to the mines. Thus a small percentage of Yaquis learned spoken Spanish in these ways;

it was also true that it became customary for Yaqui ceremonial leaders to write Spanish (and Yaqui and Latin as well) as they took over the management of their ceremonies after the Jesuits were expelled in 1767. Details as to how many Yaquis were familiar with Spanish and in what ways are, however, lacking for this late colonial period. We may guess that there were small groups of church leaders, "maestros," who maintained a specialized knowledge of written Spanish, while many individuals had superficial acquaintance with everyday Spanish as a result of work for longer or shorter periods in Sonora or Chihuahua. On the whole, prior to about 1775, more Sonoran than New Mexican Indians had learned Spanish, but except for the Opatas it was primarily an esoteric language still.

In Chihuahua, by the beginning of the 1800's Conchos were probably largely detribalized as were many Tarahumaras. But there was a population of over twenty thousand Tarahumaras, living in the mountains, whose contacts with missionaries had been relatively slight, even during the Jesuit period, and who had had almost no contacts with Franciscans subsequently. Most of these remained with no knowledge of Spanish whatever, except for a word or two introduced by Jesuits. Among them no well-trained ritual specialist group had been developed by the Jesuits, and hence they lacked the body of ritual knowledge in Spanish which characterized the Yaquis, Mayos, and Opatas. Of course, some percentage of Tarahumaras who customarily went to work on the ranches or in the mines had the speaking knowledge of broken Spanish characteristic of the Indian fringes of the Spanish settlements. These constituted some nexus with the still monolingual Tarahumaras, but to what extent they came from settlements deep in the Sierras and returned to them is unknown. At this stage in our historical knowledge, we can only guess that they were on the fringe of the main Tarahumara tribe as well as of the Spanish settlements.

Navajos, Apaches, and Seris all had some contacts with Spanish speakers up to this time. A few Navajos in the vicinity of Santa Clara Pueblo and Navajos who had allowed a mission to be set up briefly among them near Mt. Taylor—the Enemy Navajos—had had passing contacts. These along with others made contacts with Spaniards at the Taos fairs and other trade centers. There were also contacts through Navajo slaves who escaped from the Spaniards in New Mexico. Similarly, the Apaches of the Gila (Western Apaches, Chiricahuas, and Mescaleros) through warfare and the taking of Spanish prisoners in the 1700's had some fleeting contacts, so that they knew Spanish personal names, place names, and the words for various innovations. These were all very minor diffusions and in the main may be classed as so fleeting as to have produced only an occasional Spanish-speaking individual in each tribe. It is doubtful that such speakers commanded the language of the Spaniards in any effective way.

Some Seris, on the other hand, had intensive contacts with Spaniards, both in the pre-1749 mission days at Pópulo and then again during the 1770's and 1780's at Pitic, when they were herded into the Villa de Seris. It is possible that all the Seris who were left by this time had had some contact at Pitic and knew Spanish words, but it is also true that military men like Croix consistently made distinctions in the late 1700's between Seris (those who had been at Pitic apparently) and Tepocas and Tiburones (presumably, those who had not been rounded up and who may have consisted of some of those who had never had mission experience either). It may be said that Spanish was more widely known among Seris than among either Navajos or Apaches, and that ability to "get along" in Spanish existed among them to a greater extent than among Navajos or Apaches.

There were also Upper Pimas, now differentiated as Papagos, living in the desert country west of the Santa Cruz River who had had only the most fleeting contacts with Spaniards and had little or no opportunity to learn the language. In the same classification, we may perhaps put the Yuman-speaking peoples, including both upland and river Yumans, although of course the Yumas had one brief mission experience and had had contacts with Father Kino who did not speak their language at all.

The results of the impact of Spanish language on Indians of northwestern New Spain by the end of the colonial period might be summarized as follows:

Widely diffused among those tribes to which the missions had penetrated, who constituted a majority, was knowledge of sacred formulas and ritual concepts in the Spanish language. This kind of knowledge was certainly most firmly rooted in the areas of the Jesuit missions, but there was considerable such knowledge also among the Eastern Pueblos. It should be recalled, however, that there were thousands of Indians who had not been reached by the missions, namely, Apaches, almost all Navajos, most Upper Pimas, almost all Yumans, and finally the Seris whose mission history had been drastically interrupted as a result of the rash action of the commander of the first presidio of Pitic. Where the knowledge of sacred Spanish had diffused, its formulas and phraseologies were integrated into the ceremonial culture of the Indians, but in strikingly different ways.

Much less widely diffused among all the tribes, and extending to non-missionized ones, was a knowledge of a fragmentary, but usable, practical Spanish. There was the Spanish of the mine, ranch, and hacienda jobs, the content of which was limited in vocabulary and the grammar of which was probably offensive to missionaries. There was further the still more fragmentary Spanish of the trade contacts in Spanish towns and the New Mexican fairs. This kind of knowledge was most widely diffused among Opatas of all the tribes, but it existed in considerable degree among Mayos, Yaquis, most Lower Pimas, a minority of Upper Pimas, a minority of Tarahumaras, and the Rio Grande Pueblos. Among Western Pueblos, most Tarahumaras, Apaches and Navajos, Yumans, and most Gila Pimas it was even less widely known.

Narrowly diffused was a knowledge of reading and writing in Spanish. No consistent efforts of Spaniards except the Jesuits had been directed toward the diffusion of literacy. The Franciscans seem to have begun with such an objective but in New Mexico and New Biscay their efforts progressively lapsed, so that by the last quarter of the 1700's they ceased to maintain schools. The Jesuits, whose efforts had been conceived in terms of the creation of a small elite who were literate, were expelled in 1767. Their work along these lines did leave a small number of individuals among Mayos, Yaquis, and Opatas in Sonora who were in some degree literate — how many we can only guess. There is no doubt that a tradition of literacy had been established among Yaquis, a tradition which continued despite the withdrawal of the Jesuits and which became an important part of the modified Yaqui culture. The chief use of this literacy was in connection with maintenance of the Catholicized ceremonialism. As a repository of historical or any other type of knowledge besides the sacred no literate tradition had been created, in the course of the 250 years of contact, anywhere in northwestern New Spain.

On the other hand a language of intertribal contacts had been introduced which was now employed in some degree from the Colorado to the Rio Grande and from the San Juan to the Fuerte. The Spaniards had imposed their own names for geographical features widely over the region, as in the cases of the rivers mentioned, and these became fixed; Indians employed them, even though they had their own names for rivers and other places, if they wished to be understood by the increasing numbers of Spanish-derived people coming into the region. The Spaniards had further imposed their own selection of terms on the Indians as tribal names, so that Indians who formerly had had no names for distant tribes now began to speak of them by the names which the Spaniards adopted. But the place names and the tribal names used by the Spaniards had not by this time completely replaced existing Indian words, since most of the tribes still retained their own languages and had traditional terms for places and some peoples. What the Spaniards had done was to lay solid foundations, by means of a common language designation, for the linkage of the small tribal worlds with one another and with the wider world of Western civilization. A new framework for thinking about the region had been successfully implanted. Moreover, certain new elements of Spanish culture which had spread widely were accompanied by their Spanish names. Not only the words for God (Dios), Easter, saint, and other ritual concepts were now in some form a part of all the Indian languages of the region, but in addition some elements of mundane life which spread even to tribes having little direct contact with Spaniards had also been accompanied by their Spanish names. Thus work, governor, town, horse, cow, housecat, knife, and others had become parts of the vocabularies of Indian languages from Tarahumara to Tiwa. To be sure, these were altered to fit the various Indian phonetic systems, but they now constituted common elements in languages which before had had no cognates. The diffusion of Spanish was well under way.

The independence of Mexico from Spain gave rise to a new set of contrasting influences, in south and north. In New Mexico the short period between the gaining of independence from Spain and the conquest by the United States, from 1820 to 1847, saw one major new development affecting language. In these years there was even more complete isolation from Mexico City and the wider world of Spanish civilization. The Catholic Church as an organized influence dropped out of the picture completely as it had been in process of doing. Spanish military power continued to disintegrate, and the conflicts between Pueblos and Navajos, Apaches, and Comanches intensified. The important influence so far as language was concerned in this brief period was in the relations of Pueblos with the descendants of Spanish colonists, now also isolated from Mexico.

Both the Spanish New Mexicans and the Pueblo Indians were targets of raiding Indians and hence were thrown together as allies against the Navajos, those Apaches who occasionally raided into the area, and the Comanches. While the alliance was not a formal one, it was a basis for friendships and a sense of common cause. The Spanish settlements had slowly increased in size since 1700 and by the middle of the century constituted more than four thousand persons settled in the immediate vicinity of the Pueblos along the Rio Grande. Directly at the edges of Pueblo villages, with the exception of Tesuque, Jemez, Sandia, and the western villages of Laguna and Acoma, small settlements of Spanish-speaking New Mexicans had gathered. At Taos there were three hundred. Across the river east of Santa Clara there was the Spanish settlement of Santa Cruz with a population of twelve hundred. In addition, scattered along the Rio Grande and up into the hills on either side, particularly to the east, there were many Spanish villages, comparable to those of the Pueblos in size and economy. Intermarriages took place, especially involving the Tewa at Santa Clara, Nambé, and Pojoaque. Contacts occurred at the fiestas celebrating saints' days, and the godparent and compadre relations became well established between Indians and Spanish New Mexicans. Considerable visiting took place back and forth. A phase of intimate, as opposed to official and directed contacts developed. As the official contacts had steadily declined during the preceding 150 years, intimacy had increased.

The Mexican breakaway from Spain produced no important political repercussions in the area and so the opportunities for a good deal of intimate language borrowing continued into the period of Anglo-American political control. The results of this informal framework of relationships without political dominance were twofold: (1) probably every person in each of the Eastern Pueblos gained an acquaintance with Spanish through contacts of various kinds with Spanish speakers; (2) a considerable amount of borrowing of Spanish words occurred. There is much evidence that Tiwa speakers (at Taos and Isleta, for example) gained a progressively greater familiarity with Spanish phonetics as indicated in a decreasing tendency to modify the words borrowed from Spanish; familiarity with Spanish continued to increase steadily through the early 1800's. Pueblos did not necessarily become bilingual, able to command both languages; rather, a majority merely learned to understand many Spanish words, because they heard them frequently and perhaps a majority learned how to "get along" in Spanish for particular, practical purposes. The process of increasing familiarity did not involve literacy in Spanish, since there were no Spanish schools.

At the same time hundreds of words were borrowed from Spanish. This, too, was a process which had been going on since the early 1600's; it probably intensified through the 1800's. Words for material items, tools, building materials, foods, clothing were borrowed along with the Spanish words for days of the week and various Catholic ritual occasions, saints, and ritual objects. There is an indication, as will be seen below, that speakers of Tiwa at Taos and Isleta did the greatest amount of such direct borrowing of words, that perhaps Tewa speakers came next, and finally, that Keresans did the least.

In general the Eastern Pueblos, but not the Western, had moved by the

1900's into a situation in which there was more or less equal give and take in relations with Spanish-speaking persons. Practical adaptations involving borrowing and limited language learning were well worked out. Spanish was in no way replacing the Indian languages. Although more Indians were learning actually to use Spanish than vice versa, indicating some cultural dominance of the Spanish New Mexicans, there was no trend toward disappearance of the Indian languages. The borrowing on the part of the Indians was an adaptation to the contact situation in which there had been, and with less intensity continued to be, a flow of cultural elements from the Hispanic culture to the Indian ones. Spanish continued to be important as a general trade language and, even during the major part of the Anglo period, as the language of external political affairs, such as in connection with land titles and local law enforcement. Although there were these few indications of Spanish dominance in the external world of the Pueblo villages, in the main the situation could be described as one of cultural pluralism with cultural adaptation rather than assimilation as the dominant process.

In the south relations between Indians and Spanish speakers were markedly different. Isolation from Mexican political control was never so complete. The mission program of the Catholic Church was ultimately, by the 1830's, completely broken up, but a system of secular priests was maintained at least in theory, and here and there, as among the Yaquis, a few priests continued to function in influential ways in some villages. In Chihuahua the Spanish-descended Mexican settlers steadily pushed the Indians into increased isolation in the mountains. During the early 1800's Mexicans moved deeper into the lowlands of Chihuahua which were well adapted to cattle raising, usurping lands in those areas still occupied by the Indians. As they did so they absorbed many of the missionized Indians, particularly the Conchos, into their own society and pushed most of the Tarahumaras westward. A borderland existed where Mexicans constantly extended their holdings at the expense of the Indians. But in the main by the middle 1800's most Tarahumaras had more or less effectively isolated themselves. The church had entirely disappeared as a bridge between Indian and Mexican cultures and did not reappear until 1900. In this situation the Tarahumaras, rather than learning an increasing amount of Spanish, began in fact to forget what they had learned during the days of the missions. Only here and there in small Mexican mining settlements and along the still advancing frontier was contact maintained. However, there was also some degree of contact with Hispanicized Indians from Sonora in the center of the Tarahumara country, where refugees and rebels from the Indian wars in Sonora settled, as in the vicinity of Tomochic where some vigorously anti-Mexican Mayos, Yaquis, Opatas, and others congregated. Tarahumara thus did not become a completely isolated language, but continued to receive minor influences from Spanish in such areas.

In Sonora the situation was neither like that in Chihuahua or in New Mexico. It was more like the latter in that, in general, Indian villages were not isolated from settlements of Spanish-speaking settlers, but it differed sharply in that the Sonora Mexicans, even before they had the necessary military power, began to assert their political dominance. The results were active hostilities between Yaquis and Sonorans through the 1900's, a period of intermittent warfare almost as long involving the Mayos, and what amounted to social and cultural absorption of the Opatas and Eudeves. A remnant of the Seris ultimately achieved a fairly complete isolation, while the Pimans south of what became the United States border were almost as completely absorbed as were the Opatas. All the groups, except a majority of the Mayos, were by the middle of the 1900's Spanish speakers. Almost all the two hundred Seris knew a smattering of Spanish words and could "get along" in some degree with the Mexicans. The Opatas and Eudeves spoke only Spanish, having moved rapidly during the 1800's in the direction of assimilation — a direction which they had taken definitely by the end of the 1600's. They were not bilingual; Opata and Eudeve had disappeared as spoken languages, remaining only as recorded in two grammars by Jesuits who had worked among them. Pimans were generally bilingual, as were the great majority of Yaquis. On the other hand, most Mayos were not bilingual, but spoke only Mayo. Yet a third or more of the Mayos did speak Spanish, as well as their own language.

This much more extensive diffusion of Spanish in Sonora as compared with Chihuahua and New Mexico came about chiefly as a result of breakup and redistribution of the Indian communities. This applied especially in the case of the Opatas, Yaquis, and Seris, far less for Mayos and Lower Pimas. The Opata case will be discussed below. The Seris picked up their smattering of Spanish in connection with their forced relocations at Pitic (Villa de Seris) in the 1770's and again in the 1880's, and in their periodic associations with cattle ranchers and at the Mexican fishing town of Kino Bay where most of them camped during the 1930's on the shore of the Gulf of California. For the Yaquis, conditions giving rise to the learning of Spanish were somewhat more complex and resulted by 1960 in a much more intensive and more general knowledge of Spanish. After the War for Independence the state government planned, as has been seen, small day schools throughout the state, equally in the Indian as in other areas. Yaquis (and most Mayos) resisted this program as they resisted all other attempts to integrate them into the state organization. As a result, throughout the 1800's there were no schools in their country. After the first Yaqui-Mayo efforts at independence were put down by armed force, the Sonora state government attempted a program of colonization, which brought some Mexicans as settlers at various times into the Yaqui country. However, all settlers were killed or pushed out of Yaqui territory by the end of the 1830's, and no permanent Mexican settlements were established until Yaquis were defeated again in the late 1880's. Thus Yaqui contacts with the Spanish language within their own territory were very minor except during the period from about 1887 to 1910 and again after 1920 when several thousand Mexicans made their homes in the Yaqui country.

However, Yaqui contacts with Spanish speakers outside the Yaqui country were considerable throughout the 1800's and intensified during the 1900's. Yaqui and Mayo movement out of their territories to work for Spanish employers in mines or ranches and haciendas had begun after the 1740 rebellion and continued unabated for the next two hundred years. The recurrent disorders in and around the Yaqui country throughout the 1800's, and the steady increase in agricultural and ranching establishments owned by Mexicans, provided appreciable seasonal employment of Yaquis and Mayos. The Yaquis were probably most prompted to this sort of outside labor because of the greater amount of warfare and fighting in their territory, while the Mexican settlers were steadily encroaching on Mayo territory and providing opportunities nearer home for them. By the end of the 1800's there were probably few Yaqui families who had not spent considerable time working at haciendas or in the growing Sonoran towns. Many Yaqui families left the country permanently to reside among Mexicans in different parts of Sonora. Moreover, those Yaquis whose interests were focused on the winning of self-determination also left the Yaqui country to work on haciendas and provide for the guerrilla fighters who remained in the Bacatete Mountains. In addition, after the 1880's the Mexicans began the program of deportation which scattered Yaquis out through Mexico, and this continued until the 1910 revolution. Thus Yaquis and some Mayos (a small minority) were for a hundred years living among Mexicans for greater or lesser periods and thereby came to learn Spanish. The general bilingualism of Yaquis was a result of this pattern of working outside their towns and of the voluntary and involuntary leaving of their towns as a result of the conflict with Mexicans. The general effect was a practical knowledge of Spanish — almost universal among Yaquis by perhaps 1910. Familiarity with Spanish did not result, however, in the disappearance of the Yaqui language, which generally remained the language of the home. Only in some of the fringe settlements around cities in Sonora and Arizona by the 1940's had families begun to replace Yaqui with Spanish, often consciously teaching their children Spanish as a practical measure for getting along in a Spanish-speaking milieu. At the same time that Yaquis reconcentrated in their territory from the 1920's through the 1950's, there was a corresponding return to the use of Yaqui in community life and many children began to grow up with only limited contacts with Spanish speakers. Mexican federal rural schools were set up in most of the larger towns in the 1930's but these were attended by only a small minority of Yaqui children. Most Mayos, in contrast with Yaquis, remained in or near their old towns and were not forced to learn Spanish as the dispersed Yaquis were. Many Mayos, even by 1960, were monolingual in the Mayo language.

The mobility of Yaquis resulted also in a fairly widespread literacy among them by the 1950's. Literacy among a small elite had been characteristic ever since Jesuit times. The determined program of maintaining their own churches with their own independent officials had required a certain number of literate persons in every Yaqui generation, men who could read the prayers, portions of the Mass, and other written ritual. This written tradition, kept alive quite independently of the Mexican culture around them, began by some time in the 1800's to lead to some record taking, to the writing of letters to Mexican officials, and to some development of written historical knowledge. The scattering of Yaqui families apparently also led to a very considerable employment of written Yaqui in the form of letters. Thus Yaquis were generally not only bilingual by 1950, employing Spanish with some facility as a spoken language, but they were also employing Spanish orthography in writing their own language and in maintaining a traditional written knowledge of their own in Spanish.

The state of the diffusion of Spanish as a spoken language in Chihuahua and Sonora could be summed up in the figures of the Mexican census for the year 1940. Of a total population of 840,648 over 5 years of age in these two states, there were a total of 52,984 persons who spoke Indian languages, or 6.3 percent. The number speaking Indian languages in the two states were almost the same — 26,354 in Sonora and 26,630 in Chihuahua. However, in the latter state there was a far higher proportion of monolinguals, that is, persons speaking only an Indian language with no knowledge of Spanish. Monolinguals in Chihuahua, all Tarahumaras, constituted nearly half of the total of Indian language speakers — 12,304 — while there were 14,326 who spoke Spanish in addition to Tarahumara. In Sonora there were only 5,994 monolinguals as against 20,360 bilinguals. The Indian-language speakers in Sonora were scattered among Yaquis, Seris, Upper Pimas, Lower Pimas, Mayos, and some others, including Warihios. The largest numbers of monolingual Indian speakers were Mayos living in three municipalities in the vicinity of Navojoa on the Mayo River, municipalities where the percentages of Indian speakers in the populations ranged from 32 to 57 percent.

The number of speakers of Indian languages in these two states had declined by possibly half the number which had been there at the time of the coming of the Spaniards, and this decline in numbers had been chiefly in Sonora among the Opatas, Eudeves, Upper Pimas, and probably Seris. In Chihuahua the decline in absolute numbers was not so great, possibly only as much as a fourth. The Indian speakers were now, however, small enclaves in the midst of nearly a million Mexican speakers of Spanish. Nevertheless about a third (32.6 percent) of the Indian speakers knew no Spanish whatever, this being the total percentage of monolinguals. The diffusion of Spanish was not complete after 350 years, the Mayos and the Tarahumaras being primarily the groups where the process was obstructed. It is clear that the same causes were not operating in these two cases of similar results.

THE DIFFUSION OF ENGLISH

The impress of Spanish culture, duly modified by the cultures of the various Indian tribes, had extended widely in northwestern New Spain by the early 1800's when Anglo-American traders, trappers, and woodsmen came into the region. New Mexico was by that time an area where Spanish culture and language had become established in local communities side by side with Indian communities which had been strongly influenced by Spanish ways. Indian and Spanish inhabitants of New Mexico lived side by side either as military allies or as enemies. The Spanish language had become the lingua franca among these communities, a far more widely used lingua franca than Keres which to some extent had served that purpose.

The Anglos who entered New Mexico in the period before and during the Mexican War in 1846–48 were for the most part men of no formal education — provincial and ethnocentric in outlook — often inclined to look down on the Spanish New Mexicans as barbarians little less civilized than the Indians. In fact once they had determined the peaceful farming character of the Pueblo villages they tended to rate the Pueblos as at least as civilized as the New Mexican Spaniards. A few of the early Anglos came to know and to find attractive the way of life of the wealthier Spaniards and made some effort to learn the language. But there seems to have been almost as much readiness to learn the Indian languages as to learn Spanish on the part of the Anglos. This situation changed sharply, however, as soon as the United States effected its conquest of New Mexico, when the local New Mexicans began to share in the responsibilities of setting up government. It became apparent that because of their numbers, as well as the experience of the wealthier families in local government, the Anglos would have to work with the Spanish-speaking people on at least equal terms.

Thus, English did not emerge immediately in New Mexican life as the dominant language but existed for some time merely as a new language in the milieu of intermingling cultures. Top level state business was, to be sure, transacted in English, but at lower levels of government, in courts and town councils, and even in the territorial legislature Spanish continued to be widely employed.

Slowly, however, as more English-speaking people entered the territory, Spanish, while not generally displaced as the most widely spoken language of the area, became secondary in the business of government and particularly in the business of Indian relations. It was Anglos who took the leading roles in planning campaigns against the "wild" Indians, namely, the Navajos and Apaches, and in planning for the future with the "civilized" Indians — the Pueblos. In the hands of Kit Carson, Colonel Donovan, and the others who took the field against the Navajos and Apaches, the language of treaty-making became English. The Indians who had not accepted Spanish or Mexican power slowly became aware of a new ethnic group in the region and at first regarded them as allies since they had taken the field against the Mexicans. The Pueblos who continued their peaceful behavior also became aware of the new language and began to make distinctions between the Anglos and the New Mexicans.

It was not until about 1870, however, that the importance of the new language and the role that it was to assume began to be apparent. Until that time, the military and other Anglo officials who had had dealings with the Indians had been occupied with consolidating the Anglo military position, both with regard to the Civil War in the United States and with regard to the first efforts to assert and define Anglo military power over the Navajos and other Indians. After the Civil War and into the early 1870's President Grant's advisers wrestled with the problem of Indian policy. Grant established a Board of Indian Commissioners who gradually formulated the policy which came to be known as "Grant's Peace Policy." It was a response chiefly to the abuses and the high costs which had attended the subjugation of the Plains Indians. In this respect it was an attempt to correct bad administration, but it was also a response to a growing humanitarian sentiment which gave rise to spokesmen for the Indians, men who were sympathetic to the now largely defeated tribes and their sufferings, and who were opposed to continued adjustment of the Indian-White conflict entirely in terms of the United States' military power. Such men as Vincent Colyer, secretary of Grant's Indian Commission, and General O. O. Howard approached Indian-White relations with a distinct bias in favor of the Indians. They took the view that Indian leaders were good men who would respond with cooperative spirit and integrity to fair offers of rights to certain territory and protection from settlers. Colyer and Howard were often ignorant of the absence of real tribal organization among Indians and of the bitterness of settler-Indian conflict and its background. This lack of knowledge led them into what seemed fatally unrealistic positions from the point of view of old Indian fighters like General George Crook and the settler-oriented territorial governor of Arizona.

The attempt at re-evaluating Indian policy was at its height as the first military phase — the successful campaign against the Navajos — of Indian-White relations in Arizona-New Mexico ended. The major decision of Grant's new Board of Indian Commissioners was to put Indian affairs in the hands of various religious denominations who were interested in converting the Indians to Christianity.

The most important feature of this new plan for cooperation between state and church was that the churches (or their mission boards) undertook to assume responsibility for schools among the Indians, for which the government proposed to furnish funds for schoolhouses and other facilities. The teachers in the schools were missionaries, who included in their educational programs religious instruction in whatever doctrine the particular church favored. Thus the initial educational program launched by the Bureau of Indian Affairs in the Southwest was characterized by two important features: (1) it was religiously oriented and (2) it was not, except for insistence on the English language, unified with respect to what was taught in the schools, the curricula being determined by the religious denominations responsible. In the first respect it resembled the early mission program of the Spaniards; in the second respect it differed sharply but was in accord with the religious heterogeneity of American culture.

The first school established was a small one among the Papagos at San Xavier near Tucson, which as early as 1864 had received some financial help from the Arizona Territorial Legislature, and which was managed by an order of Catholic sisters. This was followed in 1869 by another small day school at Fort Defiance among the Navajos, which was established in accordance with the federal government's agreement in its treaty of 1868 to establish one school and schoolteacher for every thirty Navajo children. The Papago school continued, but the Navajo one was discontinued because of lack of interest in it on the part of the Navajos. These were followed in quick succession by two small schools on the Gila Pima Reservation in 1871 and 1873, one for the Hopis at Keams in 1872, and one near Parker, Arizona, for Mohaves and Chemehuevis in 1873. Of the Indians concerned, only the Pimas and Papagos were reported to have attended regularly and only their schools were rated as more or less successful.

Meanwhile, the Board of Indian Commissioners under the influence of the church mission boards had concluded that the kind of school most likely to get the results they wanted would be boarding schools. In large part this idea was promulgated by General Pratt ("The Red Man's Moses"). A former Army man, he conceived the idea of establishing boarding schools far from the reservations where Indian children would be removed from the influence of their parents. It was his belief that this would rapidly bring about the civilizing of the Indians. In 1878 it was arranged to open to Indians Hampton Institute in Virginia, a school established for Negroes after the Civil War. By 1881 Hampton had fifteen students from the Southwest — Pimas, Papagos, and Apaches. In 1879 General Pratt founded Carlisle Institute in Pennsylvania; through 1885, Carlisle had some two hundred students from the Southwest — six Navajos, ninety-two Pueblos, and nearly one hundred Apaches (Chiricahuas). The boarding school took hold rapidly, and in addition to the distant ones others were established closer to the Southwestern reservations — at Albuquerque in 1884, at Tucson in 1888, at Santa Fe and Fort Mojave in 1890, at Phoenix in 1891, and near Riverside, California, in 1892.

At the same time a program for establishing boarding schools on reservations was also instituted, so that by 1892 seven such schools were in operation — for Mohave-Chemehuevis on the Colorado River, for Navajos at Fort Defiance, for Pimas at Sacaton (1872), for Hopis at Keams (1887), for Yumas at Fort Yuma (1884), for Mescalero Apaches (1884), and for San Carlos Apaches at San Carlos (1880, 1887). In addition, five day schools were operating on Southwestern reservations — for White Mountain Apaches at Fort Apache, and for Pueblos at Zuni, Laguna, Jemez, and Santa Ana. Thus, within twenty years some sort of school program had been inaugurated for all the Southwestern Indians, either as day or boarding schools, except for smaller groups such as the Jicarilla, Yavapai, Havasupai, and Walapai. It had been assumed that the boarding schools at Albuquerque and Phoenix could take care of these smaller groups, but nevertheless, by 1900 the program had been supplemented with day schools for all the Eastern Pueblos, the Havasupais, and the Jicarilla Apaches, together with another boarding school for the Walapais and three additional day schools for Hopis and eight more day schools for the Gila Pimas.

Most of these schools were run under the supervision of the various religious denominations assigned under "Grant's Peace Policy," the Presbyterians having responsibility for more than any other group. Thus, the Pima, Mohave, Navajo, Hopi, and Tucson schools were Presbyterian. The San Carlos and Mescalero Apache and Zuni schools were Lutheran. The Yuma, Papago, and White Mountain were Catholic. However, the policy of placing education entirely in the hands of the religious denominations for which the federal government contributed support had become unpopular, so that after about 1887 the Bureau of Indian Affairs began to manage some of the schools and set up some for which it immediately took the full responsibility, such as those at Albuquerque, Phoenix, Santa Fe, and Riverside. After 1897 the policy of maintaining contracts with religious groups was prohibited by Congress, although some exceptions continued to be made thereafter. From that time on, the denominationally supported schools increasingly became independent of government financing.

The great majority of all Indians who attended school during this period into the early 1900's were in boarding schools. The total number from New Mexico and Arizona is not available, but in 1917 from New Mexico, Arizona, Utah, and Nevada there were 6,949 in boarding schools. In other words, thousands of Indians had attended the boarding schools and were doing so in increasing numbers. A guess might be that within fifty years after the inauguration of the school program at least one-tenth of Arizona and New Mexico Indians had been enrolled for greater or lesser periods.

The system under which they were being educated contained some very important features with reference to the diffusion of the English language. In 1887 the Commissioner of Indian Affairs reiterated a rule which had already become a part of the educational policy of the Bureau: *Instruction of Indians in the vernacular is not only of no use to them but is detrimental to the cause of education and civilization and will not be permitted in any Indian school over which the government has any control . . . . It is believed that if any Indian vernacular is allowed to be taught by missionaries in schools on Indian reservations it will prejudice the pupil as well as his parents against the English language . . . . This language which is good enough for a white man or a black man ought to be good enough for the red man. It is also believed that teaching an Indian youth in his own barbarous dialect is a positive detriment to him. The impracticability, if not impossibility of civilizing Indians of this country in any other tongue than our own would seem obvious.*

This was similar to the view expressed by the Franciscan Archbishop of Mexico, Lorenzona, nearly one hundred years before.

The viewpoint was consistent with what had by then crystallized as the policy of the Bureau of Indian Affairs. It was consistent with the Dawes Act which proposed to individualize all Indian land holdings promptly in order to "make Indians into responsible land owners" as self-supporting individuals. It was the general belief of those who were then making Indian policy that Indians could all be rapidly transformed into English-speaking citizens if only the young persons were taken away from their parents and separated from reservation influences. This view led to recruiting children for the schools, often against their parents' will. Nevertheless, a majority of the Indian children attending the schools seem even at the beginning of recruitment to have gone voluntarily and with their parents' consent. This view led also to efforts on the part of boarding school officials to keep students away from their homes even during vacations, and they were farmed out to families who would board them in return for housework or other kinds of employment. This approach, based on the view that separation of children from parents was desirable, was the one generally accepted by missionaries, government officials, and others of the period. It grew out of two conditions: first, the real acceptance of responsibility, after years of disinterest, for Indian welfare, and, second, the assumption that there could be a future for Indians only through complete acceptance of Anglo-American culture. So long as a concept of completely isolated Indian societies had prevailed in American life, responsibility was felt only here and there, and chiefly by missionaries who became individually interested. Once the complete isolation arrangement, by force of events, was seen as impracticable, the next development was the concept of complete assimilation. The boarding-school policy was perhaps the fullest expression of this conception of Indian-White adjustment developed by the Anglos. It was, although in a somewhat more extreme form, the device which Spaniards conceived — in their schools for Indians — some three hundred years previously and applied, not generally as in the U.S., but rather to a select group who were regarded as the future ruling class of the Indians under the Spaniards.

There would seem to be no question that this device was an effective one for teaching a new language. The children in the schools were from many different tribes and could employ no common language except English. This was the situation in the off-reservation boarding schools, but not, of course, in the on-reservation boarding schools. Out of touch with parents and other Indian adults, and under the instruction of men and women who were officially and usually personally antagonistic to native Indian ways including language, as well as unequipped for learning the Indian languages, the students in periods of three or four years learned how to speak English and, somewhat less effectively, to read and write it. A sort of boarding school dialect of English developed, recognizable as a "foreign" version of English, but still perfectly intelligible to non-Indians. Pimas, Papagos, Apaches, Yavapais, Walapais, and Mohaves all went in some numbers to the boarding schools. There are no adequate figures, only some suggestive items. They suggest that of the Southwestern tribes, perhaps the Papagos, the Pimas, and a few of the Eastern Pueblos, such as Santa Clara, Isleta, Taos, and Laguna were the most influenced; these had the largest percentage of students in attendance at the boarding schools. It seems also to be true that most of the men so educated did not return to their reservations immediately. Most of them went in for periods of wandering, making livings for themselves at odd jobs. Most ultimately returned to their reservations, but an unknown proportion never came back and were assimilated into Anglo society in various parts of the country. It must be remembered that those who returned to the reservations — the majority — rarely had more than the equivalent of a grade school education, for that was the level maintained by Carlisle and the other Indian schools. They also had had some experience with one or more trades, ranging from baking or plumbing to printing. Almost all had become Protestants of some denomination and generally were outspokenly antagonistic to prevailing Indian health and sanitary customs. It is probable that in 1920-30 on the Papago Reservation there were eight to twelve women in their late twenties and thirties who had completed a full course at some boarding school and there were another thirty to forty who had had from one to four or five years under the boarding-school system. Most of these had been at nearby schools, such as the Pima one at Sacaton, or at Phoenix, or Riverside. These boarding-school-trained persons constituted perhaps one percent of their age group and they were concentrated for the most part in the eastern and southern part of the Papago reservations, where contacts with Whites had been most intensive. Their knowledge of English was good and their communication with Whites at the agency at Sells was good. But none had lost their Papago language ability. They were bilinguals.

The first impact of the boarding-school program certainly resulted in producing capable English speakers. It failed to fulfill the aims of its framers chiefly in that its influence was small in terms of the numbers of Indians who actually became bilingual. Nevertheless, those individuals for the most part began to be an important influence on the Papago, Pima, Mohave-Chemehuevi, and Apache reservations as mediators between the Indian Bureau officials and the mass of Indians on the various reservations. They interpreted what was going on to their relatives and friends in the Indian communities as they heard or read about it in English. Some moved into positions of leadership, either as go-betweens with the Whites or as recognized representatives and advisers in their home communities. Increasingly, such individuals with boarding-school backgrounds became the means through which Indian Bureau officials dealt with Southwestern Indian tribes. It should not be assumed that they became generally leaders in the sense of trusted judges and speakers in their communities, although some certainly did. Rather, the characteristic role which they came to fill was that of intercessor and interpreter. On some reservations they became focuses of internal factional splits.

This first phase of about sixty years, or two generations, had the following results stated numerically. By about 1930 only the Papagos and Navajos were listed by the Indian Bureau as having more than 50 percent of their numbers who could not speak English. Fewer than 20 percent of Navajos spoke English and only 40 percent of Papagos. Both were rapidly increasing tribes, shortly to become the largest and the second largest tribes, respectively, in Arizona. The lack of knowledge of English among them, in view of the fact that they were offered the first English language schools in the Southwest, would not seem to have rested on lack of government concern. It rested rather on the inadequacy of the boarding-school system — in the sense that the boarding schools were limited in the number of students they could take. These had to serve all tribes and all turned some students away by 1930. But also their very distance from the Indian communities, especially the more remote Navajo and Papago settlements, reduced their influence. Even if there had been enough room in existing boarding schools, it would have required a systematically carried out campaign of compulsory recruiting (which the Indian Bureau tended to shy away from after its experience with the Hopis) to fill the boarding schools. Day schools plus nearby boarding schools had achieved remarkable results for the Pueblos who by 1930 had been reported to be some 85 percent acquainted with English; moreover this knowledge was a fairly full and intensive one since they were reported to be about 75 percent literate in English. The boarding school for the Mohaves (which was close to their residences) was similarly effective as was the Truxton Canyon boarding school for the Walapais. The San Carlos and White Mountain Apaches similarly had day and boarding schools within their own reservations and their rate for both English speaking and literacy was just under that for Mohaves. The Pimas had long enjoyed both day schools and a boarding school within their own reservation as well as a nearby boarding school at Phoenix for all Southwestern Indians. These had resulted in figures with regard to English language skill even higher than for the Eastern Pueblos.

The introduction of English had been a more rapid process than the introduction of Spanish. The knowledge of English was much more extensive among these tribes of Arizona and New Mexico after some seventy-five years of contacts with Anglos than was the knowledge of Spanish by even the Sonoran tribes (the most favorable area for language learning as compared with New Biscay and New

Mexico) after two hundred years of contacts with Spaniards. The device which had brought about this rapid introduction was obviously the school, both boarding and day types, aimed at all the children. By 1930 it was not yet universal, capable of serving all Indian children, but it had been moving steadily in that direction. It was clearly the aim of the Indian Bureau to make the schools, with their absolutely required English learning, universal for all Indians, and as early as 1908 the Indian Bureau began what gradually became of major importance in the Bureau's educational program, namely, the enrolling of Indian children in public schools, wherever possible. In 1908 the Indian Bureau paid the tuition in public school for six Pima children, and by 1921 in the state of Arizona there were 182 Indian children enrolled under these same conditions in Arizona state schools, including Yavapais, Apaches, Mohaves, Chemehuevis, Papagos, Pimas, Navajos, and Hopis. The Anglo-Americans had introduced an institution which the Mexicans fully visualized for Sonora and Chihuahua, but had not been able, until the late 1930's, to get under way because of the general disorder. The Anglo policy was universal secular education for Indians; what interfered with the full realization of the policy was the failure of the national Congress to support the Indian Bureau. Here the difficulty rested on a basic conflict which the existence of the Indians as conquered people had set up in Anglo-American culture.

With the degree of support which Congress gave the Indians of Arizona and New Mexico during the first sixty years of the school program only half of these Indians became acquainted with English. But the efforts of the program were accelerating. It did not appear in 1930 that it would take another sixty years to bring the Indians to the degree of English speaking that the Opatas had attained by 1930 in speaking Spanish.

In 1933 changes came in Indian policy. Chief of these was the attempt to give up the boarding schools and to emphasize day schools. The viewpoint back of this particular change was that the Bureau had been wrong in fostering isolation from parents and community. It was now held that the primary emphasis should be placed on learning to live as members of families in the mixed cultural communities of the reservations. Consistent with this approach, the curriculum of the Indian Bureau schools was modified, or at least beginnings were made. These consisted of attempting to teach Indian children something of their own historical and cultural background as well as that of the United States as a whole; relating the school programs to the existing economic problems of the reservations; and instituting instruction in the Indian languages. These efforts focused on the Navajo Reservation and reached their fullest development there but they also were applied among the Hopi, and in lesser degree among the Pueblos and the Papagos. It is not clear that much change was instituted elsewhere in the Southwest. The closing of boarding schools was already underway before 1933. The Fort Mohave boarding school was closed in 1930, the Pima in 1932, the Colorado River boarding school was converted into a day school in 1934, the Truxton Canyon boarding school for Walapais was closed in 1938, and the Fort Apache became a day school in 1939. Between 1925 and 1935 the number of Indian students in Arizona attending off-reservation boarding schools declined from 37.3 percent to 18.4 percent, and by

1955 some 25 percent of Arizona Indian children were enrolled in the local public schools. Between 1933 and 1936, in an effort to provide schools for the two tribes least fully supplied with them, six day schools were established on the Papago Reservation and forty-three Navajo schools were programmed as day schools. Among these latter were the newly-conceived "community schools" which were designed to be centers of the community life. From 1939 on, the Indian Bureau maintained specialists in the Indian languages, particularly Navajo, and primers were written in Navajo, Hopi, and Tewa. This latter development was consistent with work in the reduction of Indian languages to writing which various mission groups, chiefly Catholic and Lutheran, had been doing already, but the government efforts were more systematic for at least the Navajo and the Hopi.

This second phase of Indian education in New Mexico and Arizona gave way about 1950 to a new one. This was characterized by a return to emphasis on boarding schools for Navajos and Papagos, but not for other reservations, and by new impetus to the long-standing program for enrolling Indians in public schools of the states with the Indian Bureau paying tuition. This phase in education may be characterized in the following ways: (1) The major emphasis on learning to speak, read, and write English was continued. (2) The learning of English was probably slowed because children were less isolated from Indian-language speakers such as their parents, and because they were thrown together in the schools with other children who spoke the same Indian language. Moreover, the use of the Indian language was no longer strictly prohibited, but even encouraged and words of the Indian languages were used by some teachers in the class rooms. (3) Some knowledge of English diffused more widely than under the boarding-school system in that a far larger percentage of Indian children, especially among Papagos and Navajos, attended schools where they learned English. (4) Unquestionably, however, the schools did not produce the very competent speakers of English that the boarding schools had in their program of isolation. This became a sore point with reservation parents, especially those who had themselves been to boarding schools and were able to compare the lesser efficiency of the new day schools.

The results in terms of the diffusion of the English language may be summarized in figures as follows. In 1952 in the state of Arizona there were 100,337 Indians resident on reservations and classified by the Indian Bureau as Indians. Of these 50,081 were non-English-speaking, or about 49 percent. The overwhelming majority of these monolinguals were Navajo — some 44,000 out of the 50,000. The percentage of Navajos who spoke English had doubled since 1930, but still 61 percent of the tribe were monolingual. Only the Papagos approached the Navajos in the high percentage of monolinguals, there being 49 percent of the Papagos who spoke no English. Of the others in the state, the Apaches were about 80 percent English-speaking, the Havasupais and the Hopis about 85 percent, and all the rest, including such larger groups as the Gila Pimas, were from 98 to 100 percent English-speaking. In New Mexico the situation was similar. All the Pueblos ranged from 85 to 100 percent English-speaking, and the Jicarilla and Mescalero Apaches were within this range, being about 87 percent English-speaking, while New Mexico Navajos ranged a little higher than Arizona Navajos.

There was no reason to assume that the Navajos or Papagos would not ultimately become 100 percent bilingual. All trends pointed in that direction, including Indian Bureau aims and Congressional tendencies in providing appropriations, as well as prevailing Indian and Anglo attitudes. But it should be remembered that the figures here report bilingualism, not the disappearance of the Indian languages. While, as a result of the increase in school enrollment, bilingualism appeared inevitable for Arizona and New Mexico Indians, the relation between this condition and obsolescence of an Indian language was not known, nor was the relationship between the speaking of two languages and the disappearance of subordinate cultural values or customs understood.

The diffusion of English had almost wholly blocked the diffusion of Spanish among Indians in Arizona and appeared to be moving toward a similar situation in New Mexico. In Arizona, despite the fact that better living conditions attracted Papagos from Sonora into Arizona from the 1870's on and thus brought Spanish-speaking Papagos into Arizona, the schools were slowly turning all Papagos into English speakers. However, through frequent daily association in jobs and in residential areas where they were thrown together with Spanish speakers in Tucson and Phoenix, many Papagos continued to learn some Spanish. Elsewhere, except for the acquisition of a few Spanish words by Navajos in a largely hostile situation in northern Arizona, the learning of Spanish had ended by 1950. In New Mexico the situation was different. Spanish was intricately integrated into Pueblo culture, and the clusters of Spanish-speaking rural people around the Pueblo villages continued. Spanish thus was in use among Pueblos to a greater extent than among other Indians of New Mexico and Arizona.

THE EXTINCTION OF INDIAN LANGUAGES

The diffusion of the two European languages among the Indians did not necessarily involve the replacement of the Indian languages. In only one area of the region had there been a consistent trend for a period of some two hundred years toward extinction of the Indian languages. This was the area of the Apache frontier, where the non-Apachean languages were subject to this process. There even seemed to be a phase in the course of cultural adaptation in New Mexico when Spanish existed under circumstances in which no one culture was clearly dominant, so that Spanish was learned by Indians as one tool along with other Indian languages in a pluralistic cultural milieu. Before and following this brief period, however, the European languages were part of politically dominant cultures and during these eras there were strong factors making for language replacement. In the half century before 1950, both in the areas of Spanish and of English dominance, it appeared that only special and perhaps temporary circumstances encouraged the persistence of the Indian languages in the face of growing pressures for language replacement. The relations of Indians and European-derived peoples changed sharply in this period and the new situation appeared to affect the direction of change in language. However, in the first half of the twentieth century, population dominance of non-Indians with standard Anglo and Mexican dialects being taught in extensive school systems, suggested a new trend toward extinction.

At the time of the coming of the Spaniards, there were at least forty-one dialects of Indian languages spoken. How distinct these were from one another remains an unanswered question, and it is not likely that the question can ever be settled. Since some of the dialects became extinct without ever having been recorded, the materials for determining their nature were not preserved and cannot be resurrected. Therefore the precise number must remain doubtful. We may, however, accept the following as a probable listing of the dialects of the region during the last half of the 1500's:

In the area of what is modern Chihuahua there were possibly five languages recognized as distinct by the Spaniards, who followed the lead of Indians in distinguishing them. These were Tarahumara, Warihio, Concho, and possibly two others whose distinctness is less certain — Jano and Suma. Ranging into the eastern part of the present state were people speaking "Toboso" and Apachean languages. In the area that is now Sonora there were at least four groups of languages, which have since become differentiated in forms that were not the same as those encountered by the Spaniards: Cahita, since differentiated into Mayo and Yaqui; the Seri group, which may have been composed of five or more different dialects but which by the 1800's was consolidated into the single language known as Seri; the Opatan group, composed of Eudeve, Opata, and Jova; and the Piman group composed of Nebome, Sobaipuri, and six or seven dialects of Upper Pima, later consolidated into Papago and Pima. In New Mexico there were at least eleven groups as follows: Tompiro, Piro, Tiwa, Tewa, Towa, Keres, each of which probably consisted of several mutually intelligible dialects corresponding to the Pueblo villages called by those names by the Spaniards; Navajo, in what is now northwestern New Mexico; Apache, differentiated into Jicarilla, Mescalero, and Lipan; and Zuni, probably then comprising several different dialects very closely similar. In Arizona there were another ten or eleven different languages: Hopi, with minor dialect differences among the villages; Apache, comprising Tonto, White Mountain, and San Carlos, all dialects of Western Apache and Chiricahua; the river Yuman group consisting of Cocopa, Yuma, Halchidoma, Mohave, Maricopa, and possibly another; the upland Yuman group consisting of Yavapai and Walapai; and in addition some doubtful ones, possibly Jocome, Suma, and another language in the same area of what is now southeastern Arizona.

How distinct all of these were remains doubtful. The designations are the ones to which Spaniards had become accustomed by the early 1700's after a century and a half of acquaintance with the Indians of the region. These names used here are the ones adopted by Anglos when they came into the region. They reflect a combination of linguistic difference and locality association. They reflect, as they have come to be used in recent writings, primarily the locality association as ultimately defined by reservations. Thus, for example, the distinction between Yavapai, Walapai, and Havasupai linguistically is not great and these "tribes" have become differentiated largely through their historical experience with white men. Similarly, the linguistic difference between modern Papago and Gila Pima is also slight, the differentiation depending much more on the reservations established for each.

Perhaps a more accurate listing from the point of view of full-fledged languages would be the following: in Chihuahua two, Tarahumara and Concho; in Sonora four, Cahita, Seri, Opata, and Pima; in New Mexico seven, Tiwa, Tewa, Towa, Keres, Zuni, Eastern Apache and Navajo; and in Arizona three, Yuman, Hopi, and Western Apache. This would make a total of sixteen.

As has been indicated, of the forty-one or forty-two languages listed according to Spanish designation, perhaps twelve had become extinct by 1950. Using the more compressed grouping three out of sixteen had become extinct. Thus about 25 percent linguistic extinction is indicated, however the dialects are grouped.

Nearly all, in fact all but one of the dialects which had become extinct existed in the area of the Apache frontier or "Corridor," that is to say, in the area from central New Mexico across the southwestern part of New Mexico and northern Chihuahua into southeastern Arizona and northeastern Sonora. Those language groups which became extinct were the following: Piro, Tompiro, Concho, Lipan, Opata, Eudeve, Jova, Jano, Suma, Jocome and Halchidoma. The last was a Yuman language spoken by people who inhabited the Colorado River Valley between the Yumas and the Mohaves until sometime in the late 1700's. Through warfare their numbers were decreased and they attempted to move eastward into the Gila Valley. They either were absorbed into the Maricopa who were also moving eastward because of warfare with neighboring Yumans, or disappeared as a biological entity before the middle of the 1800's. They were thus a casualty of the traditional warfare among the Yuman groups, and it seems doubtful that their disappearance was in any way connected with the coming of white men into the region.

On the other hand, the disappearance of the other groups seems definitely connected with the arrival of the Spaniards and the stimulus to warfare which resulted. The events which led to their extinction were climaxed by the Pueblo Rebellion of 1680, but the conditions leading to the extinction arose earlier. The eastern margin of the Rio Grande Valley was subject to attacks from raiding nomads at the time of Coronado's expedition and before 1540. The Tanoan-Tewa peoples were forced out of the Galisteo Basin before 1680 as a result of such raids. At the same time the villages east of the Rio Grande between El Paso and Albuquerque were similarly subject to raiding and the Spanish governors of New Mexico made special efforts to protect them and enlisted them in retaliatory military operations. The Piros and Tompiros of this area, in fact, seem to have accepted the Spaniards as needed allies, and when the Pueblo Rebellion broke out, they remained loyal to the Spaniards, accompanying them to El Paso rather than joining the Pueblos to the north. They were re-established in the vicinity of El Paso in mission centers and never returned to their former villages, which had been subject to a failing water supply anyway. From the early 1700's on, there was a progressive cultural assimilation in the small missions around El Paso. There were not only Piros and Tompiros, but also Sumas and other Indians of the El Paso region in the missions. In 1749 there were listed· 1,484 Indians in five missions: El Paso, San Lorenzo, Senecu, Isleta del Sur, and Socorro, but living with them in the same settlements were a greater number of Whites, namely 1,646. The next hundred years saw first a succession of attacks on the missions by the Apaches of various groups and second the steady overrunning of the settlements by Spaniards and Mexicans, so that by the later 1800's the native languages had ceased to be used, intermarriage with Spanish-speaking people was general, and nearly all sense of tribal or cultural identity had disappeared. The same fate overtook the not very populous Concho communities along the Rio Grande and also in northern and eastern Chihuahua. Precisely what happened to the Sumas who were not settled at El Paso, to the Jocomes of southeastern Arizona and to the Janos cannot be said. They either were similarly absorbed by Spanish settlers or possibly even absorbed into the bands of various Apaches with whom they fought in the late 1600's and early 1700's against the Spaniards. These six groups then were early casualties of the Apache frontier, extinct within the first 150 years after the arrival of the Spaniards. Their extinction may be attributed to decimation in numbers through warfare and epidemic, combined with acceptance of the Spaniards as allies, intermingling with them and consequent rapid loss, since they were all small groups, of their distinct linguistic and cultural identity.

The story of the Apache frontier and its cultural effects farther west is somewhat different. Here the people concerned were those who spoke Opata and related languages — Eudeve and Jova. These languages, with the possible exception of Jova, were extinct by 1950, but it is unlikely that Opata and Eudeve were extinct as languages before 1900. Moreover, although the language disappeared it is not true that the Opatas everywhere lost their cultural identity as well. There were still communities in central Sonora in 1950 which identified themselves as Opatas and prided themselves on some distinctive customs. The process was parallel with, but much longer drawn out than the process of assimilation in the El Paso area, and this was correlated with the fact that rather than being in the very center of Apache raiding they were able to move back out of the focus to some extent.

Beginning in the 1680's the northern Opata villages became the object of attack of the tribes which were raiding into eastern Sonora. Opatas in these villages were forced to move south, until finally the whole northern margin of their territory was largely depopulated. This followed what had been a generally peaceful acceptance of Spanish missionaries, miners, and settlers. Never concentrated into large communities, such as those of the Yaquis even after missionization, the Opatas accepted Spaniards in their communities and even before 1700 had intermarried with them. In the face of the Apache attacks, this intermingling was intensified, partly because of the need of falling back to Spanish settlements and partly because of the need for allies against the Apaches. The friendly intermingling, including the learning of Spanish, and alliance continued on through the 1700's and into the early 1800's. Thus, for over a century the Opatas underwent relocation of their communities in many areas, and they accepted responsibility for military operations against the Apaches, several Flying Companies from the mid-1700's on into the early 1800's consisting of Opatas in the frontier presidios.

These conditions brought about the steady replacement of Opata language and culture by Spanish and Spanish-Mexican ways. The integrity of their territory and communities was not maintained as the Yaquis maintained theirs. They voluntarily moved into new settlements close to Mexicans. After their defeat in the 1820's by Mexicans in their bid for independence, their young men fought alongside Mexicans. The Opata language continued in use probably through the 1800's, but replacement was steady. It would be interesting to know the details of this process, but at present data are lacking. All we know is that the process was complete by 1950. It is also clear that a few customs, such as some connected with basket making and with spring ceremonials have survived the language, as for instance in the Batuc and San Miguel valleys. But replacement of language and other aspects of culture seem to have been almost parallel processes.

THE PERSISTENCE AND MODIFICATION
OF INDIAN LANGUAGES

Three-quarters of the Indian languages had, as seen above, persisted up to 1950, and all indications were that most of these would be spoken for indefinite periods in the future. Due to the number of speakers, there was no likelihood that Navajo, Hopi, Zuni, Keres, Tiwa, Tewa, Western Apache, Papago, Gila Pima, Tarahumara, Mayo, or Yaqui would disappear under any conditions foreseeable in 1960. There was room for doubt about the indefinite persistence of Mohave, Yavapai, Walapai, Havasupai, Seri, Maricopa, Chiricahua, Cocopa, Lower Pima (Nebome), Yuma, Chemehuevi, and Warihio, the chief reason for uncertainty about these resting on the small numbers of those speaking them. Any trend toward complete replacement could rapidly affect a group of less than one thousand. Disease could wipe out such small groups suddenly. For these reasons there was less assurance that the languages of the smaller groups would persist. Nevertheless, nothing in the record pointed to any clear basis for expecting replacement of any of the languages listed. Even such factors as drastic demographic shifts, to the point of breaking up communities, did not always result in language replacement — as the Seris and Yaquis had demonstrated. Thus, on the basis of the evidence, no such external, or noncultural factors could generally be considered as pointing toward replacement. The replacement of language was evidently a complex process, which might be triggered by such noncultural factors, but which worked itself out in the field of cultural factors. One factor which appeared to be of great importance was the growth of bilingualism. Some small groups, such as some Yavapais, Gila Pimas, and Chemehuevis, had become 100 percent bilingual, and this was further reason for thinking that these languages were likely to become extinct more rapidly than those like Papago, Navajo, Tarahumara, and Mayo where some proportion of monolinguals existed. Nevertheless, it was easy to imagine some of the small bilingual groups developing, under some circumstances, nativistic movements which would give high value to the speaking of their languages under conditions important in their lives. For this reason, then, further prediction seemed dangerous on the basis of any combination of probable factors.

It should be emphasized that the languages listed as "persisting" had not gone unchanged during the course of contact. This statement rests on facts known about only a few of the languages. Those which have been studied all indicate some degree of change in the process of adaptation to the new cultural conditions. This applies both with reference to change in form and in function of the languages. Unfortunately, neither aspect of change has been analyzed in any detail for more than three or four languages and none of these analyses is complete, every study having been concerned primarily with form rather than function.

SPANISH INFLUENCES — However, some analysis of five languages with respect to formal changes has been made and these data can be reviewed and a little insight gained thereby into linguistic adaptation under the conditions of contact. The languages about whose changes a little is known are Tiwa, Tewa, Keres, Pima, and Yaqui. As might be expected in view of the different circumstances of contact, these five have not changed in the same ways.

In their adaptation to contact all of these languages were characterized by an increase in their vocabularies by adding words derived from Spanish. The borrowing was not, however, patterned in the same way. Yaqui borrowed freely and extensively, Pima considerably less so, while the three Pueblo languages borrowed very sparingly. Nevertheless they all borrowed, as languages in contact unfailingly do. The way in which they borrowed sheds a good deal of light on the circumstances of the relationships between the Spaniards and Indians as well as on the structural characteristics of each of the languages.

Speakers of the three Eastern Pueblo languages — Tewa, Tiwa, and Keres apparently began using Spanish words for some of the new things and ideas introduced by the Spaniards at the very start of their contacts, in the first decade of the 1600's. They all adopted the Spanish words for new things that the Spaniards brought such as bull, cow, ox, horse, burro, mare, and pig, and for grape, pear, probably peach and apple, chile, melon, oats, and wheat bread, and for such utensils as bottle, sword, fork, pistol, spoon, and table. In addition, they uniformly adopted the Spanish terms for godparents (*comadre* and *compadre*), for saint, for Mass, and perhaps for captain, lieutenant governor and governor, *fiscal* (church official), bishop, the Blessed Virgin, and soldier. They also generally adopted words for measurement which covered such new concepts as, for example, the days of the week, the week as designated by the word for Sunday, numbers of large quantity such as one thousand, hour, and perhaps league and mile. Less uniformly, the various villages made use of the Spanish words for Christian festivals such as Easter and Christmas, for God, the soul, the Vespers service, and a number of others. The acceptance of these varied among villages, as did the use of other miscellaneous terms such as bridge, coffin, chair, lamp, button, hammer, ribbon and some others. But the considerable uniformity with which such adoptions were made among all the Eastern Pueblos suggests an early readiness to borrow the words along with the things and ideas themselves; it also suggests the utility immediately felt in domestic animals and plants, metal and glass artifacts, time and space measures, as well as an interest in some of the social and religious innovations, such as the liaison officers for the villages and the ritual of Mass and ceremonial sponsorship and the figure of the Catholic female supernatural — the Virgin

— although of course the acceptance of these last indicates also the importance attached to them by the Spanish innovators.

Although these early word adoptions became rooted solidly in the Eastern Pueblo languages and some others were also adopted from time to time as contacts with Spanish-speaking people continued on down to 1950, it is an interesting fact that the process of acceptance of Spanish words seems to have slowed down after the initial contacts. All observers agree that some 350 years later not more than 5 percent of Spanish words were included in the vocabulary of the three languages mentioned. We may guess that certain checks on the ready adoption of words from Spanish developed in the period leading up to the Pueblo Rebellion of 1680 and that perhaps these checks were intensified during the following period of hostile relations with Spaniards. As more friendly relations with New Mexican Spanish-speaking people developed during the early and middle 1800's more casual borrowing of words undoubtedly took place again, but by the middle of the 1900's it was clear that the dominant tendency was to curb such borrowing. In fact, it appeared that a conscious policy of avoiding the use of Spanish words among the Tewas, Tiwas, and Keresans had been adopted. Speakers of Tewa were reported to be aware that many words were borrowed from Spanish and were not part of the Indian language, and so were finding ways to avoid using them.

This consciousness of the small Spanish-derived vocabulary in Tewa existed in 1950 as a reflection of the hostile Pueblo-Spanish relations of the late 1600's and the 1700's. It existed despite the growth during the 1800's of friendly accommodation with Spanish-speaking people and a good deal of cultural borrowing during that time. It existed also in conjunction with what by 1960 was a widespread familiarity with Spanish on the part of Tewa-speakers and a general ability to use the language. Evidently there was a definite and conscious process in operation which kept the languages separate.

One effect was the employment of loan translations rather than the borrowing of words. As many items of Spanish culture became interesting to and were adopted by Pueblo Indians, instead of borrowing the words for such items as had been done rather generally at first, the tendency now was to reject the Spanish word and to coin a new expression in Tewa for the cultural element which came to be used. Thus, in Tewa, there were a good many alternate forms of this sort, which might be used on occasion rather than the Spanish loanword. There were such alternates for burro, goat, horse, and watermelon, words for which had originally been borrowed from Spanish. There were numerous loan translations for other borrowed elements for which a Spanish word probably had never been borrowed. Words of this sort in modern Tewa were those for baptism, holy water, cross, Devil, sin, and Catholic priest. There were others such as words for peach, wheat, for beets and carrots, for hammer, mirror, gun, chair, and also for airplane and automobile. Loan translation was accomplished not only through the coining of new words but also through the extension of new meanings to old word forms, as for example, the extension of the meaning "Christmas" to the old Tewa word for winter solstice, of the meaning "governor" to the Tewa term for leader, of "ammunition" or "bullet" to the Tewa word for arrow, and many others. The absence of loanwords for such recent things as airplane suggests that a type of accommodation was developed which emphasized the Tewa language as a value in itself and which operated against the borrowing of words, either from Spanish or English, although the item itself might be well known, much used and appreciated. The evidence tended to suggest that word borrowing had been more common at the beginning of the contacts with Spaniards than it was later, by the middle 1900's, in connection with either English or Spanish.

The processes of language accommodation for Tiwa and Keres were essentially similar with respect to Spanish. There is evidence of a check on the tendency to borrow words, with resultant similar effects — vocabularies of 5 percent or less derived from Spanish. But the ways in which words were handled varied. Like Tewas, Keresans made up their own words for baptism, holy water, sin, Hell, cross, and Devil, or better it should be said that they did not make up new words after the manner of Tewa speakers, but rather extended new meanings to old words. This lesser freedom with regard to new word formation was characteristic of Keres and a contrast with Tiwa. Nevertheless the two languages tended to behave in about the same ways with regard to linguistic borrowing. In connection with Tiwa it is interesting to note that, on the basis of an analysis by one linguist of a short list of borrowed words from Taos, it appears that there were three phases of borrowing; an early one in which Spanish words were very much modified, a middle phase in which they were considerably less modified, and a third phase when the Spanish words were modified hardly at all. This suggests that borrowing from Spanish continued throughout Taos history to 1960, but speakers of Tiwa became increasingly familiar with the phonetics of Spanish during the three hundred years of contact.

Phonetic modification characterized the borrowing of all three of the Indian languages discussed. Tewa lacks the Spanish *l* sound and hence in borrowing substituted usually a *t* or *r* sound. Also Tewa words do not end in consonants except *m* and *n* and hence final consonants in Spanish words were usually omitted. In Keres the Spanish *b, d,* and *g* were generally, especially at the beginning of and in the middle of words, changed to *p, t, k,* since Keres lacks the voiced stops. Spanish *h* was also often replaced by Keresan *sh*. The greatest alteration of Spanish words was in the Keresan insertion of a vowel between members of consonant clusters or the omission of one member of the cluster in order to adjust to the usual pattern of alternating vowels and consonants characteristic of Keres. In Taos, since Tiwa has no voiced stops at the beginning of words, *b* and *d* were omitted. Spanish *f* became *p*. And there were shifts in the vowels, such as *e* to *a, a* to *o,* and *o* to *u*.

In the case of all three of the Pueblo languages which have been studied it was only the names for things which were ever borrowed from Spanish. Words for doing and acting — verbal expressions — were not borrowed, nor were other kinds of words, so that the main fabric of the Indian languages was not at all affected by contact with Spanish speakers. Neither the sound patterns nor the grammatical structures of Tiwa, Tewa, or Keres appear to have been altered. It was only the vocabulary which was affected and this was simply added to in small part.

The language of the Pimas of the Gila River was affected in very similar fashion to that of the Pueblos. Despite much less intensive contacts with missionaries or with colonists, the Pimas borrowed very much the same Spanish words as did the

Pueblos — days of the week, domestic animal terms, measures and counting terms, and words for useful new artifacts such as table, knife, muslin, money, glass, and terms connected with the new Christian beliefs, such as Easter, church, saint, God, and fiesta. The list of borrowed terms for this early period varies in detail, but it is essentially the same as for the Pueblos. The list as recorded is fuller than for the Pueblos. Some of the borrowing for the Gila Pimas may have been indirect through the Papagos and Sobaipuris of the San Pedro Valley, since the Gila Pimas were not missionized, nor were they in very close contact with Spaniards. The striking similarity in the list of borrowed words to those of the Pueblos indicates the generally similar impact of Spanish culture on all the Indian groups of the region and suggests again readiness to borrow at the time of the initial contact. It is apparent from the study of Pima that has been made, however, that the borrowing from Spanish did not continue at the same rate that it had begun. After perhaps 10 percent of the nominal vocabulary of Pimas had become Spanish-derived, there was fairly complete isolation from Spaniards — during the late 1700's and early 1800's. During this period and extending into the early reservation period when Mexicans as well as Anglos were in contact with Pimas, it appears that a new process began to dominate. This was the one discussed above, namely, the making up of new words and the extension of the meaning of old ones. Pima, in fact, during this phase seemed equally as fertile in word invention as was Tewa, and many new words for new things were developed. Thus various varieties of wheat were named by Pima words, as were fruits such as bananas, lemons, and dates; unfamiliar animals such as camel, elephant, and monkey were named in Pima in this way. And some new measures had terms injected for them in Pima. It is interesting to note that of the days of the week, only Sunday, Monday, Friday, Saturday were terms borrowed from Spanish, and in the subsequent phase words were coined for Tuesday, Wednesday, Thursday. As this phase developed Spanish influences steadily declined, so that by 1960 Gila Pima was borrowing from English very heavily and not at all from Spanish.

In great contrast with the four languages discussed so far, Yaqui of Sonora was not limited in its borrowing either by the growth of antagonistic attitudes between Indians and Spaniards or by loss of contact with Spanish speakers. The outstanding result of the contact between Yaqui and Spanish speakers was by 1960 a very extensive permeation of Yaqui vocabulary by Spanish together with some less extensive, but nevertheless important modifications of the language structure.

One investigator estimated that Yaquis resident in Arizona in the 1940's employed Spanish-derived words when speaking Yaqui for as much as 65 percent of the total words used. This estimate did not mean that in the speech of Yaquis in Arizona one heard sixty-five Spanish-derived words for every thirty-five words; it meant rather that a listing of terms for artifacts, for social statuses recognized by the Yaquis, and for religious ideas and rituals resulted in showing that some 65 percent of these terms were Spanish-derived. It was true also that, in contrast with the languages just discussed, the Yaqui language in the 1940's contained a sprinkling of verbal, adjectival, and other expressions derived from Spanish. The vocabulary of Yaqui had to a large extent been remade, then, as a result of contacts between Yaqui and Spanish speakers. The situation was somewhat analogous to that of the Anglo-Saxons after the Norman Conquest, when large numbers of Norman-French terms were borrowed and supplemented the basic Anglo-Saxon vocabulary. Through the generations from 1617 on to 1950 borrowing continued and, relatively speaking, new word formation — loan translation — and extension of meaning of old words to cover new cultural items were unimportant. This borrowing went on despite the Yaqui rebellion of 1740 (which was almost as destructive as the Pueblo Rebellion of 1680) and the Yaqui-Mexican wars of the 1800's.

The list of words incorporated into Yaqui included all of those borrowed in the early phases of contact by the Pueblo and Pima languages, but it included many more not only in the realm of material culture, but also in social life and organization and in religion especially, where Catholicism permeated Yaqui life more deeply and more extensively than it did either Pima or Eastern Pueblo religious life. Thus kinship terms and nearly all the status terms of town organization and military life had been borrowed. Similarly ceremonial organization, which was so involved and important in Yaqui life, was carried on in an almost wholly Spanish-derived set of terms. Sermons and the many formal ritual speeches characteristic of Yaqui religious life were to a very large extent permeated with Spanish-derived words.

Twenty to 30 percent of the words in a sermon recorded at a Yaqui settlement in Arizona in 1941 were Spanish-derived. They ranged from particles and connectives like *if, or* and *because* through status terms like *sir, governor, captain, soldier* and all the offices of the ceremonial organizations, through ritual terms like God, Blessed Mary, Virgin, Jesus Christ, benediction, prayer, Holy Spirit, Trinity, and many others, to words which have become fixed in Yaqui religious thought as "technical" terms, such as license, presence, ceremonial work, tribulation, punishment, indulgence, dawn, and so forth. In this extensive use of Spanish-derived terms, it was apparent that many had become fixed in the Yaqui language at a time when few Yaquis knew Spanish, so that the words were very much modified as they were fitted to the aboriginal Yaqui phonetic system. Thus where *d* occurred in Spanish an *l* was substituted, since no *d* existed in Yaqui, as in Lios for Dios; initial consonant clusters not occurring in Yaqui, words like *cruz* in Spanish became *kus* in Yaqui, one member of the cluster being omitted. Many such words were an integral part of modern Yaqui, even though as borrowing had continued under conditions in which Yaquis had become thoroughly familiar with Spanish phonetics they also borrowed words which were not at all or only slightly modified. Under the conditions of general bilingualism which obtained by the 1940's Spanish words were often not adjusted to Yaqui phonetics even though an individual was speaking Yaqui.

It was difficult to determine whether Yaquis were aware of the origins of the Spanish-derived words. They seemed generally not to be so. There was certainly no reluctance to employ Spanish words and no cultural block to further borrowing. The attitude seemed to be that, even when the similarity with current Spanish was recognized, the words were as much Yaqui as Mexican. Hence the process of Hispanicization of the Yaqui vocabulary was continuing vigorously in the 1940's and promised to go on indefinitely.

The Yaqui language nevertheless remained a distinct language from Spanish in the sense that it maintained a Uto-Aztecan phonetic system and grammatical structure. The Spanish words which were borrowed were incorporated into Yaqui by the same morphological and grammatical processes which governed the arrangement of Yaqui verbs. Spanish-derived verbs, such as to invite, to think, and to attend-an-all-night-ceremony, were conjugated in the same way as Yaqui verbs, that is, were employed with the Yaqui pronominal prefixes and the Yaqui modal and aspectual suffixes. The nominal expressions were similarly treated by the use of the usual suffixes for location at, in company with, and so on. Thus, the Spanish-derived verb *velar* (to hold an all-night ceremony) was directly incorporated into Yaqui by the addition of the Yaqui suffix -*oa* and conjugated like any Yaqui verb, e.g., *nevelaroane*, "I intend to hold an all-night ceremony." The first *ne-* is the standard Yaqui prefix meaning "I" and the final -*ne* is the suffix indicating intention or expectation.

It was true at the same time that there was some influence from Spanish on both the phonetic and the grammatical structure. The Yaqui vowel system, for example, seemed in the speech of those Yaquis who were largely bilingual to be approximating that of the Spanish vowel system. Yaqui speakers tended to slur the differences between long and short vowels and to eliminate the geminate vowels, although the same speaker handled the vowels differently under different circumstances of speech. Also the semi-vowel *w* appeared to have changed in the direction of the Spanish *g* since the days of first contact. There was some influence on word order in connection with prepositional phrases by analogy with Spanish word order for equivalent phrases. There was further analogic change in connection with prepositional constructions. All of these latter changes were well fixed in the language but they were relatively slight. The basic grammatical categories were probably influenced to some extent, especially with reference to the substitution of the strongly emphasized tense categories of Spanish in translation of some of the modal categories of Yaqui unexpressed in the structural principles of Spanish. These changes, few and not well fixed in the language, had come about over a period of 350 years. They pointed to a persisting influence, the outcome of which could not be predicted, but they had not yet resulted in the alteration of the major structural features of Yaqui.

Spanish influence was much less on all the other languages still persisting. Neither Seri, Tarahumara, nor Lower Pima had been influenced lexically to the extent that Yaqui had, although all three were probably moving in that direction. The Athapaskan and Yuman, Zuni, and Hopi languages had hardly been influenced by Spanish. It was not likely in view of the change in political dominance in their areas that they would be.

ENGLISH INFLUENCES — The influence of English developed in a different way from that of Spanish. The Anglo-Americans did not come into the New Mexico country as bearers of new and wondrous things, as did the early Spaniards; they did not come first as great religious teachers. Consequently there is not a common layer of borrowed words from earliest contact, corresponding with early borrowed culture elements. The metal, the guns, the horses, and other trappings of Anglo civilization were already familiar to Indians through Spanish contacts. Hence English speakers appeared on the scene at first in roles little different from those of other Indian tribes; the Apaches of the Gila regarded the Anglos as equals rather than politically dominant people when they found that they were indeed — up until 1848 — allies against the Mexicans. The emergence of the Anglos as a new controlling power, far stronger than Spain or Mexico had shown itself to be, took place slowly, particularly because of the Civil War. By the time the intimate contacts with Indian agents began in the late sixties, the United States was already regarded as an enemy tribe. No longer were there the incentive and the favorable attitudes for borrowing from the new language that had existed at the time that the wonderful new things from Spain were introduced. Moreover, it was not until the early 1870's that intensive contacts began to develop of the nature of those that had accompanied Spanish mission life. It was then that the first schools were built. As the early day schools gave way to the boarding schools, a situation was created not for the blending of languages as had begun to take place in the Jesuit missions, but for a sharp separation of the languages, often into two quite distinct compartments in the minds of the boarding-school graduates. It was not until the later reservation period that important borrowing from English began to take place. It has been pointed out in connection with the Gila Pimas that a period began in the 1930's which in its effects on language was somewhat similar to the early Spanish period. Direct borrowing from English began to take place, superceding loan translation and new word formation which had characterized the period of earliest contacts with Anglos. This tendency increased at an accelerated rate during the next twenty years, as the Indians in Arizona and New Mexico became increasingly familiar with English and with Anglo culture. One area of life where direct borrowing became most important was the political, as tribal councils developed. In tribal council sessions there was a great deal of use of the Indian languages and many council meetings, such as the Papago, the Navajo, the Gila Pima, and the Eastern and Western Pueblo, were conducted wholly in the Indian languages except when Anglos of the Indian Bureau or others were called in specially for information. In such sessions, it was apparent that an increasing number of words from the English vocabulary of political organization and law were being introduced into the discussions. Words like democracy, contract, tribal council, president, governor, chairman, Congressional, and so on crept with increasing frequency into the vocabulary of common usage for members of the tribal councils and for many with whom they associated. The same phenomenon was to be noted in connection with the Anglo vocabulary of economic thought and activity. Tribal councils as business organizations found it necessary to employ English words in their attempts to establish types of business organization similar to those in the dominant economy. Since many, but by no means a majority, of council members spoke English fairly well, this being often one of the bases for election, the process of borrowing was accelerated. Also, by the 1920's as the Anglo missionary program intensified, another area of borrowing was in that of religious life, so that the words of hymns and the ritual vocabulary of Anglos became available in intimate contacts and many such words were taken into

the Indian languages. By the 1950's a process something like that which had
resulted in the early borrowing of Spanish had been set well in motion, and the
Indian languages were on the road to the inclusion of another layer of borrowed
words from another European language. No studies had been made which gave any
clear idea as to just how this process was working out.

INFLUENCE OF LITERACY PROGRAMS — Another major influence on some of the Indian
languages was the literacy programs in the Indian languages set up by both the
Mexican and the United States governments in the 1930's. The languages directly
affected by such programs in the Southwest were Tarahumara, Navajo, and to a
lesser extent Yaqui.

The Mexican government, under the administration of President Lázaro Cárdenas, began in the late 1930's to develop a program of literacy in Tarahumara.
Linguists were employed who devised a system of writing. Primers were prepared
and a few score Tarahumaras were taught to read and write their language. It was
expected that such individuals would spread their knowledge among the tribe. An
effort to prepare news sheets in Tarahumara was made. This program continued
into the 1940's, but no figures were available on the numbers affected or any studies
on the effects generally of this establishment of a written tradition. The program
was continued with the establishment of a National Indian Institute center in the
Tarahumara country in 1952.

The program of the U. S. Bureau of Indian Affairs for writing the Navajo language was carried out more systematically and probably with greater effect. About
1939 an alphabet of forty-five characters was worked out by an Indian Bureau em-
ployee assigned to the problem of preparing a system which would accurately distinguish the essential sounds of the language and at the same time be simple enough
for use by English-speaking typesetters and others familiar with the English alphabet. This system was arrived at after considerable study of the systems already
devised by missionaries, such as those of St. Michael's Catholic mission, and by
professional linguists who had recorded and analyzed the Navajo language. Using
this system, primers in the Navajo language were then prepared and eventually a
phrase book and lists of words in medicine, agriculture and range management,
and administration which the Indian Bureau was interested in having Navajos
understand. It was contemplated that the primers would be used by members of
the Indian Bureau staff working on the Navajo Reservation and also in Navajo
schools. Some advocates held that it would speed up and simplify the teaching of
literacy in English if children could first become literate in the Navajo language.
The use of the program in the schools was not developed or carried on because of
disagreement of the school administrators over the efficacy of the method and also
because it was not accepted by the United States Congress that government schools
should teach a language other than English to Navajo children. In 1943 the Indian
Bureau began to publish a monthly news magazine in Navajo with some English
summaries, called Adahooniligii ("Events"). For some years twenty-five hundred
copies were issued monthly and distributed to schools, to six training-in-literacy
centers, and to other subscribers. The purpose of "Events" was to provide informa-

tion concerning happenings on the Navajo Reservation for the large numbers of non-English-speaking Navajos, so that they might better be fitted into the Indian Bureau programs of development and cultural assimilation. At first there was some opposition by Navajos to this program, but by 1950 it had been accepted and the magazine continued to be issued. It had been demonstrated that a non-English-using Navajo could, after a short period of instruction, make some progress in reading the magazine. Also, it had been shown that a person already literate in English, whose first language was Navajo, could learn to read Navajo after six hours of instruction. In 1952 information with regard to the candidates for election to the Tribal Council was printed in Navajo and distributed throughout the reservation, together with other matters such as the regulations for elections, and was widely used in the various election districts. In addition, in 1949 the Indian Bureau began a series of publications in the Navajo language called the Navajo Historical Series. The first issue dealt with the history of the Ramah Navajos as told by The Son of Former Many Beads, an old Navajo man of the area. It appeared that by 1950 a written tradition had been established for Navajo. It was, however, wholly financed by the Indian Bureau and depended for its existence on money appropriated by the national Congress of the United States. A body of literature had been created and possibly several hundred Navajos were writing and reading, particularly reading, the language. With such sources as the Navajo Tribal Council minutes, it was possible that the writing of the language would be taken up more extensively and that it would be continued whether or not the Indian Bureau continued its subsidization. At any rate three requisites for a written tradition had been created — a fairly simple system of writing, a number of individuals versed in the system, and a small body of literature. The need for information about the activities of the tribal political organization which was actively drawing into its web all Navajos, whether English-speaking or not, appeared as if it might be a stimulus to further growth of written Navajo.

FUNCTIONAL CHANGE — Twenty-eight of some forty Indian languages continued to be spoken by a hundred or more people down to 1960. Those languages which persisted had changed as the speakers' interests and ways of life changed. In some cases, as in Tewa, there was relatively little change in structure through the 350 years; in other cases, such as Yaqui, the language had undergone so much change that it might have been difficult for a Yaqui who lived in 1600 to have recognized it without some study.

The changes in functions, if looked at in the perspective of 350 years, seem very great for all Southwestern Indian languages. Let us take as a single example the Tewa language of the Pueblo village of Santa Clara. In 1590 an inhabitant of this village lived his whole life entirely and literally in terms of the Tewa language. Even the nearest villages with whom some visiting or exchange took place were inhabited by people who spoke Tewa. Occasionally a trader came by from a Keresan-speaking village or sometimes one went to a Keresan or a Tiwa village perhaps, when peace prevailed, for a ceremony or gathering. But in 1950 it was no longer possible to say that any individual's life in Santa Clara was lived wholly in terms of Tewa. Every child of the village was in school and in the school there was constant pressure to learn English, whether in the day school at the village or at boarding school and most Tewa children experienced this pressure for at least eight or ten years. It resulted in their associating English with certain kinds of activities and aspects of life with which they did not associate Tewa at all — for instance, engineering and the professions, written literature, mathematics, and so on. Large areas of living or at least glimpses of such areas were opened up and the awareness of the relative smallness of scope of Tewa was suggested. So many things learned about in school, read about in newspapers, seen in moving pictures, encountered on the streets of nearby Espanola or Santa Fe or Albuquerque, or read about in English, simply did not lend themselves to being talked about in Tewa. The very use of the language was in some measure restrictive of the scope of participation in the total life round about. To the extent that one sought such restriction he or she could function better in Tewa, but to the extent that interest in the wider participation was roused by school and other influences, the use of Tewa was felt to be undesirable. In this situation individuals lived double lives to some extent as they became proficient in English and were attracted to the cultural world which it designated and expressed. There were those who moved out of the English world after having experienced it and others who constantly reduced their participation in the world expressed by Tewa.

The movement out of the Tewa world was a process influenced by status as well as cultural interests. From the time of entering school at least, it was subtly impressed on children that the Indian world was inferior in some way. This was reinforced in a thousand ways through all the institutions of the dominant culture with which an individual became acquainted. Individuals differed as to how they were affected by these inter-ethnic attitudes. Some became more sensitive to them than to the ethnocentric values of the village and in so doing became sensitive to the use of the Indian language as a symbol of inferior status. Some who became aware of the valuation reacted against it and accepted the prevailing village reverse valuation. But for all, especially as schooling became general, the awareness of language as a status symbol grew stronger. Acceptance equally with rejection of the Indian language as a status symbol indicated the changed function of the language in the complex milieu of different cultures and articulated societies.

Although no studies of the changing functions of Indian languages had been carried out by 1950, it appeared that an understanding of these functions would shed far more light on the direction of language change than would the analysis of structure and form of the Indian languages. It was not changes in form that were significant with regard to the disappearance or persistence of the language, but rather changes in the social situations of individuals using the languages. It was evident that situations in which the Indian languages were used continued to have high value for thousands of individuals, but it was also apparent that there was devaluation of such situations for hundreds more. In this sense, since no white men were moving into the Indian language situation, the European languages had become dominant and the Indian languages, however stable their forms appeared to be, were changing rapidly in regard to function.

THE INFLUENCE OF INDIAN LANGUAGES
ON SPANISH AND ENGLISH

No discussion of linguistic change in the Southwest would be complete which failed to consider the influences which Indian languages exerted on the two European languages which, by 1960, had become dominant in the region. The processes of diffusion and the restructuring of society by which the European languages became dominant have been sketched. In large part their dominance was a result of the immense increase in the numbers of speakers as compared with a relatively static population for the Indians. It was also a result of the control by the European-language speakers of political, educational, economic, and religious institutions. In the course of these developments it was clear that the influences were largely, almost exclusively one-way, that is, from the European languages to the Indian languages. The reverse influences remained very slight throughout. Nevertheless there were some.

It certainly would appear unreasonable to attribute Tewa behavior in connection with linguistic change to the structure of the language alone and to ignore the fact that English, which has borrowed readily in the course of its history, has borrowed even less from Tewa than Tewa has from English or Spanish. Obviously the nature of the relationships between individuals of societies in contact is an important factor in linguistic acculturation, and languages behave differently as conditions of contact change. The speakers of vernacular Spanish of New Mexico had borrowed a few words from various of the Pueblo Indian languages. Both Spanish and English speakers borrowed a few words from Navajo. Spanish speakers in Sonora borrowed a number of words from Yaqui and Opata. Everywhere some borrowing of this sort occurred, but it was a decelerating process by 1960.

One area of borrowing by Spanish and English which accounts for probably most of the loanwords from Indian languages is that of topographical and geographic names. This was especially notable in Chihuahua and Sonora, where the early missionaries and explorers tried repeatedly to obtain the Indian names for rivers, settlements, and mountain ranges. The result in Sonora was the naming of two major rivers with what the Spaniards thought were Indian names — Mayo and Yaqui — although neither of these words were the actual tribal names which the Spaniards thought they were. Nevertheless most of the major settlements of the Yaquis, as of the Tarahumaras, and many Mayo and Opata settlements came eventually to be called by terms derived from the Indian words for the places. Like the Indians, the Spaniards in attempting to borrow the Indian words modified them in accordance with their own phonetic patterns. Thus the eight Yaqui towns consolidated by the Jesuits became established on Spanish and Mexican maps as Cocorit (from Yaqui *ko'oko'im*), Bacum (from Yaqui *baakum*), Torin (from Yaqui *torim*), Vican or Vicam (from Yaqui *biikam*), Potan or Potam (from Yaqui *potam*), Rahum (from Yaqui *ra'um*), Huirivis (from Yaqui *wiibisim*), Belen (from Yaqui *beene*). The modification of the Indian words was very considerable in both the Yaqui-Mayo and the Tarahumara countries, so that although several hundred Indian place names are preserved on modern maps, many of these are not easily recognizable to Indian speakers and they regard them as the "Mexican names."

In New Mexico and Arizona a much smaller proportion of place names is derived from Indian languages. Spaniards renamed nearly all the rivers in Spanish, such as Rio Grande del Norte, Colorado, Pecos, as well as the mountain ranges and most of the Indian settlements. Most of the Eastern Pueblo villages were renamed with names of the saints or other Spanish designations. The Anglos when they came in adopted the Spanish names, only occasionally renaming. At first they made less effort than did the Spaniards to attach Indian names to the places of the region, although they did adopt a few Navajo and Hopi place names. Later the Indian Bureau, beginning in the 1930's, made a definite effort to place on the official United States maps the Indian place names wherever they had not been completely superceded already by Spanish or English names. The Papago area was the one in which this policy was most thoroughly applied, so that from the 1930's on Papago place names began to appear in increasing number on road and other maps. The use of Indian names, especially as a result of employment on road maps, was well established within some ten years. Similarly, many Navajo and Hopi names were introduced into the Indian Bureau maps. Elsewhere no effort of this sort was carried out, so that the Apache reservations, the Yuman reservations, and most of the Pueblo grants remained unaffected by this policy. The areas of greatest borrowing of Indian place names were those of the Tarahumara, Yaqui-Mayo, Papago, Hopi, and Navajo, and to some extent Opata. The other languages left relatively little mark on the European languages. It should be noted also that the most recent borrowings from the Indian languages, as on the Papago and Hopi reservations, showed the least amount of modification from the original Indian terms. It took over a hundred years for Anglos to learn enough about the Indian languages to record them with some accuracy. There were by that time a number of traders and some Indian Bureau employees who, together with a few linguists, were able to transcribe the Indian terms.

In other areas the borrowing from the Indian languages occurred much less often. Some terms for plants and animals peculiar to an area were borrowed by Spanish, such as the Yaqui word *ubari* for a spider, the Tewa word for greasewood, the Keresan word for the bee plant; these became a part of the local Spanish vernacular. Words for material culture items were borrowed most frequently by Spanish speakers in New Mexico in the area of equal coexistence along the Rio Grande drainage. But probably with equal frequency the words for ceremonial performers and acts and objects for which Spanish culture had no equivalents were borrowed in the Pueblo-Navajo area. Examples are *yeibichei* for a Navajo ceremony, Tiwa *chifonete* for an Isleta-type clown, *koshare* for a Keresan-type clown, *kachina* for representations of Pueblo supernaturals, *paho* for Hopi prayersticks. These borrowings in the north were paralleled by similar ones in the south, where *pascola* for a type of dancer from Yaqui became a part of Sonoran Spanish. There was indeed an increase in the area of borrowing with reference to ceremony as Anglos and Mexicans became more familiar with Indian ceremonies and linguists contributed more accurate recordings of the Indian words. These words were increasingly becoming a part of the technical language of anthropologists and some other students.

Another type of influence on the dominant languages consisted of the growth of distinct dialects of Spanish and English employed by persons of Indian background. The rapid bilingualization of Yaquis during the period of their deportation had resulted in the growth among them of a dialect of north-Mexican Spanish, characterized by a somewhat special vocabulary and phonetic pattern. It had spread into Arizona and was recognizable there as a distinct dialect of Mexican Spanish. In a different way a dialect of English was also created in Arizona and New Mexico. This was a variety of English which developed in most of the boarding schools, where Indians from many different tribes assembled, such as at Albuquerque, Santa Fe, Phoenix, Riverside, and some of those outside the Southwest. In such schools English quickly became not only the language required by the matrons and administrators but also the necessary means of communication, as the lingua franca, among the Indian students. Thus a way of speaking developed which was not wholly controlled by the teachers and administrators who were relatively few in number. The determining factors in the development of this language were the phonetic systems in which the various children had grown up. At Phoenix Indian School, where the prevailing numbers of students were usually Pimas, Papagos, and Hopis — all Uto-Aztecan speakers — the whispered syllables and some other characteristic phonetic elements strongly influenced the "boarding-school dialect" of this sub-area. On the other hand, the predominant numbers at Albuquerque consisted of Navajos, with many different kinds of speakers from the Pueblos. Here the boarding-school dialect took on influence from the Athapaskan languages. The two varieties of boarding-school dialect were nevertheless surprisingly similar. As yet, they have not been studied carefully with reference to the phonetic factors giving rise to them.

By 1960 all the surviving languages had been recorded by Mexican or Anglo professional linguists. The adequacy of these recordings varied greatly, but there was a fairly full record of most of the languages. Considerable bodies of folk literature had been collected in most of them. Thus, the social sciences of the dominant cultures were the richer for such material. And increasingly intensive studies of some of the languages, such as Hopi and Navajo, were being made. At the level of technical thought in English the analysis of Hopi was having an important influence through the brilliant papers of Benjamin Whorf analyzing the categories of space and time as expressed in Hopi.

CHAPTER SIXTEEN

Community Reorientation

THE INDIAN COMMUNITIES of northwestern New Spain, whether villages, rancherías, or bands, were economically self-sufficient, and autonomous governing units. Each local community was almost a world unto itself; each maintained its own social and moral order and only exceptionally and fleetingly admitted any common interest with any other community.

However, during the 350 year period of contact some kind of integration into wider social units came about for every Indian community. Some groups of communities bitterly resisted the wider integration; some accommodated themselves to a degree of linkage after resistance seemed useless. Some escaped, through various kinds of isolation, any very effective wider integration; and some moved steadily into the new framework with little resistance.

As all were forced into some kind of articulation with Spain, Mexico, and the United States, their internal structures did not escape change. Some of those which resisted political integration with greater determination were among those which changed their local organization most profoundly. The little worlds of a few hundred people, divided into groups of kin who cooperated closely with one another in using the land and its resources, had changed by 1960 in different ways and in different degrees. Whatever degree of political integration of a wider sort had come about, no community was any longer the self-sufficient world that it had been.

It is these changes that we shall proceed to sketch. In a sense, they are the obverse of the political changes already traced. That is to say, political integration into the dominant nations could proceed only to the extent that the narrower relations within the communities were relaxed or modified. Intense solidarity of a group of a few hundred people, such as constituted an Eastern Pueblo village, was not compatible with a national citizenship of real significance for the individuals professing it. The narrower relations of the communities of Indians were for the most part the relationships of blood relatives — of kinship as defined in a variety of ways. To the extent that these relationships were modified, the political relationships of national citizenship could grow. To the extent that the kinship and local group ties remained as at the time of the coming of the Spaniards, or to the extent that they were reinforced in response to conquest, an organization in terms of citizenship was blocked. And so long as such organization was blocked the working idea of the citizen could not develop.

It was probably true that, for the great majority of Indians, not even by the 1960's had the idea of citizenship assumed the kind of reality which it had for the invaders. It was not true, however, that the rejection or partial acceptance of European political organization was correlated precisely with any degree of preservation of an aboriginal form of community life.

CHANGES IN THE SIZE AND SHAPE
OF INDIAN COMMUNITIES

The way in which a people distribute themselves over the land reflects important features of their social structure, and probably such distribution has important influences on the view of life which the people develop. The compact rural village gives rise to individuals who view life in different ways from those who live in scattered farmsteads. The nature of the settlement pattern may reveal the character of political or administrative units in a society; it may shed light on the kinds of kinship units which exist in a society. But above all it is indicative of the extent to which civilization — in the sense of an urbanized society — has developed. Where large concentrations of people live close together in cities and towns intensive division of social and economic labor and heterogeneity of belief and custom exist.

The Spanish administrators had a very clear conception of the relationship between compact communities and the kind of civilization which they advocated. This conception was embodied in their policy of "reduction," through the institution of which they expected to bring their variety of civilization to the Indians of New Spain. Throughout the 1600's and after they sought to create, as the very foundation of Spanish culture in northwestern New Spain, compact communities centered about churches. This program, in which the missionaries heartily concurred, was pressed with great vigor and here and there it had profound influences on the life of Indians in central Mexico. Nevertheless it must be admitted that in the northwest really important effects were confined largely to central and southern Sonora and along the Rio Grande in the vicinity of El Paso. Elsewhere, as among the Eastern Pueblos, compact communities already existed or, as among the Navajos and Apaches, the program was never put into effect.

In fact, by the middle of the twentieth century the only Indian groups who had communities somewhat similar to the Spanish town were the Eastern and Western Pueblos who had developed such village plans before the Spaniards came on the scene. Others, such as the Yaquis, Mayos, and Opatas, had settlements of a mixed character, embodying both the old ranchería irregularities of plan and Spanish influence. Many lived in communities influenced by the less compact arrangements of Anglo-American settlement, but a majority of all the Indians, it may be said, lived either in communities arranged as they had been before the arrival of white men or in communities of that type accommodated in various ways to the exigencies of invasion and economic adaptation.

Reduction, in the sense of more concentrated settlements of a sort, had taken place everywhere, but no uniformity of plan corresponding to the Spanish town nor to any other single town plan prevailed over the region. The changes in the direction of generally greater concentration of population were complex and reflected for each tribe the peculiar combination of historical influences which they had experienced. The fact that the Spanish town plan, even among those Indians to whom it was introduced, did not become universal was indicative not only of the incompleteness of Spanish political domination on the northern frontier but also the tenacity of patterns which the Indians had developed over centuries in their adaptation to the physical environment of the region. Undoubtedly the Spanish settlement pattern would have prevailed much more widely after four hundred years, if there had been political continuity. The coming of the Anglo-Americans, however, resulted in the introduction of different settlement patterns, as well as a less clear and consistent conception of the relationship of settlement pattern to types of civilization.

It is interesting to look at settlement pattern change in the Southwest from the point of view of the process of diffusion. For example, to what extent did the Spanish town plan spread to the Indians and what was involved in its acceptance and rejection? And to what extent did any of several Anglo-American community patterns diffuse among Indians and what determined and limited this diffusion?

By the time that the missionization of northwestern New Spain took place, a definite emphasis on an ideal form for Indian communities had developed among the colonial administrators. Plans had been carefully developed for the resettlement of the Indians of the central plateau of Mexico and for their congregation in towns. The plans for these towns had been gleaned from Roman documents. The town plan decided on was that of a central plaza, where a church and at least a town government building were located. Radiating out from this center were to be straight streets, cross-cut at regular intervals by other streets at right angles, in short, a grid pattern. This was not a general Spanish type of town arrangement; it had been imposed in parts of Spain by Rome and was one of the elements of the "Culture of the Conquest." Although a good deal of effort was expended in the vicinity of Mexico City to introduce such grid-patterned congregations before 1600, it is by no means clear that the missionaries in the north attempted this innovation in its complete form. Certainly it was the case that both Franciscans and Jesuits sought to establish church-centered communities, but it seems doubtful that they insisted strongly on the grid pattern. Nor does it seem probable that they insisted on contiguous houses fronting on streets with patios behind. They did not mention such plans as being their objective and did not describe such plans as having been developed in the mission communities. If they were instructed to introduce this innovation, it is clear that they were nowhere successful among the Indians. It was only some Spanish settlers who followed, after a fashion, this mode of constructing their settlements. Thus in New Biscay, in New Mexico, and eventually by the 1700's in Sonora there were grid-pattern towns here and there, but these were the Spanish, not the Indian mission, communities. The Indians — including the Mayos, Yaquis, and Opatas — of Sonora built houses around the churches, but these were not contiguous, and were scattered irregularly. In New Mexico the Eastern Pueblos maintained their own form of contiguous blocks of houses surrounding plazas and allowed the mission churches to be built at the edge of the villages. Santa Fe and the other Spanish towns, however, approximated the rectangular form. By the end of the Spanish period, the plaza-grid town was well known to Indians, but it was not being copied. Moreover, many of the Spanish settlers in those small communities which were not laid out as royal towns adopted the Indian styles of building. The Spanish rural villages of New Mexico looked more like Eastern Pueblo villages than like the new towns of central Mexico. The houses were often not contiguous; they usually followed the contours of the land rather than a prearranged rectangular form. Similarly the smaller communities of Spaniards on haciendas and around mines in Sonora were irregular in plan.

The failure of the plaza-grid town to diffuse through northwestern New Spain would seem to have been a result of the Indian settlement patterns and a lack of definite planning for anything except greater concentration of houses around the churches. This objective was achieved for a majority of the Indians of Sonora but not for the Tarahumaras of Chihuahua. As for the Eastern Pueblos, they already lived in tighter concentrations than most Spaniards were accustomed to.

For the Mayos and Yaquis there was a real change in settlement pattern, and this was true for most Opatas. The change consisted in two features — a more compact arrangement of houses around the ceremonial center of the church and the grouping of houses into local communities as much as ten times the size of the usual settlement before the coming of the missionaries. For all three of these tribes concentration resulted in the growth of communities of from three or four hundred to around three thousand. This constituted a very considerable change in breadth of social integration. It further involved a centralization of focal interests such as land management and ceremonialism. It increased the need for an administrative organization. It also, under the urging of the missionaries, probably meant an increase in craft, as well as political and ceremonial specialization. The reduction program was therefore of far-reaching effect on these tribes.

However, it should not be concluded that the change was so great as the figures above may suggest. They are approximate average figures. It appears from the imperfect record that none of the three tribes mentioned entirely lacked large communities at the entry of the Spaniards. Although Francisco de Ibarra spoke of Opata settlements as generally small, he reported at least two settlements among Opatas and one among Jovas with approximately two to three thousand inhabitants. While no communities of large size are specifically reported except "Oera" for the Yaquis, certainly there were some Yaqui settlements larger than the two to three hundred average of the rancherías. The readiness of both Mayos and Yaquis to come into larger church-centered towns immediately upon the arrival of the Jesuits suggests that their local organization was of a form which was consistent with concentrated population. In other words, it appears that the Spanish program in this respect caught the Cahitas, Opatas, and Lower Pimas at a stage in which they were ripe for town development. In this sense they were affected differently and more profoundly than were the Upper Pimas, the Yumans and other rancheria Indians. Indirectly the Spanish entry also had an effect of concentration on the Upper Pimas. Aside from the creation of mission towns of several hundred people more than the usual Upper Pima rancheria, there was another effect. The stimulation of the Apache raiding toward the end of the 1600's in northern Sonora resulted in the concentration into defensive local units of Papagos and the Gila Pimas, whose rancherias were augmented both by migration of Sobaipuris westward into their country and by concentration for defense of several rancherias under a single peace-war leadership.

Not all rancheria peoples were affected similarly by Spanish efforts at concentration or reduction. The success of the reduction program among the Cahitas and Opatas is in marked contrast with its general failure among the Tarahumaras. It was pushed equally hard and for an even longer period among the Tarahumaras. Nevertheless the missionaries themselves were forced to admit by the early 1700's that reduction could not be carried out among the Tarahumaras. The Tarahumaras, although called "rancheria" people by the Spaniards, had very different settlement patterns from the Yaquis or the Opatas. They were far more scattered, and often a family lived in considerable isolation from any other family. It was this wide scattering with no pattern for close living that blocked the Jesuit reduction program. The ultimate effect of the efforts for change was a wide acceptance among Tarahumaras of the idea of the church vicinity as a ceremonial and administrative center but not as a living place. The churches became headquarters for some governmental and ceremonial activities, especially at Easter time, and in some areas for weekly meetings. People gathered around the churches only for these meetings and ceremonies, but lived permanently in their relatively isolated farmsteads which were scattered widely as far as fifteen miles or more from the church. Thus the innovation of the mission community resulted finally only in the introduction of a new ceremonial center. This was in itself an important new element of wider social integration in Tarahumara life, but it was less far-reaching as a cultural change than the Jesuit-inspired towns of the Yaquis, Opatas, and Mayos.

There is little need to discuss changes in settlement pattern which the Spanish program brought about among the Eastern Pueblos. The effects were not far-reaching. The Pueblo Rebellion of 1680 had profound influence in the over-all distribution of villages, eliminating some old sites entirely, bringing about the establishment of some new ones, such as Laguna, and reducing greatly the population of most villages. The total effect of Spanish contact among the Eastern Pueblos may be summed up as a general decrease in population and the elimination of large villages, such as Pecos. In other words, there was a somewhat reverse result from that noted in Sonora. Any tendency that may have been present among the Eastern Pueblos toward the formation of communities of several thousand was checked and the small, compact community of several hundred remained throughout the Spanish period as the type of local grouping. These communities had the same form as before, but added a new secondary ceremonial center — the Christian church building at the edge of each pueblo.

For the Western Pueblos the Spanish conquest had in general the effect of concentration of people. For example, the Zuni villages of several hundred each ultimately became consolidated into the largest of all the pueblos in historic times, with more than two thousand people concentrated in a single village. This tendency did not go so far among the Hopis, although the general effect of Spanish contact, following the 1680 rebellion, was some consolidation. The population of "renegade" Awatovi was absorbed into other villages. Below-mesa villages moved up on to the mesas and consolidated with villages already established there. The ultimate result, however, was the creation only of communities of two to four hundred people. There were no large consolidations comparable to Zuni, merely a reduction in the total number of Hopi settlements and some shift in their locations to less accessible spots.

Other tribes of the Southwest, who were organized in bands at the coming of the Spaniards, in some cases underwent some temporary change of community organization. The relocation of the Seris at Pópulo and later near Pitic (Hermosillo) where they were concentrated into mission communities had no permanent effect on local grouping. The partly successful efforts to get Western and other Apaches to settle around the presidios of the northern frontier had no lasting effects. Seris and Apaches, and also the Cebolleta Enemy Navajos, all went back to the more roving life of the bands after short periods of more settled living.

The Spanish grid-type town grew increasingly popular among settlers in Sonora during the 1800's and became the standard form for large towns and some small towns settled by Mexicans. It was introduced by Mexican settlers who moved into the easternmost Yaqui towns — Cocorit and Bacum — in the middle 1800's. Gradually the whole town plan of these two settlements became assimilated to the plaza-grid pattern. This same process of imposition of the plaza-grid affected many of the towns where Mexicans settled with relocating Opatas in formerly Opata rancherías. During the last twenty years of the 1800's, the Yaqui town of Torim was laid out by General Luís Torres to conform with the ideal Mexican type, and the town established to replace the drought-ousted town of Belem — Pitahaya — followed this plan. However, the Torim grid plan was abandoned after the Torreses left the Yaqui country following the 1910 revolution, and Pitahaya became a "ghost town." In the 1920's Potam was resettled by former Yaqui soldiers under Mexican Army direction; the greater part of the population in the 1940's were settled in blocks intersected regularly by wide streets. However, the new houses built by Yaquis along the new streets were not in contiguous Mexican style, and one large section of the town was arranged in the old haphazard fashion. The town of Vicam, a station founded by Mexican colonists on the railroad, not on an original Yaqui town site, was the only fully plaza-grid-type community in the Yaqui country proper. On the other hand, the major Mayo River towns were all largely on the grid plan, as were the formerly Opata towns.

Elsewhere in Sonora and Chihuahua there was little change in the Indian settlements. Mexican movement continuing into the Tarahumara and Lower Pima country increasingly brought the grid-type town into those areas, but most Tarahumaras, whether anti-Christian or not, utilized church areas as ceremoniopolitical centers and maintained their scattered farmstead type of settlement pattern. The Seris similarly built irregularly arranged camp sites at various points and when they camped at Desemboque, the fish-trading center, disposed themselves in the same fashion in the vicinity of the Mexican stores. Near the international border a few small scattered rancherías of the pre-Spanish form existed, inhabited by Papagos — the remnants of the Upper Pimas of Sonora.

The most significant demographic change by the 1950's in both Sonora and Chihuahua was that the Indian communities had become a part of a rural-urban condition of sharply contrasting settlements. Indian communities were rural, and whether widely scattered like the Tarahumara, or approximating Mexican forms like the Opatas, were in greater or less degree dependent economically on and subordinate politically to city-centers of fifty thousand or more people, such as Chihuahua City, Ciudad Obregón, and Hermosillo. In this sense, as parts of a larger whole, the settlement patterns of the Indians had changed profoundly over the 140 years since the Spanish withdrawal.

The most notable developments on the reservations of New Mexico and Arizona were (1) the growth of small but concentrated trade and administrative centers — the agency towns — and (2) some degree of decentralization of settlement pattern. The agency town affected all the Indians except the Eastern Pueblos. The latter on their small plots of land were all near either Santa Fe, Espanola, Bernalillo, or Albuquerque. Agency towns had never been built on their territory and the Eastern Pueblos had assumed the rural-urban trade relations directly with the large cities in their vicinity. Their own patterns of concentrated residence had not changed appreciably. On the other hand, the Indians who lived farther from the developing city-centers of the region were related to the larger centers indirectly through the agency towns built by the Indian Bureau, so that to some extent they constituted small scale rural-urban patterns within each reservation. Whiteriver and San Carlos among the Western Apaches, Sells and Sacaton among the Papagos and Gila Pimas, Keams among the Hopis, Parker Agency among the Mohave-Chemehuevi, and Tuba City, Fort Defiance, and Window Rock among the Navajos constituted a level of integration intermediate between the Indians and the nearest cities.

The agency town in each case was the seat of some governmental buildings and activities, whether hospital, school, or administrative office, or some combination of these. As the place through which federal money flowed for expenditure and as the seat of administrative authority and operations they were sources of jobs for Indians. Consequently they attracted Indians who built houses at the edges of the areas where governmental buildings were placed. To some extent arrangement was influenced by the street layouts which characterized the agency buildings, but for the most part the Indian homes were arranged in irregular fashion, making a considerable contrast with the regular streets of the government buildings and those of the government employees. In these towns there was a contrast of rich and poor, a contrast of solidity and elaborateness of construction with makeshift and simple construction. Each town exhibited a number of contrasting areas, perhaps somewhat analogous to the contrasts in the Spanish royal towns about which Indians had in an earlier period gathered for employment. There was some similarity to the most common type of United States settlement, namely, the Main Street nucleus with irregularly arranged houses in the vicinity. Agency towns ranged from several hundred to two thousand or more inhabitants, so that everywhere they represented some degree of concentration of population, contrasting with the rural parts of the reservations.

On the other hand, decentralization of communities was apparent on a number of reservations. The Papago villages which had undergone some centralization during the early and middle 1800's into "defense villages," as a result of Apache raids, began a dispersal during the late 1800's. There were thus more settlements and a return to the scattered ranchería type of arrangement. But one large community — Santa Rosa — of over one thousand had grown up in the northern part of the reservation. There was a similar less pronounced dispersal of Pima settlements. Navajos, seeking forage for their sheep and horse herds, had also dispersed widely during the early 1900's, so that the whole Navajo Reservation was widely but thinly settled in what the Spaniards would have called rancherías. The Western Pueblos likewise were undergoing some dispersal. Although Zuni retained its centralized single location, there were also temporary farm-season settlements, and Acoma and Laguna, possessed of more land than the other Eastern Pueblos, had developed small permanent settlements over farm and range land, the people maintaining ceremonial affiliation in the large centers. The dispersal of Hopis had begun by 1900; some from each of the villages had moved off the mesa tops and established permanent residence below the mesas, as at New Oraibi, Polacca, Toreva, and Moenkopi. The Western Apaches, except at San Carlos, had also dispersed, reconstituting the communities of Cibecue and some other smaller ones. The trend toward dispersal meant that in general, within the confines of the reservations, there was an increase in rural type of settlement. But this was taking place within a region where the general over-all trend was toward urban concentration, so that the reservation conditions stood in marked contrast with what was taking place in the region as a whole.

At the same time there had been since the late 1800's an increase in the density of population on all the reservations. This was most marked on the most rural of the reservations, namely, the Navajo and the Papago, but it was an important change on all the reservations. The increase in population from 1900 to 1950 was a counter-trend to the previous steady decline. It marked a movement toward a density of population which had never been approached at any time previously and which approximated the trend among non-Indians of the region.

In Sonora and Chihuahua there was no similar increase. In the 1930's, Sauer described the Indian population about as it had been three hundred years before.

THE GROWTH OF ALTERNATIVE FAMILY PATTERNS

The Spaniards and Anglos differed with regard to the importance that they attached to the form of the community, or local group. Conscious of the compact village or town as an important feature of their civilization, the Spaniards made intensive efforts to impose this form of group on the Indians, but with varying success. The Anglos on the other hand, having in their background the tradition of the isolated homestead — a community plan that resembled that of the Tarahumaras as much as anything else in the world — were not insistent on concentrations into villages. Rather they were inclined to direct development toward some equivalent of the "little red schoolhouse" neighborhood, in which most of the Indian Bureau people of the time had been brought up and which had come to be a well recognized pattern in American culture. The schoolhouse without attention to community form seemed basic in the Anglo program; but in the Spanish program the compact village was essential regardless of educational center.

These insistences in the two different programs had their marked effects and gave sharply contrasting directions to the assimilation programs adopted by each of the nations. It is an interesting fact that one can discover no such clear and conscious programs with respect to the form of the family. It is true that monogamy was the only form of marriage which either the Spaniards or the Anglos (early Mormons excepted) would tolerate and that vigorous measures were adopted immediately by Spaniards and later by Anglos to eliminate polygyny. Although there was awareness of polygyny, there seems to have been no clear consciousness of the variety of forms of family life which the Indians presented. The strongly unilateral family rules among some tribes seem barely to have become known to the administrators, or even to the missionaries. The Europeans apparently could not conceive clearly of any forms of family life different from their own, with the single exception of plural marriage. Consequently whatever one can call program in their attempts to remake Indians with respect to family life usually stemmed out of misinterpretation. The dominant peoples never gained an understanding of the family systems they faced; only special students not in touch with the bearers of the assimilation programs penetrated the mysteries.

The conscious programs with respect to the customs attending family and marriage were simple and direct. The Jesuit and Franciscan missionaries wrote as though they had little conception of family life and its relation to personality development; nevertheless they had some definite ideas about marriage. These were that marriage should be a sacrament duly presided over by the priest, that divorce must be prohibited, and that marriage might take place only between one man and one woman. Each of these prescriptions was contrary to the customs of all the tribes the missionaries encountered. Marriage was an arrangement between family groups having nothing to do with an individual's soul or spirit, a marriage arrangement could be broken off at any time when for various reasons a man and a woman no longer wished to live together, and finally any person could in the course of his or her life live with an unprescribed number of mates. Moreover, most of the tribes, the exceptions being the Pueblos, customarily allowed a man to have more than one wife at a time, when that fitted the economics of his household, and it was not entirely unknown, as among the Havasupai, for a woman under special conditions to have more than one husband. The Catholic prescriptions regarding monogamous marriage were advocated by the missionaries absolutely without compromise, being regarded as equally sacred with baptism and other features of their religious system. Their insistence on the sacred marriage rules involved them, not, as they thought, in building a system of regulated marital life where none had existed before, but rather in trying to alter complex social arrangements which had wide ramifications in Indian life. They were unaware that they were substituting a conjugal for a consanguineal system.

Since the missionaries, even those whose personal contacts became intimate and deep, learned almost nothing about how the Indian social systems worked and particularly about marriage and family, with which they had no participant experience, they remained in the position of working to introduce a few relatively unimportant forms rather than of transforming the system. They were successful in this limited sphere in those communities which were most receptive to the Catholic ritual system generally, namely, the large ranchería groups of southern and central Sonora. Here the forms of marriage on which they insisted were accepted rapidly along with other ritual forms such as baptism. Certainly by the 1700's it had become usual for Mayos, Yaquis, and Opatas to accept marriage by the missionary as the proper way to seal a marital union. It had also become accepted that this ceremony was to be performed only once for an adult. And it seems likely that the prescription of only one wife at a time had a large degree of acceptance as an ideal pattern. But there is little indication that the acceptance of these rules resulted in any basic alteration of the systems of kinship and marriage as they had existed among the Indians. Rather, the priestly sacrament was an additional rite added to the exchange of feasts and gifts between families and to the other ritual which had accompanied marriage. Moreover the formal marriage rite could be postponed until long after man and wife began to live together. Not only was this an external form, but the missionary rule that it was not to be repeated for any individual — since divorce was not permitted — was taken very literally. Individuals underwent the marriage ceremony only once but they changed mates as they had before, and when the change took place, since the parties had been previously married by the missionary they simply did not go through it again. Thus the principle of no divorce was accepted only in the letter. It was still the case for various reasons, ranging from personal incompatibility to incompetence of a wife or husband in household duties, men and women did dissolve their marriages and take new mates. It seems probable nevertheless that among these tribes an ideal pattern of monogamy became widely accepted under the teaching of the missionaries. There was, however, not universal practice of the principle even by the 1950's, when there were still polygynous unions among both Mayos and Yaquis. There had been periodically an increase in polygyny during the period of warfare when many Yaqui males lost their lives in battle. Monogamy was not universally practiced and the prevailing viewpoint, if not the ideal view, was that marriages were economic arrangements for sustaining households and rearing children. Those Tarahumaras who had close contact with the Jesuits were affected similarly by the teachings regarding marriage forms and these were renewed with intensity again when the Jesuits returned in the 1900's. But polygyny and the changing of mates without formal divorce was perhaps even more general among Tarahumaras than among the Indians of Sonora. The point to be made is that the concept of marriage as an economic arrangement between families was still, after 350 years, the dominant one. In this it not only remained consistent with the concept prior to Spanish contact, but it also was consistent with the actual practice of Spaniards and Mexicans in the rural areas of New Spain and northwestern Mexico. The Catholic ideal of marriage without divorce was a part of the cultural system, but it was only a partially accepted ideal at variance with the prevailing practice.

Among the Eastern Pueblos the early missionaries did not speak of plural wives as a problem, indicating that polygyny had not been customary there. The change of mates was, however, a general practice and the no-divorce rule of the missionaries seemed here also to have no effect. The marriage ceremony in addition to the fairly elaborate interfamily rites was widely accepted by the Eastern Pueblos and had become general by the end of the 1700's. But again the concept of marriage as a sacrament symbolizing unbreakable relations between two individuals did not replace the older concept of a relationship with practical family functions in which the two individuals were incidental. Among Seris, Navajos, Apaches, and Yumans, the Spanish-Catholic ideas regarding marriage had no influence.

The obstacles to the diffusion of the Catholic marriage ideals lay deep in the social organization of the Indians. It is possible that if the Spaniards had gained insight into the nature of the family systems they might have formulated an approach which would have more effectively struck at its roots. It seems, however, that family organization is an aspect of culture concerning which people do not easily come to any objectivity. Spaniards, Mexicans, and Anglos simply did not gain comprehension of how the kinship systems of the Indians worked. Lacking such knowledge they were in no position to attack them directly, and this they never did, although the kind of societies which they ultimately built around the Indian tribes did indirectly strike at the roots of the Indian systems.

Of fundamental importance in all the Indian societies of northwestern New Spain, even including the separate homestead-based society of the Tarahumaras, was what might be loosely called the extended family. By this we mean a group larger than a couple and their children, composed of persons who recognized blood kinship with one another and cooperated in various ways as a kinship group. The extended family did not by any means have the same composition among all the tribes. The differences depended on whether the tribes emphasized kinship connection through the male or the female line or treated both lines more or less similarly. The differences also depended on other factors, such as the relationship between the local community and the kinship groupings, for example, whether a settlement was composed of closely related kin. Whether or not the internal structure was of a matrilineal or patrilineal form or was bilateral, whether it was relatively large or relatively small, compact or dispersed, the nuclear family, a couple and their children, constituted a group whose existence was more or less submerged in a larger whole through emphasis on descent ties. Thus no nuclear family, whether among the close-knit Western Pueblos or the more loosely knit Seris or Western Apaches, had anything approaching an independent existence. It is doubtful if any of the Indians possessed the concept of the nuclear family as a distinct social unit. The very emphasis on divorce as a right and proper means of economic and social adjustment indicated this. The nuclear family produced whatever it could for its own economic support, but other nuclear families had an equal right to the use of its products. The precariously existing Seri families expected constantly to share with one another whatever they managed to forage; this expectation was a constant insurance against bad luck and hard times for each family. The grouping of people for purposes of the work of food gathering was in fact always in terms of several nuclear families, just as the group that consumed always consisted of several. Among the Hopi, where the composition of the household was strictly prescribed, this household was never under any circumstances a nuclear family, but rather several who shared a house or group of houses, fields, and the stored produce of the fields. Between the extremes of the loose aggregation of nuclear families composing the Seri gathering unit, and the tightly organized maternal family of the Hopis were many varieties. In all, the economic unit was a group of kindred whose work and whose produce were shared on the basis of the kinship relations. For these groups there was a further basis of unity in their recognition of a common ancestry and sacred obligations arising out of that common origin. Thus the nuclear family was also merged in a wider worshipping group with ritual relations to ancestral spirits or other supernaturals.

The extended family was the link between each individual life and the wider community of band or village. Basic loyalties were formed in this kinship group and induction into the life of the local group came through its operation. The Hopi maternal family of three or more generations, the family cluster of the Apaches, the bilateral cooperating groups of the Tarahumara, rather than individuals or nuclear families, constituted the foundations of any wider cooperation. The existence of a village or of a band depended on the customs and habits of cooperation between such extended family units. The customs of exchanging marriage partners between Yaqui rancherías or between unrelated maternal Hopi families were forms of wider cooperation on which unities larger than the kin group had rested.

The unity in terms of village or band which had been achieved by Southwestern Indians rested solidly first on the strength of the extended families and secondly on the traditional forms of cooperation between these groups. Leadership did not exist on any permanent basis except as it grew out of the extended families. It was never hereditary in the sense that kingship was among the Spaniards — descending from an eldest son to an eldest son regardless of ability — but it was always hereditary in the sense that some kin group either owned the traditional office, as among Pueblo clans, or that some kinship group through numbers or an acquired prestige backed one of their members, as among the "sub-chiefs" of the Western Apaches or perhaps among the Yaquis. Leadership was not sought directly by an individual but grew out of the confidence of the extended family group in an individual closely watched in his development by the whole. The individual, as husband, as farmer or hunter, as group leader, even as wrongdoer, was indistinct from his extended family or kinship group or, better, was in all his activities an expression of the group's ideals and hopes. It was in this sense that the extended family was not only the economic and religious basis of village and band but was also the matrix of individual expression and activity. One was primarily one's kinfolk and only temporarily involved in any wider loyalties in larger crises.

The very basis of the Spanish missionaries' approach was subversive of the extended family. Their approach was to the individual and their objective was to win over to the Christian way each separate individual. Their concept of individual salvation required an individual-by-individual approach. They did not recognize the extended family as the unit of the Indian societies, only the individual, and they focused their persuasion there. The individualism in their approach had far-reaching consequences for the societies which they confronted. Even though all of their doctrines and rituals were not promptly accepted, the fundamentals of their viewpoint constituted almost immediately a revolutionary influence on Indian societies. This was true despite the absence of evidence that the missionaries understood what they were doing. The paradox was that they did not appear to understand enough about the nature of society to realize what a revolutionary force for civilization their approach constituted.

Among the two tribes which the Jesuits converted almost as wholes and in the space of a few years — the Mayos and Yaquis — the force of the individualistic approach was largely lost. These peoples, as extended families, accepted the Catholic forms in large part and quickly adapted them to the traditions of their social organization. The concept of salvation of an individual quite apart from the fate of his relatives made no perceptible impression. Confession and the idea of individual sin and salvation were ignored. Family forms of worship, joint family rituals, family-focused crisis ceremonies were developed which adapted the new religion to the persisting extended-family arrangement of Yaqui life. The old emphasis on unity with the family's ancestors was continued and a variety of adaptations of the Catholic beliefs was worked out and incorporated into the newly developing ceremonial life. This was all possible because the extended families had come as units into the practice of the new religion under Jesuit tutelage. The fabric of kinship organization had been little altered in the process.

The effects of the approach were very different among those tribes where there was not a prompt, general acceptance of the missionary teachings. The reduction of the Tarahumaras began at the southern edge of their territory and progressed only very slowly, and with repeated setbacks, into the heart of the Tarahumara country. More than a century was required before the missionaries recognized that they were dealing with a situation fundamentally unlike that among Yaquis and others where reduction had been readily accepted. From the beginning, conversion drove wedges between the members of the extended family groups. Families split over the issue of becoming Christians. Some members of families came down out of the mountains to enjoy the mission life; others stayed behind. Kinship obligations pulled many back away from the missions. Individuals who came to the missions and then worked in the mines often became anti-Spanish and rejected the missionaries. The missionaries themselves were inclined to attribute this to the "character" of the Tarahumaras. It seems more likely to have been a result of the poor adaptation of the missionary methods to the structure of Tarahumara society. Their approach was constantly in conflict, without their fully realizing it, with the social system based on the scattered extended-family units. Some results of the conflict engendered by the Jesuit approach were still apparent as late as the 1950's in the existence of "pagan" and "Christian" groups among the Tarahumaras, whose religious behavior hardly differed but who preserved the antagonisms engendered in the course of the missionary program.

Somewhat similar results were apparent at first among the Opatas, but the missionary program was carried on more rapidly and ultimately reached all the Opatas, so that the final results approximated those of the Yaquis and Mayos. It nevertheless seems likely that the extended family system suffered more among the Opatas, as it did among the Tarahumaras, and that for some time the creation of Christian converts was accompanied by the creation of anti-Christian converts.

The effects of the individualized approach of the Franciscan missionaries on the Eastern Pueblos seem to have been slight. It is not indicated that there was any period when the Pueblos made sharp distinctions between Christians and adherents of the native religions. In contrast with the Mayos and Yaquis, the impact of the missionaries was sharply limited so far as reorganization of religious life went. There was no comparable widespread acceptance of forms, only some selected few which were practiced in conjunction with the existing ceremonies. The acceptance in any thoroughgoing way of missionary leadership in religion never took place. Christian behavior was merely an adjunct of the old ways. Thus all attended the church and all attended the native ceremonies, until the missionaries directly attacked the native rites. Then these were continued without missionary knowledge. The issue of being Christian or non-Christian was not accepted by or successfully forced on the Pueblos. An individual was as Christian as he felt like being or had to be in order to get along with the Spaniards. But he remained a loyal, worshipping member of his kinship group. The family schisms of Tarahumara conversion were not present here; in fact, conversion in the sense of a break with the past did not take place. Interest in the activities of the church alongside the village did not involve any separation from one's daily life and one's extended family, as it did among Tarahumaras.

Among the Lower Pimas the missionary approach had ultimately about the same effects as it did among the Yaquis and Opatas. Among the Upper Pimas the splitting of families began — much as it did among the Tarahumaras — but the missionary program was cut short or reduced in intensity. Hence the Papagos extended family was left intact by the end of the Spanish period.

Since individual landholding was not imposed, there was little else in the Spanish program which contributed to weakening the extended family beyond the idea of individual salvation and to a slight extent the introduction of individualized wage labor in the mines. The first struck at the solidarity of the kin group through suggesting that individual welfare was something independent of obligations to family, and the second did so through providing economic support apart from the extended family. Since, however, wage labor was not continuously engaged in during the Spanish period and was punctuated with long periods at home with the family group, it had little influence except perhaps on some few individuals who left Indian society altogether and became rapidly assimilated. Hence the extended family was still vigorous everywhere by the end of the Spanish period. The Spanish program had included no substitute for it.

In the subsequent period, new forces in addition to the individualism of Catholic teaching and the wage labor of the mines and haciendas came into play, although both of those, translated into different forms, continued to develop and to exert influence. In Chihuahua among the Tarahumaras wage labor strongly affected a small minority of the Indians. Mining developed rapidly during the 1800's, as did ranching, and the Indians who had been missionized continued to work frequently as laborers for the Mexicans. Among them the extended family tended to weaken, and a good deal of cultural assimilation took place. For the majority of Tarahumaras, however, there was more or less effective isolation from Mexican society, so that wage labor, rather than being a routine feature of life, was an occasional resort in times of crisis. The retirement to the mountains resulted in the maintenance of something of an independent economy — subsistence agriculture supplemented by small amounts of trade. Among the mountain Tarahumaras, therefore, the extended bilateral family remained strong into the 1900's; probably it was little different from what it had been when the Jesuits first arrived. In fact, it was probably reknit more strongly after the breakdown of the Jesuit reduction program. The situation began to resemble that of the Mayos and Yaquis in which Christian forms of religion were adapted to the persisting extended family system.

In Sonora, the Opatas increasingly intermarried with rural Mexicans, blending the two forms of family organization, with a similar trend in the Mayo country.

The Yaqui situation was different. During the early 1800's there was little change from the previous period. Within the river towns the Yaquis maintained a high degree of social isolation from Mexicans and here the extended families remained well knit and vigorously functioning units of the ever increasingly centralized town organizations. Moreover contact with the organized Catholic Church decreased to almost nothing and as a consequence the Yaqui social system reintegrated itself with little influence from the individualistic ideology of Christianity. It is true, however, that the economy of the Mexicans continued to develop, both with respect to mining and agriculture. Yaquis were drawn into this as wage laborers with increasing frequency, especially as a result of the periodic disruption of agricultural production in the Yaqui country on account of the fighting. Many individuals became independent of their families in the river towns and drifted from haciendas to Mexican town life. Nuclear families in these towns and cities became assimilated to Mexican society, and this process continued with increasing intensity through the 1800's. But in many ways this increased the solidarity of the extended families of the river towns. Their economic security was enhanced by the income of members who went out to work and came back. Although some of them lost members, this meant that those who remained were subjected to less strain. The great threat to the Yaqui social system came after the defeats of the 1880's and the inauguration of the Mexican program of deportation. Families were broken up and hundreds of individuals became isolated within Mexican society in Sonora, in Arizona, and elsewhere in Mexico. By this time, however, the solidarity of Yaquis against Mexicans had become so intense that wherever Yaqui individuals found themselves together the absence of any real blood tie did not matter. They applied the term "kinfolk" to all Yaquis and steadily formed little groups of cooperating persons in Sonora and Arizona cities. They reconstituted their ceremonial life and on these foundations the extended family came back into existence. The composition of the new units was miscellaneous and untraditional, but they assumed in the new settings the functions of the old extended family. The tie of ritual kinship, or godparenthood, was employed to cement its structure. Everywhere that Yaquis gathered during the first half of the 1900's this functional equivalent of the extended family came back into existence, and Yaqui solidarity was reinforced by its reappearance.

In New Mexico and Arizona the first twenty-five years of Anglo political control were not ones of thorough political domination. In the 1870's the program of the Anglos began to take shape. By the 1880's it appeared that a major feature of it would strike deeply at the roots of the extended family, since it was aimed specifically at breaking up the relations between children and older members of the family group. This was the boarding-school policy, which set as its objective the removal of children from their family and community surroundings in order to bring about as rapidly as possible their assimilation into the religious and economic aspects of Anglo culture. This policy seems not to have included any clear conception of a form of family to be substituted for the Indian extended family from which the child was to be saved. It is true that the "farming out" program was designed to show from the servant's angle how an American Protestant household was organized and functioned. But it is hard to see what the policy makers had in mind for the Indian children with respect to selection of mates. Obviously the program was not clearly thought through with reference to family life, but dealt with the situation in a highly abstract way based on extremely individualistic conceptions. The program foundered ultimately on this confusion of view as to what was being dealt with; it also failed because of insufficient funds from the national Congress to carry it out with rigorous thoroughness.

As it was, the deliberate attempt to disrupt family life through the boarding-school quotas had some effect. It added to each reservation a few individuals, often couples who married at school or after their return, who actually knew the nature of Anglo culture. This was a new phenomenon in the Southwest. Those who went to school and came back became instruments for the spread by slow diffusion either of Anglo viewpoints or of antagonistic views of white men and white culture. In both respects they were forces for civilization, because they constituted new sources of values and ideas within the extended families of which they were parts. Despite the fact that hundreds of Southwestern Indians had attended boarding schools by 1934, the program was not intensive enough to destroy the solidarity of extended family life. Some "educated" couples were persistent about setting up their own households and furnishing and running their houses in ways that were different from Indian tradition and which embodied Anglo domestic habits. Thus on all the reservations a new type of setting for family life had been introduced which approached closely the rural household of the United States. But these material additions and replacements did not remove the "progressive" boarding-school couple from the web of kinship obligations which constituted their extended family. In some cases by accident the couple were not part of a large and demanding group and in these instances were able to move toward the kind of independence characteristic of Anglo families. But most such boarding-school matches melted back into their extended families, some with relief to enjoy again the economic and psychological security of the group, others protestingly, convinced that the family system was the source of Indian "backwardness."

No studies have yet been undertaken of the specific effects of the attempt to destroy family relationships on the structure of any Southwestern Indian society. There is no question that it was partly successful, in the sense that some individuals trained in boarding school felt uncomfortable and unhappy and out of touch with older family members if they came back to the reservations. It is probable that such individuals became the nucleus of a new type of family, namely, the independent couple living apart from parents and primarily interested in their own solidarity and welfare regardless of the situation of other families with which they might have kinship connections. This was the type of the conjugal family, the basic kinship group toward which Anglos had steadily been tending. There were also such families, living away from reservations in many parts of the Southwest, composed of people who had become almost completely assimilated and who found it impossible to live happily on reservations as parts of extended families. There were on various reservations — Papago, Pima, Western Apache, Navajo, Mohave, Walapai, Hopi, and Laguna — but not on other Pueblo reservations — such kinship-isolated couples, but they were exceptional and chiefly a phenomenon of the agency town. On the whole the extended family in one or another of its various forms was the predominant and basic social unit everywhere. It had survived two generations of direct attack.

There were, of course, other factors which were tending to move family life in the same direction as among the Anglos, that is, towards the conjugal family type — the isolated couple and their children. The strongest factor was probably the availability of work for individuals in the Southwest. Cash income had steadily increased among Indians since 1900. By the 1940's there was a regular exodus off reservation to work in carrot, beet, or cotton fields for wages. The effect of these sources of funds independent of any cooperative activities on the reservation might be assumed to have relieved the extended family of one of its functions — economic security. Certainly some individuals and couples did move out of the sphere of family control as a result of financial independence through wages. But it was hard to see this as the general trend. At least by 1950 there had been little consistent movement in this direction. An individual's wages were for the most part spent by one's extended family rather than by oneself — among Navajos, Papagos, and all the other groups. Although production patterns might have changed under the stress of opportunities for wage work, the consumption patterns characteristic of the extended family were changing at least more slowly. There was some indication that there was a strengthening of the extended family — at least on some reservations. On the San Carlos Apache, for example, extended-family consumption patterns were characteristic not only for wage-work benefits off reservation, but also in connection with cattle sales on the reservation. There was a superabundance of leisure on the reservation and the extended-family social life and recreation patterns resulted in a great invigoration of the extended family as a determinant of any individual's behavior, to the point where young boys and girls who went to school outside the reservation felt oppressed and hopeless about efforts to "improve" themselves or the tribe. Extended families were themselves the unit which went out to work off reservation among the Papagos. There was a great variety of situations and in all certainly wage work offered some new opportunities for individuals to disengage themselves from their extended families, but it was not at all clear that wage work was an influence only for extended-family breakup; it worked also the other way.

The many other factors had not been carefully assessed on any reservation; the only generalization possible was that on every reservation the extended family was the major consumption unit and that it functioned generally in strong competition with the day and boarding schools as the moulder of the individual's goals and social attitudes. Through the schools there was some diffusion of the conjugal-family pattern which by 1950 had become so widespread among Anglos, but in general the strength of the extended family constituted a major cultural difference between all the Indian groups and the Anglos.

There existed at the time of the entry of the Spaniards several different types of larger kinship groupings among the Indians, called by anthropologists lineages, clans, and phratries. All of these emphasized one descent line, some through the mother, some through the father. These were most elaborated among the village Indians of the north and had spread from them to the invading Athapaskan Navajos and Western Apaches. The ranchería Indians seem generally not to have had strongly developed unilineal descent groups at the time of the coming of the Spaniards, except for the Papagos and Gila Pimas, who had patrilineal lineages. Thus, it seems certain that the Western Pueblos had the most widely integrated kinship units in the form of phratries combining a number of clans. The Navajos and Apaches approximated this and possibly derived the clan directly from the absorption of women from among the Western Pueblos. The Eastern Pueblos, the Pimans, and the Yumans had or had had lineal groupings of some sort, which were possibly nothing more than descent-reckoning gadgets, the names of which survived but the functions of which were very tenuous; why these should have died out before or why they died out so rapidly after Spanish contact is an interesting question; their distribution in no way coincided with intensity or type of Spanish contact. The Tarahumara, Opatas, and Cahitas, on the other hand, give no clear evidence of having had unilineal descent groups at any time; they were clearly bilateral at the time of the coming of the Spaniards and continued to be so.

The fate of the integrations of kin larger than the extended family has been varied. The patrilineal lineage of the Papagos was reported by Underhill to have been one of the most stable of all Papago institutions during the period of changes from earliest Spanish contact until about 1936. But this report is backed by little in the way of data. It appeared that whatever marriage regulation function the Papago moiety and clan units ever possessed had been eliminated. This sort of trend was strongly apparent among Navajos, Apaches, Hopis, and Zunis; just as intertribal marriages were taking place based on boarding-school contacts, so boarding-school teaching was working against the maintenance of clan exogamy traditions among boarding-school graduates. Everywhere the marriage regulation function of clan and phratry was at least being questioned, but the matrilineal lineages and maternal families among the Hopis, Navajos, and Apaches were more persistent than the patrilineal arrangements of the Pimans and they remained functional into the 1950's. Hopi Third Mesa families, for example, who moved down off the mesa top because of inter- and intra-clan disputes, re-formed promptly as matrilineal lineages, while as functioning units of clans they ceased to exist, although they still demanded land in some cases as a clan prerogative. At Ramah among the Navajos there in the 1950's half the marriages were matrilocal and perhaps nearly as large a percentage of Western Apache marriages were the same.

One of the social institutions of which the Spaniards were conscious and which they introduced as part of their religious conversion program was that of godparents and godparental cooperating groups. This became of great utility and significance in the social structure of the Yaquis and made a definite impression on Pimans, Mayos, Opatas, and Eastern Pueblos. Widespread over the Southwest had been an analogous institution, namely, one which might be designated as ceremonial sponsorship. Among Seris, Hopis, Gila Pimas, as well as Yaquis and Mayos there were two major kinds of functions which ceremonial sponsors performed — the care of the dead on behalf of the dead person's kinship group and the induction of young people into ceremonial organizations or to see them through some sort of initiation rite. The Yaquis and the Mayos took hold of godparent customs introduced by the Jesuits and transformed them into a systematized set of rights and obligations growing out of all social transition rites — thus not only for baptism and confirmation and marriage, but also for illnesses and induction into various ceremonial societies. A major obligation of the native ceremonial sponsors among the Yaquis being care of the dead, this obligation was grafted on to those prescribed for the godparents of baptism by the Catholic Church. Combined native Yaqui and borrowed Spanish names were invented to apply to the sponsors. In general a very great elaboration of the native and Spanish forms took place in the course of their combination. By what year this new elaborate system had been remoulded is unknown. But by the end of the 1800's the new sponsoring system was an integral part of Yaqui culture. It seems likely that it served a very important purpose in the period of dispersal, when the extended families were much disrupted. Certainly there is much evidence to indicate that the godparenthood or accompanying co-parent (compadre) tie was employed as frequently as a basis for reinstituting an extended-family type of household group as was real kinship. Hence the ritual kinship system served the function of reintegrating kinship groups after the breakup, and probably was elaborated and given increased cultural emphasis in the process.

Among no other Indian tribes did this degree of elaboration of godparenthood occur. The institution had a minor place among Pimans and Opatas, supplementing kinship in some degree. Similarly it was taken up by the Tarahumaras as a minor social tie. For the Eastern Pueblos, characteristically, the godparent institution remained merely a linking device between Indians and Spanish or Mexicans, not an integrating mechanism within the Indian village structures. It consequently underwent no elaboration as among the Yaquis. Elsewhere it assumed the functions of linking ethnic groups but did not develop as an important internal integrating device as among the Yaquis. Its importance was on the decline generally among groups other than Yaquis by the 1950's.

THE INDIVIDUAL IN SOCIETY

The general trend in kinship organization up to 1960 seemed fairly clear. Wherever Indians had developed a strong sense of tribal identity in contact with Whites — which was almost everywhere among the surviving tribes — the existing extended-family system had been reinforced. Among some Indians in the United States this tendency resulted in the persistence of the extended family even despite vigorous efforts on the part of the Anglo-Americans, through their governmentally directed program of assimilation, to weaken the family. At the same time these calculated efforts, together with the undirected influences of the wage system, resulted in establishing on all reservations except the Eastern Pueblos a new family pattern as an alternative to the extended family. This was the conjugal, single couple relatively isolated from other families with which it was connected by descent; it was also a neolocal family unit, maintaining its independence of a larger kinship group by establishing its residence apart from the family of either the wife or the husband at the time of marriage. The new alternative family arrangement was common in the agency towns dominated by Whites and it appeared also in new settlements which began to develop about 1900 as offshoots of older established villages, such as the below-mesa settlements of the Hopis, the Acomans, and the Lagunans. It was the most common form of family in the off-reservation settlements of Papagos, Pimas, Hopis, Navajos, and Apaches, as well as of Eastern Pueblos. It was by 1960 a well known and increasingly important alternative in Indian life. In Sonora it existed also, but among Yaquis was frequently a transitional form to a re-established extended family of some sort. Wherever the neolocal conjugal family existed it was usually a vehicle for the transmission of many elements of Anglo or Spanish culture, including language, domestic technology, educational values, and religion. It constituted an institution in which the process of individuation was taking place. It was transitional in a shift from the kinship to the territorial basis of local group organization.

Accompanying this there were other changes contributing to the individuation process. One or two of these we may attempt to trace, but it is impossible, because of inadequacy of record, to trace them very surely. Those about which something may be said are the personal naming systems of the Indians, the changes in marriage selection methods, and perhaps the changes in common law. None of our data are adequate, but at least some trends may be suggested.

PERSONAL NAMES — There was a profound difference between the personal naming systems of the various tribes of the Southwest and the personal naming systems

of the Spanish and Anglo societies. There was no Indian group without some
system for naming individuals, and these in general resembled one another. The
Pimans, for example, generally employed two distinct names for each individual.
One was a sacred name, given at birth by a ritual specialist, which was regarded
as having a relationship to the destiny of the person. The name was dreamed by
the shaman and bestowed by him in a non-public ceremony; it somehow designated
the spiritual essence of the person. The name was not employed as a term of
address, and was in fact something of a secret which none but intimate family
members, and not always they, knew. It was never changed but became the in-
violable property of the individual. In addition, however, every individual acquired another name, more or less by chance, by which other persons knew him
or her. This name was in a sense a nickname, calling attention to some physical
characteristic or to some memorable experience. Among Papagos there was a
delight in bestowing names which had to do with sexual experience, but these
were given late in life and most individuals were known for many years by some
other childhood name. The adult name, often a result of some sexual or other
experience, could be traded. Names often acquired special value and individuals
were covetous of other persons' names. Hence they bought and sold them. The
name by which a person was known and called, when he himself was not present,
was thus a highly personalizing designation. It distinguished him from all others
on a basis of his own personal characteristics. It had nothing to do with family or
other group affiliation, but gave recognition to him as a person with a unique
experience in life. In addition, among those tribes which had unilineal organizations, such as the Hopis, the Navajos, and the Western Apaches, there was also the
clan name which identified one with his kinship group. But this was never person-
alized and in no way denoted individual characteristics.

In contrast the personal names of the Spaniards and of the Anglos were, para-
doxically, impersonal. That is, they permitted the specific designation of individuals in such a way that each could be distinguished from others; but this designation had nothing to do with one's personal experiences or physical or personality
characteristics. Nicknames of special personal reference existed, but were apart
from the formal system of personal names. The Spaniards had a binomial system
which, as it were, placed an individual as a distinct entity within a family line or
lines. The effectiveness of the system did not depend on knowledge of the personal qualities of the individuals, but rather on combinations of terms which were
not likely to be repeated often enough to cause confusion. Thus the Christian
name of Juan or Juana or Jesús or Jesusa was combined with a family line name or
sometimes two such names. An individual was identified as the Juan of the Maldonado line or as the Juan of the Maldonado line by union with the Valenzuela
line, so that the name became Juan Maldonado de Valenzuela. By the employment
of such combinations an individual could be found by an outsider in a community
regardless of anyone's knowledge of the personal background of the individual.
The employment of such a highly standardized system was consistent with the
concept of citizenship and with the counting of individuals as impersonal units
for purposes of military service or the payment of tribute to a king. The system

was part of the framework of the state and in line with the impersonal designation of citizens within that state, which lent itself to the quantitative handling of persons in different communities in the same way. As such, it was functionally a very different system from those of the Indian groups and involved a quite different concept with reference to individual designation.

The adoption of this system by Indian communities in northwestern New Spain was not rapid, a fact which suggests the different bases of the Indian and the European systems and their incompatibility. The Indian systems were as integral a part of the Indian personalism in all relations within the small community as the Spanish system was an integral part of the impersonality of citizenship in the state. The adoption of the Spanish naming system proceeded in pace with the adoption of the Spanish political system. The process of political integration was not complete even by 1960 in Sonora and Chihuahua and correspondingly neither was the process of impersonalizing individual names. Among the Seris, Yaquis, Lower Pimas, and the Tarahumaras the transition to the Spanish-Mexican naming system was still in process.

Among Yaquis and Mayos the process had taken place in about the same way. The beginning point in the long transition, during which alternative naming systems coexisted for some three hundred years, was the bestowal of Christian names on individuals who were baptized by the Jesuit missionaries. This was part of the directed religious assimilation program. It is not clear that there was any consistent policy on the part of the Jesuits with regard to surnames, although of course a paper program with respect to Christian names was instituted immediately through the baptismal records. Since nearly all Yaquis and Mayos were baptized within a few years after 1617, there must have been a roster of between twenty and thirty thousand Christian names each for Yaquis and Mayos very early in their contact history. That Christian names were in general use from the beginning seems likely, especially for all those with whom the missionaries came into direct contact and for whom they required such usage. It is nevertheless true that the employment of nicknames in preference to Christian names was still well entrenched by the 1940's. Leading figures in Yaqui political life were known to Yaquis exclusively by their nicknames in the 1880's and 1890's. While all Yaquis employed "Cajeme" for the great leader of the 1880's, few knew the full name — José Maria Leyva — of that *caudillo*. The same is true for Tetabiate (Rolling Stone), the last great guerilla leader, whose Spanish name was Juan Maldonado. On the other hand, important figures of the period of military climax in Yaqui history, who sided with the Mexicans, such as Loreto Villa, were not known to Yaqui historians by any name other than the Spanish. It would seem that the old Yaqui naming system was adhered to by those who remained most devoted to other aspects of Yaqui tradition, while the alternative Spanish system was used exclusively by those who accepted Mexican standards and ways. It was probably for the latter a symbol of social status, and Yaquis were inclined to use it in the same spirit with reference to those whom they regarded as not fully Yaqui. The two systems then persisted side by side as alternatives, each with its own connotation of cultural participation. This was true also of the Mayos until the 1890's.

Nevertheless a third alternative grew up which was in use as early as the beginning of the 1700's. Apparently, the Jesuits, along with their designation of individuals by the Christian name, symbolic of the new status as Christians, also introduced surnames commonly used by Spaniards. Probably Andrés Pérez de Ribas in his first baptisms named many children Pérez, for this surname has been one of the common ones among Yaquis, and Pedro Méndez introduced Méndez among the Mayos. The long line of Jesuits which followed also introduced their own names, so that a characteristic stock of surnames for each tribe came into use derived from the Valenzuelas, Valencias, Garcias, Chavezes, Leyvas, Amari-llases, etc. among the missionaries. Later this stock was added to from the names of proprietors of haciendas and ranches for whom the Indians worked during the nineteenth and twentieth centuries. By the 1900's Yaquis who had lived among Mexicans also employed the full system of designating individuals by the surnames of both father and mother, a custom which no doubt was felt to be consistent with their own bilateral kinship system. The Mexican system was thus in use by some Yaquis, existing as an alternative to the more personal nicknaming system exem-plified in Cajeme and Tetabiate. There is a good deal of evidence, however, that even for those Yaquis who employed the system the names did not have the same meanings as for Mexicans. The Spanish name was not a fixed and unalterable designation. Children's surnames were not always repetitions of the parents' sur-names. The mother's Spanish surname was often the only surname given the child. Sometimes children of the same parents were given different surnames, some bear-ing the mother's and some the father's. How much of this variation from Mexican practice was due to attaching different meanings to the Spanish name from Mexi-cans and how much was due to efforts to disguise identity is not known. Both factors played a part. The difference in meaning consisted in the Spanish name being regarded by some Yaquis merely as an adjustment to Mexican interests. For the sake of maintaining a job and a patron relationship with an employer, a Yaqui would adopt a name which his patron used. Outside of this relationship the name perhaps had no significance to the Yaqui, and if the relationship was discontinued the name might be also. Apparently the idea of inheritance of surnames was not clearly accepted by Yaquis, just as it was inconceivable that the highly personal-ized name of Cajeme could be inherited by that leader's sons. Since the name was primarily associated with relationships with outsiders, its employment varied as those relations varied. In addition, when the Mexican program of deportation, which involved the ferreting out of Yaquis everywhere in Sonora, was adopted, it became advantageous to hide one's identity and hence there arose after the 1880's the practice of changing one's name freely and frequently.

What did persist as a fixed designation was the Christian name. While sur-names were changed and inconsistently given with reference to parental names, the baptismal Christian name of Juan, Jesusa, or José was employed usually throughout life. This of course was less personal in the sense that there were many Josés and many Juans, and it constituted no very definite means for identifying an individual by an outsider. The Christian names were employed in the listing of dead ancestors in family books of the dead, but only rarely the surname.

A type of surname other than the borrowed Spanish terms came into wide use before the Jesuit program ended. This was a Yaqui name not translated into Spanish, such a Ujllolimea, Wiikit, Buanamea, Husakamea, or Moroyoki. Some of these had simple meanings, such as Bird (Wiikit), but by the end of the 1880's the very numerous names ending in the suffix -mea or -me'a had no significance other than as surnames. The specific meaning formerly attached had become obscure, although some Yaquis insisted that the -mea suffix meant "killer." It is probable that they were a survival of some system of naming connected with the vigorous warfare interest of Yaquis. These were employed with Christian names, constituting a binomial system of the same types as the Spanish Christian and sur-name system. The -mea series seems to have been inherited from the father, but it is not clear that all Yaqui surnames were so inherited. The Yaqui-Christian name system seems to have been used with more consistency as a patrilineal naming sys-tem than the Spanish. It is likely that we have here a fusion of a Yaqui patronymic system with the Spanish system. In Arizona settlements of Yaquis in the 1950's both the Yaqui-Spanish and the full Spanish system were employed by Yaquis with increasing consistency in the Mexican manner, but with little tendency to combine both the mother's and the father's surnames in an individual name, in accord with lower-class rather than upper-class Mexicans. The practice of referring to individ-uals by nicknames within the Yaqui communities was, however, much employed, but in the manner of Anglo-Americans. The binomial system was well established as an official naming system for designating individuals in their statuses with employers and political and church officials.

Among Eastern Pueblos, as among the Cahitans, there was an initial wide-spread acceptance of both Christian names and Spanish surnames as bestowed by the priests. Certain surnames became characteristic of particular villages, such as Naranjo, Tafoya, and Gutiérrez for Santa Clara, and Cata, Martínez, and Archu-leta for San Juan. There was not the adaptation of the Spanish system by employ-ing a native language name as the surname, nor were there other variations as noted for the Yaquis. The older custom of a single designation, derived from plants, animals, or the natural environment and not inherited either matrilineally or patrilineally continued in existence unaltered up to 1950, so that individuals bore both the Spanish binomial and the Indian single term, often being best known to fellow villagers by the single Indian language name. However, after individuals began attending government schools, names were given to them in English, both Christian and surname, so that the stock of Spanish surnames was added to by English names. A later development was the translation of the native Indian name into English and the attaching to it of the English Christian name, so that by 1960 names such as Tom Whitecloud and Joseph Little Deer were not uncom-mon. Thus both the single and the binomial systems continued in use side by side, but English binomials were becoming increasingly common as official names.

Much the same condition existed among the Hopis and the Zunis, but with two differences. In the first place, especially at Hopi, the Spanish names which were introduced by the Franciscans did not continue in use after the 1680 rebel-lion, so that Spanish names in any form were rarities, especially among the Hopis, though more common among Zunis. In the second place, the tendency to translate the single Indian name into English was little apparent. Those who went to school or had contacts with Whites continued to use their Hopi names, untranslated, but with a "Christian" first name attached, such as Dan Katchongva or David Monongye. In dealings with Anglos the binomial was used and usually the Hopi surname was inherited from the father, not the mother. But in internal affairs in the villages individuals were known by their single Hopi names, and these were not ordinarily inherited in any line. In addition, a number of Hopis who became most assimilated adopted full English binomials, such as David Johnson or Fred Adams. The retention of a Hopi name and its use as a single designation, was by 1960 symbolic of membership in the "traditionalist" factions of the villages.

Among the Upper Pimas three different stages in the diffusion of the binomial naming system were apparent. The first stage, beginning with the entry of Father Kino and continuing apparently on into the late 1700's and early 1800's, was characterized by the same results as for the Cahitans and the Eastern Pueblos. The Christian names and Spanish surnames as bestowed by the missionaries and recorded in the mission records were accepted. These became common only among that minority of the Pimans who had closest contact with the Spaniards. There is little evidence as to precisely how they were adapted and used in village life. It seems likely that the Spanish surnames were largely ignored, but that a good deal of use was made of the Christian names. In a later phase, particularly during the 1800's, when mission control broke down, the Christian names were in use, at least among the southern Upper Pimans and perhaps among the Gila Pimas who had some contact with the Mexicans, and there may have been some adoption of Spanish translations of native names, such as Azul (blue) and others. But during this period, the major development was an adaptation of the Spanish system to Papago and Pima social structure. The Spanish surnames were frequently forgotten or ignored, but the Christian names were retained. These were combined into a binomial system, but one which was developed in a very different way from the Spanish-Mexican. The names were employed in addition to, not as replacements for, the Piman names and were inherited in accordance with Piman custom. Thus a man whose name was José might have a son who was baptized Juan. When José died his name was inherited by his son, but the Christian name of the son was not replaced, so that his son was called Juan José. This constituted then a binomial the last part of which was inherited patrilineally in accordance with the importance of patrilineal descent in Piman social life. However, this binomial was not handled further like the Spanish binomial. The Christian name was regarded as the heritable member, so that Juan José's son would bear as his surname his father's Christian name. If Juan José had a son named Pedro, he would be called not Pedro José, but Pedro Juan. It was, in other words, the Christian name which was inherited as surname. This gave each succeeding generation a different surname and it served no purpose whatever in designating family lines. The Christian name, which changed from generation to generation, was the designator of the patrilineal line. This adaptation of the Spanish binomial system was not universal among Pimans, but it was employed in many villages farthest from the points of Mexican contact and constituted a well-established alternative to the Spanish system, along with the native single name system.

The third phase in Piman naming consisted of the adoption of English binomials as designated in schools. Often the English-speaking teachers were unable to pronounce the Spanish Christian name or surname. They either recorded the surname in an Anglicized form, such as replacing Xavier with Harvey, or simply gave up and substituted a common English surname such as Johnson for Francisco. Along with these modifications or substitutions, they assigned English forms of Christian names or sometimes permitted students to continue to use easily pronounceable Spanish-Christian names. The Papago naming system, as it finally existed by 1960 then, was binomial, but there was a great variety in the surname part of it. Some were arbitrarily-assigned English surnames, some were Anglicized Spanish surnames, some were standard Spanish surnames, and some were Spanish Christian names. This system of mixed content had begun to be employed with some consistency, with surnames inherited in the male line by 1950. School and agency records, especially rationing cards during World War II, were the major factors tending to bring about consistency of usage. The Piman system of sacred names had by this time been replaced, but the nicknaming system was still vigorous, employed informally among the Pimans and also much used by them in designating white men with whom they were associated.

In the 1940's the Navajos were still in transition from a "power name"-nickname situation, resembling that of the ranchería Indians, to the English binomial system. Navajos generally had never accepted and employed the Spanish naming system, although various Navajos, prominent and well known to Mexicans, had come to be known to white men by Spanish names. These were in the nature of nicknames, such as Ganado Mucho (Many Cattle), or familiar forms of Spanish Christian names, such as Manuelito. Only a very few Navajos by the time of the coming of Anglos had accepted these Spanish names. Many of them were, as among Apaches to the south, translations of a nickname from the Navajo. These were adopted by Anglo military men who had dealings with Navajos, but gradually most of the Spanish names disappeared. Since the majority of Navajos were never missionized there was no systematic introduction of the binomial system among them. Instead, as they came into contact with Anglos, a rather haphazard system of bestowal of names was introduced. Early contacts were with traders, then slowly with schoolteachers, and here and there with Protestant or Catholic missionaries by the early 1900's. Traders gave names to Navajos with whom they did business, for the purpose of identifying individuals, especially in connection with giving credit. The traders followed no consistent and uniform system. Some employed whatever name a Navajo would volunteer for himself and attempted to use this in its Navajo form. The Navajo name volunteered was most often a nickname, such as was commonly used for the individual (when not present) in his extended family. Thus names like Hoskenini, Hosteen Begay, etc., came into use in some areas. Elsewhere traders or Indian Bureau persons attempted to get English translations of such names, so that names like Shorty, Silversmith, Clean Girl, etc., came into use in other areas. These names, whether English or Navajo, often were accepted by Navajos and became their fixed designations, but equally often they were known by one name in one White relationship and by another in another relationship. The situation became still more complicated as Navajos began to attend school. The need for a uniform name in school resulted either in the arbitrary bestowal by a teacher of such a name as John McCabe or Willy Smith or Joseph Morgan, or an attempt to add an English given name to what the teacher was told was the father's name. The latter might result in a child's being called William Tall Salt or Tom Begay. Frequently a child gave his father's two names, customarily used at the trading post they frequented, and would be christened Lilly John Pino or Edward Long Moustache. Sometimes the child gave the mother's name and would have an English given name added to that. Sometimes the interpreter would get the child's clan name and that would be used as the surname. Often the child already had a nickname at his family's trading post. Thus children grew up using one name in school, another at the trading post, and still another at a mission of some sort. In addition the child would also have his local group nickname, perhaps more than one in the course of attaining adulthood, and in addition the old "war name" or "power name" which remained secret. The very custom of being addressed directly by one's name, of any sort, was foreign to Navajo practice; hence the school name might never be employed even if it were known by his family. The different contexts of social life and the different functions of names in those contexts, together with the varying practice of Whites with whom they came in contact, resulted in great lack of uniformity. As some individuals came into more intensive contact with Anglos and learned the nature of Anglo naming usages, they gradually fixed on one of their names, but in general there was not by 1960 any consistent binomial naming system.

The Navajo naming system had not been replaced. It continued as the one common feature in Navajo naming. This was primarily a secret or war name which was used as little as possible, although the taboos on use of the war name were weakening, especially for women, plus one or more nicknames, none of which were used to a person's face, but only by way of reference.

Among Apaches, as a result of their rigid control on reservations from the 1870's on, the great majority used English binomials inherited through the male line. This was in spite of the persistence of the matrilineal clan and constituted an influence weakening the latter in some ways. For a time some Apache names were used, especially in the period when the Western Apaches were rationed and were first organized into "tag bands," that is, groups of families under a headman appointed by the Indian agent. The tag bands were numbered and the numbers inherited, by orders of the agent, through the fathers. Individuals and family lines came to be known by the number of the tag bands and a few such numerical names persisted as surnames into the 1940's. The use of Apache names was quickly abandoned by the agents and English surnames assigned. Although some Apache names given in the old fashion and Apache nicknames were widely employed, the use of English binomials in the Anglo manner for most purposes was so general among Western Apaches as to indicate that replacement in the naming system was almost complete. It was constantly reinforced by the numerous agency records and censuses, which were fairly complete for such concentrated populations as the Mescalero and San Carlos Apaches.

It was obvious that the impersonal naming system of the Mexicans and the Anglos had come into increasing use by all the Indian groups by 1950. It was probable that it was steadily replacing the personal naming system of all the Indian groups and that this had been taking place very clearly on the basis of competition of alternatives. The process was a complex one because on the United States reservations the introduction of the binomials had not taken place uniformly, as it had during the Spanish mission period, and this was also true among the Yaquis of Sonora. The replacement process was influenced by the functions of binomials and of the Indian personal name systems. While the functions of binomials increased steadily for Indians in connection with the political integration process, for various record purposes, as Indians were incorporated into Mexican and Anglos states, the functions of the Indian personal names declined as Indians accepted forms of Christianity and the conception of personal power declined. These were complementary processes. The pressures to standardize naming practices among specific groups mounted as more and more agencies, from the United States Public Health Service to schools and tribal government on the reservations, became more active. The uniformity of employment of the impersonal binomial was probably a good index of the effectiveness of wider political integration on any reservation. It was not necessarily, however, an index as to the extent to which replacement had taken place. This depended on another set of factors, namely, the degree of integration of extended family and community life on the Indian bases. Thus among the Pueblos the two alternatives existed, each with functions in different contexts, where the Indian communities remained well integrated. Among Navajos and Papagos the alternative usages were rather coterminous with individuals exhibiting various degrees of assimilation tendency, so that they were not alternatives for each individual as among Pueblos but rather designated two different segments of the populations. For the Gila Pimas nearly complete replacement had occurred. The Indian system had been replaced, indicating the Anglo basis of reorganization of family and community life there. The unevenness of results in this process was in line with the unevenness of political integration and disruption of family life.

We have taken the impersonal naming system as a rough indicator of the increase in individuation. We have seen that, although it may be such an indicator, its adoption does not necessarily indicate a decline in the kind of personal relations for which the Indian personal name system was functional. Thus, personal relations do not necessarily decline as impersonal ones increase.

OTHER TRENDS — Other measures of the extent to which individuals were removed from the operation of the sanctions of their extended families were even less studied and understood. One of these might perhaps be considered to be the extent to which boys and girls made their own marriage matches rather than having them made by their extended families. Because of lack of data little can be said on this point. It was certainly true that the young people who went off to government boarding schools from the reservations beginning in the 1880's began to make their own marriage matches. They fell in love, sought, and sometimes were successful in marrying, their personal choices. Western Pueblo, Navajo, and Apache parents complained sometimes that these matches disregarded clan relationships and could not be sanctioned at home. In such cases the marriages either were dissolved by parental pressure or continued outside the Indian communities. It was also true that intertribal marriage took place as a result of association in boarding schools, so that even tribes which had been enemies, such as Gila Pima and Western Apache, found their young people intermarrying, contrary to the wishes of parents and extended families. The point is that in the boarding-school milieu, clan relationships were entirely ignored, tribes were associated in ways that would never have been the case outside of the boarding schools, and children grew up during formative years with a minimum of parental influence. Consequently marriage rules became to a large extent inoperative and individual choice tended to assert itself. The general effect was to release a certain percentage — no one has recorded how many — of youths from tribal custom and to introduce free choice by the parties to the marriage as an alternative marriage arrangement. Often tribal custom and extended family influence reasserted themselves after return to reservations. Sometimes they did not and the couples became living examples to others of the possibility of the individualized marriage system of the Whites. Some of the boarding-school graduates, but by no means all of them, thus became innovators with respect to the extended family system.

Another factor making for independence of the individual from his family group was wage work, especially wage work off reservation. This too had never been fully evaluated nor analyzed as a process in relation to the persisting extended families. That individuals through the wage system were able to remove themselves from the extended-family system of obligations was certainly true, but it is also true that the wage system did not work uniformly in this way. Papago extended families often went off as units to work in cottonfields or other employment; Navajos often did the same thing, in agricultural work especially. On the other hand, individual Navajos often went out to work on railroads. Even in the latter type of male gangs in wage work it was true that pay checks were sent to traders on the reservations, so that at the time of spending the wages, an individual often had his whole extended family around him. This resulted in the continued operation of the extended family controls on consumption. The wage system then, did not uniformly operate as a factor for increasing individuation and independence of the individual Indian from his extended family obligations.

A third factor which affected individuation was the institution of tribal courts. These were in existence from earliest reservation times in the United States. At first, up until 1934, they were simply courts presided over by the superintendent, who asked advice frequently from trusted associates among the Indians. Disputes were settled and penalties levied which conformed almost entirely to the superintendent's conception of justice. As the system of elected tribal judges was introduced in the 1930's, varying practices developed. Sometimes judges operated within a system of a code of offenses written for the tribal council by an Anglo

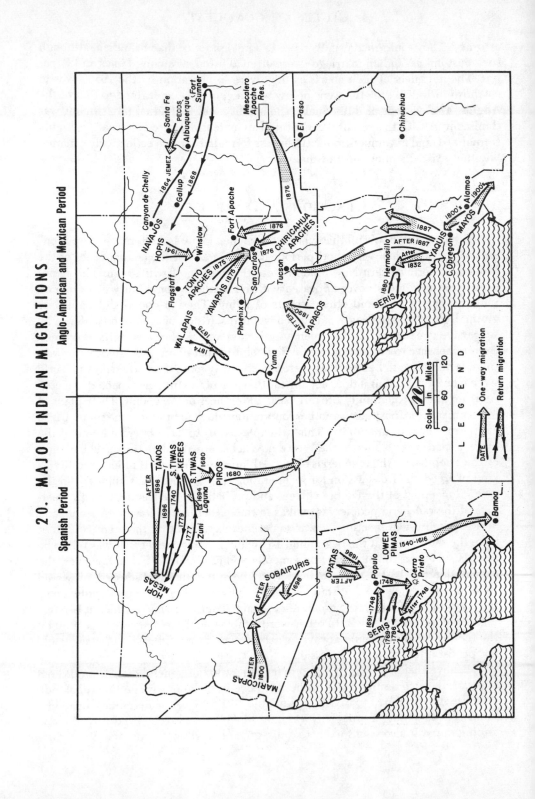

20. MAJOR INDIAN MIGRATIONS

Spanish Period

Anglo-American and Mexican Period

attorney. They conformed usually more to Anglo practice than to Indian, although such customs as "Indian marriage" were often allowed, as among Pimas and Papagos. The net effect of such courts as they were in operation by the 1950's was to establish in Indian society a type of law which generally conformed to that of the Anglos. The concept of individual responsibility and individual punishment was dominant in it. To this extent it constituted an increasingly used alternative, highly formalized, and in competition with the less formalized, more collectively oriented law that existed among most of the groups.

FACTIONS AND PARTIES

It seems very doubtful that what modern men know as "difference of opinion" existed for more than very short periods of time in any of the communities of the Indians in northwestern New Spain before the coming of white men. This is not to say that new ideas never appeared with reference to community government, religious ceremonies, and other aspects of living. They of course did appear as gradual growths, resulting from the constant discussion of community affairs by successive generations of older men and women and by the slow shifts of opinion from adherence to one strong man's viewpoint to that of another. In other words, there is no reason to believe that these societies any more than others in the world were wholly static. But it does not appear that any of the Indians expected as a constant feature of community life any basic differences of viewpoint. Their plans of government were posited on another foundation which in brief may be summarized as the principle of unanimity. This principle seems to have operated among the more nomadic bands such as the Western Apaches equally with the settled villages of the Pueblos and the rancherías of the Cahitans and Pimans. It indeed required a kind of freedom of discussion for its operation; this freedom was apparent in the general meetings of the Pueblo villages and probably in the frequent men's meetings of the ranchería peoples, as well as in the gatherings of Navajo, Apache, and Seri bands. In such meetings it was sometimes expected that the men would not have the same views at the beginning, especially in some matter that was felt to be a crisis such as a threat of war or some ceremonial failure. It was, however, the expectation that by the time the matter had been thoroughly discussed, all would be of the same view, so that statements were always turned eventually into a consensus in terms of which the group felt and acted and in terms of which it became organized to face the crisis. In other words, the general meetings were posited on the feeling that unity could always be achieved and that difference of view would not persist after thorough discussion.

It nevertheless seems true also that the method of general discussion did not always have such results. The Apaches employed a technique for getting rid of individuals who continued to dissent against the authority of the hereditary head of a family cluster or larger unit. This was banishment, a well recognized way of maintaining unity. It also seems likely that disagreement was not unusual in the tightly knit Pueblo villages and that conflicts did develop between the hereditary or elected leaders, especially over control of ceremonies. The method for restoring unity when such leadership conflicts developed was a sort of group banishment. One of the dissenting divisions was forced to leave the settlement and establish its own new village. Such fission resulted in the maintenance of unity within each of the divisions which developed. Its effectiveness depended on the availability of land and water for the banished group, as well as on the expectation of unanimity as the basis for community life. What was characteristic of the Pueblos and others aboriginally, then, was probably not an absence of the growth of dissent in any form in community life, but rather a method for settling disagreement and difference of opinion which involved the splitting of communities and the banishment of individuals. Difference of opinion was not regarded as a condition that could be tolerated. As soon as it was clear that differences were not to be resolved into the usual unanimity, then fission or banishment had to take place. There was no *modus vivendi* for government of a community with dissenters in it.

The imposition of the Spanish program — on Eastern Pueblos, Tarahumaras and Cahitans — almost immediately introduced a serious issue for dissent and agreement. Both the Franciscans and the Jesuits drew lines within the communities, beginning immediately to classify sharply into baptized and unbaptized. The effects of this procedure on the Cahitans were not schismatic in an important way, at least not in a way that gave rise to political disorder and lasting social conflict. On the contrary, it would seem that unanimity was achieved rapidly, after a few minor brushes between "witches" and the missionaries. Those men whom the missionaries called witches were opposed to the mission program. As described, they appear to have been curers and ritual specialists of various kinds. Only a few among the Yaquis and Mayos opposed the missionaries. It appears that such dissenters were in a very small minority almost from the start, that they were isolated from most other Indians in their communities, and that they had no influence on opinion generally. In other words unanimity existed on the new basis of Christian acceptance within months after the coming of Pérez de Ribas and Basilio. And yet there is more to the story than that, even if the historical record is not clear. The Yaqui myths of the 1900's often underscore the old categorization of human beings into baptized and unbaptized. After becoming acquainted with these myths, one finds it hard to believe that missionization was as simple and smooth as the Jesuit records indicate. The myths often present an opposition of ritual concepts expressed as "baptized" and "unbaptized" which received much dramatization in ceremony. The importance of "unbaptized" beings in the mythology suggests a segment of unbaptized real persons. Yet the historical data available indicate that the old basis of unanimity in the rancherías rapidly became the basis of the new mission communities. We do not hear at any time in their history of apostate Yaquis and Mayos, of anti-missionary leaders, or even of anti-clerical parties. The Christian belief and ceremonialism was apparently from the beginning so firmly integrated into Yaqui community life that it could not be separated out for hostility or devotion. Even in the later phases of Yaqui history, in the crucial 1880's and 1890's, the attitude toward Mexican priests and nuns was less hostility than indifference — "We do not need you," the old Yaqui leaders said to the priest who went to Bacum, implying that they could minister their own sacraments.

It would seem that a similar development took place among the Eastern Pueblos up through Benavides' time in the 1620's. That is, there was almost as general a rapid acceptance of the mission program in the early years, with some notable exceptions such as Jemez and Acoma. By 1625 the Franciscans were almost as happy about their success as the Jesuits were in the Cahitan country. Unanimity prevailed, but it was probably a unanimity with respect to the necessity for accepting Spanish domination, rather than agreement on the value and desirability of Christian devotions. Soldiers were in close proximity to the Rio Grande pueblos; there had been demonstrations of Spanish ruthlessness, both in Coronado's actions against the Tiwa of the south and Oñate's against Acoma. Certain it is that from the 1640's on the Eastern Pueblos presented a very different picture from the Cahitans. The Spaniards became dimly aware of change in attitudes by at least the 1650's and of what seemed to them a recrudescence of native religion, which was probably indeed to some extent a revival. The repressive measures taken by the Franciscans had an effect which indicates that unanimity was being achieved in terms of opposition to the missionary program. The leaders of the 1680 revolt were uniformly described as religious leaders — in contrast with the Yaqui-Mayo leaders of the 1740 revolt in Sonora. It was the missionaries who were promptly killed when rebellion broke out — again in great contrast with what happened in Sonora. A brief unanimity was achieved during the rebellion with reference to the restoration of the old order and independence from all aspects of the Spanish program. Then when military control was re-established, there seems to have been a general unanimity in all the villages with regard to passive resistance. This program of the Pueblos then prevailed throughout the remainder of the period of control by Spaniards and Mexicans, resulting in only superficial acceptance of Christianity. There was no growth of parties favoring or opposing aspects of the Spanish or Mexican programs, merely a consolidation of the old community life with complete agreement, apparently, on specific techniques for accommodation to Spanish administration and New Mexican neighbor relations, such as the employment of the governor system as a buffer, and secrecy with reference to ceremonial life.

The effects on Tarahumara community life of the imposition of the Spanish program were quite different from those among either Pueblos or Cahitans. Acceptance of missionaries was only at an extreme margin of the Tarahumara territory at first and large segments of the tribe remained outside the program throughout. Apostate Tarahumaras with substantial followings appeared as an important factor in Indian-White relations as early as twenty years after the beginning, and such leaders worked against acceptance of the missionaries, despite strong repressive measures for the duration of the Jesuit period. While little is known of the nature of affairs in the Tarahumara communities, it seems apparent that Tarahumaras almost from the beginning were divided into three kinds of communities, the compact mission ones where leaders strongly favored the missionaries and the colonial administrators against all other Tarahumaras, the scattered rancherías farther to the northwest where people sometimes favored the missionized leaders, and those still more remote from Spanish settlement where fairly consistently the leaders were either men who had never tasted mission life or were vigorously anti-Spanish apostates. The attitudes of Tarahumaras were affected by a more complex set of conditions than existed for the Cahitans before 1740, consisting of forced labor in the mines and ranches, land encroachment by Spaniards, periodic military depredation and punitive expeditions, and harsh discipline practiced by the missionaries. These conditions were even more complex than those existing among the Pueblos, where for at least each village more or less uniform conditions prevailed. The result seems to have been the growth of spheres of rancherías where the attitudes and views differed rather sharply, ranging from thoroughgoing acceptance of the missionary program at least through recognition of need for some kind of accommodation, so long as forced labor and other harsh measures were not too unbearable, to uncompromising rejection of everything Spanish. This territorial division of the Tarahumaras, rather than internal community division, persisted down to the 1950's, being reflected in the division into "pagan" and "Christian" communities. The basic differences here were not actually so much in terms of acceptance of Christianity as a readiness to tolerate Mexicans in contrast with a determination to isolate from Mexicans.

With the transition to the Mexican period it is possible to see a development which for the Cahitans at least looks more like the growth of parties among the Tarahumaras on the basis of favoring and opposing accommodation to Whites. In the 1820's after the first Banderas movement and continuing after the second there were clearly two parties among Yaquis — one which continued to favor the independence movement and one which opposed it, favoring political cooperation with Mexicans. The latter, headed by a man named Husakamea, enjoyed control of the Yaqui towns during the 1830's, but seems to have disappeared thereafter. Its strength in the 1820's probably was a result of Mexican support with arms in the period after the execution of Banderas. As Sonoran politics took form in the caudillo pattern, there seems to have been an alliance of most Yaquis with Gándara and his followers, but in the early 1850's, after Gándara was defeated by Pesqueira, who believed in ruthless conquest, there was again no rapprochement between Yaqui leaders and any of the Mexican parties. This meant evidently a vigorous return to the condition of town unanimity, which was the situation into which Cajeme came. The processes by which he became the military leader of Mayos and Yaquis and chief judicial functionary of at least the western Yaqui towns remain obscure. There is no question that the eight towns were all unanimously anti-Mexican by the late 1870's and that Cajeme adopted their program for an independent Yaqui country, or rather an exclusively Yaqui territory. The towns were functioning as politico-ceremonial units on the basis of unanimity until the defeat of Cajeme in 1886. There seems also to have been some draining off of individuals who became opposed to war with Mexicans and who were seeking economic security outside the Yaqui country. Cajeme's father was one among hundreds such persons. Cajeme by some means, which included struggles for power with at least one individual, forged a tribal unity among the eight towns which gave him the position not only of military commander but also of alcalde or judge. It was in the latter connection that factionalism was stimulated, resulting in many individual Yaquis becoming personally opposed to Cajeme's leadership. But no opposition to his leadership was effective and he continued as spokesman for the town governments as a whole.

Cajeme's defeat, however, resulted in a new situation. Several Yaquis, like Loreto Villa, accepted benefits from Mexicans, such as military command, visits to Mexico City, and status as advisers to the Mexican occupation forces. Once having accepted such position Loreto Villa and some followers remained loyal to the Mexican command, but they obviously were not part of a Yaqui faction, and were regarded as entirely outside the Yaqui community by all other Yaquis. The town organizations remained unanimously opposed to Mexican residence in their territory and affiliation with the Sonoran state government. From about 1900 on the town governments were completely broken up and individual Yaquis went their own ways. Effective party differentiation had not developed, nor did it develop through the 1940's. It is true that Yaquis affiliated in different ways during the resettlement period in the Yaqui country, some collaborating with Mexican military and political officials, some refusing to do so, and some attempting to stand on a sort of middle ground. But the town organizations as they re-formed in the reconstituted Yaqui settlements maintained themselves as community structures operating on the principle of unanimity and without any effective mechanism for the adjustment of opposing interests. When some leaders, such as Pluma Blanca of Bataconsica (the re-formed Bacum), became interested in the exploitation of natural resources such as firewood and charcoal or cane, they were unable to work with or through any town organization, but were led to operate in the same manner as Mexican officials through their status in the Mexican army. They thus worked as caudillo leaders, imposing their objectives and finding no means of cooperation with any but their personal followers. This continued to be the condition, with no change in the Yaqui system of town government which operated in the same towns with the imposed Mexican municipal system.

As Anglos took over political control of the north a situation similar to the Yaqui became apparent in both the Eastern and the Western Pueblos, but not among all of them. By the 1950's all of the Eastern Pueblo villages had experienced schism of some kind, although not all of these instances were well recorded. Moreover, the schisms were not all of the same kind. Most of them, as at Santa Clara, San Ildefonso, and San Juan among the Tewa, seemed to be primarily matters of religion involving dispute over proper conduct and control of ceremonies or succession to religious office. This was true also among the Hopi at Oraibi, Shongopovi, and Shipaulovi. On the other hand, some involved not only the native religious system, but arose over conflict concerning the introduction of new religions, such as Protestantism in Laguna and San Felipe among the Keresans and at Jemez or the introduction of the Peyote cult at Taos. A third form of schism arose over more purely political matters, such as an election dispute at Isleta. An analysis of some of these will indicate the nature of the issues involved and the effects of the schism on village life, as well as the conditions which gave rise to the divisions.

Although it was customary for Indian Bureau employees and other Anglos to regard the schisms in the Pueblo villages and among other Southwestern Indians as splits between progressives and conservatives, or in other words, between those favoring white man's ways and those opposing them, this view is entirely too over-simplified. In every split there was some factor deriving directly from opposing attitudes regarding one or another feature of the contact with white men, but nowhere was this the decisive basis of division. It was by no means clear even that one could attribute the beginnings of a schism to the complex impact of Anglo culture alone. A schism often seemed to grow out of the nature of the village organization itself and culture contact appeared merely as an aggravating factor. This was true, for example, of the schism in the Tewa village of San Ildefonso on the Rio Grande.

This division was one which could be classified as growing initially out of differences of opinion within the village as to supernatural influences on community welfare. In the late 1800's there had taken place a movement of the people a short distance north of the site then occupied. It came to be believed by many villagers that this move had been dictated by witchcraft designed to weaken the village. Deaths by disease and decreasing prosperity which characterized San Ildefonso life before 1910 came to be attributed to the movement. Accordingly, about 1910 or earlier, sentiment developed for returning to the earlier site. Long discussion was held, which included an archaeologist from the New Mexico Museum who had interested himself in Indian affairs, and especially in those of San Ildefonso. He encouraged the removal and about 1910 it was undertaken under the leadership of the cacique of the village. But it developed that a majority did not take kindly to the move. Those who did move, who consisted of most of the male officers in the ceremonies, re-established themselves at what came to be called the South Plaza, while the majority, including most of the female ceremonial officers, remained at what was called the North Plaza. Efforts were made by the others to persuade the North Plaza families to move, but without success. Steadily friction developed over ceremonial prerogatives, culminating in the forcible taking of some ceremonial paraphernalia by the North Plaza leaders. Moreover, the governor, a North Plaza man, refused to give up his cane of office to any South Plaza electee, so that two separate systems of village government grew up. The North Plaza people lacked a top ceremonial official, the cacique, but they continued to elect governors and their assistants and maintained a separate set of ceremonies annually. The South Plaza people had proper religious officials, the cacique, a war captain and assistants, and ceremonial society heads, but, lacking the canes of office for the secular officials, simply continued in office those who had held them at the time of the split, so that they became permanent rather than annually elected officers. The Indian Bureau gave official recognition to the North Plaza officers who held the canes of office. There were thus by the 1940's two separate village governments, now modeled on somewhat similar plans, and an atmosphere of constant bickering and bad feeling. The conflict was intensified by the superior economic position of the North Plaza people, among whom lived the most successful potters, who took a dominant part in village affairs. One of these women maintained a store through which she and her husband exercised some economic pressure on individuals to side with the North Plaza group. The schism showed no signs of healing through the 1940's. It was as though two separate villages had been created, although the people of the two plazas lived actually contiguously. They had no common community organization. There was no mechanism for establishing cooperation between the two opposing groups, no means to compromise differences within the same village unit.

A similar development took place in another Eastern Pueblo village, at Isleta near Albuquerque. This schism, however, began with a quite different series of events. There was at the start no difference of opinion over the supernaturally determined welfare of the community. Isleta was the only Eastern Pueblo which had formally adopted the Spanish custom of open election of a governor. In the 1870's it was governed by a cacique (or ceremonial head), an elected governor who appointed a number of assistants, a ceremonial officer called a war captain, and, most important next to the cacique, what was called a council of older men who had had service in one or more of the other offices. Dissatisfactions developed when one governor, in the early 1880's refused to call together all the council members, (principales), for the transaction of business. He failed consistently to call men whom he did not get along with or who did not get along with the cacique. There was at this time considerable consciousness of innovation through Anglo contacts and it appeared to persons like Pablo Abeita, educated by the Jesuits in Albuquerque and at St. Michael's College, Santa Fe, that there were some in the village opposed to the new ways and some favoring them. Abeita and others spoke of these differences as progressive and conservative contrasts. It was clear, however, that such terms were not indicative of what was taking place. A bitter feud was developing over the issue of control of village affairs, including the handling and use of money which came in from the lease of Isleta lands to Whites. The cacique and some of the men elected governor were trying to limit the participation of Isleta men in village government to those who thought as they did and with whom, consequently, they could get along. Just what was involved in thinking alike is not known, but certainly an issue of personal use of village funds was involved as well as careless accounting and also there was an issue regarding the power of the cacique. The latter held that he had the exclusive right to nominate and to install the governor in office after election annually. He also held that he had the right to call only those principales that it suited him to call in the affairs of village government. Lined up against him were a number of men who had attended Anglo schools of one sort or another, and who were to some extent under the leadership of Pablo Abeita, who served as war captain and then as judge of the Court of Tribal Offenses as long as it lasted. They were not advocates of cultural assimilation but pushed for two things, namely, regular participation of all the council in village government and the maintenance of elections for governor rather than direct appointment by the cacique. For some seventy years this condition of friction within the village went on, from the 1880's to 1950. It became focused on certain personalities, while the issue nevertheless remained that of the method of selecting the governor and the participating council members, although often it appeared wholly obscured by some other point of friction for the year. The factionalism, which increasingly disrupted social life in the village, resulted in fights and beatings on several occasions. It resulted, in the period before the 1930's, in focusing one faction as bitterly hostile to the Indian Bureau and its officers. In fact, acceptance or non-acceptance of Indian Bureau authority became entwined in the hostilities.

In the early 1940's the schism focused again around the issue of the power of the governor. Two complete sets of officers, in a series of moves involving the Indian Service and the determination of a majority of the council to oppose the governor, came into existence in 1940–41. The Indian Bureau and the All-Pueblo Council finally approved the governor who had been elected at a meeting called by the war captain, and not the one elected by a majority of the councilmen. In the course of the struggle the village gave birth to two different groups which functioned somewhat as political parties, but there was no resolution on this basis. The fundamental issue was as to where authority lay in the village; the conflict was between ceremonial offices, that of the cacique and those of the heads of ceremonial societies. As difference of viewpoint arose over this matter, conflict of personality developed and a host of differences fell into place behind personalities. The situation illustrated again, like that of San Ildefonso, the impossibility of settling serious disputes within the framework of Pueblo community organization. During the late 1940's steps were taken by the Isletans, with the cooperation of the Indian Bureau, to prepare a constitution in which the forms of political organization and the locations of power were spelled out. This was adopted in 1952.

At Laguna still another sort of schism developed which over the course of some seventy years, from the 1870's to the 1950's, had remarkable effects on the life of the Lagunans. The division among them grew out of the introduction of a Protestant religion into the village — Presbyterianism. With the exception of one at Jemez, this introduction was the only instance among Eastern Pueblos of a Protestant missionary having any important influence until the 1940's. Its influence was enhanced by the fact that the missionary married a Laguna woman, as did also his brother. Laguna was one of the more recently established Pueblo villages, having been founded in 1699 after the Pueblo Revolt, and was composed of a relatively heterogeneous population of Keresan-speaking people. The Presbyterian missionary was successful in getting a number of Lagunans to affiliate with the Presbyterian Church, but it seems doubtful that many forsook their native religious participation. He and later his brother were at different times elected to the governorship of the village. The election of the latter precipitated a serious conflict, during which two of the kivas were closed and those who opposed the White governor took ceremonial paraphernalia and left the village to take up residence at Isleta. This was in the familiar pattern of the splitting of villages. It left in political control the Presbyterian-influenced people, and while they continued affiliation with the Presbyterian Church, they also continued the native ceremonies. Nevertheless, the ultimate effect of the split was to increase the homogeneity of the village. The political structure was modified along somewhat the same lines as had been tried at Isleta. Eventually this liberalization of structure resulted in a type of representation in the village which permitted the coexistence of different viewpoints and some degree of swing from year to year from one viewpoint to another. In other words, something approaching a party type of politics was permitted to grow in village political life. But the most notable effect was the creation of homogeneity as a result of "banishment" of the conservative and uncompromising group from the village in the ancient tradition of the Pueblos.

Factionalism among the Hopis also followed the old lines, resulting on Third Mesa in the creation of three separate villages out of what had been the largest and most influential of the villages. To Anglo administrators it appeared at first to be a difference of opinion over permitting children to be taken to boarding school at the agency. And it is true that this factor was important in precipitating the splits. But the basic conflict was one over rivalry of leaders concerning control of the traditional ceremonies. One group opposed unalterably the sending of children to boarding school, the other inclined to favor it. Each group set up its own cycle of ceremonies and would admit of no compromise. After the split no one group was distinguishable as any more prone to accept Anglo elements of culture than any other; in fact, all remained uncompromising in regard to sending children to school.

Each of these cases illustrates the inability of Pueblo forms of community organization to adapt to heterogeneity of belief in religion and variety in political opinion. In 1950 the Isleta community structure was in process of replacement by constitutional local government. Laguna political structure had by small increments taken on such form. Santa Clara traditional government had likewise been replaced by constitutional government. But the Second and Third Mesa Hopi villages, San Ildefonso, and the other Eastern Pueblo villages were still organized along the old inflexible lines.

We must distinguish among the different kinds of "factions" which mark Indian community history during the Anglo and Mexican phases. Excepting only Laguna perhaps, all of the factions which we have discussed are of one type, namely, divisions growing within the aboriginal type of community structure. Such divisions became associated with particular individuals, usually hereditary leaders of some sort, as at San Ildefonso and Oraibi. There seemed to be no mechanism for resolution of the differences except by fission. However, whenever fission could not be accomplished because of lack of land, as was the case in Isleta, there was a tendency for new structural forms to be invented or borrowed. Thus, the ideas of Abeita regarding the council members or principales, whether a case of stimulus diffusion or invention, made some headway in the continuing crisis; the situation drifted on until finally the idea of a constitution was borrowed in 1947. The old principle of unanimity which resulted in the settlement of disputes by fission had been given up at least in part and replaced by the principle of majority rule and representation. However, this had occurred only after some eighty years of division-ridden life in the village and the existence of pressures which made fission impracticable if not impossible. Most Hopis were still dominated by the old form of organization, and here some fission was still possible and had been practiced.

The two other kinds of factionalism involved some of the same causal factors exemplified in Abeita bringing ideas from the Jesuit school into Isleta, or in the attitudes towards schools and association with white men which played a part in the intensification of the schism at Oraibi, but the two types developed in different ways. One type consisted of the introduction of a new form of organization into the local community, so that factionalism developed not around control of the traditional groups, whether ceremonial or political, but rather around rejection by some villages of the whole framework of traditional organization and belief. Thus, opposing organizations, one traditional and one new and borrowed, appeared in the communities and conflict grew. The Isleta conflict almost gave rise to new organization when the Isleta Union formed, but this did not persist; it was nevertheless a symptom. Wholly new organization often accompanied the introduction of new religions. Probably the Laguna trouble is to be regarded as of this type, but the resolution of conflict was worked out largely in terms of the old form of community organization with some modifications. The introduction of Protestantism among the Papagos resulted in the division into two groups in bitter conflict in a half dozen villages. Under these conditions the village organization nearly ceased to function, but as missionary activities declined in intensity and Piman clergy took over, the schism was softened, and the villages were probably by 1960 accepting a sort of party representation, at least by family groups. Among the Pimas the introduction of the Presbyterian churches with their elder form of organization resulted — in many villages — in a complete replacement in a short time of the older village organization, somewhat after the manner of the Yaquis. This kind of division in the Indian communities resulting directly from introduction of a new organization was most notable in connection with religious groups and particularly where Protestant and Catholic groups or two sharply different Protestant groups were involved in the same communities. San Carlos Apaches, Ramah Navajos, Ganado Navajos, First Mesa Hopis, Mescalero Apaches, Mohaves all suffered from this type of community factionalism, which was almost but not quite so bitter as the kind generated within the aboriginal community organization. It led usually or appeared to be leading to an approximation of the situation among Anglo communities, where religious differences and political differences were expected in the same community. At the same time it sometimes led to a kind of apathy in community life, notable perhaps among San Carlos Apaches and some of the Pima villages.

The third type of factionalism was of a kind which could be called a reflection of factions among the surrounding non-Indians, not based on the direct introduction of specific organizations into the Indian communities. For its development this sort of situation depended on the growth of interests among Indians parallel with non-Indians. Its expression in the United States was fostered through Indians who had been to boarding school or in Mexico through those who had worked in Mexican cities. This kind of development was responsible for Yaqui and Tarahumara support of various caudillos in Sonora and Chihuahua during the nineteenth-century disorders there. It was responsible for the growth of participation in state and national elections in the United States, as Indians began to line up to vote as Republicans or Democrats. The reflection of such activities, however, remained very weak indeed in the Indian communities themselves. It appeared that the heterogeneous community, as it existed among non-Indian Anglos and Mexicans, was still the exception rather than the rule among Indians in both the United States and Mexico.

CHAPTER SEVENTEEN

Religious Diversification

IN 1600 THE DREAM of a vast harvest of souls, to be ripened by Christian teaching, imbued the missionaries who contemplated the Indians of the New World. Here, they believed, simple savages, uncontaminated by the appeals of competing faiths like Islam and Buddhism, awaited enlightenment. The Franciscans and the Jesuits plunged boldly and with unbounded hopes into the desert reaches of northwestern New Spain carrying the cross and seeking the thousands to be saved. Nearly fifty Franciscans and half as many Jesuits met death at the hands of the Indians during the first hundred years, but scores more pressed on and carried the work of conversion, as far as Spanish soldiers would give them protection, into the wilderness. Perhaps two hundred thousand Indians north of Durango received baptism during the first great burst of effort — before the missionaries became entangled in the Spanish government's and their own worldly interests, and the will to convert died down along with the will to conquer.

Then for nearly one hundred years the Christian dream faded, and the Indians of the north were left largely alone to make what they could of the revelations which had been vouchsafed to them. But again after 1850, renewed in vigor under the aegis of a new military power, the Christian dream reasserted itself — this time in the minds of Baptists, Presbyterians, and Lutherans. Less well supported and far fewer in numbers, a handful of missionaries moved out among the Indians of what had been northern New Spain and began again, in somewhat different ways and language, to preach and to convert. Then, as the churches of the United States became aware of the large numbers of Indians classed as heathens, more missionaries became possessed by the four hundred year-old dream. Dutch Reformed, Episcopalians, the Franciscans again, the Mennonites, the Mormons, the Methodists, the Plymouth Brethren, the American Baptists, the Southern Baptists, the Seventh Day Adventists, the Church of the Nazarene, the Assembly of God, and the Free Methodists all took up the dream, while down in Mexico among the Tarahumaras the Jesuits, after 1900, went back to work. A considerable sample of all the variations on Christianity which now existed in America was brought to the Indians. After four hundred years the full impact of Christianity was being felt; nearly all the Indians were becoming aware of the new religions.

By 1960 they were aware of the new religions, but of different ones depending on which missionaries had happened to reach them. A considerable majority of all the Indians in the region spoke of themselves as Catholics — employing the Spanish word *católico* — the Eastern Pueblos, perhaps a majority of Tarahumaras, Yaquis, Mayos, Opatas, Lower Pimas, and many Papagos and Gila Pimas. In addition, most Yumas, some Navajos, some Apaches, and some Zunis spoke of themselves as Catholics. The next largest group calling themselves by the name of one of the Christian faiths were the Presbyterians — more than half the Gila Pimas, a fourth or more of the Papagos, many Navajos, some Apaches, Mohaves, Maricopas, and Hopis; the other sects had members in small numbers among most of the Southwestern reservation groups. Indeed the situation among the Indians paralleled that among the Mexicans and the Anglos. The Indians of the southwestern United States had church membership in about the same proportions and in nearly as many sect groups as did the population of the United States as a whole. In Mexico the Indians were nearly all, like the general Mexican population, professing Catholics. Over the four hundred years, the dream of Christian unity held by the pioneer Jesuits and Franciscans had not come true, but nevertheless extensive religious assimilation had taken place.

However, such a general statement of the results of contact ignores two facts which were important for understanding the religious life which had developed among the Indians. One was that the majority of those Indians calling themselves Catholic were not actually accepted as such by the Catholic Church. The Yaquis, the Mayos, the Tarahumaras, and the Eastern Pueblos were regarded by the Church as something less than Catholic. The fact was that they had developed variations of belief and practice which were not acceptable to the organized church. Both in regard to beliefs and practices which they preserved from their old religions and in regard to their failure to accept certain doctrine and practice which the Church regarded as essential, they deviated from Roman Catholic orthodoxy. Yet they persisted in regarding themselves as Catholic, even (in the case of the Yaquis) as better Catholics than neighboring Mexicans accepted in the Church; thus they must be considered as adherents of a variety of Christian sect which the early missionaries had unwittingly created.

Another significant fact about religious life in the Southwest was that some hundreds of Indians in every generation reacted negatively to the offerings of the missionaries and, although aware of the new sects, did not join them. Some of the Indians who thus rejected Christian ways merely maintained their old religions, in some ways slightly modified in adjustment to the life around them, but essentially preserving their own views of men and the universe. A majority of Hopis, possibly a majority of Navajos, Eastern Pueblos generally, some Papagos, and the Seris until the late 1950's did this. Other Indians who reacted negatively to the denominational offerings as presented invented new cults. Of these, the ones which did not die out showed Christian influence, usually, in belief and ritual, yet they duplicated none of the sects which missionaries advocated. These were new religions growing out of the complex influences which had impinged on the Indians, especially during the hundred years after the eclipse of Spain.

The dream of civilizing the Indians by bringing them to a unity of belief according to Roman Catholic tenets had not materialized. Instead they had been brought to a state of very considerable diversity, with a range of belief probably just a little wider than that which existed among their conquerors. A new common element had been introduced and there was a strong tendency for this common element to dominate the religious life of all, but nevertheless in the 1950's the range in religious belief was far greater than it had ever been in the region, before or after the entry of the white men. The way in which this heterogeneity grew may be traced readily through the four hundred years of contact.

THE DIFFUSION OF CATHOLICISM

The Catholic variety of Christianity was introduced to the Indians of the region through two distinct missionary campaigns separated by more than one hundred years. The first campaign accompanied the first military conquest and lasted, with waning intensity, from about 1600 to after 1750. The second followed some fifty years on the heels of the military conquest of the northern Indians and continued, with increasing intensity, from about 1900 on into the 1950's.

The first campaign took place under conditions very favorable for the spread of new ideas. The Spanish missionaries carried with them not only the new religious concepts, but also many other new ideas and materials the practical value of which was immediately obvious to the Indians. The new food plants and fruits, the domestic animals, the metal tools, the cloth which Spaniards introduced at the same time that they preached and taught were inseparably connected at first with the new ideas concerning supernatural power and the new rituals of baptism and worship. The prestige of each missionary could be high, as a kind of culture hero bringing all sorts of wonderful goods and promising innovations. It is true that at the same time missionaries brought to at least some Indians military and other forms of oppression which roused resistance, but nevertheless the Spanish power could also force acceptance of new ways which became habitual, especially for children growing up in the soldier-protected mission communities. Moreover, the Jesuit and Franciscan missionaries had a monopoly of the new religious ideas. For more than 150 years their work was not hampered by any of the Protestant forms of Christianity to distract and confuse the Indians. If there were some differences between the specific rituals and the doctrinal emphasis of the two Orders, nevertheless each Order had exclusive control of the different tribes and worked without competition in the areas to which the king assigned them. The effectiveness of individual missionaries varied according to the adaptability of each to the local conditions and according to the nature of the particular Indian leadership with which each worked, but the general conditions were far more favorable to the diffusion of Christian belief and behavior than those which prevailed during the second campaign of conversion.

Under these circumstances the Jesuits, and to a lesser extent the Franciscans, overexpanded in their zeal to make Catholics of the Indians. They overexpanded in the sense that they brought the tidings of Christianity to many Indians to whom they were unable to bring also the mission communities. It was in the organized mission communities that the indoctrination became the basis of new behavior under the direct tutelage of the missionary. The Jesuits were unable to follow through in their campaign by bringing missions to all the Tarahumaras, all the Upper Pimas, the Seris, or any of the Yumans. They acquainted these people superficially with Catholicism, but the rigorous indoctrination and daily practice of Christian ritual, characteristic of the mission communities, was not brought, and consequently those Indians remained outside the sphere of intensive diffusion.

Similarly, the Franciscans remained unable to maintain missions, after initial efforts, among the Seris, Zunis, Hopis, Navajos, and Yumans, even though they continued during the last half of the 1700's to make brief contacts and to go on short proselytizing expeditions. The Orders had both expanded beyond the power of their organizations to supply the necessary missionaries and beyond the power of the Spanish government to protect the missionaries if they had been available. The Hopis, Navajos, and Yumans, along with the Apaches whom neither Order even attempted to convert, thus lacked any but the briefest experience of the mission system and quickly forgot what little they had heard from the missionaries. However, the Zunis and some Upper Pimas, having had somewhat more intensive mission experience, did retain elements of Catholicism from these early contacts.

It was the Eastern Pueblos, the Opatas, the Lower Pimas, the Mayos and Yaquis, and some of the Tarahumaras, all of whom experienced intensive mission contacts, to whom many elements of Catholicism diffused. All of them, however, were left for 150 years, more or less, with no missionaries or priests actively among them. In the south the Jesuit expulsion in 1767 left the Sonora and Chihuahua Indians without missions and only a scattering of not very vigorous secular priests. In the north the decline in Franciscan activity had set in even before 1767 and for the next 150 years steadily faded out.

The result was that all the most strongly Catholicized tribes went their own ways. The Mayos, Yaquis, Opatas, and Tarahumaras took over the management of their own church organizations, which the Jesuits had instituted. They became independent of priests and even antagonistic in some instances, although some priests who shared the Indians' antagonism to Spaniards and Mexicans were able now and then to work among them. The functions of the priests in saying the Mass, officiating at marriages, and even in baptism ceased to be regarded as essential. Forms of ceremony changed and developed over the 150 years without the guiding standard of the priests constantly in touch with Roman orthodoxy. The Indians continued to use the prayers and other rituals which had been written down in the native languages, but interpretation was in the hands of the Indian specialists who developed as the ceremonial leaders. The seeds of Catholic behavior which the missionaries had planted continued to grow, but in nearly complete isolation from the nurture of the official Roman Church. Similarly in the north, the Eastern Pueblos continued through the late 1700's and almost throughout the 1800's with only the most passing contacts with the secular Spanish and Mexican priests. At first after the 1680 revolt priests in New Mexico tended the churches, but they did not work very hard at the difficult task of influencing the Indians. They did not work at all in the Indian languages and as their numbers decreased under the Mexican regime they paid less and less attention to the Indians. The Pueblo villagers, like the Indians of the south, proceeded to carry out without benefit of priests those Catholic rituals which they had thus far accepted, maintained the churches through their own village organizations, and bothered little about the unavailability of priests for those rituals which the missionaries had told them were essential in Catholic life.

The ultimate result of this experience of initial intensive indoctrination followed by loss of contact with Catholic Church officials for an equal length of time was the growth of religious behavior which Church officials did not recognize as Catholic. Three quite different types of religious life developed, which incorporated Catholic forms of beliefs and ritual with Indian forms. These distinctive modifications of Catholic elements in many ways paralleled the adjustment of native and Spanish forms in the political organization which grew up among the Indians following Spanish contacts. The Eastern Pueblos added some selected Catholic elements to their existing ceremonial system, while retaining the latter otherwise little changed. The Yaquis reworked the whole ceremonial system, integrating so many Catholic elements into it that a wholly new religion appeared to result. The Papagos accepted certain Catholic elements as alternative ways to their aboriginal religion, with a minimum of integration between the two. These three types of Catholic influence may be considered in some detail as representative, since the other tribes merely varied somewhat these basic types of adjustment.

The Keres, such as the Pueblos of Santa Ana, exemplify the process of additions from Catholicism in part integrated and in part kept separate from the Indian religion. They permitted the missionaries to build churches in their villages, appointed fiscales and sacristans to maintain the churches, and continued through three hundred years to hold various ceremonies in and around the churches. They accepted and continued to use images and pictures with which the missionaries furnished the churches. They permitted missionaries and then secular priests to hold Masses in the churches and accepted the rite of baptism. They included in their annual ceremonial calendar a Christmas ceremony depicting the birth of Jesus, observances at Holy Week consisting of prayers recited by the Indian sacristan and the shooting of guns, the offering of food to the ancestral dead on All Souls' Day, and the annual celebration of the Christian patron saint's day assigned to the village by the missionaries. All these elements of Catholicism were apparently incorporated into Keresan ceremonial life early in the period of Franciscan work in the villages and they have continued to the present. In addition, certain Catholic observances were adopted by many individuals, including saying standard Catholic prayers in Spanish, keeping sacred pictures or images in the house, and calling themselves "Catholics." To this extent they adopted the Catholic religious way, but did not consider themselves members of any religious organization outside the village (and hence not of the Roman Catholic Church), nor did the acceptance of these elements lead to any reorientation of their own religious life.

Rather, the elements adopted were modified in small ways to fit their existing ceremonial system, much as the governor system was taken over to serve the additional functions of relations with the Spaniards but modified to fit into the existing governmental system. Thus Holy Week and Christmas were observed regularly, but chiefly as occasions for prayers and not for the purpose of dramatizing the life of Jesus. Jesus was not in fact accepted as a central, or even important, figure in religious life, appearing merely as a companion of Santiago (St. James) in saint's day celebrations riding a wooden horse. All Souls' Day was accepted as an occasion for honoring ancestors with gifts, but not as a day to repair to the graveyard and offer prayers for or to the ancestors by way of securing happiness in heaven. The patron saint's day became an important fiesta day with a procession with the image of the saint in the Catholic manner and with dances by men representing Santiago and the Indian variant of Jesus; the saint's day, which in Catholic concept was of course a minor part of Catholic practice, became in fact the one of the accepted ceremonial occasions which most resembled Christian observance. Yet it too invariably consisted not only of a procession and the Santiago dance, but also dances in the Indian style by the ceremonial organizations of the Indians. In this way the borrowings were modified and accepted, but kept peripheral to the central core of Indian ceremonial life.

In the process the Indian religion acquired more occasions for ceremony and more supernaturals in its pantheon, but lost nothing for nothing was replaced, and its central values and orientations remained the same as before. Thus, in line with their conception of a number of deities, none of whom was supreme, the Pueblos despite specific missionary pressure never accepted the conception of the Christian God. To be sure, they began, under missionary influence, to speak of Dios, but Dios was merely another deity of minor importance whom the Pueblos most often called "the Mexican God" and who became the object of no ceremonial cult. The Pueblos maintained even less interest in the Virgin and in Jesus, some of the villages admitting them to their pantheons, but merely as minor figures like Santiago's companion and with no important functions. The whole story of Jesus remained a matter of indifference, winning no interest or sympathy from the Pueblos, perhaps because the idea of individual salvation in a tightly organized, priestly-managed collectivity like a Pueblo village could have no meaning. At any rate the missionaries seemed to find no way to make it meaningful, for down to the 1950's there developed no dramatization or symbolization of the life of Jesus or of the Passion, and Pueblos, as priests complained continually, did not take communion. Nor did the basic ideas of Heaven and Hell have any appeal; the Pueblos continued to believe in an afterlife as a sort of continuation of this life. Eternal punishment and purgatory remained unintelligible, and their governors consistently forbade all villagers, once Spanish power disintegrated, to carry out confession. The prohibition may have had something to do with the effort to maintain secrecy concerning the ceremonials which the missionaries had attacked, but whatever its cause it would seem to be rooted also in an inability to understand sin and its official absolution. It is apparent from this list of rejections that the fundamental ideas of Catholicism were resisted by the Pueblos, despite the existence of a church and a saint's day celebration in every village and the belief on the peoples' part that they were "Catholics." The details of ritual which they had accepted and incorporated into their own system embellished the latter, but did not at all bespeak a transition from a religion focused on natural growth and fertility to one preoccupied with sin and individual salvation.

The Eastern Pueblos can hardly be said to have been much influenced by Catholicism. And yet for over three hundred years they maintained churches in their villages and listened to and were baptized by official representatives of the Catholic Church. In assimilating the offerings of the latter to their own religion and continuing to accept, and pay for, their services, the Pueblos maintained a sort of compartmentalization of religions. Keeping their own organization and viewpoint quite separate from that of the Catholic Church, they nevertheless accepted and sharply defined functions of the latter in their lives. They integrated fragments of Catholicism, but not the system, and hence it is no cause for wonder that the Catholic Church regarded no Pueblo village as a Catholic community.

The Yaquis, on the other hand, were profoundly influenced in their religious life by Catholicism. Unlike the Pueblos, they did integrate the Catholic system with the religion which the missionaries found them practicing, and in the course of doing so achieved a new product, far more like that of the missionaries than was the Pueblos', but still different enough to be unacceptable to the Catholic Church. As in the case of the governmental system, there is very little reliable information about the religion of the Yaquis at the time they accepted Fathers Andrés Pérez de Ribas and Tomás Basilio. It is therefore not possible to say precisely and in detail what happened in the way of transformation during the time that the Jesuits worked peacefully in the newly established eight towns. It is nevertheless possible to gain some understanding of the transformation that took place by considering the nature of Yaqui religion as it was practiced as late as the 1950's.

In those that remained of the eight towns along the Yaqui River and in some eight smaller settlements of emigrants from the Yaqui country on the outskirts of cities in Sonora and Arizona, churches were maintained around which centered an organized religious congregation. However, the churches were by no means standard-pattern Catholic churches, nor did priests of the Catholic Church regularly attend any of the congregations. The churches in the Yaqui River towns were either rough cane shelters or ruined brick buildings, largely unrepaired for thirty years; those in the settlements elsewhere were improvised shelters often much like the houses lived in by the emigrant Yaqui population. The religious life which centered at these nondescript buildings was, however, highly organized; ceremonies were frequent; and the interest of the people was vigorous, even intense. The whole of ceremony was conducted by Yaquis, never by priests of the Catholic Church. It was in the hands of men called *maestros* who possessed little notebooks in which were written out, sometimes in Spanish and sometimes in Yaqui, large amounts of Catholic ritual material. Thus many hymns, or *alabanzas*, standard prayers such as the Our Father, Hail Mary, and the Credo, the Mass for the Dead, and the ritual of the Stations of the Cross appeared in the notebooks; the prayers were usually in Yaqui, the hymns in both Yaqui and Spanish, the ritual of the Stations in Spanish, and the Mass for the dead in a combination of Yaqui and Latin. With these notebooks, often aided by one of the Mexican books of common prayer and a Missal, maestros and their assistants conducted a regular round of ceremony according to the Roman Catholic ceremonial calendar — Lent and Holy Week, the Day of the Finding of the Holy Cross, All Saints' and All Souls', the Day of the Virgin of Guadalupe, Christmas, and the Day of the Kings. In between there were regular Sunday services and observances of some saints' days, Corpus Christi, and the Holy Trinity. The maestros, none of whom had any training other than the apprenticeship of learning from another maestro, often read Mass. In this way a kind of framework of Catholic ceremonial was maintained in the Yaqui settlements.

It was carried out by a rather elaborate organization. The maestros had assistants, men who acted as sacristans and were called by the name which the Jesuits had used for the catechists whom they trained — *temastim;* women who accompanied the maestros as singers and were called by a term — koparia — which the Yaquis had adapted from the Spanish *cofradia;* and girls called *alpesim* (Spanish, *alferez,* flagbearer) who worked with other women in tending the church images. Each of these was an organized group, or society, dedicated to church service through a lifelong vow. Similarly organized were men's societies: an organization of dancers called *matachinis* dedicated to the Virgin, and two organizations collectively called the Customs Chieftainship devoted to the enactment of the Passion of Christ during Lent and Holy Week. These societies worked as cooperating units to carry out the annual round of ceremonies, each village being organized separately from every other and each entirely independent of the Catholic Church priesthood. Yet in each community, whether in Arizona or on the Yaqui River in Sonora, the religious life differed only in details and rested on the same foundation of beliefs.

Superficially, Yaqui belief appeared to be Catholic. At least nearly the whole range of terms employed in orthodox Catholicism, as well as the occasions for ceremony, were used by Yaquis. Baptism was regarded as essential for every individual; God, Jesus, and the Virgin were not only recognized and called by the Spanish terms but also were important and the objects of special devotion; Heaven was spoken of, as were grace and penance; a large number of saints were known and honored; a sharp distinction was maintained between baptized and unbaptized persons; the cross was an all-important symbol. Yet the system of beliefs, as the Catholic Church recognized, was something distinctly Yaqui. The Catholic ideas and symbols had been modified and knitted into a view of life and its meaning which was peculiar to the Yaquis.

There were essentially three cults, although all three were closely integrated through the ritual singing and praying of the maestros who took part in all three. Probably of primary importance was a cult of Jesus, who was identified in Yaqui thought as God. Maestros were regarded as representing Jesus and were sometimes spoken of as Savior Maestros. The Customs Chieftainships, two men's organizations, were dedicated to Jesus and took over all civil and ceremonial functions in a community during the weeks of Lent and Easter each year. They undertook annually to make real to the people the last days of Jesus by the dramatization of his persecution and crucifixion. Members of one of the organizations donned masks representing Judas and Jews and enacted a search for Jesus, the capture of him and Mary, his crucifixion, and finally after losing Jesus as a result of his Resurrection, a military attack on the church. Defeated in the attack on Holy Saturday by the power of little children dressed as angels, the evil Judases were ritually destroyed, through the burning of their masks, and the community delivered from their evil power. This period of enactment of the Passion with the personification of evil by the men's organizations and the addition of a ritual battle between good and evil forces was the climax of ceremonial life each year in a Yaqui community. During the ascendancy of the Customs Chieftainship taboos on work and sexual inter-course were strictly maintained and the men's organizations acting as police forced all people to attend all the observances.

Opposed ritually to the cult of Jesus but linked through many religious mean-ings was one of the Virgin. A men's society also supported this cult with members dedicated to serving the Virgin Mary. These men were dancers called Matachinis. They owned an image of their own of the Virgin, and the mythology described how these dancers were created as soldiers by the Virgin in order to spread good influ-ences through dancing in her honor. Headdresses of the dancers were called "flow-ers" and as such were symbols of all good power. The dancing of the Matachinis with their flower headdresses supported the child angels who opposed the evil Judases on Holy Saturday and ultimately, together, the angels and the Matachinis destroyed the Judases. After Holy Week the Judases disappeared from community life entirely until the following Lent, and ceremonial life was dominated by the good Matachinis and the cult of the Virgin. The dance of the Matachinis was intro-duced by the Jesuit missionaries originally as a dramatization of the triumph of the Christians over the Aztec ruler Montezuma through Malinche, the first Christian convert in Mexico. The whole of that meaning, however, had disappeared from Yaqui belief. Although the name Malinche was still used for certain of the dancers, Montezuma had been entirely lost, and the Matachinis and Malinches were known only as the good soldiers of the Virgin.

The third cult was a cult of the dead. This received its major expression through ceremonies carried out on the days of All Saints and All Souls. At this time, the spirits of all the dead ancestors, who were believed to be present in the com-munity during the month of October, took their leave of their families and as they left, maestros prayed with them and families put out food and drink on tables in their yards. Every family kept a small book in which the names of dead family members were written. These were placed on family altars during All Saints' and All Souls' days and the prayers were regarded as making the dead happy. The books of the dead were also brought to most ceremonies during the year, because it was believed that the spirits would appreciate the prayers and singing of the maestros and the women singers. In addition, once a month families made an effort to go to the graveyard surrounding the church to burn candles and make offerings of flowers, food, or drink to the dead buried there. The Mass for the Dead, from Catholic ritual, was a frequent part of the ritual of most important ceremonies and was recited from notebooks by the maestros.

As has been indicated, these three cults were woven together into a single ceremonial system. As the foci of Yaqui religious life, they rested on very definite beliefs. Jesus, sometimes identified with God, was the creator of all things includ-ing himself. He had lived in the Yaqui country and had been known there as a great curer. He had been pursued throughout the Yaqui country by the Jews and Judas and, after performing many great deeds of curing during his persecution, was ultimately captured and crucified. But he rose again and instructed people how to honor him. His mother, who was not only the mother of Jesus but of all Yaquis, had the power of transforming herself. She thus made herself into the cross, so that Jesus was crucified in her arms, after she had failed in trying to protect him by the creation of the Matachini good soldiers. Actually, as mother of all, the Virgin was the earth itself as well as the church and the ground around the church where all Yaquis were buried. As the earth she produced the flowers which were the source of good and through whose power the persecutors of Jesus were annually destroyed. The dead continued to live in the Yaqui country and to return to the community annually. They lived neither in a heaven nor a hell, but in a place of flowers, that is, divine grace. They continued to be very much aware of what was going on and were aided in this by having their books, in which their names were inscribed, brought by the living to all ceremonial altars. They were helpful, not dangerous, and living people were obligated to please them, chiefly by maintaining the ceremonies in honor of Jesus and the Virgin.

There was a somewhat lesser cult of the Virgin of Guadalupe, who was patroness of the military society, and whose images were carried in a weekly Sunday ceremony which symbolized the marking of the sacred boundary line of the Yaqui territory. A whole set of myths, with many Biblical references, had grown up around the idea of the sacredness of the Yaqui land and the sacred locations of the eight towns. No cult of the saints had grown up among the Yaquis, although simple observances were carried out for many saints' days and every Yaqui community had a patron saint with a very elaborate secular celebration annually, an important feature of which was an enactment of the war between the Moors and the Christians of which the Jesuits had taught the Yaquis a dramatization. Closely linked also with the three major cults were non-calendrical ceremonies, or fiestas, as they were called, which took place at private houses rather than the church.

These fiestas were occasioned by deaths, by weddings, and by promises by families to honor Jesus or the Virgin for help they had given in curing or in some enterprise. At such fiestas the church organization, maestros and, depending on the ceremonial season, different men's organizations took part at a specially constructed altar. Alongside the altar was set up a temporary shelter at which dancers, who were not part of the church organization, acted as ceremonial hosts. These were the pascola dancers, "old men of the fiesta," as Yaquis called them. They wore bearded wooden masks in part of their dancing, told funny stories, gave out cigarettes and food and drink. They represented a survival of aboriginal ritual performers who had derived supernatural power from animals, but they remained a very vigorous part of Yaqui ceremonial life, and kept alive a great deal of the old mythology and point of view toward the universe. Yet they were tied in closely and in a variety of ways with the Christianized belief and ceremony. Mythologically they were held to have been derived from the Devil, but they were required to carve crosses on their masks, and to preface their sometimes sexually very expressive dances and ribald jokes by crossing themselves before the church altar. They also were required to ask God's pardon for their disrespectfulness and to offer up a Christian prayer before and after the ceremony. Under their auspices a dancer representing a deer, probably aboriginally connected with hunting magic, performed an active dance and enacted with the pascolas' help hunting scenes and funny skits. The songs to which the deer dancer danced dealt with flowers and a supernatural world of power connected with the flowers. Christian symbolism, except for the requirement of crossing himself before dancing, did not figure in the deer dancer's behavior.

It was thus apparent that Yaqui religious life constituted an intricate integration of the aboriginal beliefs and rituals with what had been learned from the Jesuits. This would be even more apparent in any detailed account of any one ceremonial occasion. The sketch presented here merely suggests the way in which the two traditions had been fused. It should be clear that many essential features of orthodox Catholicism were not present. God, a Supreme power, was not clearly recognized, although certainly such a concept was approached in the Yaqui view of Jesus. Rather there were two major deities — the male Jesus who was creator and the female Mary, Our Mother in Yaqui, who was also a creator in a more passive way. Hell was hardly recognized at all, except as a name; Heaven was identified with an afterlife to which all persons went where flowers and Our Mother's presence made things pleasant. Punishment in the afterlife was not conceived as a reality and prayer for the dead was not to improve their position in a hierarchy of levels but to add to their happiness in the place where they were. In such a view of the afterlife individual salvation could not have the orthodox Christian meaning; rather application to the prescribed forms of worship — prayer, dancing, dramatic representation, participation in the varied work of the ceremonial societies — was regarded as a return to the ruling supernaturals for their help in keeping one well through the years and keeping away evils. Religious life was essentially vigorous participation in a network of exacting relationships with Jesus and the Virgin and perhaps a few other supernaturals. "Fulfillment," which Yaquis habitually used in their religion, meant carrying out obligations to the deities with the result that both individual and deity felt well-being and remained well disposed toward one another.

This type of religious feeling led to no emphasis on sin as something which could be atoned for by any individual activities such as confession or even individual saying of prayers. Yaqui religion was primarily a group expression with emphasis on performance of roles in the established expressive ceremony. Confession was ignored. Yet penance was performed by assuming duties in the annual ceremonies, in the men's or women's societies. The ceremonies were the focus of interest and these were regarded as being quite independent of any priestly knowledge or authority. Hence the Catholic priesthood had no place in Yaqui religion, except as specialists who knew how to perform baptism. Since baptism was regarded as essential, priests were sought for this rite, but for many generations in Sonora priests were not available and hence came to be regarded as not necessarily essential even for baptism.

The Papago acceptance of Catholicism had something in common with that of the Yaquis, but differed in a few essentials. In the first place, it consisted of an adaptation made during a period when no representatives of the Catholic Church were present among Papagos and hence showed features of independence similar to those of the Yaquis. But there was far less in the way of involved integration of old and new. The Papago adaptation of Catholicism consisted almost entirely of the adoption of the cult of one saint — Saint Francis Xavier, the Jesuit founder. This cult possibly grew up quite late, even as late as the last quarter of the 1800's. Nevertheless it undoubtedly had its roots in the earlier activities of Father Kino in the Upper Pima area. By 1900 many Papago villages, which at that time had no resident missionaries or priests, had small wattle-and-daub chapels surmounted by crosses in which a weekly worship of Saint Francis was carried on. The chapels usually contained several pictures, rather than images, of St. Francis and perhaps other Christian pictures. The worship was managed usually by a particular family who owned the major picture of the saint. The women of this family with the help of others conducted services consisting of the recitation of standard Catholic prayers, in Spanish, and the singing of hymns also in Spanish in praise of the saint. Villages having such small chapels were scattered throughout the Papago country, although not all villages had them. The chapels were not visited or recognized by priests, and hence the cult was wholly in the hands of the Papagos.

Another feature of the cult was an annual pilgrimage to Magdalena, a town in Sonora, where Father Kino had died and where his remains were buried. The Saint Francis of the cult was identified by some Papagos as Father Kino. The day on which Papagos made their pilgrimage to Magdalena was October 4, the day of Saint Francis of Assisi, founder of the Franciscan Order, not December 7, the day of Saint Francis Xavier. However, the Papagos seemed unaware of Saint Francis of Assisi and considered themselves to be honoring St. Francis Xavier or Father Kino. Hundreds of Papagos made the annual pilgrimage, as did also some Yaquis and other Indians of the region. Whether it began in Kino's day is not known. The fame of the reclining image of Saint Francis in Kino's Magdalena church was very great. Every year pilgrims in large numbers passed by the image seeking to gain some of its magical power. It was from Magdalena that many of the furnishings in the Papago chapels came.

In villages where the chapels existed, not necessarily all the inhabitants participated in the weekly or other gatherings. Some remained aloof and a name grew up for those who frequented the chapels, namely "santos." Some Whites spoke of the cult as the "Sonoran Catholic" since its source seemed to be in Sonora and since it resembled other Catholic-inspired independent developments like the Yaqui religion. Most of the people in the southernmost Papago villages practiced the cult with greater or less intensity and in conjunction with it made a great deal of use of rosary services for sick persons, as a means of curing and also as a means of preparing them for the afterlife. However, the participation of an individual or family in the cult did not carry with it lack of interest in the activities of the native religion, nor were devotees of Saint Francis excluded from the latter. On the contrary, in every village where a chapel to Saint Francis existed, there existed also ordinarily a village council house where saguaro wine for the annual rain-making ceremony was prepared. Often the family which led the Saint Francis ceremonies also played a prominent role in aboriginal ceremonies. Thus, the saint's cult was a simple addition to the ceremonial life of the village which replaced nothing else in the way of ceremony. Added to the means of curing — a focus of Papago ritual interest which had always existed was another — Saint Francis and objects connected with him.

There was here no compartmentalization of two religious systems as among the Eastern Pueblos, for the Papagos did not receive regular visits of priests and they built their own chapels on their own initiative. Moreover, baptism was not a necessary part of the cult and so it required no attention from the Catholic priesthood. The cult of the saint had diffused to the Papagos without the intermediary of a planned program of introduction. On the other hand, the Papago situation did not resemble very closely that of the Yaqui. Where the Yaqui acceptance of Catholicism involved many elements and a complex combination of these with aboriginal features, the Papagos selected one element — a powerful saint — and took him pretty much as he was without elaboration: representation, attributed power, and hymns. Once taken, his cult remained formally separate from other aspects of religious life. He was indeed interpreted as a source of supernatural power similar to existing Papago mythological figures and so was conceptually integrated with the persisting aboriginal religion. But the ritual associated with him remained distinct from other ritual, employing candles, rosaries, and hymns in Spanish, where the other made use of painted sticks, feathers, and Papago songs.

In Pueblo, Yaqui, and Papago religion we thus see three different results in the diffusion of Catholicism following the first Jesuit-Franciscan campaign of introduction — compartmentalization, fusion, and simple addition.

The other tribes of Sonora, with the exception of the Seris whose contact with Catholicism was most tenuous, accepted Catholicism pretty much as had the Yaquis. The Mayo and Opata reaction was almost identical, but the Opatas' aboriginal beliefs and practices were much more deeply submerged than were the Yaquis'. The Lower Pimas and the Upper Pimas of Sonora may have experienced a fairly complete replacement of aboriginal religion, but we know too little to say. The religious life of the Tarahumaras was chiefly, even among those who before 1900 spoke of themselves as Catholics, still in the aboriginal pattern with little admixture of Christianity. Nevertheless elements of Catholicism had been adopted and were in process of being integrated with the aboriginal religion in much the manner of the Yaquis and Mayos. Those Tarahumaras who called themselves Christian, or Catholic, maintained churches as ceremonial and civic centers and most of these were visited about once a year by priests. At these churches part of the Catholic ceremonial calendar was observed — Sunday services, Holy Week, the Day of Guadalupe, Christmas, and Day of the Kings, with occasionally other saints' days. The observances, like those of the Yaquis, were carried out entirely without the assistance of a priest. Maestros who knew Catholic prayers in Spanish and some hymns directed the ceremonies. The ceremonies consisted of feasts and simple rituals similar to those of the native curing ceremonies, but they had additional features which were Catholic-derived. Thus the maestros sang and offered prayers and at each ceremony instructed the people in crossing themselves and saying the Our Father. In addition, on the Day of Guadalupe, Christmas and Day of the

Kings, an organization of men called matachines danced under the direction of another men's organization called the chapeones; and during Holy Week other groups of men called Judases and Pharisees danced. Their performances were pure dances, rather than dramatizations, and thus differed from the Judases of the Yaquis but resembled the Yaqui Matachinis. These dance groups, under the general direction of the maestros, performed dances in a sacred context of worship of church images, but apparently had no Christian meanings that were generally understood by the Tarahumaras practicing them. The Judases burned effigies of Judas on Holy Saturday, but enacted no part of the Passion. Like the Yaquis the Tarahumaras spoke of God, identified with Jesus, and the Virgin as important male and female deities but possessed no clear beliefs concerning them in the Christian pattern. They had adopted the sign of the cross and employed three crosses in numerous otherwise aboriginal ceremonies. Thus among them, the aboriginal religious system was dominant and fusion with Catholic elements was still limited.

The second Catholic campaign of conversion brought missionaries again into close and continuous relationships with some of the Indians of the region. Jesuit missions, schools, and hospitals were established among the Tarahumaras in 1903. Steadily the program expanded and orthodox Catholic behavior slowly diffused in the vicinity of the new Jesuit centers. By 1960 however the great majority of Tarahumaras were still outside this influence, being visited only annually by the priests. This process of fusion of the church-centered ceremonies proceeded.

Franciscan missionaries went to work about 1910 among the Papagos and Gila Pimas, for the first time giving the latter Catholic missions and expanding throughout the desert area of the Papagos where the Kino mission chain had never reached. Here, too, orthodox Catholic behavior slowly diffused, in some cases absorbing the Saint Francis cult of the Papagos, and in some cases creating sharp divisions in Papago or Pima villages, where Presbyterian influence had preceded the Franciscans. Similarly, Franciscans added to the sectarian heterogeneity already existing among the Apaches, Navajos, Zunis, and a few Eastern Pueblos such as the Lagunas.

The hope of the early missionaries had not been realized three centuries after the beginning. Even among those Indians where missionaries had had the best conditions for work and had been able to carry out their program intensively, there was not a quick response resulting in complete acceptance and understanding of the Catholic ideas. The Pueblos remained devoted to their native religion and found ways to limit the influence of Catholic teaching. The Yaquis, Mayos, and Opatas were certainly profoundly influenced, but the new system of beliefs was clearly not that which the missionaries themselves had held, and the Tarahumaras were even further away from the doctrines and practices which had been offered. It could definitely be said that the missionaries had been forced to stop their work at the very height of its intensity in the case of the Jesuits and that the Franciscans had had to work in New Mexico against heavy odds during the 1700's. In this sense there were obvious reasons for the failure of the dream. The conflicts in Spanish culture had interfered and had left the Indians without effective guides and teachers of the Culture of the Conquest.

It seems nevertheless relevant to ask: How long under the very favorable conditions of the early Jesuit missions would it have taken to transfer a new religion? If 150 years, five generations was not sufficient, what time period would be? And further, what evidence is there from the record in Chihuahua, Sonora, and New Mexico that a religion could be transferred and replace another at all? What were the conditions which gave rise to a solid resistance like that of the Eastern Pueblos and to the creation of a new integrated system like that of the Yaquis? Were these results caused by the working methods of the missionaries? Were they a product of the incompatibility of the religion offered with the economic and social life which the Indians continued to lead?

These questions might have been answered after the new campaign of Catholic conversion had proceeded for another hundred years, but already the conditions had completely changed. The Catholic missionaries were now working as one among many sects competing for influence among the Indians with spiritual offerings and material gifts. Equivalents of the early gifts of tools, clothing, and seeds were being offered by the Indian Bureau in the United States and by the National Indian Institute in Chihuahua, as well as by various churches. The isolated communities of the old missions with contacts with the outside world so often controlled by a single, devoted missionary could not be reproduced. If the new missionaries among the Catholics were dreaming the same dream which their predecessors had, the reading of history might be frustrating. Their predecessors created several new religious ways rather than a single one, and the new missionaries were themselves working in the midst of what the early missionaries would surely have regarded as a more difficult situation than simply savagery.

THE MANY VOICES OF PROTESTANTISM

The taking over of political control of New Mexico Territory by the Anglo-Americans brought no immediate intensification of pressures on the Indians to change their religious life. The United States Indian Bureau did not develop, until President Grant's administration in the early 1870's, any systematic program of this sort. Consequently, during the 1850's, when Anglo-American contacts with the Indians first began to occur with some intensity, it was trappers, soldiers, mining men, a few civil administrators, and settlers who gave Indians their first acquaintance with Anglo-American ways. This was, of course, a great contrast with the earliest Spanish contacts, in connection with all of which the Indians were confronted with men who immediately advanced new religious beliefs and tried immediately to persuade the Indians of their importance.

In the 1860's one tribe of Indians, the Hopis, became aware of the religious interests of some Anglo-Americans. The Mormons, through Jacob Hamblin, made a great effort to convert the Hopis to Mormonism. It was part of Mormon belief that all American Indians were descendants of the Lamanites, one of the lost tribes of Israel. In accordance with this belief they held that Indians had once practiced the Hebrew religion, but had degenerated since arrival on the American continents, producing nevertheless the prophetic book of Mormon which had been found by Joseph Smith, the founder of the Mormon religion.

It was therefore a duty of Mormons to convert Indians and bring them back to the right path. Moreover, the early Mormon settlers in Utah conceived of a new Mormon state in the west and, in the face of tendencies toward persecution by other Anglo-Americans, they wished to bring Indian tribes to their point of view and ally themselves with the Indians. It was with such aims that Jacob Hamblin tried to convert the Hopis and to persuade their leading men to go to Utah and learn the new revelations. Although Hamblin worked periodically for six years among the Hopis and gained their friendship, he made no converts and finally gave up the task. The Mormon efforts made no more lasting impression on the Hopis than had the efforts of the Franciscans.

In 1869, with President Grant's appointment of a Board of Commissioners to advise the Indian Bureau, it became the policy of the Bureau to give funds to various religious denominations for the establishment of schools on Indian reservations. The plan included giving sole jurisdiction to one denomination on each reservation, or at each agency. Prominent in the New Mexico-Arizona region were the Presbyterian and the Christian Reformed (a Lutheran denomination) churches. The Christian Reformed Church took over education and mission work among such groups as the Apaches, Navajos, Gila Pimas, and later the Zunis. This church, however, relinquished jurisdiction over the Gila Pimas by 1880 and the Presbyterians took over. Thus the first Protestant denominations in the field were the Christian Reformed and the Presbyterian churches, with the Presbyterians early becoming the sole missionary group among the Gila Pimas, sharing the Papago field with the Catholics who were established at San Xavier, and beginning work among the Mohaves and at Laguna among the Pueblos. In the 1890's, however, the Indian Bureau changed its policy. Instead of giving funds to the churches to manage schools on the reservations, the Bureau itself assumed responsibility for schools. In doing so, it did not eliminate schools already established by various church groups which were able to continue their own support of the schools. Such schools as the Presbyterian ones among the Gila Pimas and at Tucson for Papagos and the Evangelical Lutheran schools among the various Western Apache groups and continued in operation, competing for students with the Indian Bureau schools which slowly increased in numbers. The policy of giving favored position on a reservation to any one denomination was, however, abandoned. Any church which wished to set up a mission or a school on a reservation was permitted to do so by the Indian Bureau.

The result was that during the 1890's more churches entered the mission field and shortly after 1900 there began a steady increase in the number of denominations maintaining missionaries, schools, or other services on the reservations. In the 1890's the Mennonites began intensive work among the Hopis, the Episcopalians among the Havasupais and somewhat later among the Navajos. The American Baptists began to work among the Hopis, the Methodists among the Yumas and Navajos, the Plymouth Brethren among the Walapais, Eastern Pueblos, and Navajos. At the same time the Franciscans again entered the field among the Navajos, Apaches, Gila Pimas, and Papagos. There were by 1915 eight different Christian denominations conducting schools and missionary work on the reservations of New Mexico and Arizona. None any longer had a monopoly on the religious conversion of any tribe, except for the Episcopalians who were the only church working among the small, concentrated community of the Havasupais. The Mormon missionary work among the Indians was discontinued as a result of the concentration of the Mormons on a colonization program rather than any direct missionary activity.

In general, the Protestant denominations followed a similar plan in their efforts to convert the Indians. They usually established schools as a beginning and, like the Jesuits and Franciscans before them, offered whatever services they found were needed — medical and nursing help, acting as go-betweens with other Anglo-Americans, and charity for the poorest Indians. Some maintained boarding and some day schools, in all of which the effort was made not only to give elementary secular instruction but also instruction in the doctrines of the sect. Converts were recruited primarily from among their students and members of their families. The use of the native language varied greatly, but only the Evangelical Lutherans (other than the Franciscans) made much effort to translate prayers and hymns into Indian languages and to train their ministers to preach in the Indian languages. In general, although no missionary was in a position, as had been the Jesuits and early Franciscans, to suppress effectively Indian ceremonials and religious practices, vigorous condemnation of the surviving native religion was the rule. Missionaries generally refused on principle to attend any Indian ceremonials, consistently taught in the schools that they were evil, and preached regularly against those practices of which they were aware. All the missionaries also introduced taboos on certain behavior such as smoking, drinking liquor, playing cards, and dancing in couples, thereby acquainting the Indians with a different standard of behavior from that which they were aware of among soldiers, miners, ranchers, and most of the settlers with whom they were coming into contact. The sects differed somewhat among themselves on doctrine and ritual, but a common complex of behavior and belief ran through them all. Such elements as the requirement of baptism, Sunday services, exclusive sect membership, absence of concrete representation of God, Jesus, or other figures in the churches, group hymn singing, sacredness of the Bible, and annual revival meetings made it clear that these were all the same general kind of religious way and that they as a group differed from the Catholic way.

The impact of the Protestant missionary program, as it developed during the years from about 1870 to about 1920, was pronounced on a majority of the tribes; it was a major influence on all the reservations and must be considered as one of the most important factors in shaping Indian life. It did not have the same sort nor the same degree of impact on all the reservations, but everywhere it was significant. Three types of influence were important; in confining ourselves to a consideration of those we may see in what ways Protestantism constituted an aspect of the "program of civilization" which the Indian Bureau administrators conceived themselves as bringing to the Indians. These three types of impact were the following: (1) the regeneration of community life disorganized by the reservation system, (2) the stimulation of political factionalism and community disorganization, and (3) the growth of new Christian sectarianism.

There is a certain rough similarity between what happened to the Yaquis as a result of Jesuit contacts and what happened to the Gila Pimas as a result of Presbyterian contacts. The Gila Pimas constituted the clearest example of a tribe regenerated up to a point through Protestant influence. By the 1880's they had lost much of their irrigation water to white settlers on the Gila River upstream from their reservation. From farmers with an abundant surplus selling wheat and other agricultural products to starving Anglo emigrant trains in the 1850's and 1860's, the Gila Pimas on the reservation had become twenty-five years later barely subsisting, poverty-stricken people. In the 1850's they had been spoken of as the "most civilized Indians" in the United States, not only because they were well off for food and land but also because they lived in peaceful, well-organized villages with strong and wise leadership, tribally expressed in the person of Antonio Azul. But by the 1880's the villages had become largely demoralized. The reservation system had been put into operation among them, a superintendent and his aides had unwittingly undermined many of the funtcions of the village headmen, drunkenness had vastly increased, and an attitude of dependency on the "government" had begun to take root. Into this situation of general community disorganization had come in 1870 a man named C. H. Cook. At the request of the tribal headman, Antonio Azul, he had started a school which had by 1878 become very well known to Pimas and Papagos alike, with a fairly regular enrollment of forty students. Cook's ambition was to convert all Pimas to Presbyterianism. This he was able to begin in 1880 when the Christian Reformed Church gave up its right to missionize them.

Cook, with his already long experience among the Pimas, went to work as a full-time missionary. He worked slowly and probably therefore all the more solidly. His period of most intensive building of congregations took place nearly twenty years after his first arrival among the Pimas. This was in the ten years from 1889 to 1899 when he baptized eighteen hundred Pimas. By 1911 when he relinquished his missionary post to another he had organized two-thirds of all the Pimas into active church congregations. He not only taught doctrine, conferred English names at baptism, persuaded people to cut their hair short and give up other minor customs which were different from Anglo-Americans, he also successfully altered the whole social organization. He gave the village headmen, who had been declining into listlessness as the Indian Bureau personnel took over many of their functions, a new lease on life. He instituted a system of church organization in the villages, appointing such leaders as elders of the churches. Each church had its board of elders who not only managed specific church affairs but also constituted a village council. The head elder was encouraged to preach good moral behavior to the congregation and thus the old moral exhortation function of the village headman was revitalized. The head elder and his assistants acting as a board or council sat on cases of misbehavior, meted out advice, and when they thought necessary, punishment, such as suspension from church activities. Although the Pimas did not accept the Presbyterian doctrine in regard to the nature of Hell and Heaven, they did rapidly reorganize their villages around the institution of the church. The social control applied through the old daily evening meetings now was exercised through the weekly Sunday meetings and the actions of the boards of elders. The elders through their training in English and Anglo ways in the Presbyterian school became increasingly able to deal with Indian Bureau personnel and other Anglos as representatives of their villages. Missionary Cook took an interest in practical problems such as the loss of water for irrigation and encouraged his church leaders to think about and seek action for betterment. The total effect of Cook's activities, which emphasized so strongly the development of leadership through their own organizations, was a strong movement toward cultural assimilation of the Pimas and the regeneration of a dying community organization. In 1906 he introduced annual revival meetings which brought the people of all the villages together once a year and gave impetus on the tribal level to religious feeling and to the whole church organization.

Considered from the tribal point of view, there is no other example of constructive transformation through Protestant mission work remotely comparable to that of the Pimas. Some Papago villages, through Presbyterian influence, developed vigorous leadership. In the southeastern part of the Navajo Reservation, where Presbyterians founded a mission in 1903, there was a similar stimulation of leadership sometimes able to deal with the outside world. And on many reservations the Christian Reformed, Episcopal, and other churches strongly influenced individuals who became constructive leaders in community or even tribal affairs. But in other situations the unity of church influence, as it had developed among the Pimas, was interfered with by the existence of competing sects, the organized vigor of native religion, or other factors.

Elsewhere almost uniformly, the Havasupais being the only clear exception, Protestant missions stimulated factionalism which split families and communities. Such factionalism was not necessarily permanently destructive of community life; on the contrary it appears in several instances to have been a stage in the growth of communities which, through resolution of the conflict, reached a more stable equilibrium in the heterogeneous society of which they had become a part.

One of the earliest of these factional splits came about through the settlement of an Anglo man named Marmon at Laguna village in 1871. He married a Laguna woman and set about with her converting other Lagunas to Presbyterianism. He was successful with a majority of the families in the space of ten years and, when he was elected governor of Laguna, proceeded to tear down, with the approval of the converted Lagunans, two kivas. This precipitated a conflict over the ownership of ceremonial objects and ultimately resulted in one-fourth of the population leaving the village permanently. Those who left were not the Presbyterian converts, but those who were opposed to the new sect and devoted to the old religion. Making up a group of about one hundred they left Laguna and were given land for permanent settlement at Isleta on the Rio Grande. They took with them the disputed sacred objects and resumed their ceremonies at the settlement at Oraibi on the outskirts of Isleta. The remaining Lagunans continued in a state of schism, between the Presbyterians and the Catholic-native religionists, but were able to reconcile differences sufficiently, with the removal of the most conservative, to maintain a village organization. The ultimate result of the split was the breakdown of the control of the village organization by the cacique, or village ceremonial leader, and the growth of a more purely secular village government.

A factional split with equally serious consequences developed in the Hopi village of Oraibi as a result of missionary work of the Mennonites which began in 1893. The Mennonites were a European sect which opposed war and participation in civil government, maintained no priesthood, and regarded baptism and the celebration of the Lord's Supper as fundamental rites. A missionary established himself near Oraibi in 1893 and began to preach and offer instruction to children. He gained influence with a number of families and was not opposed until after 1906 by the village chief, Tewakwaptewa. The latter, then, after having turned anti-Christian as a result of his forced stay in an Indian Bureau boarding school, discouraged further activity by the Mennonite missionary. Those families who had been influenced moved out of Old Oraibi below the mesa where the mission was established and set up a new settlement where they then centered their lives around the Mennonite church. They still held their land, however, by virtue of assignment from the Old Oraibi village chief and this led to conflict. Some families attempted to extricate themselves from the conflict by adopting individual landholding as urged by the Indian Bureau officials, but such arrangement was not recognized by the village chief. The dispute over land continued through the years and further disputes developed over the Mennonite Hopis' efforts to carry out some ceremonies of the Hopi religion apart from official Old Oraibi sponsorship. The Mennonite Hopis, following the tenets of their new religion, also rejected participation in the Hopi Tribal Council when it was formed later as well as service in the United States armed forces.

A somewhat different sort of factionalism resulted among the Papagos when Presbyterians began to work intensively among them in 1910. The Presbyterian missionary work was carried out only in the southeastern part of what later became the Sells reservation, affecting directly only a quarter of the population. Here the Presbyterians built four churches between 1910 and 1920 and carried on an active proselytizing campaign. They made use of ministers who spoke the Papago language, having been trained by C. H. Cook, the Presbyterian missionary on the Pima Reservation. They rapidly gained several hundred converts and instituted an organization of elders similar to that among the Pimas. The converted Papagos not only accepted basic Presbyterian ritual and doctrine, but also gave up smoking, drinking, and card playing and became actively hostile to the native religious practices, such as the annual saguaro wine rain ceremony and others. This vigorous rejection of the native religion was required by the Presbyterian missionaries. The implacably hostile attitude toward native religion as well as toward the cult of Saint Francis and other Catholic practices resulted in friction with other Papagos of the area. The Presbyterian congregations consisted of only parts of the population of a half dozen villages, never of whole villages. The other residents of the villages were ones who called themselves Catholics for the most part, and practiced the Saint Francis cult along with some features of the Papago religion. The friction grew into serious schism as the Presbyterians expressed their hostility to other religious practices and as some Presbyterians emerged as vigorous leaders in tribal affairs in connection with the Indian Bureau program. All the villages in which a Presbyterian church existed were torn with conflict, and there was no cooperation for any purpose between the Protestant and the Catholic factions. The Presbyterian missionary campaign was not, however, extended beyond this area and hence the factionalism did not spread among all the Papagos. After 1930 the friction lessened, although the Presbyterian congregations continued vigorous.

Internal factionalism not resulting in migration and in less intense form than that which characterized the Papago villages appeared on many other reservations. At the time when the Presbyterian churches had reached their peak of development on the Pima Reservation, the Franciscan Order built missions there and rather quickly gained many converts, as many as a third of the tribe. This division into two sects did not result, however, in the intensity of factional conflict which had characterized the Presbyterian conversion of the Papagos. Christian Reformed and Catholic factions sometimes opposed each other on Apache and Zuni reservations, as did Baptist and Mennonite on the Hopi Reservation. Generally speaking, where Protestant conversion was well established before the growth of Catholic missions, as among the Gila Pimas and the San Carlos and White Mountain Apaches, factional bitterness did not develop with much intensity. But where Catholicism in some form had been the rule and Protestantism was introduced, as among Papagos, Eastern Pueblos, and Zunis, some serious conflict developed. The process of Protestant replacement carried with it greater stimulus to factional discord.

A third feature of the Protestant impact on Indian life was the separation of new sects out of those introduced on the reservations. The new sects formed in this way consisted of groups of Indians already converted as Presbyterians, Baptists, or Lutherans who rebelled against being a part of a national organization and wanted more local control of their church. Sometimes they had their origin in the leadership of a particular personality serving as minister. Most of them centered around Indians who had received training as ministers, but occasionally an Anglo minister was employed. Independent churches grew up from Baptist congregations on the Hopi and Pima reservations, from Lutheran congregations on the San Carlos Apache Reservation, and from Presbyterian congregations on the Mohave Reservation. In all of these, church affairs and the treasury were administered by the various local congregations on the reservations, all of the ties with the denomination out of which they had grown being severed. They abandoned the denominational names and adopted new ones containing the tribal name, such as Hopi Mission Church, Mohave Mission Church, San Carlos Apache Independent Church, and Pima Independent Church. In all cases they constituted small minorities of the reservation population. Each church usually had a minister who was widely known as an effective preacher and who visited frequently the other independent churches to preach and to hold revival meetings. An important feature of these churches' activities was annual camp meetings in which the congregations of all or several got together for a week or more at a time and conducted revivals in the manner of one or another of the churches from which they had been derived. Necessarily the preaching at such meetings was in English, since those in attendance spoke different Indian languages. However, the local congregations employed the native Indian language as frequently as English in their own services.

The independent churches represented a tendency toward local autonomy in religious life, yet they were not composed of those Indians who had been least influenced by Protestantism. On the contrary, the congregations consisted of persons who had been most affected by the Protestant principle of exclusive sectarianism. They were usually persons who were most deeply opposed to the practice of the native religions and most uncompromising in their denunciation of native curing and other practices. They were usually noted on their reservations for the strictest religious discipline — as the most regular church-goers — and as the strictest observers of the taboos on smoking, drinking, card-playing, gambling, and couple dancing. They, in fact, represented the extreme in the development of Protestant behavior on the reservations and the rejection of all those behaviors about which Anglos were most articulate in their disapproval.

The diffusion of Protestantism was characterized by different results from that of Catholicism in respect to the modification and reintegration of basic doctrines and rituals. Although the social effects were somewhat similar in that Catholic conversion resulted in the unification of some tribes, the sometimes paralyzing splitting of others and the growth of new forms of Catholicism, the new varieties of Protestantism differed fundamentally from those of Catholicism. The Eastern Pueblo, Yaqui, and Papago types of modification of Catholic ritual and doctrine did not occur in the case of Protestantism. It is clear enough that there had been in the seventy-five years of Protestant contact no repetition of those conditions which were major determinants of the Yaqui and Papago varieties of Catholicism, namely, the departure of priests after an initial intensive indoctrination. We should not therefore expect similar results, unless perhaps they might be looked for as future developments in the independent churches which have split off from the nationally organized denominations.

However, there were basic characteristics of Protestant belief and missionary procedure which inhibited such results. The sects mentioned which were active in the field for the first fifty years of Protestant contact instructed their missionaries in a wholly uncompromising attitude toward native religions. They refused to attend native ceremonies and probably learned less about them than did even the early Franciscan missionaries. They insisted that their converts reject entirely all participation in the native religion and confine their religious life exclusively to the simpler and less colorful ritual of the introduced Protestant church. They tended to regard the greater Catholic tolerance for persisting Indian belief and ceremony as a compromise with evil. Later, after the 1920's, some missionaries began to show more tolerance and some recognition of the need for a slower transition from the old to the new, but even in the later period the Protestant missionary attitude was predominantly one of no compromise. Thus a Christian Reformed missionary working at Zuni in the 1940's expressed the prevailing viewpoint: *Differences of opinion naturally arise whether in the realm of religion one should try to use existing concepts. Paul did make reference at Athens to an Unknown God, of whom he said, "Whom, therefore, ye ignorantly worship, Him declare I unto you." But it is questionable whether Paul gained much by this introduction. The most common reaction of well-meaning Zunis to the gospel message is that the Jesus-way and the Zuni-way are "hi-ni-na," the same. To identify our God, "eternal, incomprehensible,*

invisible, immutable, infinite, almighty, perfectly wise, just, good, and the over-
flowing fountain of all good " [Article I of The Confession of Faith] *with an indefi-*
nite Holder of the Path proves rather a stumbling block than an aid to the full con-
ception of the Christian message.

This missionary further expressed the ideal result in the conversion of Zunis.
Louis Chavez and family . . . no longer attend native ceremonies. Their beloved
dead lie in a graveyard remote from those who have been given pagan burial. By
the grace of God they have learned that one cannot walk upon two roads. He contrasted this family with another Zuni whom he described as "a faithful friend to
the missionaries." *Oldest among the Indians was Telesee . . . Decade after decade,*
Telesee has faithfully come to church . . . It was he who would blow into the ears
of the new-comers and say, "Now you will understand our language." . . . Telesee
heard the message directly in his own language from Rex Natewa . . . . He has been
especially valuable in translation work the last few years . . . . Telesee may not have
liked the message of that Sunday. Rex made it very clear that the Holy Spirit toler-
ates no other spirit within. Telesee in all these years that he has attended church
has never come to the point where he was ready to give up his own religion. When
he visited the missionary at Thanksgiving time, with one breath he would ask for a
Jesus story, with the next he would ask for some feathers, that is if the missionary
had been fortunate enough to have had turkey. They were for his plumes. But
Telesee also said he wanted to pray to Jesus. Of late, as he was hearing Sunday after
Sunday that he must give up his own gods, he seemed less interested.

Such attitudes on the part of the missionaries generally resulted in little or no
blending of Indian religious concepts with the Protestant. The Indian convert had
to make a complete break. There was no combination of Protestant ritual with
Indian ritual, no assumption of new ceremonial functions by existing Indian organizations, and consequently no fusion of the old and the new such as took place
among the Yaquis. What the missionaries sought was sudden and complete replacement of the Indian religious behavior.

This result was obtained for the congregations who accepted missionary leadership and remained under direct missionary tutelage. Some modifications of a
minor sort did take place. The kinds that resulted were exemplified by some of the
Papago congregations. For the Papagos song had always been an important accompaniment of religious activity as well as a constant feature of daily life. Supernatural
power was acquired in the form of songs. Songs brought rain and transformed wine.
The first Presbyterian missionaries among the Papagos taught choral singing,
which was the form — combined male and female voices — of song characteristic of
the major Papago ceremonies. The Papagos took up the choral singing of hymns
with great enthusiasm; the congregations vied with one another in singing. Choral
groups went from their own church to sing at others. Protestant hymns were
translated into Papago, although the music remained as the missionaries taught
it. Churches had choral meets in which the different congregations sang competi-
tively. The Papagos had chosen to emphasize an aspect of church behavior which
appealed especially to them and fit in well with their own religious heritage. Emphasis on choral singing made their church life a little different from that of Anglo

Presbyterian churches, but in other respects the ritual was the same. There was further a different emphasis in the big revival meetings which the Presbyterians stimulated among the Papagos. The sins publicly confessed were most frequently failures to live up to the traditional kinship obligations in Papago culture. Tearful church members rose and spoke not of sins against the Holy Spirit, but of neglect of aunts and uncles on the father's side. The framework of morality was the old kinship system, but the sanctions for it were expressed through the new medium of the revival meeting.

It was also difficult for Papagos, and Pimas as well, to think in terms of eternal punishment in the afterlife, since that concept had not been part of their native religious system. Rewards and punishments in an afterlife were conspicuously absent in the sense of sin which developed among them. There were also attempts, certainly not sanctioned by the missionaries but nevertheless indulged in by individual Papagos, to make parallels between their old culture hero — I-itoy, creator of men — and Jesus. Such reinterpretations were not conspicuous in the thinking of the most devoted church-goers, but as the numbers of the latter increased and Jesus became better known to other Papagos who maintained some belief in the old myths, adjustments in their thinking were made to the Christian concepts. In these ways the same process developed by which the introductions of the Jesuits had been adjusted to Papago world views.

There were similar differences in emphasis in what was being taught among other tribes who formed Protestant congregations, but like those among the Papagos and Pimas they constituted only small departures. In general, Protestantism was not fundamentally altered in its process of transference and by virtue of that very fact a sharper distinction was created between those who embraced it and those who tended to cling to the Indian religions than had been the case in the diffusion of Catholicism.

Following World War I came some new developments in the diffusion of Protestantism. In the United States generally there were new trends in religious life. One of these was the proliferation of new Protestant sects such as the Holiness Church and the Assemblies of God, sects which emphasized the individual conversion experience, "speaking in tongues," and the supreme importance of religion over other aspects of life. During the 1920's and 1930's new missionaries representing such sects appeared on the reservations in New Mexico and Arizona — the Church of the Nazarene, the Free Methodists, the Assembly of God, the Southern Baptists, and a number of independent groups such as the Good News Mission, the Navajo Gospel Mission, the Navajo Bible School, and the Brethren in Christ. These raised the total number of Christian sects at work converting Indians on the reservations of the two states to twenty-six. While to some extent the older established denominations had altered their uncompromising attitude toward Indian religion and had settled down to a more patient and tolerant approach, at the same time increasingly emphasizing social and medical services, the new sects reintroduced the approach of no compromise with strict religious behavior. Their representatives were obviously often at odds with the longer established groups and hence sectarian exclusiveness was given a new impetus among the Indians. The

new missionaries were working in a general situation of increasing poverty among
the Indians, increasing clash between Indian ways and Anglo ways, and increasing
attitudes of dependency on government or resources outside of Indian society. In
this atmosphere all of the new sects gained adherents. They made extensive use
of charity, collecting and giving out to poorer Indians clothing and various other
goods. They worked among all the tribes of the Southwest except the Havasupai
and one independent revivalist carried his operations among the Seris in Sonora.
The impact was primarily the increase of sectarian feeling among the tribes where
they worked. Usually the sects gained influence quickly at first, as among the San
Carlos Apaches and in some Navajo areas, then tended to lose adherents as the
strictness of their behavior code became apparent and Indians became aware of
their implacable opposition to most Indian customs of family life. Small numbers
wherever they worked, however, remained devoted converts. Their greatest influence was attained among segments of Apaches, Navajos, and some Pimas, the
poorest and most disorganized and conflict-torn groups. The Eastern Pueblos,
Zunis, Hopis, and those Yaquis who had settled in Arizona among whom they
worked appeared to remain almost impervious.

A second influence following World War II was also an integral part of United
States religious trends generally. Quakers and Unitarians had developed during
the 1920's and 1930's a conception of secular social service as a part of what they
called their Service Committees. These groups set up "Indian Centers" in cities
where many Indians came as transients, in an effort to provide a place to stay other
than the streets or the cheap rooming houses. During the 1940's and 1950's these
centers in Gallup, Phoenix, and Los Angeles became important influences of the
nature of the "settlement house" where young Indians of all the Southwestern
tribes became acquainted with one another. In addition, the Quakers instituted
what they called self-help programs among the Papagos, Maricopas, and Apaches.
These consisted of encouraging local committees to discuss and take action on
practical problems. Participation did not entail the adoption of any religious beliefs or practices, but the Quaker representatives introduced a new type of religious
believer to Indians — Protestant-like in many ways, but less exclusive and non-
proselytizing.

THE RISE OF NEW RELIGIONS

New religions have often arisen among defeated and oppressed people, people
looking for a new hope in the midst of ruin. Christianity arose in this way and
became, through a remarkable series of circumstances, one of what we call the
world religions. No one knows how many religions have arisen under similar conditions — and died out. The Cargo Cults of the natives of New Guinea, the Messianic movements of oppressed Jews of the ghettos of eastern Europe, and the Ghost
Dance of the North American Indians we know something about, but there must
have been many more about whose hopes and whose struggles nothing is known,
for conquest and oppression have not been rare in human history.

The entrance of the Spaniards into northwestern New Spain was heralded by a new religious movement on the borders of the Tarahumara country. The Tepehuanes, rapidly missionized by the Jesuits, fell enthusiastically under the leadership of a prophet after some twenty years of apparent acceptance of the Christian missions. A stone image was believed to speak and to foretell the destruction of the Spaniards. The Indians fought to fulfill the prophecies and only gave up their hopes after a bloody war that lasted through the year of 1618. The Tarahumaras from time to time for the next hundred years listened to similar prophecies and sometimes killed missionaries and soldiers in the belief that they had supernatural power which made them invulnerable to Spanish bullets. These beliefs, promulgated by an occasional prophet, never became organized into a religious movement even as unified as that of the Tepehuanes. It was possible for the missionaries to regard the outbreaks as inspired merely by isolated "witches" rather than as a concerted movement based on a new set of beliefs, which they had recognized in the Tepehuan rebellion. The wisps of information available concerning the Tarahumara uprisings suggest nevertheless that the conditions set up in the form of forced labor in the mines of Chihuahua, the determined missionary effort to force people to live under strict discipline in concentrated towns, the suppression of ceremonies, and the repeated devastation of rancherías by the soldiers encouraged religious leaders of the prophet type. No "new religion" arose, probably because of the unintegrated nature of Tarahumara religious life as well as of their social organization, but the need for it was evidently sufficiently there to inspire an occasional prophet.

Other major uprisings of Indians in northwestern New Spain during the 1600's and 1700's cannot be attributed to new religious movements. The Pueblo Revolt of 1680 was a political-military effort to preserve an old religion. It was a revolt against political and religious oppression, but its leaders were offering nothing new in the way of religious belief. The old religion had not been destroyed, and it was in its name that the revolt was carried through. Nor can the destructive Mayo-Yaqui revolt in 1740 be attributed to newly-inspired religious beliefs; insofar as we know what happened it appears to have been set off by a conflict of authority in town government, and there was definitely no tendency before or after toward any deviation from the century-long growth of Catholicism which had become rooted among the Yaquis and Mayos. The Seri revolt a little later was over the appropriation of land and deportation of women, with no religious aspects, except marked continuing respect for Jesuits, and the Upper Pima rebellions can be classed as political rather than religious movements.

The Spanish conquest period, north of the Tepehuanes, was indeed singularly free of any instances of the rise of new religions. It was only during the last phases of the conquest, carried out by Mexicans and Anglo-Americans, that such movements began to appear. The earliest of which there is clear record was the appearance of the Ghost Dance among the Walapais in 1889. The Ghost Dance originated among the Paiute Indians whose territory bordered on the Walapais to the north. It was a Messianic cult preached by a Paiute named Wovoka, or Jack Wilson, who claimed to have received a revelation of supernatural power. The hopes involved in the cult obviously had their origin in the changes wrought by the Anglo-American advance into the western United States. The cult focused on the elimination of white men and the return of the Indian country to the Indians, with the return of the wild game and the restoration of old ways. The means for removal of the white men consisted in the performance of a dance, based on an old type of social dance. Men and women dancing in a circle with hands clasped moved round and round to the music of voice and drum. The prophet, Wovoka, held that the constant performance of the dance would restore all the dead Indians as well as bring back the old conditions of freedom and good hunting. No military or other forcible action was urged. The mere regular carrying out of the dance would bring the results that the Indians hoped for. The movement was called the Ghost Dance because of its hopes for the return of the dead ancestors. During the 1880's the new cult spread rapidly and widely. Most of the Indians of the western United States, who had experienced the steady encroachment of white men and often battles with the Whites, took it up. It was danced for six or seven years even more vigorously by many newly conquered tribes of the Plains region than by the mountain Indians of the far west.

In 1889 the Walapais took it up. This was at a time when they were in the midst of conflict with white cattlemen. As a scattered, unorganized tribe, they had been largely ignored by white settlers. But it was possible to raise cattle to advantage in their territory, and Whites moved in. They appropriated waterholes, pushed Indians out of their way, shot them when necessary, and thus seriously threatened the very existence of the Indians. The government had tried to move the Indians to the Colorado River Reservation, but the Walapais had refused to stay. At the time the Ghost Dance appeared among them most had become hangers-on around the mining town of Kingman, poverty-stricken and despised by the white settlers. At some distance from Kingman, in 1889, they began a long series of Ghost Dance ceremonies. The participants included more than half the tribe. The ceremonial was to last until the desired results came. The Whites, as they did elsewhere in the western United States, became frightened that the dancing was preliminary to armed rebellion. It became apparent, however, that only magical means were to be used for the destruction of the Whites and the Indians were permitted to carry on their ceremonials unmolested. After several weeks, food supplies had all been used up by the dancing Indians and gradually group by group they gave up their efforts, slowly returning to their state of dependency on the mining-town Whites. Bringing no clear, positive results the cult was short-lived and within three years completely died out.

From the Walapais the Ghost Dance spread to the Havasupais, where, however, it lasted only a year. Here its leader lost prestige when he made an effort to restore to life a particular dead man, without result. At the same time many Navajos were aware of the Ghost Dance. They, too, like the Walapais at this time, were experiencing White encroachment and sporadic violence. Yet no Navajos embraced the cult. The hope of bringing back the dead, an essential element in the Ghost Dance, was one which Navajos would not entertain. In Navajo belief the dead as ghosts were to be feared. Navajos feared a dead body from the moment of death, were reluctant to handle one for burial, and tore down the hogan in which anyone died. Most evil witch power was believed to come from corpses. Thus the Navajos would have regarded the return of the dead as a great calamity. The Ghost Dance influenced some Apaches on the Fort Apache Reservation, but elsewhere in Arizona and New Mexico Indians had no interest whatever in the new religion.

About the same time — from 1890 to 1892 — another prophet cult arose among the Mayos in southern Sonora. It had no ritual features whatever in common with the Ghost Dance, but it shared a similar hope. In 1890 on the Cocoraqui Wash at Cabora, which was the traditional boundary line between the Mayo and Yaqui territory, a girl named Teresa Urrea began to experience visions which she explained to her father in the Mayo language. Her father, Tomás, encouraged her once he learned the nature of the visions. One of the important myths in the Mayo-Yaqui mythology which had developed since the entrance of the Jesuits was a flood myth which described how the whole Yaqui-Mayo country had been flooded at the beginning of things. A few beings were saved by taking refuge on mountain tops, and these became the ancestors of the Indians. Teresa had begun to dream that a flood was coming to the Mayo country and that all who did not take refuge on certain spots, which were revealed to her in her visions, would be destroyed. The Mayos at this time had just been reconquered by the Mexicans after participation with the Yaquis in the series of battles that had begun about 1875, under the leadership of the Yaqui Cajeme. Mayo towns had been occupied by Mexican troops and most able-bodied Mayos had been forced to go to work on the haciendas of Mexicans in and beyond the Mayo country. The people were short of food and times were extremely hard.

The news of Teresa's visions spread everywhere in the Mayo country. Minor prophets began to have visions of the same sort and, taking up positions on high ground designated by Teresa, began to preach the new revelation. During 1890 seven or eight additional prophets or preachers appeared. So many Mayo laborers gathered to hear them, staying night and day, that the Mexican army officials began to fear that an uprising was brewing. They found instead that the people were gathering in expectation of the flood on the points of refuge and that they were listening peacefully to the preachers and expecting that the flood would destroy the hacendados and all other Mexicans. The Mexicans broke up the meetings and jailed the preachers, but the movement was not stopped. Teresa was not jailed and went on dreaming. Her influence continued strong among the Mayos. The rough treatment of the preachers inspired violence. In 1892 a nondescript party of armed Mayos attacked Navojoa, the largest Mexican settlement in the Mayo country, shouting, "Long Live the Saint of Cabora." The Mayos were promptly repulsed and punished by the Mexicans, and Santa Teresa and her father were taken into custody along with other sympathizers. There were repercussions of the movement in the Tarahumara country at Tomochic. Ultimately Teresa was deported out of the Mayo country and went to Arizona, where she took up residence near Tumacacori. For a time she lived there and gained fame as a curer, but her prophetic visions ceased, and the religious movement she had inspired on the

Mayo River died out altogether. Although thousands of Mayos had listened and believed what Teresa said, her visions made no impression whatever on Yaquis. This was true despite the fact that conditions of poverty and oppression were even worse in the Yaqui towns than among the Mayos. The Yaquis apparently were not relying on magical means for removing Mexicans from their territory.

Another short-lived prophetic cult took hold of a small group of Papagos in 1906. It differed from the Ghost Dance and Saint of Cabora cults in that it envisioned the destruction of the whole world, not merely the white men. It probably had its origin in the preaching of an itinerant Protestant revivalist in Phoenix who may have preached the end of the world. At any rate a group of fairly well-to-do families living in the southeastern part of the Papago country, where Presbyterianism later made its entry, began to believe that the world was coming to an end and that therefore it was useless to work anymore. They assembled their cattle and all food resources they could muster and retired to the Comobabi Mountains. They expected the end to come before their food ran out but this was not the case. With all their stores gone and the fulfillment of the prophecy not indicated, they left the mountain and returned to their homes. The beliefs did not spread beyond this small group of families from a single village, nor had they appeared again up to 1960.

Another movement which affected some Papagos, but was chiefly influential among Gila Pimas, went by the name of the Montezumas. Strictly speaking, it was not a religious movement in the sense of resting on supernatural belief. Yet it had religious repercussions and in some ways affected Pimas and Papagos as a religious movement. About 1918 a man of Yavapai ancestry who had in childhood been captured by Pimas and sold as a slave came to Sacaton on the Pima Reservation and began to hold meetings. He was Dr. Carlos Montezuma. Since his early childhood, after being brought up by a frontier photographer of Italian descent, he had lived as an Anglo-American. He had gone to Chicago, where he worked his way through medical school and later became a successful practicing physician. He had become increasingly interested in the condition of Indians on United States reservations and especially in the serious economic plight of the Pimas, whose loss of irrigation water and consequent poverty had been given publicity widely over the United States by various Indian defense organizations. Montezuma began to publish a small magazine in which he advocated the abolition of the Indian Bureau and the elimination of government authority from Indian affairs. About 1918 he came to Arizona to preach his viewpoint among the Pimas, Papagos, Yavapais, and Western Apaches. His meetings at Sacaton on the Pima Reservation gained him many adherents, who were deeply dissatisfied with reservation conditions; at the same time he incurred the disapproval of the Indian Bureau. After several years of preaching he died of tuberculosis on the Salt River Reservation.

His influence survived him for some twenty-five years, but was most marked during the 1920's. His appeal had been based chiefly on the dignity and worth of the Indian racial and cultural heritage. He preached that Indian ways were fundamentally sounder than white man's ways and that Indians should cleave to their traditions in religion and moral behavior and not look to the Whites for guidance.

The oppressive and demoralizing program of the Indian Bureau was a prime example of White immorality. Indians should reassume the independence they had practiced before the Indian Bureau had taken them over, take up their land again in their own name, and demonstrate the fundamental greatness of the Indian way of life. The preaching was not wholly anti-White, it was rather completely anti-Indian Bureau; and its positive feature consisted in the assertion of the great value of Indianhood. The ideas of Dr. Montezuma were not unique in the United States; they were to a considerable extent parallel with ideas which had been discussed and advocated for thirty or forty years by the various Indian defense organizations. Dr. Montezuma's influence differed from that of any of the organizations in that he made a personal and direct appearance among some Indians and spoke with the authority of an Indian who had accepted wholly and with success the white man's way, but who had returned to the clear view of the worth of the Indian way.

With Dr. Montezuma's death in 1922, no organized movement came into existence. It was apparent that his influence had been very diffuse, but it had been powerful here and there. Some older Pima leaders had listened to him with eagerness and had accepted thoroughly his view of the destructive and evil role of the Indian Bureau; the idea fell into fertile ground among such elders who had lived through the period of the steady destruction of Pima agriculture by White farmers and the inability of the Indian Bureau to prevent it. On into the 1930's there were older men on the Pima Reservation who refused to deal with the Indian Bureau superintendent, who were called "Montezumas" by others, and who preached the necessity for the old Indian morality. Even stronger through the northern part of what had become the Papago Reservation, Montezuma's ideas became the basis of a conservative faction which remained unorganized, but probably had at least initial influence on the formation of the League of Papago Chiefs. The "Montezumas" of the northern Papago Reservation were older village headmen, men who were still maintaining the office of the Keeper of the Smoke, who still tried to keep up the practice of frequent moral exhortation. They wished for and advocated less contact with white men; many advised their children not to go to schools and attempted to scare them into not going by asserting that the children would be boiled to turn them White. There were among such men and their followers some attempts to adjust the tribal mythology; they believed that Jesus was really I-Itoy and some held that both Jesus and I-Itoy were Montezuma and that Montezuma would one day return and restore better times and good moral behavior. The Montezumas were not inclined to have any dealings with the Indian Bureau agency and tried to ignore it. Similarly, Dr. Montezuma's ideas gave support and sanction to older leaders among Yavapais on the Fort McDowell and San Carlos reservations and to Apaches at San Carlos. No organization of any sort developed however, and by 1950 Dr. Montezuma the man was but a vague memory to the Indians with whom he had come in contact. His ideas persisted under the general label of "Montezumas" among a few "conservative" old men on the Papago Reservation.

Only the Apaches, among all the Indians of the region, conceived a new religion which persisted for more than a few years. In contrast with the ephemeral and unorganized cults which have thus far been described, a religion now generally called by Apaches The Holy Ground religion grew up after 1920 among both Fort Apache and San Carlos Indians. Thirty-five years later it was still vigorous and its influence had spread beyond the Western Apaches to the Yavapais of central Arizona and the Mohaves and some other Yumans. The Holy Ground religion had a series of predecessors which had some of the characteristics of cults described above. Thus, in 1880 an Apache medicine man, Nocadelklinny, became the prophet of a short-lived movement which seems to have been inspired in part by the Ghost Dance. Nocadelklinny lived at Cibecue where he was widely known as a man with considerable supernatural power. In 1881 he announced that he would bring back to life not all the ancestral dead, but two formerly important war leaders — Diablo and Eskiole — of the Coyotero or White Mountain Band. Dances and rituals such as he prescribed were performed with no results. The chiefs did not come back to life. Nocadelklinny then said that his supernatural power had given him to understand that all Whites would have to be exterminated before the transformation of the dead leaders could be brought about and that this should begin with certain dances. Hundreds of Apaches in the vicinity of Cibecue and Fort Apache became interested and began to listen to Nocadelklinny and to dance. This was a period of tension and trouble on the Apache reservations. Miners and Mormon settlers had been encroaching on the reservations. Indian agents, in a succession following Clum, had been corrupt. Army officers at Fort Apache feared that Nocadelklinny's activities presaged a general uprising. They attempted to arrest him at Cibecue, precipitating a battle with his followers. Nocadelklinny was killed. Nantiatish, another Cibecue medicine man, then assumed leadership and tried to organize an uprising, which however failed to gain a general following after attacks on the San Carlos agency and the mining town of McMillenville were put down in 1882. The Nocadelklinny movement died out.

Subsequently, before 1910, another general movement led by several medicine men gained influence in the Fort Apache area, but little is known about this. It no doubt provided some foundations for the third movement which began just before 1920 and persisted down through 1960. This movement had a leader from near Fort Apache who was known as Silas John. He had gained supernatural power in the usual Apache manner; it took the form of special power with snakes. He held ceremonies in which many snakes were used and which were rendered powerless in Silas John's hands. The ceremonies were designed to cure illness and many miraculous cures were believed to have come about. Silas John's reputation increased and his ceremonies were widely attended. He is said to have been a member of a Catholic congregation and introduced some features of Catholic ritual into his ceremonies. By 1921 his influence had spread throughout both the Fort Apache and the San Carlos reservations. The period was one of hard times for Apaches: influenza epidemics in 1918 killed many Indians; in the depression of 1920-21 mines where Apaches worked were shut down; agriculture was curtailed when settlers upstream from the San Carlos agency diverted water; food was scarce; and Mormon settlers were encroaching on the northwestern part of the Fort Apache reservation near Show Low. Under these circumstances the Silas John movement gained many adherents.

Some of the viewpoint of his followers is indicated in the following letter sent to the superintendent at the San Carlos agency and signed by twenty-five San Carlos Apaches and Yavapais in August, 1921:

We the undersigned hereby request that we be permitted to hold Indian Prayer Service every Sunday on our Prayer Grounds. One year ago we began trying to do away with all evil habits, such as drinking, stealing, and finally to influence them to live a clean life, a Godly life; so far, we have, by talking to all the Indians, induced them to do away with drinking, gambling; we have about three hundred or more who come to our meetings and seem anxious to hear, and take home each Sunday what we try to have them do.

The purpose of this meeting is to teach every one of our Creator and the life of Jesus Christ, and that each one must worship only two highest beings.

As heretofore we have been worshipping things such as the sun, the different movements of clouds, winds, stars and many other things which God created, the same as we are; at the same time we are rapidly doing away with the medicine men, who in years past have been among us, and from practicing medicine have taken from us the best we had in horses, cattle, saddles and money.

This we are dealing with. We have been all our lives and have accomplished nothing in the way of advancement; the Missionaries have been among us, a failure it seems. They tend more to learn our language and tend more to introduce our singing.

So in the year 1920, we ... called together a few of our leading Indians and decided to take this step, to hold a Prayer Meeting every Sunday which is open to all our Indians who desire to come here.

The Indians (Apache) of this Reservation are now coming to our meeting from Peridot, and few from Bylas. All of the Indians of San Carlos attend. Seeing that we have been able to induce many of our Indians, we desire to continue our service as we see the Indians have and are listening. They go about now different what it used to be one year ago, no tulapai, stealing not fighting and less trouble.

We are pleased with the advance movement, and we are pleased to learn that many Indians are in hearty accord with continuing our Prayer Meeting. It means an aid to our Indian Bureau and to our Government, and the coworkers of the Government in the field.

We, the Undersigned, also are putting forth every effort to safeguard every man, woman, boy and girl, and have on the ground men and women, known by all who help along with our work not only there but at the camps, and away from home wherever they may be. The Service is conducted in the Indian tongue, as the leaders are non-English speaking.

Believing that it will not be well to force civilized church work on our people, who have for past unknown ages, been untouched by such proceedings; we desire to take step by step, and if fate does not interfere hope to induce our Apache Indians to live a pure Christian life, such as they never dreamed of. Those who come and help along with our work are all expressing a feeling of Brotherly Love and cooperation, we are,

Very respectfully ...

This letter was followed by another five months later, addressed likewise to the superintendent and signed by twenty-four Apaches from the settlement north of the San Carlos agency at the boarding school of Rice. It requested the same privileges as those the San Carlos agency people had asked for, namely, "to have our Religious Sermonies and without being molested by Agitators."

Permission to maintain the "Prayer Grounds" and to hold regular Sunday meetings was granted. The new movement was challenged by the minister of the Lutheran mission as a return to paganism, but when he refused to debate with Silas John publicly his opposition was ignored by Apaches. Hundreds of Apaches continued to attend the Sunday services and an annual ceremony attended by all adherents from both reservations was instituted. The strength of the movement was established, so well in fact that various missionaries began to regard it as a threat to their work. Their antagonism to Silas John became definite and open. In 1933 he was accused of murdering his wife and was convicted. His followers remained convinced that he was innocent. During the twenty years that he spent in jail from 1934 to 1954 they maintained communication with him. He continued to think about and develop the ritual, and followers who come to visit him went back to the reservations with diagrams and instructions for carrying on the various ceremonies. He remained a vigorous source of inspiration throughout his years in jail, and many leading Apaches became adherents. On his return to the San Carlos Reservation in 1954 he was enthusiastically welcomed and began immediately to lead and take part in the annual round of ceremonies on the reservations.

The Holy Ground religion was a combination of concepts, rituals, and moral rules from Protestant and Catholic Christianity and the old Apache religious system, with the latter predominating. Although it centered in the leadership of Silas John, it was carried out by Apache men and women, called "disciples," who constituted an organized group. They permitted medicine men, whose power was derived from the old Apache sources of animals and features of the natural world, to practice their curing ritual as a part of ceremonies; but the medicine men had to conform to certain requirements of the new religion, the most important of which was the performance of their ritual within the space ceremonially defined as "The Holy Ground," which was the scene of all the ceremonies. The fundamental beliefs consisted in the belief in God, spoken of as a supreme power, and in Naiyenesgani. The latter was the name for one of the Twin War God Monster Slayers of old Apache mythology, who were sons of the sun, as the result of a virgin birth. Naiyenesgani was associated in the new religion with *goshlatagoletn*, "sitting above the clouds," who was identified by some as Silas John who was also, therefore, the Son of God. Silas John had the power of this Son of God or Monster Slayer, rather than being the Son of God himself. This power could be used for curing either directly by Silas John himself or by other men with supernatural power who derived it through the Son of God. The power could be used also for a variety of other purposes, such as bringing rain and eliminating evil feelings.

In each community the ceremonies centered about a specially designated area which was rectangular, the four sides of which were marked by crosses colored according to the old Apache four directional associations — black for east, green for south, yellow for west, and white for north. The four-directional arrangement and the color associations in a ceremonial circuit in the order given above ran through most ceremony. A sign of the cross similar to a Catholic hand movement and the raising of the right hand with palm forward were prescribed individual actions punctuating ceremony. Circular ground paintings with different colored earth and sand were employed as an important part of many ceremonies. Processions with a variety of standards, singing of songs in Apache to the accompaniment of the Apache water drum, and the use of colored hoops were all features of ritual. Also the use of pollen as a sacred substance characterized the ceremonies.

By 1955 the ceremonies had come to be guarded from Anglo interference with a good deal of care, although it was not unknown for Anglos resident on the reservation to participate in the Sunday meetings, joining in the religious processions and the social dancing in the Apache style, which punctuated the ceremonies. Apache leaders of the movement maintained that the religion was a universal one, not only for Apaches. Nevertheless, Apaches were aware of the disapproval of missionaries and other Anglos and there had been occasional attempts to interfere in the services after Silas John had been sent to jail. The general summer ceremony was held as far as possible from the agency town and although Whites were not forcibly kept away, they were discouraged from coming. The annual ceremony drew five to six hundred people and continued for four days and nights.

The Holy Ground movement was the only vigorous and persisting new religion devised by the Indians of the region, unless we classify the Yaqui variation of Catholicism as a new religion. The blend of Christianity and old religion which the Apaches achieved, however, was very different from the Yaqui. In the first place it was a much simpler system of belief and practice, lacking the elaborate organization, very great degree of specialization of ritual, and large number of complexly interrelated concepts which characterized Yaqui religion. Moreover, Christian concepts penetrated only to the extent of accepting nominally the supreme position of God (and even this was not clear), the likewise not too clear identification of Jesus and Naiyenesgani, and the acceptance of a Protestant-like moral system and behavior taboos; Christian ritual was manifest only in the use of a modified hand sign of the cross and the prominence of the cross as a symbol which also had a native precedent in four-directional symbolism. Beliefs were explained by Apaches primarily with reference to the old mythology dealing with the sun, his monster-slaying twin sons, and other Apache myths. Parallels were certainly drawn between Jesus and other Christian figures, but this was merely auxiliary. The story of Jesus, the role of Mary, and Old Testament world-beginning stories were not accepted. The old basis of belief had been only slightly modified. The new religion was a new one primarily in its organization into a church form of congregation with a regular ceremonial calendar centering in the week and the efforts of its leaders constantly to relate its teachings to the moral problems of its adherents. In these respects it was very different from the old unrelated curing ceremonies which had constituted the elements of Apache religion. In these respects also it certainly showed the influence of the church organizations which had become established on the Apache reservations. Perhaps also in its universal character, it revealed some influence from Christian teaching, but it did not require a personal experience of conversion for participation in its activities.

The other new religion which was active in the region in the 1950's was the Native American Church. This was not an invention of any of the tribes in the region but had diffused to them from Indians in Oklahoma who had organized the church in the 1890's. The Native American Church was a religious group which employed as its central rite the eating of the cactus button, peyote. The system of beliefs and rituals combined some Christian-derived elements, such as the belief in Jesus as a source of spiritual inspiration, and other elements derived from the old ceremonial systems of the Delaware and other Indian tribes who had been sent to Oklahoma by the United States government. The moon as a female deity and ground altars were examples of such elements. The religion centered around the practice of group eating of the peyote buttons. Such a group gathered in a house or other structure, sat in a circle, and consumed the buttons. The effect of the peyote consisted in the inducement of visions of various kinds and, when eaten in the group, feelings of well-being and group identification. A usual accompaniment of peyote-eating was the passing of a drum to each participant successively, who then accompanied himself while singing songs known as the peyote songs. A session was ordinarily an all-night affair and was terminated with forced vomiting about dawn by each member of the group. The Native American Church existed as early as 1900 as an organized institution with a national head and staff of officers. It carried on missionary work among many Indian groups, proselytization which steadily increased through the 1950's.

The first New Mexican tribe to show interest in the Native American Church was Taos village among the eastern Pueblos. Peyote buttons had been used there traditionally as a specific cure against illnesses caused by witchcraft, but the use of peyote had never developed into a cult. In the 1890's a young Taos man who had been educated in Pennsylvania at Carlisle took an interest in the peyote ceremony and introduced it to other young men in the village. Soon a group was established which regularly carried out the peyote-eating ceremonies. Their activities were opposed by the village leaders, especially as the "peyote boys," as they were called, began to curtail their participation in the traditional village ceremonial life.

Attempts were made by the village hierarchy to forcibly suppress the new rites and oust the peyote-eaters from the village. These were unsuccessful and a feud developed between the families of the "peyote boys" and other families. The peyote cult became more entrenched in the lives of the group that had adopted it, but it did not spread as the opposition to it by the ceremonial leaders crystallized. It continued to exist, and its practitioners increasingly withdrew from other religious activities, constituting a source of conflict for fifty years at Taos. Its attempted introduction was resisted at San Juan village, and it spread nowhere else among the Eastern Pueblos, except for its adoption by a lone practitioner in Santa Clara village.

Although Native American Church missionaries worked as far west and south as the Papagos, nowhere else in the Southwest was the religion adopted for the forty years following its introduction at Taos. But during World War II in the early 1940's, it began to be taken up by Navajos, chiefly in the extreme north-eastern part of the reservation where many different religious sects had concentrated their activities and where the Indian Bureau had instituted a resettlement project on newly irrigated land. Here, in the vicinity of Fruitland, New Mexico, peyote-eating groups of Navajos were formed. Gradually the religion spread westward until by 1955 there were some two thousand members of the Native American Church. Its spread was opposed by the Navajo Tribal Council, on the ground that peyote was a habit-forming drug, until it was pointed out that medical opinion in the United States was not in agreement on the matter. The Tribal Council then on the principle of religious freedom ceased to oppose it. Nevertheless, the fact that the use of a drug was a necessary feature of the religious ritual constantly brought the practitioners of the religion into conflict with Anglo-Americans. Navajo groups who carried on their ceremonies off the reservation were raided by police, and newspapers took up campaigns against the religion. Nevertheless, by 1960 the influence of the Native American Church was rapidly growing among Navajos. As a religion which combined some elements of Christian belief with generalized Indian traits it fitted well into the mixed culture patterns of many Navajos who had worked extensively off the reservation, and appealed as well to many Navajos who felt antagonistic towards Anglos and saw in the Native American Church an institution which they themselves could control locally. It also fit into the growing awareness on the part of Navajos of many other Indians in the United States with similar reservation background and relations with Anglos. Its spread was related to a pan-Indian type of feeling which had grown up widely over the Southwest as a result primarily of large public performances such as the Gallup Ceremonials participated in by Indian dancers and musicians from many reservations. Yet by 1960 the Native American Church had spread nowhere else among Southwestern Indians. It was confined to a declining cult in Taos and a rapidly growing movement among the Navajos.

The new religions which took hold in the Southwest affected with greatest intensity the Mayos, the Navajos, and the Apaches. The Mayo new religion was very short-lived once forcible suppression of its leaders had been applied. The other groups, with the exception of Walapais, Havasupais, some Papagos, and Tarahumaras who embraced cults very briefly, did not develop intense interest in new religions. By the middle of the 1900's the Apache Holy Ground religion seemed the strongest rooted and most influential. Yet it, too, seemed to be giving way in the late 1950's to a new type of evangelistic Protestant movement, a few years after the return from jail of Silas John.

THE PERSISTENCE OF INDIAN RELIGIONS

The great variety in Indian religious belief and practice which was characteristic of the states of New Mexico, Arizona, Chihuahua, and Sonora by the middle of the twentieth century was partly a result of the persistence of the native religions as whole systems or surviving parts. Religious diversity was greater in this region than in any other part of the United States or Mexico because of the special geographical, political, and economic factors which had operated to permit or to foster the survival of the native cultures in the face of both Catholic and Protestant invasion. Elsewhere in North America there were not so many culturally distinct peoples at the time of Spanish entrance, and conquest and post-conquest conditions had forced a far greater leveling of cultural differences.

The survival of Indian religion in the face of the systematic missionary efforts of Christians was by no means a matter only of the persistence of odds and ends of belief. There were among all the groups such piece-meal survivals, sometimes compartmentalized in the minds of converted Christian Indians and tagged by them as superstitions, sometimes held as respectable beliefs the inconsistency of which with new ideas had somehow not become apparent to the holders. There were also Indians who had not become members of Christian congregations who lived by a medley of beliefs which derived mostly from the old religions but which were no longer held together by a clear sense of the values which they had expressed. There were in other words survivals of the old which Indians had not been able to adjust to the new conditions of life and which accordingly existed in their minds as unrelated ideas and customs. Every Christian congregation on the reservations was, as it were, surrounded by and partly interpenetrated with such no-longer-functional remnants.

But there were also Indian religions which functioned as systems of belief and daily practice which ordered the universe and gave meaning to life for their participants. The Seris on the margins of the civilizational advance on their desert coast believed in spirits and maintained a view of the universe which could in no sense be said to have been inspired by the Jesuit missionaries and which contained, even after a few years of Protestant evangelization in the 1950's, only superficial Christian influence. A considerable number, although perhaps a minority by 1960, of Navajos, shielded from the ever-intensifying and multi-form missionary attack in the isolated parts of their large reservation, saw the world still as bounded by four sacred mountains and their place in it as influenced by spirits who had come up from an underworld. In the Hopi Mesa villages a round of dramatic ceremonies continued year after year, the meaning of which was well preserved in old beliefs that held deep significance for many people. Among Zunis and the Eastern Pueblos there were likewise, even though Catholic churches existed in all the villages, a round of ceremony and a system of belief that constituted vital religions, quite distinct from and in some ways wholly incompatible with the beliefs which the visiting priests expounded to them at periodic intervals.

CHAPTER EIGHTEEN

Economic Integration

A MAJOR FEATURE of cultural development in the Southwest was the lag of economic behind political, religious, and other aspects of change in Indian cultures. After some four hundred years of contact, the one aspect of the situation on which segments of Anglo and Mexican population showed greatest agreement was the economic. It was widely accepted that Indians were economically backward.

In the 1950's programs for change in Indian life by the Mexican and the United States governments were concerned chiefly, although not exclusively, with accelerating the rate of economic change. This was partly a result of the prevailing high valuation of economic development by the classes who controlled the governments of those countries and their consequent intense awareness of differences in standards of material life within the nation. The focus of governmental interest had steadily shifted to economic development during the hundred years between 1850 and 1950. At the level of government planning the Spaniards had emphasized religious and social aspects of life. This emphasis had also appeared at the very first among Anglos concerned with Indian affairs. Since 1900, however, religious emphasis has steadily given way to economic concern among both Mexicans and Anglos.

In the 1950's there were sharp differences between the economic life of groups identifying themselves as Indians and the invading peoples. It was not to be denied that Spaniards, Mexicans, and Anglos had always shown some concern about the differences and had all along paid some attention to remaking the Indian economic life. The differences that did exist in the 1950's were not only a result of the failure in the application of such programs but also of contradictions in the economic and political life of Mexicans and Anglos. The federal governments and the settlers in Indian country repeatedly came into conflict over the issue of the place of Indians in the national economies. These conflicts often resulted in decisive shifts in policy, so that adjustments veered in different directions, and Indian economies had less stability even than the rapidly changing national economies of Mexico and the United States. The lack of consistent policy with reference to economic development in the programs for civilization was one of their most conspicuous features; and this was rooted deeply in inherent conflicts in the invading cultures.

The lag in the development of Indian economies was in part also a result of rapid changes in Mexican and Anglo economies in the fifty-year period preceding 1950. With increasing acceleration, the basis and the nature of agriculture underwent profound changes, shifting from small- to large-scale production with corresponding changes in economic organization. At the beginning of these changes the Indian communities were operating at a low level of production on a very small scale; as the Mexicans and Anglos rapidly outstripped them the gap between Indian and White economic life widened. As industrialization of the region proceeded, especially in the late 1940's after World War II, the Indians not only became backward farmers in contrast with Whites but also poorly integrated participants in the new industrial developments.

A major influence affecting the economic position of the Indians had been a relative lack of interest of the invaders in the exploitation of either Indian labor or resources until late in their contact with the natives. The conquerors at first showed interest in Indian labor for the production of some goods, but this turned out not to be profitable except in the Chihuahua and Sonora mines — and here not for very long — so that labor exploitation, in contrast with colonial developments in central Mexico, was of minor influence. Gradually the interest of the invaders focused down simply on the agricultural land of the Indians. This resulted in pushing the Indians on to the less productive land wherever possible, with consequent isolation of the Indians from the economy developing around them.

The isolative tendency was the dominant trend from the early 1700's until the 1940's. This expressed itself in many ways and with greatly varying results in different parts of the Southwest. With small beginnings in the 1890's and early 1900's, however, a new tendency developed. This was a growing interest on the part of both Mexicans and Anglos in the Indians, small as their groups were, as a labor supply in connection with, first, the transportation requirements of the developing civilization, then the mines contributing to the industrial expansion of the United States, and finally the growing large-scale agricultural production in the region. The shift from isolation of the Indians which characterized the long middle period of contact to their incorporation into the general economy as laborers was well along by the mid-1900's and seemed to be steadily accelerating. It impinged on the groups differently and at different times according to geographical position.

The later phase of economic integration was marked by great complexity rather than uniformity of process, in contrast with the earlier phase, during which a fairly consistent development had taken place. It was marked by greatest variation in the United States, where special forms of economic integration took place on reservations, usually inconsistent with the general trend of surrounding economic development. Further complicating the new phase was the discovery in the 1950's of mineral resources on some reservations, giving rise to yet another trend.

THE DECLINE OF FARMING

In the 1500's, among all the tribes of northwestern New Spain except the Seri coastal bands, agriculture had a secure place. For the Eastern and Western

Pueblos the raising of corn, beans, and squash had been fundamental for centuries, and farming was therefore knit intricately into their lives. It was in a sense their religion, since their major ceremonials were directly or indirectly agricultural rites, and the central values of their religious view were expressions of the agricultural way of life. To raise a field of corn annually was to live.

It is less clear that agriculture had so deep a place in the lives of the ranchería peoples. There is no question that the basic subsistence of most of them was derived from planting. But it is also clear that there was nothing like the close integration of religion and agriculture among them that existed for the Pueblos. Even the Pimas of the Gila River Valley, whose agriculture was technically elaborated at least to the same extent as the Rio Grande Pueblos, seem not to have focused their religious values so definitely around the growing of crops. Whether this was due to a relative recency, as compared with Pueblos, in the adoption of agriculture, or whether it was due to a relative ease of producing crops along large river courses such as the Mayo, Yaqui, Sonora, Gila, and Colorado rivers we do not know. Neither explanation would seem to hold generally for all the ranchería peoples. But this difference from the Pueblos did not mean that agriculture was unimportant in the lives of the ranchería peoples. It is true that many of the Upper Pimas gained more than half their subsistence from other sources than domestic crops, as did many of the Yumans, and all the ranchería peoples made extensive use of the abundant mesquite beans, cactus fruits, small game, and other wild products of their areas. But agriculture was nevertheless the pivot of their settlements and crops were a mainstay. Even for the Navajo and Western Apache bands the raising of corn was important and was becoming more so at the time of the coming of the Spaniards. The region was basically agricultural, and nearly all the people were farmers.

It was on those tribes who were most deeply committed to the agricultural way of life that the impact of the Spanish program fell most heavily. But it was probably their agricultural activities which were the least affected of all aspects of their lives. The program of the missionaries included the introduction of crops and tools not possessed by the Indians. These were accepted, almost *in toto* as offered, but their influence on the Indian systems of agricultural production was minor. What the Spaniards had to offer in the way of agricultural technology was, in the first place, two important tools, namely, the metal hoe and the plow. Iron gradually replaced stone hoes and wooden digging sticks among the Cahita, Lower Pimas, Opatas, and Eastern Pueblos. Perhaps the plow was only slowly accepted; it seems that digging sticks were still employed through the Spanish period and that metal for hoes was not abundant.

The effects of these technological improvements were not very far-reaching; the agriculture of the Eastern Pueblos remained on a small scale. Tribute in the form of agricultural produce was not exacted after the 1680 rebellion and the villages did not increase in size. Agricultural produce for the Spanish towns along the Rio Grande was supplied not by the Indian villages but rather by the haciendas and village lands of the colonizing Spaniards. Thus Pueblo agriculture was not forced or stimulated into any larger scale production and continued on the same basis as before the entry of the Spaniards, despite the more efficient tools employed.

There is no record that Eastern Pueblo standards of living increased during the Spanish period, or that agricultural production increased in any degree. The addition of new crops brought by the Spaniards was also without revolutionary effect. Fruits such as peaches, apples, grapes, and apricots were quickly adopted. But the agricultural staples of the ancient complex were not replaced as the basis of diet by the introduction of wheat and barley. It may be said that an increase in the variety of foods, without replacement of the basic dietary standard, and some increase in the efficiency of cultivation methods, were the only effects. The basic pattern of subsistence agriculture of the Eastern Pueblos was not altered.

In a general way this was the story in regard to Indian agriculture as influenced by Spanish culture everywhere in northwest New Spain. This was to be expected in view of the Spanish system which did not focus on agricultural development and which in Sonora and Chihuahua, as well as New Mexico, increasingly relied on Spanish colonists to furnish the towns with meat and grain beyond what was imported from farther south. But there were some exceptions. Thus we have seen that there was a temporary shift of some magnitude in Yaqui agricultural production under stimulus of the Jesuits, and this shift also involved not a replacement but a very important addition to the staple native crops, namely wheat. Yaqui wheat production was raised under Jesuit management to the point of a considerable surplus — how much we do not know — but certainly to the amount necessary for supplying beginning missions in the Upper Pima country and the unproductive missions of Lower California. Precisely how this came about is not known, but there is a suggestion that the surplus resulted from bringing more lands under cultivation. There is also an indication that the organization of Yaqui production for export was a very temporary condition, lasting perhaps not more than fifty years. For some time after the 1740 rebellion production returned to a low subsistence level and continued to decline after the expulsion of the Jesuits.

Another exception was the influence of the Spaniards on the one nonagricultural people, the Seri bands. The exposure of a small minority to mission life produced a vigorous interest in farming and settled life. Those who came in to the mission of Nuestra Señora de Pópulo were reported as being devoted to farming, to the point that they protested bitterly when their land was taken from them by the soldiers from the presidio of Pitic. After ruthless punishment for their protest, they left the mission. There is no record of interest in farming by Seris since then.

Elsewhere the impact of the mission community on Indian agriculture was confined to the improvement in efficiency noted. There was no trend toward integration with a larger economy. Indians neither produced special commodities nor raised greater quantities of crops for trade. As we shall see, the introduction of livestock was a significant factor for change in the total culture, but in general Spanish agricultural introductions had the effect of enhancing the existing agricultural orientations of the village and ranchería Indians, of reinforcement of the existing economies rather than of revolutionary change.

It was not until the late nineteenth century that the farming of the Yaquis and the Mayos, the Eastern and Western Pueblos, and the Upper Pimas began to be a part of a larger system of agricultural production. The decisive factor in the economic situation of the region was the increase in White population over the whole region. This began in Sonora and Chihuahua in the 1820's and continued slowly but steadily with accelerating migration into this frontier area from other parts of Mexico. Cities like Chihuahua and Hermosillo quadrupled their populations from 1820 to 1910 and thereafter increased even more rapidly. In New Mexico and Arizona the growth began later, in the 1870's and '80's, but at a far more rapid rate of acceleration. Albuquerque, El Paso, Phoenix, and Tucson were all cities of over 100,000 by 1950. And in the 1950's Chihuahua and Sonora cities began to match them in rate of growth. This urban expansion was accompanied by a great increase in cattle raising, in mining, and in irrigated agriculture. Although Indian population growth also increased after 1890, the total numbers of Indians remained small in comparison with the numbers of Mexicans and Anglos, constituting by 1960 less than one-ninth of the total. The agricultural production which developed in Chihuahua, Sonora, New Mexico, and Arizona was not only to supply the growing city-centers but also, and increasingly as irrigation projects expanded, for the national markets. Fruits, wheat, and cotton began to be important cash crops.

In this development the Indian farmers were not at first completely bypassed. The Gila Pimas during the 1850's and 1860's were important suppliers of food to the incoming Anglos; but they steadily lost their place in the market to the new settlers. Water for irrigation and land itself was appropriated not only from the Gila Pimas, but also from San Carlos Apaches who had begun a promising agricultural development in the early 1900's, from Eastern Pueblos, from Navajos, and from Mayos and Yaquis. The interests of Anglos and Mexicans became focused on acquiring Indian land and water, which they justified on the ground that Indian farming was too inefficient to warrant the Indians holding even as much land as remained to them. Indian holdings in the United States had been sharply limited by the assignment of reservations. In Sonora, reservations had not been set up for Mayos and Yaquis, but colonists in their territory were in constant conflict with them throughout the 1800's over water for the agricultural land. The result was that Indians wherever they engaged in farming ceased to produce for the expanding market, and in fact, as they were limited to smaller and more marginal tracts, produced less and less even to the point of not being able to supply their own needs. By the early 1900's few were any longer even reasonably secure subsistence farmers. Even the Eastern Pueblos who continued to hold good farm land along the Rio Grande River suffered a decline in production as the result of destructive floods caused by the uncontrolled use of range land and by encroachment of squatters on their lands. The Yaquis in Sonora were steadily pushed off their farm lands along the south side of the Yaqui River delta and confined to land on the north bank, which at the same time was deprived of the river floodwaters by the expanding Mexican irrigation projects to the south. There was, in short, not only an absence of Indian participation in the general agricultural expansion, but in most cases a real decline from the fairly adequate subsistence farming which they had developed during the Spanish period.

In Sonora in the 1890's there were some attempts by the state government, with federal aid, to develop the Yaqui lands through irrigation. Assignment of the lands so developed was made to the Yaquis, an especial effort being exerted to provide all Yaqui families. At the same time lands were also assigned to Mexican colonists in Yaqui territory with the aim not only of providing them with resources for development of the state but also of breaking up Yaqui tribal solidarity and thus eliminating the constant conflict. Conflict was not however eliminated but rather intensified. The ultimate result through flight and deportation was the destruction of agricultural production in the remaining Yaqui land, so that most Yaquis from the 1890's until the 1920's became agricultural laborers on haciendas in Sonora outside the Yaqui country. At the same time Mayos who did not become agricultural laborers continued as small-scale marginal farmers on the small acreages left to them scattered through the Mayo country. This condition continued until the 1920's, when the federal government made efforts to resettle Yaquis in the Yaqui country. Irrigation development planned by the federal government lagged; it was not until the late 1950's that water became available for production on a scale beyond that of small subsistence farms and a few scattered tracts where wheat was produced for a national market. After the completion with federal funds of an irrigation system on the north bank in 1956, some ejidos were organized, and production for the national market began to increase. Much hostility had developed, however, between Yaqui leadership and government organizers. It appeared that years might pass before agricultural production would be on a comparable basis with Mexican farmers.

In the United States, faced with the problem of increasing populations on limited and (with the exception of the Eastern Pueblos) generally marginal farm lands, the Indian Bureau sought to develop new land through irrigation and to improve production through the introduction of better crops and farm machinery. In the 1920's these efforts became well organized, through a division of the Bureau of Indian Affairs concerned exclusively with irrigation development. The general approach was that of providing all Indian families with plots of irrigated land of not more than ten acres. In some cases, as among the San Carlos Apaches, the efforts were directed toward providing "garden plots" of two or three acres for as many assignees as there was land. In other words, the conception behind the work was to entrench the small subsistence type of farming which had been traditional with the Pimas, Papagos and Pueblos and to introduce such farming more widely among the Apaches and some Navajos. The program generally consisted of the provision of the water source, through dams or wells, by government funds and government planning and execution; the preparation of the land by similar means; and, to get the Indians started, the provision of credit for purchase of seed and tools. The land was assigned or reassigned by the reservation superintendent.

This improvement and provision of farms resulted in general either in the abandonment of farming almost completely, as among the San Carlos Apaches, or in an uncertain attempt by Indians to accept what was given them. The uncertainty resulted from their having been removed from the planning and management of the land use and the inconsistent administration of the credit and other provisions. While a few Indians managed to make a living under these circumstances of subsistence farming, most went at it halfheartedly and found greater security in other forms of employment. By the 1940's programs of subsistence farming were completely inconsistent with the type of farming which had become dominant in the vicinity of the Indian reservations. That was a system of large-scale agriculture producing certain specialized cash crops such as cotton for a national market. This was the form of agriculture best suited to the expensive irrigation projects which had been developed. The subsistence farm plots of the Indians provided at best an ultimate slight security against failure to find off-reservation employment and an adjunct to cattle or stock raising or wage employment on the reservation.

The chief exception to this kind of low-level production on subsistence farms was to be found among the Eastern Pueblos and the Zunis, where Indian Bureau efforts resulted in a reconsolidation of the old Pueblo subsistence farming. Land was fertile here, water supply sufficient, and Bureau aid in land conservation more or less effective, so that Pueblo farming, both East and West, moved again on to the old basis, chiefly as subsistence farming, but with some slight production of a few crops for the local market among the Eastern Pueblos. By 1950 some Pueblos on the Rio Grande were deriving income by lease of some of their land to White farmers. After initial resistance in most Pueblos to the use of farm machinery, harvesters and tractors were being used and agricultural production was maintained at a level of efficiency comparable to that on surrounding farms. Only here did farming continue as the basic source of subsistence and only here was the economic life of the Indians not completely altered from its aboriginal state. The result, together with utilization of other income resources, was a fairly well-to-do farm population.

But this adjustment was within a larger economy. The Pueblos had been forced into the position of an aberrant group in a society to whom farming was no longer a vital orientation. At the same time, Pueblo children were subjected to forces similar to those moulding the majority of children in the United States and they did not by any means always look toward subsistence farming as the proper and ideal way of life. In this sense, there had been much change and the Pueblos were to be regarded as an enclave of farming people within the United States economy, comparable to such enclaves as the Old Order Amish and similar sectarian groups but with the important difference that they did not have their own schools.

One other exception to the general rule consisted of the Mohaves and Chemehuevis on the Colorado River Reservation, which remained one of the few truly large-scale potentially irrigable areas still held by Indians. This area was developed in the 1940's as an Indian Bureau program designed not only to provide large tracts for Mohaves and Chemehuevis to raise cash crops of alfalfa, but also to provide farms for resettled Indians from crowded reservations, such as Hopi, Navajo, and Papago. The efforts were successful in introducing Mohaves into the wider economy as alfalfa producers and leasers of land to White farming companies. However, the program of resettlement was blocked as the Colorado River tribes protested what they regarded as invasion of their land by other Indians. Resettlement was discontinued in 1957.

It appeared therefore in 1960 that insofar as farming was concerned, Indians with the exception of some Mohaves had nowhere been moved into the agricultural economies of the United States or Mexico. Nor, with the exception of the Eastern

Pueblos, had they continued as successful subsistence farmers marginal to that economy. Rather, farming had been disrupted as a satisfactory economic pursuit and had steadily lost its meaning as a way of life.

THE INTRODUCTION OF LIVESTOCK

The Indians, as farmers, were progressively isolated from the economic systems which grew around them, first under the Jesuit system of transition mission communities, then as they lost out in the competition for land with the Anglo and Mexican settlers and finally in the United States, through government efforts to re-establish them as enclaves of subsistence farmers. However, the isolative trend was counterbalanced for some of the larger groups as a result of the introduction of livestock.

The immediate effects of the introduction of livestock were not in the direction of linkage with the national economy of Spain so much as in the strengthening of Indian subsistence farming. Cattle and sheep were introduced in small numbers to the Eastern Pueblos and very gradually assumed a solid place in Pueblo economic life. In the 1700's they were made use of throughout the Pueblo villages, meat and wool being staple products, but in no Pueblo village had livestock assumed the place of more than an adjunct to the still dominant small-scale farming. Livestock, for a time at least, probably had more far-reaching effects on the economy of the Mayos and Yaquis. Here some large herds of cattle had been developed by the late 1600's and evidently constituted an important addition to the food supply, but again with the decline of the Jesuit agricultural establishments in the late 1700's they ceased to be important, although they were still utilized. Livestock did not become important among the Upper Pimas generally until the Anglo invasion in the late 1800's, although domestic animals were allowed to range and were killed for meat in various parts of the Upper Pima country following Father Kino's introduction of them at the mission centers. The Tarahumaras accepted cattle and goats and, to a lesser degree, sheep from the first arrival of the Jesuits and continued on into the 1900's to raise them on a small scale as an addition to their corn, beans, and squash. The effects on the economic life of the village and ranchería peoples were thus important as an addition to the farming economy, but did not result in any considerable shift in the economic activities or way of life.

The effects of the initial introduction of livestock on the band peoples were far more remarkable. They could in fact justifiably be called revolutionary. The impact on the more nomadic band peoples, such as the Navajos and the Apaches, continued to build up slowly for nearly 150 years after the first Spanish entradas. As the state of Sonora opened up to mining in the latter part of the 1600's, and after the suppression of the Pueblo Revolt in the 1690's it became apparent that the ways of life of these Athapaskan-speaking peoples had begun to undergo a radical readjustment from their aboriginal patterns. The presence of livestock — sheep, goats, cattle, horses — in New Mexico and Sonora stimulated the Athapaskan-speaking people to a predatory, parasitic way of life. It is possible that before this they were living to some extent as periodic raiders of the Eastern Pueblo villages, but it is certain that they undertook to live to a large degree by raiding in the period marked by the beginning of the 1700's. They knew of and now wanted horses, and proceeded to acquire them in small numbers by raiding the Spanish settlements, ranches, and haciendas that had begun to appear in New Mexico, Sonora, and Chihuahua. Those Athapaskans who became differentiated from the others as Navajos in the north also became interested in sheep and goats, as well as horses, sheep having thrived in the New Mexico environment since their introduction by the Spanish. On the other hand, the Athapaskans of the south, later called the Apaches, were raiding settlements which had begun some cattle, rather than sheep, raising.

The Navajos thus became raiding robbers of the horse and sheep herds of New Mexico, the Western and Eastern Apaches raiders of the horse and cattle herds of Sonora and Chihuahua. As they grew more accustomed to the use of horses as riding animals, the Navajos became, by the middle 1700's, highly skilled raiders, who carried off increasing numbers of sheep as well as horses. The sheep were used not only immediately as a source of meat supply, but also were accepted as domestic animals which the Navajos began to raise with an increasing interest in developing their own herds. Steadily the size and number of flocks of sheep increased among them, so that by the early 1800's, a century after their first serious interest in livestock had occurred, herding had assumed a place in their lives of at least equal importance with farming. On the other hand, the Apaches in the south never developed an interest in herding. It is true that they kept strings of horses, for use in their raids into Sonora and Chihuahua, but they never developed herds of cattle. They rather promptly killed and cured most of their booty from a raid, whether horses, burros, or cattle and used the meat. They became, in other words, more completely parasitic on the Spanish sources of supply and failed to develop a livestock economy of their own. Among both Navajos and Apaches horses became to some extent a standard of wealth and an individual's status within his band was often measured in terms of the numbers of horses he possessed. This, however, was much more marked among Navajos than among Apaches, who tended to subsist on horses rather than to save them. This difference probably was a reflection of a basically more settled way of life connected with the greater importance of farming among the Navajos as compared with the Apaches, as well as a country better adapted in the north to sheep raising as compared with a less well-adapted livestock country in the south and the greater complexity of cattle over sheep raising.

The raiding economies of the Navajos and Apaches were well developed by the middle 1800's, at the time of the coming of the Anglos. The raids were directed primarily toward the taking of livestock, not toward killing, and especially not toward driving out the White men. The relationship was a symbiotic one in which it was to the interest of the raiders to maintain their source of supply, in other words to keep the Whites in a position to supply them with horses, sheep, and cattle. As the raiding continued, both Navajos and Apaches began to follow the custom of the Spaniards in taking captives who then were kept or sold as slaves. This resulted in some interbreeding not only with Spaniards and Mexican slaves whom they captured and who grew up in the Indian bands, but also with Indians of other tribes who became the object of the raids. Thus the Navajos raided Eastern and Western Pueblo villages and Paiute camps, taking food and livestock as well as women and children as prisoners. Similarly the Apaches raided the settlements of Opatas, and Upper Pimas, as well as Spanish and later Mexican settlements. Racial mixture and also cultural mixture took place as a result of harboring captives — especially women. Moreover, settled Indians who were hostile to Spaniards were also absorbed into the Navajo and Apache bands, such as Jemez people from among the Eastern Pueblos and the various small groups of Indians of the northern Chihuahua-Sonora borderlands, as well as Pimans. The raiding economy therefore had complex results culturally and racially and transformed the Athapaskan groups in many subtle ways.

The Navajos experienced a continuity in their economic development in the transition from the Spanish period to political control by the Anglos. After their imprisonment at Fort Sumner they were issued sheep on their return to their old territory. They were moreover encouraged by Indian Bureau agents to increase their flocks, and efforts were made to develop a market. This policy continued in effect on through the 1940's. The products which first brought Navajo herders into the regional market were blankets made from the wool of the sheep, blankets which had a fairly wide sale before the end of the nineteenth century. As the flocks increased, Navajos also came into the regional market by the sale of lambs, wool, and hides. This trade became of increasing importance through the 1920's. It was carried out through Anglo traders who established themselves in the Navajo country at permanent trading posts, bought the Navajo products, and sold the coffee, sugar, canned foods, clothing, knives, axes, wagons, blankets, and other goods which Navajos would buy. Navajos were probably reached more systematically by such outposts of Anglo material culture than was any other Southwestern tribe from the 1880's on through the 1920's. The trade was geared to what the Navajos were producing and so they became more integrated into the general American economy than any other group. At the same time their population was increasing rapidly but within a sharply defined area against which Anglo cattlemen and sheepherders were pressing in competition for the grazing land and water sources. Moreover, by the 1920's it was apparent to agents of the Indian Bureau and others that Navajo stock was, like that of Anglo stockmen in northwestern New Mexico, increasing at a rate which the range could not stand. There was a steady decline in the amount of forage, as the numbers of sheep, goats, and horses increased. In the 1930's the Indian Bureau and another government bureau, the Soil Conservation Service, instituted a program for soil and range conservation on the Navajo Reservation. This was put into effect with federal money and with no participation by Navajos in the planning. It involved a heavy reduction in the existing herds and flocks, for which few Navajos understood the meaning. By 1948 the stock had been reduced to what the range technicians regarded as a proper carrying load, but this had been accomplished largely by force, the educational measures undertaken by the Indian Bureau having been instituted only after the reduction of stock and limitation of herds had been put into effect. By 1950 Navajo sheep raising was reportedly on a sound basis for continuance, which meant at a dead level of production, and it was, in common with much other stockraising in the region, a marginal enterprise. The income of the majority of Navajo families was extremely low as compared with Anglos, perhaps the lowest of any Indian group and far lower than any other group in the Southwest. Thus the transformation of Navajos into sheepmen and their integration on this basis into the general American economy had not brought an economic adjustment which compared so far as income went with the pastoral economy of the region generally. Moreover, it provided at a low level for only some 30 percent of the whole tribe and could by no means be regarded as the basis of adjustment of the whole tribe. The Navajo tribe as a whole was constantly being bolstered by federal subsidies through the Indian Bureau for road and school construction and all other public works. Sheep raising could provide income for only a little over a third of the tribe at a standard of living comparable to that of most rural families of New Mexico and Arizona, but as a matter of fact this income was distributed among some two-thirds of the population, who were forced to add to their income through other means including wage work off the reservation and the small returns from very small-scale subsistence agriculture.

Stock raising became an important part of the economic life of several other tribes, namely, the Western and Eastern Apaches, the Walapais, and the Papagos and Pimas. There was, however, no continuity among the Western Apaches such as characterized Navajo economic history. The raiding economy with its slight emphasis on possession of horses was cut off sharply with confinement to the reservation in the 1870's and 1880's. As this took place the plan for economic development of the Apaches entertained by the Army and Indian Bureau officials consisted of the encouragement of farming and the discouragement of wild-food gathering. The gathering of acorns, mescal, and other wild foods together with hunting had been a mainstay among Apaches, ranking as a greater source of food supply than their small-scale farming. The encouragement of farming was carried out under conditions of close supervision by Indian Bureau agents. The four thousand Apaches on the southern, or San Carlos, reservation were to be supported by fields along the Gila River irrigated from the flow of that river. From the first there was insufficient land for full support, although Apaches went to work with some diligence to follow out the plan. Gradually more land was brought under cultivation, but for a whole generation until 1903 the Indian Bureau issued rations as the basic subsistence for all of the San Carlos Apaches. Some efforts before 1920 to get Apaches to raise cattle resulted in only two or three families successfully developing small herds. Meanwhile Mormon settlers on the Gila River upstream from the San Carlos reservation steadily reduced the supply of water for irrigation and Apaches were generally forced, with the stopping of rations, to subsist by wage work off reservation, a means greatly encouraged by the Indian agents. At the same time the rangeland, which was very suitable for cattle, was leased increasingly by the Indian Bureau to Anglo cattlemen, so that by 1925 nearly the whole reservation was under lease. Nevertheless, a superintendent who took charge in the late 1920's held the dream of turning Apaches into cattlemen. By not renewing leases he slowly eliminated the large cattle companies and secured cattle which he urged Apaches to manage. By the end of the 1930's, this superintendent and subsequent ones who followed his program had eliminated all Anglo lessees, secured good stock and Anglo foremen, and launched the Apaches in a cattle business, which under Anglo management and Indian Bureau supervision increased in effectiveness through the 1940's. Good breeding programs and intelligent management resulted in the San Carlos Apache cattle bringing fairly consistently the highest prices in the region. Most families had some cattle, which were managed by associations of Apache men under the close supervision of Indian Bureau technicians. A program for taking over the management of the cattle by the Apache Tribal Council was instituted and proceeded during the early 1950's. Similar developments took place among the Apaches of the Fort Apache Reservation on the north and among the Walapais. The net effect of these developments on the San Carlos Reservation was to provide, as compared with Anglo cattle-raising families in the vicinity, a low-level subsistence with an average income per year of about $800 in 1950. Since only a small percentage of Apaches actually took part in the care and handling of the cattle under the group enterprise system, this left the majority of Apaches with a great deal of leisure time. Some merely enjoyed the leisure; others added to their income by taking off-reservation employment casually and intermittently.

The cattle industry developed somewhat differently on the Papago reservations. Papagos had at first allowed cattle to run wild in their territory; then they were hunted down and killed for meat. During the 1880's, in competition with Anglos who were steadily encroaching on their land and appropriating water holes, a number of families in the southeastern part of the territory began to learn the techniques of cattle raising. They, too, appropriated water sources from the village lands and slowly developed large herds. These successful cattle-raisers became a fairly well-to-do group, whose standard of living was above that of the majority of Papagos. When the Sells reservation was established in 1917, more Papagos began to raise cattle, but on a small scale, so that by the time of the establishment of the Tribal Council in 1937 the whole reservation was divided into cattle range districts. By 1950 some dozen families were well established in the cattle business, another fourth of the tribe or less were running a few small herds in a casual way, but the majority were without cattle. Those who maintained small herds used them as something to fall back on when other sources of subsistence, such as wage work, failed them. Altogether, only about a fifth of the total income of the Papagos was derived from cattle raising by 1950. In addition, however, the Tribal Council maintained as a business enterprise a tribal herd which brought in a small income used to defray expenses of the tribal business through the Tribal Council. In contrast with the San Carlos Apaches, only a small percentage of all the Papagos were actually in the cattle business, marketing their cattle on the regional market and thus participating in the national economy in the same way as the Anglo cattlemen.

THE GROWTH OF ECONOMIC INTERDEPENDENCE

In view of the immense opportunities which the Southwest eventually offered to the expanding industrial economy of the European-derived nations, it was to be expected that the dominant trend in economic life would be one of increasing inter-dependence among all the Indian tribes and the invading peoples. Even the small stimulus to subsistence agriculture given by the Spanish crop, tool, and domestic animal introductions was not without features promoting some degree of inter-dependence. The subsistence economies of the Pueblos remained almost wholly self-sufficient, since the new seeds and the new animals were self-perpetuating once the Indians learned how to plant and rear them. The taste for woolen garments, in addition to the native cotton ones, could be served by the sheep and goats as Pueblo care of these developed. The one Spanish innovation which most rapidly replaced its Indian counterpart and came into general demand was the one for which Indians were wholly dependent on Spanish techniques. This was, of course, metal for blades. Trade for metal became the most basic nexus between the Pueblo villages and the Spanish towns. How important the Pueblos felt this to be and by what time the replacement of stone blades in general had taken place we do not know with any precision. Probably by the later 1700's most Pueblos of the East would have regarded it a serious hardship to do entirely without metal which only the Spaniards could provide them, since they themselves, of course, developed no metal production techniques. Along with trade for metal goods, which remained nevertheless minor in terms of volume of interest and activity, inevitably went the stimulus of interest in other Spanish goods, such as cloth, glass, and a few other luxury items. In other respects, however, the Pueblo community economies re-mained self-sufficient throughout the Spanish period and well on into the period of Anglo control, when fairly rapid change began.

The position of the Tarahumara and Sonoran Indian communities was about the same until the early 1800's, except for one very important factor. This was the factor of wage work, chiefly at first in the mines but increasingly on ranches and haciendas. Wage work assumed a more important position here than it ever did in the north for the village Indians. For the Tarahumaras it began with forced labor and was probably stimulated considerably by the recurrent disruption of com-munity life during the 1600's resulting from the Tarahumara revolts. Individuals were frequently forced to seek work as a result of the repeated laying waste of fields and breakup of rancherías by punitive expeditions of the Spaniards, so that some-thing of a pattern developed for this kind of dependence on the Spanish settle-ments. It was not, however, universal among Tarahumaras and affected them in a very uneven way. Since the majority of Tarahumaras moved in the direction of iso-lation from the economic system growing up in Chihuahua, with the raising of their own livestock as a subsidiary food source to their farming, the main nexus with Spanish-Mexican society continued throughout the 350 years of contact to be the need felt for metal goods and the luxury trade which accompanied this. The great majority of Tarahumaras remained self-sufficient in regard to food from farm-ing and livestock, clothing, shelter, and all other necessities just as did the Eastern and Western Pueblos until well along in the Anglo period.

For the Cahitans, Opatas, and Pimas of Sonora a greater dependence on the Mexican economy developed by the middle of the nineteenth century. Precisely in what way this came about is not wholly clear. It appears that there was little in the way of forced labor required by the Spaniards from these people, yet "Sonorans," supposedly Opatas, were reported in some numbers in the Parral mines in Chihuahua at their very beginning, and there is indication that as mining developed in the late 1600's in central and northern Sonora Opatas worked frequently and regularly in the Spanish mines. Also Yaquis are reported as working in the mines before 1700 and by the 1760's hundreds of Yaquis were so employed — in the Sonora mines, as at Soyopa. It seems probable that the aftermath of the destructive revolt of 1740 included a stimulus to Yaqui wage work in mines, haciendas, and ranches which had by that time begun to appear throughout Sonora. Certainly, whatever the causes, Yaquis and to a lesser extent Mayos were well known from the 1760's on as laborers in the whole area. The Yaqui-Mexican wars during the nineteenth century intensified this tendency rather than curtailed it. Again it was a matter of devastating punitive expeditions, such as General Pesqueira's in the 1840's, which forced Yaquis for very survival to go out and work on the expanding Mexican haciendas. In the late 1800's many Yaquis left to do this simply because they preferred peace to fighting and still later it was a matter of being deported out of the Yaqui country to work on the haciendas. By 1900 Yaqui labor had become important for the Sonora hacendados and they were as much dependent on Yaquis as the latter were on the hacendados. The situation was similar for Mayos and for Opatas, except that since Mexican ranchers and hacendados had moved directly into their territories the wage work did not necessarily carry the Indians away from their own rancherías. The whole of Sonora had become the range for the Yaquis, but not for the other Indians. There was a far greater measure of economic self-sufficiency in most Mayo communities than for any community of Yaquis. In fact, from the 1820's on probably no Yaqui community was continuously self-sufficient. Whereas the Mayos continued such production as that of woolen textiles in the same way that Tarahumaras did, the art of weaving was entirely lost among Yaquis by the late 1800's. Yaquis not only had developed a high degree of dependence on the Mexican settlements for wages to secure food, but in their own villages on the Yaqui River they were also dependent on the Mexican market for nearly all their clothing. They had, more generally than Mayos, adopted Mexican cooking methods and so were dependent also for coffee, sugar, lard and other Mexican foods and condiments. Their dependence on such things had led by the early 1880's to a lively trade regionally. Guaymas was a trade center for Yaqui products and boats plied between that town and Medano, a port on the Yaqui River. Also burro trains were constantly made up in the Yaqui country and taken with Yaqui goods to Guaymas. This led to an exploitation of certain Yaqui resources for commerce, chiefly salt from important beds in the Yaqui River banks, parakeets and other birds. These were traded for food, textiles, pottery (which had also become something of a lost art), metal goods, guns, and gunpowder. Thus, while perhaps a majority of Mayos continued into the twentieth century to live in largely self-sufficient agricultural communities, the Yaquis moved into a much closer interdependence with Mexican society, and developed important trading activities in conjunction. This was the condition also in the 1940's during the period of Yaqui resettlement — in probably an even more pronounced way — which led to a growing interest in cash crop production in the form of wheat, ajonjolí (sesame), and beans. The persistence of distinctive forms of social and ceremonial life among the Yaquis seemed in no way dependent on the maintenance of an isolated subsistence farming economy. They persisted in conjunction with rather full participation in the general Mexican economy in Sonora and in the economically integrated Yaqui settlements in Arizona.

The Seri remnants had by 1950 also undergone a growth toward interdependence with the Mexican economy comparable to that of the Yaquis, but let us say at a less intense level of interaction. Although their society suffered severe disruption in the 1700's as a result of incarceration at Villa de Seris near Hermosillo, they nevertheless refused to participate in the plan which Spaniards had for them of developing a settled life on irrigated farm land. Wandering again out into the still isolated country of the coast, they attempted to re-establish themselves as food gatherers and fishers. However, two more expeditions against them with again temporary incarceration at Villa de Seris seemed to disrupt their economy still more. After breaking away from their last incarceration in 1880 they turned to small-scale raiding, apparently subsisting almost as much from the killing of cattle now being grazed by Mexican cattlemen on their lands as from wild products. They also sporadically accepted employment on the cattle ranches which had been established at the edge of their country. Their level of living was appallingly low in the view of the Mexican ranchers who came to know them. An attitude of disgust and a conception of them as depraved beings grew up among Mexicans. A condition of partial parasitic living on the invading cattle herds and partial small-scale utilization of sea turtle, fish, and other wild products prevailed until the 1920's; accompanying this adjustment was a steady population decline. In the 1920's they had largely ceased any raiding of cattle — as a result of severe measures taken against them by cattlemen. They settled on the coast at a Mexican fishing site called Kino Bay and began to replace their reed balsas with wooden fishing boats. They gradually assumed a position as fishermen, trading what they caught for clothing, Mexican foods, and fishing equipment. In their taste for cotton clothing and for wheat flour, lard, coffee, and sugar they had become as dependent as the Yaquis on the Mexican economy. Moreover, their increasing participation in commercial fishing activities increased this dependence as a result of their need for fishhooks, metal for turtle harpoon heads, knives, and other tools for making their boats. In the 1930's the Seris had become full-fledged participants in the fishing economy of Sonora and this was intensified as an active market grew up for shark livers for the purpose of making vitamin preparations. Although as a result of synthetic vitamins this market collapsed in the early 1940's, the Seris continued firmly established as suppliers along with Mexican fishermen of the rapidly growing market for fish in the cities of Sonora, Arizona, and California. By 1950 they began to use dynamite in fishing and outboard motors on their boats, so that their integration into the national economy of Mexico, and the United States (much of their product was marketed in the United States) was fairly complete. Although fishing equipment, clothing, and food were the chief nexus of their interdependence, other wants were developing rapidly which reinforced the linkage — for medicines, liquor, marijuana, and other luxuries, and a desire to learn arithmetic for account keeping.

The general trend, as we have seen, among the Eastern Pueblos through 1950 was one of isolation, or parallel development, in relation to the Anglo economic system. The more or less successful agricultural subsistence economy pursued by the Pueblo villages became increasingly stabilized through the first half of the twentieth century, as the land base was protected from encroachment by the federal government and as conservation measures preserved the soil. Interdependence with the Anglo economy rested not on fitting into the system through either labor skills or specialized production, with a minor exception as will be noted below, but rather on slowly increasing desire for miscellaneous specialties obtainable only through retail trade in the Anglo city centers. As Pueblo youth went through Anglo schools and became familiar with Anglo ways, demand on their part for certain goods, ranging from baking powder and cosmetics through metal and enamelware utensils to farm machinery and window glass brought Pueblos increasingly into the retail stores of the region, where they traded chiefly for cash and only in a minor way for any produce of their farms and livestock. The cash came from the lease of land to Whites in some instances, such as at Isleta, in others from craft specialization and sale, and from wage work. This trade thus rested on and encouraged a threefold integration into the general economy. The basic adjustment of the Eastern Pueblos remained that of subsistence farming, although young men and women were increasingly moving out of the villages to take wage work in the cities. The adjustment was essentially that of small farm areas, marginal to the general economy, with population constantly emigrating to the urban centers.

For the Western Pueblos the economic adjustment was somewhat different, involving by the 1950's a considerably greater importance of wage work. This was especially true of the Lagunas and the Hopis. In the case of the Hopis land resources were more limited than for the Eastern Pueblos and the land was more marginal. One result was that the expanding population was even less able to rely on the reservation for subsistence. Consequently, many Hopis beginning in the 1930's and with greater frequency after World War II took jobs in neighboring towns, chiefly Winslow, working in the railroad yards or in small industries. By 1950 a colony of several hundred grew up in Winslow, Arizona, the inhabitants of which were linked with families on the reservation and who maintained their social and ceremonial relations in the reservation villages. There were similar small colonies of Hopis, Lagunas, Acomas, and Zunis scattered along the Santa Fe railroad from Albuquerque, New Mexico, to Barstow, California. In a sense these, especially the Winslow colony, were extensions of the reservation communities, wholly dependent on the general economy and constituting to some extent a source of subsistence for the people remaining on the reservations.

The Indians of the Southwest who came earliest in an important way into the wage system of the Anglos were the Western Apaches, more especially those of San Carlos. Restricted by the Indian Bureau from the continuance of their raiding and gathering economy and confined to a reservation which admittedly had insufficient farming resources, they early were introduced to wage work on the reservation. As scouts in the campaign against fellow Apaches which continued through 1887 and as policemen on the reservation following the surrender of Geronimo, most of the younger men drew wages which supplemented the rations of their families and the agricultural produce. They also learned some building skills in the construction of the agency buildings at old San Carlos and the boarding school on the San Carlos River at Rice. But in 1903 rations were discontinued because in the opinion of the agent there was sufficient in the way of wage work in the surrounding area to take care of Apache needs. Apaches had been hired for the construction of the railroad across their reservation from Globe to Safford and Bowie and a number had learned semiskilled trades in this experience. Following the completion of the railroad in the 1920's, there were increasing demands for labor in the area. Not only the growing number of ranches required hands, but road construction and the construction of the Roosevelt Dam as a federal reclamation project took place. Apaches worked in large numbers on the dam and the related road construction, such as the Apache Trail. The greater part of San Carlos Apache subsistence in the period just before and after World War I came from wage work. Apaches participated in these operations maintaining their own camps with their families apart from the other workers. They also began to work in the Globe-Miami and Clifton-Morenci copper mines, which had been sliced off the west and east margins respectively of their reservation. To some extent they also worked as farm laborers on the Mormon-owned farms of the Safford area east of their reservation and in the sawmills which Anglos had built on the two reservations. It appeared by the time Coolidge Dam was constructed at the end of the 1920's and the agricultural land of old San Carlos had been flooded that the basic adjustment of Apaches in the enveloping economy had been made in terms of wage work off the reservation. But the coming of the economic depression of the 1930's brought a sharp change. One shift was wage work on the reservations in connection with the numerous projects undertaken by the federal government in soil conservation and public works. The other was the development of the cattle industry on the San Carlos Reservation. Nearly all Apaches resettled on the reservations as these opportunities appeared and thereafter wage work off the reservation remained of minor importance through the 1940's. More than 60 percent of Apache income came from the tribal enterprises of cattle and trading posts by 1950, and Apaches worked only sporadically and occasionally off the reservation, although one colony of two to three hundred became more or less permanent in the vicinity of the Miami copper mines. The Apache economy had become integrated with the regional economy through cattle raising. Apaches could live on the reservation and buy goods which they had universally come to want with money from cattle sales and tribal enterprises. But the standard of living was low as compared with Anglos.

The Papagos, as we have seen, had not developed a cattle industry which was tribal-wide in its benefits, except insofar as a small tribal herd contributed something. Rather, a few families derived a living from cattle, while the majority of Papagos were forced to other pursuits. Most families derived a very small amount of food from tiny floodwater farms and the running of a few cattle on deteriorating ranges. Several hundred Papagos became established in Tucson as a permanent colony, with changing personnel, which worked at odd jobs and domestic service for Anglos. This colony continued, much like the Hopi segment of Winslow of a later date, as a sort of way-station for Papagos who found living off-reservation better than on. Other Papagos subsisted by supplying wood and to a limited extent pottery to Tucson, but the major adjustment which developed during and after World War II was one which straddled the reservation and the world outside. After World War II cotton growing developed with great rapidity, following a start during the 1930's in the Santa Cruz and Gila valleys. At the same time a large copper mine at the western edge of the Papago reservation at Ajo went into large-scale production. The great majority of Papagos by the 1950's were working chiefly as mine laborers at Ajo or as agricultural laborers on the cotton ranches on the eastern margins of their reservations. They maintained their homes on the reservations, but derived only small parts of their subsistence from resources there. Rather, the major source of income for all but those few families which had developed cattle herds of some extent came from this wage work in the area. The agricultural labor came seasonally, with cotton chopping in the spring and early summer and cotton picking in the fall. Most families had regular employment with the same ranches year in and year out. They came and went seasonally from their homes on the reservation to the ranches. A permanent colony of several hundred Papagos grew up in the mining town of Ajo. Thus the Papago adjustment was one which involved for the great majority an acceptance of the wage system of the Anglo economy, with minor additions from their own meager resources on the reservations. There was a similar general adjustment for the Gila Pimas, but with a considerably greater amount of subsistence derived from small-scale farming which the curtailed water supply permitted.

Somewhat later than either Apaches or Papago-Pimas, the Navajos entered the labor market of the Southwestern region. Their considerable employment as wage laborers — on the Santa Fe railroad which ran through the southern edge of their reservation — did not begin until World War II. Nevertheless, from the time of the Fort Sumner incarceration, a few Navajos worked on the ranches or, after 1880, in the towns growing up along the railroad. For the most part, however, until after 1900 there was room to raise sheep and roam widely on the reservation. It was only as population density increased heavily from about 1910 that Navajos began to seek outside work in any numbers. Moreover, it was only after the depression years and with the outburst of industrial operations and vast expansion of Anglo population in the 1940's that any large demand for Navajo labor grew up. There was great demand with the beginning of World War II. The Indian Bureau established an employment division by the end of the war which devoted itself to securing jobs for Navajos off the reservation. Steadily during the 1940's more and more Navajos began to be employed. The greatest volume of employment annually was with the railroads which in 1956 employed sixty-five hundred of the eighty thousand Navajos. In addition, large numbers went to work seasonally in the beet fields of Colorado, in the carrot fields near Grants, New Mexico, and Phoenix, Arizona, and in agricultural harvests elsewhere. A smaller percentage were employed in various light industries which had been established in towns along the southern edge of the reservation and in the larger cities such as Albuquerque, Phoenix, Tucson, and El Paso. During the 1950's the vast majority of the

Navajos retained permanent residence on the reservation and a considerable proportion of the families there derived some support from flocks of sheep and extremely small-scale farming. Rug production by women was also of some importance. But the overwhelmingly major part of subsistence for nearly all the families was from wages earned by some member of the extended family who was employed for from three to eight or nine months a year off the reservation. In contrast with the Papagos, the families did not usually go as units to work but rather the men, and usually the younger ones, went off in gangs and lived apart from their families during the working seasons. The women and children and older men tended to stay at their home sites on the reservation, although various arrangements were worked out for the wife and some children to live off-reservation with the man for short periods. This also meant that families had a supply of cash which was spent at the trading posts in the vicinity of their homesites. It meant that much of the subsistence was derived from store-bought goods as supplements to the mutton which many families produced. It meant that there was cash to use to secure new things in which interest was developing, such as small trucks. The basic economic type of adjustment was similar to that of the Papagos, but also the difference between the two was important.

The Papagos, living off the reservation for most of the year as family groups and trading in stores near the labor camps were for much of the time deep in the milieu of the Anglos. A cotton pickers' camp, composed of a variety of ethnic groups, was a very different milieu for children from a Papago village. On the other hand, it was the men among the Navajos, for the most part, who lived this white man's life. Most Navajos remained in their familiar rural environment, having their economic wants and habits controlled and channeled by a familiar Anglo trader. The processes of cultural change set in motion by these economic adjustments were very different ones. At the same time that this was taking place there was also during the early 1950's a very considerable program of construction financed by the United States government, including schools and roads, which held many Navajos on the reservation and brought back many who had settled either permanently or temporarily off the reservation. This was an economic adjustment like that which had taken place on most reservations during the depression years of the 1930's.

The basis of integration into the general economies of the two nations was primarily that of wage work. Except for a few Mohaves on the Colorado River, Indians were nowhere engaged in farming which paralleled that of Anglo farmers. A conception of protected, transitional communities like that of the Jesuits had been put into operation among the tribes of the United States, but wage work was increasingly establishing links between the Indians and the general economy. It could be said that in the 1950's all the Indians except the most remote Tarahumaras were intimately involved in the general industrial economy of North America. Superficially it may have appeared that the Eastern and Western Pueblos — the only ones who as whole communities still conceived of farming as a dignified and valuable way of life — had somehow worked out an adjustment which left them relatively independent of this general economy. There were, however, two aspects of their adjustment which indicated interdependence. One was the well-developed taste for a great variety of material goods not produced by themselves ranging from window glass, sugar and coffee, to shovels and enamelware pots. As rather well-to-do farmers they were able to buy such goods and had become devoted to them. Of deeper significance, however, was the small but steady flow of individuals out of the Pueblo communities to work and take up residence permanently elsewhere. This possibility for an outward flow into the general milieu of the Southwestern region was one of the major stabilizing factors in Pueblo life, permitting it to continue with relatively little religious and political change.

The interdependence which had developed was based chiefly on the labor power of individual Indians, to only a very small extent on their natural resources or on any distinctive specialization in production. There was, however, the possibility that at any moment new resources would be discovered on the reservations, as they were beginning to be in the 1950's, which would revolutionize the interrelations developed up to that time.

CRAFTWORK – THE DISTINCTIVE INDIAN SPECIALIZATION

For a very small percentage of Indian men and women living on the reservation and to some extent for those living off the reservations there was an exception to the general rule that there was nothing distinctive in the nature of the Indian integration into the regional economy. Among all the Pueblos, Eastern and Western, and the Navajos there were individuals who maintained what might be called a tourist industry, that is, the manufacture of goods for sale to tourists coming through their country. Members of other tribes of New Mexico and Arizona, with the exception of the Gila Pimas and most of the Yumans, also made and sold some goods for this special trade, but on a very small scale as compared with the Pueblos and Navajos. The chief forms of goods were pottery, woolen blankets, silver jewelry, and baskets. The tourist trade began almost simultaneously with the completion of the transcontinental railroads in the 1880's and 1890's. Navajo blankets had become well known regionally even before this time and were traded widely. Through the twenty-five years following the opening of the railroad the market for Navajo blankets outside their territory steadily increased, at the same time that blankets made by machinery in Oregon almost completely replaced Navajo-made blankets among Navajos in their own daily life. Perhaps less widely known and used, the pottery of the Eastern Pueblos and of the Hopis met a steady market during the first half of the 1900's. There developed two different traditions in pottery, one which was a response to a mass market and one in response to a highly specialized trade. The tourists came in increasing numbers, with only minor recessions during the World Wars, on highway and railroad and demanded souvenirs and colorful mementos. Most of the Pueblos responded by producing small and brightly colored pieces of pottery. The basic techniques continued to be hand, but the general tendency was toward the quickest methods and the greatest possible uniformity consistent with hand methods. The result was a steady sale in roadside stands and at curio stores throughout the Southwestern region of the United States. The sales from this mass-produced pottery amounted however to only a tiny percentage of all income for the Eastern and Western Pueblos. It was a source of cash for buying the material goods which the Pueblos increasingly had come to want. In Santo Domingo and Acoma about 15 percent of the families made pottery and sold it; the percentage manufacturing pottery was considerably less in other villages.

There was another tradition which developed and which was in fact largely responsible for the revival of the whole pottery industry. This grew out of the interest of archaeologists in persuading potters to revive the lapsed prehistoric designs and forms of their ancestors. The School of American Research at Santa Fe and the Bureau of American Ethnology, through Edgar B. Hewett and Walter Fewkes respectively, played an important part in providing models and encouraging particular potters to revive this nearly lost art. The immediate results were that one family at the Tewa Pueblo of San Ildefonso and one family at the Tewa Pueblo of Hano undertook to begin to reproduce the prehistoric designs and techniques. Nampeyo on First Mesa, the site of the Hopi villages most friendly to Anglo contacts, and Maria Martínez of San Ildefonso went on to develop steady markets for their pottery. As this market grew other women copied what had been started. At San Ildefonso the men took part as decorators of the pottery manufactured by the women, and in 1911 Maria invented a new type of pottery — black polished ware with a black matte design — which became very popular. By 1920 a third of the families of San Ildefonso were supporting themselves by the manufacture and sale of pottery, and their pottery, under the stimulus of the standards set by Maria and her tutor Hewett, was in a different category from that of the cheaper wares being sold at the roadside stands. It was going into museums and reaching an upper-income clientele throughout the United States. Its marketing was further stimulated in the 1930's when the Indian Bureau encouraged the formation of the Indian Arts and Crafts Commission. This commission composed of Anglos familiar with the crafts market encouraged and found markets for many different Indian products. It served as a bridge between the Indian craftsmen and the taste in such specialized goods over the United States. It gave the pottery tradition of Maria and Nampeyo a distinct push in the direction of nonpopular art, toward the taste of more sophisticated and esthetically conscious buyers. In the 1940's the sale of pottery was an important source of income in the Tewa pueblo of San Ildefonso, but only there did it assume a major role in Indian economy.

The Navajo production of blankets increased steadily after 1900, and similarly two traditions—of cheap and rapid production to meet the tourist trade and production for a sophisticated and esthetically conscious taste — developed. The latter was given impetus especially by the Indian Arts and Crafts Commission in the 1930's when it encouraged the use of native vegetable dyes and publicized in a world's fair certain sophisticated standards of production. The great mass of Navajo blanket production, however, was not influenced by this tradition and continued to be just that which the tourist trade demanded. Navajo blanket production reached a high level in volume of trade in 1955, but this constituted less than 10 percent of total Navajo income. The blanket trade was a minor source of cash for most women of families who engaged in raising sheep. The blanket trade was more spectacular than functional. Weaving developed not at all for an external market among any other tribes of the region. The Navajos were also unique for a while in their development of the specialty of silverwork. The manufacture of silver jewelry over a hundred years grew into a small but important industry. In 1935 there were some forty Navajo silversmiths exporting their products and this number increased three-fold in the next twenty years. The total income from silverwork in 1950 was only a small percentage of total Navajo income, but silverwork and weaving had become a source of knowledge about the Navajos which extended widely through the United States and to other countries. As arts of high quality, those traditions fostered by the Commission had become famous at least in the museum world and they were a source of tribal pride. The success of Navajo silverwork as a market product in the Anglo world led to the development of silvercraft traditions also among the Hopis and the Zunis. As in the production of pottery, the Hopis were encouraged by an Anglo institution, the Museum of Northern Arizona at Flagstaff. A dozen Hopis by 1955 were making something of a living as silversmiths. Another style distinctive from the Navajo grew up in silverworking at Zuni, where an increasing number of smiths after the 1930's produced for an outside market. Zuni silverwork was characterized by a lavish use of turquoise and other semiprecious stones as insets. This small development of a specialty in metal jewelry among three tribes appeared to be well established, but nevertheless it was in process of being strongly affected by attempts at mass production by non-Indians in response to the increasing tourist market. Small factories were set up in Santa Fe and Albuquerque at which stamping and other mass production techniques were employed. It seemed apparent that a certain number of tourists would continue to buy the mass produced articles as readily as the handmade. They were interested in something made by an Indian and Indians were employed in these factories. But the staple product continued to be the handmade articles, usually manufactured by individual silversmiths off the reservation at curio stores and "trading posts" where tourists and others could see them as they worked.

There were similar, even smaller, developments in the making and selling of baskets, not as utilitarian, but rather as decorative objects. Trade in baskets was built up by the Indian Arts and Crafts Commission especially among the Papagos, the Hopis of Second Mesa and Third Mesa, the Walapais, and to a lesser extent among Pimas and Western Apaches. Basketry, like pottery, was a woman's art among all the tribes and provided some slight cash income. Nowhere did any one woman or family, as in the case of San Ildefonso and Hano pottery manufacture, build up a trade which became the only or chief source of income for the family. The most vigorous producers of baskets by the 1950's were the Papagos with the Walapais close behind. Pima basketry was obviously becoming a lost art, and Apache basketry seemed also to be on the decline. A few Hopis on Second and Third Mesa continued to make a few baskets, but the interest was not vigorous. Basketry remained even less important as a source of income than any of the other crafts, but as in the case of the others it was also true that the craft goods contributed to a sense of tribal identity and were encouraged by tribal council leaders.

In Sonora, the last surviving crafts which found some market in the general economy were blanket-weaving by the Mayos and basketry by the Seris. Nearly every Seri woman knew how to make baskets and on the average, during, for example 1953, some two hundred baskets were made in a year. These were used for household tasks of storing and carrying but each basket was also for sale and various individuals and organizations drummed up temporary interest in a market. It was apparent however that the basket style did not attract many Anglos and even fewer Mexicans, so that a temporary spurt in production in the early 1950's subsided to a trickle within a few years. Mayo blanket-weaving seemed also to be on the decline, but the opening of tourist travel on a large scale through Sonora promised possibly to revive it. Much better established, because it continued to have a root in Indian life itself, was the Tarahumara blanket-weaving industry. Tarahumaras, employing handlooms like those of the Navajos, except that they were horizontal in layout, produced blankets of wool for their own use and also found a small market for a few blankets in the Mexican cities of Chihuahua and Creel. No one knew how much income was derived from this source, but it was very small.

These craft specialties were mostly revivals, stimulated by an Anglo interest in the esoteric qualities of "primitive" art and goods. They nevertheless appealed to a constant, if small, number of persons. The existence of "Indian curio shops" was assured for as long as Indians were interested in producing their distinctive crafts.

Another specialty, affecting a very small number of individuals, but important from the view point of tribal identity, was that of watercolor painting. This, like the crafts traditions, had been stimulated at first by Anglos—in this case teachers in the Santa Fe Indian boarding school who influenced children to paint the life of the tribe from which they came. Certain young men and women developed distinctive styles of their own, such as Alan Hauser, a Western Apache; Harrison Begay, a Navajo; numerous Pueblos; and Fred Kabotie, a Hopi. These decorative paintings began also to be sold in curio stores and some Indian artists were able to make a living in the 1940's and 1950's by their art alone. Most of these artists ceased almost all participation in reservation life, seeking the company of artists or others in Anglo society. Like their lives, their art was a fusion of two cultures.

CORPORATE ENTERPRISE

Another feature of Indian economics which gave it some distinctive quality, at least in the United States' portion of the region, consisted of special forms of economic enterprise. These were set in motion by the Indian Reorganization Act of 1934, which authorized tribes to organize as business corporations and pursue business activities. Thus, for example, the Tribal Council of the San Carlos Apaches was not only a political unit but also had a charter as a business corporation. Under this dual organization the Tribal Council served as a board of directors for a tribal cattle herd and also for the large retail stores at the towns of San Carlos and Bylas which were tribally owned. The Tribal Council hired or delegated the hiring and firing of employees for these enterprises, determined basic policy for management, and held proceeds in a tribal fund which was employed in various ways including the meeting of welfare benefits for tribal members. The Fort Apache Tribal Council similarly conducted business as a corporation. The Gila Pimas ran a tribal farm on this basis; the Walapais ran a tribal herd, as did the Papagos. The tribes were functioning economic units, as well as political entities, formally organized and chartered. Such units nominally consisted of all individuals who met whatever requirements a tribal council laid down as necessary for tribal membership. This was not of course a measure of actual participation.

To many Anglo observers these units of business management seemed anomalous. They were corporations with collective division of proceeds like any other corporation, and they appointed managers, like any other corporation, subject to the policies of the board of directors of the corporation. What seemed anomalous was the basis of membership in the corporation, namely, genealogical descent or place of residence or a combination of these. This was in contrast with the usual basis of shareholding in a corporation, namely, investment in the enterprise with an accompanying financial interest. Another difference lay in the fact that tribal councils, which served as boards of directors, were composed of individuals elected as political representatives, individuals who did not necessarily have any kind of business experience. The basis of the Indian corporation lay in the legal right of each individual Indian in the total natural resources of a reservation — a right embodied in the tribal title held in trust by the United States government.

The tribe which had gone the farthest in the development of its business interests as a collective enterprise by the early 1950's was the Navajo. This tribe was engaged in the production of lumber from its timber resources, in the leasing of its oil and mineral resources to Anglo companies engaged in exploring and developing them, and in such other enterprises as a tourist court. The annual income of the tribe from these various activities by 1955 had reached into the tens of millions of dollars. The Navajo Tribe was a large business enterprise with a very considerable range of activities and interests. Up to 1955 it had not made any per capita distributions of income but was putting income back into the tribal enterprises, providing scholarships for training in special skills for tribal members, and other collective benefits, such as weather control. The Navajo Tribe had hired a number of managers and employees and attorneys to take care of these interests. The Tribal Council remained the policy-making body. One of the issues which arose, that of per capita distribution of tribal income, would be fought out on the Tribal Council floor as part of its deliberations, where political and economic functions were more closely interlocked even than in surrounding communities.

Numerous problems had beset this kind of organization among the smaller tribes which lacked new large sources of income. The Papago Tribal Council, in an effort to develop tribal stores, had become insolvent. The San Carlos Tribe was constantly on the brink of insolvency, as was the Walapai. All the tribes had the power of taxation of their membership, but this power had been used sparingly and the taxation of land was not undertaken. Taxes were levied on the sales of individual cattle raisers, as among the Papagos. All tribal corporations except the Navajo were in a chronic state of precarious existence, sometimes as a result of poor management practices associated with both the inexperience and political character of the leadership, sometimes inextricably connected with the lack of capital and other business facilities. The tendency was strong in all the tribal organizations to hire Indians in the available jobs. That it was possible to improve the management practices, providing there was capital to work with was demonstrated in the case of the Navajos, who as income increased employed experienced members of the tribe returned from off reservation or else qualified Anglo Americans.

In Sonora, too, there had been some governmental effort to stimulate collective enterprises. In 1938 a fishing cooperative was organized by the Department of Indian Affairs among the Seris. Some government subsidy resulted in the building of a weighing and icing station and most members of the tribe became members of the cooperative, which, however, remained under the management of a Mexican paid partly by the federal government. With his retirement from the scene in 1945 the cooperative broke apart and all the business began to be handled by private entrepreneurs from the Sonoran cities. Yaquis and Mayos as ultimately the beneficiaries of the government-subsidized land development along their rivers were organized into ejidos and by the early 1940's were producing some grain, chiefly wheat, for export from their country. It was also true that President Cárdenas of Mexico had by decree created a sort of reservation out of the territory occupied by the Yaquis on the north side of the Yaqui River. By the terms of this decree only members of the "Yaqui Tribes" could own land in this area. Others might be permitted to work tracts of the land but were required to pay rent to the village government which had title to it. This arrangement was not revoked but its terms were repeatedly broken through various forms of encroachment during the 1940's. The ejidos which were organized in the Yaqui country were of the collective type and thus conflicted in some measure with the traditional form of working the land, which had been on an individual basis despite the collective control and assignment of farmlands. Among the Tarahumaras tribal management of timberlands was begun about 1952.

In the course of the four centuries of contact the economic life of the Indians was profoundly altered. The economic base shifted from subsistence agriculture, supplemented by varying amounts of hunting and wild food gathering, to wage work, supplemented among some groups by livestock raising and among a few others by cash-crop farming on a small scale. The scene of daily life changed from economically independent to thoroughly interdependent communities existing as parts of industrialized national economies. The shift to interdependence took place largely during the first half of the twentieth century. It was accompanied by a decline and, in most instances, a disappearance of native crafts, a major feature of the new economic adjustment being a steadily intensifying interest in and reliance on material goods produced outside the Indian communities. It remained to be seen whether the Indians, through forms of corporate enterprise encouraged by the national governments, would achieve a type and level of participation in the national economies comparable to that of the dominant people, and at the same time maintain a sense of distinct identity.

PART IV

PATHS TO CIVILIZATION:
THE PROCESSES OF CULTURE CHANGE

CHAPTER NINETEEN

The Processes of Acculturation

THE CONQUEST of the American Southwest set in motion trains of events which resembled those in the wake of other conquests in human history. At the end of 430 years it was clear that, despite intensification of communication among all the peoples of the region through the adoption of common language and a great deal of cultural borrowing and interchange, most of the conquered people had retained their own sense of identity. Moreover there was little or no ground for predicting that even by the end of half a millennium of contact the native peoples would have ceased to exist as identifiable ethnic groups. An abundance of evidence indicated that two different and opposing processes set in motion by the conquest had attained a balance which favored the persistence of the Indian entities.

On the one hand conquest stimulated native peoples to a vigorous borrowing of new ideas and ways of doing things at the same time that it stimulated the invaders to active imposition of their ways. This resulted in a steady growth of common culture over the whole region. The Europeanization of the Indians became an accelerating process and from its inception far overshadowed the relatively minor tendency of the newcomers to borrow from the Indian cultures. Almost from the beginning military and political control by the Europeans had insured that the cultural interchange would take this direction.

On the other hand the political domination also stimulated the Indians in a variety of ways to resist submergence in the conquering societies. Moreover, in the dominant nations themselves the tendency was ultimately reinforced by recognition of the Indian entities and even encouragement of their continued existence as distinct ethnic groups. The result after four hundred years was the balance between processes of assimilation and differentiation which made extremely unlikely in the foreseeable future the disappearance of such native groups as the Navajos, the Western Apaches, the Tarahumaras, the Yaquis, and the Eastern and Western Pueblos.

The survival of native groups in the face of successful conquests, followed by vigorous programs for cultural assimilation, has been by no means exceptional in the course of human history. On the contrary it is probably the most common result.

It has been difficult to gain perspective on the European conquests of various parts of the world during the eighteenth, nineteenth, and twentieth centuries because until very recently we have been immersed in that phase of triumphant dominance which has made cultural assimilation appear to be the inevitable result of conquest. As the events of the twentieth century unfold it becomes ever clearer that conquest can be best understood as only the first part of a recurring cycle. Conquest and the processes it inaugurates are to be viewed as a phase in the periodic expansion and withdrawal of nations. Expansion with accompanying political incorporation of other tribes or nations brings about some degree of transfer of cultural elements from the dominant nation to the dominated peoples. But the urge to expansion eventually spends itself and withdrawal of dominance takes place. The withdrawal may leave in its wake newly invigorated political entities, enriched by the cultural interchange and stimulated to a new self-consciousness. In mid-twentieth century it is possible to see clearly the withdrawal as well as the expansion phase in the western European cycle.

Such cycles are familiar in earlier conquests known to history. It is helpful to view the conquest of the Southwest from the standpoint of expansion and withdrawal. For example, the Roman conquest of Western Europe had, up to a certain point, consequences which paralleled those of the Spanish and Anglo-American conquest of the Southwest. The Romans established military and political control over the Teutonic, Frankish, Iberian, and British tribes. To be sure, the domination was not complete or thorough everywhere; as in the Spanish advance into the Southwest, some tribes were held well under control for several hundred years while others were never wholly conquered. The Romans, then, like the Spaniards built towns to which the colonial administrators and the soldiers and their families came to live. Outposts of Roman civilization grew up widely over western Europe, but there were no extensive migrations of Romans into the area. Plans were formulated for more thoroughgoing civilizing of the barbarians, and the resident Romans, with natives whom they forced or persuaded to cooperate, worked at the formidable task. Town plans, architecture, and roads were introduced as far west as Hadrian's Wall, so that the tangible framework of Roman culture became well known to the European tribes. Writing and the Latin language began to be used not only by the Roman invaders but also by the native elite who worked with the conquerors in their towns. Military organization, governmental procedures, and law were imposed wherever possible. Even some temples with their cults were introduced here and there, and eventually Christian church organization. The influences of Roman language and culture were deep and lasting among Frankish and Iberian tribes, less so among the others. But the Roman impetus to conquest died down and after four hundred years in the Iberian peninsula could be said to have spent itself. There emerged after that with increasing definiteness the new self-conscious peoples out of which Spain was later forged — the Catalonians, the Castilians, the Basques, and the others. While farther north, the British, the Welsh, the Scots, and the Irish took form as vigorous bearers of the new fusion of Mediterranean and north European cultural traditions.

The essential difference between the Roman conquest of western European tribes and the Spanish-Anglo conquest of southwestern American tribes was that the latter was eventually followed up with mass migrations of the conquerors which completely enveloped the native peoples. Thus, by the time the conquering spirit of the Europeans and their descendants had waned there was no possibility of physical withdrawal. Enclavement had taken place and the opportunity for any independent renaissance of native peoples, such as followed in the wake of the Roman conquest, was impossible.

THE GROWTH OF COMMON CULTURE

The spread of religious ideas, of forms of government, of language, of tools and techniques, and of other elements of culture from the people of Western cultural backgrounds to the Indians of the Southwest has appeared to most non-Indian observers as unexpectedly slow. There is implicit or explicit in most considerations of the matter by persons involved in native administration, by historians, by anthropologists, and by others an assumption that Indians have generally been backward in acceptance of a better way of life. There is also generally implicit the assumption that ultimate complete replacement of Indian ways is inevitable. Such assumptions seem hardly justified in view of the results of most other conquests and moreover, with respect to the speed of assimilation, are not based on the application of any clear standard.

The Romanization of western European tribes, which never was completed, took place over periods of four to five hundred years. The spread of Arab civilization attendant on conquests beginning in the 700's went on for five hundred years in the vast area from Spain to the Philippines; and Moslemization like Romanization left a great variety of independent and unevenly influenced groups in its wake. The Hinduization of tribes in southern Asia has been going on for two thousand years. The Europeanization of peoples in Africa and Oceania has likewise been in process for more than four hundred years. These processes of cultural assimilation based on conquest and rarely resulting in the complete assimilation of any people have gone on at markedly different rates. How fast they have proceeded has depended on the kinds of conditions set up by the conquerors, the political institutions through which they have maintained dominance, the kinds of organizations permitted or stimulated by the invaders among the native peoples, the compatibility of the cultures thrown into contact, and a host of other circumstances. The speed of assimilation of American Indians has not been measured by any careful comparisons with other situations in which the contact conditions were similar. Hence it remains meaningless to speak of cultural assimilation in the Southwest as rapid or slow. We may merely point out the nature and results of those particular processes of assimilation which came into operation, namely, the processes of Hispanicization, Mexicanization, and Anglicization.

The assimilation programs of the Spaniards, Mexicans, and Anglo-Americans were, inevitably, products of their particular traditions and their conceptions of what was important in life. Each program sought to impose on Indians as much as possible of the way of life of the bearers. Each of the three ways of life was advanced unquestioningly by its various bearers — administrators, missionaries, technicians, settlers — as the best of all possible ways and identified as "civilization." The three conceptions of civilization were, as has been seen, remarkably different; they gave to the programs which embodied them strikingly divergent orientations. The Spaniards, whatever may have been the special concerns of particular governors and missionary orders, inaugurated a program for civilization which was guided most definitely by a religious orientation. Obviously there were also strong economic interests which influenced high policy and affected the local administration of the program. But the basic conception of what Spaniards wanted to accomplish in New Spain was clearly defined as religious conversion, and repeatedly when that purpose was seriously intefered with by the local development of economic interests the conflict was resolved in favor of the missionary program. This was especially true in the northwest of New Spain where there was relatively small scope for the economic objectives of individual Spaniards. The guiding framework determining the major features of the process of Hispanicization was the conversion of the Indians to Christian practice and a new world view, and this obtained most positively during the whole initial impact of Spanish culture on the Indians — for a century and a half through the middle 1700's. In contrast, the later phase of Hispanicization which we may call Mexicanization proceeded from a very different ruling purpose. The emphasis in Mexican policy was on political, rather than religious, values. Insofar as any organized program of assimilation developed it was oriented toward the implantation of new political behavior and the integration of Indians as individuals or in communities into the Mexican republican system. The Anglo-American program of assimilation is more difficult to characterize in terms of any persistent focus. Its basic orientation shifted fundamentally at least twice and in its latest phase lost sharp focus. Nevertheless, it seems fair to define it as a program guided primarily by an economic orientation. Each of these emphases — religious, political, and economic — was a reflection of dominant values in the societies which conceived them and particularly of the dominating interests of those who participated in the formulation of high political policy. The means by which each was expected to attain the objectives of the assimilation programs also varied in ways that were consistent with the orientations of each of the three different national cultures.

Although the ultimate orientation in Christianity was individualistic and hence the aim of Hispanicization was the transformation of individual Indians into Christian individuals, nevertheless there can be no doubt that the view of process held by the Spaniards was a community one. The formulators of Spanish policy thought in terms of the creation of a certain type of community in which the mechanism of change in the direction they sought would automatically come into operation. The necessary changes were to be wrought by the key figures in their program — the missionaries — working in this kind of community. The immediate practical objective, therefore, was the formation of such communities everywhere in Indian country. This was the reduction program, which aimed at gathering the presumably scattered Indians into compact communities with a physical and spiritual focus in a very tangible church building. A basic feature was, of course, continuously resident Spanish agents of change. The cross-culturally managed mission communities, rather than the intrusive Spanish towns, were the basic mechanism for setting the processes of assimilation in operation.

The technique of community reorganization turned out to be a very effective means for cultural assimilation. Wherever the Spaniards succeeded in putting it into effect, the Indians began to adopt numerous Spanish ways. This took place among the great majority of ranchería peoples. Among them new communities were organized and missionaries went to work. They succeeded within a hundred years in implanting religious, political, and some economic forms of behavior. Moreover assimilation appeared to be an accelerating process in the mission communities, especially in those areas where Spanish towns grew in numbers in proximity to them, so that the second hundred years saw an intensification of Hispanicization among Opatas, Mayos, Yaquis, Lower Pimas, and a minority of Tarahumaras. Only those ranchería peoples to whose communities the missionaries failed to penetrate were not deeply influenced by Hispanicization — the more remote Tarahumaras, Upper Pimas, and the Yumans. The failure here may be assumed to have been a function of geography and the general weakening of the total Spanish program, rather than of the community reorganization technique.

However, it is also apparent that there were certain circumstances under which the reduction program was ineffective. The clearest example is that of the Pueblos. Although the Spaniards attempted the same approach among them, community reorganization was not brought about. The Pueblos were already living in compact communities with their own well-established religious centers. The missionaries worked in vain to refocus the villages around themselves and their mission churches, but the villages remained almost impermeable. There was no restructuring, no new fluid organization which could be controlled in process of reorganization by the purposeful missionaries. The Pueblo villages were already "reduced," and the Spanish agents of change remained peripheral, not only in a geographical sense at the edge of the Indian community, but also in terms of their roles in the community life. The result was blockage of the processes of assimilation — almost complete among the Western Pueblos — in a manner to limit assimilation to the special form of compartmentalization among the Eastern Pueblos.

The other instance in which the reduction program was not effective was that of the band peoples — the Seris, Navajos, and Apaches. It might be said that it was never actually put into operation among them but the fact is that it was on a small scale. There are in these instances indications that something more was involved than the lack of a foundation of Spanish military control to back up the program. Reduction was attempted with Seris and Navajos. They were brought to mission centers for concentration, and Apaches late in the 1700's were gathered about presidios. It is true that Spanish military strength was not exerted to keep them in place as it was in the case of the various ranchería peoples, but it is also true that the reactions of the Indians suggest that some very different technique would had to have been employed to involve them effectively in a cultural reorientation comparable to that which appeared among the ranchería peoples. Perhaps such an approach was being evolved by the Jesuits in the last years of their experience with the more resistant and more remote Tarahumaras.

It appears, therefore, that the basic method employed by the Spaniards in their program encouraged processes of assimilation only among peoples of one type of culture in the region. It cannot be regarded as a universally effective method and was clearly badly adapted for establishing favorable conditions for assimilation among the compact village and the band peoples. Only among the Indians in the middle range of the cultures of the Southwest was the Spanish technique for community reorganization adapted to the objectives of the Spaniards.

The most effective Hispanicization, then, took place among the Opatas, Mayos, Yaquis, Pimas, and Tarahumaras, pretty much in that order and with the reservation that some Pimas and Tarahumaras remained almost unaffected. Among this majority of Indians 250 years of contact resulted in introducing certain fundamental elements of Spanish culture. The most effectively implanted were probably the use of domestic animals and metals, a large number of religious concepts and rituals such as the Virgin and the saints with their appropriate ceremonials, forms of local government, and the use of spoken and written Spanish as a ritual language. These and some other elements described above were adapted in various ways to the persisting core cultures of the Indians, but the integration was so intricate that it may be said they fundamentally transformed the Indian cultures most affected. The Indians in some degree adopted a new religious orientation which carried them beyond the tribal horizon and gave them in some measure a world view in common with other tribes, including the Spaniards. Similarly the Indians most affected had clearly begun to move to a higher level of political organization. The process of political incorporation had not yet resulted in a clear and full participation in the national system of the Spaniards, but foundations in the form of Spanish town organization had superceded the looser and narrower ranchería governmental forms. Among the Pueblos of the villages, on the other hand, the acceptance of ceremonial usages and governmental forms resulted in no very fundamental change. No new levels of local organization or new range of religious orientation were established. The particular Jesuit techniques under the fluid conditions of ranchería reorganization constituted a highly favorable combination for Hispanicization. On the other hand, the Franciscan techniques, in combination with preexisting highly organized and compact communities, were conditions in which the processes of Hispanicization resulted in relatively little assimilation.

The Spanish method of directing cultural change was not destined to continue and the Mexican approach was very different. The Mexican policy makers proceeded on new assumptions and discarded the over-arching religious objective of the Spanish program. They nevertheless retained the objective of political incorporation and made it the focus of their early efforts. The initial plan for immediate political incorporation of the Indians was based on the assumption that the processes of Hispanicization had been completed. When the attempt to execute this plan resulted only in vigorous resistance, no coordinated program comparable to that of the Spaniards was developed. Mexican policy remained bogged down at the level of military domination insofar as any plan for dealing with the Indian communities was applied at all. The major feature of relations between Mexicans and Indians was the persistent infiltration of Indian country by settlers. This was seen by some persons in government as a program and was sometimes given a little government subsidy. Under these circumstances settler infiltration was called colonization. This approach to civilizing the Indians was the major one in northwestern Mexico during the nineteenth century and it continued to operate throughout the first half of the twentieth.

The major results of infiltration and colonization with respect to cultural assimilation were the following: renewed resistance on the part of the better organized groups such as Yaquis and Mayos, a great deal of individual assimilation among all groups, and extensive detribalization. The effects of resistance will be considered below. The individual assimilation took place in the cities and towns of the region among those Indians who were pushed off their land and in the small communities of settlers in Indian country. Among Indians who sought a means to live in the cities there was much mingling with low-income Mexicans from whom they hardly differed in racial features. Thousands of Indians pushed off their land by cattle ranchers augmented the population of the cities and gradually moved into and were accepted in Mexican urban society. At the same time a good deal of intermarriage took place in Mexican settlements in Indian country which resulted most often in identification of the children with the dominant Mexican families. Detribalization was a somewhat different process and took place most characteristically on the large haciendas which grew up in Sonora and eastern Chihuahua during the last half of the nineteenth century. These agricultural establishments employed large groups of laborers, recruited chiefly from dislocated Indian communities and refugee families from those parts of Indian country where open warfare was recurrent. Often there were Indians from several different tribes so that there was no common language and a minimum of common custom. Under the regime of the haciendas, characterized by absence of local government, attendance at the church supported by the owner of the hacienda, and dependence on the food and other goods supplied by the management, Indians usually became well assimilated into the cultural life of the rural Mexican peon. Tribal identification lapsed, notably among Opatas and Upper Pimas, even though the general identification as Indians continued. The process might be described as a sort of suspended assimilation resulting in a minimum of cultural differences between Indians and Mexicans without full acceptance into Mexican society. In general it may be said that infiltration and colonization, proceeding from the base of extensive assimilation established by Hispanicization, resulted in a high degree of Mexicanization among a majority of the Indians, but these developments also hardened the resistance of many Indians and among them Mexicanization was effectively blocked, particularly with respect to that feature of the program most valued by Mexicans, namely, political incorporation.

After more than a century of infiltration and border warfare a centrally directed program began to take form again in Mexico. Formulated in the face of great resistance from Mexicans who despite all that had taken place continued to view Indian assimilation as already accomplished, the new program readopted the older Spanish view of the Indian community as the mechanism for bringing about adjustment. Only the Tarahumaras among the Indians of northwestern Mexico were affected in an important way. In 1960 it was still too early to assess results.

The processes by which Anglicization took place among the Indians duplicated neither those of Hispanicization nor of Mexicanization, although there were some superficial similarities. Thus the directing of cultural change by a central government was a common feature of the Spanish and the Anglo-American programs. Moreover there was an apparent similarity in the approach of Spaniards and Anglo-Americans in that they both recognized Indian communities as distinct from settler communities. Nevertheless the guiding concepts of the Anglo-Americans were fundamentally different from those of the Spaniards and it would be a mistake to equate as instruments of assimilation the reservations in the United States with the mission communities of New Spain. The mission communities were conceived by the Spanish policy makers as places where Indians were to receive instruction in the Christian world view and to gain experience with the Spanish forms of local government. As the Indians learned to participate in the reorganized communities it was expected that their pueblos would become functioning units in the Spanish political system. Such a view of Indian settlements as transitional political communities did not develop in the United States until the 1930's and did not then gain full acceptance by those responsible for Indian administration. Meanwhile during the crucial sixty or seventy years of initial contact no program was established designed to reorganize the Indian communities with a view to fitting them into the Anglo-American political system. Instead, they were appended to the executive branch of the central government purely as administrative units. The effect of this feature of the program was to create conditions under which political assimilation could not take place. Indians were isolated from the growing number of Anglo-American communities surrounding them and gained no experience whatever of the Anglo-American type of local government or acquaintance with its principles. At the same time the superintendency form of administrative control, which was responsible only upward in a bureaucratic hierarchy and not to the Indians, undermined the existing community organization and system of authority. The result was not only a failure to move Indians progressively toward political integration but even to bring about a loss of the institutions through which they had traditionally governed themselves. This effect was directly proportional to the degree of control which the United States government was able to establish. On larger reservations like the Navajo and later the Papago, the great majority of Indians escaped for many years direct interference in their communities and, consequently, while not becoming politically assimilated, retained in considerable degree their traditional forms of community organization. On small reservations where the Indians were concentrated in or near agency towns such as the San Carlos Apache and Gila Pima the loss of community organization was almost complete. An important exception during the first seventy years of contact were the Pueblos. Their communities remained almost as impermeable to the superintendencies as they had to the mission system. Both Eastern and Western Pueblos maintained their traditional organization, not intact but in basic pattern.

Other techniques of the first phase of Anglicization brought about much cultural assimilation. These were consistent with the policy which ignored Indian communities as training grounds for political assimilation. In great contrast with the Spanish policy they proceeded from a conception of the assimilation processes as operating at the individual rather than the community level. The boarding-school program took individual Indians out of all the social units in which they participated on the reservations, from family to community and tribe. The missionary program, for which the central government took no responsibility in planning, opened up each reservation to two or more religious denominations within a short time after the reservations were established and ultimately to an indefinite number. The two programs resulted in a progressive increase of heterogeneity among the populations of the reservations. The percentages of Indians from each reservation who underwent the boarding-school type of training varied widely. The number of years of boarding-school attendance also varied for those who were enrolled. Moreover, for a great variety of reasons, the impact of the schools on individuals varied greatly with respect to influencing them toward assimilation. In short, the boarding-school experience was very far from uniform for the Indians of even any one reservation. The program resulted in creating a very wide range of attitudes, interests, and occupational skills among Indians. Similarly, the missionary programs as they reached more Indians increased the diversity of outlook. By the time of the shift in policy in the 1930's the majority of Indian communities exhibited a degree of diversity in their members which could be matched only in the Anglo-American cities, not in settlements of comparable size. While individual heterogeneity was beginning to approach that of Anglos, this did not of course mean that assimilation was nearly complete. On the contrary, assimilation of those Indians who lived on the reservations, and their numbers had begun accelerating rapidly, was blocked at every point by the very nature of the reservation in the polity of the states where they were located.

The shift in Indian policy which took place in the 1930's was actuated by a view of acculturation processes similar to that of the Spaniards who built the transitional mission communities. The changed approach was based on a conception of Indian communities as places where experience could be gained in political and economic institutions similar to those in the larger society and that the communities could on this basis be integrated eventually into the political organization of the United States. This was of course much like the idea of the missionary reorganizing Indian communities for ultimate equal place in the Spanish state. However, the breakdown of community life on the reservations as a result of the administrative system and of the heterogeneity produced by other features of the assimilation program imposed great odds against the successful carrying out of the new policy. The result was some amount of political assimilation over a period of twenty years and the creation of a small number of individuals on every reservation who became in some measure able to work in Anglo-American type political organization. However, by 1960 a fundamental change in the character of the political life of the reservations had only begun to take place. The tribal councils had slowly initiated the widening of the integration of Indian communities with Anglo-American political structure, but they still functioned basically only as appendages of the executive branch of the federal government, and the Indian Bureau exhibited decreasing interest in working toward any other objective. It was an important fact that the hitherto impermeable Pueblos for the first time exhibited a tendency toward fundamental change — at Isleta, Santa Clara, and among the Hopi.

By the 1960's policy was reverting to the purely individualistic conception on which it had usually been based in the past. Educational and religious assimilation were still so focused and the programs in operation in these aspects of culture resulted in an ever increasing degree of heterogeneity among the people on the reservations. Family types, religious behavior, and economic attitudes and skills ranged a wide gamut on most reservations from patterns very close to what they had been when white men arrived to completely Anglicized forms. Moreover, these patterns were combined in the behavior of particular individuals in such a variety of ways that it often seemed that the residents of reservations lacked anything that could be called a common culture. Anglicization had proceeded in a manner far more uneven than had Mexicanization.

THE SENSE OF IDENTITY

In the American Southwest the results of conquest were less striking with respect to the growth of common culture than to the continued existence of Indian groups as identifiable and self-conscious entities. In the middle of the twentieth century Navajos, Yaquis, Papagos, Seris, Hopis, Tarahumaras, and a score more of Indian groups had a vivid consciousness of themselves as distinct peoples from Mexicans and Anglo-Americans. This persistence of ethnic identification in the region seemed remarkable because of the smallness of the groups at the beginning of contact, their military weakness, and the ultimate invasion of their territory in overwhelming numbers by the European and European-derived peoples. The explanation of the persistence, despite such apparently unfavorable conditions, requires us to consider as much the effects of contact on the dominant peoples as on the Indian societies. The intensity with which a sense of distinct identity was maintained by any given Indian group was quite unrelated to the extent to which its customs and beliefs had been replaced by those of the conquerors; the sense of identity was not at all proportional to the number of aboriginal traditions persisting. The processes of cultural assimilation were in fact distinct from the processes of group identification.

The factors affecting the Indian sense of identity were numerous and no one factor among those operating within the Indian societies can be said to be decisive in all instances. A major influence in all cases, however, was the conditions affecting the relationship of Indians to the land. At the time of the entrance of the Spaniards all the Indians held in some form a belief in a sacred and indissoluble bond between themselves and the land in which their settlements were located. For the village Indians the land areas were well defined and the village locations well established. Among them only small dislocations took place. It may be said that only one group of village Indians — the Piro-speaking or southern Pueblos — was much affected in its relation to the land. The Piros were early removed from their village locations and then rapidly lost their sense of identity. The other Pueblos, with the exception of some Tanoan-speaking people who moved to the Hopi country, were not required to change their locations and consequently were able to maintain their sense of intimate and indissoluble identification with their traditional areas. Moreover this relationship was not fundamentally disturbed in later phases of contact.

The ranchería Indians on the other hand were stimulated to develop a more definite and stable relationship with their land than they had maintained before. The coming of the Spaniards resulted in the establishment of more stable boundaries between tribal groups such as the Tarahumaras and Tepehuanes, Yaquis and Mayos, and Lower Pimas and Opatas. Furthermore, within these newly stabilized territories, the locations of settlements became more fixed. The result was an intensification of the sense of sacred identification with the land in the service of which the sanctions of Christian mythology were sometimes employed. The Yaquis are the classic instance of the operation of the Spanish conditions of contact to stabilize and intensify the man-land relationship. A major exception would seem to have been the Opatas, whose stability of location was disrupted by the Spanish-stimulated warfare with the Apaches. It seems probable that this factor played some important part in the Opata loss of distinct identity following the Spanish period.

The band peoples were also probably to some extent stabilized in their relation to the land as a result of the Spanish drawing of boundaries. However, the Navajos, Apaches, and upland Yumans were not influenced in an important way in this respect until they came under the domination of the Anglo-Americans. They were then like the other Indians of the northern area assigned to reservations which were in each instance within the range of their traditional territories. Only those Yavapais placed on the San Carlos Apache Reservation constituted an exception. The whole reservation program may be seen as a major factor in the maintenance of the sacred man-land relationship for those Indians who resided in the United States.

Thus a basic circumstance affecting group identification in the Southwest was the maintenance of residence by the Indians within their traditional territorial ranges. This condition promoted the continuance of a tribal identification which had strong sacred sanctions. It stood in the way of the development of that separation of men from particular localities on which the growth of modern states has depended. Nevertheless it was apparent in mid-twentieth century that social mobility was steadily growing among Indians. As their populations increased a great inconsistency developed between their recognized land base and their population distribution.

The retention of land bases was an important basic condition permitting a continuity of tribal sense among Indians and, in later phases of contact, constituting fixed boundaries in an increasingly mobile enveloping society. An equally important factor consisted of conditions which promoted working solidarity among tribal members. Chief among such conditions were successful warfare vis-a-vis the invaders, continuity in community structure, and enforced consolidation of previously disparate units within a tribe. Warfare against the invaders played a part in promoting solidarity in the case of almost every tribe. In many instances its effect was not of primary importance, as among Pueblos and Upper Pimas. In others warfare lasted long enough and was sufficiently successful to reinforce feelings of solidarity and to implant a strong common sense of hostility against the invaders. The Yaquis and Seris are notable instances of people whose solidarity was intensified through warfare to the point that they were able to maintain identity even in the face of removal from their sacred lands. In all instances of extended warfare stimulating solidarity among Indians, there followed an enforced consolidation of bands or rancherías which became a stimulus to the development of a new sense of common destiny. The clear instances of this are to be seen in the history of the Navajos, the Western Apaches, the Seris, and perhaps the Walapais and some Tarahumaras. Among these groups consolidation followed bitter and devastating common experiences of defeat, out of which grew a new sense of solidarity in the face of aggression from the invaders.

In addition to the factors mentioned there were non-military reactions against the dominant peoples. These reactions, taking the form of religious movements of various types, were often responses to defeat in warfare. They reinforced solidarity through new faith in magical means for destruction of the invaders or in some concept of spiritual regeneration. The nativistic movements of this sort which arose among Tarahumaras, Mayos, Western Apaches, and Walapais represented culminations in feelings of hostility and in exaltation of the Indians' moral basis of life. They had the effect of defining and giving meaning to symbols of Indian common purpose and Indian pride in their distinctness from their conquerors. The symbols so defined then took permanent place in the belief systems of the Indians, especially among the Mayos and Apaches. It is to be expected that similar movements will arise among Yaquis, Eastern and Western Pueblos, Seris, and Tarahumaras during the coming phase of contact.

In different combinations the factors discussed have contributed in various tribes to the maintenance and reinforcement of feelings of separateness from others and to a sense of common destiny among themselves. Continued residence on their land and common experiences in the struggle for autonomy have resulted in the definition of beliefs and values which are peculiar to their history and which they are aware are not understood in their terms by members of the dominant societies. These beliefs and values have been symbolized in different ways. Certain elements of the traditional cultures were selected and as a result of the special circumstances of a given tribe's history imbued with special significance in connection with that tribe's identifications in the milieu of other Indian groups and the dominant society. Various features of dress became important symbols, such as headbands for males among Pueblos and full-skirted dresses for women among Western Apaches. These were not of aboriginal materials or styles. Hairdress also took on significance among some groups for both men and women. Songs and dances, selected from the surviving complexes of ceremony, became extremely important as symbols of group solidarity. Certain forms of ceremonial dress came to have great importance as tribal symbols because, in addition to the significance attached to them through associations with Indian traditions, non-Indians became especially conscious of them.

Through this process their function as symbols of distinct identity for Indians in the White milieu was intensified. The Pueblo kachina doll, the Apache crown dancer's paraphernalia, and the Yaqui deer dancer were examples of such symbols which gained increasingly wide significance in the larger societies.

The group identifications of the Indians rested solidly in their historical experiences with white men and were symbolized in elements of their cultures which were, like their experiences, products of contacts between Indians and white men. It was true also that the Indian sense of identity was stimulated and reinforced through the reactions of white men to the contact situation. A sense of identity depends not only on a distinction made by the group possessing it, but also on distinctions made by other groups excluded from the identification. The original Spanish approach to the Indians had a profound effect on their future, particularly with reference to their place in the political entity of New Spain. The official viewpoint was that in Indian country there existed a plural society, that is, two distinct categories of communities. The mission communities where the transition to civilized society was to be engineered by the missionaries were not to be forced immediately into the mould of the empire. Residents in these had a relationship to the king and his representatives different from that of the residents in the Spanish towns. There were two sets of laws, one for the full-fledged Spaniard, another for the Indians in transition. The Spanish conception of the time that would be necessary for the transition — ten years — now seems surprisingly naive, but the missionaries, particularly the more zealous Jesuits, saw to it that more time was allowed. Thus the Indians lived in a plural society, as a specially defined legal entity, for almost the whole of the Spanish period. The foundations were laid for a persisting emphasis on the distinctness of Indians.

The Mexican viewpoint was antithetical to the conception of plural society. Nevertheless, the effort to force political integration had the effect of intensifying the solidarity and hence the sense of identity of the Indians, especially of those who had been most Hispanicized. The warfare, moreover, resulted in forcing upon the Mexicans an awareness of the intensity with which Indians insisted on their distinctness. The century of conflict gave rise to the indigenist movement in Mexico, as elsewhere in Latin America; some intellectuals and scholars came to realize that there were Indians who still thought of themselves as Indians and that the idea of a unitary society was unrealistic. The new Indian policy which emerged, somewhat uncertainly during the 1930's, embodied a conception not unlike that of the Spaniards. Indian rights to land were re-emphasized and the Cárdenas administration even went so far as to decree exclusive Indian ownership over what was left of the Yaqui territory. The policy which ultimately crystallized into the formaton of the National Indian Institute was based in the conception of transitional communities, that is, of indigenous communities where a special relationship with the federal government was required for satisfactory movement toward greater integration with the nation as a whole. The spokesmen of the new policy had much to say about the importance of fostering pride in the Indian background, at the same time that they insisted on the necessity of political and economic integration with the Mexican people generally. The viewpoint of the administrators in the National

Indian Institute, as an expression of *indigenismo,* was a clear indication of the Mexican government's reaction against its own earlier roughshod assimilation program.

In the United States the reservation policy from the first stages of contact fixed the concept of Indian separateness. Moreover, since for a long time the approach was not tempered with a program for gradual transformation of the Indian communities, the concept of a plural society became very solidly established. Accepted as a fact by policy makers and settlers, the idea became steadily embodied in a host of laws and administrative regulation. In the hands of the Jesuits the transitional mission communities were steadily given longer and longer life than had been called for in the original planning. In the hands of the government bureau for Indian affairs, the reservations in the United States took on the form of permanent arrangements. The effect on the Indian sense of identity was profound, regardless of the extent to which any reservation residents became culturally assimilated.

The reservation policy profoundly influenced not only Indians, but also many non-Indians. Organizations grew up in the United States, such as the Indian Rights Association, which brought pressures to bear on the federal government for maintenance of the reservation system. Like the Mexicans who supported the indigenist movement, members of these organizations accepted the existence of the Indians as distinct entities and much of their influence was directed toward preserving the concept of plural society as a basis of policy.

CHAPTER TWENTY

Enclaves and Cultural Evolution

A MAJOR THEME of this study is that plans for changing the ways of life of Indians in the Southwest did not work out as those who conceived the plans expected them to. The objectives of military and political domination over the Indians were eventually achieved, after about 350 years, but even given the control that this made possible, most of the Indians simply did not respond as the conquerors thought they would and should. As late as 1960 it was still true that the expectations of the dominant peoples were not being realized in any consistent manner.

Various theories were proposed to account for the Indian "resistance" to change. The Jesuit Nentuig in the eighteenth century, after years of close contact with Indians in Sonora, reached the conclusion that Upper Pimas and Seris by their very nature could not be changed and hence should be removed to "distant countries." It should be noted that this was not a general explanation for all Indian behavior. Nentuig did not hold that other Indians were incapable of change. Essentially he was saying that those Indians with whom the Spanish program had been most successful in achieving its ends could be changed and those with whom it had not been successful could not be. In other words, the Spanish program was in the main beyond criticism; it was accepted as the only possible means for achieving the ends desired by the Spaniards. Implicit in Nentuig's proposal was the proposition that there are sharply distinct types of human beings, some capable of being civilized and some not. This view, it should be emphasized, was contrary to that which guided the policy makers of the early Spanish program. It seems nevertheless to have become the prevailing viewpoint among Spaniards in northwestern New Spain, as exemplified not only by Nentuig but also, for example, in the Gálvez Apache policy.

In the nineteenth century the historian Bancroft, preoccupied chiefly with facts concerning the Indians of Sonora and Chihuahua when many of them were in periodic revolt against Mexican domination, put forth an explanation which was somewhat similar. He wrote: *Again the work of the padres was like that of most, perhaps all, missionaries, a failure, unless perchance their theories respecting future salvation should prove true, because they did not civilize the Indians, nor could they have civilized them even if not interfered with, since savages cannot be civilized under the tuition of superior races* . . . In this explanation of the continuing cultural differential between Indians and white men, Bancroft was working with two ideas not quite consistent with each other. On the one hand, he seems to have believed in the inherent superiority and inferiority of races, a conception which was widespread among Europeans and Anglo-Americans of his day. At the same time Bancroft appears also to have adopted another current idea, namely that of evolutionary development by stages. Savagery and civilization were the terms often applied to the earliest and latest stages. However, the idea that mankind has moved progressively through three or more cultural stages to a state of civilization was believed in by men who generally held that all races had the capacity for such development; the idea of innate limited capacity was inconsistent with the evolutionary view. Bancroft did not develop his explanation systematically, and hence we do not know how he dealt with the inconsistency. What he did say was that savages cannot be civilized. In that respect he agreed with Nentuig. They both believed that no matter what type of program might be adopted, certain people could not be changed to behave like Europeans. The major difference between the two views was with respect to which peoples should be included in the category of uncivilizable. The Jesuit included only a selection of Indians known to him. The historian appeared to class all the Indians of northwestern Mexico as incapable of civilization. Moreover, Bancroft's position was based on an attempt to apply a general theory, peculiar though his application may have been. He held, in substance, that evolutionary stages in cultural development cannot be jumped, but did not commit himself concerning the mechanism by which civilized peoples attained their position in the scale.

There had developed in the United States, even at the time Bancroft wrote, an approach to Indian affairs which was diametrically opposed to Bancroft's. Those who formulated the Dawes Act in 1887 worked from the same assumption that had actuated the makers of early Spanish policy, namely, that all Indians could be civilized. The important consideration in this view was the type of program. If only the right means could be found, the desired changes in the way of life of the Indians could be brought about. This general approach to Indian affairs prevailed in the United States from the 1880's through the 1950's. Moreover, by the 1930's the same basic viewpoint was adopted by government policy makers in Mexico and continued there also to underlie the programs for directing Indian cultural change. The issues in Indian policy did not center on the possibility or impossibility of bringing about change, but only on which means could be expected to produce the results aimed at by the government programmers.

About 1900 a new assessment of the causes of Indian backwardness in Sonora began to be made. The phenomenon which concerned government officials and other Mexicans was the continued Yaqui resistance, despite disastrous battles, to the well-intentioned government program for peaceful resettlement of the Indians, along with Mexican colonists, on their land. The military historian Troncoso recorded the views which led to the deportation program. It was essentially a consideration of the long list of armed conflicts between Spaniards and Mexicans on the one hand and Yaquis on the other. The listing of these led to the conclusion that Yaquis were inherently warlike and that the women particularly could not be changed and that they instilled hostility into their children. Thus a subsidiary feature of the solution was the separation of mothers and children. This analysis, of course, ignored the long period of peace under the Jesuits and the very extensive Hispanization which had taken place. It was, nevertheless, an effort to arrive at a reasonable program based on an intensive study of Yaqui history. The weakness was that the historical study was one-sided and incomplete and never attained objectivity with reference to Spanish and Mexican behavior. The examination did have the virtue of considering at least three alternative means, the two others being extermination and colonization.

There was, however, another viewpoint among Mexicans familiar with the Yaqui situation. A military medical officer, Manuel Balbas, looked at the problem differently from the war department officials. About 1900, after serving in a number of campaigns against Yaquis, he wrote as follows: *The Yaqui tribe is half savage. It is necessary to civilize them. But to accomplish that two diametrically opposed courses present themselves: that of peaceful and that of armed conquest ...*

The first is very slow and would necessitate several generations for its realization. Success would be practically impossible if it were applied to the adults. ... It is true that all people are susceptible of civilization; beginning their education and instruction however not through adults but through children. ... There is a great difference between dominating a people and civilizing them. ...

... the campaign against this tribe is nothing else than a war of conquest, in which the government is the aggressor and the Yaqui people the attacked. ...

Schools! Schools!

In this regard Balbas took the position of the formulators of the early Spanish program. Seeing military conquest at first hand he reacted against it and held the belief that education of the young was the course which would work to the end of getting the Indians to behave like Mexicans. He gave no indication of thinking through the organization of an educational program. It appears that he conceived an educational program in terms of individualized instruction which would substitute the influence of Mexican schoolteachers for that of Yaqui parents over the children.

This acceptance of the early Spanish approach gained ground in Mexico steadily during the twentieth century and ultimately became the basis for federal governmental policy with respect to Indians. The idea of removal of children to boarding schools for Mexicanization was still a part of the early Cárdenas program, but in the 1940's a different means was conceived and this became the actuating policy of the National Indian Institute. *The work of the National Indian Institute has been conceived for dealing with the problems of the indigenous communities in integral fashion, preserving and encouraging the positive aspects of the culture of these communities and extending the means for raising the cultural level in all aspects of the collective life. To accomplish that we believe that it is fundamental to acquire the confidence of the communities and never to employ methods of coercion.* . . . In this plan of action is clearly expressed a theory of relationship between a particular means and an end desired. In this case the end is an integration of Indian life into the national cultural life, not simply replacement of Indian ways with Mexican ways. The means for integration of the two is community restructuring through a variety of techniques but with a focus on persuasion.

In the United States meanwhile, the issue of Indian policy tended to be decided, as we have seen, in the opposite direction — although it would be more just to say that shifts of policy followed no very clear path. Nevertheless, the clear acceptance of the view at the official level that all Indians could be changed to behave like Anglo-Americans hardly altered from the 1880's to the 1960's. The objective generally accepted was fairly consistently defined as cultural assimilation, despite the view of upper-level officials during the Collier administration that assimilation ought to be considered only with reference to the degree necessary for satisfactory adjustment between Indians and Whites and not in terms of absolutes. The issues in Indian policy, then, focused on the means for achieving some degree of assimilation. Discussion of issues centered around precisely the points raised in Mexico: Should Indian communities be regarded as units of adjustment or should individuals? Should programs rest on forms of coercion or on Indian choice? The features of the first broad program beginning in the 1880's were an outgrowth of the assumption that cultural assimilation should and could be brought about in individuals in isolation from their families and communities. On the other hand, the program initiated in the 1930's was based on the belief that changes could best be brought about by establishing conditions for stimulating Indian communities to choose and develop their own patterns of adjustment. In the 1950's Indian Bureau programs were compounds of features inherited from both earlier periods and often therefore showed striking contradictions.

In both Mexico and the United States, despite the over-all trends in policy, officials involved in the administration of Indian programs were still asking whether Indians could be civilized. Some, like the Dominican las Casas, believed they could; others, like the Jesuit Nentuig, believed they could not. The fact that it was possible to cite many instances past and present to support either position indicated that the practical efforts to solve Indian problems as conceived by the dominant peoples had not yet given any overwhelming demonstration of how to achieve what the conquerors desired. The puzzling question to which Bancroft had sought an answer remained: Can people at one level of economic and political development be raised to another level through planned programs?

We may pose the question in the following way and suggest an answer. Why did Indians not progressively reorganize their communities in such a way as to participate in the higher level of political and economic organization made available to them and, parallel with such change, adopt the European type of world view?

A possible explanation, in line with theories of the economic interpretation of history, has great plausibility. We have pointed out the "economic lag" which characterized every phase of change in the Southwest. Indians simply were not brought into the production and market system of the Spaniards during the Spanish colonial period. To a considerable extent, through the hacienda system they were, however, brought into the later Mexican economy, and to the degree that they were so incorporated cultural assimilation began to take place. In the United States a significant degree of participation in the general economic life did not take place until the 1940's, but even then the reservation system stood in the way of full participation.

These facts suggest that fundamental to the whole process of change in the direction of the European way of life was the bringing of Indian land, labor, and resources into a fully functioning role in the developing market economy. If that had taken place in each phase of contact, it may be assumed, other changes in the direction of the adoption of the European ways of life would have followed. But this did not take place; rather the attention of the dominant peoples in New Spain and Mexico was focused on religious and political change and in the United States on a peculiar sort of protected economic development.

We might frame an explanation in the following way: because Indian land, labor, and resources were of so little importance for the economies of the dominant peoples, the Indians were not brought into these economies and hence the programs for cultural change did not affect them in consistent or progressive fashion. Given the small Indian populations, the lack of resources valuable to the invaders, and the possibility of concentrating the Indians on small parts of the less valuable land, the Indians were forced, as it were, into an evolutionary *cul de sac*. They remained localized communities with the essential world view, as well as customs, of primitive people, and hence in the main resistant to assimilation programs.

This economic explanation of cultural development among Southwestern Indians seems to explain much. Compared with efforts at religious and political integration, economic integrative efforts lagged very far behind throughout the four hundred years of contact. Given that lag, there was small basis for development among Indians in their own communities of a culture and world view of the type of those of their conquerors. The economic life of a people is an important limiting factor with respect to the growth of higher levels of organization and greater cultural differentiation. We have here an explanation for the failure of the Indian cultures to change their type.

There are, nevertheless, several respects in which this explanation remains unsatisfactory. If we wish to explain the formation and persistence of the cultural enclaves, it is true that an important factor has unquestionably been the relative lack of economic interest on the part of the dominant people in the Indian communities. But we cannot employ the economic factor very far in explaining the similarity and variety in types of enclave which have characterized Southwestern Indians. As a very broad sort of explanation outlining a general limiting condition, the economic interpretation may be valid, but it suggests a closer functional relationship between, for example, market economy and the Christian religion than has so far been demonstrated. No doubt full-scale economic integration of Indians would have resulted in a greater degree of cultural assimilation, but would not also full-scale political integration? Why should we not take political or family organization as equally determining factors as the economy?

At any rate, if we wish to gain some understanding of the variety in responses to contact, it would seem that we must then take another factor in addition to the economic into account. This factor is social structure. As we review the patterns of change in Indian life through the various phases, it appears that in those instances where there was greatest continuity in social structure there was the least degree of cultural replacement and hence the least change in the direction of the dominant cultures.

By continuity in social structure, we refer specifically to persistence of the Indian forms of family and community, or local group, organization. Where these were little altered under the conditions of contact, cultural assimilation was at a minimum; where they were much altered the dominant peoples proceeded with greater success to bring about replacement of custom and belief. Where there was continuity the Indian-type family continued as the major institution for inducting children into the cultural life of the group; where there was continuity the Indian form of local community was the regulator of change and the effective mechanism of cultural adaptation. If we look at the course of change from this point of view many of the differences and many of the similarities with respect to the results of contact among the various tribal groups become intelligible. Together with the economic, the factor of continuity in family and community structure can be employed to good advantage for understanding the complex forces of change as they operated in the past and as they will continue to operate in the future.

BIBLIOGRAPHIC NOTES TO CHAPTERS

INTRODUCTION

The conception of "civilization" employed in this book and introduced here in the section, "The Overlapping Conquests of North America," is essentially that developed at some length in Robert Redfield, *The Primitive World and Its Transformations* (Ithaca: Cornell University Press, 1953).

For more extended descriptions of the Indian cultures of the region, see the following general surveys:

Basauri, Carlos. *La población indígena de México.* 3 v. México: Secretaría de educación pública, 1940.

Beals, Ralph L. *Preliminary Report on the Ethnography of the Southwest.* Berkeley, Calif.: National Park Service, 1935.

Goddard, Pliny E. *Indians of the Southwest.* New York: American Museum of Natural History, 1927.

Hernández, Fortunato. *Las razas indígenas de Sonora y la guerra del Yaqui.* México: Talleres de la Casa Editorial "J. de Elizalde," 1902.

Hodge, Frederick Webb (ed.). *Handbook of American Indians North of Mexico.* 2 v. Bureau of American Ethnology, Bulletin 30. Washington, 1907–1910.

Kroeber, A. L. *Cultural and Natural Areas of Native North America.* Berkeley: University of California Press, 1939.

Sauer, Carl O. *The Distribution of Aboriginal Tribes and Languages in Northwestern Mexico.* (Ibero-Americana: 5). Berkeley: University of California Press, 1934.

CHAPTER ONE

This account leans most heavily on Decorme and Dunne for the Spanish period, on Peña and Plancarte for the Mexican period. Dunne is certainly the most readable, in English or Spanish, for the entire colonial phase of Tarahumara history. He may be recommended, but with the reservation always that he is a Jesuit writing about, primarily, Jesuit activities; he inevitably exhibits a Jesuit bias in his selection and emphasis. Moreover, it is not easy to find a corrective for this, for the only other broad narrative accounts of the period are also by Jesuits — Decorme and Alegre. Within the limits of secondary sources, the best correctives that can be recommended are Bancroft, Saravia, and perhaps West.

The Mexican phase of Tarahumara history remains to be written as a unit. There is no published book which contains it, and I have not heard of any pile of notes on any scholar's desk which would constitute the material for the narrative. This is unfortunate; it would be of immense interest in view of the large size of the tribe, the wide variety of contacts, and the probability of important factional splits and contrasts — contrasts which are suggested in Bennett and Zingg and in Lumholtz. It is these last two books which, although they lack adequate historical perspective, give the best insights into Tarahumara life in the Mexican phase. For narratives of events, almost exclusively from the narrow official Mexican viewpoint, we must turn to Plancarte and Peña. Basauri has a few notes, Ocampo is good for the recent Jesuit activities, but there is nothing for the whole Mexican period comparable to Dunne for the Spanish. Somewhere in the records Tarahumara viewpoints must show through, at least to the extent that they do in the Jesuit accounts of the colonial period, but so far they have not been found and compiled.

Acción Indigenista. Boletín mensual del Instituto Nacional Indigenista. Numbers 22 (April 1955), 43 (January 1957), 48 (June 1957), 59 (May 1958), México.

Alegre, Francisco Javier. *Historia de la Compañía de Jesús en Nueva España.* 3 v. México, 1841–42.

Almada, Francisco R. *Diccionario de historia, geografía y biografía chihuahuenses.* Chihuahua, 1945.

Bancroft, Hubert Howe. *History of the North Mexican States and Texas.* 2 v. San Francisco, 1884–89.

Basauri, Carlos. *Monografía de los Tarahumaras.* México: Talleres Gráficos de Nación, 1929.

Bennett, Wendell C. and Robert M. Zingg. *The Tarahumara, An Indian Tribe of Northern Mexico.* Chicago: University of Chicago Press, 1935.

Decorme, Gerard. *La obra de los Jesuitas mexicanos durante la época colonial, 1572–1767.* 2 v. México: Antigua Librería Robredo de J. Porrua e Hijos, 1941.

Dunne, Peter Masten. *Early Jesuit Missions in Tarahumara.* Berkeley: University of California Press, 1948.

Gómez González, Filiberto. *Rarámuri, mi diario Tarahumara.* México: Tall. Tip. de Excelsior, 1948.

González Navarro, Moisés. "Instituciones indígenas en México independiente," in *Métodos y resultados de la política indigenista en México.* Instituto Nacional Indigenista, Memorias, Vol. VI. México, 1954.

Lumholtz, Carl. *Unknown Mexico.* 2 v. New York: Charles Scribner's Sons, 1902.

México. Departamento del Trabajo. *La raza Tarahumara.* México, 1936.

Ocampo, Manuel. *Historia de la misión de la Tarahumara, 1900–1950.* México: Editorial "Buena Prensa," 1950.

Peña, Moisés T. de la. "Extranjeros y Tarahumares en Chihuahua," in Miguel Othón de Mendizábal, *Obras completas.* Vol. I. México, 1946.

Plancarte, Francisco M. *El problema indígena Tarahumara.* Instituto Nacional Indigenista, Memorias, Vol. V. México, 1954.

Saravia, Atanasio G. *Apuntes para la historia de la Nueva Vizcaya.* Tomo 3, "Las sublevaciones." México, 1956.

West, Robert C. *The Mining Community in Northern New Spain.* (Ibero-Americana: 30). Berkeley: University of California Press, 1949.

CHAPTER TWO

The most important publications for piecing together Yaqui-Mayo history are Andrés Pérez de Ribas' *Triumph of Our Holy Faith among the Most Wild and Barbarous Nations* . . . ; Decorme's history of Jesuit work in Mexico; Ignacio Zuñiga's *Rapid Glance over the State of Sonora;* Fortunato Hernández' story of the final phases of the Mexican-Yaqui struggle in the nineteenth century; and perhaps Alfonso Fabila's description of the Cárdenas administration's program for Yaquis in the late 1930's. With the exception of Decorme's chapters, these are all firsthand accounts of happenings during crucial periods in the lives of the Indians. Peréz de Ribas tells of his own adventures as the first missionary to work among the Yaquis beginning in 1617. Decorme has tried to reconstruct, primarily from Jesuit accounts, the clashes of personality and purpose which brought about the bloody revolt of 1740, and Zuñiga reports unusually vivid impressions of the causes and results of the attempt of Juan Banderas to force an independent Indian nation in the 1820's. Hernández knew the principal actors in the climactic struggle of Cajeme and Tetabiate to fend off Mexican domination at the close of the nineteenth century. Fabila was a participant in the hopeful efforts of the federal government to construct a new basis of cooperation between Indians and Mexicans. From these accounts a picture emerges of attitudes which guided the dominant people, and, between the lines, one gets some glimpses of the Indian viewpoints. Each gives insight into a major crisis period. The intervals between, when events were building toward the crises, remain shadowy.

Curiously enough, perhaps the most valuable publication for illuminating some of these shadowy phases of Yaqui-Mayo history is the straightforward military history compiled at the request of the Mexican government by Francisco P. Troncoso. His history is ostensibly a year-by-year record of all military activities by Yaquis and Mayos from 1533 to 1900. It was prepared as an effort at gaining understanding of and finding a solution for "the Yaqui problem." In its pages,

and only here, some of the deeper causes and more far-reaching effects of Mexican-Indian relations come into focus, such as, for example, the religious prophet movement among the Mayos in the 1890's and the economic forces at work in the Sonoran state legislature in the mid-nineteenth century. The other publications which succeed in some measure in being history in the sense that they relate succeeding events to one another are Acosta's interesting, if not too well integrated narrative of the colonial period, and Hernández' account of events during the 1800's.

In addition to the books mentioned, the bibliography includes a selection of the available publications most heavily relied upon in this account. Bancroft, Calvo Berber, and Villa, dealing with the history of the whole region in which Mayos and Yaquis live, have made beginnings at the necessary background for an understanding of the remarkable struggle of the Yaquis for autonomy. The others listed give valuable insights into particular aspects of the dramatic series of events. Balbas, a doctor serving with the Mexican troops who fought the Yaqui guerrillas in the final phase of the Yaqui wars, expressed rather clearly the emerging viewpoint of sympathy with the Indians which began to be important in Mexico by the end of the nineteenth century. Ezell discusses the hopefully formulated legal basis for Indian integration in Sonora during the 1820's, when the problem seemed quite simple to the Mexicans. Hrdlička describes in sketchy fashion the broken families and some of the miseries resulting from the deportation program, while Turner, actuated by deep moral indignation, reports impressionistically the mechanics of deportation, going as far as Yucatan to gather miscellaneous facts and rumors. Carleton Beals gives glimpses of some of the foundations of policy of the Díaz government with respect to the Indians, and the Weyls in a few brief passages give details of the military program of the Obregón government in the Yaqui country toward the close of the Revolution of 1910. Spicer reports the nature of the Yaqui River towns in the 1940's, attempting to give background for the Yaqui viewpoints of their historical relations with Spaniards and Mexicans.

The definitive history of these tribes remains to be written. What we have up to now are glimpses, although it seems probable that we do know the main outlines. The materials are abundant for particularly the last 150 years. They await the historian who is willing to work with living informants as well as with the documentary record.

Acosta, Roberto. *Apuntes históricos sonorenses: la conquista temporal y espiritual del Yaqui y del Mayo.* México, 1949.

Balbas, Manuel. *Recuerdos del Yaqui: principales episodios durante la campaña de 1899 a 1901.* México, D. F.: Sociedad de Edición y Libreria Franco Americana, 1927.

Bancroft, Hubert Howe. *History of the North Mexican States and Texas.* 2 v. San Francisco, 1884–1889.

Beals, Carleton. *Porfirio Diaz, Dictator of Mexico.* Philadelphia: J. B. Lippincott Co., 1932.

Calvo Berber, Laureano. *Nociones de historia de Sonora.* México, D. F.: Librería de M. Porrua, 1958.

Decorme, Gerard. *La obra de los Jesuitas mexicanos durante la época colonial, 1572–1767.* 2 v. Tomo 2, "Las misiones." México: Antigua Librería Robredo de J. Porrua e Hijos, 1941.

Ezell, Paul H. "Indians Under the Law. Mexico, 1821-1847," *América Indígena,* Vol. 15, Num. 3 (1953), pp. 199–214.

Fabila, Alfonso. *Las tribus Yaquis de Sonora: su cultura y anhelada autodeterminación.* México: Departamento de asuntos indígenas, 1940.

Hernández, Fortunato. *Las razas indígenas de Sonora y la guerra del Yaqui.* México: Talleres de la Casa Editorial "J. de Elizalde," 1902.

Hrdlička, Aleš. "Notes on the Indians of Sonora, Mexico," *American Anthropologist,* n.s., Vol. 6, No. 1 (1904), pp. 51–89.

Métodos y resultados de la política indigenista en México. Instituto Nacional Indigenista, Memorias, Vol. VI. México, 1954.

Pérez de Ribas, Andrés. *Historia de los triunfos de nuestra santa fe entre gentes las más bárbaras y fieras del Nuevo orbe* . . . México: Editorial Layac, 1944.

Spicer, Edward H. *Potam, A Yaqui Village in Sonora.* American Anthropological Association, Memoir 77, 1954.

Troncoso, Francisco P. *Las guerras con las tribus Yaqui y Mayo del estado de Sonora.* México, 1905.

Turner, John Kenneth. *Barbarous Mexico.* Chicago: C. H. Kerr & Co., 1911.

Villa, Eduardo W. *Historia del estado de Sonora.* 2. ed. Hermosillo: Editorial Sonora, 1951.

Weyl, Nathaniel and Silvia. *The Reconquest of Mexico: The Years of Lázaro Cárdenas.* London: Oxford University Press, 1939.

Zuñiga, Ignacio. *Rápida ojeada al estado de Sonora.* México, 1835.

CHAPTER THREE

This chapter rests essentially on Bannon's careful summary of events for the early colonial period and, for the later Spanish period, the description of the Opatas and their country given in *Rudo Ensayo,* supplemented with details from the always useful general histories of Decorme and Bancroft. There is little information of any importance about Opata life during the nineteenth and twentieth centuries until the 1950's, when the studies by Hinton and Owen give us some clear facts regarding the cultural assimilation of the descendants of Opatas. A history of the Opatas during the late eighteenth and nineteenth centuries will probably be difficult to obtain material for, simply because of the rapid loss of identity by the group, and the consequent difficulty of separating their history from that of the Sonoran Mexicans generally. It would probably be an artificial procedure to attempt to do so. Nevertheless the processes of assimilation in central Sonora can undoubtedly be illuminated by some intensive work with the records which may still be obtainable. On the other hand, the Lower Pimas, although a small group, have maintained a sharper sense of identity. Their history would be well worth writing, particularly if the conception actuating the study included the Upper Pimas.

Bandelier, A. F. *Final Report of Investigations Among the Indians of the Southwestern United States* . . . *1880–1885.* Archaeological Institute of America, Papers, "American Series," Nos. 3 and 4. Cambridge, Mass., 1890–1892.

Bannon, John F. *The Mission Frontier in Sonora, 1620–1687.* United States Catholic Historical Society, Monograph Series 26. New York, 1955.

Dunne, Peter Masten. *Pioneer Black Robes on the West Coast.* Berkeley: University of California Press, 1940.

Escudero, José Agustín de. *Noticias estadísticas de Sonora y Sinaloa* . . . México: Tip. de Rafael, 1849.

Hardy, R.W.H. *Travels in the Interior of Mexico.* London: H. Colburn & R. Bentley, 1829.

Hinton, Thomas. *A Survey of Indian Assimilation in Eastern Sonora.* Anthropological Papers of the University of Arizona, No. 4. Tucson, 1959.

Hrdlička, Aleš. "Notes on the Indians of Sonora, Mexico," *American Anthropologist,* n.s., Vol. 6, No. 1 (1904), pp. 51–89.

Johnson, Jean B. *The Opata: An Inland Tribe of Sonora.* University of New Mexico Publications in Anthropology, No. 6. Albuquerque, 1950.

Ocaranza, Fernando. *Parva crónica de la Sierra Madre y las Pimerías.* Instituto Panamericano de Geografía e Historia, publicación num. 64. México: Editorial Stylo, 1942.

Owen, Roger C. *Marobavi: A Study of an Assimilated Group in Northern Sonora.* Anthropological Papers of the University of Arizona, No. 3. Tucson, 1959.

Rudo Ensayo, by an Unknown Jesuit Padre, 1763. Tucson: Arizona Silhouettes, 1951.

Treutlein, Theodore (ed. & trans.) *Sonora: A*

Description of the Province, by Ignaz Pfefferkorn. (Coronado Cuarto Centennial Publications, Vol. 12). Albuquerque: University of
New Mexico Press, 1949.

CHAPTER FOUR

I have relied heavily on a letter written
by Father Adam Gilg in 1692 for the earliest
events in Seri contacts with the Spaniards.
His statements do not always agree with what
has been published by McGee and others. I
have not discussed the disagreements, but
have attempted a narrative which is probably
biased from the Jesuit point of view. McGee
has put together the most useful set of documents for understanding Seri history through
the nineteenth century, but there remain
many obscure phases which deserve further
intensive research. McGee is also responsible
for a firsthand account of the significant
epoch of the "Encinas Wars" and what led
up to them. The whole twentieth-century
history of the Seris could be worked out in
detail from living informants in Sonora.

Bancroft, Hubert Howe. History of the North
Mexican States and Texas. 2 v. San Francisco,
1884–1889.

Decorme, Gerard. La obra de los Jesuitas mexicanos durante la época colonial, 1572–1767.
2 v. Tomo 2, "Las misiones." México: Antigua
Librería Robredo de J. Porrua e Hijos, 1941.

Coolidge, Dane and Mary. The Last of the Seris.
New York: Dutton, 1939.

Eckhart, George B. "The Seri Indian Missions,"
The Kiva, Vol. 25, No. 3 (1960), pp. 37–43.
(Arizona Archaeological and Historical Soci-
ety, Tucson).

Gilg, Adam. "Letter to the Reverend Father
Rector of the College of the Society of Jesus
at Brunn in Moravia. Written in Pópulo in the
Seri District in the country of Sonora, in February, 1692." Number 53. In microfilm. Translated by Daniel Matson.

Griffen, William B. Notes on Seri Indian Cul-
ture, Sonora, Mexico. School of Inter-American
Studies, Latin American Monographs, 10.
Gainesville, Florida, 1959.

Hernández, Fortunato. Las razas indígenas de
Sonora y la guerra del Yaqui. México: Talleres
de la Casa Editorial "J. de Elizalde," 1902.

Kino, Eusebio F. Kino's Historical Memoir of
Pimería Alta. 2 v. Herbert E. Bolton, trans.
Berkeley: University of California Press, 1948.

Kroeber, A. L. The Seri. Southwest Museum
Papers, No. 6. Pasadena, Calif., 1931.

McGee, W. J., "The Seri Indians," Annual Report,
Bureau of American Ethnology, No. 17. Washington, 1898.

Ocaranza, Fernando. Los Franciscanos en las
provincias internas de Sonora y Ostimuri.
México, D. F., 1933.

Reyna de León, Carmela. Dolores o la reina de
los Kunkaks. Pitiquito, Sonora, 1943.

Rudo Ensayo, by an Unknown Jesuit Padre,
1763. Tucson: Arizona Silhouettes, 1951.

Treutlein, Theodore (ed. & trans.). Sonora: A
Description of the Province, by Ignaz Pfefferkorn. (Coronado Cuarto Centennial Publications, Vol. 12). Albuquerque: University of
New Mexico Press, 1949.

CHAPTER FIVE

We are fortunate in having a succession
of personal documents which take us in an
intimate manner into the heart of events in
the lives of the Upper Pimas from their first
contacts with the Spaniards to recent times.
Father Kino's own record of his explorations
and visits with Indians in their rancherías,
Captain Manje's account of many of the same
events, the Franciscan Garcés' diaries, the
fascinating autobiography of the Papago
woman Chona, Carl Lumholtz' vivid narrative
of his travels throughout Papago country in
the early twentieth century, the account of
the kindly matron Janette Woodruff immersed in Papago personal problems, and
Superintendent Kneale's record of his accomplishments and frustrations in attempting to
solve the Gila Pima water problems — these
deal with major phases in the history of the
Upper Pimas and give us rare insights. But
they do not in themselves constitute a coher-
ent history of Indian life. Bolton, relying on
Kino and Manje, has provided what has become the standard guide to the early phase
of Upper Pima-Spanish contacts. He has been
followed here with supplementary details
from Decorme, Ezell, Ewing, and Pfefferkorn. Engelhardt, from the viewpoint of the
Franciscans, carries us on through the Spanish and into the early Anglo-American period.
Hackenberg's as yet unpublished work gives
us a useful summary of Gila Pima history from
the particular viewpoint of economic and
political developments. There is, however, no
full history of the Mexican and Anglo-American periods. We are forced to piece together
the accounts of personal experiences mentioned above with the aid of the Papago calendar-stick record published by Underhill,
and the reports of the United States Commissioner of Indian Affairs. Much specialized
data has been accumulated, but the connected story, at least as fascinating as that of
the Kino phase, awaits a new Bolton.

Bolton, Herbert Eugene. Rim of Christendom:
A Biography of Eusebio Francisco Kino, Pacific Coast Pioneer. New York: Macmillan, 1936.

Decorme, Gerard. La obra de los Jesuitas mexicanos durante la época colonial, 1572–1767.
2 v. México: Antigua Librería Robredo de J.
Porrua e Hijos, 1941.

Engelhardt, Zephyrin. *The Franciscans in Arizona*. Harbor Springs, Mich.: Holy Childhood Indian School, 1899.

Ewing, Russell C. "The Pima Revolt of 1751," in *Greater America: Essays in Honor of Herbert Eugene Bolton*. Berkeley: University of California Press, 1945.

Ezell, Paul H.*The Hispanic Acculturation of the Gila River Pimas*. Unpublished Ph.D. dissertation, University of Arizona, Tucson, 1956.

Geiger, Maynard. *The Kingdom of St. Francis in Arizona, 1839–1939*. Santa Barbara, Calif., 1939.

Hackenberg, Robert A. *Economic and Political Change Among the Gila River Indians*. Unpublished manuscript, Bureau of Ethnic Research, University of Arizona, Tucson, 1955.

Hamilton, J. *A History of the Presbyterian Work Among the Pima and Papago Indians of Arizona*. Unpublished M.A. thesis, University of Arizona, Tucson, 1948.

Joseph, Alice, Rosamond B. Spicer, and Jane Chesky. *The Desert People, A Study of the Papago Indians of Southern Arizona*. Chicago: University of Chicago Press, 1949.

Kneale, Albert H. *Indian Agent*. Caldwell, Idaho: Caxton Printers, 1950.

Lumholtz, Carl. *New Trails in Mexico*. New York: Charles Scribner's Sons, 1912.

Manje, Juan Mateo. *Luz de tierra incógnita: Unknown Arizona and Sonora, 1639–1721*. Harry J. Karns and Associates, trans. Tucson: Arizona Silhouettes, 1954.

Russell, Frank. "The Pima Indians," *Annual Report*, Bureau of American Ethnology, No. 26. Washington, 1908.

Treutlein, Theodore (ed. & trans.). *Sonora, A Description of the Province, by Ignaz Pfefferkorn*. (Coronado Cuarto Centennial Publications, Vol. 12). Albuquerque: University of New Mexico Press, 1949.

Underhill, Ruth M. *A Papago Calendar Record*. University of New Mexico Bulletin, Anthropological Series, Vol. 2, No. 5. Albuquerque, 1938.

———. (ed.) *Autobiography of a Papago Woman*. American Anthropological Association, Memoir No. 48, 1936.

Wagoner, J. J. *History of the Cattle Industry in Southern Arizona, 1540–1940*. University of Arizona, Social Science Bulletin No. 20. Tucson, 1952.

Woodruff, Janette and Cecil Dryden, *Indian Oasis*. Caldwell, Idaho: Caxton Printers, 1939.

CHAPTER SIX

Scholes's studies, of which only one is mentioned in the bibliography, give incomparable insights into the nature of Indian-Spanish relations in New Mexico during the period leading up to the Pueblo Rebellion. The documents on early New Mexico lack a type which is the richest for the Chihuahua-Sonora region, namely, the reports and memoirs of the missionaries themselves. Aside from Benavides' report, there are no comparable documents — at least so far generally available — of the nature of the narratives of such men as Pérez de Ribas, Gilg, Nentuig, Pfefferkorn, Kino, and the other Jesuits who worked in the southern region. Therefore, in what can be written of the early Pueblo story there is lacking the intimate quality which we have for the Jesuit area. The best sources are not personal narratives but court records. These have their value certainly, but do not make up for the details of personality so often revealed in the Jesuit documents. Were the Franciscans less well trained for reporting their observations than the Jesuits? Were there regulations which restricted them? Even though we may infer that their relations with the Indians were not so intimate and friendly as were those of the Jesuits, their experiences must still have seemed to them just as interesting and important to write about. At any rate, there is a bias in the record. The formal documents dealing with the Rebellion of 1680 and the reconquest, and the interesting, but relatively superficial and hurried reports of the official Visitors such as Tamarón y Romeral are full of information, but they leave us in the dark with respect to the interplay of personalities.

The best later material consists of studies by anthropologists. It is they, many of whom have been attracted to the Pueblos over the past hundred years, who have compiled the historical data with reference to each village, and brought together historical and ethnographic facts in a manner to enable us to re-create Pueblo life quite vividly during the Anglo-American phase. The historical sections of White's monographs on the Keresan pueblos are most useful and satisfactory. But there are also others, such as French, Fenton, and Marriott, which provide understanding of Pueblo life in historical perspective for which there is nothing comparable in any anthropological studies of the southern Indians so far. There are, moreover, three studies by Indian administrators — those by Crane, Collier, and Aberle — which give another perspective. The many-sided telling of the story for the recent phase among the Pueblos has begun to make possible the fullest sort of understanding. What we need now are commentary and autobiography by Indians.

Aberle, S. D. *The Pueblo Indians of New Mexico: Their Land, Economy, and Civil Organization*. American Anthropological Association, Memoir No. 70, 1948.

Adams, Eleanor B. (ed.). *Bishop Tamarón's*

Visitation of New Mexico, 1760. Historical Society of New Mexico, Publications in History, Vol. 15. Albuquerque, 1954.

Collier, John. *Indians of the Americas.* New York: W. W. Norton, 1947.

Crane, Leo. *Desert Drums: The Pueblo Indians of New Mexico, 1540–1928.* Boston: Little, Brown, 1928.

Fenton, William N. *Factionalism at Taos Pueblo, New Mexico.* Bureau of American Ethnology, Bulletin 164 (Anthropological Papers, No. 56). Washington, 1957.

French, David H. *Factionalism in Isleta Pueblo.* American Ethnological Society, Monograph 14. New York, 1948.

Hackett, C. W. and C. C. Shelby. *Revolt of the Pueblo Indians of New Mexico and Otermin's Attempted Reconquest, 1680–1682.* (Coronado Historical Series, Vols. 8 and 9). Albuquerque: University of New Mexico Press, 1942.

Hodge, Frederick W., George P. Hammond, and Agapito Rey (eds.). *Fray Alonso de Benavides' Revised Memorial of 1634.* Albuquerque: University of New Mexico Press, 1945.

Marriott, Alice. *María, The Potter of San Ildefonso.* Norman: University of Oklahoma Press, 1948.

Parsons, Elsie Clews. *Pueblo Indian Religion.* 2 v. Chicago: University of Chicago Press, 1939.

Scholes, France V. *Troublous Times in New Mexico, 1659–1670.* Historical Society of New Mexico, Publications in History, Vol. II. Albuquerque, 1942.

Vogt, Evon Z. "A Study of the Southwestern Fiesta System As Exemplified by the Laguna Fiesta," *American Anthropologist,* Vol. 57, No. 4 (1955), pp. 820–39.

White, Leslie A. "The Acoma Indians," *Annual Report,* Bureau of American Ethnology, No. 47. Washington, 1932.

———. *The Pueblo of Santa Ana, New Mexico.* American Anthropological Association, Memoir No. 60, 1942.

Whitman, William. *The Pueblo Indians of San Ildefonso.* New York: Columbia University Press, 1947.

Underhill, Ruth M. *First Penthouse Dwellers of America.* New York: J. J. Agustin, 1938.

CHAPTER SEVEN

Like the Eastern Pueblos, the Zunis and Hopis have now become of intense interest to anthropologists and others. As a result there is a growing abundance of materials which approach Western Pueblo life from many different angles. Laura Thompson's *Culture in Crisis* is in many ways the best single account in print for giving us in small compass the whole story of the Hopi contacts and their effects on Hopi culture, but this should be balanced, especially with the writings of Hopis themselves, such as Nequatewa and "Sun Chief."

Bartlett, Katherine. "Spanish Contacts with the Hopi, 1540–1823," *Museum Notes,* Vol. 6, No. 12 (June, 1934), pp. 55–60. (Museum of Northern Arizona, Flagstaff).

———. "The Navajo Wars – 1823–1870," *Museum Notes,* Vol. 8, No. 7 (January 1936), pp. 33–37. (Museum of Northern Arizona, Flagstaff).

Cushing, Frank H. *My Adventures in Zuni.* Santa Fe: The Peripatetic Press, 1941.

Dockstader, Frederick J. *The Kachina and the White Man: A Study of the Influences of White Culture on the Hopi Kachina Cult.* Cranbrook Institute of Science, Bulletin 35. Bloomfield Hills, Michigan, 1934.

Eggan, Fred. *The Social Organization of the Western Pueblos.* Chicago: University of Chicago Press, 1950.

Hodge, Frederick W. *History of Hawikuh, New Mexico.* Los Angeles: The Southwest Museum, 1937.

Jones, Volney H. "The Establishment of the Hopi Reservation, and Some Later Developments Concerning Hopi Lands," *Plateau,* Vol. 23, No. 2 (1950), pp. 17–25. (Museum of Northern Arizona, Flagstaff).

Kroeber, A. L. "Zuni Kin and Clan," *American Museum of Natural History Anthropological Papers,* Vol. 18, Part 2. New York, 1917.

Kelly, Henry W. "Franciscan Missions of New Mexico, 1740–1760," *New Mexico Historical Review,* Vol. 16 (1941), pp. 41–69.

Kuipers, Cornelius. *Zuni Also Prays.* Christian Reformed Board of Missions, 1946.

Montgomery, Ross Gordon, Watson Smith, and J. O. Brew. *Franciscan Awatovi: The Excavation and Conjectural Reconstruction of a 17th-Century Spanish Mission Establishment at a Hopi Indian Town in Northeastern Arizona.* Papers of the Peabody Museum of American Archaeology and Ethnology, Vol. 35. Cambridge, Mass., 1949.

Nequatewa, Edmund. *Truth of a Hopi and Other Clan Stories of Shung-opovi.* Museum of Northern Arizona, Bulletin No. 8, Flagstaff.

———. "A Mexican Raid on the Hopi Pueblo of Oraibi," *Plateau,* Vol. 16, No. 3 (1944), pp. 45–52. (Museum of Northern Arizona, Flagstaff).

Simmons, Leo W. (ed.). *Sun Chief, The Autobiography of a Hopi Indian.* New Haven, Conn.: Yale University Press for the Institute of Human Relations, 1942.

Smith, Watson and John M. Roberts. *Zuni Law, A Field of Values.* Papers of the Peabody Museum of American Archaeology and Ethnology, Vol. 43, No. 1 (Reports of the Rimrock Project Values Series, No. 4). Cambridge, Mass., 1954.

Thompson, Laura. *Culture in Crisis: A Study of the Hopi Indians.* New York: Harper, 1950.

Titiev, Mischa. *Old Oraibi: A Study of the Hopi Indians of Third Mesa.* Papers of the Peabody Museum of American Archaeology and Ethnology, Vol. 22, No. 1. Cambridge, Mass., 1944.

CHAPTER EIGHT

Most of what is offered here as Navajo history is to be found in Underhill's excellent, richly detailed, and marvelously illustrated, *Here Come the Navaho!* This chapter is perhaps the only historical one in this volume which is unnecessary, unless it is some help to have a very short version of Underhill's history.

My reliance on Underhill has been very considerable. I have, nevertheless, read other materials which I hope have, here and there, enriched my telling of the story of the Navajos. I have listed those publications which seemed to me most successful in conveying the historical development of Navajo life. The three volumes in the Navajo Historical Series are especially to be recommended, as giving us bits of Navajo history from authentic Navajo viewpoints, not passed through the Anglo-American or Spanish filter at all. The autobiography of Son of Old Man Hat has some of the same quality, but it has been filtered at least with respect to Anglo-American canons of narrative conventions. I have included the article by Fryer because it reveals so well the hopeful spirit and the attitudes of Anglo-Americans who were dedicating themselves in the late 1930's and 1940's to the solution of the desperate problems of the Navajos. This phase in Navajo history was a crucial one and we might well devote years to the understanding of it. The recent work by Sasaki deserves special mention, because it tells vividly the story of what has been happening right up to the present in one Navajo community. This is not representative for all Navajos, but it suggests the rapidity and the revolutionary effect of changes that are currently taking place. Vogt's study of Navajo veterans gives also, in a different way, the feeling of the changes of the post-World War II period.

Brewer, Sallie Pierce. "The 'Long Walk' to Bosque Redondo, As Told by Peshlakai Etsedi," *Museum Notes,* Vol. 9, No. 11 (May 1937), pp. 55-62. (Museum of Northern Arizona, Flagstaff).

Dyk, Walter (recorder). *Son of Old Man Hat, A Navaho Autobiography.* New York: Harcourt, Brace, 1938.

Fryer, E. R. "Navajo Social Organization and Land Use Management," *Scientific Monthly,* November, 1942, pp. 408-422.

Hill, W. W. *Navaho Warfare.* Yale University Publications in Anthropology, No. 5, 1936.

Kluckhohn, Clyde and D[ ] *The Navaho.* Cambridge, [ ] versity Press, 1946.

Landgraf, John L. *Land-Us[ ] of New Mexico: An Anth[ ] [ ]pproach to Areal Study.* Papers of the Peabody Museum of American Archaeology and Ethnology, Vol. 42, No. 1. Cambridge, Mass., 1954.

Left-Handed Mexican Clansman and others. *The Trouble at Round Rock.* U.S. Bureau of Indian Affairs, Indian Life Readers: Navajo Historical Series, No. 2. Phoenix, Ariz.: United States Indian Service, 1952.

Rapoport, Robert N. *Changing Navaho Religious Values.* Papers of the Peabody Museum of American Archaeology and Ethnology, Vol. 42, No. 2. Cambridge, Mass., 1954.

Sasaki, Tom T. *Fruitland, New Mexico: A Navaho Community in Tranisition.* Ithaca, N. Y.: Cornell University Press, 1960.

Son of Former Many Beads. *The Ramah Navahos.* U. S. Bureau of Indian Affairs, Indian Life Readers: Navajo Historical Series, No. 1. Phoenix, Ariz.: United States Indian Service, 1949.

Underhill, Ruth. *Here Come the Navaho!* United States Indian Service: Indian Life and Customs, No. 8. Lawrence, Kansas, 1953.

Van Valkenburg, Richard. *A Short History of the Navajo People.* (Mimeographed). Window Rock, Arizona, 1938.

————. "Navajo Naat'aani," *The Kiva,* Vol. 13, No. 2 (January 1948), pp. 14–23. (Arizona Archaeological and Historical Society, Tucson).

Vogt, Evon Z. *Navaho Veterans: A Study of Changing Values.* Papers of the Peabody Museum of American Archaeology and Ethnology, Vol. 41, No. 1. Cambridge, Mass., 1951.

Wilken, Robert L. *Anselm Weber, O.F.M., Missionary to the Navaho, 1898–1921.* Milwaukee, Wis.: Bruce Publishing Co., 1953.

Young, Robert W. (ed.). *The Navajo Yearbook.* Report No. 6, Fiscal Year 1957. Window Rock, Arizona, 1957.

———— and William Morgan (eds.). *Navajo Historical Selections.* U.S. Bureau of Indian Affairs, Indian Life Readers, Navajo Historical Series, No. 3. Phoenix, Ariz.: United States Indian Service, 1954.

CHAPTER NINE

Curiously enough, the Western Apaches are one of the most written-about peoples of the Southwest and yet they remain, in my opinion, the most poorly understood by white men. Apaches complain constantly that all the history which is in print misrepresents them, yet so far no Apache autobiographer or even rough chronicler has emerged. Perhaps we may expect that development within the next few years. The Geronimo period has given rise to thousands of pages of reminiscences, a few of which, such as Cruse's,

, e some rare insights into Apache-White relations, and even here and there Apache viewpoints. For the most part, however, the nontechnical writings on Apaches tell more about the colorful personalities of American military men and Indian agents than they do about the Apaches. There simply is no book which tells the story of the changing Apache life during the past hundred years. Even less is there represented in the literature anything which relates the facts about the crystallization of the Apache raiding complex during Spanish times to the strange sequence of later events.

Adams, William Y. *A Study of San Carlos Apache Wage Labor*. Unpublished manuscript, Department of Anthropology, University of Arizona, Tucson, 1955.

Bancroft, Hubert Howe. *History of Arizona and New Mexico, 1530–1888*. San Francisco: The History Co., 1889.

———. *History of the North Mexican States and Texas*. 2 v. San Francisco, 1884–1889.

Bolton, Herbert Eugene. *Rim of Christendom: A Biography of Eusebio Francisco Kino, Pacific Coast Pioneer*. New York: Macmillan, 1936.

Bourke, John C. *On the Border with Crook*. New York: Scribner, 1891.

Clum, Woodworth. *Apache Agent: The Story of John P. Clum*. Boston: Houghton Mifflin, 1936.

Cremony, John C. *Life Among the Apaches*. Tucson: Arizona Silhouettes, 1951.

Crook, George. *General George Crook: His Autobiography*. Martin F. Schmitt, editor. Norman: University of Oklahoma Press, 1946.

Cruse, Thomas. *Apache Days and After*. Caldwell, Idaho: Caxton Printers, 1941.

Goodwin, Grenville. *The Social Organization of the Western Apache*. Chicago: University of Chicago Press, 1942.

Keleher, William A. *Turmoil in New Mexico, 1846–1868*. Santa Fe, N. M.: Rydall Press, 1952.

Lockwood, Frank C. *The Apache Indians*. New York: Macmillan, 1938.

Matson, Daniel S. and Albert H. Schroeder. "Cordero's Description of the Apache—1796," *New Mexico Historical Review,* Vol. 22 (1958), pp. 335–56.

Ogle, Ralph H. *Federal Control of the Western Apaches, 1848–86*. New Mexico Historical Society Publications, Vol. 9. Albuqerque,1940.

Rudo Ensayo, by an Unknown Jesuit Padre, 1763. Tucson: Arizona Silhouettes, 1951.

Sauer, Carl. *The Distribution of Aboriginal Tribes and Languages in Northwestern Mexico*. (Ibero-Americana: 5). Berkeley: University of California Press, 1934.

Thomas, Alfred Barnaby. *Teodoro de Croix and the Northern Frontier of New Spain, 1776–1783*. Norman: University of Oklahoma Press, 1941.

CHAPTER TEN

This brief sketch of the history of Yuman peoples is obviously inadequate. It is only within the last few years that basic facts essential for an understanding of the Yumans have begun to be published, and much excellent research, notably that of Dobyns, Euler, and Schroeder is still in process of publication. The adequate telling of the Yuman story is still a matter for the future.

Bolton, Herbert Eugene. *Rim of Christendom: A Biography of Eusebio Francisco Kino, Pacific Coast Pioneer*. New York: Macmillan, 1936.

Castetter, Edward F. and Willis H. Bell. *Yuman Indian Agriculture: Primitive Subsistence on the Lower Colorado and Gila Rivers*. Albuquerque: University of New Mexico Press, 1951.

Devereux, George. "Mohave Chieftainship in Action: A Narrative of the First Contacts of the Mohave Indians with the United States," *Plateau*, Vol. 23, No. 3 (1951), pp. 33–43. (Museum of Northern Arizona, Flagstaff).

Dobyns, Henry F. *The Walapai Ghost Dance*. Unpublished manuscript, Department of Anthropology, University of Arizona, Tucson, 1955.

——— and Robert C. Euler, "A Brief History of the Northeastern Pai," *Plateau*, Vol. 32, No. 3 (1960), pp. 49–57. (Museum of Northern Arizona, Flagstaff).

Forde, C. Daryll. *Ethnography of the Yuma Indians*. University of California Publications in American Archaeology and Ethnology, Vol. 28, No. 4, 1931.

Iliff, Flora Gregg. *People of the Blue Water*. New York: Harper, 1954.

Kelly, Dorothea S. "A Brief History of the Cocopa Indians," in *For the Dean: Essays in Anthropology in Honor of Byron Cummings on his Eighty-Ninth Birthday*. Tucson: Hohokam Museums Association, 1950.

Kroeber, A. L. (ed.). *Walapai Ethnography*. American Anthropological Association, Memoir No. 42, 1935.

Schroeder, Albert H. "A Brief History of the Yavapai of the Middle Verde Valley," *Plateau*, Vol. 24, No. 3 (1952), pp. 111-18. (Museum of Northern Arizona, Flagstaff).

———. "A Brief History of the Havasupai," *Plateau*, Vol. 25, No. 3 (1953), pp. 45–52. (Museum of Northern Arizona, Flagstaff).

Schwartz, Douglas W. "The Havasupai, 600 A.D.–1955 A.D.: A Short Culture History," *Plateau*, Vol. 28, No. 4 (1956), pp. 77–85. (Museum of Northern Arizona, Flagstaff).

Spier, Leslie. *Yuman Tribes of the Gila River*. Chicago: University of Chicago Press, 1933.

Woodward, Arthur, "Irataba–'Chief of the Mohave,'" *Plateau*, Vol. 25, No. 3 (1953), pp. 53–68. (Museum of Northern Arizona, Flagstaff).

CHAPTER ELEVEN

The sketch of basic features of what the Spaniards sought to change in Indian life rests on a wide variety of sources. The conception of a "culture of the conquest" is taken directly from the writings of George Foster, who has done a great service in pointing out the relationships between the culture of the Spaniards in old and in New Spain. For the very sketchy and highly selected material on "bearers of Spanish culture" I have relied on all too few sources; nevertheless, I believe that in each case the reality of a particular contact situation is well reported. The material on Father Neumann is taken largely from Dunne's *Early Jesuit Missions in Tarahumara*, Chapters XVII–XXI, pp. 137–197. The quotations regarding Adam Gilg among the Seris are taken from his letter of 1692 reporting his early impressions of the Indians. The sketch of aspects of Father Kino's relations with the Upper Pimas and Yumans utilizes quotations from Bolton's *Rim of Christendom*, from sections LXXI–CXXVIII, pp. 249–487. While I have attributed the material in *Rudo Ensayo* to Father Juan Nentuig, the authorship of this volume is still in some doubt; it of course makes no difference for our purposes precisely who the missionary was who wrote this volume. It is the type of contact that is important, and the *Rudo Ensayo* is one of the most revealing of such accounts. The quotations are taken from Chapters V and VI, pp. 53–91. I feel that I have, especially in the section of the chapter dealing with bearers of Spanish culture, merely suggested the possibilities for interpretation of well-known and much used documents from a point of view growing out of the question: How much mutual understanding of each other's ways of life really grew out of the contacts between Europeans and Indians? I am indeed hesitant to present these sketches, but if they are understood not as purporting to give the range of, but rather some preliminary insights into, contacts which had profound influence on the future of various Indian groups, my purpose will have been realized.

Adams, Eleanor B. (ed.). *Bishop Tamarón's Visitation of New Mexico, 1760*. Historical Society of New Mexico, Publications in History, Vol. 15. Albuquerque, 1954.

Barber, Ruth Kerns. *Indian Labor in the Spanish Colonies*. Historical Society of New Mexico, Publications in History, Vol. 6. Albuquerque, 1932.

Bolton, Herbert Eugene. *Rim of Christendom: A Biography of Eusebio Francisco Kino, Pacif-ic Coast Pioneer*. New York: Macmillan, 1936.

——. *Wider Horizons of American History*. New York: Appleton-Century, 1939.

Decorme, Gerard. *La obra de los Jesuitas mexicanos durante la época colonial, 1572–1767*. 2 v. Mexico: Antigua Librería Robredo de J. Porrua e Hijos, 1941.

Dunne, Peter Masten. *Early Jesuit Missions in Tarahumara*. Berkeley: University of California, 1948.

Foster, George M. *Culture and Conquest: America's Spanish Heritage*. Viking Fund Publications in Anthropology, No. 27. New York, 1960.

Gilg, Adam. "Letter to the Reverend Father Rector . . ." [see notes for Chapter Four for full title].

Hanke, Lewis. *The First Social Experiments in America: A Study of the Development of Spanish Indian Policy in the Sixteenth Century*. Cambridge, Mass.: Harvard University Press, 1935.

Hodge, Frederick W., George P. Hammond, and Agapito Rey (eds.). *Fray Alonso de Benavides' Revised Memorial of 1634*. Albuquerque: University of New Mexico Press, 1945.

Kelly, Henry W. *The Franciscan Missions of New Mexico, 1740–1760*. Historical Society of New Mexico, Publications in History, Vol. 10. Albuquerque, 1941.

Mendizábal, Miguel Othón de. "La evolución del noroeste de México," in *Obras completas*, Vol. 3. México, 1946.

Métodos y resultados de la política indigenista en México. Instituto Nacional Indigenista, Memorias, Vol. VI, México, 1954.

Pérez de Ribas, Andrés. *Historia de los triunfos de nuestra santa fe entre gentes las más bárbaras y fieras . . .* México: Editorial Layac, 1944.

Phelan, John Leddy. *The Millenial Kingdom of the Franciscans in the New World: A Study of the Writings of Geronimo de Mendieta (1525–1604)*. University of California Publications in History, Vol. 52. Berkeley, 1956.

Rudo Ensayo, by an Unknown Jesuit Padre, 1763. Tucson: Arizona Silhouettes, 1951.

Scholes, France V. "Civil Government and Society in New Mexico in the Seventeenth Century," *New Mexico Historical Review*, Vol. 10 (1935), pp. 71–111.

——. *Troublous Times in New Mexico, 1659–1670*. Historical Society of New Mexico, Publications in History, Vol. 11. Albuquerque, 1942.

Simpson, Lesley Byrd. *The Encomienda in New Spain*. Berkeley: University of California Press, 1929.

Stanislawski, Dan. "Early Spanish Town Planning in the New World," *Geographical Review*, Vol. 37, No. 1 (1947), pp. 94–105.

Thomas, Alfred Barnaby. *Forgotten Frontiers: A Study of the Spanish Indian Policy of Don Juan Bautista de Anza, Governor of New Mexico, 1777–1787*. Norman: University of Oklahoma Press, 1932.

———. *Teodoro de Croix and the Northern Frontier of New Spain, 1776–1783.* Norman: University of Oklahoma Press, 1941.

Treutlein, Theodore (ed. & trans.). *Sonora, A Description of the Province by Ignaz Pfefferkorn.* (Coronado Cuarto Centennial Publications, Vol. 12). Albuquerque: University of New Mexico Press, 1949.

West, Robert C. *The Mining Community in Northern New Spain.* (Ibero-Americana: 30). Berkeley: University of California Press, 1949.

Zavala, Silvio. *New Viewpoints on the Spanish Colonization of America.* Philadelphia: University of Pennsylvania Press, 1943.

CHAPTER TWELVE

Adequate materials for understanding the latest phase of Indian policy in Mexico became available only during the writing of this chapter, notably the National Indian Institute's various publications since 1954. It seemed better to offer the present brief introduction rather than to attempt a hurried analysis of a complicated subject, still by no means fully reported. Objective analysis based on adequate information of Mexican Indian policy is only in its beginning stages. Certainly the best introduction to the subject at present is *Methods and Results of Indian Policy in Mexico,* published by the National Indian Institute in 1954.

Balbas, Manuel. *Recuerdos del Yaqui: principales episodios durante la campaña de 1899 a 1901.* Mexico, D. F.: Sociedad de Edición y Librería Franco Americana, 1927.

Ezell, Paul H. "Indians Under the Law. Mexico, 1821–1847," *América Indígena,* Vol. 15, No. 3 (1955), pp. 199–214.

Fabila, Alfonso. *Las tribus Yaquis de Sonora: su cultura y anhelada autodeterminación.* México: Departamento de asuntos indígenas, 1940.

Hernández, Fortunato. *Las razas indígenas de Sonora y la guerra del Yaqui.* México: Talleres de la Casa Editorial "J. de Elizalde," 1902.

Métodos y resultados de la política indigenista en México. Instituto Nacional Indigenista, Memorias, Vol. VI. México, 1954.

Peña, Moisés T. de la. "Extranjeros y Tarahumares en Chihuahua," in *Obras completas* of Miguel Othón de Mendizábal, Vol. 1. México, 1946.

Plancarte, Francisco M. *El problema indígena Tarahumara.* Instituto Nacional Indigenista, Memorias, Vol. V. México, 1954.

Troncoso, Francisco P. *Las guerras con las tribus Yaqui y Mayo del estado de Sonora.* México, 1905.

Villa, Eduardo W. *Historia del estado de Sonora.* 2. ed. Hermosillo: Editorial Sonora, 1951.

CHAPTER THIRTEEN

The subject of Indian policy in the United States appears to be so complicated and so entangled — quite justifiably, certainly — in the emotions of the people of the United States that there is no standard (that is, generally acceptable) single historical analysis in print. This is in itself a highly significant fact and makes it unnecessary to offer any kind of apology for the particular interpretation presented here. The section of this chapter dealing with "bearers of Anglo culture" is even less adequate than the corresponding section of the chapter on the Spanish program. The few selections are weighted on the side of the reservation superintendents, just as those dealing with Spaniards were weighted on the side of the missionaries. This is indicative of my view that these were key roles during initial highly significant periods of contact, albeit roles which operated in completely different institutional frameworks. The quotations in the sketch of Leo Crane are taken from pp. 37, 136, and 204–05 of his *Desert Drums.* I feel that a much longer account of Crane would have been justified because he represented a most influential type of superintendent, but perhaps this introduction will lead the reader to look at both his books from the point of view adopted here. The quotations from the less articulate, but equally representative superintendent, Kneale, are taken from his autobiography, *Indian Agent,* pp. 329, 332, 333–34, 362–63, and 422. The quotations in the account of the Dutch Reformed missionary at Zuni are taken from that most sincere and revealing little book by Cornelius Kuipers, *Zuni Also Prays,* pp. 51–3, and 150–51.

Brown, Estelle Aubrey. *Stubborn Fool: A Narrative.* Caldwell, Idaho: Caxton Printers, 1952.

Collier, John. *Indians of the Americas.* New York: W. W. Norton, 1947.

Crane, Leo. *Desert Drums: The Pueblo Indians of New Mexico, 1540–1928.* Boston: Little, Brown, 1928.

———. *Indians of the Enchanted Desert.* Boston: Little, Brown, 1925.

Dale, Edward Everett. *The Indians of the Southwest: A Century of Development under the United States.* Norman: University of Oklahoma Press, 1949.

Haas, Theodore H. *The Indian and the Law.* United States Indian Service, Tribal Relations Pamphlets, Nos. 2 and 3. Lawrence, Kansas, 1949.

Kelly, William H. *Indians of the Southwest.* Tucson: University of Arizona, Bureau of Ethnic Research, 1953.

Kneale, Albert H. *Indian Agent.* Caldwell, Idaho: Caxton Printers, 1950.

Kuipers, Cornelius. *Zuni Also Prays.* Christian Reformed Board of Missions, 1946.

Leupp, Francis E. *The Indian and His Problem.* New York: Charles Scribner's Sons, 1910.

Lindquist, G. E. E. *Indians in Transition: A Study of Protestant Missions to Indians in the United States.* New York: Division of Home Missions, National Council of Churches of Christ in the U.S.A., 1951.

McNickle, D'Arcy. *They Came Here First: The Epic of the American Indian.* Philadelphia: Lippincott, 1949.

Meriam, Lewis and others. *The Problem of Indian Administration.* The Brookings Institution Studies in Administration, No. 17. Baltimore: The Johns Hopkins Press, 1928.

Simpson, George E. and J. Milton Yinger (eds.). *American Indians and American Life.* The Annals of the American Academy of Political and Social Science, Vol. 311. Philadelphia, 1957.

CHAPTER FOURTEEN

Aberle, S. D. *The Pueblo Indians of New Mexico: Their Land, Economy, and Civil Organization.* American Anthropological Association, Memoir 70, 1948.

Beals, Ralph L. *The Aboriginal Culture of the Cahita Indians.* (Ibero-Americana: 19). Berkeley: University of California Press, 1943.

Bennett, Wendell C. and Robert M. Zingg. *The Tarahumara, An Indian Tribe of Northern Mexico.* Chicago: University of Chicago Press, 1935.

Bunker, Robert. *Other Men's Skies.* Bloomington, Ind.: Indiana University Press, 1956.

Dobyns, Henry F. *The Yavapai Fighters: The Kinship Structure and Territorial Range of a Hualapai Congery.* Unpublished manuscript, 1957.

Forde, C. Daryll. *Ethnography of the Yuma Indians.* University of California Publications in American Archaeology and Ethnology, Vol. 28, No. 4, 1931.

Gill, Mario. *La conquista del valle del Fuerte.* México: 1957.

Goodwin, Grenville. *The Social Organization of the Western Apache.* Chicago: University of Chicago Press, 1942.

Hackenberg, Robert A. *Economic and Political Change Among the Gila River Pima Indians.* Unpublished manuscript, Bureau of Ethnic Research, University of Arizona, Tucson, 1955.

Hill, W. W. "Some Aspects of Navaho Political Structure," *Plateau,* Vol. 13, No. 2 (1940), pp. 23–28. (Museum of Northern Arizona, Flagstaff).

Hinton, Thomas B. *A Survey of Indian Assimilation in Eastern Sonora.* Anthropological Papers of the University of Arizona, No. 4. Tucson, 1959.

Johnson, Jean B. *The Opata: An Inland Tribe of Sonora.* University of New Mexico Publications in Anthropology, No. 6. Albuquerque, 1950.

Kluckhohn, Clyde and Dorothea C. Leighton. *The Navaho.* Cambridge, Mass.: Harvard University Press, 1946.

Maine, Henry S. *Ancient Law.* London, 1861.

Plancarte, Francisco M. *El problema indígena Tarahumara.* Instituto Nacional Indigenista, Memorias, Vol. V. México, 1954.

Rudo Ensayo, by an Unknown Jesuit Padre, 1763. Tucson: Arizona Silhouettes, 1951.

Spier, Leslie. *Yuman Tribes of the Gila River.* Chicago: University of Chicago Press, 1933.

Spicer, Edward H. *Potam, A Yaqui Village in Sonora.* American Anthropological Association, Memoir No. 77, 1954.

Spicer, Rosamond B. *An Outline of Papago Society in the Baboquivari District.* Unpublished manuscript, 1943.

Thompson, Laura. *Culture in Crisis: A Study of the Hopi Indians.* New York: Harper, 1950.

————. *Personality and Government: Findings and Recommendations of the Indian Administration Research.* Ediciones del Instituto Indigenista Interamericano, México, 1951.

Underhill, Ruth. *Social Organization of the Papago Indians.* Columbia University Contributions to Anthropology, Vol. 30. New York, 1939.

White, Leslie A. *The Pueblo of Santa Ana, New Mexico.* American Anthropological Association, Memoir 60, 1942.

CHAPTER FIFTEEN

Adams, Eleanor B. (ed.). *Bishop Tamarón's Visitation of New Mexico, 1760.* Historical Society of New Mexico, Publications in History, Vol. 15. Albuquerque, 1954.

Dale, Edward Everett. *The Indians of the Southwest: A Century of Development under the United States.* Norman: University of Oklahoma Press, 1949.

Densidad de la población de habla indígena en la república mexicana. Instituto Nacional Indigenista, Memorias, Vol. 1, Num. 1. México, 1950.

Dozier, Edward P. "Two Examples of Linguistic Acculturation: The Yaqui of Sonora and Arizona and the Tewa of New Mexico," *Language,* Vol. 32, No. 1 (1956), pp. 146–57.

Herzog, George. "Culture Change and Language: Shifts in the Pima Vocabulary," in *Language, Culture, and Personality,* edited by Leslie Spier and others. Menasha, Wis.: Sapir Memorial Publication Fund, 1941.

Johnson, Jean B. "A Clear Case of Linguistic Acculturation," *American Anthropologist,* Vol. 45, No. 3, Part 1 (1943), pp. 427–34.

Officer, James E. *Indians in School.* Tucson: Bureau of Ethnic Research, University of Arizona, 1957.

Spencer, Robert F. "Spanish Loanwords in Keresan," *Southwestern Journal of Anthropology,* Vol. 3, No. 2 (1947), pp. 130–46.

Spicer, Edward H. "Linguistic Aspects of Yaqui Acculturation," *American Anthropologist,* Vol. 45, No. 3, Part 1 (1943), pp. 410–26.

Swadesh, Morris. "Observations of Pattern Impact on the Phonetics of Bilinguals," in *Language, Culture, and Personality,* edited by Leslie Spier and others. Menasha, Wis.: Sapir Memorial Publication Fund, 1941.

Trager, George L. "Spanish and English Loan-words in Taos," *International Journal of American Linguistics*, Vol. 10 (1944), pp. 144–58.

Treutlein, Theodore (ed. & trans.) *Sonora: A Description of the Province, by Ignaz Pfefferkorn*. (Coronado Cuarto Centennial Publications, Vol. 12). Albuquerque, University of New Mexico Press, 1949.

Van Well, Sister Mary Stanislaus. *The Educational Aspects of the Missions in the Southwest*. Milwaukee, Wis.: Marquette University Press, 1942.

Young, Robert and William Morgan. *A Vocabulary of Colloquial Navaho*. Phoenix, Ariz.: U.S. Indian Service, 1951.

CHAPTER SIXTEEN

Bennett, Wendell C. and Robert M. Zingg. *The Tarahumara, An Indian Tribe of Northern Mexico*. Chicago: University of Chicago Press, 1935.

Bunker, Robert. *Other Men's Skies*. Bloomington, Ind.: Indiana University Press, 1956.

Eggan, Fred. *The Social Organization of the Western Pueblos*. Chicago: University of Chicago Press, 1950.

Fenton, William N. *Factionalism at Taos Pueblo, New Mexico*. Bureau of American Ethnology, Bulletin 164 (Anthropological Papers No. 56). Washington, 1957.

French, David H. *Factionalism in Isleta Pueblo*. American Ethnological Society, Monograph No. 14. New York, 1948.

Goodwin, Grenville. *Social Organization of the Western Apache*. Chicago: University of Chicago Press, 1942.

Ellis, Florence Hawley. "An Outline of Laguna Pueblo History and Social Organization," *Southwestern Journal of Anthropology*, Vol. 15, No. 4 (1959), pp. 325–47.

Hernández, Fortunato. *Las razas indígenas de Sonora y la guerra del Yaqui*. México: Talleres de la Casa Editorial "J. de Elizalde," 1902.

Dunne, Peter Masten. *Pioneer Jesuits in Northern Mexico*. Berkeley: University of California Press, 1944.

Kaut, Charles R. *The Western Apache Clan System: Its Origins and Development*. University of New Mexico Publications in Anthropology, No. 9. Albuquerque, 1957.

Kluckhohn, Clyde and Dorothea C. Leighton. *The Navaho*. Cambridge, Mass.: Harvard University Press, 1948.

Parsons, Elsie Clews. "Isleta, New Mexico," *Annual Report*, Bureau of American Ethnology, No. 47. Washington, 1932.

Spicer, Edward H. *Potam, A Yaqui Village in Sonora*. American Anthropological Association, Memoir No. 77, 1954.

Stanislawski, Dan. "Early Spanish Town Planning in the New World," *Geographical Review*, Vol. 37, No. 1 (1947), pp. 94–105.

Stubbs, Stanley A. *Bird's-Eye View of the Pueblos*. Norman: University of Oklahoma Press, 1950.

Titiev, Mischa. *Old Oraibi*. Papers of the Peabody Museum of American Archaeology and Ethnology, Vol. 22. Cambridge, Mass., 1944.

White, Leslie A. *The Pueblo of Santa Ana, New Mexico*. American Anthropological Association, Memoir No. 60, 1942.

Whitman, William. *The Pueblo Indians of San Ildefonso*. New York: Columbia University Press, 1947.

CHAPTER SEVENTEEN

Beals, Ralph L. *The Contemporary Culture of the Cahita Indians*. Bureau of American Ethnology, Bulletin 142. Washington, 1945.

Bennett, Wendell C. and Robert M. Zingg. *The Tarahumara, An Indian Tribe of Northern Mexico*. Chicago: University of Chicago Press, 1935.

Bunzel, Ruth. "Introduction to Zuni Ceremonialism," *Annual Report*, Bureau of American Ethnology, No. 47. Washington, 1932.

Coolidge, Dane and Mary. *The Last of the Seris*. New York: Dutton, 1939.

Cushing, Frank H. *My Adventures in Zuni*. Santa Fe: The Peripatetic Press, 1941.

Dobyns, Henry F. *The Walapai Ghost Dance*. Unpublished manuscript, Department of Anthropology, University of Arizona, Tucson, 1953.

Engelhardt, Zephyrin. *The Franciscans in Arizona*. Harbor Springs, Mich.: Holy Childhood Indian School, 1899.

Forde, C. Darryl. *Ethnography of the Yuma Indians*. University of California Publications in American Archaeology and Ethnology, Vol. 2, No. 4, 1931.

Geiger, Maynard. *The Kingdom of St. Francis in Arizona, 1839–1939*. Santa Barbara, Calif., 1939.

Goodwin, Grenville. "White Mountain Apache Religion," *American Anthropologist*, Vol. 40, No. 1 (1938), pp. 24–37.

——— and Charles R. Kaut. "A Native Religious Movement Among the White Mountain and Cibecue Apache," *Southwestern Journal of Anthropology*, Vol. 10, No. 4 (1954), pp. 385–404.

Hamilton, J. *A History of the Presbyterian Work Among the Pima and Papago Indians of Arizona*. Unpublished M.A. thesis, University of Arizona, Tucson, 1948.

Kluckhohn, Clyde. "The Philosophy of the Navaho Indians," in F. S. C. Northrup, *Ideological Differences and World Order*. New Haven, Conn.: Yale University Press, 1949.

Kroeber, A. L. (ed.) *Walapai Ethnography*. American Anthropological Association, Memoir No. 42, 1935.

Kuipers, Cornelius. *Zuni Also Prays*. Christian Reformed Board of Missions, 1946.

Lindquist, G. E. E. *Indians in Transition: A Study of Protestant Missions to Indians in the United States*. New York: Division of Home Missions, National Council of Churches of Christ in the U.S.A., 1951.

Ocampo, Manuel. *Historia de la misión de la Tarahumara, 1900–1950.* México: Editorial "Buena Prensa," 1950.

Parsons, Elsie Clews. *Pueblo Indian Religion.* 2 v. Chicago: University of Chicago Press, 1939.

Reichard, Gladys. *Navajo Religion: A Study of Symbolism.* (Bollingen Series, Vol. 18). New York: Pantheon Books, 1950.

Russell, Frank. "The Pima Indians," *Annual Report,* Bureau of American Ethnology, No. 26. Washington, 1905.

Spicer, Edward H. *Pascua, A Yaqui Village in Arizona.* Chicago: University of Chicago Press, 1940.

———. *Potam, A Yaqui Village in Sonora.* American Anthropological Association, Memoir No. 77, 1954.

Spier, Leslie, "Havasupai Ethnology," *American Museum of Natural History Anthropological Papers,* Vol. 19, Part 3. New York, 1928.

———. *Yuman Tribes of the Gila River.* Chicago: University of Chicago Press, 1933.

Thompson, Laura and Alice Joseph. *The Hopi Way.* Chicago: University of Chicago Press, 1950.

Titiev, Mischa. *Old Oraibi.* Papers of the Peabody Museum of American Archaeology and Ethnology, Vol. 22, No. 1. Cambridge, Mass., 1944.

Underhill, Ruth. *Papago Indian Religion.* New York: Columbia University Press, 1946.

Wilken, Robert L. *Anselm Weber, O.F.M.: Missionary to the Navaho, 1898–1921.* Milwaukee, Wis.: Bruce Publishing Co., 1953.

CHAPTER EIGHTEEN

Aberle, S. D. *The Pueblo Indians of New Mexico: Their Land, Economy, and Civil Organization.* American Anthropological Association, Memoir No. 70, 1948.

Adams, William Y. *San Carlos Apache Wage Labor.* Unpublished manuscript, Department of Anthropology, University of Arizona, Tucson, 1957.

———.*Shonto: The Role of the Trader in Navajo Culture Change.* Unpublished Ph.D. dissertation, University of Arizona, 1959.

Castetter, Edward F. and Willis H. Bell. *Pima and Papago Indian Agriculture.* School of Inter-American Affairs, Inter-Americana Studies: 1. University of New Mexico, Albuquerque, 1942.

———. *Yuma Indian Agriculture:Primitive Subsistence on the Lower Colorado and Gila Rivers.* Albuquerque: University of New Mexico Press, 1954.

Fabila, Alfonso. *Las tribus Yaquis de Sonora: su cultura y anhelada autodeterminación.* México: Departamento de asuntos indígenas, 1940.

Getty, Harry T. "Development of the San Carlos Apache Cattle Industry," *The Kiva,* Vol. 23, No. 3 (Feb. 1958), pp. 1–4. (Arizona Archaeological and Historical Society, Tucson).

Kelly, William H. *The Changing Role of the Indian in Arizona.* Circular 263, Agricultural Extension Service, University of Arizona, Tucson, 1958.

Kluckhohn, Clyde and Dorothea C. Leighton. *The Navaho.* Cambridge, Mass.: Harvard University Press, 1946.

Marriott, Alice. *Maria, The Potter of San Ildefonso.* Norman: University of Oklahoma Press, 1948.

Plancarte, Francisco M. *El problema indigena Tarahumara.* Instituto Nacional Indigenista, Memorias, Vol. V. México, 1954.

Robison, Edward and others. *The San Carlos Apache Indian Reservation: A Resources Development Study.* Stanford, Calif.: Stanford Research Institute, 1951.

Spicer, Rosamond B. *An Outline of Papago Society in the Baboquivari District.* Unpublished manuscript, 1943.

Sasaki, Tom T. *Fruitland, New Mexico: A Navaho Community in Transition.* Ithaca, N.Y.: Cornell University Press, 1960.

Tanner, Clara Lee. "Contemporary Southwest Indian Silver," *The Kiva,* Vol. 25, No. 3 (Feb. 1960), pp. 1–22. (Arizona Archaeological and Historical Society, Tucson).

Thompson, Laura. *Culture in Crisis: A Study of the Hopi Indians.* New York: Harper, 1950.

Wagoner, J. J. *History of the Cattle Industry in Southern Arizona, 1540–1940.* University of Arizona, Social Science Bulletin No. 20, Tucson, 1952.

Whitman, William. *The Pueblo Indians of San Ildefonso.* New York: Columbia University Press, 1946.

Young, Robert W. (ed.). *The Navajo Yearbook of Planning in Action.* Window Rock, Arizona, 1955.

———. *The Navajo Yearbook.* Report No. 6. Fiscal Year 1957. Window Rock, Arizona, 1957.

CHAPTER TWENTY

Balbas, Manuel. *Recuerdos del Yaqui: principales episodios durante la campaña de 1899 a 1901.* México, D. F.: Sociedad de Edición y Librería Franco Americana, 1927.

Bancroft, Hubert Howe. *History of the North Mexican States and Texas.* 2 v. San Francisco, 1884–1889.

¿Qué es el I.N.I.? Instituto Nacional Indigenista, México, 1955.

Rudo Ensayo, by an Unknown Jesuit Padre, 1763. Tucson: Arizona Silhouettes, 1951.

Simpson, George E. and J. Milton Yinger (eds.). *American Indians and American Life.* The Annals of the American Academy of Political and Social Science, Vol. 311. Philadelphia, 1957.

Troncoso, Francisco P. *Las guerras con las tribus Yaqui y Mayo del estado de Sonora.* México, 1905.